Child Support Handbook

19th edition

Updated by Mark Brough, with Will Hadwen

Child Poverty Action Group

CPAG promotes action for the prevention and relief of poverty among children and families with children. To achieve this, CPAG aims to raise awareness of the causes, extent, nature and impact of poverty, and strategies for its eradication and prevention; bring about positive policy changes for families with children in poverty; and enable those eligible for income maintenance to have access to their full entitlement. If you are not already supporting us, please consider making a donation, or ask for details of our membership schemes, training courses and publications.

Published by Child Poverty Action Group
94 White Lion Street, London N1 9PF
Tel: 020 7837 7979
staff@cpag.org.uk
www.cpag.org.uk

A CIP record for this book is available from the British Library

ISBN: 978 1 906076 51 1

Child Povery Action Group is a charity registered in England and Wales (registration number 294841) and in Scotland (registration number SC039339), and is a company limited by guarantee, registered in England (registration number 1993854). VAT number: 690 808117

Cover design by Devious Designs
Content management system by Konnect Soft
Typeset by David Lewis XML Associates Ltd
Printed in the UK by CPI William Clowes Beccles NR343 7TL
Cover photo by Joanne O'Brien/Photofusion

The authors

Mark Brough is a freelance writer. He previously worked for many years as a welfare rights adviser for people with learning disabilities.

Will Hadwen is a freelance trainer and consultant on welfare rights and related areas.

Acknowledgements

A huge debt is owed to all the authors of previous editions. Thank you to Yvonne Snape and Sarah Alcock for their helpful suggestions.

Thanks are also due to Alison Key for editing and managing the production of the book, Katherine Dawson for updating the index and Kathleen Armstrong for proofreading the text.

The law described in this book was correct at 1 May 2011.

Contents

Appendices

Abbreviations

AA	attendance allowance
CA	carer's allowance
CMEC	Child Maintenance and Enforcement Commission
CMED	Child Maintenance and Enforcement Commission for Northern Ireland
CSA	Child Support Agency
CSAC	Child Support Agency Centre
CTB	council tax benefit
CTC	child tax credit
DEO	deduction from earnings order
DER	deduction for earnings request
DLA	disability living allowance
DSDNI	Department for Social Development Northern Ireland
DWP	Department for Work and Pensions
ECJ	European Court of Justice
ECHR	European Convention on Human Rights
ESA	employment and support allowance
EU	European Union
HB	housing benefit
IB	incapacity benefit
ICE	Independent Case Examiner
IMA	interim maintenance assessment
IS	income support
JSA	jobseeker's allowance
MAF	maintenance application form
MEF	maintenance enquiry form
NI	national insurance
PC	pension credit
RPC	regular payments condition
SDA	severe disablement allowance
the Revenue	HM Revenue and Customs
WTC	working tax credit

Child support rates 2011/12

Note: many assessments in force during this year will have been calculated on the basis of earlier year's rates.

	£
Dependent child's personal allowance	
Under 20	62.33
Adult's personal allowance	
Single	67.50
Couple	105.95*
** This is only used in the protected income calculation*	
Premiums	
Family	17.40
Disabled child	53.62
Carer	31.00
Disability (single)	28.85
Severe disability (single)	55.30
Enhanced disability (single)	14.05
Enhanced disability (child)	21.63
The following premiums are only used in the protected income calculation:	
Disability (couple)	41.10
Severe disability	
couple (if one qualifies)	55.30
couple (if both qualify)	110.60
Enhanced disability (couple)	20.25
Pensioner/enhanced/higher pensioner	
single	69.85
couple	103.75
Child benefit	
Only or eldest child	20.30
Other children	13.40

	£
Child support	
Minimum payment of child maintenance ('old rules')	6.80
Contribution towards child maintenance deducted from income support ('old rules')	6.80
Minimum payment of child maintenance ('new rules')	5.00
Income tax (per year)	
Personal allowance (under 65)	7,475
Married couple's allowance (minimum)	2,800
Blind person's allowance	1,980
National insurance contributions	
Lower earnings limit	102.00
12% on earnings between £139 and £817	
2% on earnings above £817	
Bands of taxable income	
Basic rate – 20%	£0 – £35,000
Higher rate – 40%	over £35,000
Additional rate – 50%	over £150,000

Part 1

Introduction

Chapter 1

Introduction to child support

This chapter covers:

1. What is child support

Child maintenance paid by parents who do not live with their children is intended to reflect their legal responsibility to provide financial support for their children. Some people make voluntary arrangements to pay maintenance, others have arrangements made following a court order, and some people have maintenance calculated and enforced by the government's Child Support Agency (CSA), which is now managed by the Child Maintenance and Enforcement Commission. Some people may pay or receive child maintenance in more than one of these ways.

Child support is the name given to child maintenance calculated and enforced by the CSA. This *Handbook* deals mainly with the rules of the child support scheme and the work of the CSA. It is intended to help parents who use the CSA and their advisers.

Note: in this *Handbook*, we generally use the term 'child support' for child maintenance calculated by the CSA and the term 'child maintenance' for all types of child maintenance, including child support, voluntary agreements and payments made under a court order.

The child support system administered by the CSA has been in operation since 1993. This calculates the amount of child support people have to pay in different situations. The original complex formula for calculating child support (the 'old rules' formula) was replaced by a simpler calculation from 3 March 2003. This 'new rules' calculation mostly applies to applications made on or after this date (but see Chapter 7 for details of when 'old rules' cases convert to the 'new rules'). An even simpler system of calculating child support is expected to be introduced in 2012 (see p8).

Responsibility for child maintenance

It is a legal principle that both parents of a child have a duty to contribute to the maintenance of that child.[1] This duty is fulfilled when a parent who does not have the main care of a child makes payments of child maintenance assessed under the formula or calculation.[2]

This duty applies whether or not:

- the child is living with the other parent or with someone else who is not legally her/his parent; *or*
- the child is living with a lone parent or with a couple; *or*
- the child's parents are on benefit.

This duty only becomes enforceable if there is a court order or an application to the CSA.

Calculating child support: 'old rules' and 'new rules'

Whether a case comes under the 'old' or 'new' rules for calculating child support is important, not only because it dictates how much maintenance should be paid, but also because there are some differences in how other aspects of child support apply – eg, enforcement. In addition, the legislative references are often different. The **'new rules'** are those that came into force on 3 March 2003 (not the proposed simplified system, planned to be introduced in 2012). The **'old rules'** are those introduced with the child support system when it started in 1993. Both sets of rules have been amended since they were introduced.

The 'old rules' use a complicated formula with several steps to work out how much child support should be paid (see Chapter 8). An application can be made for departure from the formula in certain circumstances (see Chapter 15). The 'new rules' use one of four rates of child support maintenance for each non-resident parent, based on his income (see Chapter 5). The calculation can be varied in certain circumstances (see Chapter 6). The fact that people in the two systems are treated differently in terms of the amount of maintenance received and paid, even though their circumstances may otherwise be the same, is probably not discriminatory and does not breach human rights law.[3]

Generally, if an application for child support is made on or after 3 March 2003, it is a 'new rules' case, and if the application was made before that date, it is an 'old rules' case. However, there are some exceptions to this, and some 'old rules' cases that are connected to a 'new rules' case may be converted to the new rules (see also Chapter 7). Apart from these cases, however, it is now unlikely that 'old rules' cases will convert to 'new rules' because the government intends to introduce a third, and even more simple, calculation. This is expected to be introduced in 2012 (see p8). In the meantime, existing cases will continue to fall under either the 'old rules' or the 'new rules'.

2. The Child Maintenance and Enforcement Commission and the Child Support Agency

The Child Maintenance and Enforcement Commission (CMEC) is a non-departmental public body that came into being on 24 July 2008. It took over responsibility for the child maintenance system in Great Britain, including the Child Support Agency (CSA), from the Department for Work and Pensions (DWP) on 1 November 2008.

CMEC has a much wider remit than the CSA previously had. CMEC's main objective is to maximise the number of effective child maintenance arrangements in place, whether these are made by agreement between parents, by court order or through the statutory schemes operated by the CSA. This main objective is supported by two subsidiary objectives:

- to encourage and support parents to make and keep appropriate voluntary maintenance arrangements;
- to support applications to the statutory child support scheme, and enforce liability.[4]

CMEC is also required to take whatever steps it thinks appropriate to promote awareness among parents of their responsibility for the maintenance of their children and for making appropriate arrangements for the maintenance of any of their children who live apart from them.[5]

CMEC has two delivery bodies: the CSA (see below), which continues to administer the statutory child support scheme, and the Child Maintenance Options service (see p6), which provides information and support. For this reason, this *Handbook* continues to use the term 'CSA' when referring to applications, calculations, decisions, and collection and enforcement procedures under the statutory schemes.

The Child Support Agency

The CSA is responsible for calculating child support payments and, in some cases, their collection and enforcement. This includes tracing non-resident parents and investigating parents' means. Although now part of the responsibilities of CMEC, the CSA remains the delivery body continuing to administer the current statutory child maintenance schemes. This means that individuals continue to apply to the CSA if they cannot reach an agreement for maintenance themselves and wish to use the statutory collection scheme. Current users of the CSA will continue to deal with, and receive letters from, the CSA, not CMEC.

The CSA works closely with Jobcentre Plus, which is responsible for identifying when a parent with care claims benefit. Jobcentre Plus staff pass the parent with care's details to CMEC's Child Maintenance Options service, which then contacts her to discuss the different options for pursuing child maintenance.

The CSA has wide powers to gather information. These are covered in Chapter 4. If a parent is unhappy with a child support decision, there are procedures for challenging these (see Chapter 17), and for appealing most sorts of decisions (see Chapter 18).

Structure of the Child Support Agency

The CSA is divided into six regional business units. Apart from the one for the east of England, they are all based in the areas they serve (see Appendix 1). Each business unit has a Child Support Agency Centre, which assesses child maintenance.

The CSA also has local offices around the country, called local service bases or field offices. These may be used to conduct face-to-face interviews with parents.

In February 2006, the government announced a twin-track approach to the reform of child maintenance. The first was an Operational Improvement Plan, which ran from 2006 to 2009 and attempted to stabilise the work of the CSA. This saw the CSA move towards the following structure:[6]

- new client teams supporting new applications;
- client service teams managing ongoing cases and processing changes of circumstances;
- debt management teams taking action when a payment is missed;
- legal enforcement teams ensuring that payment is enforced.

There should also be specialist client teams for different areas of work, usually determined by the employment status of the non-resident parent – eg, teams dealing with benefit claimants, employed clients and self-employed clients.

The second task was to undertake a longer term redesign of the child maintenance system, which will see the proposed introduction of a new, simplified, calculation in 2012.

Child Maintenance Options

CMEC is required to provide information and guidance to assist parents to make effective maintenance arrangements.[7] Child Maintenance Options was set up by CMEC to offer free, impartial information and support to help both parents make informed choices about child maintenance arrangements. Child Maintenance Options is intended by CMEC to be the first port of call for anyone seeking information on child maintenance, although at present there is no requirement to contact the Child Maintenance Options service before applying to the CSA. It can be used by separating and separated parents, as well as family, friends, guardians and anyone with an interest in child maintenance.

Child Maintenance Options can provide information and assistance with:[8]

- setting up a child maintenance arrangement following separation;

- establishing child maintenance arrangements for parents who are not in a relationship;
- switching from a private arrangment to a CSA calculation, or *vice versa*;
- situations in which an exisiting child maintenance agreement has broken down or is not working well.

The service is delivered by phone, via a website and through a face-to-face service where required. See Appendix 1 for contact details. It seeks to encourage voluntary maintenance arrangements by offering estimated calculations based on the statutory schemes and other guidance to help parents decide on maintenance arrangements and amounts. It also provides information on other related areas such as housing, employment and money, and can put people in touch with specialist advice agencies.

Child Maintenance Options aims to give impartial information to any party involved in child maintenance arrangements. It can be used anonymously and records are not linked, so that if two parties contact the service independently in relation to the same child(ren), no information regarding one party would be divulged to the other. The website includes leaflets explaining how personal information will be used[9] and how to complain about the service (see Chapter 20).[10]

Arrangements in Northern Ireland

The child support system is the same throughout the UK, but there is a separate Child Maintenance and Enforcement Division (CMED) for Northern Ireland, which is part of the Department for Social Development (DSDNI). There is an Information and Support Service which provides impartial information and support in a similar way to Child Maintenance Options. CMED's powers are the same as those of the CSA in England, Scotland and Wales. Before 1 April 2008, child support was dealt with by the Northern Ireland Child Support Agency. For the time being, cases will be dealt with in the same way as before this date. The future changes proposed for England, Scotland and Wales (see p8) will also apply in Northern Ireland. See www.dsdni.gov.uk for updates. Also part of DSDNI is the Social Security Agency, the Northern Ireland equivalent of Jobcentre Plus.

If this *Handbook* is being used in Northern Ireland, references to the DWP should be read as references to DSDNI and references to Jobcentre Plus should be read as references to the Social Security Agency. **Note:** some legislative references are different in Northern Ireland.

3. Future changes

In recent years there have been significant proposals for further changes to the child support system, prompted in part by persistent problems with the existing system, particularly delays in assessments, difficulties in enforcing payment and weaknesses in IT systems.

Some changes originally planned for 2010 and 2011 have not yet been introduced. These include:

- further changes in enforcement powers, including the power to disqualify non-resident parents from holding passports and the power to apply for curfew orders; *and*
- the new simplified maintenance calculation (see p9).

In January 2011, the government published proposals for the future of child maintenance.[11] The consultation states that 'conflict is inherent' in the current child support system, and that it needs to be rebalanced towards supporting parents to work collaboratively to agree family-based arrangements wherever possible. The government's intention is that the statutory child support system should be for only those families who are not able to come to their own arrangements.

The proposals include initiatives to improve the integration of support services for separating families. The main proposed changes to the statutory system include:

- a new 'gateway' process that will require parents to take reasonable steps to make family-based arrangements first and allow them to be directed to support if needed, before an application to the statutory scheme will be permitted;
- a calculation-only service to provide parents who are able to make family-based arrangements with an authoritative calculation on which to base decisions, but without that calculation creating any formal liability;
- the new simplified statutory maintenance calculation scheme, underpinned by a new IT system;
- introducing charges to use the new services, with some provision for reductions and exemptions. The proposals cover one-off charges for the calculation-only service and for an application to the statutory scheme, and ongoing administration charges on both the person with care and the non-residents parent when the Child Support Agency (CSA) collection service is used;
- giving non-resident parents control over the choice of paying maintenance direct to avoid ongoing administration charges.

The consultation on these proposals ended in April 2011. At the time of writing, legislation to provide for some of the changes was still undergoing parliamentary scrutiny. The government is expected to publish a response to the consultation in summer/autumn 2011, and then to consult on the detail of the regulations required to implement the system before introducing a single package of regulations before the end of 2011. For updates, see CPAG's *Welfare Rights Bulletin*.

The proposals are intended to be introduced in 2012. The new service will initially be available only to new applicants. A process of closing all existing CSA cases will begin at a later date, with parents then treated in the same way as new applicants if they wish to apply to the new statutory scheme. There is no information yet on how this process of closing cases will take place in practice, but it is expected to take around two years.

It is also not yet clear how the services will be delivered in the future. The consultation says that there is no assumption about who should deliver the gateway or what connection that body should have to the statutory scheme organisation and other services. The government has also proposed that the Child Maintenance and Enforcement Commission should cease to be a non-departmental public body and become an executive agency of the Department for Work and Pensions. This is also still subject to parliamentary scrutiny and no date has yet been set for the change of status.

The new maintenance calculation

A new scheme for calculating child maintenance is expected to be introduced in 2012. All new claimants will have their claims calculated under these new rules. At a later date, a process of closing all existing CSA cases will begin, and any parents who wish to apply to the new scheme will have to do so in the same way as new applicants.[12]

The new calculation will be based on information from HM Revenue and Customs on the non-resident parent's gross income for the latest available tax year. The amount will be fixed for one year unless his income varies by 25 per cent.

As the new calculation will be based on gross income rather than net income, as currently used, the percentage amount that the non-resident parent will be expected to pay will change.[13]

For a non-resident parent whose weekly income is £800 or less, the rates will be:

- 12 per cent for one child;
- 16 per cent for two children;
- 19 per cent for three or more children.

If the non-resident parent's income is over £800 a week, the following rates will apply to the excess over £800:

- 9 per cent for one child;
- 12 per cent for two children;
- 15 per cent for three or more children.

The gross weekly income taken into account will be reduced if the non-resident parent has other relevant children.

The flat rate will increase from £5 to £7.

4. Using this *Handbook*

This *Handbook* covers the child support scheme in England, Wales and Scotland as at 1 May 2011. Northern Ireland has a similar scheme, although some of its legislative references and guidance are different. Separate chapters detail how maintenance is worked out under the 'old' and 'new' rules. All other chapters relate to both 'old' and 'new' rules chapters.

Structure of the book

Part 1 is an introduction to child support, the Child Support Agency (CSA) and how to use this *Handbook*. **Part 2** explains the key principles and terms of the child support scheme, how applications are made (including for parents treated as applying) and how the CSA seeks information. Once all the information is available, the amount of maintenance can be worked out – **Part 3** does this under the 'new rules' and **Part 4** under the 'old rules'. The transitional rules on the conversion of 'old rules' cases to the 'new rules' are also covered in Part 3 (Chapter 7). **Part 5** covers CSA decisions, how to change, query or challenge them (by review, supersession and appeal), collection and enforcement of maintenance, and how to complain.

The **appendices** contain useful addresses, information about reference materials and an explanation of income support premiums. For child support rates, see pxi.

The best way to find the information you need is to use the index at the back of the book.

Footnotes

At the end of each chapter are the footnotes. These contain the legal authorities and other sources of information which support the text, and some further information. Parents and advisers can quote the reference to the CSA if the statement in the text is disputed. Appendix 6 explains the abbreviations used in the footnotes, with information on how to obtain the sources.

Different guidance applies to 'old rules' and 'new rules' cases. The Child Maintenance and Enforcement Commission (CMEC) does not publish the guidance used by CSA decision makers. As the guidance is not readily available, this *Handbook* does not use it as a source. The guidance can, however, be obtained by making a request to CMEC under the Freedom of Information Act 2000. Anyone concerned about the application of a particular aspect of the law may wish to ask the CSA to provide a copy of any guidance taken into account by the decision maker.

This *Handbook* also includes references to relevant caselaw.

Definitions and terms used

The following terms are used throughout this *Handbook*. For more detailed definitions, see Chapter 2.

A parent who does not live with her/his own child is a **'non-resident parent'**.

A child who does not live with both her/his parents is a **'qualifying child'**.

The person with whom the child is living and who provides her/him with day-to-day care is the **'person with care'**. If a person with care is also a parent of the qualifying child, s/he is a **'parent with care'**.

A child living with the non-resident parent, for whom s/he or any new partner receives child benefit, is a **'relevant child'**.

As the latest statistics from the CSA show that 95 per cent of people with the care of a qualifying child are women, this *Handbook* uses **'she'** to describe the person with care and **'he'** to describe the non-resident parent. However, the law applies in the same way if the person with care is a man or the non-resident parent is a woman, or if both parents are men or both women.

The term **'second family'** is used loosely to describe the situation where a parent of a qualifying child (usually the non-resident parent) also has children who live with her/him. This could be a third or fourth family, or even a first family where, for example, a married man remains with his wife despite having a child with another woman. It may also apply where a parent is living with a same-sex partner who has responsibility for a child.

The term **'stepchild'** is used to describe the child of a person's partner, whether or not they are a married couple or in a civil partnership.

Notes

1. **What is child support**

1 s1(1) CSA 1991

2 s1(2) and (3) CSA 1991

3 In CCS/1077/2006 the commissioner stated that, even if discrimination could be shown, 'it is an objective and reasonable justification that parents are treated differently as new legislation is tested as it is brought into force'. See also R(CS) 3/07 in which the commissioner decided there was no breach of the European Convention of Human Rights, even though it is now clear that the 'new rules' scheme will not be implemented for all 'old rules' cases as had originally been intended.

2. **The Child Maintenance and Enforcement Commission and the Child Support Agency**

4 s2 CMOPA 2008

5 s4 CMOPA 2008

6 CSA Operational Improvement Plan 2006-2009

7 s5 CMOPA 2008

8 *Child Maintenance: getting started*, Child Maintenance Options, April 2010

9 *How Will the Child Maintenmance Options Service Use My Personal Information?* Child Maintenance Options, October 2008

10 *How Can I Complain About the Child Maintenance Options Service?* Child Maintenance Options, October 2008

3. **Future changes**

11 DWP, *Strengthening Families, Promoting Parental Responsibility: the future of child maintenance*, Cmnd 7990, January 2011

12 DWP, *Strengthening Families, Promoting Parental Responsibility: the future of child maintenance*, Cmnd 7990, January 2011

13 Sch 4 CMOPA 2008

Part 2

Using the Child Support Agency

Chapter 2

Who is covered by the scheme

This chapter covers:

1. The duty to maintain

Both parents of a 'qualifying child' (see p18) are responsible for maintaining her/him.[1]

The Child Support Agency (CSA) can only require a 'non-resident parent' (see p21) to pay child support for a qualifying child. A 'parent with care' (see p19) cannot be required to pay child support for the child for whom s/he is caring, unless s/he is treated as a non-resident parent because s/he provides care for less time than someone else or, in some cases, for the same amount of time (see Chapter 15).

The CSA can only make a calculation (or assessment in 'old rules' cases) if the person with care, non-resident parent and qualifying child meet the rules on habitual residence (see p25).

2. Parent

A **'parent'** is a person who is legally the mother or father of the child.[2] This includes:

- a biological parent;

- a parent by adoption;[3]
- a parent under a parental order (used in surrogacy cases).[4]

If a child was conceived by artificial insemination or *in vitro* fertilisation:

- the mother is the woman who gave birth to the child (wherever in the world the insemination or fertilisation took place),[5] unless an adoption order or parental order is made;[6]
- the father is the man who provided the sperm. However, there are exceptions depending on when the insemination or *in vitro* fertilisation took place (see below).

If the insemination took place on or after 1 August 1991 but before 6 April 2010, the father is:[7]

- the mother's husband, unless he did not consent to[8] or died before insemination;[9] *or*
- if the insemination was during licensed treatment services provided for the mother and a man, that man.[10] The man and woman must have received treatment services together.[11] This rule does not apply to a woman inseminated/fertilised outside the UK.[12]

From 6 April 2009, in the case of assisted reproduction:[13]

- if married to the mother, the man is the father unless he did not consent;
- if a man and woman are not married and the woman has a child as a result of licensed treatment, the man is the father if there is a notice of consent between them.

Female civil partners are treated in the same way as married couples – ie, if one partner gives birth to a child as a result of donor insemination (anywhere in the world), she is the mother of the child and her civil partner will automatically be the other parent, unless she did not consent to the mother's treatment.[14]

If a person denies being the parent of a child, the Child Support Agency (CSA) must *assume* that the person is a parent of the child, unless the child has subsequently been adopted by someone else (see p17), if:[15]

- in England, Wales or Northern Ireland, a declaration of parentage or, in Scotland, a declarator of parentage, is in force about that person. This includes situations where the person with care or the CSA has applied to court for a declaration on whether the person is a parent of the child;[16]
- in Scotland,[17] England and Wales,[18] the person is a man who:
  - was married to the mother at any time between the child's conception and birth; *or*
  - acknowledged his paternity *and* was acknowledged by the mother *and* was named as the father on the birth certificate issued in the UK;

- the person is a man who was found to be the father by a court in England or Wales in proceedings under certain legal provisions (see Appendix 3). The court decision usually states the legal provision under which it was made;[19]
- the person is a man who was found by a court in Northern Ireland to be a father in proceedings under similar legal provisions to those in Appendix 3;[20]
- the person is a man who was found by a court in Scotland to be the father in any action for affiliation or aliment;[21]
- the person is a man who refuses to take a DNA test, or where the results of the test show that he is the father (even if he refuses to accept it);[22]
- a parental order has been made in favour of that person following an application made within six months of a birth which is the result of a surrogacy arrangement;[23]
- certain types of fertility treatment have been carried out by a licensed clinic and the person is treated as a parent of the child under the Human Fertilisation and Embryology Act 1990.[24]

These rules apply even if paternity was not disputed in the proceedings.[25]

If none of the above applies, the CSA cannot make a calculation until parentage is admitted by a person or decided by a court.

An **adoption order** means the child is, in law, the child of the adopter(s).[26] The liability of a biological parent to maintain her/his child ends on adoption and the parent(s) by adoption become the only people liable to maintain the child.

A person who has legal parental responsibility[27] is not necessarily a parent for child support purposes.[28] For example, a step-parent who has acquired parental responsibility (except one assumed to be a parent under the rules above) cannot be required to pay child support maintenance, but the courts could order maintenance (see p30).

A foster parent is not a parent for child support purposes because the child has been placed with her/him by a local authority (see p19).

Parentage disputes

If the parent with care does not name the other parent, or if the alleged non-resident parent denies parentage, the CSA investigates to identify the other parent and, if possible, show that he can be assumed to be a parent under the above rules (see pp58 and 61). If the alleged non-resident parent disputes that those rules apply (eg, he says the person named in a court order is someone else), he can appeal against the CSA decision. This appeal is dealt with by a magistrates'/sheriff court rather than by the First-tier Tribunal (see also p61).[29]

However, if the alleged non-resident parent accepts that those rules apply, but disputes the correctness of the court order referred to by the CSA (ie, the court was wrong to name him as the father), he cannot dispute parentage through the CSA appeals system. Instead, he should consider applying to the court to set aside its order and/or making a late appeal against it.

If no one is assumed to be the other parent under those rules, the CSA usually attempts to arrange voluntary DNA testing or applies to court for a declaration/declarator of parentage (see p65).

3. Qualifying child

Child support maintenance is only payable for a 'qualifying child'. A child is only a **'qualifying child'** if one or both of her/his parents are non-resident parents (see p21).[30]

A **'child'** is defined as a person who is under 16 years of age.[31] In some circumstances, a young person is also a qualifying child for child support maintenance purposes until s/he reaches 19 years of age.[32]

Therefore, a qualifying child is someone who is:

- under 16; *or*
- 16–18 years old inclusive and receiving full-time, non-advanced education; *or*
- 16 or 17 years old and who has recently left education and who is registered for work or work-based learning for young people (see p19).

Even if a person falls into one of these groups, s/he is *not* a child if s/he is, or has been, married or in a civil partnership. This applies even if the marriage or civil partnership has been annulled or was never valid – eg, s/he was under 16.[33]

Note: not all young people for whom child benefit is received count as children for child support purposes. However, sometimes, receipt of child benefit may be important – eg, if a 16/17-year-old has recently left education (see p19). The definition of 'qualifying child' for child support purposes is not the same as the definition of a child or young person in respect of whom child benefit can be paid. At present, a young person aged 19 cannot be a 'qualifying child'. The definitions are, however, expected to be aligned as part of forthcoming changes to the child support system (see Chapter 1).[34]

Full-time, non-advanced education

A course is **non-advanced** if it is up to A level or higher level Scottish Certificate of Education (this includes a Scottish certificate of sixth year studies and a national diploma or certifcate from BTEC or ScotVEC). Courses of degree level and above (and DipHE, higher national diploma, or a higher diploma or certificate from BTEC or ScotVEC) count as advanced education.[35]

The child must attend a recognised educational establishment (such as a school or college) *or* the education must be recognised by the CSA.[36]

The CSA must treat a child as receiving **full-time** education if the child attends a course where the weekly contact time is more than 12 hours. Contact time includes teaching, supervised study, exams and practical or project work which are parts of the course. It does not include meal times or unsupervised study, whether on or off school premises.

If a child is not attending such a course (eg, where contact is for less than 12 hours), the CSA must look at all the facts and decide if the education is full time.[37]

After leaving school or college, a child still counts as being in full-time education until child benefit stops being paid. This is known as the 'terminal date'.[38]

Breaks in full-time education

Someone at school or college still counts as a child if there is a temporary break in full-time education.[39] It does not matter whether s/he is under or over 16 when education is interrupted.

For someone to continue to count as a child, any breaks in full-time education must not be followed by a period during which child benefit stops being payable.[40]

16/17-year-olds not in full-time education

A 16/17-year-old who is no longer in full-time education still counts as a child for child support purposes if s/he is registered for work or work-based learning for young people and child benefit is payable for her/him.[41] This can last for the child benefit 'extension period' of 20 weeks after a young person leaves education. The person with care can request that child benefit continues, provided the young person is registered for training with a qualifying body such as Connexions or the Careers Service.[42] Child benefit is still payable for a young person who does paid work, provided it is for less than 24 hours a week.[43] See CPAG's *Welfare Benefits and Tax Credits Handbook* for more information on this child benefit extension period.

4. Person with care

A **'person with care'** is the person with whom a child has her/his home (see p20) and who usually provides day-to-day care (see p20) for the child.[44] This means a person who actually and usually provides day-to-day care in practice, and may not necessarily be someone who has parental responsibility for the child. What is 'usual' is a question of fact and takes time to evolve.[45] There may be more than one person with care of a particular child.[46]

A person with care is usually a parent of the child or another individual, but could also be, for example, an organisation such as a children's home. However, a person with care *cannot* be a local authority, or someone looking after a child who has been placed with her/him by the local authority.[47] The only exception to this rule is if someone in England and Wales is the child's parent and the local authority has allowed a child it looks after to live with her/him.[48]

Day-to-day care

The Child Support Agency (CSA) normally looks at how many nights of care a person provides when deciding who is a person with care. To count as providing day-to-day care, a parent must provide care of at least 104 nights per year on average.[49] The amount of care can be averaged over a different period if this will be more representative of actual arrangements. The CSA considers the total time a child spends with each parent and decides who is the principal provider of care. In some cases where care is shared equally, other factors may be taken into account to determine which parent is treated as a non-resident parent – eg, the parent who does not receive child benefit.[50]

A person who is responsible for a child's daily routine may be providing day-to-day care even if some things are done by another person – eg, a childminder. It may not be necessary for a person to be *with* the child for at least 104 nights a year if she is nevertheless the person responsible for overall care during that time. What matters is the degree to which a person continues to exercise control over the child and to be responsible for the child's behaviour and protection.[51]

Example 2.1

A mother on night shifts leaves her son in the care of grandparents for 22 nights a month. She decides what he will eat and when he will go to bed, and each morning she dresses him and takes him to school. Using the 104 nights average, she does not provide day-to-day care, but, using the ordinary meaning of those words, she is the principal provider of day-to-day care.

In two situations, the care actually being provided does not matter. If a child is placed with her/his parent by a local authority in England and Wales, even though the local authority is legally responsible, the parent is treated as providing day-to-day care.[52] If a child is a boarding-school boarder or a hospital inpatient, the person who would otherwise provide day-to-day care is treated as providing day-to-day care.[53]

If the CSA cannot identify one person with whom the child spends the most time, it may decide that the person not receiving child benefit is the non-resident parent.[54] The result can be that someone who would otherwise be a parent with care is treated as the non-resident parent (see p21). On the other hand, in some cases, there may be no one providing day-to-day care and so there is no one who can be treated as a person with care.

Home

The person with care must have a home with the child. A home is the physical place where the child lives. It is different from a household (see p21). Where a child has her/his home is usually clear. A child may have more than one home, in which case the CSA decides which is the principal home.[55]

Parent with care

A 'parent with care' is a person with care who is also a parent (see p15) of a qualifying child (see p18).[56]

However, where there is a shared care situation, someone who might otherwise be a parent with care may be treated as a non-resident parent (see p96 in 'new rules' cases and p268 in 'old rules' cases).

5. Non-resident parent

A **'non-resident parent'** ('absent parent' is the terminology used in 'old rules' cases, but 'non-resident parent' is used throughout this *Handbook* for simplicity) is a parent (see p15) who is not living in the same household (see below) as his child, and the child has her/his home with a person with care (see p19) – eg, where the parents of a child have separated.[57] In cases where people share the care of a child, a person who would otherwise be a parent with care may be treated as a non-resident parent (see p96 in 'new rules' cases and p268 in 'old rules' cases).[58] If a parent thinks that a decision identifying him as a non-resident parent is wrong, he should seek advice. If the non-resident parent begins living in the same household as the parent with care, the calculation immediately ceases to have effect in 'new rules' cases. However, in 'old rules' cases it may not be cancelled completely and will depend on the length of the reconcilliation.[59]

Both parents can be non-resident parents, in which case they can both be required to pay child support maintenance (see p279) to a person with care – eg, to a grandparent who provides day-to-day care for a child.[60]

Household

'Household' is not defined in child support legislation. A household is something abstract, not something physical like a home (see p20). It is either a single person or a group of people held together by social ties.[61] In many cases, whether or not people are members of the same household is obvious. If it is not obvious, the Child Support Agency (CSA) considers other factors. No one factor on its own should be conclusive. There does not need to be any settled intention about future arrangements for a household to exist.[62]

The meaning of household has been considered in family law and social security cases as well as child support cases, and this caselaw may be used to help make child support decisions. For some of the social security caselaw, see CPAG's *Welfare Benefits and Tax Credits Handbook*.

Some guidelines from the caselaw are as follows.

- There can be two or more separate households in one house.[63]
- One or more members of a household can be temporarily absent from the home without ending their membership of the household.[64]
- There does not need to be a relationship like marriage for people to share a household – eg, two sisters can form a household.[65]

If there is a polygamous marriage, the CSA decides whether the qualifying child lives in a different household from at least one of the parents when establishing whether there is a non-resident parent. There can only ever be two legal parents, regardless of the number of partners either parent may have.

A couple may become members of the same household even if they get back together only briefly, assuming that they are hoping the relationship and, therefore, the domestic set-up will be indefinite.[66] In this case, a new household could be formed immediately, whether or not it then ceases to exist a few weeks or months later. A household can be formed as soon as people live together intending to form a household, and before they have arranged joint domestic and financial matters.

Advisers should be careful when arguing that a supposed non-resident parent shares a household with a parent with care on benefit. A decision by the CSA or First-tier Tribunal that the couple share a household for child support purposes is likely to mean that the couple share a household for benefit or tax credit purposes. For more information about cohabitation decisions for benefits and tax credits, see CPAG's *Welfare Benefits and Tax Credits Handbook*.

6. Relevant child

A **'relevant child'** is the term used by the Child Support Agency (CSA) in 'new rules' cases for a child, other than a qualifying child, for whom the non-resident parent or his partner receives child benefit.[67] This can include a child who does not live with the parent all the time – eg, because s/he is at boarding school or there is a shared care arrangement for her/him.

If a relevant child is cared for by a local authority either for part or all of the time, s/he continues to count as a relevant child if the non-resident parent or his partner receives child benefit for her/him.[68]

The number of relevant children is important because it affects the calculation of child support. In 'old rules' cases, the term is not used, but children who live with the non-resident parent may affect the maintenance assessment in different ways.

Relevant non-resident child

'Relevant non-resident child' is a term used by the CSA in 'new rules' cases to refer to a child of the non-resident parent for whom an application for child support cannot be made because the non-resident parent is liable to pay maintenance under a court order for her/him.[69] This is a child who would be considered a qualifying child if an application for child support maintenance could be made for her/him. It could be a child who does not live with the non-resident parent, or a child whose care is shared between the non-resident parent and someone else in a situation in which the child would be regarded as a qualifying child but for the court order. See p27 for more information about when a court order prevents an application for child support being made.

The number of relevant non-resident children is important because it also affects the calculation of child maintenance in 'new rules' cases. Although the term 'relevant non-resident child' is not used in 'old rules' cases, child maintenance paid under a court order may affect the calculation.

7. Welfare of the child

Whenever the Child Support Agency (CSA) makes a discretionary decision about a case, it must take into account the welfare of any child likely to be affected by the decision.[70] This also applies to discretionary decisions made by the First-tier Tribunal and Upper Tribunal.

Many child support decisions involve choosing between alternatives, such as whether a person is habitually resident or not, but these are not usually discretionary decisions. A person has discretion only if, once s/he has decided on the facts of a case and what the law requires, s/he still has a choice about what decision to make. An example of a discretionary decision in child support is how to collect or enforce maintenance, including whether to make a deduction from earnings order.

Only the welfare of a child has to be taken into account (see definition of a child on p18), not that of any adults involved. However, it is not just qualifying children or those named in the maintenance application who must be considered. The situation of any child likely to be affected by the decision must be looked at[71] – eg, a child of the non-resident parent's new family, known under the 'new rules' as a 'relevant child', or another child of the non-resident parent who does not live with him.

The duty to have regard to the welfare of children is 'a general principle' in child support law.[72] The legislation does not make it the paramount consideration, or impose a duty on the CSA or First-tier Tribunal/Upper Tribunal to promote the welfare of any children.[73] Considerable weight should, however, be given to this duty.[74] In general, the principle should be considered along with the other principles of child support.[75]

Because there is usually no discretion about whether or not to make a calculation (or 'old rules' assessment), or about the amount of maintenance due, there are only a limited number of cases in which the welfare of a child can make a difference. It is important to give the CSA full details at the earliest stage about the effect a discretionary decision may have on a child's welfare.

'Welfare' includes the child's physical, mental and social welfare. For example, if a deduction from earnings order (see p415) would prevent a non-resident parent from visiting a child, that child's emotional welfare may be affected. However, an order may mean the parent with care has more money coming in, which may improve the child's physical and social welfare.

Generally, the welfare of a child has to be balanced with the benefits of receiving maintenance for that child or other children. This is why it is usually only in certain situations that the welfare of a child will be deemed more important than the principle that parents should maintain their children. For example, if the non-resident parent has a child in his household who is disabled and who would be adversely affected if there were less money to spend on her/his living costs, or by the implications of enforcement action, this might mean that certain enforcement action should not be taken. However, when deciding on enforcement action, decision makers must not use the welfare of the child principle to avoid full use of the CSA's powers of enforcement unless it is genuinely appropriate.[76]

Reasoning on the welfare of all children who could be affected has to be fully documented, and it may be useful to ask to see the welfare of the child considerations. If a decision has been made in ignorance of its effect on a child, the information should be supplied and the CSA asked to reconsider. It is possible for some decisions which should involve the welfare of the child principle to be revised or superseded (see Chapter 17), or appealed (see Chapter 18). If the decision cannot be appealed (eg, if it is about enforcement), a CSA client should consider making a complaint or applying for a judicial review (see p343).

In addition to the general principle of the welfare of children in child support law, the UK is also bound to comply with international obligations, including a commitment to the welfare of children under the United Nations Convention on the Rights of the Child. This means that in instances where more than one interpretation of the law is possible, the one chosen should be that which more closely complies with protecting the welfare of children.[77]

8. **Family**

'Family' is defined as a couple or a single person and any children in the same household for whom the single person or at least one member of the couple is responsible.[78]

A couple is:[79]

- a man and a woman who are married to each other and living in the same household;
- a man and woman who are living together as husband and wife but are not married to each other;
- a couple registered as civil partners who live in the same household;
- a same-sex couple living together as if they were civil partners.

The definition of family includes those living in polygamous marriages. For information on when a couple are living together as husband and wife, or as civil partners, see CPAG's *Welfare Benefits and Tax Credits Handbook*. The children living with a couple or lone parent do not have to be biological or adopted children to count as family members, but foster children are not included. A person under 16 cannot be a member of a couple.[80]

Partners

A partner in the context of this *Handbook* means a married partner living with her/his spouse, a man or woman living with his/her civil partner, or someone living with a partner 'as husband and wife' or 'as if they were civil partners' (see above). Since December 2005, same-sex couples have been able to register as civil partners, and various aspects of the law have been changed to reflect this.[81] Child support legislation was amended from 5 December 2005 to take account of these provisions.[82] From this date, civil partners who are parents (including those who have adopted a child) are treated, for most child support purposes, in the same way as married partners. Parents who are living with a same-sex partner but have not formed a civil partnership are treated in the same way as couples of the opposite sex who are living together but have not married. Before 5 December 2005, same-sex couples were *not* treated as partners. However, it has been decided that this treatment, which under the 'old rules' could have resulted in a non-resident parent in a same-sex partnership paying higher child support contributions than someone in an opposite-sex partnership, did not constitute unlawful discrimination.[83]

9. **Habitually resident in the UK**

The Child Support Agency (CSA) cannot make a maintenance calculation unless the person with care, non-resident parent and qualifying child are all habitually resident in the UK.[84] Relevant children do not have to be habitually resident in the UK.[85] The requirement for the person with care to be habitually resident does not apply if that 'person' is an organisation.[86]

The UK means England, Scotland, Wales and Northern Ireland (including coastal islands like the Isle of Wight). It does not include the Isle of Man or the Channel Islands.[87]

Habitual residence is covered fully in CPAG's *Welfare Benefits and Tax Credits Handbook*.

If a person is not habitually resident in the UK, see p31.

Meaning of habitual residence

A person is habitually resident if s/he is ordinarily resident and has been for an appreciable period of time.[88] For child support purposes, habitual residence is to be considered bearing in mind that the purpose of child support is to require non-resident parents to contribute to the maintenance of their children.[89] Ordinary residence means 'residence for a settled purpose'.[90]

While each case is different and a decision has to take into account all of the person's circumstances and intentions, some of the most important factors to consider when deciding on habitual residence are:

- the person's normal centre of interest or connections to a particular place;
- the length, continuity and purpose of residence in the UK;
- the length and purpose of any absence from the UK; *and*
- the nature of the person's work.

Although the cases do not directly concern the jurisdiction of the CSA, caselaw gives the following guidelines.

- A person can habitually reside in more than one country or in none.[91]
- Habitual residence can continue during an absence from the UK.[92]
- A person cannot be habitually resident in the UK if s/he has never been here.
- A person who leaves the UK intending never to return to reside will stop being habitually resident in the UK on the day s/he leaves.[93] The intention never to return must be a settled intention and not to see how things will work out in that country.[94]
- A person held in a country against her/his will may not be habitually resident there, even after long residence (but see below).[95]
- A person unlawfully in the UK may be habitually resident.

If a non-resident parent is not habitually resident in the UK, the CSA still has jurisdiction to make a maintenance calculation if he is employed by the civil service, the armed forces, a UK-based company, a local authority or the NHS (including trusts).[96]

A person returning to the UK after an absence may have remained habitually resident in the UK during her/his absence.[97] When deciding whether a person has ceased to be habitually resident in the UK for child support purposes, the emphasis should be on the nature and degree of past and continuing connections with the UK, and any future intentions.[98]

Children

For a child, habitual residence depends on where the parent or person with parental responsibility lives. If there are two such people who live apart, one person should get the consent of the other to a change in the residence of the child, otherwise the child may be considered to have been abducted. If there is only one parent or person with parental responsibility, the child's residence changes with that person's.[99]

If a child has been abducted, s/he is considered still to be resident with the person with whom s/he was lawfully living, unless that person later agrees to the move.[100] Agreement might be assumed if that person does not act.[101] However, if a child is of sufficient maturity, her/his views may prevail in a child abduction case.[102]

10. The role of the courts

Note: you should seek legal advice about any court proceedings. The following is not intended to be a comprehensive guide to the law.

In general, the courts cannot make, vary or revive an order for periodic payments of child maintenance if the Child Support Agency (CSA) has jurisdiction to make a calculation.[103] The CSA has jurisdiction if a child is a qualifying child and all the relevant parties (child, person with care and non-resident parent) are habitually resident in the UK, even if the CSA *would not* in fact make a maintenance calculation.[104]

However, the courts do have the power to make certain orders in relation to maintenance – eg, consent orders, orders on special expenses or maintenance orders if the young person is no longer considered a child by the CSA. Courts can also vary orders in situations where an application to the CSA cannot be accepted (see p28). The courts cannot vary an order if a maintenance calculation has actually been made or an application to the CSA is possible.[105]

A **'consent order'** is an order made by the court with the written consent of both parties. It is legally binding and can be enforced like any other court order and cannot be changed by one party without the court's permission. Orders made before 3 March 2003 prevent an application to the CSA. Orders made on or after this date prevent an application for up to one year unless the parent with care applied for income support (IS) or income-based jobseeker's allowance (JSA) before July 2008. In these cases, the consent order would have been replaced by a CSA calculation.

Parents who want a consent order can agree with each other what should go in it, but should seek assistance from a family law solicitor to turn that agreement into a draft order to be submitted to the court. This is because a consent order must be made as part of a formal application to the court and must refer to the family law provisions under which it is made. The wording of the order is important – eg, a consent order containing an order to provide maintenance for the parent with care and undertakings to provide maintenance for the children may not prevent a calculation by the CSA.[106] However, in some circumstances both undertakings and orders as a whole can be interpreted as a whole without any distinction.[107]

From 3 March 2003, an application to the CSA, whether made by an adult or by a qualifying child in Scotland (see p35) cannot be accepted (ie, the CSA will refuse to make a calculation) if there is in force:[108]

- a written maintenance agreement made before 5 April 1993 (see p36);
- an order made before 3 March 2003; *or*
- an order made after 3 March 2003 that has been in force for less than a year.

The child support scheme does not change the court's powers in relation to other aspects of relationship breakdown – eg, contact and residence orders, maintenance for a spouse or civil partner and property division, or the court's jurisdiction to deal with parentage disputes (for which, see p17).

A CSA decision refusing to make a calculation can be appealed to the First-tier Tribunal (see Chapter 18). A court ruling that the court has no jurisdiction can be appealed or judicially reviewed (see p343).[109] No case should be outside the jurisdiction of both the CSA and the courts.

If a court order is cancelled because it was made by mistake when a CSA calculation was in force, any payments made under the order are treated as payments of child support maintenance.[110]

If a court order ceases to have effect because of a maintenance calculation (see p324), but the CSA revises the decision and decides no maintenance is payable as the previous decision was made in error, the court order revives and any child support maintenance already paid counts as paid under that order.[111]

If the Child Support Agency has jurisdiction

Until a calculation is made

Even if an application could be made to the CSA (but has not been), an agreement for periodical payments for a child (in Scotland, aliment) can be entered into.[112] However, any clause included which claims to prevent anyone from applying to the CSA is void.[113] Anyone who considers s/he would get a better deal from an agreement than under the maintenance calculation may wish to try to enter into one. If it is made into a consent order (registered agreement in Scotland) after 3 March 2003, it only stops a party to the agreement from voluntarily applying to the CSA for one year from the date it was made.[114]

The court can also use its powers to vary an existing agreement (whenever made) by *increasing* periodic child maintenance due under that agreement,[115] but not by *adding* a requirement to pay periodic child maintenance, unless the parties give their written consent.[116] A person who does not want to apply to the CSA, or who is waiting for a CSA decision, can go back to court to increase (or reduce) maintenance. This is especially important if it is unclear whether the CSA has jurisdiction (eg, if the non-resident parent may no longer be habitually resident in the UK), as it allows the level of child maintenance to be reconsidered quickly by the court and not left unchanged until any CSA decision is finally made.

Effect of a calculation on existing court orders and agreements

When a maintenance calculation is made, any existing court order or maintenance agreement either ceases to have effect or has effect in a modified form in relation to periodic payments.[117] The existence of a court order or agreement may mean that the amount of the calculation is 'phased in' (see p322). Before July 2008, if there was a pre-2003 court order, the CSA could make a maintenance calculation following an application from a parent with care on IS/income-based JSA or, if the order was made after 3 March 2003 and had been in force for more than one year, an application was made to the CSA. **Note:** since July 2008, parents with care on IS/income-based JSA are no longer treated as applying to the CSA.

These rules apply even to 'clean break' orders/agreements. There are conflicting court decisions on whether the child support scheme (or changes made to it) allows the court to re-open the capital/property part of such an order.[118] The arrangement may be self-adjusting to address the effect of any maintenance calculation which may be made. This could mean, for example, a legal charge on the transferred home so that the non-resident parent could recover any sums paid under the child support scheme from the transferred asset.[119] It could also mean an order that the non-resident parent top up any future calculation to a certain total amount of maintenance.[120]

If a child maintenance calculation is made for all of the children still covered by a court order, that order ceases to have effect on the effective date of the calculation – ie, two months and two days after an application to the CSA if the court order was made on or after 3 March 2003 and has been in force for at least a year (see p324).[121]

If the order includes provisions for additional maintenance, such as a child's education or training expenses or for a disabled child's special needs, only the elements for periodical maintenance for a qualifying child should cease to be in force. If the order is made solely for these additional expenses, it remains in force.[122] Parts of the order for matters other than periodic maintenance for the children named in the calculation (eg, other children or spousal maintenance) remain in force.[123]

In Scotland, if the CSA ceases to have power to make a calculation in respect of a child, the original order revives from the date it ceases to have that power.[124]

The same is not explicitly stated for England and Wales, which means that the original order does not revive when CSA involvement ceases. However, it could be argued that it should apply since the court order has not been revoked but simply ceased to have effect for the duration of a maintenance calculation. If the original order does not revive, a new agreement or consent order will need to be negotiated. If this is no longer possible, a parent may have no other option but to use the CSA to calculate and enforce child maintenance.

Maintenance agreements are unenforceable from the effective date (see p332) of the calculation.[125] Again, this only affects the part of the agreement to pay periodic maintenance for the children named in the calculation. The agreement remains unenforceable until the CSA no longer has the power to make a calculation.[126]

Notifications

As well as notifying the parties about the calculation (see p321), the CSA must notify the court in which the order was made or registered.[127] Similarly, if a court makes an order which affects, or is likely to affect, a maintenance calculation, the relevant officer of the court (see p54) must notify the CSA of this if s/he knows a calculation is in force.[128]

Additional maintenance

Even where the CSA has jurisdiction, the courts may still be able to make orders for children who are no longer qualifying children, and can still make orders for:[129]

- maintenance for stepchildren of the non-resident parent – ie, children who were accepted by him as members of his family when they used to live with him, but who are not qualifying children;[130]
- maintenance for expenses of a child's education or training for a trade, profession or vocation;[131]
- maintenance to meet expenses of a child's disability – a child counts as disabled if s/he is getting disability living allowance (DLA) or does not get DLA but is blind, deaf, without speech, or is substantially and permanently handicapped by illness, injury, mental disorder or congenital deformity.[132] The courts may even extend payments beyond the child's 19th birthday;[133]
- maintenance for a spouse or civil partner;
- maintenance from the person with care;[134] *and*
- child maintenance in excess of the maximum worked out under child support rules.[135]

The courts can backdate these maintenance orders to the effective date (see p332) of a maintenance calculation, if the application is made within six months of that date.[136] Backdating is at the court's discretion and can ensure that other maintenance is in step with child support.

The court's power to make a lump-sum award for a child will not be used to provide regular support for the child, but only to meet a need for a particular item of capital expenditure – eg, acquiring a home.[137]

If the Child Support Agency has no jurisdiction

If the CSA does not have jurisdiction (eg, because one parent or the qualifying child is not habitually resident in the UK), the court may make, vary or revive a maintenance order. In addition, if there is a pre-3 March 2003 court order for child maintenance, a post-3 March 2003 order which has been in effect for less than a year, or a pre-April 1993 agreement (see p36), the courts have the power to vary such orders and agreements.[138]

In the past, many courts used calculations under the 'old rules' CSA formula as a guide when setting levels of child maintenance. They may now decide to do so using the 'new rules' calculation, so parents seeking a variation of an order or agreement can ask their solicitors to prepare a calculation. The calculation currently used for new CSA applications is likely to be seen as 'highly' persuasive but not legally binding on courts (as the 'old rules' formula was in the past).[139] This principle has been emphasised in relation to the 'new rules' scheme in Scotland.[140] The courts also have the power to enforce orders and agreements, including those made by courts in other countries.[141]

If an application to the CSA by an adult cannot be made because of a pre-April 1993 written maintenance agreement (see p36), the courts cannot make or revive an order, except with the parties' consent (see p27).[142]

Although the courts can revoke child maintenance orders, this is not usually done simply to allow an application to be made to the CSA.[143] If revocation is being considered, advice should be sought on the likely child maintenance calculation.

In England and Wales, applications for maintenance are made to the family proceedings (magistrates') court, the county court or High Court. In Scotland, they are made to the sheriff court or Court of Session.

If a maintenance calculation is cancelled because one of the parties moves abroad (see p329), an application for maintenance can be made to the court. If the application is made within six months of the end of the maintenance, the order can begin from that date.[144]

Notes

1. The duty to maintain

1 s1(1) CSA 1991

2. Parent

2 s54 CSA 1991
3 s39 AA 1976; s39A(S)A 1978; s26(2) CSA 1991 Case A
4 s30 HF&EA 1990; s26(2) CSA 1991 Case B
5 s27(3) HF&EA 1990
6 ss27(1) and 29(1) HF&EA 1990
7 s29(2) HF&EA 1990
8 s28(2) HF&EA 1990; *Re CH (Contact: Parentage)* [1996] 1 FCR 768, [1996] 1 FLR 569, [1996] Fam Law 274
9 s28(6) HF&EA 1990
10 s28(3) HF&EA 1990
11 See *Re D (a child appearing by her guardian ad litem)* [2005] UKHL 33
12 Because such a clinic would not have a UK licence: *U v W (A-G intervening)* [1997] 3 WLR 739, [1997] 2 CMLR 431 [1997] 2 FLR 282
13 HF&EA 2008
14 s42 HF&EA 2008
15 s26 CSA 1991
16 Under ss55A or 56 Family Law Act 1986, Art 32 Matrimonial and Family Proceedings (Northern Ireland) Order or s7 LR(PC)(S)A 1986
17 s26(2) CSA 1991 Case E and s5(1) LR(PC)(S)A 1986
18 s26(2) CSA 1991 Cases A1 and A2
19 s26(2) CSA 1991 Case F(a)(i) in 'relevant proceedings' under s12(5) Civil Evidence Act 1968 or affiliation proceedings
20 s26(2) CSA 1991 Case F(a)(i) in 'relevant proceedings' under s8(5) Civil Evidence Act 1968 (Northern Ireland) or affiliation proceedings
21 s26(2) CSA 1991 Case F(a)(ii) in affiliation proceedings
22 s26(2) CSA 1991 Case A3
23 s26(2) CSA 1991 Case B
24 s26(2) CSA 1991 Case B1
25 *R v Secretary of State for Social Security ex parte Shirley West*, CO/568/1998, 30 April 1999, unreported
26 **EW** s67 A&CA 2002
S s40 A&C(S)A 2007
Both s54 CSA 1991 'parent'
27 **EW** CA 1989
S C(S)A 1995
28 **EW** s3(4) CA 1989
S s3(3) C(S)A 1995
29 Arts 3 and 4 CSA(JC)O ('old rules') and Arts 3 and 4 CSA(JC)O 2002 ('new rules'); Art 3(1)(s) and (t) C(AP)O

3. Qualifying child

30 s3(1) CSA 1991
31 s55(1) CSA 1991
32 The Child Support (Miscellaneous Amendments)(No.2) Regulations 2009, No.2909
33 s55(2) CSA 1991
34 s42 CMOPA 2008
35 Sch 1 para 2 CS(MCP) Regs; CCS/12604/1996
36 s55(1)(b) CSA 1991
37 Sch 1 para 3 CS(MCP) Regs; CCS/1258/2009 [2010] UKUT 39
38 See CPAG's *Welfare Benefits and Tax Credits Handbook* for more details.
39 Sch 1 para 4(1) CS(MCP) Regs
40 Sch 1 para 4(2) CS(MCP) Regs
41 s55(1)(c) CSA 1991; Sch 1 para 1 CS(MCP) Regs
42 Reg 5 The Child Benefit (General) Regulations 2006, No.223
43 Sch 1 paras 1(1)(b) and 6 CS(MCP) Regs; reg 5(c) Child Benefit (General) Regulations 2006, No.223

4. Person with care

44 s3(3) CSA 1991
45 *GR v CMEC (CSM)* [2011] UKUT 101 (AAC)
46 s3(5) CSA 1991
47 s3(3)(c) CSA 1991; reg 21 CS(MCP) Regs
48 Reg 21(1)(b) CS(MCP) Regs; s23(5) CA 1989
49 **Old rules** Reg 1(2) CS(MASC) Regs
New rules Reg 1(2) CS(MCSC) Regs, 'day-to-day care'
50 Reg 8(2) MCSC Regs
51 R(CS) 11/02; *GR v CMEC (CSM)* [2011] UKUT 101 (AAC)

52 Reg 13 CS(MCSC) Regs. This applies where a child is placed under s23(5) CA 1989.
53 Reg 12 CS(MCSC) Regs
54 DMG para 2034; reg 8(2) CS(MCSC) Regs
55 Reg 1(2) CS(MCSC) Regs, 'home'
56 s54 CSA 1991

5. **Non-resident parent**

57 s3 CSA 1991
58 Reg 8 CS(MCSC) Regs
59 *SL v CMEC* [2009] UKUT 270 (AAC)
60 s1(3) CSA 1991
61 *Santos v Santos* [1972] 2 WLR 889, [1972] All ER 246, CA
62 CCS/2318/1997
63 CSB/463/1986
64 R(SB) 4/83
65 R(SB) 35/85
66 CCS/2332/2006

6. **Relevant child**

67 Sch 1 para 10C CSA 1991
68 Reg 10 CS(MCSC) Regs
69 Reg 11 CS(MCSC) Regs

7. **Welfare of the child**

70 s2 CSA 1991
71 CCS/1037/1995
72 s2 CSA 1991
73 *Brookes v SSWP* [2010] EWCA 420
74 *R v Secretary of State for Social Security ex parte Biggin* [1995] 2 FCR 595, [1995] 1 FLR 851
75 *Brookes v SSWP* [2010] EWCA 420
76 *Brookes v SSWP* [2010] EWCA 420
77 *Smith v SSWP* [2006] UKHL 35

8. **Family**

78 Reg 1(2) CS(MCSC) Regs; the 'old rules' definition in Reg 1(2) CS(MASC) Regs is equivalent, but specifies children for whom the single person, or at least one member of the couple, has day-to day-care.
79 Reg 1(2) CS(MCSC) Regs
80 CFC/7/1992
81 CPA 2004
82 CPA 2004; CP(PSS&CS)(CP)O; CPA 2004 (RACP)O
83 *SSWP v M* [2006] UKHL 11

9. **Habitually resident in the UK**

84 s44(1) CSA 1991
85 CCS/2314/2008; [2009] UKUT 3 (AAC)
86 s44(2) CSA 1991
87 Sch 1 Interpretation Act 1978
88 *Nessa v Chief Adjudication Officer* [1998] 2 All ER 728, [1998] 2 FCR 461, [1998] 1 FLR 879, [1998] Fam Law 329, CA applying *Re J (A Minor) (Abduction: Custody Rights)* [1990] 2 AC 562, [1990] 3 WLR 492, [1990] 2 All ER 961, [1991] FCR 129, [1990] 2 FLR 442, [1991] Fam Law 57, HL; *Cruse v Chittum* [1974] 2 All ER 940; *Brokelmann v Barr* [1971] 3 All ER 29; *Langford Property Co. v Athanassoglou* [1948] 2 All ER 722
89 R(CS) 5/96; CCS/7207/1995
90 *Shah v Barnet LBC* [1983] 2 AC 309, [1983] 2 WLR 16, [1983] 1 All ER 226, HL
91 CCS/2314/2208; [2009] UKUT 3 (AAC)
92 *Lewis v Lewis* [1956] 1 WLR 200, [1956] 1 All ER 375
93 *Re J (A Minor) (Abduction: Custody Rights)* [1990] 2 AC 562, [1990] 3 WLR 492, [1990] 2 All ER 961, [1991] FCR 129, [1990] 2 FLR 442, [1991] Fam Law 57, HL
94 CCS/3574/2008; *H v CMEC* [2009] UKUT 84 (AAC)
95 *Shah v Barnet LBC* [1983] 2 AC 309, [1983] 2 WLR 16, [1983] 1 All ER 226, HL; *Re Mackenzie* [1940] 4 All ER 310
96 s44(2A) CSA 1991; reg 7A CS(MAJ) Regs
97 R(CS) 5/96
98 R(CS) 5/96
99 *Re J (A Minor) (Abduction: Custody Rights)* [1990] 2 AC 562, [1990] 3 WLR 492, [1990] 2 All ER 961, [1991] FCR 129, [1990] 2 FLR 442, [1991] Fam Law 57, HL
100 *Re M (Minors: Residence Order: Jurisdiction)* [1993] 1 FCR 718, [1993] 1 FLR 495, [1993] Fam Law 285, CA
101 *Re A (Minors: Abduction: Acquiescence)* [1992] 2 WLR 536, [1992] 1 All ER 929, [1992] 2 FCR 97, [1992] 2 FLR 14, [1992] Fam Law 381, CA
102 *Re M (A Minor) (Abduction: Child's Objections)* [1995] 1 FCR 170, [1994] 2 FLR 126, [1994] Fam Law 366, CA

10. **The role of the courts**

103 s8(1) and (3) CSA 1991. It has been decided that this lack of access to the courts is not inconsistent with art 6(1) European Convention on Human Rights – see *R v SSWP ex parte Kehoe* [2005] UKHL 48
104 s8(2) CSA 1991
105 s8(1) and (3A) CSA 1991
106 CCS/316/1998; CCS/8328/1995
107 CCS/316/1998

108 ss4(10) and 7(10) CSA 1991; reg 2 CS(APD) Regs
109 rs 8.1(2)-(6), 10.24 and 10.25 Family Proceedings Rules
110 Reg 8(2) CS(MAJ) Regs
111 Reg 8(1) CS(MAJ) Regs
112 s9(2) CSA 1991
113 s9(4) CSA 1991
114 ss4(10) and 7(10) CSA 1991; reg 2 CS(APD) Regs
115 s9(6) CSA 1991. Applies unless a calculation is made in an s6 case, when the agreement becomes unenforceable.
116 ss8(5) and 9(5) CSA 1991
117 s10(1) and (2) CSA 1991
118 *Crozier v Crozier* [1994] 1 FLR 126; *Mawson v Mawson* [1994] 2 FLR 985
119 *Smith v McInerney* [1994] 2 FLR 1077. However, an arrangement like this might be void under s9(4) CSA 1991 because it would 'restrict the right to apply for a maintenance assessment', though the commissioner in CCS/2318/1997 thought not.
120 See the arrangement in CCS/2318/1997
121 Reg 3(2) CS(MAJ) Regs
122 Reg 3(3) CS(MAJ) Regs
123 Reg 3(2) CS(MAJ) Regs
124 Reg 3(4) CS(MAJ) Regs
125 Reg 4 CS(MAJ) Regs
126 Reg 4(3) CS(MAJ) Regs
127 Reg 5(1) CS(MAJ) Regs
128 Reg 6 CS(MAJ) Regs
129 s8 CSA 1991
130 **EW** MCA 1973
S FL(S)A 1958
131 s8(7) CSA 1991
132 s8(8) and (9) CSA 1991
133 Sch 1 para 3(2)(b) CA 1989. In *C v F* [1997] 3 FCR 405 the court held that where s8(1) CSA 1991 applies, s8(8) CSA 1991 limits this power to children aged under 19. However, this seems to be wrong because the fact that the CSA 1991 only applies to those aged under 19 can hardly prevent an order being made under the CA 1989 for a person aged over 19.
134 s8(10) CSA 1991
135 s8(6) CSA 1991
136 s29(7) MCA 1973; s5(7) DPMCA 1978; Sch 1 para 3(7) CA 1989 as amended by Sch 3 paras 3, 5, and 10 CSPSSA 2000 respectively
137 Sch 1 CA 1989; *Phillips v Pearce* [1996] 2 FLR 230
138 ss8(3A) and 9(6) CSA 1991; *McGilchrist v McGilchrist* [1997] SCLR 800
139 *E v C* [1996] 1 FLR 472; *GW v RW* [2003] EWHC 611 (Fam), [2003] 2FLR 108
140 *Sutherland v Sutherland* [2004] GWD 20-436
141 MO(RE)A 1992
142 s8(3) and (3A) CSA 1991
143 s8(4) CSA 1991; *B v M (Child Support: Revocation of Order)* [1994] 1 FLR 342, [1994] 1 FCR 769, [1994] Fam Law 370
144 s29(7) MCA 1973; s5(7) DPMCA 1978; Sch 1 para 3(7) CA 1989

Chapter 3

Applications

This chapter covers:

1. Who can apply to the Child Support Agency

Any person with care (see p19) or non-resident parent (see p21) can apply to the Child Support Agency (CSA) for child support, unless barred by an existing maintenance arrangement (see p36).[1] In Scotland, children aged 12 or over can apply to the CSA for child maintenance, provided no application has been made or treated as made by the person with care or the non-resident parent.[2]

If there is more than one person with care of a qualifying child and at least one, but not all, of them has parental responsibility for the child, only those persons with parental responsibility can apply for maintenance.[3] For example, if a child is cared for partly by her/his mother who has parental responsibility and partly by her/his grandmother who does not have parental responsibility, only the mother can apply to the CSA. Parental responsibility has the same meaning as in other areas of law.[4] Parents who were married to each other when the child was born automatically have parental responsibility, which continues even if they divorce.[5] If the parents are not married, the mother can make a formal agreement giving the father parental responsibility.[6] In addition, in England and Wales, if a child's parent is married to (or in a civil partnership with) someone who is not the child's other parent (ie, a step-parent), the parent (or if both biological parents have parental responsibility, both parents) can make a parental responsibility agreement with the step-parent, giving her/him parental responsibility for the child.[7] The courts can also give parental responsibility to a person(s) (including a non-parent or step-parent) who apply/ies for it.[8] In England and Wales, if an unmarried father's name appears on a birth certificate on or after 1 December 2003, he has parental responsibility. In Scotland, this applies if an unmarried father jointly registers a birth on or after 4 May 2006. Unmarried fathers who signed a birth certificate before these dates cannot acquire parental responsibility without going through one of the other routes – ie, arranging a formal agreement with the mother or applying for a court order.

A female partner of the mother of a child conceived on or after 6 April 2009 automatically has parental responsibility if her details are included in the birth registration on or after 1 Septemeber 2009. If they are not civil partners, the non-birth parent must be present at the registration.

If a birth certificate was issued before these dates, a female partner or unmarried father can only aquire parental reponsibility through one of the other routes.

Written maintenance agreement

A written maintenance agreement for a child prevents an application being made for that child.[9] **'Maintenance agreement'** means a written agreement for making (or securing the making of) periodic payments of maintenance (or aliment in Scotland) to or for the benefit of a qualifying child.[10] An agreement only counts for this purpose if it:[11]

- was made before 5 April 1993. It does not need to have been in force before 5 April 1993, and it may have been varied after that date;
- is in writing. This can include an agreement made in correspondence headed 'without prejudice'.[12] While it need not be formal or prepared by lawyers, a spoken agreement is not enough, even if payments were made;[13]
- is an agreement. An offer that is never accepted in writing does not constitute a written agreement.[14] An undertaking made in court proceedings can be an agreement;[15]
- is made by the non-resident parent. The person with care does not have to be a party to the agreement. An agreement between the non-resident parent and the qualifying child does not count;[16]
- is for periodic payments. An agreement to pay mortgage interest charges and fuel bills as they fall due can count, even though the amounts to be paid are not written down and are not paid at regular intervals;[17]
- is for the benefit of the child(ren). The child(ren) need not be named in the agreement and an agreement to pay the mortgage for the home where they live counts as for the benefit of those children;[18]
- is 'in force'. The meaning of 'in force' is not defined in the legislation. An agreement to pay only a nominal amount counts.[19] An agreed change to the arrangement may mean the original agreement is no longer in force.

A maintenance agreement that does not meet these conditions cannot prevent any of the parties or any other person from applying for a maintenance calculation for a child who is the subject of the agreement.

Maintenance order

A maintenance order made by a court before 3 March 2003 prevents an application for the child(ren) concerned.[20] If the order was made after 3 March 2003 and has been in force for less than one year, it also prevents an application.[21] A **'court order'** only counts for this purpose if it:

- requires the making (or securing the making) of periodic payments of maintenance (or aliment in Scotland) to or for the benefit of a qualifying child.[22] Orders for payment of the costs of education or training of the child, or because the child is disabled, or to 'top up' maintenance all count as maintenance orders.[23] Such top-up orders may be made in addition to any liability worked out by the CSA. For details of these, see p30. Because an order only prevents an *application* to the CSA, an order made *after* the application does not stop the CSA making a calculation ('old rules' assessment) or revising or enforcing an existing one. A court order directing capital payments (ie, not periodic payments) does not count as an order.[24] The wording of the order is important – eg, a consent order with provision for maintenance of the parent with care and undertakings to provide maintenance for the children may not prevent an application;[25]
- is in force. The meaning of 'in force' is not defined in the legislation, and applicants may wish to seek advice as this can be a complex issue. The fact that parties may have waived their rights under an order or agreed to make different arrangements does not affect the status of the order itself.[26] It may be arguable that an order is 'in force' only if it is still relevant – eg, the non-resident parent against whom the order was made is still a non-resident parent.[27] An order is in force if some undertakings or arrangements, such as for residence of the child, are still in effect, even though there is no further liability for maintenance payments[28] or the liability for child maintenance under the order has not yet begun.[29] If a court decides that it has no power to vary or enforce an order, an application can be made to the CSA;[30]
- is made under one of certain legal provisions (see Appendix 3).[31] The order usually states the legal provision under which it was made.

Note: the CSA treats a Minute of Agreement (a form of legal agreement in Scotland) in relation to child maintenance in the same way as maintenance orders made by a court.

An application is not prevented by the existence of a type of order known as a 'Segal order'. This is one that makes specific provision for an award of maintenance to reduce at a later date because a child support calculation is made.[32]

A decision by the CSA that a written maintenance agreement or maintenance order prevents an application being made can be challenged by seeking a revision or appeal.[33]

Summary of who can apply to the Child Support Agency

Is there a pre-1993 written maintenance agreement?	→ Yes →	There cannot be an application by a person with care or non-resident parent, or by a child in Scotland.
↓ No ↓		
Is there a consent order or, in Scotland, a registered minute of agreement?	→ Yes →	There cannot be an application by a person with care or non-resident parent, or by a child in Scotland.
↓ No ↓		
Applications may be made to the CSA by a person with care or non-resident parent, and by a child in Scotland.*		

* Alternatively, the parties may make an informal arrangement or draw up a written agreement that may be formalised into a consent order or, in Scotland, registered in the Court of Session.

A person who cannot apply to the CSA because of an agreement/order can:

- ask the court to vary or enforce the amount of maintenance under the order or agreement (see p28);
- where there is an agreement, agree with the other party to end the maintenance part of the agreement or possibly even unilaterally break the agreement so it is no longer in force;
- where there is an order, ask the court to revoke it so that a CSA application can be made (but see p31);

People with court orders or agreements can use the CSA's collection and enforcement service for amounts due under those orders/agreements, but this facility is currently only available if child support maintenance is also being collected (see p401).

2. Communicating with the Child Support Agency

The first point of contact with the Child Support Agency (CSA) will usually be the Child Support Agency Centre (CSAC) which applies to the parent's area. You can write to or telephone the CSAC. It is advisable to keep copies of letters and make a note of the date, time and content of telephone calls. Telephone numbers and addresses are in Appendix 1.

Dates of postage

Under the 'new rules', if the CSA posts a document to you, it will usually be treated as sent on the day of posting.[34] If you send a document to the CSA, it is treated as being sent on the day the CSA receives it.

Under the 'old rules', documents are treated as being sent to you by the CSA on the second day after the day of posting (unless this day is a Sunday or bank holiday).[35] If more than one document is required to be sent and they are posted on different days, or they need to be sent to different people and this is done on different days, they are treated as having been posted on the latest of the dates concerned (and so sent on the second day after this).[36] If you send a document to the CSA, it is treated as being sent on the day the CSA receives it, but in some cases the CSA can treat documents as having been sent earlier if there was unavoidable delay.[37]

It is important to bear these rules in mind, especially where time limits are concerned.

Representatives

Anyone dealing with the CSA can appoint a representative to act on her/his behalf.[38] If the person is not legally qualified, authorisation for her/him to act needs to be confirmed in writing, although if the client is with the representative during a telephone call, s/he can authorise the representative verbally for the duration of the call. An authorised or legally qualified representative can complete forms, receive documents and supply information. A person with care may also choose to have payments of child support made to a representative.

A representative who understands the law and/or is experienced in dealing with the CSA may find it easier to get a quick response and clearer information from the CSA. S/he can also help you to understand your rights and what options are open to you. For information about how to find independent advice, see Appendix 4.

Representatives with legal authority to act for a CSA client (eg, someone with power of attorney, a receiver or a mental health appointee/Scottish mental health custodian) are able to act for the client in every respect, as if they were the client.

The legal help scheme (advice and assistance scheme in Scotland) can cover child support cases. A client does not have to pay back any money out of sums recovered if the money is for maintenance. **Note:** the government has announced its intention to remove welfare benefits and some other areas of public law (but not child support) from the scope of the legal help and representation scheme in England and Wales.[39]

What to expect when you contact the Child Support Agency

If you contact the CSA by telephone, you should be able to get through. The CSA's Business Plan states that it aims to answer telephone calls within one minute.[40] If you write to the CSA, it aims to reply to your letter, resolving the issue or agreeing what will happen next, within three weeks.[41] If you have difficulty in contacting the CSA or obtaining a response within a reasonable time, you should complain. For more information about standards of service and how to complain, see Chapter 20.

The CSA has staff in local offices who are able to conduct interviews, face to face if necessary. A parent or the CSA may request a face-to-face interview. A parent's request should be considered seriously if the CSA agrees that it is the most effective way to make contact or if all other ways of progressing the case have been exhausted.

The CSA should also meet any accessibility or language needs of the applicant – eg, if English is not her/his first language or if s/he has difficulty using the telephone.

---

3. How to apply to the Child Support Agency

Before applying to the Child Support Agency (CSA), parents can seek information from the Child Maintenance Options service to help them make arrangements for child maintenance (see p6).

If there is no assessment under the 'old rules' in force, a new application to the CSA will always be treated under the 'new rules'.

However, there may be some cases outstanding in which an 'old rules' application has not yet been decided (see p46).

Making the application

Applications under the 'new rules' can be made orally or in writing.[42] In some cases, the CSA may direct that the application must be in writing, in which case a form may be provided. If the CSA issues a form or requests information, this must be provided within 14 days unless the CSA is satisfied that there was unavoidable delay.[43] Applications in 'old rules' cases had to be made on a maintenance application form.[44]

The wide provisions for 'new rules' applications mean they can be made over the phone, in person, or on an application form sent to the applicant, downloaded from the CSA website, or online via the CSA website. Note that downloaded forms must be printed, signed and returned by post to the Child Support Agency Centre (CSAC). Signing the form confirms that the information given is correct. This is important since there are penalties for knowingly providing false information (see p56).

If the form is completed over the phone, it will be sent to the applicant to be checked. The application forms used are slightly different depending on whether it is a person with care, child in Scotland or non-resident parent who is applying. There is no time limit to return the form – if it is not returned, there is no effective application (see p42). If the non-resident parent wishes to apply at a point when the parent with care has already applied, he will be directed to complete a maintenance enquiry form rather than a maintenance application form.

If the CSA requests further information or reissues the application form, the information requested should be provided within 14 days.[45] If this does not occur and the CSA is not satisfied that there was unavoidable delay, this may bring forward the date of an effective application (see p42), or where no information is received, cancel the application (see p43).

The application for child maintenance form

This form may be used to gather information to pursue child support maintenance. It includes sections on:[46]

- personal details – name, address, national insurance (NI) number, date of birth, phone numbers and the best time to phone, armed forces service number;
- child(ren) being applied for – name, date of birth, NI number if over 16, who gets child benefit for the child, maintenance arrangements, shared care arrangements (or local authority care);
- if the parent/person with care is applying, whether the non-resident parent knows s/he is being named as the parent;
- child's education (if aged between 16 and 19) – school/college, course, type of course, hours a week;
- local authority details (if the child is being cared for by it);
- non-resident parent details – name (other names), address or last known address and when lived there, NI number, date of birth, employment details, phone numbers, whether the parent is the father or mother of the child;
- if the parent/person with care is applying, whether the non-resident parent knows where the applicant lives;
- payment details – whether maintenance is to be collected by the CSA, preferred method and frequency of payment to the person with care, bank/building society details;
- representative details – name, address, phone numbers and the best time to phone. If the representative is not a solicitor, an attorney under a power of attorney, Scottish mental health custodian, mental health appointee or receiver, the applicant must sign the client authority declaration on the form;
- further information – a blank page to add other relevant information.

Any relevant court order or written maintenance agreement (original documents) and the representative's authority (eg, power of attorney document) should be sent with the form and will be returned.

Signing the form confirms that all the information given is correct and complete. This is important since there are penalties for knowingly providing false information (see p56).

Applications with more than one non-resident parent

An applicant can choose from which non-resident parent she wishes to apply for child support maintenance. Thus, an application may be made for maintenance from some, but not all, non-resident parents.

When to apply

There are no time limits for making an application to the CSA. One can be made as soon as someone becomes a person with care or a non-resident parent, or at any later date. However, liability to pay child support usually runs from the date the non-resident parent is notified and this cannot occur until an effective application (see below) is received by the CSA. Parents with care should be aware that the non-resident parent's liability will not start until after an application to the CSA is made, even if the Child Maintenance and Enforcement Commission has given them information about setting up voluntary arrangements. This means that delaying the application may delay the start of liability. There is no provision for applying in advance – eg, before the birth of a baby.

Refusal to accept an application

The CSA may decide not to accept an application – eg, because it believes an existing maintenance agreement prevents an application or because it does not have jurisdiction. If this happens, the would-be applicant should write to the CSA explaining why she believes she is entitled to apply and asking for a written CSA decision. If a written decision is issued, she can try to appeal this to the First-tier Tribunal (see Chapter 18). If this does not work or if the CSA refuses to respond in writing, a complaint (see p441) and/or judicial review (see p343) should be considered.

Effective applications

Only an effective application allows the CSA to make a maintenance calculation. An application is effective if it is made by phone or in writing according to the CSA's direction.[47] All applicants must provide information to enable the non-resident parent to be identified and traced, and the amount of child maintenance payable by him to be calculated and recovered (see Chapter 4).[48] If an applicant does not supply the information, the CSA may refuse to process the application (see p44).

The CSA may ask the applicant to provide further information or evidence to make an effective application; this may be done over the phone or in writing. The

CSA may issue an application for child maintenance form to the applicant. If a form has been previously sent to the applicant, another may be issued. If the information or evidence is received within 14 days of the request, the application takes effect from the date the earlier application was treated as received by the CSA.[49]

Once an effective application has been made, any other relevant person (non-resident parent or person with care) is informed of the application either by phone or in writing.[50] The relevant person is asked to provide information to enable the maintenance calculation to be made. This can be done over the phone or the person may be asked to complete a form. This form is known as a child maintenance enquiry form. Non-resident parents are informed of the effective date of the calculation and rules on default maintenance decisions at the same time as they are informed of the application.[51] The CSA cannot refuse to deal with an effective application, even if it considers that processing it would be against the welfare of the children concerned.[52] If it refuses to accept an application, see p42.

For delays in dealing with applications, including where the non-resident parent is not co-operating, see p318.

Amending the application

An application can be amended at any time before a maintenance calculation is made, but not to take into account a change which occurs after the effective date (see p332).[53] For details of this and of changes after the effective date, see p319.

4. Withdrawing or cancelling an application

Request to cease acting by the applicant

An applicant may request that the Child Support Agency (CSA) ceases to act on her/his application for child support.

The CSA cannot refuse this request.[54] The request can be made at any time, whether or not a calculation (or 'old rules' assessment) has been made. For more information on cancelling calculations, see p327.

Requests to cease acting can be made by phone or in writing to the CSA office processing the application, or to the Child Support Agency Centre if it is not clear which office has responsibility.

An application is withdrawn or cancelled by the Child Support Agency

The CSA may withdraw or cancel an application before a calculation is made if:

- the applicant does not provide information; *or*
- the qualifying child dies.

An applicant does not provide information

An application can be withdrawn or cancelled by the CSA if insufficient co-operation is received from the person with care.[55] If a person with care does not provide sufficient information, the CSA can close the case, and the person with care will not receive child support.

Cases can be cancelled only where no 'effective application' has been made (see p42). If there is an effective application, a decision must be made and notified, even if it is a decision not to make a calculation (see p320). If an effective application is cancelled against the wishes of the applicant, advice should be sought.

The qualifying child dies

If a qualifying child dies before a calculation has been made, the application is treated as if it had never been made with respect to that child.[56] If the child was the only child named in the application, any calculation ceases to have effect. Otherwise, any calculation is superseded because of a change of circumstances (see p350).

5. **Multiple applications**

If more than one application for child maintenance is made in respect of the same qualifying child, only one can go ahead.[57] Only an effective application (see p42) counts.[58] If a calculation has not yet been made, the applications are either treated as a single application or one is selected to be considered (see p45).[59] For applications made after a calculation has been made, see p46. For applications, some of which were made before 3 March 2003 (including where there is an existing 'old rules' assessment), see p46.

The decision on whose application goes ahead only determines which applicant has the power to withdraw an application or to request a cancellation of any resulting calculation. It does not affect the outcome of any calculation or have any effect on who is liable to pay any resulting child support. Information included on any competing applications can be taken into account by the Child Support Agency (CSA).

If an application with priority is made by an applicant in Northern Ireland, the CSA there (see p317) deals with the application.[60]

Before a calculation has been made

The rules below apply unless a request is received to cease acting in relation to all but one of the applications.[61] See p46 if there is an existing application to which the 'old rules' apply.

Same person applies more than once

If a person applies and then applies again in the same circumstances before a calculation is made, both applications are treated as if they were the same application.[62]

If more than one application is made by the same child in Scotland and child support has not yet been calculated, it counts as a single application as long as it is made in respect of the same non-resident parent and person with care.[63]

More than one applicant

The CSA decides which application to deal with as follows.[64]

Applicant	*Priority application*
Only one person with care	
Person with care and non-resident parent.	Person with care.
Person with care or non-resident parent applies following an application by a child in Scotland.	Person with care/non-resident parent.
More than one qualifying child applies in relation to the same person with care and non-resident parent.	Elder or eldest child.
Both parents are non-resident parents and both apply.	Treated as a single application.
More than one person with care	
More than one person with care with parental responsibility (or, in Scotland, parental rights) applies, and one person is treated as a non-resident parent for calculation purposes (see p267).	Person with care not treated as a non-resident parent.
More than one person with care applies and none of the applicants has parental responsibility/rights, or all do and either none can be treated as a non-resident parent, or even after one of the applicants has been treated as a non-resident parent under the calculation, there is still more than one application.	The principal provider of day-to-day care (see p20) in the following order of priority: – the person who gets child benefit for the child(ren); – the person who, in the CSA's opinion, is the principal provider of day-to-day care.

If the applications are treated as a single one under these rules, that application covers all the children named in either, and the effective date (see p332) is set by the application which was made first.[65]

If more than one person with care applies and each application refers to different children, the CSA treats each application as covering all the children mentioned in all the applications.[66] If the same person with care does not provide the principal day-to-day care for all the qualifying children mentioned in the applications, separate calculations are made in relation to each person with care.[67]

Once the calculation is in force

A calculation in force in respect of a person with care does not prevent the CSA making a new calculation because she becomes a parent with care. Once a calculation is in force, any subsequent application for child support made in the same circumstances in respect of the same person with care, non-resident parent and qualifying child(ren) will not be dealt with.[68] It may, however, be treated as a request for a supersession (see p350) or, depending on the circumstances and information contained in the application, as a request for a variation (see Chapter 6).[69]

Applications for additional children

If there is an existing calculation and there is an application for an additional child(ren) of the same non-resident parent cared for by the same person with care, this is a relevant change of circumstances and a new calculation is made which supersedes the existing calculation.

One application before 3 March 2003, and one on or after 3 March 2003

If no assessment is in force

If no assessment is in force, there are transitional provisions for determining how to proceed if there is an existing application under the 'old rules' and a further application is made under the 'new rules' in respect of the same person with care, non-resident parent or qualifying child.[70] These determine whether the applications are treated as a single application or only one is to proceed. The applications do not have to be received at exactly the same time. If one application is not determined by the time the other is received, the following rules apply.[71]

Applicant	*Priority application*
Person with care applies under the 'old rules' and then under the 'new rules'.	Treated as a single application.
Non-resident parent applies under the 'old rules' and 'new rules' in relation to the same qualifying child.	Treated as a single application.

Child in Scotland applies under the 'old rules' and then under the 'new rules'.	Treated as a single application.
Person with care applies under the 'old rules' or under the 'new rules' and the non-resident parent applies under either the 'old' or 'new' rules.	Person with care's application has priority.
Child in Scotland applies under the 'old rules' and a 'new rules' application is made by either the person with care or non-resident parent.	Person with care or non-resident parent's application has priority.
More than one child in Scotland applies under either the 'old' or 'new' rules in relation to the same person with care and non-resident parent.	The application of the elder or eldest child has priority.
More than one person with care with parental responsibility applies, one under the 'old rules', the other under the 'new rules', and one person is treated as a non-resident parent for calculation/assessment purposes.	The application of the person with care not treated as a non-resident parent has priority.
More than one person with care applies (as above) but none has parental responsibility, or they all do and either none can be treated as a non-resident parent or, even after one of the applicants has been treated as a non-resident parent for the calculation/assessment, there is still more than one application.	The application of the principal provider of day-to-day care in the following order of priority: the person who gets child benefit for the child(ren), otherwise the person who, in the CSA's opinion, is the principal provider of day-to-day care.

Whether the case is proceeded with as a 'new rules' or 'old rules' case then depends on the effective date of the application with priority, or whether a maintenance assessment was previously in force in relation to the same person with care, qualifying child(ren) and non-resident parent. If an assessment was in force within the previous 13 weeks, the application is treated as an application for a child support maintenance assessment regardless of whether the effective date of the application is before or after 3 March 2003.[72]

A parent with care may cancel her application for a maintenance assessment and reapply after more than 13 weeks in order to have child support calculated under the 'new rules' instead. If, within 13 weeks of the cancellation of the 'old rules' assessment, the non-resident applies, his application will be dealt with under the 'old rules'. However, if the parent with care's 'new rules' application arrives before the non-resident parent's application has been assessed, the parent with care's application takes precedence under the above rules for multiple applications. The result will be to ignore the non-resident parent's application and treat the situation as a single 'new rules' application.

However, this is not a reason for the CSA to delay processing the non-resident parent's application under the 'old rules' before the parent with care's application is received. He may be entitled to compensation for the difference between his 'old rules' and 'new rules' liability (if the latter is more) for the period between the effective date of his application and the effective date of the parent with care's 'new rules' application.[73]

If a maintenance assessment is in force

If a child support assessment is already in force and an application is made or treated as made under the 'new rules' in relation to the same person with care, qualifying child(ren) and non-resident parent, the calculation application will not proceed.[74]

If a child support assessment is already in force and a new application is made for an additional child(ren) of the same non-resident parent cared for by the same person with care, this will not trigger conversion to the 'new rules', even if the additional child did not become a qualifying child until after 3 March 2003. It is treated as a relevant change of circumstances and a new assessment, which supersedes the existing assessment, is made under the 'old rules'.[75] It is only if the maintenance assessment has ceased, and a new application is made after at least 13 weeks, that it can be dealt with under the 'new rules' (see Chapter 7).

If a new application is made in relation to other people, it is likely to trigger conversion (see below).

New applications that trigger conversion of an existing case

Existing cases will continue to be dealt with under the 'old rules', unless there is a related decision that causes a conversion to the 'new rules'.[76] In many cases, this will be triggered by a new application from another person that involves either the non-resident parent or parent with care in the existing assessment. In addition, parents who form new partnerships with people on benefit, or partners who each have maintenance but move onto benefit, may be affected.

When an existing case converts to the 'new rules', transitional phasing may apply. For more information on when conversion is triggered, and on transitional phasing, see Chapter 7.

Notes

1. **Who can apply to the Child Support Agency**
   1 ss4(1) and 6(1) CSA 1991
   2 s7(1) CSA 1991
   3 ss5(1) and 54 CSA 1991
   4 As in CA 1989 and C(S)A 1995
   5 s3(1) CA 1989; C(S)A 1995
   6 s4(1)(b) CA 1989; C(S)A 1995
   7 s4A CA 1989, as amended by s75 CPA 2004
   8 ss4(1)(a), 4A(1)(b) and 5(6) CA 1989; C(S)A 1989
   9 ss4(10)(a) and 7(10) CSA 1991
   10 s9(1) CSA 1991
   11 ss4(10)(a) and 7(10) CSA 1991
   12 CCS/12767/1996
   13 CCS/12797/1996
   14 CCS/11052/1995
   15 CCS/8328/1995
   16 CCS/2908/1995
   17 CCS/8328/1995
   18 CCS/8328/1995
   19 CCS/12849/1996
   20 ss4(10)(a) and 7(10)(a) CSA 1991; reg 2 CS(APD) Regs
   21 ss4(10)(aa) and 7(10)(b) CSA 1991; reg 2 CS(APD) Regs
   22 s8(11) CSA 1991
   23 Otherwise s8(6)-(8) CSA 1991 would be unnecessary.
   24 CCS/4741/1995, upheld by the Court of Appeal in *AMS v CSO* [1998] 1 FLR 955
   25 CCS/316/1998
   26 CCS/4049/2007
   27 CCS/4049/2007. This and other cases have disagreed with the conclusions reached in R(CS) 4/96. The Court of Appeal in *Kirkley v Secretary of State for Social Security* ruling on an application for leave to appeal aginst R(CS) 4/96 also disagreed with the reasoning. Authorities differ as to whether changes in child(ren)'s residence (eg, from the parent with care to the non-resident parent) mean that an order ceases to have effect (CCS/3127/1995) or not (CCS/2567/1998). In the latter case, the commissioner suggested that it would instead be grounds to seek to vary the court order.
   28 CCS/4741/1995
   29 CCS/11364/1995
   30 Reg 9 CS(MAJ) Regs
   31 s8(11) CSA 1991; reg 2 CS(MAJ) Regs. Provisions repealed before 1 April 1980 are not listed.
   32 CCS/4047/2007, citing *Dorney-Kingdom v Dorney-Kingdom* [2000] 2 FLR 855
   33 R(CS)3/97

2. **Communicating with the Child Support Agency**
   34 Reg 2 CS(MCP) Regs
   35 Reg 1(6) CS(MAP) Regs
   36 Reg 1(8) CS(MAP) Regs
   37 Reg 1(7) CS(MAP) Regs
   38 Reg 22 CS(MCP) Regs; reg 53 CS(MAP) Regs
   39 Ministry of Justice, *Proposals for the Reform of Legal Aid in England and Wales,* Cm 7967, 2010
   40 CSA Business Plan 2008/09
   41 CSA Business Plan 2008/09

3. **How to apply to the Child Support Agency**
   42 Reg 3(1) CS(MCP) Regs
   43 Regs 3 and 4 CS(MCP) Regs
   44 Reg 2(1) CS(MAP) Regs
   45 Reg 3(4) and (5) CS(MCP) Regs
   46 CSA maintenance application forms, CSF 001, CSF 003 and CSF 004
   47 Reg 3(2) CS(MCP) Regs
   48 ss4(4), 6(7) and 7(5) CSA 1991
   49 Reg 3(4) CS(MCP) Regs
   50 Reg 5(1) CS(MCP) Regs
   51 Reg 3(2) CS(MCP) Regs
   52 R(CS) 4/96; CCS/14/1994; CCS/17/1994; CCS/16535/1996
   53 Reg 3(6-7) CS(MCP) Regs

4. **Withdrawing or cancelling an application**
   54 ss4(6) and 6(5) CSA 1991
   55 *How is Child Maintenance Worked Out?* CSL 303 (new rules)
   56 Reg 6 CS(MCP) Regs

5. **Multiple applications**
   57 s5(2) CSA 1991
   58 Sch 2 paras 1, 2 and 3 CS(MCP) Regs

59 s5(2) CSA 1991; reg 4 and Sch 2 CS(MCP) Regs
60 Sch 1 para 6 CS(NIRA) Regs
61 Reg 4(2) CS(MCP) Regs
62 Sch 2 para 1(1) CS(MCP) Regs
63 Sch 2 para 2 CS(MCP) Regs
64 Sch 2 para 3(1) CS(MCP) Regs
65 Reg 4(3) CS(MCP) Regs
66 Sch 2 para 3(12) CS(MCP) Regs
67 Sch 2 para 3(13) CS(MCP) Regs
68 Sch 2 para 4 CS(MCP) Regs
69 *DB v CMEC* [2010] UKUT 356 (AAC)
70 Sch 3 CS(MCP) Regs
71 CCS/3868/2004
72 Reg 28(1) CS(TP) Regs
73 R(CS) 1/06
74 Sch 3 para 4 CS(MCP) Regs
75 Sch 2 para 6(1) CS(MAP) Regs
76 Reg 3 CSPSSA (Comm12)O; reg 15 CS(TP) Regs

Chapter 4

Information

This chapter covers:

1. Information-seeking powers

The Child Support Agency (CSA) has wide powers to obtain information from (among others) parents, employers, local authorities and HM Revenue and Customs (the Revenue).[1] The CSA can require information to be provided in order to make any child support decision.[2]

In addition, the CSA can appoint inspectors who have extensive powers to obtain information (see p70). Staff at the regional Child Support Agency Centres (see p6) ask for information by telephone; those at local offices also conduct face-to-face enquiries.

Jobcentre Plus may also seek information in order to identify a parent with care (see Chapter 19).

Although, legally, the powers to obtain information are now given to the Child Maintenance Enforcement Commision, it is the CSA that currently exercises them (see Chapter 1).

When the Child Support Agency can request information

All applicants are under a duty to provide information to identify and trace a non-resident parent, and calculate, collect or recover maintenance.[3] The information may also be required to verify whether information already gathered is correct.

After an application has been made, the non-resident parent will be contacted, usually by phone, to notify him of the application and gather information. In some cases, a face-to-face interview may be arranged or, if there is no phone number, a form called the 'child maintenance enquiry' is issued. The child maintenance enquiry form can be used to gather the information needed to calculate and collect maintenance (see p59). In 'old rules' cases, the original maintenance enquiry form issued sets the effective date of the maintenance assessment (see p332). A further form will not usually be issued, and as much additional information as possible will be collected by telephone.

Information can be requested in order to:[4]

- determine an application for child support and any issues which arise under that application – eg, to establish which parent receives child benefit and thus who is the parent with care in shared care cases;
- make any other decisions under child support law – eg, to contact an employer in order to determine the income of the non-resident parent;
- enable the collection and enforcement of child support.

See p53 for who can be required to give information and p56 for the effects of failing to provide it.

Information the Child Support Agency can ask for

The CSA can request information on anything that is needed to determine a child support application, to make any other child support decisions, to calculate the amount of child support, and to decide how child support should be collected and enforced.[5] Issues on which information may be requested include:

- the habitual residence of the person with care, the non-resident parent and any child covered by the application to determine jurisdiction (including if the individual works abroad);
- the name and address of the person with care and non-resident parent, their marital or civil partnership status, and the relationship of the person with care to any child covered by the application;
- the name, address and date of birth of any child covered by the application, the child's marital or civil partnership status and any education the child is undergoing;
- if there is more than one person with care:
  - who has parental responsibility (or parental rights in Scotland) for any qualifying child; *and*
  - how much time is spent by that child with each person with care;
- if parentage is disputed, whether someone can be assumed to be a parent (see p15) and, if not, who is the parent of a child;
- the name and address of any current or recent employer of a non-resident parent and the gross earnings from any such employment;
- if the non-resident parent is self-employed, the address, trading name, gross receipts and expenses, any other outgoings of the trade or business and taxable profits;
- any other income of the non-resident parent;

- how much is paid or payable under a court maintenance order or maintenance agreement;
- details of anyone who lives in the same household as the non-resident parent, their relationship to him and to each other, and the date of birth of any child of those people;
- details and statements of any account in the name of the non-resident parent, including bank and building society accounts;
- whether a person counts as a qualifying child for the purposes of child support (see p18);
- information needed to decide whether a calculation should end (see p336).

In 'old rules' cases, additional information may be needed and can be required in order to work out child support liability, including, for example, housing costs, and the employment and income of other people who live with the non-resident parent or parent with care.

Who has to give information to the Child Support Agency

Information can be required from the people listed below. It can only be required from a person who has that information or evidence in her/his possession or can reasonably be expected to acquire it and provide it as soon as reasonably practicable.[6] Information or evidence can also be given to the CSA when there is no obligation to provide it – eg, from a relative, neighbour, GP or landlord. However, any such voluntary disclosure of information or evidence made without the permission of the person(s) concerned could break professional codes of practice, civil contracts or the Data Protection Act 1984. Information supplied to the CSA can give rise to a libel action.[7] For information on disclosure by the CSA, see p72.

The relevant persons

The person with care,[8] a non-resident parent[9] (or a parent treated as non-resident for the purposes of the calculation) and, in Scotland, a child applicant, must provide the information (except information enabling the non-resident parent to be identified[10]) listed on p52 if requested.

If information is not provided by a person with care or child applicant in Scotland, an application may be treated as withdrawn (see p43). If a non-resident parent does not supply requested information, a default maintenance decision (or, in 'old rules' cases, an interim maintenance decision) may be made.

It is a criminal offence to fail to provide information, or knowingly provide false information. It is also an offence for a non-resident parent to fail to notify a change of address within seven days of that change.[11]

Someone who denies parentage of a child

Someone who denies parentage of a child named in a maintenance application is required to give information:[12]

- to decide whether or not all the relevant persons are habitually resident in the UK and, therefore, whether the CSA has jurisdiction to make a calculation; *or*
- to identify a non-resident parent.

This means, for example, that if the CSA only wants to identify a person as the non-resident parent, employment details would not normally be necessary and so should not be requested until parentage is established.

Employers

The current or recent employer of the non-resident parent can be required to give information needed for the puposes listed on p52.[13]

The same rules apply if the employer is the Crown – eg, a government department.[14]

In 'old rules' cases, the parent with care's employer may also be required to provide information which is needed in order to make a maintenance assessment.

Companies or partnerships

A company or partnership for whom a non-resident parent has, or has had, a contract for goods or services can be required to provide information for the purposes listed on p52.[15]

This means, for example, that a self-employed IT consultant could be traced through companies for which he provides a service and his income investigated.

Accountants

The person who acts as the non-resident parent's accountant, or who has done so in the past, can be required to give information for the purposes listed on p52.[16]

Court officials

The following court officials can be required to give information.[17] In **England and Wales:**

- the senior district judge of the High Court Family Division or, at a district registry, the district judge;
- the district judge of a county court, or the chief clerk or other officer who may be acting on her/his behalf;[18]
- the justice's chief executive for a magistrates' court.

In **Scotland:**

- the deputy principal clerk of the Court of Session;
- the sheriff clerk of a sheriff court.

Court officials can be required to give information for the purposes listed on p52 to:

- identify how much is payable under a court maintenance order;
- collect child support maintenance or maintenance under a court order;
- identify any proceedings about a court maintenance order;
- decide whether there is in force either a pre-April 1993 maintenance agreement (see p36) or a maintenance order made after 3 March 2003 which has been in force for a year; *or*
- decide, if there is more than one person with care, who has parental responsibility for the qualifying child.

Crown employees

Some Crown employees can be required to give information for the puposes listed on p52.[19]

The Driver and Vehicle Licensing Agency

In addition to requiring information needed to trace the non-resident parent, the CSA can request information from the Driver and Vehicle Licensing Agency needed to collect and enforce maintenance payments.[20]

Government benefit departments

Any Department for Work and Pensions (DWP) agency or anyone providing services to the DWP may give information held for benefits purposes to the CSA.[21]

Local authorities

Local authorities can be required to give information to the CSA for the purposes listed on p52.[22]

This applies only to the local authority for the area in which either the person with care or the non-resident parent lives or used to live.

This means the CSA may require a local authority to give information concerning housing benefit or council tax benefit – eg, the parent's bank account details if s/he pays by direct debit.[23]

HM Revenue and Customs

The Revenue can be required to disclose information or evidence for the purposes listed on p52.[24] Information provided can be used for any function related to child support. If the parent is self-employed, this also includes details of the taxable profits, gross receipts and expenses. Any information disclosed must not go any further than authorised CSA staff, unless it is about civil or criminal proceedings under the Child Support Act 1991. However, where information is obtained under the Social Security Administration Act 1992, no such restriction applies. Information may also be obtained under the Tax Credits Act 2002.[25] It is unlawful for the Revenue to give the CSA any other information.[26]

In its 2006–2009 Operational Improvement Plan, the CSA stated that, in the future, it would work more closely with the Revenue to trace non-resident parents and make more use of information held by the Revenue to locate non-resident parents who owe maintenance.[27]

Credit reference agencies

The CSA can require information from credit reference agencies for the purposes listed on p52.[28]

Banks and building societies

The CSA can require 'deposit takers' (eg, a bank or building society) to provide information for the purposes listed on p52.[29]

Gas and electricity providers

Gas and electricity suppliers to the non-resident parent must disclose information if and when requested by the CSA.[30]

When information must be supplied

If information is requested from the person who made the maintenance application, in order to make an effective application, this information must be supplied if it is in her/his possession or as soon as s/he can reasonably be expected to acquire it.[31]

Information requested from all other parties must be supplied as soon as it is reasonably practicable.[32]

The CSA can allow information to be provided by a later date if it is satisfied that the delay was unavoidable.

See p39 for when documents are treated as sent and received.

Failing to provide information and providing false information

If a person fails to provide information, s/he will face a range of consequences:

- the application may not be processed (see p43);
- if he is a non-resident parent, a default maintenance calculation may be made;
- a criminal fine of £1,000 may be imposed.[33]

A person charged with an offence of failing to provide information may be able to avoid conviction if there is a good reason why the information cannot be provided.[34] However, a non-resident parent who fails to return a child maintenance enquiry form or provide information may have both a default maintenance decision and a fine imposed. This also means that if a non-resident parent makes an application and the parent with care fails to provide information, she can be fined, though this would be extremely rare.

If the person knowingly provides false information, or allows it to be provided, this is also a criminal offence.[35] The CSA can go to court and a fine of up to £1,000 can be imposed. This is paid to the court, not to the CSA.

The CSA must notify the person that it is a criminal offence to refuse to supply, or knowingly supply, false information.[36] All forms and requests issued contain this notification to ensure the fine may be pursued.

If a parent fails to give information, the CSA may ask another person for that information – eg, a parent's employer or accountant. As they are required to give information, the criminal sanctions apply. This gives the CSA greater powers to investigate and pursue other sources of information. The CSA had been criticised in the past for failing to seek information from other sources when the parent did not return a form despite reminders.[37] The legislation has now been amended to allow the CSA to obtain details of self-employed earnings from the Revenue (see p55).

Change of address

The non-resident parent has a duty to notify the CSA if and when he changes his address. This must be done within seven days of the change.[38]

If the non-resident parent fails to report a change of address, he may have committed a criminal offence and could be fined up to £1,000.[39]

Disputing the information required

If the CSA requires information:

- not relevant to the reason for the request;
- of a very different kind from the examples given in the Regulations;
- from a person who cannot be required to give it; *or*
- despite having sufficient information to make a full calculation,

the request should be queried. If the CSA insists, a challenge should be considered (see p343).

If a person in this situation refuses to give information, in order to avoid a penalty s/he should explain that decision, preferably in writing. A complaint could also be made (see p441).

2. **Contacting the non-resident parent**

If the Child Support Agency (CSA) has the non-resident parent's phone number and knows that he is aware of the existence of the child, it will contact him by phone. If the telephone number is not known, a child maintenance enquiry form may be issued (see p59). The date of contact with the non-resident parent is the date liability for child maintenance usually starts – this is known as the 'effective date' (see p332). In some cases, there have been long delays in setting the effective date and the person with care could be owed compensation. [40]

Tracing the non-resident parent

The CSA can use its information-seeking powers to identify and trace the non-resident parent.[41] CSA staff can use the various departments listed on pp54–56 to do so.

Finding a reliable address

The fact that an address is a non-resident parent's current address does not have to be established beyond all reasonable doubt (see p324) for the CSA to decide that it is a sufficiently reliable address for it to use. If the Department for Work and Pensions computer gives the non-resident parent's address and it is the same as that of the person with care, this is not considered reliable.

Information from the person with care

If the person with care has not given an address for the non-resident parent, she is contacted by telephone (or, if this is not possible, by letter) and, if she does not know the address, she is asked to give any information that could help trace the non-resident parent. This could include:

- middle name(s) and any other names by which he may be known;
- other addresses at which he may have lived;
- his place of work and any previous employers;
- the name and address of his accountant;
- any benefit claims made; *and*
- if he has a car, the registration or make, model, colour and other details.

In addition, a face-to-face interview may be arranged. At this, the person with care may be asked to confirm a potential address or provide further information to allow a trace to be made. A parent may be asked to give a recent photograph of the non-resident parent where DNA testing may be involved. She is asked to bring any relevant documents, such as a marriage certificate or expired passport, and is warned that the CSA may contact friends and relatives with whom the non-resident parent may be living. The CSA must preserve confidentiality where this occurs and should not disclose the CSA's interest.

At the interview, the person with care could be asked other detailed questions – eg, whether the non-resident parent ever lived with the person with care. Contact with these parents by the CSA is only likely where additional trace action is required – eg, to obtain details of the non-resident parent's car or where parentage is disputed.

Initial contact with the non-resident parent

Once an effective application (see p42) has been made, the CSA should give notice of that to any person(s) with care, the non-resident parent and any person treated as a non-resident parent, other than the applicant, as soon as reasonably practical.[42] The CSA may attempt to phone a non-resident parent to notify him of the application and gather information. If it is not possible to phone and the non-resident parent is aware of the child, a child maintenance enquiry form may be issued. If the parent is unaware of the child or not named on the birth certificate, the CSA will try to arrange a face-to-face interview.

There are special rules for young non-resident parents (see p60).

During the initial phone call, the non-resident parent may be asked questions to confirm the CSA's jurisdiction and whether he accepts parentage. He may also be asked to confirm any information needed to make a maintenance calculation.

The non-resident parent should be warned that a default maintenance decision may be issued if he fails to provide sufficient information to make a calculation. At various stages, he will be given the opportunity to provide more information and be given a time limit of at least seven days in which to provide it.

The child maintenance enquiry form

The CSA intends that all, or most, of the information needed to work out child support will be provided or collected over the phone. This means a child maintenance enquiry form will only be issued when the non-resident parent requests it or if he has not co-operated. If the non-resident parent does not know he is an alleged non-resident parent, a face-to-face interview should be arranged.

In simple terms, a form cannot be issued unless:

- a 'confident' address for the non-resident parent is established (see p58);
- an alleged non-resident parent is aware that he is considered to be the father of the child;
- an alleged non-resident parent is at least 16 years old and, if 16–19 years old, is not treated as a child. If the non-resident parent is 16–19 years old, an interview will take place (see p60).

When a child maintenance enquiry form is issued, the parent is usually allowed seven to 14 days to return it, depending on what stage of the procedure has been reached. The CSA may only allow seven days or phone the parent after this period of time to check when the information will be returned.

Even if a form is issued, the non-resident parent may instead choose to phone with the information.

Any notice sent to a non-resident parent must tell him the effective date (see p332) of any calculation to be made, and inform him about default maintenance decisions (see p320).[43]

The maintenance enquiry form asks for information on:

- personal details – name, address, other names used, phone number (work and mobile), national insurance (NI) number, date of birth, best contact times;
- whether he accepts paternity for all, or some, of the qualifying children named;
- any income support, income-based jobseeker's allowance, income-related employment and support allowance or pension credit being claimed by or for him;
- student details, if appropriate – ie, college, course, qualification, full- or part-time status (evidence is requested);
- child(ren) who live with him – ie, date of birth, NI number (if appropriate), who gets child benefit for the child (evidence is requested);
- details of any shared care, average per week and any other special arrangements;
- employment details – title, employer (name, address and phone number), start and end dates (if appropriate);
- income details – frequency of pay, gross pay, bonus, expenses (pay slips are requested);
- self-assessment form or tax calculation notice if the parent is self-employed;
- tax credits in payment;
- other income – eg, pension;
- other payments made to a personal or private pension;
- collection details – when the CSA wants to collect, bank details such as account number and sort code. Direct debit is the preferred method but standing order, deductions from wages, Transcash or bank giro credit are also available;
- representative details, name address, phone number and best contact times (signed authorisation is needed in certain circumstances).

The form may also ask for further information. The non-resident parent will have to sign a declaration, and parents are informed that failure to provide the information requested or knowingly to provide false information is a criminal offence (see p56).

Information given can be amended at any time before a calculation is made, but not about changes after the effective date.[44] For changes after the effective date, supersession should be sought.

If the form is returned fully completed and no indication is made that paternity is denied, the CSA assumes that the alleged non-resident parent accepts paternity. If a parent disputes that he is non-resident and maintains that he has day-to-day care of the child (see p20), this is not a proper reason for refusing to return the form (this decision was made in reference to the 'old rules' maintenance enquiry form but would equally apply under the 'new rules').[45]

Young non-resident parents

It is understood that a face-to-face interview will be arranged with a young non-resident parent – ie, one under 16 years of age (or aged 16 or over but under 19 and treated as a child – see p18). He will be asked to confirm parentage, but no calculation can be made until he ceases to be treated as a child. An adult must be present at the interview. This is because, although there is no calculation for under-16-year-olds (and some 16–19-year-olds), a paternity statement is needed.

3. Parentage investigations

Where parentage is denied, a child support maintenance application cannot be decided unless the Child Support Agency (CSA) can assume parentage (see p15). In the vast majority of cases, it will be a non-resident father who is disputing paternity. Paternity is also investigated where there is some doubt about it – eg, more than one possible father is named.

Paternity investigations can take place before or after the calculation. For example, an alleged non-resident parent may deny paternity on the initial phone contact or on a child maintenance enquiry form (see p59). The dispute can be about one or all of the qualifying children. The CSA can proceed with the calculation, or collection in post-calculation cases, for those children for whom paternity is accepted or assumed while investigations are taking place for others. Once a calculation has been made, the person named as the non-resident parent of the child will have to pay child support until he provides conclusive evidence that he is not the parent.[46]

In pre-calculation cases, if a presumption of parentage cannot be made, the CSA cannot make a calculation until paternity has been resolved. For details of when paternity may be assumed, see p15. The CSA will carry out investigations to determine whether paternity may be assumed or established. This may involve interviewing both the non-resident parent and person with care. It may also include interviewing the other parent if s/he is not a person with care. The CSA may seek a DNA test or court action to establish paternity (although this is unlikely, given the presumptions and consequences of failure to take DNA tests). Court action may also be pursued by the person with care or alleged non-resident parent at any time.

In post-calculation cases, the non-resident parent may dispute paternity and seek a revision. If the decision is not revised, the non-resident parent may have to apply to court for a declaration/declarator of parentage. A decision to refuse to revise can be appealed, but paternity can only ultimately be established by the court.

If the non-resident parent disputes parentage, he will be asked to provide evidence.[47] It is not sufficient in post-calculation cases simply to deny paternity; evidence must be given to raise doubt – eg, the parent with care was having another relationship when the child was conceived. In all cases, documentary evidence is preferred. If the evidence is a previous negative DNA test or declaration/declarator of parentage, this will be sufficient proof.[48] The calculation will be cancelled and any payments made refunded. The person with care may be re-interviewed to identify another alleged non-resident parent.

If a doubt is raised, the parent with care will be contacted by phone or in a face-to-face interview for her comments on the non-resident parent's evidence. If the parent with care:

- accepts that there may be doubt about paternity, a DNA test may be offered;
- disputes the non-resident parent's evidence, the decision will not be revised. The non-resident parent will be advised to obtain a DNA test or declaration/declarator of non-parentage; the CSA will not offer a DNA test in this case.[49] He will also be informed of his right to appeal to a court.

Interviews where parentage is disputed

Interviews can be carried out by phone or in person. If paternity is denied after initial contact or the issue of a child maintenance enquiry form, the parent with care may be interviewed in order to establish the case to be put to the alleged non-resident parent. In other cases, sufficient information may already be available to contact the non-resident parent. However, both parties are interviewed before offering DNA tests (see p67) and, even if the parent with care has already been interviewed or paternity is assumed, she may be re-interviewed to see how she responds to the alleged non-resident parent's version of events. If the parent with care has already filled in a paternity statement, she will only be re-interviewed if the alleged non-resident parent introduces new evidence.

In the case of a face-to-face interview, if the interviewee does not want to come to the local office, s/he can be interviewed at home or at a friend's or relative's house.

It is understood that, if the parent with care or alleged non-resident parent is under 16 (or under 19 and treated as a child), her/his parent or guardian must consent to the case progressing. The young person must have a face-to-face interview in the presence of a parent or guardian. A calculation is not made for a non-resident parent under 16 (or aged 16 and over but under 19 and treated as a child – see p18), but a paternity statement is required for future use. Additional information may be sought about an alleged non-resident parent aged between 16 and 19 to determine whether or not he should be treated as a child – eg, details of his current education/training and, in 'old rules' cases only, his marital/civil partnership status.

It is not compulsory to attend any interview, but see p53 for who can be required to provide what information.

Interview with an alleged non-resident parent

When the non-resident parent is unaware of the qualifying child, a face-to-face interview may be arranged to notify him of the application.

If paternity is denied, the alleged non-resident parent will be asked if he has evidence that he is not the parent. There is no guidance on whether oral or documentary evidence should be required. The alleged non-resident parent may ask for further time to obtain documentary evidence; seven days are usually allowed.

If documentary evidence cannot be supplied, the person with care may be interviewed to gather her evidence. If no evidence can be provided to assume paternity, the case may progress to DNA testing.

The CSA could ask a non-resident parent:

- whether he was in the country at any time between the date of conception and the child's birth;
- whether he had sex with the mother and, if so, over what period of time;
- where conception was assisted, was he in agreement with the treatment;
- how long the relationship lasted and whether he lived with the woman as husband and wife;
- whether or not he has had any contact with the child(ren);
- his reasons for thinking that he is not the father; *and*
- any other information which might support his view.

These questions are not an exhaustive list, so others may also be asked. The non-resident parent need only answer such questions if he denies paternity and the information is needed to decide if he is the father.

The alleged non-resident parent is sent information about disputing parentage and the reduced-cost DNA test (see p65) before the interview. At the interview, the possibility of DNA testing will be explained and the alleged non-resident parent's agreement sought.[50] The alleged non-resident parent will be told that he will be responsible for the costs of the tests for the parent with care and child(ren), as well as his own, if he is found to be the father. He will also be told that if he is found not to be the father, he will be able to reclaim from the CSA any costs he has incurred. If the alleged non-resident parent states that he cannot afford to pay for the test, the CSA will pay. However, the fee will have to be paid back if the test shows that he is the parent of the child.[51]

If the alleged non-resident parent accepts paternity, a child maintenance form is completed at the interview.

Interviewing officers should take notes and details of the interview , including any statement made by the non-resident parent, should be recorded.

If the non-resident parent does not attend an interview, the interviewing officer attempts to arrange another and, if he does not attend the second one, the officer could consider a home visit or court action at this point.

Interview with a parent with care

If someone has been named as the parent of a qualifying child and denies it, the CSA contacts the parent with care to tell her of this and explain the procedures which follow. The interview can be conducted by phone or, if the parent does not want to be interviewed in this way, in the office or at her home.

The parent with care is asked if she has documentary evidence from which the CSA could assume parentage – eg, birth or marriage certificate.[52] She is also questioned about her relationship with the alleged non-resident parent at the time of conception to establish whether he could be the father.

If no evidence can be provided to assume paternity, the parent with care is asked if she is willing to take a DNA test (see p65).

The CSA will enquire about the alleged relationship and the circumstances of conception and birth. The parent with care is likely to be asked personal questions. For example, the officer may ask about:

- the place the child was born and whether the pregnancy was full term;
- whether the man is named as the child's father on the birth certificate;
- the man's reaction to the pregnancy;
- whether she and the alleged non-resident parent ever lived together and, if so, when and where;
- whether she considered them to be a couple at the time the child was conceived;
- whether the alleged non-resident parent has ever acknowledged the child;
- whether the alleged non-resident parent has ever paid any maintenance;
- whether there is, or has been, any contact with his family;
- whether she has any letters or cards acknowledging the child, or witnesses to her association with the alleged non-resident parent;
- whether the child's conception was assisted and, if so, whether the man was in agreement with the treatment and gave notice of this;
- whether she has any photographs of him; *and*
- whether she is willing to give evidence in court.

If a person considers the question(s) inappropriate, she should ask the interviewer about the point of them. If the interviewer insists, the person with care could ask to end the interview to consider whether to give the information requested. She can ask the interviewer to write down the questions and the reason for them. If, at the interview or later, she refuses to answer any of the questions, she should indicate that she has given all the information that is necessary to trace and identify the father.

The parent with care may also be asked to make a parentage statement. She can refuse to sign this and the refusal will form part of the evidence, along with any reasons she gives. The parent may ask for a copy of the parentage statement or reasons for failing to sign the statement. This statement is added to the report of the interview and can be used in court proceedings (see p67).

Interviewing a person with care who is not the mother

If both parents are non-resident and an alleged non-resident parent continues to deny paternity after an interview, the person with care may be interviewed. The questions depend on the person with care's relationship with the alleged parents

– eg, a mother or sister is likely to know the length of the relationship between the parents. She is asked for the addresses of both parents, and any letters or cards from them. She is also asked why she is looking after the child(ren), whether there is any documentation regarding the care arrangements and whether she gives her consent for the child(ren) in her care to undergo a DNA test (see below) if she has parental responsibility.

DNA testing

DNA testing involves taking a cell sample from the parent with care, alleged non-resident parent and qualifying child. The test establishes the genetic fingerprint of the individual and is virtually conclusive. The test is usually done by taking a cheek cell sample, which is gathered from the inside of the mouth using a swab. It is possible for blood to be taken for the DNA test instead, but all parties must use the same method. If young children are involved, a cheek cell sample will usually be preferred. The use of cheek cell samples means that a fear of needles could not be used as a reason not to take the test.

DNA testing is used in cases where parentage cannot be presumed and the parties involved give consent. In cases where the CSA has applied to court for a declaration/declarator of parentage, the court may order DNA testing.

The CSA has special arrangements with a private testing agency called Cellmark and reduced testing rates may apply.[53] There are special rules that apply if an alleged non-resident parent wishes to arrange his own test.

Consent

If there is a dispute about parentage, both the parent with care and the alleged non-resident parent are asked to agree to a DNA test. Written consent must be obtained before a test can be carried out. If an alleged non-resident parent refuses to consent to a DNA test, the CSA can presume that he is the parent.[54] If the qualifying child is under 16, the parent or guardian must give consent.

Refusal to take the test will have consequences.

- If the parent accepts DNA testing for herself, but refuses her consent for the child, a court can direct DNA testing if it is in the best interests of the child, but it cannot force the child to take the test.
- An alleged non-resident parent may be assumed to be the parent (see p15).[55]
- If a non-resident parent already assumed to be the parent refuses to take a test, the CSA will not revise the calculation.
- If an applicant refuses consent for herself and/or a qualifying child, the case may be closed.
- There is no guidance on when a parent or guardian of a child applicant in Scotland refuses consent, but Department for Work and Pensions policy indicates that action may be taken to get a declarator of parentage.

The reason for any refusal must be explored. As the DNA test now usually involves taking a cheek cell sample, any objections on medical or religious grounds which applied to blood tests may no longer be viable.

If the alleged non-resident parent agrees to the test, but fails to attend the appointment, parentage will be assumed unless there are good reasons – eg, he was in hospital, did not receive test notification or was ill.

Paying for the DNA test

The CSA offers discounted tests to alleged non-resident parents who are prepared to take it in advance. These are known as voluntary cases. The cost varies depending on the number of people tested. In the latest edition of the CSA's leaflet on disputed parentage and DNA testing, the fee for testing three people in voluntary cases is £215.69.[56] The alleged non-resident parent must agree to the results being passed to the CSA.

In cases where the court directs the DNA test to be taken, the non-discounted fee is charged. Rates vary according to the number of people tested. In the latest edition of the disputed parentage leaflet, the non-discounted cost of a test for three people is £281.05.

The CSA website is updated more regularly than the leaflet and, at the time of writing, states that the discounted fee is now £187.20 and the non-discounted fee is £252.[57]

If the alleged non-resident parent is found not to be the parent, a full refund of the cost of the test is made.[58]

If the alleged non-resident parent says he cannot afford to pay for the test in advance, the CSA may pay for the test initially if the alleged non-resident parent agrees to accept the results and to repay the fee should the test show that he is the father. If the alleged non-resident parent still refuses to take the DNA test, parentage may be assumed (see p15).

The CSA can recover the costs of the test from the alleged non-resident parent if the test does not exclude him from being the parent and:[59]

- he does not now deny that he is the parent; *or*
- a court has now made a declaration that he is a parent (in Scotland, a declarator of parentage).

Private testing

An alleged non-resident parent may arrange the test himself either through Cellmark or another firm. In the meantime, the CSA may still assume parentage if the CSA test has been refused.[60] In this case, there would be no discount or CSA non-discounted rate offered. Prices vary depending on which firm is used but are likely to be at least £400. This fee may not be refunded if the test proves negative.

The test must be carried out by an approved agency and proper security measures must be in place, otherwise even where the test is negative, the CSA and court may not accept the result.

Tests must involve the mother; a test with only the alleged non-resident parent and the qualifying child will not be accepted. The CSA will not provide the address of the parent with care to the alleged non-resident parent or the independent testing company. If the parent with care does not consent to a private test, no action can be taken against her.

DNA test results

Once the DNA-testing company has received all the samples, the test usually takes 10 days. The results are sent by post to the parent with care, the alleged non-resident parent and the CSA. The results are confidential and will not be given over the phone.[61]

If the alleged non-resident parent is shown to be the parent, he will also be sent notification by the CSA. The CSA will also contact the non-resident parent to gather any additional information needed, or a child maintenance enquiry form may be issued. (If a form has been issued earlier, the date of liability for child maintenance is the date of the first contact – see p332.) If the alleged non-resident parent still does not accept paternity, he will have to take court proceedings to obtain a declaration/declarator of non-parentage. The CSA may make a calculation or refuse to revise because a positive DNA test is grounds to assume parentage.

If the DNA tests confirm that the person who took the test as the alleged non-resident parent is not the father, action is taken to confirm that the identity of the person tested was the alleged non-resident parent. If this is not the case, the CSA will pass the case to the fraud team if the alleged non-resident parent sent someone else, or will pursue further tracing if the wrong person has been traced. If the identity is confirmed, the parent with care may be re-interviewed about any other possible non-resident parent.[62]

Court proceedings

When all possible action and investigations have been completed, a CSA supervisor decides whether to apply to a court for a declaration of parentage (in Scotland, declarator of parentage).[63] It is understood that court action is rare, as there are other ways by which parentage can be assumed. Examples of situations where court action may be possible include:

- if a DNA test is inconclusive;
- cases involving fertility treatment where the alleged non-resident parent denies he gave notice of consent to the treatment;
- in post-calculation cases, where the parent with care disputes the non-resident parent's non-conclusive evidence. In this instance, the non-resident parent must apply to court (the CSA may not be involved in this action but may be informed of the outcome).

If the CSA decides not to take court action, the person with care may initiate proceedings.[64] The person with care or non-resident parent may raise court proceedings at any time.

The CSA *or* the person with care can apply to court for a declaration/declarator of parentage. However, if the CSA is willing to do so, the person with care should normally not also apply, because she would probably have to pay her own legal costs (and those of the alleged non-resident parent) if she loses (see below). If the CSA suspends the case, but the person with care wants to go to court herself, she should consider taking legal advice.

Only the courts have the power to order blood tests (including DNA tests – see p65) in any civil proceedings in which paternity is an issue.[65] If convinced that blood testing would be against the child's interests, the court should not order it.[66] A court can direct that blood tests be used to ascertain whether or not a party is excluded from being a parent of the child, but cannot force anyone to give a blood sample. It can, however, overrule a child's lack of consent if it believes it is in the child's interests.[67] However, the court may draw its own adverse inferences if a person fails to comply, depending on all the circumstances of the case.[68] Courts can only order DNA or blood testing if a party applies for it and agrees to pay. However, if that party wins the case, the court will usually order the losing party to pay costs, which can include the costs of any test. In Scotland, if an alleged non-resident parent applies for a declarator of non-parentage or illegitimacy and the CSA does not defend the action, no expenses can be awarded against the CSA.[69]

Outcome of the court proceedings

Once a declaration/declarator of parentage is issued, if no calculation has been made, the CSA telephones the non-resident parent to gather the information needed to make a calculation.[70]

If the court finds that the person is not the parent, the parent with care is approached to establish whether a different alleged non-resident parent can be named.[71] Unless the parent can name an alternate alleged non-resident parent, the case may be closed.

The court can order any party to pay some, or all, of the legal costs of another party. Usually, the losing party is ordered to pay the other party's costs. However, an order for costs cannot normally be made against a party who is legally aided. In addition to the costs of any test, the CSA usually asks the court to order the losing party to pay towards its own presentation costs – eg, a solicitor's fees and witnesses' costs.

4. Further investigations

The Child Support Agency (CSA) may make further enquiries when considering an application, revision or supersession. In practice, the CSA normally makes no further investigation if:

- parentage is accepted; *and*
- information is provided to make a calculation; *and*
- any documents requested are provided – eg, copy of maintenance agreement, pay slips or tax calculation notice.

The CSA decision maker is not under a duty to investigate. Decision makers should have regard to the nature of an application rather than whether it is in the correct legal form. For example, if a parent with care provides information to the CSA, a decision maker may treat it as an application for a variation if the information and circumstances justify that, even if the application did not expressly ask for a variation.[72] Decision makers may be under a duty to obtain information that is available to them but not to the applicant.[73] Decision makers may also be under a duty to investigate if there is a contradiction in the evidence (see below).

Even if one parent challenges the details provided by the other, the CSA may be reluctant to make any further enquiries unless the parent can provide evidence to trigger a revision/supersession. Enquiries are normally made by telephone, if possible.

The need for evidence

Corroboration of evidence (ie, other evidence to support what the CSA already has) should not be requested unless the evidence the CSA has is self-contradictory, improbable or contradicted by other evidence.[74] For example, if a self-employed parent says s/he has not worked for six months, this is normally accepted without any written evidence.

Evidence can include documentary, written and oral information.

Verifying information

Verification of housing costs (in 'old rules' cases) and earnings is routinely sought by the CSA. However, if every effort to obtain verification of earnings has failed, the amounts provided are accepted as long as they are reasonable.

Verification of earnings from a non-resident parent's employer can only be requested if the employee cannot or does not provide it (see p54).

Self-employed earnings are usually taken from the self-assessment return to HM Revenue and Customs (the Revenue), or from a tax calculation notice. If not supplied, attempts will be made to obtain the information through phone calls, accountants, companies or partnerships with or for whom the parent works, a face-to-face interview, an inspector's visit, or a request to the Revenue for self-assessment details where all other means to obtain the information have failed.

Verification of benefits, other income and costs (the latter where needed to make an 'old rules' assessment) is only sought where the amounts appear to be disproportionate or there is another reason to doubt them.

It is an offence for a person who is required to provide information to fail to do so (see p54).

When the Child Support Agency does not investigate

In some cases, the CSA fails to investigate to the satisfaction of one party. This situation does not usually arise until the calculation is made because the parent with care is only then notified of the non-resident parent's income (see p321). If, at any stage, a person believes that the CSA ought to make more enquiries, the CSA should be asked to do so. The most effective way is to phone the CSA explaining all the information the person has, asking what enquiries have already been made and suggesting further enquiries. Reference should be made to the CSA's power to require information (see p51) and use an inspector to conduct investigations (see below). If the CSA refuses to say what steps have been taken or to make further enquiries, judicial review may be possible (see p343). The First-tier Tribunal can make enquiries as soon as an appeal is made. It has more powers than the CSA and it may be easier to persuade it to use them.

A person who is dissatisfied with CSA enquiries can also make her/his own enquiries and pass the information to the CSA. For example, a person with care applying for a court order for spousal or civil partner maintenance (see p30) may obtain information about the non-resident parent's income.

The inspectors

The CSA can appoint inspectors to obtain information required.[75] The inspector must have a certificate of appointment, which must be produced when entering premises.[76]

If an office in Great Britain needs to appoint an inspector in Northern Ireland, or *vice versa,* an inspector can be appointed in the other territory.[77]

Powers of inspectors

Inspectors have the power to enter premises (except those used only as a home),[78] to make enquiries and to inspect documents.[79] Premises can include vehicles, aircraft, moveable structures and offshore installations.[80] The power to enter premises does not include any power to enter by force. Premises include ones where: [81]

- the non-resident parent is, or has been, employed;
- the non-resident parent carries out, or has carried out, a trade;

- there is information held by someone whom the inspector has reasonable grounds for suspecting has information about the non-resident parent acquired in the course of her/his own trade, profession, vocation or business.

An inspector can question any person aged 18 or over found on the premises s/he has entered[82] and request all such information and documents s/he might reasonably require from:[83]

- an occupier of the premises;
- an employer or employee working there;
- anyone else whose work or business is based at those premises;
- an employee or agent of any of the above.

An inspector can enter Crown premises in order to obtain information as long as the Queen is not in residence. Crown employees or anyone carrying out Crown functions on the premises can be questioned and asked for information in the same way as anyone else.[84]

No person is required to give any evidence or answer any question that might incriminate her/him or her/his spouse or civil partner.[85] Deliberately delaying or obstructing an inspector carrying out her/his duties is an offence. Failing or refusing to answer a question or to provide evidence requested is also an offence, unless there is a good reason for not doing so.[86] The maximum fine is £1,000.[87]

A solicitor is entitled to claim privilege as regards information about a client's confidential affairs and can refuse to give information. Also, the CSA has given assurances that the powers of inspectors will not be used in relation to other representatives, except if information is required from an employer about an employee.

5. Duty to disclose changes

There is no general duty to volunteer information about any change of circumstances to the Child Support Agency (CSA), except if the non-resident parent changes his address.[88]

However, a person with care has a duty to tell the CSA if she believes that a calculation has ceased to have effect because:[89]

- the person with care, non-resident parent or qualifying child has died;
- the person with care, non-resident parent or qualifying child is no longer within CSA jurisdiction – ie, habitually resident in the UK or working for a relevant employer and treated as habitually resident (see p26);
- the non-resident parent is no longer a non-resident parent of the child or, if there is more than one, all the children named in the calculation – eg, because the child has been adopted;
- a child no longer counts as a child, or as a qualifying child (see p18); *or*

- she has stopped being a person with care in relation to the child or, if there is more than one, all the children named in the calculation.

The person with care is required to give the reasons for her belief in writing. She may be required to give further information to allow a decision to be made.

The person with care is not required to inform the CSA until the change has taken place. There is no duty to disclose information to the CSA except in the circumstances described above and where the CSA has the right to request the information – eg, a non-resident parent does not have to disclose a change of income. This is different from social security benefits, where there is a continuing duty to disclose any relevant change of circumstances.

For the consequences of failing to disclose information when required, see p56.

6. Disclosure of information by the Child Support Agency

In the course of its investigations, the Child Support Agency (CSA) collects information and evidence about people affected by maintenance applications. Some forms of disclosure are part of the CSA's duties, such as giving information to courts, the First-tier Tribunal, the Department for Work and Pensions (DWP) and local authorities. The non-resident parent, person with care and a child applicant in Scotland must be given details of how the calculation has been worked out (see p321).

The CSA may disclose information given to it by one party (see below) to a maintenance calculation to another party to explain:[90]

- why an application for child maintenance or for revision or supersession has been rejected; *or*
- why an application cannot proceed or why a calculation will not be made; *or*
- why a calculation is cancelled or ceases to have effect; *or*
- how a calculation has been worked out; *or*
- why a decision has been made not to arrange for, or to stop, collection of child maintenance; *or*
- why a particular method of enforcement has been used; *or*
- why enforcement methods have not been used or enforcement has ceased.

For the purposes of the CSA's disclosure of information, the **'parties'** are the person with care, the non-resident parent and a qualifying child. If one of these people has died, a person appointed to represent that person or a personal representative handling a revision/supersession or appeal is also a party.[91] Any request for the above information must be made in writing to the CSA, giving reasons, but the CSA can provide the information without a request.[92]

The CSA must not disclose a person's address or other information which could reasonably be expected to lead to that person being located. This disclosure can only be made when the person concerned has given written permission. (This may not apply if a case is appealed – see Chapter 18.[93]) Also, the CSA must not disclose information which could reasonably be expected to lead to the identification of any person other than a person with care, non-resident parent, person treated as non-resident or a qualifying child.[94]

The CSA can disclose any information it has (but not the address or anything which could lead to the location of any person other than the recipient of the information or the office dealing with the request, unless that person has given written consent[95]) to the First-tier Tribunal, court and, in 'new rules' cases, to anyone with a right of appeal, if it is for proceedings under the child support or benefits legislation.[96]

In practice, in a child support appeal, CSA papers are included in the CSA submission sent to each party (see p360). The CSA can also disclose information to a court which has made, varied or revived a maintenance order or agreement if that information is required in relation to those proceedings or other matters arising from them.[97] The CSA can also disclose information it has to local authorities for their use in administering housing benefit or council tax benefit.[98] Otherwise, information cannot be given to third parties without the written permission of the person to whom it relates. Any unauthorised disclosure of information is a criminal offence (see p74).

Anyone wishing to see a copy of the information on her/him held by the CSA can apply in writing. This information must normally be supplied within 40 days.[99] If anyone has concerns about the collection, retention, accuracy or use of this information, the Information Commissioner's Office can be contacted.

Disclosure to other government departments

The CSA can disclose information to government departments dealing with benefits, including DWP agencies.[100] This includes information obtained using its powers or that which has been disclosed to the CSA voluntarily.

As the DWP has close links with the Home Office, disclosure may create problems for people from abroad, in particular possible illegal entrants and those prohibited from having recourse to public funds. If there are any doubts about whether information ought to be disclosed to the CSA, you should get advice first from a law centre or independent advice centre dealing with immigration issues (see Appendix 4). You cannot be prosecuted for refusing to give information unless it was requested by the CSA or an inspector (see p70).

CSA staff can exchange information with their counterparts in Northern Ireland and *vice versa*. Once disclosed, the information is subject to local rules about unauthorised disclosure.[101]

Unauthorised disclosure

Unauthorised disclosure of information is a criminal offence. This offence applies to anyone who is or has been a child support officer, a CSA employee, a civil servant carrying out a function under the Child Support Acts (eg, a Jobcentre Plus officer helping the CSA make enquiries), First-tier Tribunal staff, various ombudsmen and their staff, staff at the National Audit Office, those employed as a member of a Child Maintenance Enforcement Commission committee or sub-committee and anyone who, whether or not a civil servant, is providing services to the DWP.[102] It does not apply to members of the First-tier and Upper Tribunals.

It is not an offence to disclose information if:[103]

- the CSA can do so under the disclosure Regulations;
- the CSA has already done so under those Regulations;
- it is in the form of a summary or statistics and it cannot be related to any particular person; *or*
- the person to whom the information relates gives consent or, if that person's affairs are being dealt with under a power of attorney, a receiver under the Mental Health Act, a mental health appointee or a Scottish mental health custodian, the attorney, receiver, custodian or appointee gives consent.

A person who has broken these rules will have a defence if s/he can prove that s/he believed s/he was making the disclosure under these rules, or believed that disclosure under these rules had already been made, and had no reason to think otherwise.[104]

On summary conviction (ie, where a case proceeds without a trial), the maximum prison sentence is six months and the maximum fine is £5,000. On conviction or indictment, the maximum prison sentence is two years.[105] No prosecutions have been brought.

Disclosure of information about spent convictions, other than as part of an official duty, is also a criminal offence.[106]

Notes

1. **Information-seeking powers**
1 s14 and Sch 2 CSA 1991
2 s12 CSPSSA 2000
3 ss4(4), 6(9) and 7(5) CSA 1991; reg 3 CSI Regs
4 Reg 4(1) CSI Regs
5 Regs 3 and 4 CSI Regs
6 Reg 7 CSI Regs
7 *Purdew v Seress-Smith* [1992] 23 September 1992 (QBD)
8 Reg 3 CSI Regs
9 Reg 4(2)(a) CSI Regs
10 Reg 3(2) CSI Regs
11 Reg 9 CSI Regs
12 Reg 5 CSI Regs
13 Reg 3(2)(b) CSI Regs
14 Reg 4(3) CSI Regs
15 Reg 4(2)(c) CSI Regs
16 Reg 4(2)(d) CSI Regs
17 Reg 6 CSI Regs
18 Order 1 r3 CCR 1981
19 Reg 4(3) CSI Regs
20 Reg 4(h)(i) CSI Regs
21 See s3 SSA 1998
22 Regs 2(2)(d) and 4(2)(g) CSI Regs
23 s122D SSAA 1992
24 Sch 2 para 1 CSA 1991; Sch 6 para 2 CMOPA 2008
25 Sch 5 TCA 2002
26 s6 and Sch 1 Taxes Management Act 1970; s182 Finance Act 1989
27 CSA Operational Improvement Plan 2006-2009
28 Reg 2(h) CS(MCP) Regs; credit reference agencies are as defined by s145(8) Consumer Credit Act 1974; reg 4(2)(f) CSI Regs
29 Reg 4(2)(i) CSI Regs
30 Reg 4(j) and (k) CSI Regs
31 Reg 7(1) CSI Regs
32 Reg 7(2) CSI Regs
33 s14A CSA 1991
34 s14A(4) CSA 1991
35 s14A CSA 1991
36 Reg 8 CSI Regs
37 CCS/16535/1996 reported as R(CS) 2/98; CCS/12686/1996 reported as R(CS) 8/98
38 Reg 9 CSI Regs
39 s14A CSA 1991; s36 CMOPA 2008

2. **Contacting the non-resident parent**
40 CSA Operational Improvement Plan 2006-2009
41 Reg 3(1)(a) CSI Regs
42 Regs 1(2) and 5(1) CS(MCP) Regs
43 Reg 5(2) CS(MCP) Regs
44 Reg 5(3) and (4) CS(MCP) Regs
45 R(CS) 8/98

3. **Parentage investigations**
46 *What Happens if Someone Denies They Are the Parent of a Child?* CSL304, April 2010
47 s26 CSA 1991
48 *What Happens if Someone Denies They Are the Parent of a Child?* CSL304, April 2010
49 s26 CSA 1991
50 *What Happens if Someone Denies They Are the Parent of a Child?* CSL304, April 2010
51 *What Happens if Someone Denies They Are the Parent of a Child?* CSL304, April 2010
52 *What Happens if Someone Denies They Are the Parent of a Child?* CSL304, April 2010
53 *What Happens if Someone Denies They Are the Parent of a Child?* CSL304, April 2010
54 *What Happens if Someone Denies They Are the Parent of a Child?* CSL304, April 2010
55 s26 CSA 1991, Case A3(b)
56 *What Happens if Someone Denies They Are the Parent of a Child?* CSL304, April 2010
57 www.csa.gov.uk/en/case/dna-testing.asp
58 *What Happens if Someone Denies They Are the Parent of a Child?* CSL304, April 2010
59 s27A CSA 1991
60 *What Happens if Someone Denies They Are the Parent of a Child?* CSL304, April 2010
61 *What Happens if Someone Denies They Are the Parent of a Child?* CSL304, April 2010

62 *What Happens if Someone Denies They Are the Parent of a Child?* CSL304, April 2010
63 s27 CSA 1991
64 s27 CSA 1991
65 s20 FLRA 1969; *Re H (Paternity: Blood Test)* [1996] 2 FLR 65
66 *W v Official Solicitor* [1972] AC 24
67 s21 FLRA 1969
68 s23 FLRA 1969; *Re A (Paternity: Refusal of Blood Test)* [1994] 2 FLR 463
69 s28(2) CSA 1991; s7 LR(PC)(S)A 1986; r152 AS(CSA) (AOCSCR)
70 *What Happens if Someone Denies They Are the Parent of a Child?* CSL304, April 2010
71 *What Happens if Someone Denies They Are the Parent of a Child?* CSL304, April 2010

4. **Further investigations**
72 *DB v CMEC* [2010] UKUT 356 (AAC)
73 *DB v CMEC* [2010] UKUT 356 (AAC), citing R1/04(SF)
74 *DB v CMEC* [2010] UKUT 356 (AAC)
75 s15(1) CSA 1991
76 s15(8) CSA 1991
77 Sch 1 para 8 CS(NIRA) Regs
78 s14(4A) CSA 1991
79 s15(4) CSA 1991
80 s15(11) CSA 1991
81 s15(4A) CSA 1991
82 s15(5) CSA 1991
83 s15(6) CSA 1991
84 s57 CSA 1991; reg 11 CSI Regs
85 s15(7) CSA 1991
86 s15(9) CSA 1991
87 s15(9) CSA 1991

5. **Duty to disclose changes**
88 Reg 9 CSI Regs
89 ss44 and 55 and Sch 1 para 16 CSA 1991; reg 10 CSI Regs

6. **Disclosure of information by the Child Support Agency**
90 Reg 13 CSI Regs
91 Reg 13(2)(c) CSI Regs
92 Reg 13(3) CSI Regs
93 r19(3) TP(FT) Rules
94 Reg 13(4) CSI Regs
95 Reg 13(4) CSI Regs
96 Reg 12 CSI Regs
97 Reg 12(3) CSI Regs
98 s3 SSA 1998
99 s7 Data Protection Act 1998
100 s3 SSA 1998
101 Sch 1 para 7 CS(NIRA) Regs
102 s50 CSA 1991; reg 14 CSI Regs
103 s50 CSA 1991
104 s50(3) CSA 1991
105 s50(4) CSA 1991
106 s9 Rehabilitation of Offenders Act 1974

Part 3

Amount of maintenance: 'new rules'

Chapter 5

The maintenance calculation ('new rules')

This chapter covers:

1. Maintenance calculation rates

To carry out a child maintenance calculation, the following information is needed:[1]

- the number of qualifying children;
- the number of relevant other children (see p22);
- the number of any relevant non-resident children (see p85);
- the number of persons with care;
- benefits (if any) received by the non-resident parent;
- whether the non-resident parent meets the conditions for the nil rate (see p80);
- the income of the non-resident parent (see p86);
- the number of nights (if any) that the non-resident parent has care of a qualifying child (see p98);
- the number of nights (if any) that a local authority has care of a qualifying child (see p105).

If a non-resident parent fails to provide sufficient information to calculate child support maintenance, a default maintenance decision may be made (see p320). A penalty for failing to provide information may also be imposed (see p56).

There are four rates of child support maintenance that can be applied:

- nil rate (see p80);
- flat rate (see p81);
- reduced rate (see p82);
- basic rate (see p83).

Child support maintenance is calculated for each non-resident parent separately. This means a person with care may receive the flat rate of maintenance from one non-resident parent and an amount from the other non-resident parent worked out using the basic rate.

In all cases, the amount of child maintenance calculated is a weekly amount.[2] Rounding rules apply to the different rates as follows.[3]

- In basic-rate and reduced-rate cases, fractions of a pound are disregarded if less than half or rounded up to the next pound if a half or over.
- In all other cases (ie, where there is apportionment or shared care), fractions of a penny are disregarded if less than a half or rounded up to the next penny if a half or over.

There is a maximum amount of income which can be taken into account for child support maintenance purposes (see p93).

If there is more than one person with care

If there is more than one person with care in relation to a non-resident parent, the amount of child support due may be apportioned between them in relation to the number of qualifying children of each person with care.[4]

Where apportionment occurs and rounding provisions would result in the total amount of maintenance being different from the total amount before any apportionment, the maintenance due is adjusted.[5] This may mean that maintenance due to one of the persons with care has to be reduced by a penny, so that no one person with care is disadvantaged. This reduction will be reallocated between the persons with care from time to time.[6]

Apportionment occurs after the calculation of maintenance at the appropriate rate and before any decrease for shared care (see p102).[7]

In basic- and reduced-rate cases, if an adjustment is made which reduces the non-resident parent's liability to less than £5 (eg, because of shared care or a variation), the amount payable will be £5 apportioned between the people with care.

If there is more than one person with care in relation to a qualifying child, the maintenance due for this child may be further apportioned between the persons with care, but only if a request to apportion maintenance has been agreed by the Child Support Agency (CSA) – see p83.

Nil rate

This applies if the non-resident parent is:[8]

- a full-time student;[9]
- a child;
- a prisoner;

- a 16/17-year-old and receiving income support (IS), income-based jobseeker's allowance (JSA) or income-related employment and support allowance (ESA) (or his partner is);
- receiving an allowance for work-based training for young people or for Skillseekers training in Scotland. Work-based training includes schemes such as Entry to Employment and Modern Apprenticeships. Young people may receive an education maintenance allowance or a training allowance;
- resident in a care home or independent hospital, or is being provided with a care home service or/and independent healthcare service and who receives one of the prescribed benefits (as for the flat rate – see below) or has the whole/part of the cost of his accommodation met by a local authority;
- a person with net income (including that from any of the prescribed benefits for the flat rate listed below), of less than £5 a week.

Example 5.1

Kerry is a parent with care of two children, Mia and Lewis. Her ex-partner, Craig, is in prison. In this case, the nil rate applies. However, even though Craig is in prison, he is still sent a child maintenance enquiry form to complete. When he comes out of prison Kerry could ask for a supersession.

Flat rate

The flat rate of £5 applies if the non-resident parent does not qualify for the nil rate and:[10]

- his weekly income is £100 or less; *or*
- he receives one of the following:[11]
  - bereavement allowance;
  - retirement pension;
  - incapacity benefit or contributory ESA;
  - carer's allowance;
  - maternity allowance;
  - severe disablement allowance;
  - industrial injuries benefit;
  - widowed parent's allowance;
  - widow's pension;
  - contribution-based JSA;
  - a training allowance (other than for work-based learning for young people or Skillseekers);
  - war disablement pension;
  - war widow's, war widower's or surviving civil partner's war pension;
  - payments under the Armed Forces Compensation Scheme;
  - a social security benefit paid by a country other than the UK;

– IS, income-related ESA or income-based JSA (or his partner does);[12]
– pension credit (PC).

The flat rate can be halved for couples if the non-resident parent's partner is also a non-resident parent with a child support maintenance application in force, and receives IS, income-based JSA, income-related ESA or PC.[13] If the non-resident parent is in a polygamous relationship and there is more than one partner who is also a non-resident parent and the non-resident parent or his partner receives IS, income-based JSA, income-related ESA or PC, the flat rate is apportioned between them.

There are special rules about shared care in flat-rate cases (see p98).

Example 5.2

Craig has now come out of prison and gets income-based JSA. Kerry requests a supersession and Craig has £5 a week flat-rate maintenance deducted from his benefit.

If Craig moved in with Josie and claimed income-based JSA as a couple, the flat rate of £5 would still apply and Kerry would receive £5 a week. However, if Josie were also a non-resident parent, the flat rate would be halved. In this case, Kerry would receive £2.50 a week.

In the situation above, if Josie had two persons with care (Alison and Penny) each caring for one qualifying child, they would find their maintenance reduced as the flat rate applies at £2.50 and is then apportioned. Alison and Penny would each receive £1.25 each.

Reduced rate

This applies if neither the flat or nil rate applies and the non-resident parent has income of less than £200 but more than £100.[14] The flat rate of £5 is added to a percentage of the parent's income between £100 and £200.[15] This means that only the income above £100, but under £200, is used in the calculation – eg, if net income is £150, the percentage is applied to £50. The percentage depends on the number of qualifying children and the number of relevant children – ie, one for whom the non-resident parent or his partner receives child benefit.[16] Rounding is to the nearest pound.

Reduced-rate percentages

Number of relevant other children	*Number of qualifying children (including relevant non-resident children)*		
	1	2	3 or more
0	25%	35%	45%
1	20.5%	29%	37.5%
2	19%	27%	35%
3 or more	17.5%	25%	32.5%

Step 1

Work out the net income over £100 but less than £200.

Step 2

Work out the relevant percentage depending on the number of relevant children and qualifying children. Apply this percentage to the income worked out at Step 1 and add this to £5, rounding to the nearest pound.

Step 3

If there is more than one person with care, apportion this amount between them depending on the number of qualifying children each cares for, rounded to the nearest penny. (If there is more than one person with care in relation to a qualifying child, maintenance may only be apportioned if a request to do so has been agreed by the CSA.)

Example 5.3

Simon is due to pay maintenance to Fiona for two qualifying children, John and Margaret. Simon lives with a new partner, Julie, and their baby, Paul. Simon's net income is £180 a week. The reduced rate of maintenance applies.

Step 1 Net income = £180
Income between £100 and £200 = £80

Step 2 Relevant percentage for one relevant child and two qualifying children is 29%.
£5 + (29% x £80) = £5 + £23.20 = £28.20 (rounded to £28)

Simon is due to pay £28 maintenance to Fiona.

If the situation were as above except that Margaret was cared for by Fiona and John stayed with his grandmother, there would still be two qualifying children but now there would be two persons with care. The maintenance calculated would need to be apportioned between them.

Step 3 Each person cares for one qualifying child, so the maintenance is divided by two.
£28 ÷ 2 = £14

Simon now pays Fiona £14 and the grandmother £14.

If the non-resident parent shares the care of any qualifying children, the reduced rate may be decreased further by applying the shared care rules (see p93).

Basic rate

The basic rate applies if none of the other rates (nil, flat or reduced) apply.[17] Thus, if the non-resident parent has a net weekly income of £200 or more, maintenance will be calculated under the basic rate. The basic rate is a percentage of net income depending on the number of qualifying children. How much is paid will also depend on the number of relevant children. There may be other relevant non-resident children who are taken into account (see p85).

Basic-rate percentages

Number of qualifying children (including relevant non-resident children)	*Percentage of net income*	*Number of relevant children*	*Percentage by which net income is reduced*
1	15%	1	15%
2	20%	2	20%
3 or more	25%	3 or more	25%

If the non-resident parent has one or more relevant children, his net income is reduced by an equivalent percentage (see p82) before the basic rate is calculated. Therefore, the basic rate may be worked out in two steps, depending on the circumstances.

Step 1

Work out the net income of the non-resident parent. Depending on the number of relevant children, reduce this by a percentage – ie, 15 per cent, 20 per cent or 25 per cent.

Step 2

Depending on the number of qualifying children, maintenance is a proportion of this remaining net income, rounded to the nearest pound.

Step 3

If there is more than one person with care, apportion this amount between them depending on the number of qualifying children each cares for, rounded to the nearest penny. (If there is more than one person with care in relation to a qualifying child, maintenance can only be apportioned where a request to do so has been agreed by the CSA.)

Example 5.4

Simon now has a net income of £240 a week. Paul is a relevant child, and John and Margaret are the qualifying children.

Step 1 Net income is £240. One relevant child means this is reduced by 15%.
15% x £240 = £36
£240 – £36 = £204

Step 2 There are two qualifying children, so maintenance is 20% of remaining net income.
20% x £204 = £40.80 (rounded to £41)

Simon therefore pays £41 in maintenance to Fiona.

If Margaret were cared for by Fiona and John stayed with his grandmother, this £41 would be split equally between Fiona and the grandmother.

Step 3 £41 is apportioned between two persons with care. Each would receive £20.50 in maintenance from Simon.

If the non-resident parent shares the care of any of the qualifying children, the maintenance calculated may be decreased further by applying the shared care rules (see p93).

Relevant non-resident children

A non-resident parent may have other children in respect of whom an application for child support maintenance cannot be made because he is paying maintenance for them under a maintenance order (or in Scotland, registered maintenance agreement), the order of a court outside Great Britain, or under the legislation of a country outside the UK.[18] The CSA calls these children 'relevant non-resident children', although they are treated like qualifying children in relation to the calculation.

If child support is payable at either the basic rate or the reduced rate, or is calculated at one of these rates after applying a variation (see Chapter 6) and would otherwise have been the flat or nil rate, the child is counted as a qualifying child.[19] The amount of maintenance calculated is then apportioned between the persons with care in relation to the number of qualifying children they care for, including any adjustment for shared care.[20] If the total amount payable by the non-resident parent would be less than £5, the non-resident parent will instead pay £5, apportioned between the persons with care as appropriate.[21]

No payment is actually made for the relevant non-resident child. There is also no adjustment of the notional amount worked out for the non-resident child because of the non-resident parent sharing care or the child being in local authority care for part of the time.[22]

Example 5.5

James lives with his new partner, Amanda, and her son, Liam. He has three other children. Two (Emma and Joshua) are cared for by Elizabeth; one (Rachel) is cared for by Hilary. James has a court order for child maintenance for Rachel. Hilary cannot apply for child maintenance as the court order is in force (if it was made after 3 March 2003, she could apply for child maintenance if the order has been in force for one year; otherwise the order must cease before she can apply). In this case:

Emma and Joshua are qualifying children.

Liam is a relevant child (even though he is not James's child, James's new partner, Amanda, gets child benefit for him).

Rachel is a relevant non-resident child.

If James had a net income of £275 a week, his maintenance worked out using the basic rate would be as follows.

Step 1 £275 – (15% x £275) = £275 – £41.25 = £233.75

Step 2 25% x £233.75 = £58.44 (rounded to £58)

Step 3 Apportionment applies between Elizabeth and Hilary. Elizabeth receives two-thirds of the maintenance calculated – ie, £38.67 (when apportioning, rounding applies to the nearest penny).
Hilary receives her normal court order maintenance.
Note: if Hilary could apply for child maintenance, she would receive £19.33.

2. Net income

The non-resident parent's net weekly income includes earned income, self-employed earnings, tax credits and payments from a pension scheme, retirement annuity or other such scheme for provision of income in retirement,[23] less any relevant deductions. Only these forms of income are included. All other income is ignored.

Relevant week

The concept of the 'relevant week' is important in a child support calculation, particularly when calculating income.[24] The relevant week is:[25]

- on application by the non-resident parent, the seven days immediately before the application is made;
- on application in any other case, the seven days immediately before the date the non-resident parent was first given notice that an application for child support maintenance had been made;
- if the original decision is revised (or superseded because of ignorance, a mistake in material fact or error in law), the relevant week for the new decision is the same as the original decision;
- if the original decision is superseded because of a change of circumstances, the seven days immediately before the date on which the application to supersede was made;
- if the original decision is superseded by the Child Support Agency (CSA) on its own initiative (except for ignorance, a mistake in fact or error), the seven days immediately before the date of notification of that intention.[26]

In some cases, the CSA may make separate maintenance calculations for different periods in a particular case.[27] If this is because of a change of circumstances, the relevant week for each separate calculation made to take account of the change is the seven days immediately before the date of notification of the change.[28]

Disregarded income

If a payment is made in a currency other than sterling, banking charges or commission for changing the payment into sterling are disregarded.[29] In addition, a payment made in a country outside the UK that prohibits currency transfer to the UK is ignored.[30]

Earnings from employment

Earnings means 'any remuneration or profit from employment' and, as well as wages, includes:[31]

- payments for overtime;
- profit-related pay;
- bonuses or commission;
- royalties or fees;
- holiday pay (except that payable more than four weeks after ending employment);
- retaining fees;
- statutory sick pay, statutory maternity pay, statutory adoption pay and statutory paternity pay;
- pay in lieu of notice.

Earnings do not include:[32]

- payments of expenses 'wholly, exclusively and necessarily' incurred in carrying out the duties of the job. It may be possible to argue that such expenses can be apportioned between private and work use if they are necessary to carrying out the duties of the job;[33]
- tax-exempt allowances paid by an employer;
- gratuities paid by customers – ie, tips;
- payments in kind;
- advance earnings or loans made by the employer;
- payments made by an employer when the employee is on strike;
- payments for duties as an auxiliary coastguard, part-time firefighter, or within the lifeboat services, territorial army or reserve forces;
- payments made by a local authority to local councillors for performing their duties;
- payments made after employment ends which relate to a specific period of time, provided that a period of equal length has elapsed between the job ending and the effective date;
- earnings from a previous job if they are paid in the same week or period in which earnings from a second job are received.

Calculating normal weekly earnings

Averaged earnings are used in the child support calculation.[34] When calculating or estimating average earnings in the relevant week, the CSA considers the evidence of the person's earnings over any appropriate period, beginning not more than eight weeks before the relevant week and ending not later than the date of the calculation. The CSA may also consider cumulative earnings in the tax year in which the relevant week falls to the date of the calculation.

If the CSA believes that the amount of weekly earnings does not accurately reflect the person's normal amount of earnings, another period can be used, taking into account earnings received and those due to be received (from past, present or future employment) and the duration and pattern (or expected duration and pattern) of any employment.[35]

The CSA must be satisfied that the calculation of earnings in the relevant week produces a figure which is not normal,[36] and that the period chosen reflects the parent's usual pattern of work – eg, the amount of overtime worked or sick leave.[37] A future period can be used to take into account, for instance, earnings from a job which has not yet begun. The CSA must also consider the expected duration and pattern of any employment. A parent may want to suggest an alternative period to the CSA, giving reasons, as the CSA cannot be expected to consider this without substantial grounds and a prompt by one of the parents.[38] The CSA must use one continuous period.[39] If earnings during a year ending with the relevant week include a bonus or commission which is paid separately from, or for a longer period than, the other earnings with which it is paid, those payments are totalled over the year and divided by 52.[40]

The CSA has to take into account any change of circumstances it is aware of between the relevant week and the effective date (see p332).[41] However, it must first calculate earnings as above for the relevant week in order to determine whether there has been a material change of circumstances.[42] For changes after this date, see p319.

The calculation of earnings is one of the areas where errors are frequently made and it should, therefore, be checked carefully.

Calculating net earnings

Net earnings from employment are counted as net income in full. Net earnings mean gross earnings less:[43]

- income tax;
- Class 1 national insurance (NI) contributions;
- all of the contributions made to an occupational/personal pension scheme (unless the scheme is intended partly to pay off a mortgage on the parent's home, in which case 75 per cent of contributions).

Income tax will be the actual amount deducted, including any tax in relation to payments not included as earnings.[44]

Pension contributions are only deducted if they are made to a scheme approved by HM Revenue and Customs (the Revenue).

Earnings from self-employment

Income from self-employment is assessed on the basis of either:

- taxable profits from self-employment shown on a tax calculation notice issued by the Revenue; *or*
- in a small number of cases, the income from self-employment as calculated from gross recepits less relevant deductions.[45]

The non-resident parent must provide a tax calculation notice (or any revised notice) on demand.[46] The demand should explain the consequences of failing to provide the information. This may be an offence (see p56).

If there is evidence of a change of circumstances in the normal or long-term average income of a self-employed parent, the CSA can make a supersession decision without waiting for the end of the relevant accounting period and the submission of the tax return.[47]

Earnings calculated using taxable profits less deductions

The net earnings taken into account will be the total taxable profit from self-employment less:[48]

- income tax (calculated using the personal allowances and tax rates applicable at the effective date[49]);
- NI (Class 2 and Class 4 contributions at the rates applicable at the effective date[50]);
- any personal pension premiums or retirement annuity contract premiums (but only 75 per cent of such premiums where the scheme is intended to pay off a mortgage).

Net weekly earnings can only be worked out as outlined above if they are for a period not more than 24 months before the relevant week.[51]

Earnings calculated using gross receipts less deductions

Earnings can be calculated by using gross receipts less deductions if:[52]

- the 24-month condition is not met (see above); *or*
- the CSA accepts it is not reasonably practicable for the non-resident parent to provide the forms submitted to, or issued or revised by, the Revenue.

It is relatively rare for a case to be assessed based on gross receipts rather than using figures submitted to the Revenue. The CSA will not consider revising or superseding a decision based simply on the fact that using the gross receipts method would produce a greater amount of maintenance due to the person with care than that calculated using the tax calculation notice. However, if a non-resident parent's earnings were assessed by the gross receipts method, but he now has self-assessment details or a tax calculation notice, the CSA may supersede the maintenance decision.

Net earnings are the gross receipts less:[53]

- income tax;
- NI;
- any premiums paid in respect of a pension or retirement annuity contract (or 75 per cent of such premiums if the scheme is intended to pay off a mortgage);
- any VAT paid in excess of VAT received in the same period as that over which the earnings are assessed; *and*
- any expenses which are reasonably incurred and which are wholly and exclusively for the business. If the CSA is not satisfied that the full expense was appropriate or necessary to the business, it will allow that part considered reasonable. If an expense is part business and part private (eg, a car), the CSA decides on the breakdown between the two uses on the evidence available.

If a non-resident parent is a self-employed earner who provides board and lodgings, his gross earnings include all of any board or lodgings payments if this is his only or main source of income.[54]

Income tax and NI are calculated in the same way as for taxable profit.[55]

Business expenses include:[56]

- repayments of capital on loans used to replace or repair a business asset (but not for loans taken out for any other business purpose or if the costs are met by payments from an insurance policy);
- any income used to repair a business asset;
- any payment of interest on loans taken out for business purposes (this does not include loans taken out to acquire a share of a business, nor to pay business tax liabilities).[57]

Business expenses do *not* include capital expenditure, nor any expenses incurred in providing business entertainment.[58]

The net weekly income of the self-employed earner is averaged over the 52 weeks up to and including the relevant week or, if the person has been self-employed for less than a year, over the period during which the person has been self-employed (including the relevant week).[59]

The self-employed person may be asked to provide other evidence of business receipts and expenses, such as business books, receipts of bills, bank statements, records of wages paid, Revenue forms and VAT bills.

If the CSA believes that the above calculation would produce an amount which does not accurately represent the parent's true earnings, another period can be used.[60] This should not be used just because earnings fluctuate, receipts are irregular, trade is slow at times or work non-existent for a period, nor should a different period be used just because it is known that earnings will subsequently change.[61] In such cases, the CSA will take into account earnings received or due to be received, and the duration and pattern (or expected pattern) of any self-employment.[62]

Since most calculations are based on the self-assessment form or tax calculation notice, this alternative method is only used if there has been a major change in trading which has resulted in higher or lower earnings, or if a person has recently become self-employed.[63]

A person may still be classed as a self-employed earner even if her/his profits are not taxable – eg, if s/he spends a significant amount of time gambling. In such a case, it may be very difficult to calculate gross receipts and allowable deductions and, in practice, a person with care may have to consider applying for a variation from the calculation on the grounds that a non-resident parent's lifestyle is inconsistent with his income (see Chapter 6).[64]

Challenging self-employed earnings

There have often been delays in the self-employed parent producing all the information necessary to work out the maintenance due. The CSA can impose penalties and a default maintenance decision (see p320) while waiting for the information. The person with care may want to request that this is done if there have been problems in the past, and may want to consider complaining (see Chapter 20) if the CSA refuses to do so. However, she cannot force the imposition of a penalty.

Some persons with care may allege that the self-employed non-resident parent, sometimes with the help of an accountant, is disguising his true income. If a person with care wants to challenge the earnings, once a calculation has been made she can seek a revision (see p344) and ask the CSA to use an inspector (see p70) to obtain more detailed information. In practice, if the non-resident parent's accounts have been accepted by the Revenue, it is very unlikely that the CSA would consider it worthwhile to undertake further investigations. However, caselaw has established that the Revenue's declaration of income is not necessarily conclusive, and the CSA is not required to use the figures used by the Revenue in the tax calculation if there is evidence that they are not reliable.[65] The CSA may also refuse to revise the calculation if the person with care cannot substantiate her allegations. This can be challenged if the belief is reasonably held as it is very difficult for one party to obtain definitive details of the other's income. The CSA is much better placed to obtain such details.

If the person with care takes the case to the First-tier Tribunal (see Chapter 18), she will see details of the income in the appeal papers and she may be able to argue that some of the expenses included are not reasonable or not wholly connected with the business. The First-tier Tribunal may adjourn the hearing for further information to be collected. Alternatively, it can estimate net earnings based on the available evidence, including oral evidence from the person with care.[66]

The person with care can apply for a variation from the calculation on the grounds that a person's lifestyle is inconsistent with his level of income or that assets which do not currently produce income are capable of doing so (see Chapter 6).

Tax credits

Working tax credit

Working tax credit (WTC) is counted as the income of the non-resident parent if it is solely based on his work and earnings.[67] The rate of WTC used is that payable at the effective date.[68]

If both members of a couple meet the conditions for WTC, they can choose who receives it, but this is not reflected in the rules for child support maintenance calculations. If both members of a couple are working, WTC is treated as the income of the partner with the higher earnings over the period used for assessing earnings for tax credit purposes, or halved if their earnings are equal.[69] The earnings used for determining WTC are the ones used to determine who is treated as having WTC included in their income.[70] This means that, should the earnings change later, the non-resident parent could be treated as having more income than he has. For example, if he is earning more than his partner when WTC is worked out, WTC counts in full as his income. If his partner's income later increases, but he does not notify the Revenue during the tax year and waits for an end-of-year adjustment, he will still have WTC counted as his income even though his partner currently earns more than he does. (It is not compulsory to report changes of income during the tax year, although it may be advisable if there is a large increase.)

If a non-resident parent's income becomes lower than his partner's (because either his partner's income increases or his decreases), he can ask for a revision of the tax credit award to reflect the new income during the year. Otherwise, the tax credit award will be based on the previous tax year. If he does ask for a revision, he can then seek a supersession of the maintenance calculation on the basis that WTC should no longer be treated as his income. However, he should seek advice before asking for the tax credit award to be revised. As income for the current tax year is an estimate, asking for an in-year income revision of a tax credit award can lead to overpayments as well as underpayments. For full details of tax credits, see CPAG's *Welfare Benefits and Tax Credits Handbook*.

Child tax credit

Child tax credit paid to the non-resident parent or his partner counts in full as income, at the rate payable at the effective date.[71]

Other income

Periodic or other payments from an occupational or personal pension, retirement annuity or other scheme to provide income in retirement count in full as income.

Payments to compensate for the failure of pension schemes (Financial Assistance Scheme and Pensions Protection Fund payments) are treated in the same way. Income is calculated or estimated on a weekly basis by considering the 26-week period ending in the relevant week (see p205).[72] If the income has been received during each week of the period, the total received over the 26 weeks is divided by 26. In other cases, the total received is divided by the number of complete weeks for which the payment was received. However, the CSA can use a different period if the amount produced by the above calculation does not accurately reflect actual income.[73] Furthermore, a change occurring between the relevant week and the effective date (see p332) must be taken into account by the CSA if it is aware of the change, in the same way as for earnings (see p208).

Maximum amount of net weekly income

The maximum amount of net weekly income that can be included in the calculation of child maintenance is £2,000.[74] This includes all income, whether from earnings, tax credits, self-employment or pension and other payments. Even if a variation is being applied, the amount of net income cannot exceed this maximum figure.

Basically, this means that the maximum amount of child maintenance that can ever be paid is £500 – ie, where the non-resident parent has three or more children and no other relevant children.

Maximum maintenance payable (using the basic rate)

Number of relevant children	*1 qualifying child*	*2 qualifying children*	*3 or more qualifying children*
0	£300	£400	£500
1	£255	£340	£425
2	£240	£320	£400
3 or more	£225	£300	£375

3. Shared care

Shared care is the term used to describe a situation in which there is more than one person looking after a particular qualifying child and those people live in different households. If the people providing care live in the same household (see p21), this is not shared care.[75]

A number of individuals may, in fact, be involved in caring for a qualifying child – eg, parents, grandparents and babysitters. For the shared care rules to apply there must be either:

- a non-resident parent who shares care – ie, looks after the qualifying child at least 52 nights a year on average (see p98);
- a parent with care (ie, with day-to-day care of a qualifying child because she cares for the child at least 104 nights a year on average) who is treated as a non-resident parent (see p96); *or*
- a qualifying child cared for by a local authority for part of the time (see p280).

One, or all, of these situations may apply in any individual case.

The Child Support Agency (CSA) will make a decision on shared care by looking at all the evidence. As far as possible it will seek written evidence, although oral evidence may be accepted if the parents agree. Normally, this information is obtained on application – ie, from relevant forms or phone contact with the person with care and non-resident parent. The CSA calculates the amount of shared care by looking at regular weekly patterns, exceptional weeks and other occasional nights within a 12-month period. It is actual care provided which counts, whether or not it is authorised or agreed. This means that contact arrangements ordered by a court or agreed to in writing are only evidence and not decisive proof of the care situation.[76] If the evidence of the person with care and non-resident parent conflicts, further evidence may be required to resolve the issue.

A court should determine contact arrangements and the amount of shared care without regard to the effects on child support liability.[77] Therefore, neither parent can argue that a court should vary an order due to the amount of child support payable.

Parents should keep a note of the nights the child(ren) spends with them and, in case of dispute, be willing to supply further evidence – eg, a diary. The CSA (and any subsequent appeal at the First-tier Tribunal) must then determine the number of nights spent in each person's care over the period.[78]

If a non-resident parent provides some care but not sufficient for it to qualify as shared care, an application for a variation may be made on the grounds that the contact costs are 'special expenses' (see p111).

Note: there are some differences between shared care under the 'new rules' and under the 'old rules'. The most significant of these differences is that, under the 'new rules', to be classed as sharing care a non-resident parent must look after the qualifying child for at least 52 nights a year on average, whereas under the 'old rules' he must look after the qualifying child for at least 104 nights a year. See Chapter 14 for details of shared care in 'old rules' cases.

What is day-to-day care

A person is treated as having day-to-day care of a child only if s/he cares for the child for at least 104 nights in the 12-month period ending with the relevant week.[79] See p205 for the definition of 'relevant week'.

Another period ending with the relevant week may be used if that would be more representative of the current arrangement.[80] The number of nights of care in that period must be in the same ratio as 104 nights is to 12 months – ie, 52 nights in six months, 26 nights in three months, 17 nights in two months, nine nights in a month. It might be appropriate for the CSA to use a period other than 12 months because no pattern of care can be gathered from a 12-month period, or because there is an intended change. If the arrangement has simply been renegotiated between the two parents, written acceptance of this should be provided so that the CSA knows this is now the current arrangement and not a temporary change. A future period cannot be used but, if there is an intended change, a period before the relevant week may include a care distribution which is closer to the intended new arrangement, and the CSA can use this period rather than the 12 months.[81]

If there is a pattern of care over a period of 12 months, even if it is occasionally disrupted, a shorter period cannot be used unless there is an intended change in the pattern.[82]

Example 5.6

Joan's maintenance application was made on 5 February 2009. The effective date is 7 April 2009 (the effective date is later than the relevant week because Joan had a court order which was made after 3 March 2003 and which had been in force for more than one year when she applied for child support; this means that the effective date is two months and two days after the application was made). Serge was notified on 19 February 2009. The relevant week for Joan's maintenance application is, therefore, 12 February to 18 February 2009 – the seven days immediately before the non-resident parent was given notice of Joan's application (see p86).

Serge will begin caring for their daughter, Chloe, two nights a week from 14 March 2009. The alternative period used will then be 14 March to 7 April 2009 – from the date of change to the effective date.

If a change occurs after the relevant week, the CSA should be informed, as this may be grounds for a supersession. If it refuses to use an alternative period, an appeal can be sought.

Example 5.7

A father who only looks after the children for six weeks in the school holidays would not be accepted as a person with care. However, he could request a supersession during the summer holidays on the grounds that he is now a parent with care and a shorter period should then be used to calculate who has day-to-day care to reflect the current arrangement. It is unlikely that this would be grounds for supersession if the six-week period had already been taken into account. However, if the arrangement for the holiday had not been known at the time, this may be successful. If day-to-day care were to be reassessed over the summer holidays, the father would become the parent with care and the mother the non-resident parent. Indeed, the father may be able to apply for maintenance from the mother. (**Note:** the relevant week in this case is the seven days preceding the request for a supersession – see p350. The request, therefore, should not be made right at the beginning of the summer holiday.)

If it is held that a supersession cannot take place, the father remains the non-resident parent over the holiday when he has the children full time. He would be liable to continue paying the mother the full level of maintenance even for those weeks the children spent with him. The parents may be able to come to a voluntary arrangement to reflect the father's level of care over this time, but this may not be financially viable.

The parent does not have to provide continuous care throughout a period of 24 hours, but must provide care during the night.[83] If a child is a boarder at boarding school, a hospital inpatient, or temporarily in someone else's care, whoever would otherwise have day-to-day care is treated as providing care.[84] For example, if a babysitter or grandparent looks after the child one night a week, this would count as a night spent with the principal provider of day-to-day care. In the case of boarding school, the person who is treated as having day-to-day care for such periods need not be the person who pays the school fees.[85] However, a non-resident parent who pays school fees for a qualifying child may be able to apply for a variation (see p110).

Parent with care treated as non-resident

If there are two or more persons with care (of a child for whom an application has been made) and at least one of them is a parent, special rules are applied.[86] In this case, a parent with care may be treated as a non-resident parent if s/he provides care:[87]

- to a lesser extent than the other parent or persons with care;
- to the same extent as the other parent but does not get child benefit; *or*
- to the same extent as the other parent and neither parent receives child benefit but the CSA decides she is not the principal provider of day-to-day care.

Example 5.8

Robert looks after Geraldine from Friday afternoon to Monday morning. Nikki looks after Geraldine from Monday afternoon to Friday morning. Each is a parent with care, but Robert cares for Geraldine to a lesser extent so he is treated as the non-resident parent.

A year later, Robert has moved onto shift work. One week he has Geraldine four nights, the second week three nights. Nikki cares for Geraldine the rest of the time. They now share care equally but, as Nikki receives child benefit, Robert is still treated as the non-resident parent.

Note: as the right to receive child maintenance follows receipt of child benefit, this may lead to competing claims for child benefit. If more than one person who is entitled makes a claim for child benefit, an order of priority is used to decide who will receive it.[88] For example, the person with whom the child is living has priority over other claimants. If the priority rules do not decide the matter and the entitled claimants cannot come to an agreement, HM Revenue and Customs makes the decision. Priority can be conceded by a higher priority claimant to someone else, in writing. For more information on entitlement to child benefit and the priority rules, see CPAG's *Welfare Benefits and Tax Credits Handbook*.

In cases where a parent with care is treated as non-resident, a calculation is carried out to find out how much child maintenance s/he has to pay. This is worked out in the same way as for a non-resident parent who shares care.

If the situation includes a remaining parent with care who does not have to pay child maintenance, this assignment of non-resident parenthood can result in one parent paying child maintenance to another who has equal responsibility for the child.

Who receives maintenance

If there are two or more people in different households who both have day-to-day care of a qualifying child, either can make an application for child maintenance as long as both or neither of them has parental responsibility.[89] If only one of them has parental responsibility, the person with parental responsibility must be the applicant. This means that if the person with parental responsibility decides not to apply, the other person with care could lose out on child maintenance, unless there is an application from the non-resident parent or a child in Scotland.

If both/all the persons with care make an application, only one will be accepted, depending on the order of priority (see p44). This may include a parent with care who is subsequently treated as a non-resident parent for the calculation.

If none of the persons with care is a parent who is treated as a non-resident parent, the person whose application is accepted will receive all the maintenance calculated.[90] The applicant or other person with care may request that the payment is apportioned between them.[91] In making the decision, the-CSA considers all the circumstances of the case and representations from the persons with care.[92] If agreed, the maintenance payable will be apportioned in relation to the amount of care provided. See *Example 5.12*.

If one of the persons with care is treated as a non-resident parent, this apportionment cannot take place. The deemed non-resident parent is liable to pay child support maintenance, and the entire amount of this child maintenance is paid to the person with care whose application has been given priority (see p44) or who provides care for the greater amount of time. In other words, a person with care who provides care for the lesser amount of time can never receive child maintenance from a deemed non-resident parent, irrespective of the amount being paid. The person with care who does receive child support maintenance could decide on an informal basis to pass some of it on to the other person(s) with care, but this cannot be enforced.

This may seem illogical, particularly if the application has been made by a parent with care who is then treated as the non-resident parent, or if applications have been made by both persons with care but one is then treated as the non-resident parent. A parent with care who applies to the CSA for maintenance from the non-resident parent but ends up being deemed non-resident and paying maintenance can request a withdrawal (see p327). However, she may find that the other person with care makes another new application (if that person has parental responsibility).

When a non-resident parent shares care

A non-resident parent shares care if he looks after a qualifying child at least one night a week on average.[93] The care must be provided overnight and the non-resident parent must stay at the same address as the child.[94] This means that the care could be provided away from the non-resident parent's normal home – eg, while on holiday or at another relative's homes. It also includes the situation where the non-resident parent looks after the child overnight in the parent with care's home when the parent with care is away from home during the relevant nights.[95]

The number of nights is averaged over the 12 months ending with the relevant week.[96] A shorter period may be used – eg, because there is no pattern for the frequency or there is an intended change in frequency.[97] The number of nights of care in that period must be in the same ratio as 52 nights is to 12 months (52 weeks) – ie, 26 nights in six months (26 weeks), 13 nights in three months (13 weeks).[98]

The effect of shared care on the flat rate

As with basic or reduced-rate maintenance, the non-resident parent may share care with one or more persons with care. In these cases, it must be established whether the non-resident parent is liable for the flat rate because he has income of under £100. If the answer to this question is yes, there will be no adjustment of his maintenance liability regardless of how many nights of shared care there are. However, if the non-resident parent:

- is liable to pay the flat rate because he is in receipt of a relevant benefit (see p81) or he or his partner receives income support (IS), income-related employment and support allowance, income-based jobseeker's allowance or pension credit (including cases where a reduced flat rate of £2.50 applies); *and*
- cares for a qualifying child for at least 52 nights a year,

the amount of child maintenance due to the person with care of that qualifying child is nil.[99]

If there is more than one person with care, the flat rate is apportioned in relation to the number of qualifying children before any adjustment for shared care is made. This may mean that the non-resident parent's liability reduces to nil for one person with care because of shared care. However, he is still liable for the remaining amounts to the other person(s) with care, in which case he will pay an amount which is less than £5. The process is as follows.

- **Step 1.** Check the reason why the flat rate applies.
- **Step 2.** Apportion the flat rate between the persons with care on the basis of the number of qualifying children. Where appropriate, apply any apportioning in relation to a qualifying child if there is more than one person with care.
- **Step 3.** Apply any reduction to nil because of shared care.

Note: apportioning and rounding may result in adjustments of a penny in some calculations done by the CSA – see p79.

Example 5.9

Alistair is the non-resident parent of Keith, who lives with his older brother Neil, and Katie, who lives with her mum, Rachel. Alistair looks after Katie one or two nights a week but Keith and he do not get on. Both Neil and Rachel apply for maintenance. Alistair receives incapacity benefit (IB) and IS.

Step 1 Alistair is due to pay maintenance at the flat rate of £5, as he receives IB and IS.

Step 2 Apportion the flat rate of £5 between the persons with care in relation to the qualifying children each cares for – ie, the amount is halved.
To Neil for Keith = £2.50
To Rachel for Katie = £2.50

Step 3 Alistair cares for Katie over 52 nights a year so the amount due reduces to nil.
Alistair remains liable to pay £2.50 in maintenance to Neil for Keith.

The situation is as above but now Keith goes to stay with his grandfather two nights a week. Neil asks for maintenance to be split between them and the CSA agrees to do this.

Step 1 Remains the same.

Step 2 Rachel is due £2.50 but now the £2.50 for Keith will be split between Neil and his grandfather.
Neil looks after Keith five nights out of seven; his grandfather looks after him two out of seven, therefore:
5/7 x £2.50 is due to Neil = £1.79
2/7 x £2.50 is due to the grandfather = £0.72

Step 3 The amount due to Rachel reduces to nil as Alistair cares for Katie over 52 nights a year.
Alistair remains liable to pay £1.79 to Neil and £0.72 to Keith's grandfather.

In total, this would mean that Alistair is due to pay £2.51. This is more than the amount before apportioning because of the rounding provisions. Therefore, in this case, the maintenance will be adjusted by one penny to one of the persons with care. Neil has his adjusted to £1.78 for a period, after which the adjustment is made to the grandfather's and he will receive £0.71 and Neil will receive £1.79.

The effect of shared care on the basic and reduced rate

A non-resident parent (or parent with care treated as non-resident) may share care in a number of situations – ie, be:

- caring for different qualifying children at different times; *or*
- caring for qualifying children with more than one person with care.

There may be any number of variations and permutations. Indeed, in any one family situation there may be a number of non-resident parents and children.

If a non-resident parent, or parent with care who is treated as a non-resident parent, shares care of a qualifying child for 52 or more nights a year, the amount of maintenance he is due to pay is reduced by a suitable fraction depending on the number of nights of shared care.[100] The amount depends on the relevant band.[101]

Number of nights	*Fraction to subtract*
52 to 103	One-seventh
104 to 155	Two-sevenths
156 to 174	Three-sevenths
175 or more	One-half

If the non-resident parent shares care of a qualifying child for a sufficient number of nights for the one-half fraction to apply, an additional £7 decrease in maintenance must also be applied.[102] This is known as **'abatement'**. Abatement will be applied for each child for whom at least 175 nights of shared care applies.

If the decreases applied because of shared care result in the non-resident parent being liable to pay the person with care less than £5, the non-resident parent will instead pay the flat rate of £5.[103] This includes the situation where the total amount of maintenance due to all persons with care is decreased to less than £5, in which case the £5 is apportioned between the persons with care in relation to the number of qualifying children. For more details on situations involving more than one person with care, see p267.

When applying the decrease for shared care, the rounding provisions apply to the nearest penny.[104]

Example 5.10: shared care with one person with care

Alex shares care of Mark with the person with care, Diane. He looks after Mark on average two nights at the weekend and a couple of weeks in school holidays. Although Alex is a parent with care, he is treated as a non-resident parent as he is not the principal provider of care. Alex's net income is £240.

Step 1 **Basic rate** = 15% x £240 = £36

Step 2 **Apply decrease for shared care**
Alex shares care in the 104–155 band (two-sevenths).
£36 maintenance must be decreased by two-sevenths – ie, £36 – £10.29 = £25.71

Alex pays Diane £25.71.

Alex increases the amount of time he shares care of Mark to three nights one week and four nights the next. In this case, Alex shares care for over 175 nights and the one-half fraction is applied. Alex's maintenance calculated under the basic rate remains £36.

Step 2 £36 decreased by one-half and a further £7 subtracted – ie, £18 – £7 = £11

Because of the increase in shared care, Alex pays £11 maintenance to Diane.

Alex's circumstances change and he now has income of £160.

Step 1 **Reduced rate** of maintenance = £5 + (25% x £60) = £5 + £15 = £20

Step 2 **Apply decrease for shared care**
The fraction to apply remains at one-half and there is an abatement of £7.
(50% x £20) – £7 = £10 – £7 = £3

Step 3 **Maintenance due** is below £5 so Alex will pay £5 a week to Diane.

More than one qualifying child

If the person with care and non-resident parent have more than one qualifying child, the fractions that apply for shared care for each qualifying child are added together, then divided by the number of qualifying children.[105] This applies where care is shared for some, but not all, of the qualifying children or there are different shared-care arrangements for each qualifying child.

Example 5.11: shared care with more than one qualifying child

Pat is the non-resident parent of Lea and Dylan. Both are cared for by their grandmother, Jean. Lea does not like staying with Pat and only does so occasionally. However, Dylan stays with him on Friday and Saturday nights. Both children stay with him for a few days at Christmas and during the school holidays. Pat has net income of £220.

Step 1 **Basic rate** for two children = 20% x £220 = £44

Step 2 **Apply decrease for shared care**
Lea does not stay with Pat sufficient days for it to count as shared care.
Dylan is in the 104 – 155 band (two-sevenths).
The fractions which apply are added together and divided by two, as there are two qualifying children for whom Jean cares.

(0 + 2/7) ÷ 2 = 2/14

Pat's maintenance is decreased by 2/14 (ie, £6.29).

Because of the shared care, Pat must pay £37.71 (£44 – £6.29) to Jean in maintenance.

Note: if Pat has costs for keeping in contact with Lea, he may be able to apply for a variation (see Chapter 6).

Lea increases the amount of time she spends with her dad and now this counts as shared care.

Step 2 Lea is in the 52 – 103 band (one-seventh).
Dylan is in the 104 – 155 band (two-sevenths).
The fractions are added together and divided by two – ie, 3/7 ÷ 2 = 3/14
The maintenance due is, therefore, decreased by 3/14 because of shared care.
Pat's maintenance is decreased by 3/14 (ie, £9.43).

Because of shared care, Pat must pay £34.57 (£44 – £9.43) to Jean in maintenance.

Dylan stays with his dad more often and increases the amount of care, so that:

Step 2 Lea is in the 52 – 103 band (one-seventh).
Dylan is in the 175 or more band (one-half).
The decrease will be (1/7 + 1/2) ÷ 2 = 9/28; 9/28 x £44 = £14.14
£44 – £14.14 = £29.86. However, because care is shared equally for one qualifying child, the abatement of £7 applies and maintenance due is decreased by a further £7.

Pat now pays Jean maintenance of £22.86 (£29.86 – £7).

More than one person with care: apportionment

A non-resident parent may be due to pay maintenance to more than one person with care because there:

- are several qualifying children with different persons with care (known as multiple maintenance units);
- is more than one person with care in relation to a qualifying child(ren).

One or both of these situations may apply in any one case, and the non-resident parent may share care with only one or all of the persons with care. In these cases there may be apportioning and shared-care adjustments made throughout the calculation (see p80).

Example 5.12: shared care in multiple maintenance units

Ivan is the non-resident parent for two children – Holly, whose parent with care is Ellen, and Jamie, whose parent with care is Laura. Ivan looks after Holly when Ellen is on night shifts, which is every other week apart from holidays, and takes her camping with him on the odd weekend. Jamie and Laura live further away so Ivan only sees Jamie for a long weekend once a month when he visits his parents and two weeks in the summer holidays. Ivan's net income is £230.

Step 1 **Basic rate** applies for two qualifying children, there are no relevant children and net income is £230.

20% x £230 = £46

There is apportionment between the persons with care. They each care for one qualifying child so halve the maintenance between them.

To Ellen for Holly = £23

To Laura for Jamie = £23

Step 2 **Apply decrease for shared care**

Maintenance paid to Ellen for Holly

Holly is in the 156 – 174 band (three-sevenths).

3/7 x £23 = £9.86

£23 – £9.86 = £13.14

Maintenance paid to Laura for Jamie

Jamie is in the 52 – 103 band (one-seventh).

1/7 x £23 = £3.29

£23 – £3.29 = £19.71

Step 3 **Total maintenance due** is £13.14 (to Ellen) + £19.71 (to Laura) = £32.85.

The situation is as above but now Laura has a new job which means she is away from home on average two nights a week and the occasional weekend. Her sister (Alice) looks after Jamie and Laura asks the CSA to split the maintenance between her and Alice.

Step 1 **Basic rate** is £46.

Apportion between the persons with care (there are two qualifying children but three persons with care – Ellen for Holly, and Laura and Alice for Jamie).

To Ellen for Holly = £23

Between Laura and Alice for Jamie = £23

Alice looks after Jamie two nights a week on average (2/6 – ie, one-third).

To Alice for Jamie = £7.67 (1/3 x £23)

Laura looks after Jamie for the remaining four nights (4/6 – ie, two-thirds).

To Laura for Jamie = £15.33 (2/3 x £23)

Step 2 **Apply decrease for shared care**

Maintenance paid to Ellen for Holly

Ivan's care for Holly is in the 156 – 174 band (three-sevenths).

3/7 x £23 = £9.86 (ie, £23 – £9.86 = £13.14)

Maintenance paid to Alice for Jamie

Ivan's care for Jamie is in the 52 – 103 band (one-seventh).

1/7 x £7.67 = £1.10; £7.67 – £1.10 = £6.57

Maintenance paid to Laura for Jamie

Ivan's care for Jamie is in the 52 – 103 band (one-seventh).

1/7 x £15.33 = £2.19; £15.33 – £2.19 = £13.14

Step 3 **Total maintenance due** is £13.14 (to Ellen) + £6.57 (to Alice) + £13.14 (to Laura) = £32.85.

Overall, Ivan pays exactly the same amount of maintenance as before, but it is split between three people.

Qualifying child is in hospital or at boarding school

If a qualifying child is in hospital or at boarding school, any night spent there will count as a night with the person who would normally provide care at that time.[106] This includes nights normally spent with the:

- non-resident parent;[107]
- person with care;
- local authority.[108]

These nights count in determining whether the non-resident parent or local authority shares care. They are also counted when establishing who is a person with care or which parent is to be treated as non-resident.

Example 5.13

A child who has been living with his mother during the week and spending Friday nights with his father goes to boarding school. The time as a boarder would continue to be treated as if he were living with his mother. Even if the care arrangement alters so that he spends alternate weekends with his father, the nights at school still count as spent with his mother.

If the parents agree, or the periods involved are infrequent, the case may be straightforward. However, if the normal arrangements break down, a normal pattern cannot be established or the parents disagree, the CSA must make a decision on shared care.

Example 5.14

Ella is a qualifying child cared for most of the time by her mother, Sarah, although her father, Stuart, looks after her on Wednesday and Saturday nights. Over the past year Ella has undergone treatment for cancer, which has resulted in her spending periods in hospital. Because of the periods in hospital, Stuart has actually only looked after Ella for 42 nights in the year. On 16 of the remaining nights that Ella should have stayed with him she was in hospital. On the other nights that Ella should have stayed with Stuart, she was unwell and wanted to stay with Sarah. The CSA would have to decide whether to consider Ella as staying with Stuart for 58 nights or accept that the intention was for her to stay with Stuart on 104 nights in the year. Either parent would have the right to appeal against the CSA's decision on this.

If, having counted these nights, a person is not a:

- person with care;
- non-resident parent who shares care;
- local authority who has part-time care,

the night is treated as if the child is in the care of the principal provider of day-to-day care.[109] For example, if a babysitter looks after a child one night a week, then the child goes into hospital, the babysitter is not a person with care, non-resident parent or local authority. Therefore, that night is treated as one normally spent with the principal provider of day-to-day care.

Care provided in part by the local authority

Part-time local authority care has no effect on the flat rate of maintenance. This section only applies if:

- the non-resident parent is liable to pay maintenance at the basic or reduced rate (including where a variation has been made which results in the non-resident parent paying maintenance at either of these rates);[110] *and*
- the qualifying child is cared for by the local authority at least one night a week on average but not more than five (see below).

A local authority cannot be a person with care.[111] Therefore, if a child is in the care of the local authority for more than five nights a week, no child maintenance is payable by the non-resident parent because there is no person with care.

If the local authority cares for the child for 52 nights or more in the 12-month period ending with the relevant week, the maintenance to be paid by the non-resident parent will be decreased.[112] As in deciding day-to-day care, the CSA may use a period other than 12 months which it considers to be more representative of current arrangements. A future period may also be considered if the qualifying child is to go into local authority care on, or after, the effective date.[113] If an alternative period is used, the number of nights of care must be in the same ratio as 52 nights to 12 months.[114] (Nights spent in hospital or at boarding school which normally would have been spent in care are included – see p104.)

Local authority care only affects the calculation of maintenance when it applies to a qualifying child. If a relevant other child is in local authority care (whether full or part time), this will not affect how s/he is treated so long as the non-resident parent or his partner receives child benefit for her/him.

The decrease for part-time local authority care

If the local authority has part-time care of a qualifying child, the basic or reduced-rate maintenance calculated from the non-resident parent is decreased in relation to the number of nights the qualifying child spends in local authority care.

This calculation may be carried out either on its own, where the non-resident parent does not share care, or alongside one carried out because the non-resident parent shares care (see p98).

The effect of part-time local authority care

Number of nights	*Fraction to subtract*
52 to 103	One-seventh
104 to 155	Two-sevenths
156 to 207	Three-sevenths
208 to 259	Four-sevenths
260 to 262	Five-sevenths

If the person with care and non-resident parent have more than one qualifying child, the fractions that apply for each qualifying child in local authority care are added together and divided by the number of qualifying children for whom maintenance is calculated.[115] This applies where the local authority cares for one or all qualifying children or there are different care arrangements for each qualifying child.

If the decrease because of part-time care by the local authority would reduce the amount of maintenance to less than £5 for the only or all persons with care, the amount due will be £5.

Example 5.15: local authority provides part-time care

Jake is the non-resident parent for Michael and Leanne. Michael has just been placed under local authority supervision, which means that over the next six months he is to spend four nights a week in a residential unit. The rest of the time he spends with his mum, Naomi. Jake has net income of £280 and currently pays maintenance of £56 (basic-rate maintenance). This must be superseded because of local authority care. The CSA supersedes the decision, considering the ratio in the six-month period.

Step 1 **Work out amount of maintenance due**
Basic rate = 20% x £280 = £56

Step 2 **Work out the decrease because of part-time local authority care**
Local authority care for Michael is in the 208 – 259 band (four-sevenths).
The fractions which apply are added together and divided by the number of qualifying children – ie, (0 + 4/7) ÷ 2 = 4/14
Jake's maintenance is decreased by 4/14 (ie, £16).

Jake now pays Naomi £40 (£56 – £16) in maintenance.

If Leanne were also in care for two nights a week:

Step 1 Same as above.

Step 2 Local authority care for Leanne is in the 104 –155 band (two-sevenths).
Local authority care for Michael is in the 208 – 256 band (four-sevenths).
The fractions are added together and divided by two:
(2/7 + 4/7) = 6/7 ÷ 2 = 6/14

Jake's maintenance decreases by 6/14 = £24

Jake now pays Naomi £32 (ie, £56 – £24) in maintenance.

The non-resident parent shares care and local authority has part-time care

If the non-resident parent shares care of a qualifying child and the local authority has part-time care of a qualifying child in relation to the same person with care, the appropriate fractions are worked out under each provision and are added together.[116] The amount of maintenance due from the non-resident parent is then decreased by this fraction.

If this decrease would result in the non-resident parent being due to pay less than £5 to the only or all persons with care, he will pay £5.[117]

This calculation is carried out at Step 2.

Example 5.16: shared care and part-time local authority care

The situation is as in *Example 5.15*, except that Leanne spends one night a week with Jake, but Michael does not.

Step 2 Jake cares for Leanne in the 52 – 103 band (one-seventh).

The fractions which apply are added together and divided by the number of qualifying children:

(0 + 1/7) ÷ 2 = 1/14

Jake's maintenance because of shared care should be reduced by 1/14.

Because Michael is in local authority care, the maintenance due should be reduced by 4/14. This is added to the amount because of shared care.

1/14 + 4/14 = 5/14

Jake's maintenance is reduced by £20 (5/14 x £56).

Jake now pays Naomi £36 (£56 – £20) in maintenance.

If Leanne is also in care two nights a week but still spends one night a week with Jake:

Step 2 Jake's maintenance because of shared care should reduce by 1/14 (as above).

Local authority care for Michael and Leanne should reduce maintenance by 6/14 (see *Example 5.15*).

These fractions are added together:

1/14 + 6/14 = 7/14 = 1/2

Jake's maintenance is reduced by £28 (1/2 x £56).

Jake now pays Naomi £28 (ie, £56 – £28) in maintenance.

Notes

1. **Maintenance calculation rates**
1 Sch 1 CSA 1991; reg 2(5) CS(MCSC) Regs
2 Reg 2(1) CS(MCSC) Regs
3 Reg 2(2) and (3) CS(MCSC) Regs
4 Sch 1 Part 1 para 6 CSA 1991
5 Reg 6 CS(MCSC) Regs
6 Reg 6 CS(MCSC) Regs
7 Sch 1 Part 1 para 1(2) CSA 1991
8 Sch 1 Part 1 para 5 CSA 1991; reg 5 CS(MCSC) Regs
9 Reg 1(2) CS(MCSC) Regs
10 Sch 1 Part 4 CSA 1991
11 Reg 4 CS(MCSC) Regs
12 Reg 4(1)(c) CS(MCSC) Regs
13 Sch 1 Part 1 para 4(2) CSA 1991; reg 4(3)(a) CS(MCSC) Regs
14 Sch 1 Part 1 para 3 CSA 1991
15 Reg 3 CS(MCSC) Regs
16 Sch 1 Part 1 para 10C CSA 1991
17 Sch 1 Part 1(1) CSA 1991
18 Reg 11(1) CS(MCSC) Regs
19 Reg 11(2) and (3) CS(MCSC) Regs
20 Reg 11(3) CS(MCSC) Regs
21 Reg 11(5) CS(MCSC) Regs
22 Reg 11(4) CS(MCSC) Regs

2. **Net income**
23 Sch Part I para 1 CS(MCSC) Regs
24 Sch Part I para 3(1)(a) and Part III para 7(6) CS(MCSC) Regs
25 Reg 1(2) CS(MCSC) Regs
26 Reg 7C SS&CS(DA) Regs
27 Sch 1 Part II para 15 CSA 1991
28 Reg 1(2) CS(MCSC) Regs
29 Sch Part I para 2(a) CS(MCSC) Regs
30 Sch Part I para 2(b) CS(MCSC) Regs
31 Sch Part II para 4(1) CS(MCSC) Regs
32 Sch Part II para 4(2) CS(MCSC) Regs
33 CCS/137/2007
34 Sch Part II para 6(1) CS(MCSC) Regs
35 Sch Part II para 6(4) CS(MCSC) Regs
36 CCS/16/1994; CCS/11873/1996
37 CCS/6810/1995
38 CCS/511/1995
39 CCS/7312/1995; CCS/556/1995; CSCS/1/1996; CSCS/6/1996
40 Sch Part II para 6(3) CS(MCSC) Regs
41 Reg 2(4) CS(MCSC) Regs
42 CCS/2750/1995
43 Sch Part II para 5 CS(MCSC) Regs
44 Sch Part II para 5(2) CS(MCSC) Regs
45 Sch Part III para 7(1) and (1A) CS(MCSC) Regs
46 Sch Part III para 7(2) CS (MCSC) Regs
47 *LW v CMEC* [2010] UKUT 184 (AAC)
48 Sch Part III para 7(3) CS(MCSC) Regs
49 Sch Part III para 7(4) CS(MCSC) Regs
50 Sch Part III para 7(5) CS(MCSC) Regs
51 Sch Part III para 7(6) CS(MCSC) Regs
52 Sch Part III para 8(1) CS(MCSC) Regs
53 Sch Part III para 8(2) CS(MCSC) Regs
54 Sch Part III para 10 CS(MCSC) Regs
55 Sch Part III para 8(4) CS(MCSC) Regs
56 Sch Part III para 8(3)(a) CS(MCSC) Regs
57 CCS/15949/1996
58 Sch Part III para 8(3)(b) CS(MCSC) Regs
59 Sch Part III para 9(2) CS(MCSC) Regs
60 Sch Part III para 9(3) CS(MCSC) Regs
61 CCS/3182/1995; CCS/6145/1995
62 Sch Part III para 9(3) CS(MCSC) Regs
63 *How is Child Maintenance Worked Out?* CSL303, April 2010
64 *HH v CMEC* [2011] UKUT 60 (AAC)
65 CCS/1263/2008; *KB v CMEC* [2010] UKUT 434 (AAC)
66 CCS/7966/1995
67 Sch Part IV para 11(1) CS(MCSC) Regs
68 Sch Part IV para 11(1) CS(MCSC) Regs
69 Sch Part IV para 11(2) CS(MCSC) Regs
70 Sch Part IV para 11(2A) CS(MCSC) Regs
71 Sch Part IV para 13A CS(MCSC) Regs
72 Sch Part V para 16 CS(MCSC) Regs
73 Sch Part V para 16(2) CS(MCSC) Regs
74 Sch 1 para 10 CSA 1991

3. **Shared care**
75 Reg 8(1) CS(MCSC) Regs
76 CCS/2885/2005
77 *Re B (A Child)* [2006] EWCA Civ 1574
78 CCS/11728/1996
79 Reg 1(2)(a) CS(MCSC) Regs
80 Reg 1(2)(b) CS(MCSC) Regs; CCS/6/1994
81 Reg 7(4) CS(MCSC) Regs
82 *SO v CMEC* [2011] UKUT 149 (AAC)
83 Reg 1(2) CS(MCSC) Regs; CCS/449/1995
84 Reg 1(2)(b)(i) CS (MCSC) Regs
85 CCS/12686/1996

86 Reg 8 CS(MCSC) Regs
87 Reg 8(2) CS(MCSC) Regs
88 s144(3) and Sch 10 SSCBA 1992
89 s5(1) CSA 1991
90 Reg 14(2)(a) CS(MCSC) Regs
91 Reg 14(2)(b) CS(MCSC) Regs
92 Reg 14(2)(c) CS(MCSC) Regs
93 Sch 1 Part 1 paras 7 and 8 CSA 1991
94 Reg 7(1) CS(MCSC) Regs
95 R(CS)7/08
96 Reg 7(3) CS(MCSC) Regs
97 Reg 7(4) CS(MCSC) Regs
98 Reg 7(5) CS(MCSC) Regs
99 Sch 1 Part 1 para 8 CSA 1991
100 Sch 1 Part 1 para 7 CSA 1991
101 Sch 1 Part 1 para 7(4) CSA 1991
102 Sch 1 Part 1 para 7(6) CSA 1991
103 Sch 1 Part 1 para 7(7) CSA 1991
104 Reg 2(2) CS(MCSC) Regs
105 Sch 1 Part 1 para 7(5) CSA 1991
106 Reg 12 CS(MCSC) Regs
107 Reg 7(6) CS(MCSC) Regs
108 Reg 9(10) CS(MCSC) Regs
109 Reg 1(2)(b)(i) CS(MCSC) Regs
110 Reg 9(1) CS(MCSC) Regs
111 Reg 21(1)(a) CS(MCP) Regs
112 Reg 9(2) and (4) CS(MCSC) Regs
113 Reg 9(2)(c) CS(MCSC) Regs
114 Reg 9(5) CS(MCSC) Regs
115 Reg 9(7) CS(MCSC) Regs
116 Reg 9(8) CS(MCSC) Regs
117 Reg 9(9)(a) CS(MCSC) Regs

6

Chapter 6

Variations ('new rules')

This chapter covers:

This chapter only applies to 'new rules' cases, including cases that have been converted to the 'new rules'. There are additional provisions which must be read with this information in conversion cases where there is an existing departure direction or application for a departure (see Chapter 7).

An application for a variation to the maintenance calculation may be made before a calculation is made or once a maintenance calculation is in force.[1]

A variation to the calculation can only be made under a ground laid out in the legislation and only if it would be just and equitable to do so (see p129).

An application may be automatically rejected in certain specific circumstances, either at preliminary consideration or at a later stage (see p125). In certain cases, the Child Support Agency may refer the application to the First-tier Tribunal for a determination (see p130).

If an application is successful, it may result in a maintenance calculation being made, or, where a calculation already exists, being revised or superseded with the variation incorporated (see p134).

There is no separate variation decision; the decision is whether to revise/supersede the maintenance calculation or to refuse to revise/supersede the maintenance calculation with or without a variation element. This means that any appeal is simply against the revised or superseded decision or against the refusal to revise/supersede.

1. Grounds for a variation

A variation can be made for:[2]

- special expenses (see p111);
- property or capital transfers made before 5 April 1993 (see p116);
- additional cases (see p118).

Special expenses

A variation can be considered on special expenses grounds where there are:[3]

- costs of maintaining contact with the child(ren) for whom the calculation is, or will be, in force;
- costs of long-term illness or disability of a relevant child;
- prior debts, incurred before the couple separated;
- boarding school fees being paid for the child(ren) for whom the calculation is, or will be, in force;
- costs from paying a mortgage on the person with care's and child(ren)'s home.

Except for costs associated with an illness or disability of a relevant child, there is a threshold level, which must be exceeded.[4] If the net income of the non-resident parent is:

- £200 or more, the threshold is £15;
- below £200, the threshold is £10.

The threshold applies to one ground or, where there is more than one relevant ground, the sum of those costs. This also means that the first £10 or £15 of these special expenses are disregarded when calculating the variation and any subsequent adjustment to the calculation.[5] The disregard, like the threshold, does not apply to the costs associated with an illness or disability of a relevant child.

The Child Support Agency (CSA) can also substitute a lower amount for any special expenses costs that it thinks are unreasonably high or have been unreasonably incurred.[6] This may be below the threshold amount or nil. In the case of contact costs, any reduced amount must not be so low that it makes it impossible for contact to occur at the level of frequency stated in any court order, so long as those visits are taking place.[7]

The effect of a variation on special expenses grounds will be to reduce the net weekly income of the non-resident parent to be taken into account in the calculation.[8]

Contact costs

The costs related to the non-resident parent's contact with the qualifying child can be included.[9] They can be for the non-resident parent or the child. The cost of a travelling companion can also be included – eg, because of disability, long-term illness or the young age of the child.

Costs of contact cannot include those that arise if the non-resident parent shares care of the child and which are already taken into account under the shared-care provisions.[10] This means, for example, that the cost of travel to collect the child from an overnight stay which counts as a night of shared care cannot be grounds for a variation, as the non-resident parent already has that contact taken into account in his maintenance calculation.[11]

The following count as contact costs:[12]

- tickets for public transport;
- fuel for a private car;
- taxi fares, but only if the illness or disability of the non-resident parent or qualifying child makes it impractical to use another form of transport;
- car hire, if the cost of the journey would be less than by public transport or taxis, or a combination of both;
- accommodation costs for the parent or the child for overnight stays, if a return journey on the same day is impractical, or the pattern of care includes contact over two or more days;
- minor incidental costs, such as tolls or fees for roads/bridges. It may include parking fees and ticket reservation fees if it was necessary to incur these to maintain contact with the child.

The costs are based on an established pattern of visits, if one exists.[13] If there is no current established pattern, a previous one may be referred to if contact is to begin again, or an intended pattern, agreed between the non-resident parent and person with care, may be used. The pattern set out in a court order may also be used.

The costs are calculated as an average weekly amount. This is based on a 12-month, or shorter, period which ends just before the first day of the maintenance period in which the variation would take effect.[14] In other cases, it can be based on anticipated costs. If it is based on a pattern which ends before the maintenance calculation, the CSA will consider the costs incurred between the effective date of the variation and the date on which it would cease (ie, the date on which the circumstances giving rise to the variation ended) and the date of the interim maintenance decision/maintenance calculation.[15]

When contact is set out in a court order, it may only specify an upper limit on visits.

To determine whether the cost for fuel is reasonable, the CSA may compare the amount claimed with an average figure.

If the non-resident parent returns from abroad and contact is only one reason for the trip, the CSA may limit costs to those of travel from his home in the UK. The CSA may only allow those costs that are a necessary and integral consequence of maintaining contact with the child.

Overnight costs only include reasonable accommodation costs if an overnight stay is necessary. They do not cover the cost of meals and sundries.

Changes in contact may mean changes to the variation element. If contact stops, even through no fault of the non-resident parent, the calculation may be superseded to reflect this change (see p134).

Example 6.1

Bronwen has a net income of £428 and pays basic rate maintenance of £86 to Ivan for Ursula and Gretchen. She claims a special expenses cost for contact with her children, amounting to £450 over a six-month period since the girls attend boarding school. This includes travel from Northern Ireland by ferry, petrol and overnight stays in hotels, amounting to 18 nights over the six-month period.

The amounts included are deemed reasonable in the circumstances and the weekly amount is calculated:

£450 ÷ 26 = £17.30 a week on average.

This is above the threshold of £15. Therefore, a variation of £2.30 (£17.30 – £15) for contact costs may be considered, and Bronwen's net income reduced by this amount.

The number of nights Bronwen sees the children is 18 (ie, less than 26 nights in six months), so the contact costs are not for nights that could be classed as shared care (see p93).

Costs of a long-term illness or disability of a relevant child

A variation can be considered on the grounds of the costs of a long-term illness or disability of a relevant child – ie, a child for whom the non-resident parent or his new partner receives child benefit.

A long-term illness is one current at the date of the variation application or from the date the variation would take effect. It must be likely to last for at least a further 52 weeks or to be terminal.[16] The child is considered disabled if:[17]

- disability living allowance (DLA) is paid for her/him;
- s/he would receive DLA but for the fact that s/he is in hospital; *or*
- s/he is blind or registered as blind.

Costs allowable are the reasonable additional costs of any of the following:[18]

- personal care, attendance or communication needs;
- mobility;
- domestic help;
- medical aids which cannot be provided on the NHS;[19]
- heating, clothing and laundry;
- food essential for a diet recommended by a medical practitioner;
- adaptations to the non-resident parent's home;
- day care, respite care or rehabilitation.

If an aid or appliance can be provided on the NHS (by health services or local authorities) a variation will normally not be agreed, even if the item is not available due to a lack of funds at a particular time. However, a variation may be considered if there is likely to be a serious delay in supplying an item which would prevent the child's condition from seriously deteriorating. The decision maker may also consider the cost of the aid and whether it can be obtained at a cheaper price.

Any financial help towards these costs from any source, paid to the non-resident parent or a member of his household, is deducted.[20] This includes DLA, but only if it relates to the expense claimed – eg, if costs for personal care are claimed, DLA care component could be deducted, but not the mobility component. If DLA has been applied for, but is not in payment, it can be included if, when awarded, it will cover the date the variation starts. In other cases where no financial assistance is in payment, no amount will be offset against the costs.

Debts of the relationship

A non-resident parent may be repaying debts incurred *before* he became a non-resident parent (see p21) of the qualifying child (whether before or after April 1993). The repayments can count as special expenses, but only if the debt was incurred when the non-resident parent and person with care were a couple (see p25). The debts must have been taken out for the benefit of at least one of the following: [21]

- the non-resident parent and person with care, jointly;
- the person with care alone, if the non-resident parent is liable for the repayments;
- a person who is not a child but at the time the debt was incurred:
  - was a child;
  - lived with the non-resident parent and person with care; *and*
  - was the child of the non-resident parent, person with care or both of them;
- the qualifying child;
- any child other than the qualifying child who at the time the debt was incurred:
  - lived with the non-resident parent and person with care; *and*
  - is a child of the person with care.

Loans only count if they are from a qualifying lender, or from a non-resident parent's current or former employer.[22] Qualifying lenders include banks, building societies or other registered lenders (eg, hire purchase).[23]

The following do *not* count as debts for the purposes of variations:[24]

- debts incurred to buy something which the non-resident parent kept for his own use after the relationship ended;[25]
- a debt for which the applicant took responsibility under a financial settlement with the ex-partner or a court order;
- a debt for which a variation has previously been agreed, but which has not been repaid in the period for which the variation has been applied to the calculation;
- debts of a business or trade;
- secured mortgage repayments, except for amounts incurred to buy or repair/improve (see p185) the home of the person with care and qualifying child;
- endowment/insurance premiums, except for mortgage/insurance incurred to buy or repair/improve (see p185) the home of the person with care and qualifying child.

Payments on a debt taken out to pay off any negative equity on the former joint home once it has been sold do not count as debts, as the person with care no longer lives there.

The following also do *not* count as debts:[26]

- gambling debts;
- legal costs of the separation, divorce or dissolution of the civil partnership;
- credit card repayments;
- overdrafts, unless taken out for a specified amount repayable over a specified period;
- fines imposed on the applicant;
- any debt incurred to pay off one of these;
- any other debt the CSA considers reasonable to exclude.

A debt incurred to pay a former debt which would have counted may be included. However, only that part which could have counted is included as special expenses.[27]

A variation is normally based on the original debt repayment period; any rescheduling of the debt is usually ignored. However, if the applicant has been unemployed or ill and the creditors have agreed to extend the repayment period, the CSA can take the extended period into account. There is discretion on the length of time over which the debt may be considered to be extended when setting the period for which the variation for prior debt applies to the calculation.

Boarding school fees

The maintenance element of boarding school fees incurred, or expected to be incurred, by the non-resident parent for the qualifying child may be considered.[28] Only term-time costs for non-advanced education at a recognised educational establishment can be included.[29]

If the maintenance element cannot be distinguished from other costs, the CSA can decide what to include, but this should not exceed 35 per cent of the total fees.[30]

If the non-resident parent receives financial help to pay the fees, or only pays part of the fees with someone else, a proportion of the costs are included. This is calculated in the same ratio as the maintenance element to overall fees.[31]

In all cases, a variation for boarding school fees should not reduce the amount of income to be considered for calculating maintenance by more than 50 per cent.[32]

Example 6.2

Bronwen claims special expenses for her contribution to boarding school costs for Ursula and Gretchen. She pays the school £1,500 a term – ie, £4,500 a year. Ivan pays the rest of the fees – ie, £4,500 a year. Her weekly net income is £428.

The fees for each child per term are £1,500 and the maintenance element is £500 a term.

Bronwen's contribution to maintenance is worked out as £250 a child each term – ie, £500. Over the three terms this amounts to £1,500, which is converted into a weekly figure (£1,500 ÷ 365 x 7 = £28.77). This is above the threshold of £15 so a variation for a contribution to boarding school fees of £13.77 may be considered. (If this were to be accepted, it would not reduce her net income by more than 50 per cent.)

Payments for certain mortgages, loans or insurance policies

A variation can be considered on the basis of payments made to a mortgage lender, insurer or person with care for a mortgage or loan if:[33]

- it was taken out to facilitate the purchase of, or repairs/improvements to, the property by someone other than the non-resident parent;
- the payments are not made because of a debt or other legal liability of the non-resident parent for the period in which the variation is applied;
- the property was the person with care's and non-resident parent's home when they were a couple, and it is still the home of the person with care and qualifying child; *and*
- the non-resident parent has no legal/financial rights in the property – eg, a charge or equitable interest.

Payments may also be considered for an insurance/endowment policy taken out to discharge a mortgage or loan as above, except where the non-resident parent is entitled to any part of the proceeds when the policy matures.[34] See p400 for more information.

Property and capital transfers

A variation on property or capital transfer grounds is only possible if a pre-5 April 1993 court order or written agreement was in force between the non-resident parent and the person with care and/or the child(ren) in the child maintenance application.[35] The court order must have been to transfer property/capital in lieu of maintenance for the child either wholly or in part.[36] If the court order specifies that it is in lieu of spousal maintenance only, the variation will be disallowed.[37]

The court order must be made under one of the Acts listed in Appendix 3.[38]

The transfer must mean that the non-resident parent has transferred any beneficial interest in the property/capital to:[39]

- the person with care;
- the qualifying child; *or*
- trustees, if the trust is set up solely, or as one of its objectives, to provide maintenance for the qualifying child.

If the transfer does not satisfy any of these conditions but the CSA is satisfied that some or all of the property subsequently transferred to the person with care, the transfer will be accepted.[40]

The CSA first works out the value of the transfer, ignoring any part which was not in lieu of child maintenance.[41] (Allowance is also made for any compensating transfer from the person with care to the non-resident parent.) Unless there is evidence to show otherwise, the CSA assumes that:[42]

- the property covered by the order/agreement was held in equal shares by the non-resident parent and person with care;
- if those parties had been married, half of the value of the transfer was for the person with care's benefit, and not for the child(ren);
- if those parties were *never* married, *none* of the value of the transfer was for the person with care's benefit.

The minimum value of the transfer must be £5,000.[43]

The equivalent weekly value is then worked out. The number of years of liability is deemed to begin on the date of the order/agreement and to end on the date it sets for maintenance to end (for the youngest child if there is more than one), or, if no date is given, when the youngest child reaches 18.[44] Using that figure and the interest rate at the date of the order/agreement, a multiplier is given by a table.[45] That gives an equivalent weekly value.

The effect of a variation on property or capital transfer grounds is that the equivalent weekly value of the transfer will be deducted from the amount of maintenance that the non-resident parent would otherwise be required to pay to the person with care with respect to whom the transfer was made.[46]

If using the equivalent weekly value in the variation would lead to an amount of maintenance of less than the child maintenance payable under the order/agreement, a lower weekly value can be set.[47]

Example 6.3

Marcus and Helene divorced in 1992, when their youngest child, Robert, was one. Marcus transferred his share in the home to Helene, in lieu of maintenance for her and the children. Marcus applies for a variation on property transfer grounds.

The value of the house at that time was £46,000 but there was a mortgage of £14,000. The CSA considers that of the £16,000 transferred (£46,000 – £14,000 ÷ 2 as they each had equal shares) only £8,000 can be considered to be in lieu of child maintenance. This is above the threshold of £5,000.

The number of years of liability is worked out as 17 – ie, from the date of the order until Robert is 18. The interest rate for a judgment debt at the time of the order was 15 per cent. Based on the table of equivalent values this gives a multiplier of 0.00323.

The equivalent weekly value of the property transfer to be considered is £8,000 x 0.00323 = £25.84.

A variation to reduce the amount of maintenance Marcus is due to pay by £25.84 a week can, therefore, be considered.

Additional cases

There are additional cases in which a variation may be applied for by a person with care or child applicant in Scotland. These are if the non-resident parent has:[48]

- assets over £65,000;
- income which has not been taken into account in the calculation;
- diverted income; *or*
- a lifestyle which is inconsistent with his stated income.

The effect of a variation on additional cases grounds will be to increase the net weekly income of the non-resident parent to be taken into account in the calculation.[49] The maximum net weekly income, after adding any amount for additional cases variation(s), cannot exceed the capped amount of £2,000.

If the non-resident parent is in receipt of a benefit that attracts the flat rate (other than income support (IS), income-based jobseeker's allowance (JSA), income-related employment and support allowance (ESA) or pension credit (PC)), even though he may not pay this because of shared care or because he qualifies for the nil rate (but not on income grounds), there are special rules on the maximum amount payable when a variation is agreed on additional cases grounds.[50] This is known as the 'better-buy' provision (see p131).

Assets over £65,000

For a variation to be possible in this case, the CSA must be satisfied that the asset:[51]

- is under the non-resident parent's control, or is one in which he has a beneficial interest;
- has been transferred to trustees, but the non-resident parent is the beneficiary of the trust, and the transfer was made to reduce the amount of assets which could be considered under a variation application;
- is subject to a trust of which the non-resident parent is a beneficiary.

Assets include:[52]

- money – actual cash or deposits in banks, building society, Post Office accounts, premium bonds or savings certificates;
- legal estate, interest in, or rights over, land;
- stocks and shares;
- claims it would be reasonable to enforce;
- in Scotland, money due or an obligation owed which it would be reasonable to enforce; *and*
- any of the above located outside Great Britain.

The CSA will not count assets if any of the following apply:[53]

- their total value is £65,000 or less after repaying any mortgage/charge on them. Any asset in respect of which income is taken into account following

the application of the next type of variation described (see below) is deducted from the non-resident parent's total assets before this test is applied;
- it is satisfied the non-resident parent is holding them for a reasonable purpose – eg, cash from the sale of a home that is intended to purchase a new home;
- they are compensation for personal injury;
- they are used for a trade or business (except a legal estate or interest in or rights over land, which produces income which is not part of the non-resident parent's net weekly income). Shares are not used in the course of a business or trade if the trade or business is not that of the non-resident parent – eg, if he has invested in a company or even owns one, but it is not his trade/business;[54]
- the asset is the home of the non-resident parent or his child; *or*
- they are payments from certain trusts (eg, Macfarlane Trust or the variant CJD compensation trust), which would be ignored if the non-resident parent were on IS.[55]

If an asset is held in joint names, the CSA assumes that each person has equal shares, unless there is evidence to suggest otherwise.[56]

The weekly value of the assets is worked out by multiplying the value of the assets by the statutory rate of interest and dividing the resulting figure by 52.[57] The statutory rate of interest is that which applies on the effective date in the non-resident parent's country of habitual residence (ie, England, Wales, Scotland or Northern Ireland); this is currently 8 per cent.[58] If the non-resident parent works abroad for a UK-based employer, the rate is based on the locality of the employer. The weekly value is added to other income, including benefits, and bearing in mind the better-buy rules for those on benefit (see p131).[59]

Example 6.4

Graham has a net income of £480 a week and pays maintenance to Andie of £96 a week. Andie applies for a variation on the grounds that Graham has substantial assets – ie, a holiday home in Spain and savings.

The property in Spain has a value of £52,000 and Graham has savings and investments of £17,000. The total value of his assets is £69,000, which is above the threshold of £65,000. This is calculated to have a weekly value of £106.15 (ie, £69,000 x 8% ÷ 52). A variation may, therefore, be considered on the basis of Graham having £106.15 more net income.

If Graham had owned the property in Spain jointly with his new partner, Nadia, the total value of his assets would have been £26,000 + £17,000 = £43,000, which is below the threshold.

Income not taken into account and diversion of income

Income not taken into account covers situations where the non-resident parent is on the nil rate (except where this is because income is below £5) or the flat rate because of receipt of a prescribed benefit (other than IS, income-based JSA, income-related ESA or PC), even though he may pay less because of shared care.[60] The CSA must be satisfied that the non-resident parent receives income which would be taken into account in the maintenance calculation if he were not due to pay the nil rate or the flat rate for these reasons.

A variation may also be agreed for income not taken into account if:[61]

- the non-resident parent has the ability to control the amount of income he receives from a company or business, including earnings from employment or self-employment, or is able to control the amount that is taken into account as his net weekly income;[62] *and*
- the income from that company or business would not otherwise be taken into account in the maintenance calculation.

This variation could, for example, apply if income in the form of dividends is received by a company director.[63] However, it can also apply to other forms of income received from a company or business. Reimbursement to the non-resident parent of legitimate business expenses is ignored. This variation can also apply if a non-resident parent is held to have reduced his net income by an unreasonable extent by making substantial pension contributions.[64] The additional income received from the company or business is added to the non-resident parent's net weekly income for the purposes of the maintenance calculation.

For a variation for income not taken into account to be made, the income not taken into account must be net weekly income of over £100. This can be from either of the situations described above or, if a variation is considered under both cases, income from both can be added together.[65]

When working out the earnings of students, the total income for the year, ending with the relevant week, is added together and divided by 52 to give a weekly amount. An alternative period may be used if the CSA considers it more representative.

The weekly value of any additional income is added to other income from benefits, bearing in mind that the better-buy provision applies to those on benefit when calculating the maximum maintenance due.[66] Benefits include those prescribed for the flat rate (except IS/income-based JSA/income-related ESA/PC), less any disregards.[67] For an explanation of disregards for these purposes, see the better-buy provision on p131.

Example 6.5

Joel is a mature student who works part time in a care home. He is on the nil rate for maintenance. Kaliani applies for a variation on the ground of income not taken into account. Kaliani looks after one child, Selim.

Joel's student grant and loan do not count as income, so only his part-time earnings are considered. Over the year Joel's net earnings are £9,367.80, which is converted into a weekly amount (ie, £9,367.80 ÷ 52 = £180.15). As this is over £100, a variation may be considered using a weekly value figure of £180.15. Therefore, if the variation to the calculation is agreed, instead of paying nothing, Joel will now be due to pay a reduced rate of £25 (£5 + (25% x £80.15) = £25.04 rounded to the nearest pound).

Diversion of income is considered where:[68]

- the non-resident parent has the ability to control the income he receives, including earnings from self-employment; *and*
- the CSA is satisfied that the non-resident parent has unreasonably reduced the amount of income he would have received (and which would have been taken into account in the maintenance calculation or under a variation for income from a company or business – see p119) by diverting it to someone else. The diversion does *not* have to have been arranged specifically to avoid child maintenance responsibilities.

Diversion of income may be made:

- to a third party, such as a new partner or close family member;
- to a business, such as where the non-resident parent takes a lower income, or to a pension scheme from which the non-resident parent will benefit later. It would, however, have to be reasonable to make a variation in such circumstances;
- towards other purposes, such as where the non-resident parent uses company assets for private use or business funds for day-to-day expenditure.

Example 6.6

Marcus runs his own import/export business, employing his new partner, Shamira, and his brother. Each has a company car, in his case a Jaguar. His brother is paid £600 a week and he and Shamira each receive £400. His ex-wife, Helene, gets basic-rate maintenance of £80 for their two children. Helene applies for a variation because she thinks Marcus is diverting income via the company, especially as Shamira does not seem to do any work. Part of Marcus's day-to-day expenses are included in business expenses – eg, the car and business lunches. Shamira's salary could also be a token payment, as Marcus takes less from the business than he pays his brother. The CSA considers that, on balance, there could be diversion of income via the company and Shamira's wages. Given its contentious nature, the case is referred to the First-tier Tribunal.

The full amount of any diverted income will be added to net weekly income when working out maintenance.[69]

Lifestyle inconsistent with declared income

The person with care, or a qualifying child in Scotland, may apply for a variation on this ground if the CSA is satisfied that the income used (or which would have been used) in the calculation is substantially lower than that needed to support the non-resident parent's lifestyle.[70] This variation may be granted in cases where the flat rate applies because of benefit income, but not where the flat rate is payable because of receipt of IS, income-based JSA, income-related ESA or PC.

However, a variation will not be allowed where it is clear that the lifestyle is paid for by:[71]

- income which is, or would be, disregarded in the maintenance calculation;
- income which could be considered under the diversion of income ground;
- income which could be considered under a variation for income not taken into account from a company or business (see p119);
- assets, or income from assets; *or*
- a partner's income or assets, except if the non-resident parent is able to influence or control the amount of income, assets or income from the assets.

A variation cannot be granted where an inconsistent lifestyle is financed by borrowing, as this would not meet the requirement that the variation decision be just and equitable (see p129).[72]

In addition to these situations, if the calculation is not based on net weekly income, a variation will not be allowed where the lifestyle is paid for from income of £100 or less, or which could be considered to be in the ground of income not taken into account (see p119).[73]

The amount of income which is taken into account is the difference between the amount:[74]

- the non-resident parent needs to support his overall lifestyle; *and*
- taken into account (or which would have been taken into account) in the maintenance calculation.

This includes any income from benefits (ie, except for IS/income-based JSA/ income-related ESA/PC, benefits prescribed for the flat rate, less disregards), bearing in mind the better-buy rules for those on benefit. See p131 for an explanation of the better-buy rules and the disregards of benefit income.

This ground is most likely to be used in situations where the non-resident parent is self-employed or where it is suspected that he is working without fully declaring income for tax and national insurance purposes.

It would not be enough to show that the non-resident parent pursued one extravagant activity, as there may be good reasons for this. The non-resident parent must have an overall lifestyle that, in most respects, is inconsistent with his declared income – eg, a large, expensively furnished home, expensive car, frequent foreign holidays and expensive leisure activities would all be considered. The use of declared capital to finance an otherwise inconsistent lifestyle, or a lifestyle supported by a partner's wealth or income, cannot lead to a successful variation.

Example 6.7

Marcus lives with his new partner, Shamira, in a townhouse in central London. He runs his own import/export business. His ex-wife, Helene, gets basic-rate maintenance of £80 for their two children. Helene applies for a variation because Marcus is able to afford to live in central London and drive a new Jaguar (changing cars every two or three years), he plays polo (keeping three ponies in stables), is a member of an exclusive golf club, and he and Shamira frequently travel abroad.

Part of the expenses are included in business expenses – eg, the car and travel abroad on business trips, and the golf club membership is used for corporate entertaining. Shamira is also an employee of the company, meaning her income is under Marcus's control, though her wages are equivalent to those of other staff. The CSA considers that, on balance, his lifestyle does appear inconsistent with his income. However, it also considers that there could be a diversion of income. Given its contentious nature, the case is referred to the First-tier Tribunal.

Had the situation been reversed, with Shamira being independently wealthy, owning the business and paying for the lifestyle, including paying Marcus's wages, the case may have been refused. Helene could appeal such a refusal, although it may be that a variation would not be possible on this ground. The CSA would also have to consider whether there had been a diversion of income or assets which Marcus could control.

2. Applying for a variation

An application for a variation may be made before or after a maintenance calculation has been made.[75] Only a relevant person may apply – ie, a person with care, a non-resident parent or a qualifying child in Scotland. An authorised representative may also make an application. The Child Support Agency (CSA) also has the discretion to reinstate a previous variation without an application in certain prescribed circumstances (see p136).

The application for a variation can be made either orally or in writing.[76] This means an applicant may give details over the phone, although the CSA may ask for a written application – eg, because complicated special expenses are being asked for which could not be explained over the telephone. A form may be provided by the CSA, or the applicant can send the application in another written form which the CSA may accept as sufficient, depending on the circumstances.[77] If a written application is required, this should be provided within 14 days. If the time limit is exceeded without good cause, the effective date of the variation may be affected.

The application must state the grounds on which it is made.[78] If the application does not state the grounds, or at least give a reason, it will not be accepted as properly made.

Example 6.8

Joe applies for a variation because he believes his maintenance is too high. The CSA does not accept it as a properly made application.

Joe applies for a variation because he believes his maintenance is too high and he cannot afford it because of the high cost of pet food. The CSA accepts the application as properly made, but then rejects the application on preliminary consideration, as it is not on a regulated ground.

Joe applies for a variation because he believes his maintenance is too high because he cannot afford the kennel costs he incurs when he travels to see his children. The CSA accepts the application as properly made and it is given preliminary consideration. It rejects the application as kennel costs are not a recognised ground. However, had Joe referred to other contact costs (eg, tickets or fuel), his application would probably have proceeded.

If a maintenance calculation is already in force and a new application is made by the same person, the CSA may (but is not obliged to) treat it as a request for a variation, depending on the circumstances and the information contained in the application.[79]

If an application is made, but there is insufficient information to decide whether to progress it, the CSA may request further information.[80] The applicant is given one month from the date of notification in which to supply the information.[81] This time limit may be extended in special circumstances – eg, if the applicant is in hospital. If the information is not provided, the CSA may either reject the application or proceed with it at its discretion.[82]

An application for a variation may be amended or withdrawn at any time before a decision is made.[83] This may be done orally or in writing. No amendment can be made if the change relates to a period after the effective date of the application.[84]

3. Procedure

Once an application has been made, the procedure is as follows.

- There is a preliminary consideration of the application (see p125).
- Unless rejected, other parties may be notified and asked to make representations ('contest') – see p126.
- An interim maintenance decision may be made (see p127).
- A regular payment condition may be imposed (see p128).
- The decision will be considered (see p129).

In addition, the case may be passed to the First-tier Tribunal after preliminary consideration for a determination (see p130).

The application will proceed for determination unless it has already failed.[85] It may fail (ie, the Child Support Agency (CSA) may refuse to consider it further before this point) because, for example:

- one of the grounds for rejection is established on preliminary consideration (see below);
- it is withdrawn; *or*
- the regular payment condition has not been met.

Two or more applications for a variation may be considered at the same time.[86] In addition, if appropriate, an application made on one ground may be treated as an application on a different ground.[87]

Preliminary consideration

Once an application is properly made, there is a preliminary consideration of the case.[88] At this point, the CSA may reject the application and decide:

- to revise or supersede the maintenance calculation, or to refuse to revise or supersede;[89] *or*
- make the maintenance calculation, or make a default maintenance decision.[90]

Any decision carries the normal appeal rights.[91]

Grounds for rejecting or refusing a variation

An application for a variation may be rejected because:[92]

- the requirements of the stated ground are not met;
- in special expenses cases, the threshold is not exceeded;
- in property/capital transfer cases, the £5,000 minimum value is not exceeded;
- in additional assets cases, their value does not exceed £65,000;
- in income not taken into account cases, this does not exceed £100;
- information requested by the CSA has not been provided within the one-month time limit;
- a default maintenance decision is in force;
- the application is made by the person with care or qualifying child on additional cases grounds and the capped amount of income is already applied, or the non-resident parent or his partner are in receipt of working tax credit;
- the application is made by the non-resident parent on special expenses grounds and, after deducting these, net income exceeds the capped amount;
- the non-resident parent is on the flat rate as he or his partner is on income support (IS), income-based jobseeker's allowance (JSA), income-related employment and support allowance (ESA) or pension credit (PC) (including if the partner is also a non-resident parent), but is due to pay less than the flat rate, or nil because of shared care or the transitional rules on conversion;
- the non-resident parent is due to pay the flat rate (or the lower prescribed amount) under the transitional rules on conversion, or a property or capital

transfer reduces maintenance below the flat rate or because of part-time care by a local authority;

- the application is made by the non-resident parent; *and*
  - he is on the nil rate; *or*
  - he is on the flat rate because he receives a prescribed benefit (other than IS/ income-based JSA/ESA/PC) or has income of £100 or less; *or*
  - he pays the flat rate of £5 (or less if apportioned) because of shared care, including care by a local authority.

In some cases, if a default maintenance decision applies, an application for a variation may contain sufficient information to revise the default decision and replace it with a maintenance calculation.

Rejecting an application for a variation at preliminary consideration for one of the above reasons is a power and not a duty.[93] However, an application must be refused if it would not be just and equitable to agree to it (see p129).[94]

Contesting the application

If the application has not been rejected on preliminary consideration, the other relevant parties will usually be notified. However, in some situations where the CSA has discretion to reinstate a previous variation, it does not need to notify or invite representations (see p136).

The notification may be done orally or in writing and must:[95]

- state the grounds on which the application has been made and provide any information or evidence the applicant has given to support it;
- invite parties to make representations about the circumstances within 14 days; *and*
- not contain information that should not be disclosed.

In practice, non-applicants are informed in writing and supplied with the evidence. Where the application has been via a phone call, the evidence may be a transcript of the telephone conversation.

In some cases, the applicant may be late in supplying further evidence or information (ie, outside the one-month time limit) but the CSA may have decided to proceed with the application in the meantime and notify the other parties. This information may be passed to the other parties later and a further 14 days for representations allowed from the date of this later notification.[96] If the CSA is satisfied that it is reasonable, this time limit may be extended.[97]

The other parties may respond orally or in writing, although the CSA may require them to make a written submission. If no contesting information is provided, the CSA may make a determination on the application as it stands.[98]

Any information which the other party provides, other than that which may not be disclosed (see p127), may be forwarded to the applicant if the CSA considers this reasonable.[99] The applicant is given 14 days to comment on the evidence or information supplied by the other party.

Additional non-disclosure rules

There are additional rules on non-disclosure in variations cases. Supporting evidence or information from one party will not be notified to the other party if it contains:[100]

- details of an illness or disability of a relevant other child if the non-resident parent has requested that this is not disclosed and the CSA agrees;
- medical evidence which has not been disclosed to the applicant or a relevant person (person with care, non-resident parent or qualifying child in Scotland) which would be harmful to that individual;
- the address of a relevant person or qualifying child, or information which could lead to that individual or child being located, and there is a risk of harm or undue distress.

If an applicant requests that information is not disclosed, this will be discussed with her/him. It may be possible to make an amended application which does not include details s/he does not wish to be disclosed. If an applicant refuses to disclose information that is relevant for the other party to contest the application, the application could be rejected. However, there may be a good reason for non-disclosure and each case should be considered on its own merits.

When representations are not required

Representations from the other relevant parties are not required if:[101]

- the CSA is reinstating a variation at its own discretion (see p136);
- there is a property/capital transfer variation and a change of circumstances meant that the CSA no longer had jurisdiction, but a subsequent change means it does and an application for variation is made on a further application for a maintenance calculation;
- a variation is agreed and the non-resident parent has the maintenance calculation replaced by a default decision, but subsequently this is replaced with a maintenance calculation.

Interim maintenance decision

If an application for a variation is made before the maintenance calculation, an interim maintenance decision may be made.[102] This means an interim maintenance decision can be made if the first calculation has not been made or if the process is complete except for an outstanding variation application. The amount of the interim maintenance decision will be the maintenance calculated in the normal way, ignoring the variation. This is to allow the variation application to be considered. An interim maintenance decision may be replaced by a maintenance calculation, which is made whether or not a variation has been agreed. The effective date of the maintenance calculation will be the same as the interim maintenance decision.

The interim maintenance decision can be appealed in the normal way. However, when a maintenance calculation is made which replaces this, any appeal may lapse.[103] If the interim maintenance decision is superseded, the normal 5 per cent change in net income tolerance rule (see p351) does not apply.

Regular payment condition

If a non-resident parent has applied for a variation, he may have a regular payment condition imposed after the preliminary consideration.[104] It is intended that this will be used if a non-resident parent has:

- a poor payment record or arrears;
- failed to make payments while the variation application is being contested and considered; *or*
- special expenses which make it hard for him to meet the maintenance liability.

The amount due under a regular payment condition will be either:[105]

- the maintenance calculated, including that set under an interim maintenance decision; *or*
- the amount of maintenance which would be due if the variation was agreed.

This means that if the CSA believes that the variation application will be successful, it may set a regular payment condition that adjusts the maintenance calculated to reflect the variation, reducing the financial burden on the parent. However, if it believes that the application will be unsuccessful and a regular payment condition is imposed, it will be set at the calculation rate.

A regular payment condition does not affect the amount of maintenance the non-resident parent is liable to pay. Therefore, if the set amount is lower than the amount due, there will be arrears if the variation application fails.

The condition is set independently of any other arrears arrangement the parent may have and ends either when the CSA makes a final decision on the maintenance calculation (whether or not the variation is agreed to), or when the application is withdrawn.[106]

When a regular payment condition is imposed, the non-resident parent, person with care and/or qualifying child applicant in Scotland will be sent written notification.[107] This makes it clear that if the condition is not met, the application may lapse.[108]

If a non-resident parent does not meet the regular payment condition within one month of this notification, the CSA will refuse to consider the application for a variation.[109] Written notification of this refusal will be sent to the non-resident parent, person with care and/or qualifying child applicant in Scotland.[110] A refusal to consider the application cannot be appealed.

Considering the decision

The CSA can exercise discretion in variations to the maintenance calculation. In addition to the normal rules, the CSA must be satisfied that:[111]

- the grounds are met; *and*
- it is just and equitable to agree to the variation.

When considering the decision, the CSA must bear in mind the general principles that:[112]

- a parent is responsible for maintaining her/his children when s/he can afford to do so;
- a parent is responsible for maintaining all her/his children equally;
- the welfare of any child affected by an application for a variation must be taken into account.

A decision may be made to agree to the variation in full or to refuse it. This may result in a revision or supersession of the decision or replacement of the interim maintenance decision.[113] The revision/supersession decision is dealt with under the normal rules (see p134).

Just and equitable

Even though the grounds are met, a variation decision will only be agreed if it is just and equitable.[114] Certain factors must be taken into account when making the decision. These include:[115]

- whether agreeing to a variation would lead the non-resident parent or parent with care to give up employment;
- if the applicant is the non-resident parent, whether there is any liability to pay child maintenance under a court order or agreement prior to the effective date of the maintenance calculation; *or*
- if the non-resident parent has applied for a special expenses variation, whether he could make financial arrangements to cover those expenses or could pay for them from money currently spent on non-essentials.

This list is not exhaustive and other factors may be considered when deciding what is just and equitable. As the child support legislation expressly leaves it to the courts to make orders that a parent pay towards tuition fees, the fact that a non-resident parent pays for school fees cannot be taken into account when deciding whether it is just and equitable to agree to a variation.[116]

The following must *not* be taken into account:[117]

- whether or not the child's conception was planned;
- who was responsible for the breakdown of the relationship between the non-resident parent and the person with care;
- whether the non-resident parent or person with care is in a new relationship with someone who is not the qualifying child's parent;

- any contact arrangements;
- the income or assets of anyone other than the non-resident parent, and/or, if an application is made on the grounds of a lifestyle inconsistent with declared income, his partner;
- any failure of the non-resident parent to pay child maintenance under CSA arrangements, a court order or written agreement; *and*
- representations from individuals other than the person with care, non-resident parent, or a qualifying child applicant in Scotland.

Referral to the First-tier Tribunal

Once the application has passed the preliminary consideration and contest stage, the case may be passed to the First-tier Tribunal for a determination on whether or not to agree to the variation.[118] This will normally only occur if a novel or particularly contentious issue is being considered. The First-tier Tribunal should consider the grounds stated in the following order:[119]

- assets over £65,000;
- income not taken into account;
- diversion of income;
- lifestyle inconsistent with declared income.

The First-tier Tribunal applies the same rules as a CSA decision maker and determines that the variation should be either agreed to or refused.[120] Its determination will be passed back to the CSA to make the decision. This decision by the CSA (ie, to revise/supersede, or refuse to revise/supersede, the maintenance calculation) may then be appealed in the normal way (see p137).

4. The decision

A variation is an element of the maintenance calculation. The Child Support Agency (CSA) may agree to, or refuse, the application for variation. In either case, it may result in a decision to:[121]

- revise or supersede the maintenance calculation/replace the interim maintenance decision, or refuse to revise or supersede;
- make a maintenance calculation (this may replace an interim maintenance decision) or default maintenance decision.

In some cases, a variation may be agreed which makes no difference to the amount of maintenance calculated. A revision or supersession will still be carried out, as each decision gives further appeal rights.

Once a variation is made, it will continue to be considered each time there is a revision or supersession of the maintenance calculation, under the normal revision/supersession rules (see Chapter 17). Because of some changes in circumstances, the variation may cease to have effect, in which case the calculation may be suspended or cancelled in order to remove the variation element. When there is a further change in circumstances, the variation may be reinstated by the CSA without an application. In other cases, a new request for a variation may need to be made.

Following variation to the maintenance calculation, as with other maintenance calculation decisions, the amount of maintenance paid may be affected by the special rules on court order phasing (see p322) or conversions (see Chapter 7).

The effect of the variation

The effect of the variation should not reduce the total amount of maintenance to less than £5,[122] and the maximum amount of net income that can be taken into account is the capped amount of £2,000.[123] The following sections examine the effect of a variation on different grounds, including where there is more than one ground – eg, special expenses and additional cases. The CSA calls these 'concurrent variations'.

Additional cases

If a variation is made on additional cases grounds, the amount of any additional income is added to the net income of the non-resident parent.[124] If this would result in a net income figure above the capped amount, the net income is restricted to the capped amount of £2,000.

Example 6.9

The case in *Example 6.6* is referred to the First-tier Tribunal. The First-tier Tribunal determines that there should be a variation for additional income, with a weekly value of £360 for both diversion of income and a lifestyle inconsistent with declared income. This is added to Marcus's net income, as used in the maintenance calculation, of £400. His net income is now £760. The amount he is now due to pay Helene is £152.

If the non-resident parent is in receipt of a benefit (other than income support (IS), income-based jobseeker's allowance (JSA), income-related employment and support allowance (ESA) or pension credit (PC)) that attracts the flat rate, even though he may not pay this because of shared care or because he qualifies for the nil rate (but not on income grounds), there are special rules on the maximum amount payable when a variation is agreed on additional cases grounds.[125] This is known as the 'better-buy' provision (see below).

Better-buy

The maximum amount of maintenance a non-resident parent on benefit (other than IS, income-based JSA, income-related ESA or PC) will have to pay after a variation on additional cases grounds is the lesser of:[126]

- the flat rate plus the amount calculated under the normal calculation rules on additional income (exclusive of the benefit income); *or*
- the amount calculated under the normal calculation rules on total income (including any benefit that attracts the flat rate liability, less disregards).

The amounts disregarded in benefit income are:[127]
- constant attendance and exceptionally severe disablement allowances in industrial injuries benefits;
- constant attendance, exceptionally severe disablement, severe occupational and mobility supplement allowances in war disablement pensions;
- unemployability allowances in service pensions.

Example 6.10

Adam gets retirement pension of £97.65 and is due to pay Carol the flat rate of £5 for one child. He has an occupational pension of £97.50 a week and a personal pension of £39 a week, providing a further £136.50 a week. Adam's total income is £234.15. Carol applies for a variation on the ground of income not taken into account. As he has income over £100, the better-buy calculation is carried out:

Flat rate (£5) + £5 + (25% x £36.50, rounded to the nearest pound = £9) = £19

Normal rules calculation on total income: £97.65 + £136.50 = £234.15

Basic rate maintenance is 15% x £234.15 = £35.12 (rounded to £35)

Better-buy will mean a variation may be considered which would result in maintenance of £19 – ie, the lesser of the two amounts.

Special expenses

The total amount of any special expenses (less any threshold amounts) is deducted from the net weekly income of the non-resident parent and the calculation is carried out as normal using this amount.[128] If there is more than one special expense included, the amounts are aggregated and only one threshold is applied (where applicable).[129]

If the net income is the capped amount, the effect of the variation is worked out by subtracting the special expenses from the actual net weekly income.[130] If this results in a figure above the capped amount of £2,000, the special expenses variation will be refused.

Example 6.11

Bronwen has a net income of £428 a week and pays basic rate maintenance of £86 to Ivan for Ursula and Gretchen. She claims special expenses costs for contact with her children, which amounts to £450 over a six-month period, and for the contribution to their boarding school fees of £1,500 a term.

Her special expenses are worked out as £17.30 for contact and £28.77 for boarding school costs, totalling £46.07. The threshold of £15 applies and £15 is deducted from the total, leaving £31.07.

This is deducted from her weekly net income: £428 – £31.07 = £396.93

Her maintenance is now worked out in the usual way: 20% x £396.93 = £79.39 (rounded to £79)

Her variation for special expenses has reduced her maintenance from £86 a week to £79.

Property and capital transfers

The transfer is treated as in lieu of periodical payments of maintenance.[131] If the CSA is satisfied that a transfer was in lieu of periodical payments of maintenance, the equivalent weekly value is subtracted from the maintenance calculated to produce the amount due after a variation on property/capital transfer grounds.[132]

Example 6.12

Marcus has a property transfer variation agreed with a weekly value of £25.84. His net weekly income is £400, and under the maintenance calculation he is due to pay Helene maintenance of £80 a week for Robert and Heather. There is no reduction for shared care and so the weekly value of the property transfer is subtracted from the amount he is due to pay:

£80 – £25.84 = £54.16, the amount he must pay following the variation.

Concurrent variations

If there is more than one variation element (ie, special expenses and additional cases) to be applied, the calculation is carried out using the following steps.

Step 1

Work out the amounts of each element.

Step 2

Apply the additional cases element, capping the income at £2,000.

Step 3

Apply the special expenses element.

Step 4

Work out the maintenance due, applying any apportionment or reduction for shared care or part-time local authority care.

Step 5

Apply any property transfer element (only that which applies to the parent with care who benefited from the transfer).

Step 6

Check that the total amount of maintenance is not less than £5. If so, apportion this between the persons with care.

Example 6.13

The situation is as in *Example 6.3*. In this instance, both the property transfer and the additional cases variation are applied to work out how much Marcus must pay Helene for Robert and Heather. His net income before variation is £400, as before.

Step 1 The additional cases variation is that £360 additional income should be included. The property transfer variation has a weekly value of £25.84.

Step 2 £360 + £400 = £760, which is below the capped amount.

Step 3 Does not apply.

Step 4 Basic maintenance due is 20% x £760 = £152

Step 5 Maintenance due is reduced by the property transfer (ie, £152 – £25.84 = £126.16).

Therefore, instead of receiving £80 from Marcus, Helene will now be due £126.16 a week.

Revisions and supersessions

A variation is not a separate decision to be challenged; it is a variation of the maintenance calculation. If a variation is agreed and applied to the calculation, this decision may be challenged by seeking a revision within one month. Any change of circumstances, whether in relation to the variation or other factors, can result in a revision or supersession of the maintenance calculation under the normal rules, depending on the circumstances (see Chapter 17). This also applies to decisions referred by the CSA to the First-tier Tribunal for a decision – eg, contentious cases.[133]

The variation will be taken into account in any reconsideration. However, there may be changes of circumstances which mean that the variation ceases to have effect. In certain circumstances, a previous variation to the calculation may be reinstated, without an application, at the discretion of the CSA (see p136).

Date the variation takes effect

If the ground existed at the effective date of the maintenance calculation (ie, when the non-resident parent was notified of the application or the application was treated as made), the date the variation takes effect will be the effective date of the maintenance calculation if either:

- the application is made before the calculation is made;[134] *or*
- the application is made within one month of the maintenance calculation, or meets the other normal rules applying to revisions (eg, misrepresentation or failure to disclose information that meant the decision was to the person's advantage) or erroneous decisions.[135]

The exception to this rule is if the non-resident parent is applying for a variation on the grounds of prior debts or payments in respect of certain mortgages, loans or insurance policies, and payments towards these are treated as voluntary payments in the initial payment period.[136] In this case, the variation takes effect from the maintenance period following the date on which the non-resident parent was notified – ie, the start of the second week of liability.

If the ground did not apply at the effective date of the maintenance calculation, the variation is effective from:

- the first day of the maintenance period in which the ground arose, where this is after the effective date but before the maintenance calculation is made;[137]
- the first day of the maintenance period in which the relevant person requested the variation.[138] However, if the CSA requests that the application is made in writing, and this is not supplied within 14 days, the date the request was made will be the date the application is received, unless the CSA accepts that the delay was unavoidable;[139]
- the first day of the maintenance period in which the ground will arise, if the application for variation is made in advance.[140]

A case may have a number of different grounds, agreed over time, and each may have different dates from which they take effect.

Example 6.14

Tara claims maintenance. The effective date is 26 August 2003. She is notified of her maintenance calculation on 19 September 2003. She takes advice and applies for a variation on the basis that an additional cases ground applied on 26 August 2003. She makes this application on 8 October 2003 – ie, within one month of her notification of the decision. The variation is agreed and the maintenance calculation is revised on 14 November 2003, with effect from 26 August 2003.

Juan takes advice and on 3 December 2003 applies for a variation on the grounds that he has been paying off the car which they bought before splitting up and which Tara needs, as she lives in a secluded cottage. He is also just about to start paying boarding school fees for their eldest child in late December. The variation is agreed and a revision is made on 3 January 2004 in which the elements for prior debts take effect from 2 December and the boarding school fees take effect from 16 December 2003.

However, even though the variation for prior debts only applies from December, Juan could ask that the amounts he paid toward the car before the calculation was made be considered as voluntary payments to offset initial arrears. Had Juan taken advice at the same time as Tara and applied for a variation at the same time as she did on the grounds of prior debts and that his repayments on the car were voluntary payments, then there could have been a further variation to the calculation, with the decision taking effect from 26 August 2003.

When a variation ceases to have effect

A variation will cease to have effect when the ground no longer applies or any other of the reasons for refusing a variation is met. For example, a variation in favour of the person with care will always cease to have effect when the non-resident parent or his partner starts to receive working tax credit (WTC).[141] When a variation ceases, a supersession is carried out, which takes effect from the first day in the maintenance period in which the change occurred.

If there is a later change, unless the CSA has discretion to reinstate the variation, a further application may need to be made.

Situations in which a further application for variation is required

Ground	*When variation ceases*	*When a further application could be made following a later change*
Additional cases	Net income before any variation is greater than £2,000.	Net income before variation would be less than £2,000.
	The non-resident parent or his partner receives WTC.	Neither receives WTC.
Special expenses	Net income after any variation is greater than £2,000.	Net income after variation would be less than £2,000.

Discretion to reinstate a previous variation

In some cases, the CSA may revise or supersede a maintenance calculation to reinstate a variation that has previously been agreed. This discretion may be applied if there is:[142]

- a change of circumstances which means the non-resident parent's liability is reduced to nil or another rate and the variation cannot be taken into account; *then*
- a subsequent change of circumstances means his liability can now be adjusted to take the variation into account.

Examples of situations where this could apply include if:

- the non-resident parent becomes a full-time student and so becomes liable for the nil rate, but subsequently returns to a basic or reduced rate;
- a variation is agreed and on a subsequent application for revision/supersession the non-resident parent fails to provide information. Therefore, the maintenance calculation is replaced by a default decision. Later on, the information required is provided and this default maintenance decision is replaced with a maintenance calculation. The variation may then be reapplied without a fresh application.

Had the maintenance calculation ceased, this discretion would not apply. For example, if the parent had moved abroad and the CSA ceased to have jurisdiction, then s/he returns to the UK, a subsequent application would need to be made for a maintenance calculation, including an application for variation. However, in some circumstances, the CSA may be able to reinstate the variation without contest (see p127).

In exercising the discretion to reinstate, the CSA must be satisfied that there has been no material change in circumstances which affects the earlier variation.[143] If this is satisfied, the previous variation can be reinstated without an application or any further contact with the relevant persons – ie, s/he is not invited to make representations. There is no obligation to investigate, so decisions are made based on the information available to the decision maker. There is no time limit on the period between the variation ceasing to apply and being reinstated, as long as the circumstances that gave rise to the variation remain unchanged. This is most easily satisfied in pre-1993 property/capital transfers.

Example 6.15

Joe applies for, and obtains, a variation from his basic-rate maintenance on the grounds of contact costs with his children. He is later convicted of a criminal offence and sentenced to six months in prison. He becomes liable to pay the nil rate. On his release, three months later, he again becomes liable, this time at the reduced rate. The CSA is not satisfied that the circumstances relating to eligibility are still the same and does not reinstate the variation. Joe will need to make a new application for a variation on the grounds of contact costs.

Had the variation been granted on the grounds of a pre-1993 property/capital transfer, the CSA could probably have reinstated the variation without Joe having to make a further application, as there is no reason why this ground and its effect should be altered by his intervening imprisonment.

Revision and supersession of a previously agreed variation

If a variation has been agreed, it may be subsequently revised or superseded. When a request is received to revise or supersede such a decision, the CSA may notify the other relevant parties and invite them to make representations.[144] This need not be done if the CSA thinks it would not agree to vary the calculation or that a revision/supersession would not be to the advantage of the applicant.

If contest does take place, the usual procedure is followed (see p126).[145]

The CSA may decide to revise/supersede, or not to revise or supersede, the decision and notify the applicant and any relevant parties, as appropriate.

Appealing a decision

Decisions on the maintenance calculation in response to a variation application, or where a variation element is reinstated into a maintenance calculation, may be appealed under the normal procedure. As with other appeals, if, following the appeal application, there is a revision of the appealed decision that is to the advantage of the appellant, the appeal will lapse.[146] For further details on appeals, see Chapter 18.

Notes

1 s28A(1) CSA 1991 (note the modifications under the CS(V)(MSP) Regs only apply in cases where the application is made after a maintenance calculation is in force)

1. **Grounds for a variation**

2 Sch 4B CSA 1991, as substituted by s6 CSPSSA 2000
3 Sch 4A para 2(3) CSA 1991, as substituted by s6 CSPSSA 2000
4 Reg 15 CS(V) Regs
5 Reg 15(1) CS(V) Regs
6 Reg 15(2) CS(V) Regs
7 Reg 15(3) CS(V) Regs
8 Reg 23 CS(V) Regs
9 Reg 10(1) CS(V) Regs
10 Reg 10(4) CS(V) Regs
11 CCS/821/06
12 Reg 10(1) CS(V) Regs
13 Reg 10(3)(a) CS(V) Regs
14 Reg 10(3)(b) CS(V) Regs
15 Reg 10(3)(b) CS(V) Regs
16 Reg 11(2)(c) CS(V) Regs
17 Reg 11(2)(a) CS(V) Regs
18 Reg 11(1) CS(V) Regs
19 Reg 11(2)(b) CS(V) Regs
20 Reg 11(3) CS(V) Regs
21 Reg 12(2) CS(V) Regs
22 Reg 12(3)(k) and (6)(a) CS(V) Regs
23 Reg 12(6)(a) CS(V) Regs (see also CCS/3674/07, para 23); s376(4) ICTA 1988
24 Reg 12(3) CS(V) Regs
25 CCS/3674/07, para 19
26 Reg 12(3)(c)-(g), (j) and (m) CS(V) Regs
27 Reg 12(5) CS(V) Regs
28 Reg 13(1) CS(V) Regs
29 Reg 13(5) CS(V) Regs
30 Reg 13(2) CS(V) Regs
31 Reg 13(3) CS(V) Regs
32 Reg 13(4) CS(V) Regs
33 Reg 14(2)(a) CS(V) Regs
34 Reg 14(2)(b) CS(V) Regs
35 Sch 4B para 3(1) CSA 1991; regs 16(1) and (2) and 17(4) CS(V) Regs
36 Sch 4B para 3(2) CSA 1991
37 Reg 17(5) CS(V) Regs
38 s8(11) CSA 1991; reg 16(1)(a) CS(V) Regs
39 Reg 16(2) CS(V) Regs
40 Reg 16(3) CS(V) Regs
41 Sch 4B para 3 CSA 1991; reg 17(1) CS(V) Regs
42 Reg 17(2) CS(V) Regs
43 Reg 16(4) CS(V) Regs
44 Sch para 1(3)(b) CS(V) Regs
45 Sch para 2 CS(V) Regs
46 Reg 24 CS(V) Regs
47 Sch para 3 CS(V) Regs
48 Sch 4B para 4 CSA 1991
49 Reg 25 CS(V) Regs
50 Reg 26 CS(V) Regs
51 Reg 18(1) CS(V) Regs
52 Reg 18(2) CS(V) Regs
53 Reg 18(3) CS(V) Regs
54 CCS/1026/2006
55 Reg 18(3)(f) CS(V) Regs
56 Reg 18(4) CS(V) Regs
57 Reg 18(5) CS(V) Regs
58 Reg 18(6) CS(V) Regs
59 Regs 18(5) and 25 CS(V) Regs
60 Reg 19(1) CS(V) Regs
61 Reg 4 CS(MCA) Regs
62 Reg 19(4) CS(V) Regs
63 CCS/2979/2008
64 *DW v CMEC* [2010] UKUT 196 (AAC), following CCS/2707/2007 and CCS/2708/2007 and disagreeing with CCS/289/2008
65 Reg 19(2) CS(V) Regs
66 Regs 19(5)(a) and 25 CS(V) Regs
67 Reg 26(3) CS(V) Regs
68 Reg 19(4) CS(V) Regs
69 Regs 19(5)(b) and 25 CS(V) Regs
70 Reg 20(1) and (2) CS(V) Regs
71 Reg 20(3) and (4)(a) CS(V) Regs

72 CCS/2018/2005
73 Reg 20(4) CS(V) Regs
74 Reg 20(5) CS(V) Regs

2. **Applying for a variation**

75 s28A CSA 1991 (note the modifications under the CS(V)(MSP) Regs take effect if the application is made when the maintenance calculation is in force); s28G CSA 1991
76 s28A(4) CSA 1991 (note the modifications under the CS(V)(MSP) Regs take effect if the application is made when the maintenance calculation is in force)
77 Reg 4(1) CS(V) Regs
78 s28A(4)(b) CSA 1991
79 *DB v CMEC* [2010] UKUT 356 (AAC)
80 Reg 8(1) CS(V) Regs
81 Reg 8(1) CS(V) Regs
82 Regs 6(2)(c) and 8(2) CS(V) Regs
83 Reg 5(1) CS(V) Regs
84 Reg 5(2) CS(V) Regs

3. **Procedure**

85 s28D CSA 1991 (note the modifications under the CS(V)(MSP) Regs take effect if the application is made when the maintenance calculation is in force)
86 Sch 4B para 5(1) CSA 1991; reg 9(9) CS(V) Regs
87 Reg 9(8) CS(V) Regs
88 s28B(1) CSA 1991
89 Reg 6(1) CS(V) Regs
90 s28B CSA 1991 (note the modifications under the CS(V)(MSP) Regs take effect if the application is made when the maintenance calculation is in force); reg 7 CS(V) Regs
91 *RB v CMEC* [2009] UKUT 53 (AAC)
92 s28B CSA 1991(note the modifications under the CS(V)(MSP) Regs take effect if the application is made when the maintenance calculation is in force); regs 6 and 7 CS(V) Regs
93 *CR v CMEC* [2009] UKUT 111 (AAC)
94 Reg 30(b) CS(V) Regs
95 Reg 9(1) CS(V) Regs
96 Reg 9(4)(a) CS(V) Regs
97 Reg 9(1) CS(V) Regs
98 Reg 9(5) CS(V) Regs
99 Reg 9(4) CS(V) Regs
100 Reg 9(2) CS(V) Regs
101 Reg 9(3) CS(V) Regs
102 s12 CSA 1991
103 s28F(5) CSA 1991 (note the modifications under the CS(V)(MSP) Regs take effect if the application is made when the maintenance calculation is in force)
104 s28C CSA 1991(note the modifications under the CS(V)(MSP) Regs take effect if the application is made when the maintenance calculation is in force)
105 s28C(2) CSA 1991(note the modifications under the CS(V)(MSP) Regs take effect if the application is made when the maintenance calculation is in force); reg 31(1) CS(V) Regs
106 s28C(4) CSA 1991(note the modifications under the CS(V)(MSP) Regs take effect if the application is made when the maintenance calculation is in force)
107 s28C(3) CSA 1991(note the modifications under the CS(V)(MSP) Regs take effect if the application is made when the maintenance calculation is in force)
108 s28C(5) CSA 1991 (note the modifications under the CS(V)(MSP) Regs take effect if the application is made when the maintenance calculation is in force)
109 Reg 31(2) and (3) CS(V) Regs
110 s28C(7) CSA 1991(note the modifications under the CS(V)(MSP) Regs take effect if the application is made when the maintenance calculation is in force)
111 s28F(1) CSA 1991 (note the modifications under the CS(V)(MSP) Regs take effect if the application is made when the maintenance calculation is in force)
112 ss28E and 28F(2)(a) CSA 1991
113 ss28D(1) and 28F CSA 1991 (note the modifications on both sections under the CS(V)(MSP) Regs take effect if the application is made when the maintenance calculation is in force)
114 s28F(1) CSA 1991
115 Reg 21(1) CS(V) Regs
116 *DB v CMEC* [2010] UKUT 356 (AAC)
117 Reg 21(2) CS(V) Regs
118 s28D(1)(b) CSA 1991
119 *HB v SSWP* [2009] UKUT 66 (AAC)
120 s28D(3) CSA 1991 (note the modifications under the CS(V)(MSP) Regs take effect if the application is made when the maintenance calculation is in force)

4. **The decision**

121 ss28B(2) and 28F(3) and (4) CSA 1991 (note the modifications to both sections under the CS(V)(MSP) Regs take effect if the application is made when the maintenance calculation is in force)
122 Reg 27(5) CS(V) Regs
123 Reg 25 CS(V) Regs
124 Reg 25 CS(V) Regs
125 Reg 26 CS(V) Regs
126 Reg 26(1) CS(V) Regs
127 Reg 26(3) CS(V) Regs
128 Reg 23(1) CS(V) Regs
129 Reg 15(1) CS(V) Regs
130 Reg 23(2) CS(V) Regs
131 Reg 17 CS(V) Regs
132 Reg 24 CS(V) Regs
133 ss16(1A)(c) and 17(1)(d) CSA 1991
134 Reg 22 CS(V) Regs
135 s28G CSA 1991; reg 3A SSCS(DA) Regs
136 Reg 22(2) CS(V) Regs
137 Reg 22(1)(b) CS(V) Regs
138 s28G CSA 1991; regs 6A(6) and 7B(6) SS&CS(DA) Regs
139 Reg 4 CS(V) Regs
140 Regs 6A(3) and 7B(5) SS&CS(DA) Regs
141 Regs 7(5)(b) and 27(6) CS(V) Regs
142 Reg 29 CS(V) Regs
143 Reg 9(3) CS(V) Regs
144 Reg 15B SS&CS(DA) Regs
145 Reg 15B SS&CS(DA) Regs
146 s16(6) CSA 1991

Chapter 7

Conversions

This chapter covers:

1. When 'old rules' cases convert to the 'new rules'

The two systems of calculating child support maintenance normally operate independently of each other. There are, however, circumstances in which an 'old rules' case is converted to a 'new rules' case.

As a new simplified scheme is expected to be introduced from 2012, the previous policy intention to convert all 'old rules' cases to the 'new rules' at a future date is no longer being pursued. The current arrangements are expected to continue in the meantime, unless the circumstances in which conversion is triggered apply. The policy intention is now that all 'old rules' and 'new rules' cases will eventually be closed, and parents are expected to make private arrangements or apply under the new simplified rules (see Chapter 1).

An 'old rules' case may convert because there is a connection to a 'new rules' case.

If an 'old rules' case converts, there may be transitional phasing to increase or decrease the old amount to the new amount due (see p144).

If an 'old rules' assessment ceases to be in force, an application may be decided under the 'new rules' if it is made more than 13 weeks after the assessment ceases (but see below). This is not a conversion as such and, therefore, transitional phasing does not apply.

There is one key exception to the general rule that an application will be dealt with under the 'new rules' if it is made more than 13 weeks after the assessment ceases. This applies to cases that ended between 10 April 2006 and 9 November

2009 because a child over the age of 16 was no longer in full-time education. If the child was on an approved training course instead, the person with care would have continued to receive child benefit. From November 2009, a change in the rules for qualifying children means that all young people for whom child benefit is payable are qualifying children for the purpose of child support until their 19th birthday.[1] From this date, some young people (such as those not in full-time education but on an approved training course) become qualifying children again and a person with care can reapply for child support. Applications for child support in these circumstances are not subject to the 13-week rule. If such a case was previously under the 'old rules', it will generally remain under the 'old rules'.

Conversions

Conversion occurs where a maintenance assessment is in force and a related decision is made.[2] The related decision may be that a maintenance calculation is made or there has been a change involving a new or existing partner who also has maintenance. A conversion will occur if:[3]

- a maintenance calculation is made in respect of someone who is a relevant person (person with care or non-resident parent) in the existing assessment, whether or not this is for a different qualifying child;
- an application is made that would result in a maintenance calculation but there is an assessment in force, the non-resident parent in the new application is the non-resident parent in the existing case but the person with care in the new application is different from the one in the existing case. However, if it is the non-resident parent who applies for the maintenance calculation and the person with care in the new application does not wish to co-operate, there will be no conversion of the existing case (see also p44).

For information on conversions made before July 2008, see previous editions of this *Handbook*.

The conversion of one case may set off a chain of conversions of other cases if the relevant person in a conversion is also a relevant person in an existing maintenance assessment. The CSA calls these 'linked cases'. This may result in a lengthy sequence of interrelated decisions that need to be made. Whenever an 'old rules' case is converted, transitional phasing may apply (see p144).

Example 7.1

Celine is the parent with care of two children, Michelle and Francis. Franco is their non-resident parent in the 'old rules' assessment. After 3 March 2003 Francis goes to live with Franco and his new partner, Helen. Franco applies, as the parent with care of Francis, for maintenance from Celine, as the non-resident parent. A maintenance calculation is made. As a relevant person in the old assessment is a relevant person in the new calculation (ie,

Celine is a person with care in the old and a non-resident parent in the new), the old maintenance assessment converts to the 'new rules' (transitional phasing may apply).

2. The calculation and transitional phasing

The new amount is worked out applying the new calculation rates, using the information that the Child Support Agency (CSA) has at the calculation date (see p141).[4] If there are decisions outstanding on the maintenance assessment at conversion, the calculation may be carried out and, once those decisions are made, the maintenance calculation may be revised or superseded (see p154). There are additional rules for calculating the new amount at conversion where a relevant departure direction or relevant property transfer was applied to an 'old rules' case (see p147).

If there is an interim maintenance assessment (IMA) in force when the conversion decision is being made, this may be:

- used to make the conversion decision;[5] *or*
- replaced with a default maintenance decision, if there is insufficient information to make a maintenance assessment or conversion decision. [6]

In either case, if information is subsequently provided by the non-resident parent to make a maintenance assessment, the conversion decision or default maintenance decision may be superseded.[7]

At conversion, the new rate will either be paid immediately or transitional phasing may be applied.[8] There are some situations in which the new amount is always applied. In other cases, the CSA checks whether transitional phasing applies. If it does not, the new amount is paid.

When the new amount is always applied

The new amount of maintenance will be applied immediately (ie, without checking whether transitional phasing applies) if the:[9]

- 'new rules' amount is nil;
- 'old rules' amount was nil and the 'new rules' amount is the flat rate reduced to nil because of shared care (see p146);
- 'old rules' amount was more than nil but the 'new rules' amount is the flat rate (or halved flat rate where there is a partner who is a non-resident parent);
- 'old rules' amount was a Category A or D IMA;
- 'new rules' amount is a default maintenance decision.

If none of the above apply, the CSA checks whether transitional phasing should be applied (see p144). If it does not apply, the new amount will be payable.

Example 7.2

Sally is due to pay Mark maintenance at the minimum amount before conversion. After conversion she is liable for the flat rate. She pays the new amount from conversion.

Kieran pays Leah a maintenance assessment worked out under a Category A IMA. At conversion, as there is insufficient information to make a maintenance calculation, a default decision replaces the IMA and the new amount applies immediately.

If Kieran had been assessed under a Category B IMA, sufficient information would have been available to make a maintenance calculation.

Transitional phasing

Transitional phasing will apply (unless the situation is one in which the new amount is always applied – see p143) if the difference between the old amount and new amount is greater than the phasing amount.[10] If there is more than one assessment in relation to the same non-resident parent, apportionment occurs, in which case the amounts referred to are those after the apportionment has been made.[11] If there is an application from a new person with care which triggers conversion of an existing assessment (see p142), the apportionment in the new calculation will occur as normal and the previous assessment amount is compared with the new amount due after apportionment.[12] There are special rules in some flat-rate cases (see p146).

The phasing amount depends on the net income of the non-resident parent. This is:[13]

- £2.50, if income is £100 or less;
- £5, if income is more than £100 but less than £400; *or*
- £10, if income is £400 or more.

Net weekly income is as worked out under the 'new rules'. (This includes where a relevant departure direction is converted and treated as a variation.) If the difference between the old and new amounts is greater than the phasing amount, the old amount is increased or decreased by the phasing amount as appropriate.[14] This increase or decrease occurs on an annual basis during the **'transitional period'**, with the amount changing on the anniversary of the date of conversion. The transitional period lasts until the new amount is reached or for up to five years from the date of conversion, unless there is a subsequent decision which affects this.[15]

If transitional phasing applies, the **maximum transitional amount** that the non-resident parent may pay in maintenance (to all persons with care) is 30 per cent of his net income (see p249).[16] This is worked out under the normal rules and, if there is a relevant additional cases departure, the net income is taken to be the total of the additional income plus the income from prescribed benefits (excluding those disregarded). If there is an additional cases variation, this means the total income after variation.[17]

In some situations, there may be a new case being calculated and an old case converting at the same time. If this happens, apportionment of the maintenance calculation is carried out as normal. Transitional phasing may be applied to the 'old rules' case and the total amount of maintenance is checked against the 30 per cent maximum. This means adding together the apportioned amount due for the 'new rules' case and the phased amount due for the 'old rules' case. If the 30 per cent maximum is breached, the maintenance is capped at this amount. The amount for the person(s) with care in the new case is deducted from the maximum, and the remainder is the amount due to the person(s) with care in the converting 'old rules' case.[18] Rounding is to the nearest penny (amounts can be adjusted where rounding would result in inequalities over time).[19]

Example 7.3

Under her 'old rules' assessment, Celine is due to get £68.40 in maintenance from Franco for Michelle and Francis. Franco lives with his new partner, Helen, and their son, Damien. Celine remains living on her own, but has a baby with a different non-resident parent. She applies for maintenance after 3 March 2003, and it is worked out under the 'new rules'. Franco's case will convert as a linked case. If Franco's net income is £360 a week at the conversion date, Celine's new amount from Franco is worked out under the basic rate.

Step 1 15% reduction for relevant child – ie, £360 – £54 = £306

Step 2 Maintenance is 20% x £306 = £61.20 (rounded to £61)

Does transitional phasing apply?

The phasing amount is £5, as Franco's income is between £100 and £400. Since there is more than £5 difference between the old and new amounts, transitional phasing applies. Celine is paid £63.40 (£68.40 – £5) in maintenance from Franco.

If Franco and Helen split up and Helen applied for maintenance for Damien after 3 March 2003, Celine's case would convert at this point, assuming this is before she has her third child. In this case there are now no relevant children living with Franco and three qualifying children.

Step 1 No reduction.

Step 2 25% x £360 = £90

Step 3 Apportionment between two persons with care (£90 ÷ 3 = £30)

Helen is due to receive £30.

Celine's new amount is £60.

Does transitional phasing apply?

As there is more than £5 difference between the old amount (£68.40) and the new amount (£60), phasing applies.

Year 1 £68.40 – £5 = £63.40

Year 2 £60

Therefore, the total amount of maintenance due is £93.40. This is less than the 30 per cent maximum (£108) so it does not affect maintenance.

If Celine's 'old rules' assessment was £100 a week, transitional phasing would mean that she received the following amounts during the transitional period:

From the date of conversion to the first anniversary	£100 – £5 = £95
First anniversary to second anniversary	£95 – £5 = £90
Second anniversary to third anniversary	£90 – £5 = £85
Third anniversary to fourth anniversary	£85 – £5 = £80
Fourth anniversary to fifth anniversary	£80 – £5 = £75

The transitional period ends on the fifth anniversary of the date of conversion.

In the first year, this means Franco would pay £30 (Helen) + £95 (Celine) = £125

As this is greater than the 30 per cent maximum (£108), the calculation is adjusted. Helen still receives £30 (as she is the person with care in the new case) but Celine receives £78 (£108 – £30).

In the second year, Franco would pay £30 (Helen) + £90 (Celine) = £120

As this is still greater than the 30 per cent maximum (£108), the calculation is adjusted. Helen still receives £30 and Celine again receives £78 (£108 – £30).

This continues through years three and four as the combined amount of maintenance to Helen and Celine remains above the 30 per cent cap. It is only in year five that Celine receives the full transitional phasing amount of £75, as £75 + £30 = £105, which is below the 30 per cent maximum so both persons with care get the full amount of child support due.

Transitional amount in certain flat-rate cases

If the old amount was nil and the new amount is the flat rate (because of receipt of a prescribed benefit), transitional phasing is £2.50 in the first year and then £5 in the second.[20] In cases where the non-resident parent's partner is also a non-resident parent with a maintenance calculation in force and either the non-resident parent or his partner is in receipt of income support (IS), income-based jobseeker's allowance (JSA), income-related employment and support allowance (ESA) or pension credit (PC), transitional phasing is £1.25 in the first year and £2.50 in the second.[21]

Except where the old amount was nil, if the flat rate is due but reduces to nil because of shared care, the transitional amount due will be £2.50 in the first year and £5 in the second.[22] (In cases where the flat rate is halved because a partner is a non-resident parent, the phasing amount will be £1.25.[23]) This will occur if the non-resident parent shares care with the only (or all) person(s) with care.

If the amount due reduces to nil for some, but not all, of the persons with care, transitional phasing will only apply if:[24]

- the old amount is less than the new amount and the difference is more than £2.50; *or*

- the old amount is greater than the new amount but the new amount is less than £2.50.

Apportionment of the transitional amount takes place between those persons with care for whom the amount due does not reduce to nil because of shared care.[25]

Example 7.4

Andrew has four qualifying children. Claire and Hannah are each a person with care for one qualifying child, Millie is a person with care for two. Andrew has one child living with him and also shares care with Claire. Andrew's case converts because it is a linked case.

Under the 'old rules' he was exempt from paying the minimum amount. Under the 'new rules' he is liable for the flat rate of £5. This is apportioned between the persons with care: Hannah and Claire are due £1.25 each and Millie is due £2.50.

Because of shared care, Claire's maintenance is reduced to nil. This means £3.75 is now due in maintenance. As this is greater than the old amount and there is more than a £2.50 difference between old and new amounts, phasing is applied. The £2.50 phased amount is apportioned between Hannah and Millie: Hannah receives 83p and Millie £1.67.

In the second year, the new amount is reached and the transitional period ends – Hannah receives £1.25 and Millie receives £2.50.

Relevant departure directions and property transfers

In 'old rules' cases where there is a departure direction or an allowance for a property/capital transfer in the exempt income calculation, these may be taken into consideration when working out the new amount used in the conversion calculation.[26] Only a relevant departure and relevant property/capital transfer affect the calculation.

If a departure direction can be considered as a variation, it is known as a **'relevant departure direction'**. A relevant departure direction is one for:[27]

- contact costs;
- prior debts;
- illness and disability costs of a relevant child – ie, if the non-resident parent or his partner receives child benefit for the child;
- a property or capital transfer;
- diversion of income;
- when lifestyle is inconsistent with stated income; *or*
- assets, where the value of the assets is greater than £65,000.

In the case of contact costs and prior debts, the £15 and £10 thresholds that apply to special expenses variations must be met for either amount or the sum of both where they apply.[28] In the case of diversion of income or an inconsistent lifestyle, the amount of additional income must exceed £100 in cases where the new amount would otherwise be:

- the flat rate because of receipt of a prescribed benefit (other than IS, income-based JSA, income-related ESA or PC);
- the flat rate as above, but reduced to nil because of shared care; *or*
- the nil rate (other than on income grounds).[29]

If there is a relevant departure direction, an equivalent variation will be applied to the calculation of the new amount without any separate application for a variation.[30]

Example 7.5

Joan has a maintenance assessment with a special expenses departure direction of £22 for contact costs and £18 for travel-to-work costs. When her case is converted because of a linked case, her special expenses for contact costs count as a relevant transfer but her travel-to-work costs do not.

A **'relevant property transfer'** is distinct from a property/capital departure. A relevant property transfer is where an allowance is included at the exempt income stage (see Chapter 10) of the 'old rules' assessment formula.[31] It may be advisable, where a relevant property transfer is applied, also to seek a variation on property/capital transfer grounds.[32] If this application is successful, the conversion decision will be revised or superseded, depending on when the application was made.

Adjustments to the conversion calculation

The adjustment made to the conversion calculation depends on the grounds under which the departure direction has been granted – ie, special expenses, additional cases or property/capital transfer. The effect of an adjustment for departure directions and relevant property transfers (or the aggregate of those that apply) are listed below and are carried out in the following order.[33]

- **Additional cases departure direction.** The amount of the departure is added to the net income figure. If this takes net income over the capped amount of £2,000, the net income figure used is £2,000.[34] If the non-resident parent is on benefit there is a maximum amount payable – ie, a conversion 'better-buy' (see p149).
- **Special expenses departure direction.** The amount of the departure is deducted from the net weekly income.[35] If the net income is the capped amount of £2,000, deduct the expenses from the actual net income, not the capped amount. If this reduces the net income figure to below £2,000, this is the net income figure to use in the calculation. Otherwise it is still the capped amount.

- **Relevant property transfer.** The amount of the transfer is deducted at conversion from the net income of the non-resident parent used to work out maintenance. If the net income is the capped amount of £2,000, the transfer is deducted from this capped amount.[36]
- **Property/capital transfer departure direction.** The amount of the departure is deducted from the maintenance due to the person with care.[37] This deduction can only be completed after any reduction for shared care (or part-time local authority care) has been applied.[38]

If these adjustments reduce the amount of maintenance due to below the £5 flat rate, the amount due will be the £5 flat rate. This may be apportioned between the persons with care as appropriate.[39]

Conversion 'better-buy'

If the non-resident parent is on benefit, the maximum amount payable where there is a relevant departure on additional cases grounds is the lesser of:[40]

- the flat rate plus the appropriate rate (reduced or basic) calculated on the basis of the additional income under the departure; *or*
- the amount calculated by applying the appropriate rate to the total of the additional income under the departure and the income payable under any prescribed benefits (excluding amounts that are disregarded).

The conversion calculation is carried out in the normal way. However, the conversion 'better-buy' provision is applied and may cap the amount to be paid.

Outstanding overpayments at conversion

Outstanding overpayments on conversion are now dealt with in the same way as other overpayments (see p399).

Offsetting arrears

If there are arrears of child support due in an 'old rules' case and the CSA has allocated other payments of child support against the arrears, this attribution of child support payments can be applied to the new amount, or the transitional amount, which applies on conversion.[41] This will be done if the arrears remain outstanding on the case conversion date and the CSA has used its discretion to offset the arrears against the payment of child maintenance in accordance with the regulations, as they apply to a conversion decision (see also p399).

The CSA now has additional powers to offset arrears, which may also be applied in this situation (see p408).

3. The conversion decision

At conversion, the Child Support Agency (CSA) carries out a conversion calculation (see p143).[42]

There is no requirement to seek more up-to-date information;[43] if the information used at the calculation date is incorrect, a revision can be requested. This may be particularly important in cases where there have been significant changes, which could increase or decrease the 'old rules' maintenance assessment. The policy intention is not to supersede maintenance assessment decisions routinely before conversion.

The new rate will either be paid immediately (ie, the maintenance calculation comes into force) or transitional phasing may be applied (see p144).[44] There are some situations in which the new amount is always applied. In other cases, the CSA checks if transitional phasing applies and, if it does not, the new amount is paid.

The effective date of the conversion decision

The effective date of the conversion decision is normally the beginning of the first maintenance period on or after the conversion date.[45] This is known as the **'case conversion date'**. If a case converts, the effective date may be the beginning of the first maintenance period on or after the effective date of the new calculation or another period depending on the circumstances.[46]

Effective date of conversion decisions

Situation	*Effective date*
A maintenance calculation is made in respect of a relevant person in relation to the maintenance assessment, whether or not in respect of a different qualifying child.	The beginning of the first maintenance period on or after the effective date of the new calculation.
A is the non-resident parent in relation to the maintenance calculation, whose partner B is the absent parent in relation to the maintenance assessment and either A or B is in receipt of income support (IS) income-based jobseeker's allowance (JSA) or income-related employment and support allowance (ESA).	The beginning of the first maintenance period on or after the effective date of the new calculation.

An application is made that would result in a maintenance calculation but there is an assessment in force. The non-resident parent in the new application is the non-resident parent in the existing case, but the person with care in the new application is a different one from the one in the existing case.	The beginning of the first maintenance period on or after the date of notification of the conversion decision.
All other circumstances.	The beginning of the first maintenance period on or after the conversion decision.

For situations in which a conversion took place before July 2008, see previous editions of this *Handbook*.

Notification

Once the conversion decision is made, the non-resident parent, person with care and Scottish child applicant are notified in writing.[47]

This notification states the:

- new amount;
- transitional amount, if appropriate;
- length of the transitional period;
- date the conversion decision was made and the date from which it is effective;
- non-resident parent's net weekly income;
- number of qualifying and relevant children;
- adjustments for apportionment or shared care;
- details of departure directions or relevant property transfers taken into account;
- adjustments because of the maximum transitional amount rule.

The conversion decision is treated as a maintenance calculation decision, so requests for a revision, supersession, variation or an appeal may be made.[48] However, when considering subsequent decisions, there are additional rules to determine the amount of maintenance to be paid (see p156).

After notification of the conversion decision, there may be an application for a departure direction or a variation.

When does the conversion end

Transitional phasing may be applied for up to five years from the case conversion date or until the maintenance calculation amount is reached.[49] If there are subsequent decisions that result in the new amount being paid immediately (ie, nil rate or default rate), these may be applied. If the calculation is cancelled, conversion will end. However, in some cases where linking applies (see below), a second subsequent decision or new application may be dealt with as if the conversion decision still applied. This may affect the amount to be paid under any subsequent decision.

4. The linking rules

The linking rules cover a range of situations where an 'old rules' assessment or a transitional amount has been in force and there are applications and subsequent decisions made after 3 March 2003. Whether or not linking is applied depends on the timescales and circumstances. In each instance there are two key factors.

- A 13-week linking period is used.
- If there is another application in the interim that involves either the person with care or non-resident parent (but not both) there is no linking.

If linking applies, the rules on working out how much maintenance is paid are adjusted.

The linking rules and their effect

Scenario	*Maintenance is worked out as if:*
After 3 March 2003 there is an application, but within 13 weeks there was a maintenance assessment in force for the same parent with care, non-resident parent and qualifying child.	it is a maintenance assessment. All the 'old rules', including the formula, are applied to the case.
The conversion calculation ceases to have effect, but within 13 weeks there is an application for the same parent with care, non-resident parent and qualifying child.	the conversion calculation is still in force and subsequent decision rules are applied.
A transitional amount is being paid. There is a subsequent decision where the £5/£2.50 flat rate, nil rate for shared care or nil rate is paid. Within 13 weeks of the effective date of this, a second decision is made where none of these rates apply for the same parent with care, non-resident parent and qualifying child.	the first subsequent decision had not been made (ie, the transitional amount is still in force) and the subsequent decision rules are applied.

Applications on or after 3 March 2003

An application for a maintenance calculation made on or after 3 March 2003 can be treated as an application for a maintenance assessment if it is:[50]

- made within 13 weeks of a maintenance assessment being in force; *and*
- in relation to the same person with care, non-resident parent and qualifying child,

unless there is a new application which includes either the 'old rules' case person with care or the non-resident parent (but not both) before the new application is made, in which case there is no linking and it is dealt with as a new case.[51]

If linking applies, maintenance is worked out using the 'old rules' maintenance assessment.

If a new application is linked to an old assessment and there is then a new application which involves the person with care or non-resident parent, the old case will be converted and a conversion calculation will be done.

If an application is made after a gap of more than 13 weeks since a maintenance assessment was in force, it is treated as an application under the 'new rules' and a calculation is carried out. No transitional phasing will apply. A parent with care has the right to opt out if she wishes, and to reapply at any time, whether or not the reason for doing so is to increase her maintenance.[52]

Example 7.6

Celine is the parent with care of Michelle and Francis (see *Example 7.1*). Franco is the non-resident parent in an 'old rules' assessment. Celine asks the Child Support Agency to stop acting – ie, she opts out. After six weeks she applies for a 'new rules' maintenance calculation. Since her 'old rules' assessment was in force within the last 13 weeks, her application is treated as an application for a maintenance assessment.

If Celine opts out and waits for 14 weeks and then applies, her case will be dealt with as a 'new rules' case.

Celine opts out, but before she reapplies Franco and his partner, Helen, split up. Helen makes an application for a maintenance calculation as the parent with care of Damien, with Franco the non-resident parent, three weeks after Celine opts out. Helen is a 'new rules' case and when Celine reapplies three weeks later, her case is dealt with as a new case (as it is another application that involves the non-resident parent – ie, Franco) and no linking or conversion rules apply.

Francis has now moved to live with Franco. If Celine opts out but, before she reapplies Franco applies as the parent with care of Francis, Franco is a 'new rules' case. When Celine reapplies six weeks later, the linking rules apply and a conversion calculation will be done. Transitional phasing may apply to her maintenance.

5. Revisions, supersessions and appeals

At conversion there may be decisions outstanding on a maintenance assessment or departure direction. In other cases, decisions may have been made but the time limits for challenging them may not yet have expired (see below).

Once the conversion decision has been made, it may be challenged in the normal way (revision, supersession, appeal and application for variation) since it is treated as if it were a maintenance calculation.[53] Adjustments of the amounts payable under the transitional phasing rules (see p144) may also be revised or superseded.[54] However, there are some conversion decisions that cannot be revised, superseded or appealed (see p155). There are also additional rules to be applied when working out how much maintenance should be paid on any subsequent decision (see p156).

Applications may also be made for a departure direction or variation that may result in decisions being revised or superseded (see p158).

Outstanding decisions and time limits at conversion

In some cases, a decision may have been made on a maintenance assessment or departure direction and the time limit for seeking a revision or making an appeal has not expired at conversion.[55] In these cases, a revision or appeal may still be sought using the 'old rules'.

Alternatively, at the conversion date there may be outstanding decisions on:[56]

- the maintenance assessment;
- a departure direction;
- a revision or supersession (including those initiated by the Child Support Agency (CSA)[57]);
- an appeal.[58]

If this is the case, a conversion decision may be made using the information held at the conversion date.[59] In the case of an outstanding maintenance assessment this may mean an interim maintenance assessment (IMA) is made and, at conversion, a default maintenance decision becomes due. The outstanding decision may be determined using the 'old rules' as if they still applied.[60] Once the outstanding decision is made or the appeal is decided, the conversion decision may be revised or superseded.[61]

Outstanding decisions on revision and supersession may themselves be appealed when they are made using the 'old rules'.[62] This means a decision not to make a departure direction may be appealed under the 'old rules'.[63] An appeal decision may be challenged on a point of law to the Upper Tribunal.

Conversion and subsequent decisions

Conversion and subsequent decisions can be revised, superseded and appealed in the same way as maintenance calculations,[64] except that the following apply.

- There are certain conversion decisions that may not be revised, superseded or appealed (see below).
- When appealing against a conversion decision, the time limit for making an appeal is either from the date of notification to one month after the case conversion date, or the usual one month from the notice of the decision, whichever is the later.[65] In practice, this means that the normal time limit applies unless there is advance notification of the conversion.
- The effective date of a revision or supersession of a conversion decision is either the conversion date or the date worked out under the normal rules, whichever is the later.[66]
- Notifications contain details of the amount in any subsequent decision rather than the new amount and details of any variations taken into account.
- A conversion decision may be revised or superseded because of a revision/supersession/appeal of a maintenance assessment (including an IMA) or departure direction after the calculation date.[67]
- When further decisions are made, the linking rules may be applied (see p152) and the rules on working out the amount of maintenance due on a subsequent decision are applied.

After notification of the conversion decision, there may be an application for a departure direction or a variation. If this is made after the calculation date but before the case conversion date, it may result in a series of supersession decisions.

Decisions that cannot be revised, superseded or appealed

Conversion decisions cannot be revised, superseded or appealed on the grounds:[68]

- that the CSA used the information it already had at the calculation date;
- that the CSA took into account a relevant departure direction – ie, one that counts as a variation under the 'new rules';
- that the CSA failed to take into account a departure direction – ie, where it does not count as a variation under the 'new rules';
- that the CSA applied a phasing amount;
- of the length of the transitional period;
- that the CSA took into account a relevant property transfer, except if the person with care or Scottish child applicant asks for it to be removed as it did not reflect the true value of the transfer, or a relevant person applies for a variation.

How much is paid on a further decision after conversion

There are special rules on how to work out how much is paid when there are further decisions after conversion. These are applied to conversion cases where there is transitional phasing (or there has been in cases where the linking rules apply – see p152). These are in addition to the normal rules on revisions and supersessions.

When considering a revision of the conversion decision (ie, where the effective date is the case conversion date, not the revision of a later supersession), the rules for working out an initial conversion are used.[69]

If there is a supersession of the conversion decision, or revision of such a decision, the additional rules explained below are used to determine the amount of maintenance to be paid.[70]

These apply to such decisions on appeal.

The amount to be paid under a further decision could be:

- the nil rate, or £5/£2.50 flat rate (or a lesser amount if it is reduced because of shared care);
- the transitional amount (see below);
- a new transitional amount (see below); *or*
- the subsequent decision amount.

If the decision is the nil rate, flat rate or flat rate reduced to nil because of shared care (including if the amount due is less than £5/£2.50), this is the amount that is paid and transitional phasing ceases.[71] However, if there is a subsequent decision after this and the linking rules may apply (see p152), the rules below may be applied and transitional phasing may be revived (see *Example 7.7*).

In all other cases, the subsequent decision amount is compared with the former assessment and the new amount due under the maintenance calculation. If there is more than one person with care, the apportioning rules apply to the calculation (including any adjustments to the maximum transitional amount).[72] The subsequent decision amount and new amount are the amounts worked out using the maintenance calculation, including adjustments for apportionment and shared care, before any transitional phasing is applied. If linking applies (see p152), this may mean the new amount referred to is in a conversion calculation that has ceased to be in force or is in a previous decision. If, at the date of the subsequent decision, there was more than one person with care in relation to the same non-resident parent but, as a result of the subsequent decision, there is only one, the new amount and the transitional amount used are the apportioned amount payable to that person with care immediately before the subsequent decision. The subsequent decision amount is the full amount payable under the subsequent decision.[73]

Unless the conditions in the table below are met, the amount due will be the subsequent decision amount. If this applies, transitional phasing ceases and cannot be revived for any further decisions, and only the normal supersession rules apply.

If the original transitional phasing or a new transitional amount applies, transitional phasing then continues until the subsequent decision amount is reached or the five-year transitional period ends, whichever is earlier (see p144).

Any further decisions in the meantime will be worked out under these rules.[74] There are provisions to allow this where the subsequent decision (Decision B) replaces an earlier subsequent decision (Decision A) or one made with an incorrect effective date, so that in effect Decision A is ignored in applying the rules.[75] However, the rules do not apply in this situation if the decision before Decision A took effect from the case conversion date.

Other cases where the amount due is not the subsequent decision amount

Condition one	*Condition two*	*Amount due*
The new amount is greater than the former assessment.	Subsequent decision is greater than the new amount.	A new transitional amount is worked out, increasing the previous transitional amount by the difference between the new amount and the subsequent decision.
The new amount is greater than the former assessment.	Subsequent decision is less than or equal to the new amount and greater than the previous transitional amount.	The amount is the previous transitional amount.
The new amount is less than the former assessment.	Subsequent decision is less than the new amount.	A new transitional amount is worked out, decreasing the previous transitional amount by the difference between the new amount and the subsequent decision.
The new amount is less than the former assessment.	Subsequent decision is greater than or equal to the new amount and less than the previous transitional amount.	The amount is the previous transitional amount.

Example 7.7

Kevin is due to pay an assessment of £68. His net income is £248. When his case converts following a linked case, he is due to pay a basic rate of £50. This has transitional phasing applied, so he is due to pay £63. Four months later he gets a promotion and his ex-wife requests a supersession. As Kevin's net income has increased to £270, the 5 per cent tolerance level is breached and the CSA considers supersession. The amount he would now be due to pay is £54. The new amount of £50 was less than the assessment (Condition one) and the subsequent decision amount (£54) is greater than this and less than the previous transitional amount, £63 (Condition two). This means he continues to be due to pay the previous transitional amount of £63.

If Kevin's net income had increased to £325, the amount due would be £65. In this case he does not meet Condition two as this is greater than the previous transitional amount (£63). This means he is due to pay £65. There is no more transitional phasing. If Kevin reduces his working hours and his income decreases to £270, his maintenance due would be £54 with no transitional phasing applied.

If the situation were different, the linking rules may apply. If the case converts, but instead of a promotion Kevin is made redundant and claims contribution-based jobseeker's allowance, he is now due to pay at the flat rate of £5. Ten weeks later he gets a new job and has a net income of £210 a week. As this is within 13 weeks, the linking rules apply (see p152). The maintenance decision at the flat rate is ignored. The new amount in Condition one is, therefore, £50 and the subsequent decision amount is £42. As this is lower than the new amount a new transitional amount is worked out. The difference between the two, £8 (£50 – £42), is subtracted from the first transitional amount (£63). Kevin now has to pay £55 (£63 – £8). Unless there are further decisions, a year later transitional phasing will mean he becomes due to pay £50 (£55 – £5).

Applications for a departure direction or variation

After notification of the conversion decision, a relevant person may apply for a variation, in which case the conversion decision may be revised or superseded accordingly (see p154).

Departure directions are more complex. To be taken into account at conversion, a departure direction must apply to the maintenance assessment used in the conversion calculation.

If an application for a departure direction is made after the calculation date but before the case conversion date, this may result in the maintenance assessment being superseded to take account of the departure direction and the conversion decision would be revised to reflect the change.[76] If it is a relevant departure direction, this revision of the conversion decision will include a variation.[77] A departure direction application cannot be made after the case conversion date. However, it may be possible to seek a revision or appeal a refusal to agree a departure direction if the relevant time limits have not expired.[78] For more information on decisions and time limits outstanding at conversion, see p154.

Conversion decision made in error

If a conversion decision, or subsequent decision on a conversion, has been made and it is found that the conversion grounds did not apply (see p142), the case will be treated as if those decisions had not been made.[79] This means the maintenance assessment will be reinstated, bearing in mind any revisions, supersessions or appeals made in the meantime which would have affected that assessment.

Example 7.8

Amy's maintenance assessment is converted because of an administrative error, which is discovered two months later. When the error is discovered, the maintenance assessment is reinstated. However, the non-resident parent notified changes in housing costs and travel-to-work costs that could not be taken into account under the 'new rules' but were relevant in the previous assessment. The assessment is superseded, the effective date being linked to the relevant date of notification of the changes by the non-resident parent, as there was a significant change under the 'old rules'.

6. Conversion, benefits and collection

All the provisions relating to 'new rules' maintenance calculations apply to old cases that convert, even though transitional phasing may apply. This section clarifies how certain issues are dealt with at conversion.

Person with care on benefit

Child maintenance bonus and child maintenance premium

Under the 'old rules' scheme, parents with care in receipt of income support or income-based jobseeker's allowance accrued a child maintenance bonus. This was replaced by a child maintenance premium in 2004 (now abolished). From 27 October 2008, all parents with care covered by the 'old rules' stopped accruing the child maintenance bonus. Before this date, a child maintenance bonus could be accrued until an existing maintenance assessment converted to the 'new rules'.

For more information on the child maintenance bonus, see previous editions of this *Handbook*.

Non-resident parent on benefit

A non-resident parent on benefit may be due to pay the flat rate of maintenance or a transitional amount if, under the 'old rules', he made a contribution to maintenance or was exempt. Under the 'new rules', deductions may be made from benefit for maintenance and arrears (see p336). There is no right of appeal against a decision to make deductions from benefit for flat-rate maintenance or to recover arrears in this way (see p155). However, a non-resident parent can appeal against decisions on both his liability to pay maintenance and the amount that is to be deducted .

Collection and enforcement

Maintenance worked out under a conversion decision is collected and enforced in the normal way, since it is treated as a maintenance calculation.[80]

Arrears built up under the 'old rules' may be recovered using a deduction from earnings order or via the normal enforcement action. An existing deduction from earnings order may be cancelled and a new one issued.

A penalty payment (see p411) may also be imposed, but only on arrears or late payments that fall due after conversion. In practice, however, the Child Support Agency (CSA) does not use this power.[81] All references to penalty payments have been removed from its leaflets and letters to clients, although the CSA could change its policy on this.[82]

Notes

1. **When 'old rules' cases convert to the 'new rules'**

1 Reg 3(4) Child Support (Miscellaneous Amendments)(No.2) Regulations 2009, No.2909
2 Reg 15 CS(TP) Regs; reg 3 CSPSSA (Comm 12) O
3 Reg 15 CS(TP) Regs

2. **The calculation and transitional phasing**

4 Reg 16(1) CS(TP) Regs
5 Reg 3(1)(c) CS(TP) Regs
6 Reg 3(4) CS(TP) Regs
7 Reg 3(5) CS(TP) Regs
8 s29 CSPSSA 2000; reg 9 CS(TP) Regs
9 Reg 14 CS(TP) Regs
10 Reg 10 CS(TP) Regs
11 Reg 11(2) CS(TP) Regs
12 Reg 11(3) CS(TP) Regs
13 Reg 24 CS(TP) Regs
14 Reg 11(1) CS(TP) Regs
15 Reg 2(1) CS(TP) Regs
16 Regs 2(1) and 25(1) CS(TP) Regs
17 Reg 25(5)-(7) CS(TP) Regs
18 Reg 25(3) CS(TP) Regs
19 Reg 25(4) CS(TP) Regs
20 Reg 13(2) CS(TP) Regs
21 Reg 13(1) CS(TP) Regs
22 Reg 12(1) CS(TP) Regs
23 Reg 12(2) CS(TP) Regs
24 Reg 12(3)-(5) CS(TP) Regs
25 Reg 12(6) CS(TP) Regs
26 s29(3)(b) CSPSSA 2000
27 Reg 17 CS(TP) Regs
28 Reg 17(2) CS(TP) Regs
29 Reg 17(6) CS(TP) Regs
30 Reg 17(9) CS(TP) Regs
31 Reg 17(8) CS(TP) Regs
32 Reg 17(10) CS(TP) Regs
33 Regs 23 and 23A CS(TP) Regs
34 Reg 20 CS(TP) Regs
35 Reg 18 CS(TP) Regs

36 Reg 21 CS(TP) Regs
37 Reg 19 CS(TP) Regs
38 Reg 23(4) CS(TP) Regs
39 Reg 23(5) CS(TP) Regs
40 Reg 22 CS(TP) Regs
41 Reg 9B CS(TP) Regs

3. **The conversion decision**

42 Regs 3(2) and 16(1) CS(TP) Regs
43 Regs 3(2) and 16(1) CS(TP) Regs
44 s29 CSPSSA 2000
45 Reg 15(1) CS(TP) Regs
46 Reg 15(2)-(3G) CS(TP) Regs
47 Reg 3(3) CS(TP) Regs
48 Reg 16(2) CS(TP) Regs
49 Reg 2 CS(TP) Regs

4. **The linking rules**

50 Reg 28(2) CS(TP) Regs
51 Reg 28(2A) CS(TP) Regs
52 See comments in R(CS) 1/06

5. **Revisions, supersessions and appeals**

53 Reg 16(2) CS(TP) Regs
54 Reg 4A CS(TP) Regs
55 Regs 14(2)(b) and (c) and 15(b) CS(D&A)(A) Regs
56 Reg 5 CS(TP) Regs
57 Reg 5A CS(TP) Regs
58 Reg 8 CS(TP) Regs
59 Regs 5(b) and 8(1) CS(TP) Regs
60 Regs 14(2) and 15(1) CS(D&A)(A) Regs
61 Regs 4(3) and 8(2) CS(TP) Regs
62 Regs 14 and 15 CS(D&A)(A) Regs
63 Reg 15(1) CS(D&A)(A) Regs
64 Reg 4(1) CS(TP) Regs
65 Reg 4(5)(b) CS(TP) Regs
66 Reg 4(4)(a) CS(TP) Regs
67 Reg 4(3) CS(TP) Regs
68 Reg 7 CS(TP) Regs
69 Reg 26 CS(TP) Regs
70 Reg 27 CS(TP) Regs
71 Reg 27(6) CS(TP) Regs
72 Reg 27(7) and (8) CS(TP) Regs
73 Reg 27(7A) and (7B) CS(TP) Regs
74 Reg 27(9) CS(TP) Regs
75 Reg 27(10) CS(TP) Regs
76 Reg 6(1)(a) and (2)(a) CS(TP) Regs
77 Reg 6(1)(b) and (2)(b) CS(TP) Regs
78 Reg 15 CS(D&A)(A) Regs
79 Reg 33 CS(TP) Regs

6. **Conversion, benefits and collection**

80 Reg 16(2A) CS(TP) Regs
81 s41A CSA 1991
82 *Independent Case Examiner's Annual Report 2006/07*

Part 4

Amount of maintenance: 'old rules'

Chapter 8

The 'old rules' formula

This chapter covers:

1. Introduction

For 'old rules' cases there is a statutory, non-discretionary formula for calculating child maintenance. An 'old rules' case is generally one where the application was made before 3 March 2003 (although some cases may be transferred to the 'new rules' – see Chapter 7). The amount of the child maintenance assessment cannot be negotiated. There is a right of appeal against the assessment, but the First-tier Tribunal is bound by the same law as the Child Support Agency (CSA), so an appeal is only likely to be successful if the CSA has made a mistake or there is room for interpretation in the law.

The amount of child maintenance payable depends largely on the circumstances and the income of both parents, but particularly the income of the non-resident parent. It may be difficult for parents and advisers to obtain all the information needed from the other parent in order to carry out an exact calculation, particularly if the other parent is the non-resident parent.

However, understanding the way in which the formula works is important for explaining the result of an assessment as well as forecasting the effect of any change of circumstances, and deciding whether to seek a revision or supersession.

When the 'old rules' formula is not used

A number of people have a duty to provide information to the CSA. If the CSA does not have sufficient information to carry out a full assessment, an interim maintenance assessment can be imposed (see p331). These are usually penalty assessments, which are set a higher rate than the final assessment.

The formula is not used to calculate the contribution towards child maintenance if the non-resident parent is on income support (IS), income-based jobseeker's allowance, income-related employment and support allowance or pension credit (PC) (see p170).

Non-resident parents with second families have the assessment phased in if there would be an increase in the payments of over £20 a week, compared with a pre-April 1993 maintenance agreement. The maximum phasing-in period is 18 months, so this should only apply to a non-resident parent whose 'old rules' case has still not been assessed, or who still has an interim maintenance assessment (see p336).

Departure

It may be possible to request a change to the standard 'old rules' formula in certain circumstances. This is called 'departure'. Departure is a way of taking into account a financial factor particular to that family – eg, the costs of the non-resident parent travelling to visit the children, or a partner's contribution towards housing costs. Although the decision on whether to take the factor into account (and to what extent) is discretionary, an adjusted statutory formula is then used to obtain the final assessment. See Chapter 15 for further details of departure.

Weekly rates and rounding up

The child maintenance payable under the 'old rules' formula is given as a weekly rate and all stages of the calculation use weekly figures.[1] Fractions of a penny are disregarded if less than one-half or rounded up to the next penny if equal to or more than one half-penny (except when calculating 70 per cent of net income for the protected level (see p249), when any fraction of a penny is ignored).[2]

Income support rates

The formula for assessing child maintenance is based on IS personal allowances and premiums. The 2011/12 rates are given at the front of this *Handbook*. **Note:** although some of the rules on entitlement to allowances and premiums have changed for IS claimants, they still apply for the purpose of working out 'old rules' child support assessments (see Appendix 2).

The IS rates used in the calculation are those which apply on the date the maintenance assessment comes into effect, known as the 'effective date' (see p332).[3] As the effective date is usually some time before the date on which the assessment is being made, assessments may be made in 2011/12 using a previous year's rates. Benefit rates increase in April each year. The maintenance assessment is not automatically altered at the annual April uprating, but if a reassessment is requested after a change of circumstances, the new rates would then be used.

Changes to the formula

Since the 'old rules' formula for setting assessments was introduced in April 1993, there have been several changes to it. Unless there is a specific provision, the general rule is that the calculation must be done using the regulations which applied on the effective date (see p332) of the assessment.[4] This edition of the *Handbook* covers the formula in effect during 2011/12; make sure you refer to the appropriate earlier edition for assessments with earlier effective dates.

2. The five steps of the 'old rules' formula

It is tempting to skip steps of the 'old rules' formula as it is long and complex, and you might think certain steps do not apply. However, you should not skip any steps without checking them unless you are very familiar with the formula.

Although only a non-resident parent is liable to pay child maintenance, the calculation involves the income of both parents. The term 'parent' applies to both the non-resident parent and the parent with care.

As elsewhere in this *Handbook*, for the sake of simplicity the parent with care is referred to as 'she' and the non-resident parent as 'he'. However, all aspects of the formula apply in the same way if the parent with care is the father and the non-resident parent the mother. If the person with care is *not* the legal parent of the child, the income of that person does not affect the amount of child maintenance payable.

Step 1: the maintenance requirement

The maintenance requirement represents the minimum day-to-day expenses of maintaining children. However, the maintenance requirement is neither the minimum nor the maximum amount of child maintenance payable. Under the formula, a non-resident parent might be assessed as liable to pay less or more than the maintenance requirement.

The main significance of this step is that a non-resident parent pays 50 per cent of his assessable income (see Chapter 11) in child maintenance until the maintenance requirement figure has been met. At this point he pays a lower percentage of any remaining assessable income.

For full details of the maintenance requirement, see Chapter 9.

Step 2: exempt income

Exempt income represents the minimum day-to-day living expenses of the parent and covers the housing costs of the family with whom s/he lives. However, it only includes amounts for living expenses of any of the parent's *own* children who are living with her/him, *not* the living expenses of a new partner or stepchildren. An allowance in recognition of property/capital settlements pre-dating April 1993 may also be included in exempt income.

Each parent is allowed to keep income equal to the exempt income before being expected to pay any child maintenance.

For full details of exempt income, see Chapter 10.

Step 3: assessable income

Assessable income is income which is available to pay child maintenance. It is the amount of the parent's income which remains after exempt income has been taken into account. If a non-resident parent has no assessable income, he may still have to pay the minimum payment.

For full details of assessable income, see Chapter 11.

Step 4: proposed maintenance

Proposed maintenance is the amount of child maintenance the non-resident parent is expected to pay, provided it does not bring his income below the protected income level (see Step 5).

A non-resident parent pays 50 per cent of his assessable income in child maintenance until he has met the maintenance requirement figure of Step 1. Once the maintenance requirement is met, he pays 15, 20 or 25 per cent of any further assessable income, depending on the number of children for whom he is being assessed to pay maintenance.

The assessable income of the parent with care can reduce the proposed maintenance.

There is an upper limit to the amount of child maintenance payable under the formula, but it may be possible for the parties to go to court to seek additional child maintenance (see p30).

For full details of proposed maintenance, see Chapter 12.

Step 5: protected income

The protected income step ensures that a non-resident parent's disposable income does not fall below a certain level as a result of paying the proposed maintenance. At this stage, the whole family's expenses and income are taken into account, including those of a new partner and stepchildren.

A non-resident parent is not expected to pay more than 30 per cent of his own net income.

For full details of protected income, see Chapter 13.

3. Minimum child maintenance

There is a standard minimum of child maintenance that a non-resident parent must pay if the formula results in an amount less than this minimum.[5]

The amount of the minimum payment is currently £6.80. This is calculated by rounding 5 per cent of the income support (IS) personal allowance for someone aged 25 or over (£67.50) up to the next 5 pence and doubling it.[6]

The minimum payment must be made unless the non-resident parent falls into a category which is specifically exempt (see below). This means that a non-resident parent who has been assessed under the formula as liable to pay less than £6.80 must pay child maintenance of £6.80 a week unless he is exempt, in which case he pays nothing.

Only one minimum payment is due if the non-resident parent has qualifying children being looked after by more than one parent or person with care.[7] For example, if a non-resident parent has children with two or more women with whom he does not live, or if the qualifying children are being cared for by different people in different households, the minimum payment is divided between the persons with care in the same ratio as their respective maintenance requirements (see Chapter 9).

Exempt non-resident parents

A few non-resident parents do not have to pay any child maintenance at all. If a non-resident parent has been assessed under the formula as having to pay £6.80 or less, he is exempt from paying any child maintenance if he:[8]

- has the family premium (see Appendix 2) included in the calculation or estimation of his protected income level – ie, a child is a member of his family for at least two days a week;
- is a prisoner;
- receives (or would receive if he satisfied the national insurance contribution conditions or did not receive an overlapping benefit):
  - incapacity benefit, employment and support allowance or statutory sick pay;
  - maternity allowance or statutory maternity pay;
  - severe disablement allowance;
  - disability living allowance or attendance allowance;
  - an industrial disablement benefit;
  - a war disablement benefit or payment from the Armed Forces Compensation Scheme;
  - carer's allowance; *or*
  - payments from the Independent Living Funds;
- is under 16 years old, or under 19 and in full-time non-advanced education – ie, a child for child support purposes (see p18);
- has a net income of less than £6.80 (for details of what is net income, see Chapter 11). Trainees on approved training (eg, Entry to Employment, or Skillseekers in Scotland) whose income consists solely of a training allowance/ education maintenance allowance,[9] or students whose only income is a grant

or student loan,[10] have these payments ignored when calculating net income for child support purposes. This means they are usually exempt from paying child maintenance.

4. Non-resident parents on certain benefits

If the non-resident parent is in receipt of income support (IS), income-based jobseeker's allowance (JSA), income-related employment and support allowance (ESA) or pension credit (PC), the formula is not used. Instead, the Secretary of State can make a deduction from the IS/income-based JSA/income-related ESA/PC of a non-resident parent as a contribution towards child maintenance.[11] The deduction can be made from a partner's IS/income-based JSA/income-related ESA/PC if the partner of a non-resident parent is claiming for the couple.[12]

Who cannot have the deduction made

Deductions cannot be made if the non-resident parent is exempt. In these cases, a non-resident parent will pay nothing. A non-resident parent will be exempt if he:[13]

- is aged under 18; *or*
- qualifies for the family premium (see Appendix 2) and/or has day-to-day care (see p20) of any child; *or*
- receives any of the following benefits (or would receive one except for the national insurance contribution requirements or overlapping benefit rules):
  - statutory sick pay;
  - incapacity benefit or contributory ESA;
  - severe disablement allowance;
  - attendance allowance or disability living allowance;
  - carer's allowance;
  - maternity allowance;
  - statutory maternity pay;
  - an industrial disablement benefit;
  - a war disablement benefit or payment from the Armed Forces Compensation Scheme; *or*
  - payments from the Independent Living Funds.

Amount of the deduction

A non-resident parent on IS/income-based JSA/income-related ESA/PC who is not exempt may have an amount equal to the minimum payment (see p168) deducted from his benefit by the Department for Work and Pensions (DWP), irrespective of his age.[14] This is currently £6.80 a week. No more than one deduction of £6.80 can be made from an IS/income-based JSA/income-related

ESA/PC claim at any one time.[15] In some cases, half of this amount may be deducted. Whether the deduction is actually made by the DWP, and how much is deducted, depends on the number of other deductions of higher priority being made from benefit. For more information about how deductions are made, see p397.

Only one deduction for child support can be made, even if there is more than one person with care looking after the non-resident parent's qualifying children. In this case, the minimum payment is apportioned between the persons with care in the same ratio as their respective maintenance requirements.[16]

What the deduction is for

Technically, deductions from benefit are not payments of child support maintenance, but payments in lieu of child maintenance.[17] Deductions are not the result of a maintenance assessment and the rules that apply to assessments do not apply to these contributions. In particular, liability for the contributions will not be backdated to the effective date and arrears will not accrue if the DWP is unable to make the full deduction because there are other deductions with higher priority.

No more than one deduction of £6.80 can be made from an IS/income-based JSA/income-related ESA/PC claim at any one time,[18] and because deductions can only be made where there is a non-resident parent with current liability, no amount for child maintenance arrears can ever be deducted from these benefits. Arrears of child maintenance could still be collected by other methods (see Chapter 19), but usually the arrears will just be held in abeyance until the non-resident parent comes off IS/income-based JSA/income-related ESA/PC. However, if a non-resident parent is in receipt of contribution-based JSA, an amount can be deducted from this benefit towards arrears (see p407).

Challenging decisions

Child Support Agency (CSA) decisions about the liability of non-resident parents on certain benefits can be challenged in the same way as other CSA decisions[19] – ie, by seeking a revision[20] or supersession[21] (see Chapter 17) or by appealing to the First-tier Tribunal (see Chapter 18).[22] If the DWP's decision is being contested (ie, whether the non-resident parent can have £6.80 or some other amount deducted from his IS/income-based JSA/income-related ESA/PC, given other higher priority deductions), it can be challenged in a similar way. See CPAG's *Welfare Benefits and Tax Credits Handbook* for more details.

5. Special cases

The child support legislation uses the phrase 'special cases' to cover situations that are not as straightforward as when one non-resident parent has left one family and there is one person with care looking after all the children from that family.[23] However, in order to enable you to carry out calculations for all family situations, these situations are integrated in this *Handbook* into the relevant steps of the formula – eg, where:

- both parents are non-resident (see pp176 and 237);
- more than one person with care applies for child maintenance from the same non-resident parent (see p239);
- a person cares for children of more than one non-resident parent (see pp177 and 244).

If care of a child is being shared between different people, several modifications of the formula are necessary. Shared care under the 'old rules' is, therefore, treated separately (see Chapter 14).

'Shared care' is different from the situation where different children of the same family have different homes. If the children of a family are divided between two households (eg, if one child lives with one parent and another child with the other parent), this involves two maintenance assessments. In one assessment, the first parent is the parent with care and the second parent is the non-resident parent. In the second assessment the roles are reversed. This situation is referred to as 'divided families' in this *Handbook* (see p243). The Child Support Agency may refer to this as 'split care'.

Notes

1. **Introduction**

1 Reg 33(1) CS(MAP) Regs; reg 2(1) CS(MASC) Regs
2 Reg 2(2) CS(MASC) Regs
3 Regs 3(2), 9(5) and 11(5) CS(MASC) Regs
4 Reg 2(3) CS(MASC) Regs; CCS/7312/1995

3. **Minimum child maintenance**

5 Sch 1 para 7 CSA 1991
6 Reg 13 CS(MASC) Regs
7 Reg 22(4) CS(MASC) Regs
8 Reg 26 and Sch 4 CS(MASC) Regs
9 Sch 2 paras 21 and 36 CS(MASC) Regs
10 Reg 7(3) CS(MASC) Regs

4. **Non-resident parents on certain benefits**

11 s43 and Sch 1 para 5(4) CSA 1991
12 Sch 9 para 7A(1) SS(C&P) Regs
13 Reg 28 CS(MASC) Regs
14 Reg 28(2) CS(MASC) Regs; Sch 9 para 7A(3) SS(C&P) Regs
15 Reg 28(3) and (4) CS(MASC) Regs
16 Sch 9 para 7A(2) SS(C&P) Regs
17 s43(2)(a) CSA 1991
18 Sch 9 para 7A(2) SS(C&P) Regs
19 s43(3) CSA 1991
20 Sch 4C para 1(a) CSA 1991
21 Sch 4C para 2(1)(a) CSA 1991
22 Sch 4C para 3(1)(a) CSA 1991

5. **Special cases**

23 Part III CS(MASC) Regs

Chapter 9

The maintenance requirement ('old rules')

This chapter covers:

1. What is the maintenance requirement

The maintenance requirement is intended to represent the minimum weekly cost of caring for a child(ren) for whom child maintenance is being assessed.[1] The maintenance requirement is based on income support (IS) rates. For information on the conditions of entitlement to the IS premiums, see Appendix 2. **Note:** some of these premiums may no longer be paid with IS (eg, because parents get child tax credit instead), but are still used in the child support formula.

Both parents' incomes affect the maintenance requirement. In the case of the parent with care, a notional contribution towards the maintenance requirement is calculated, which may reduce the amount of child maintenance a non-resident parent has to pay.

The parents may not have sufficient income to be able to pay the full maintenance requirement. If this is the case, the non-resident parent pays 50 per cent of his available income, known as 'assessable income'. Equally, the maintenance requirement is not the total amount of child maintenance that may be expected from a non-resident parent. However, once the maintenance requirement is met, the non-resident parent then pays a lower percentage of any further income (see Chapters 11 and 12).

The maintenance requirement is also used where child maintenance has to be apportioned between two persons with care. This occurs if a parent is a non-resident parent for two different maintenance assessments (see p243).

Interim maintenance assessments

When the Child Support Agency does not have sufficient information from the non-resident parent to carry out an assessment, it can make an interim maintenance assessment. If the non-resident parent is withholding information, other than information about his partner or another member of the family's income, the interim maintenance assessment is set at 1.5 times the maintenance requirement (see p331).[2]

2. How much is the maintenance requirement

The maintenance requirement includes an allowance for each qualifying child (see p18) being looked after by that person with care. The person who is being assessed to pay child maintenance *must* be the parent (see p15) of that qualifying child. If a person with care is looking after children of different non-resident parents, a different maintenance requirement is calculated for each of the assessments (see p177).

The maintenance requirement calculation

The maintenance requirement is calculated as follows:[3]

- for each qualifying child, the amount of the income support (IS) personal allowance for a child (£62.33); *plus*
- the amount of the IS family premium (£17.40); *plus*
- a 'parent as carer' element (see also p175):
  - if at least one qualifying child is under 11 years of age, the amount of the adult IS personal allowance at the rate for a person aged 25 years or over, irrespective of the age of the person with care (£67.50); *or*
  - if none of the qualifying children are under 11 but at least one is under 14 years of age, 75 per cent of this adult allowance (£50.63); *or*
  - if none of the children are under 14 but at least one is under 16 years of age, 50 per cent of the adult allowance (£33.75); *less*
- an amount of child benefit for the qualifying child(ren) (see below).

This is the basic maintenance requirement calculation, which is adapted in situations where more than one non-resident parent is involved (see p177).

The rates used in the calculation are the IS and child benefit rates applicable at the date on which the maintenance assessment takes effect, known as the 'effective date' (see p332).[4] The figures given above are those for 2011/12 .

Deduction of child benefit

The amount of child benefit deducted is:[5]

- £20.30 for the only, elder or eldest child for whom child benefit is payable; *and*

- £13.40 for all other children.

The amount of child benefit deducted from the maintenance requirement may be different from that actually paid to the person with care, perhaps because she has not claimed it or because someone else (eg, the non-resident parent) is receiving it. In such cases, the person with care should consider claiming child benefit or asking the non-resident parent to make the payment of child benefit in addition to the maintenance payment (see *Example 9.4*). If more than one eligible person claims child benefit, the person with whom the child lives has priority. See CPAG's *Welfare Benefits and Tax Credits Handbook* for more details.

If child benefit is not payable for a child because s/he is in the care of an institution, an amount of child benefit is still deducted.[6] However, in other situations where no one is entitled to child benefit for that child (eg, because of the rules about residence in the UK) no deduction is made. For more information about child benefit, who is entitled and when it is payable, see CPAG's *Welfare Benefits and Tax Credits Handbook.*

The parent as carer element

When the 'old rules' assessment was designed, the inclusion of the adult personal allowance was intended to represent the care costs of the child. The reduction of the allowance for children over 11 years of age is based on an assumption that care needs reduce as children grow up. This means that the maintenance requirement as a whole can reduce immediately after a child's birthday.

The parent as carer element is not maintenance for a former spouse or civil partner.[7] Spousal or civil partner maintenance is separate from child maintenance calculated by the Child Support Agency. Any application for maintenance for the parent with care must be made to the courts (see p27).

Couples

The personal allowance for couples is never included in the maintenance requirement. This is because the non-resident parent is not responsible for maintaining a partner of the person with care.

Children with disabilities

The disabled child premium is not included in the calculation of the maintenance requirement and neither is any related carer premium. A court may be able to consider a top-up maintenance award for a child who is disabled (see p30).[8]

The maintenance requirement calculation for one non-resident parent and one parent with care

The most common situation in which the maintenance requirement needs to be calculated is where there is one parent with care and one non-resident parent.

Example 9.1: maintenance requirement for one non-resident parent and one parent with care

Anita and Bob have two children. They split up, and Anita remains in the family home with Carol (13) and David (8).

		£
Personal allowances	Anita	67.50
	Carol	62.33
	David	62.33
Family premium		17.40
Sub-total		209.56
Less child benefit		33.70
Maintenance requirement		**175.86**

Five years later, Anita remarries. David is 13; Carol is 18 and still at school.

		£
Personal allowances	Anita	50.63 (75% x 67.50)
	Carol	62.33
	David	62.33
Family premium		17.40
Sub-total		192.69
Less child benefit		33.70
Maintenance requirement		**158.99**

3. **Both parents are non-resident**

An application for maintenance can be made by a person with care who is not a parent – eg, if a child lives with her/his grandparents or another relative. Both parents of that child are then non-resident parents and liable to pay maintenance. An assessment can be carried out for each non-resident parent if an application is made in respect of her/him, and each contributes to the maintenance requirement (see p237 for the calculation of the proposed maintenance).

An application may be made for maintenance from only one of the non-resident parents. In this case, the maintenance requirement for the one non-resident parent is halved.[9] However, it is not halved when an application is made for maintenance from both non-resident parents, even if an assessment cannot be made for both – eg, one parent cannot be traced or is habitually resident outside the UK.

Example 9.2: maintenance requirement if both parents are non-resident

Beverley (15) lives with her grandmother, who is a widow.

		£
Personal allowances	Grandmother	33.75 (50% x 67.50)
	Beverley	62.33
Family premium		17.40
Sub-total		113.48
Less child benefit		20.30
Maintenance requirement		**93.18**

This maintenance requirement will be halved to £46.59 if the grandmother applies for child maintenance only from her son-in-law and not her daughter.

4. More than one non-resident parent

A person with care may look after qualifying children who have different parents – eg, a mother is looking after her children who have different fathers, a grandmother is looking after children of two of her sons, or a lone parent is also looking after a friend's child. In these cases, if applications are made for child maintenance from each non-resident parent, a number of different assessments must be carried out, one for each non-resident parent.

The maintenance requirement for each non-resident parent includes only the child(ren) who are his own responsibility. However, the adult personal allowance and the family premium are divided among the non-resident parents[10] in proportion to the number of non-resident parents and not in proportion to the number of children who are their responsibility.[11] This apportionment should occur whether or not child maintenance is being pursued from all the non-resident parents.[12] For example, a person with care may apply for child maintenance from one father and not another, or one of the parents may be resident abroad and outside the Child Support Agency's jurisdiction. However, a deceased parent is not treated as a non-resident parent and there is no reduction in the maintenance requirement for the living non-resident parents.[13]

The apportioned 'parent as carer' element is then further reduced if the children in the individual assessment are aged 11 or over – ie, 75 per cent of the apportioned amount is used if the youngest child is aged 11 to 13, and 50 per cent of the apportioned amount if s/he is 14 or 15 years old.[14]

Example 9.3: maintenance requirement if children have different fathers

Zoe is a single parent and has three children, all of whom live with her. Wayne is the father of Yvonne (12) and Veronica (10). Terence is the father of Scott (3).

Wayne's assessment:

		£	
Personal allowances	Zoe	33.75	(50% x 7.50)
	Yvonne	62.33	
	Veronica	62.33	
Family premium		8.70	(50% x 17.40)
Sub-total		167.11	
Less child benefit		33.70	
Maintenance requirement		**133.41**	

Terence's assessment:

Personal allowances	Zoe	33.75	(50% x 67.50)
	Scott	62.33	
Family premium		8.70	(50% x 17.40)
Sub-total		104.78	
Less child benefit		13.40	
Maintenance requirement		**91.38**	

Two years later, Zoe is living with Bob and her four children. Wayne is the father of Yvonne (14) and Veronica (12). Terence is the father of Scott (5). Bob is the father of Ricky (1). However, as Bob is not a non-resident parent, the apportionment occurs between Wayne and Terence only. Terence's assessment remains as above.

Wayne's assessment:

		£	
Personal allowances	Zoe	25.31	(75% x one-half of 67.50)
	Yvonne	62.33	
	Veronica	62.33	
Family premium		8.70	(50% x 17.40)
Sub-total		158.67	
Less child benefit		33.70	
Maintenance requirement		**124.97**	

If a person with care is looking after children of different parents, but two of the non-resident parents are parents of the same child (ie, the person with care is *not* a parent of that child), those two non-resident parents will be treated as one person for the purposes of apportioning the relevant elements of the maintenance requirement.[15]

Example 9.4: maintenance requirement if there is more than one non-resident parent and both parents of one child are non-resident

Zoe's niece, Rebecca, who is aged 17 and still at school, comes to live with Zoe and Bob when her parents split up. Rebecca joining the household alters the maintenance requirement for the other children. For the four qualifying children Zoe is now looking after, there are four non-resident parents (Wayne, Terence, and both of Rebecca's parents).

However, Rebecca's parents count as one unit for this purpose and therefore the amounts are divided by three.

Wayne's assessment:		£	
Personal allowances	Zoe	16.88	(75% x one-third of 67.50)
	Yvonne	62.33	
	Veronica	62.33	
Family premium		5.80	(one-third of 17.40)
Sub-total		147.34	
Less child benefit		26.80	
Maintenance requirement		**120.54**	

Terence's assessment:			
Personal allowances	Zoe	22.50	(one-third of 67.50)
	Scott	62.33	
Family premium		5.80	(one-third of 17.40)
Sub-total		90.63	
Less child benefit		13.40	
Maintenance requirement		**77.23**	

Rebecca's parents' assessment:		
Personal allowance for Rebecca	62.33	
Family premium	5.80	(one-third of 17.40)
Sub-total	68.13	
Less child benefit	20.30	
Maintenance requirement	**47.83**	

An assessment is carried out separately for both of Rebecca's parents, each using the maintenance requirement of £47.83. If Zoe chose to apply for child maintenance only from one of Rebecca's parents, the maintenance requirement would be halved to £23.92. **Note:** if she chose to apply for child maintenance for Rebecca on or after 3 March 2003, this would prompt conversion of the other assessments, and all her child maintenance would be dealt with under the 'new rules' (see Chapter 7).

We have assumed that Zoe has claimed child benefit for Rebecca, which means that under the child benefit regulations the higher rate applies to Rebecca and the lower rate now applies to Yvonne. As the person with whom Rebecca is living, Zoe takes priority over the mother for child benefit purposes (see p269).[16]

If Rebecca's mother had continued to claim child benefit, the higher rate would be payable for Rebecca as the only child for whom her mother is claiming. At the same time, the higher rate would still be payable for Yvonne as she is the eldest child for whom Zoe is claiming child benefit.[17] If this were the case, the child benefit of £20.30 would be deducted for both children in the calculation, even though Zoe would not actually be receiving child benefit for Rebecca.

In this scenario, if Rebecca's mother did not give £20.30 each week to Zoe, whether as child maintenance or on top of the maintenance assessment, she would no longer be entitled to child benefit.[18] In this case, the maintenance requirements would be as shown above, as child benefit would not legally be payable to Rebecca's mother, even though in practice it may still be being paid. It would be to Zoe's advantage to claim the child benefit for Rebecca in this situation.

Notes

1. What is the maintenance requirement
1 Sch 1 para 1(1) CSA 1991
2 Regs 8(3)(a) and 8A(1) CS(MAP) Regs

2. How much is the maintenance requirement
3 Sch 1 para 1 CSA 1991; reg 3 CS(MASC) Regs
4 Regs 3(2) and 4 CS(MASC) Regs
5 Reg 4 CS(MASC) Regs
6 Sch 1 para 1(2) CSA 1991
7 CCS/11729/1996
8 s8(8) and (9) CSA 1991

3. Both parents are non-resident
9 Reg 19(2)(d) CS(MASC) Regs

4. More than one non-resident parent
10 Reg 23 CS(MASC) Regs
11 Reg 23(3) CS(MASC) Regs
12 Reg 23(1) CS(MASC) Regs
13 CCS/7436/1999
14 Reg 23(2A) CS(MASC) Regs
15 Reg 23(3) CS(MASC) Regs
16 Sch 10 para 2 SSCBA 1992
17 Reg 2 CB&SS(FAR) Regs
18 s143(1)(b) SSCBA 1992

Chapter 10

Exempt income ('old rules')

This chapter covers:

1. What is exempt income

Exempt income is income a parent can keep for her/his own essential expenses before any child maintenance is expected. The expenses are based on income support (IS) rates, but also include housing costs.

When the 'old rules' assessment was designed, exempt income was intended to represent the minimum day-to-day living expenses of parents and their *own* children who are living with them. If the parent has a partner, the partner's personal expenses are *not* included in exempt income. However, the housing costs for the whole family, including any partner and stepchildren, are covered in exempt income.

'Own child' means a child for whom the parent is, in law, a parent – eg, the biological or adoptive parent (see p15). Exempt income does *not* include amounts for any other children in the family – eg, stepchildren. Allowances for other children are not even initially included if the child is the primary responsibility of the parent – eg, if the stepchild's other parent is dead or cannot afford to pay any child maintenance. In some cases, departure from the 'old rules' assessment can be sought on these grounds (see p288).

Exempt income applies to *both* the non-resident parent and the parent with care, as both are liable to maintain their children. If the parent with care has any income available to maintain the children, this might reduce the non-resident parent's contribution (see Chapter 12). However, if the parent with care is on IS, income-based jobseeker's allowance (JSA), income-related employment and support allowance (ESA), pension credit (PC) or working tax credit (WTC), it is assumed that she has no income available for child maintenance[1] and the exempt income step is carried out for the non-resident parent only. This applies both where the parent with care is the benefit claimant and where her partner is making the claim.

If the non-resident parent is on IS/income-based JSA/income-related ESA/PC, there is no need to calculate exempt income for either parent, as the formula is not used in this situation. Instead, the non-resident parent may have deductions made from his IS/income-based JSA/income-related ESA/PC as a contribution towards child maintenance (see p170). If the non-resident parent is on WTC, the child support calculation is still carried out unless there is also an assessment being considered or in force for a child for whom he is the parent with care (see p19).[2] If he is a parent with care in this position, he is not liable to pay any child maintenance as a non-resident parent. This does not apply if a 'new rules' calculation is being considered. If a 'new rules' calculation is carried out, the assessment as a non-resident parent is converted and carried out as a 'new rules' calculation. In this case, WTC is counted as income. See also Chapter 7.

If the person with care is not a parent, the exempt income step does *not* apply to her/him, as only parents have a liability to maintain their children. In this case, there will usually be two non-resident parents, and a maintenance assessment (including the exempt income step) is carried out for both.

2. How much is exempt income

Exempt income is generally calculated in the same way for parents with care as for non-resident parents.[3] Any reference to 'parent' below applies equally to the parent with care and the non-resident parent.

The rates used in the calculation are the income support (IS) rates applicable on the date on which the maintenance assessment takes effect, known as the 'effective date' (see p332).[4] The rates given below are for 2011/12.

For the qualifying conditions for the IS premiums, see Appendix 2.

The exempt income calculation

Exempt income is calculated as follows for each parent:[5]

- the amount of the IS personal allowance for a single person aged 25 or over, irrespective of the age of the parent (£67.50); *plus*
- if there is a child (ie, the parent's own child – see p181) living with the parent, the amount of the IS personal allowance for such child (£62.33);*†*plus*
- if an allowance for a child is included, the amount of the IS family premium (£17.40);*†*plus*
- if any of the children included would qualify for the IS disabled child premium, the amount of that premium for each child entitled (£53.62);*†*plus*

- if any of the children included would qualify for the IS enhanced disability premium, the amount of that premium for each child entitled (£21.63);*† *plus*
- if the parent would qualify for the IS disability premium even if s/he is over the qualifying age for pension credit, the amount of the premium for a single person (£28.85); the disability conditions must be satisfied by the parent her/himself; *plus*
- if the parent would qualify for the IS carer premium, the amount of that premium (£31); *plus*
- if the parent would qualify for the IS severe disability premium, the amount of that premium (£55.30); *plus*
- if the parent would qualify for the IS enhanced disability premium, the amount of that premium (£14.05); *plus*
- housing costs (see p184); *plus*
- where applicable, an allowance for a pre-April 1993 property settlement (see p192); *plus*
- if an employee travels more than 240 kilometres a week to and from work, an amount towards travel costs (see p196).

* If the child's other parent also lives in the family and has sufficient income to help support the child, these amounts may be halved (see p198).

† These amounts are included at a proportionate rate if the parent looks after the child(ren) for less than seven days, but at least two nights on average per week (see Chapter 14). For parents with care, this apportionment only takes place if another person also has day-to-day care of the child.[6] Special expenses can be added to exempt income after a departure direction.

Example 10.1

Bob and Anita have split up. Anita is looking after Carol and David, and remains in the family home. There is no need to calculate Anita's exempt income as she is in receipt of IS. Bob is living on his own in a bedsit, paying rent of £48 a week. He is not entitled to any housing benefit. He does not qualify for any premiums. He travels less than 240 kilometres a week to work.

Bob's exempt income is therefore:	£
Personal allowance	67.50
Housing costs	48.00
Total exempt income	**115.50**

If Bob had moved in with his parents, his exempt income would be £67.50. If Bob was in receipt of long-term incapacity benefit, his exempt income would then be:

	£
Personal allowance	67.50
Disability premium	28.85
Total exempt income	**96.35**

3. Housing costs

Housing costs for the parent and any of her/his family (see p25) living with her/him are included in exempt income. If the other party believes that the parent's partner can afford to contribute to the housing costs, s/he may be able to apply for a departure direction (see p294).

To be included in exempt income, housing costs must be eligible (see p185) and payable in respect of the parent's home (see p186). Housing costs which are excessive may not be included in full (see p190).

Responsibility for housing costs

Eligible housing costs for the parent's home are included if the parent or partner is responsible for the costs and the payment is made to a person who is not a member of the same household.[7] Therefore, if a parent lives with a new partner, the housing costs are accepted, even if they are the partner's responsibility. The amount of the housing costs included in exempt income can be reduced if it is reasonable to expect the partner to contribute.[8] Otherwise, the full eligible costs are covered and not the amount paid by the parent towards the housing costs.[9]

In addition to when s/he is actually liable for the costs, a parent is treated as responsible for housing costs if:[10]

- s/he has to meet the costs in order to live in the home; *and*
- the person liable to make the payments is not doing so; *and*
- either the parent is the former partner of the liable person or is someone else whom it is reasonable to treat as liable.

If costs are shared with another person who is not a partner, only the parent's actual share of the costs is used (unless the parent is treated as liable because the other person(s) is not paying her/his share).[11] This means that if the non-resident parent continues to pay his liability for the housing costs on the former joint home in which the parent with care remains, this amount cannot be included as the parent with care's housing costs.[12] If the non-resident parent stops paying his liability, the full amount is treated as the parent with care's housing costs.[13] If three friends are joint tenants and share the rent equally, one-third of the rent is considered to be the responsibility of the parent, unless the Child Support Agency (CSA) believes that such a division would not be reasonable – eg, one of the joint occupiers is not paying her/his share (in which case, the amount the parent actually pays may be used), or they have unequal shares in the accommodation. However, a parent is not be treated as responsible for housing costs which a member of her/his family (see p25) is not paying.[14]

From 1 December 2005, eligible housing costs should include payments made by a same-sex partner of a parent. Before 1 December 2005, same-sex couples were not treated as partners, and so if a same-sex partner of a parent was paying or contributing to housing costs, these costs would not automatically be treated as the parent's. This has, however, been successfully challenged on the basis (among others) that it infringed the parent's rights under Article 14 and Protocol 1 of the European Convention on Human Rights. Exempt income for periods before 1 December 2005 should, therefore, include such costs.[15]

The parent may be treated as responsible for housing costs that s/he shares with other members of the household, even if s/he makes those payments via another member of the household and not directly.[16] This applies if:

- it is reasonable for a parent to be treated as responsible for a share of the costs; *and*
- the person with responsibility is not a close relative of the parent or her/his partner (see p21); *and*
- the person with responsibility either has an equivalent responsibility for housing costs as the parent or that person is meeting the costs because the liable person is not.

However, if a parent is a non-dependent member of a household (see p253), no housing costs are included in exempt income, even if s/he is paying a contribution for housing costs to another member of the household.[17] In order for a parent to be a non-dependant, not only can there be no commercial arrangement, but s/he has to be a member of the same *household* as the person liable to make the payments (see p21).

If a parent is living with her/his parents as a non-dependant, s/he is therefore not entitled to have her/his contribution to the housing costs included in exempt income.[18] However, where costs are shared with other people who are not close relatives and the parent is not a non-dependant, even if the parent is contributing to housing costs on a voluntary basis, it might, depending on the circumstances of the case, be arguable that it is reasonable to treat the parent as responsible for a share of the costs. This is most likely to succeed in cases where the costs have previously been shared with someone else and the parent has taken over that person's share. If the parent becomes a co-owner or joint tenant, half of the housing costs are treated as the parent's responsibility. If the parent becomes a sub-tenant, s/he is responsible for the costs specified in the tenancy agreement.

Eligible housing costs

Eligible housing costs are costs which have to be incurred in order to buy, rent or otherwise secure possession of the parent's home or to carry out certain repairs and improvements.[19] Eligible costs are:[20]

- rent (after deduction of any housing benefit (HB) – see p187);[21]
- mortgage interest payments;
- capital repayments under a mortgage;
- premiums paid under an endowment or other insurance policy, or a personal pension plan that was taken out to cover the cost of the mortgage (see p187);

- interest payments on any loans for repairs and improvements to the home taken out before the maintenance application or enquiry form is sent to the parent;
- interest payments on loans for major repairs necessary to maintain the fabric of the home and for measures which improve its fitness for occupation, such as: the installation of a bath, shower, wash basin or lavatory; the provision of heating, electric lighting and sockets, drainage facilities or storage facilities for fuel and refuse; improvements to ventilation, natural lighting, insulation or structural condition; or any other improvements considered reasonable by the CSA (the previous 'unfitness' which necessitated the improvement needs to be demonstrated[22]);
- interest payments under a hire purchase agreement to buy a home;
- payments in respect of a licence or permission to occupy the home;
- payments in respect of, or as a result of, the occupation of the home. (This is intended to cover payments made by a former licensee who occupies premises unlawfully – eg, after a notice to quit has expired. It does not include property and contents insurance,[23] payments in respect of the purchase of a home[24] or council tax[25]);
- ground rent or feu duty;
- payments under co-ownership schemes;
- service charges if they are a condition for occupying the home (but see p189);
- mooring charges for a houseboat;
- site rent for a caravan or mobile home;
- payments for a tent and its site;
- payments under a rental purchase scheme;
- payments in respect of croft land;
- payments in respect of a home made to an employer who provides the home;
- payments for a Crown tenancy or licence;
- payments in respect of a loan taken out to pay off (in full or in part[26]) another loan that covered eligible housing costs;
- the fees (after deduction of any HB) if a parent or a partner lives in a care home or an independent hospital, or is being provided with a care home service or independent healthcare service.[27]

Repayments of an advance of salary (see also p205) used to purchase a home are not housing costs.[28]

Home

For the purposes of housing costs, the parent's home is either the dwelling in which s/he normally lives or, if s/he normally lives in more than one home, her/his principal home.[29] Therefore, if a non-resident parent is paying the costs of the family home in which the parent with care remains with the child(ren), these costs cannot be included in the non-resident parent's exempt income as this is not the non-resident parent's own home.[30] Before deciding which dwelling is the principal home, the facts must show that the parent lives in more than one home.[31]

The test of a principal home is not simply the parent's own view nor a calculation of the time spent at each home.[32] For example, an army officer's own home where s/he spends her/his leave could be her/his principal home over and above army married quarters. Expenditure on army accommodation in addition to the principal home could not in this situation also be taken into account as expenses, but army officers serving abroad may be able to have the costs of both a home in the UK and quarters overseas included in exempt income.[33]

The only other exception to the rule on only including one set of housing costs is where the parent is in a care home. The residential fees can be included as well as the costs of the parent's own home if the parent has been in the residential accommodation for less than a year or if the CSA believes that the parent intends to return home.[34]

If the payments for the property cover accommodation used for other purposes (eg, business use), the CSA must identify the proportion of the cost attributable to housing.[35]

Housing benefit

HB is subtracted from housing costs if the parent has claimed and been awarded it.[36] In this situation, the housing costs are the weekly amount treated as eligible rent for the purposes of HB minus the amount of HB calculated by the local authority.[37] (Because of rent restrictions and local housing allowance rules, eligible rent may be less than the non-resident parent's actual rent, even allowing for the deduction of ineligible charges. For more information, see CPAG's *Welfare Benefits and Tax Credits Handbook*.)

If a parent delays claiming HB until after completing the maintenance enquiry or application form, full housing costs are included as exempt income (unless they are excessive – see p190). If a parent is awaiting a decision on an HB claim, the excessive housing costs rule does not apply, but the CSA may later seek further information about the claim.

Mortgage and other loan payments

Unlike for income support (IS), most payments connected to mortgage repayment, whether directly as capital repayments or through certain policies, are eligible housing costs for exempt income purposes.[38] However, such payments are not eligible at the protected income stage (see p253).

As well as endowment policies, other insurance policies taken out to pay off a mortgage on the home are eligible housing costs. These include premiums paid into a mortgage protection policy to cover the mortgage in the event of unemployment, sickness or disability.[39] Life assurance policies taken out with the mortgage in order to discharge the debt on death are also included.[40] However, neither building nor contents insurance is included.[41] The mortgage which any such policy is intended to discharge need not exist at the time of the assessment.[42]

Only loans for the provision of a home are eligible. A loan used to buy out a former partner's interest in a property is only be eligible if it can be shown that the loan is necessary to secure possession of the home or protect the right of occupancy.[43]

If a loan is partly for the provision of a home (see p186), only that part is an eligible housing cost.[44] If only part of the mortgage is eligible, the nature of any insurance policies should be investigated. It should not be assumed that the proportion of the premiums allowed follows the proportion of the mortgage interest allowed.[45]

Personal pension plans taken out, at least in part, to discharge a mortgage on the parent's home are eligible housing costs.[46] If a personal pension plan has been obtained both to discharge the mortgage and to pay a pension, 25 per cent of the contributions made are included as housing costs in exempt income.[47]

If the mortgage is under £60,000, all the premiums paid to an endowment policy are eligible housing costs.[48] If the policy was also taken out to produce a lump sum and the mortgage is over £60,000, 0.0277 per cent of the mortgage is taken to be weekly housing costs, unless the CSA can establish what proportion of the premium is actually paid to cover the mortgage. If the parent's endowment premium is larger than this 0.0277 per cent figure, it is worth pursuing the issue of how much capital is likely to be produced, especially as many endowment policies may not produce any capital in excess of the mortgage. Any payments made in excess of those required by the mortgage agreement are not eligible housing costs.[49]

There is nothing to prevent repayments to a member of the family or friend on a loan to purchase a home being considered as housing costs, as long as a mortgage or charge has been created by depositing the title deeds or a land certificate which prevents the borrower disposing of the property without the lender's consent.[50] Repayments on a loan to purchase a home can be considered as housing costs if the mortgage or charge is created against the interest of one or more, but not all, co-owners of a property.[51]

Repayments made under an agreement for a loan taken out for eligible repairs and improvements (see p185) or a service charge to cover these items are included in exempt income as housing costs,[52] as are insurance policies associated with such a loan or which are taken out to pay off another loan for an eligible housing cost.[53]

Ineligible charges

Charges made for food, fuel, water or sewerage services do not count as eligible housing costs.[54] If the housing costs payments include an ineligible charge, an amount attributable to the service must be deducted.

If meals are provided, a standard weekly deduction is made:

2011/12	*Aged 16 or over*	*For each child under 16*
Full board	£24.05	£12.15
Half board	£16.00	£8.05
Breakfast only	£2.95	£2.95

If the parent provides information about the level of the fuel charge included in the housing payment, this actual or estimated amount can be deducted. Otherwise standard weekly deductions are made. For 2011/12, these are: heating £21.55; hot water £2.50; cooking £2.50; and lighting £1.75.[55] If the parent has exclusive use of only one room, the deduction for heating, hot water and/or lighting is £12.90 a week.

If the amount for water and sewerage charges is not separately identifiable, an amount will be attributed.

If other service charges are included in the rent payments, the amount deducted is any amount higher than the following, whichever is greater:[56]

- the total of eligible charges included in the rent; *or*
- 25 per cent of eligible housing costs.

If it is not clear what amount for ineligible service charges is included, the CSA attributes a reasonable amount. Ineligible services include:

- personal laundry service;
- sports and other leisure facilities, including TV rental and licence fees, but excluding children's play areas;
- cleaning, other than communal areas or where no one in the accommodation is able to do it;
- transport;
- medical or nursing services; *and*
- any other charge not connected with the provision of adequate accommodation.

Weekly amount of housing costs

The amount allowed for housing costs is usually the amount payable at the effective date (see p332), converted into a weekly amount.[57] If the costs are monthly, the amount at the effective date must be multiplied by 12 and divided by 52. If the housing costs are paid on any basis other than weekly or calendar monthly, the CSA considers the amount and payment period of the housing costs payable on the effective date and:[58]

- divides 365 by the number of days in the payment period, rounding to the nearest whole number;
- multiplies this figure by the amount of the costs due in the payment period; *and then*
- divides this figure by 52 to give the weekly costs.

If rent is payable to a local authority or housing association on a free-week basis, the rent payable in the relevant week (see p205) is used unless that was a free week, in which case the last non-free week is used.

If the housing costs are a repayment mortgage and the parent has failed to provide information on repayments and interest on the effective date but has provided a mortgage statement from the lender for a period ending less than a year before the relevant date, this statement can be used to calculate the capital repayments and, where possible, the interest payments.[59]

The calculation of housing costs should be carefully checked as this is an area where the CSA often makes mistakes.

Excessive housing costs

Housing costs of a non-resident parent are not generally allowed in full if they are excessive. Parents are exempt from restrictions on their excessive housing costs if they:[60]

- have day-to-day care of any child;
- have claimed or been awarded HB;
- would qualify for an IS disability premium, even if over the qualifying age for pension credit (see Appendix 2);
- remain in a home previously occupied with a former partner;
- have high housing costs because money which would otherwise be available is tied up in the former family home, which is still occupied by an ex-partner;
- have been meeting high housing costs for over 52 weeks before the application for child support, and there has been no increase in those costs other than an increase in the rate of mortgage interest or rent;
- have higher housing costs than the usual restricted amount (see below) only because of an increase in the rate of mortgage interest or rent.

Departure can be sought by the other parent if the exemption applies and the housing costs are unreasonably high (see p294).

Unless the parent is exempt, eligible housing costs are otherwise only allowed up either £80 or half of the parent's net income, whichever is greater.[61] (See p204 for the calculation of net income.) Therefore, parents who have a net income of less than £160 can include housing costs of up to £80, while those with higher net incomes can include housing costs of up to half the parent's income.

The excessive housing costs rule does not apply to parents with care and it is unlikely that the notional income or capital rules could be used where a parent with care takes on excessive housing costs (see p220).[62]

Example 10.2

Bob goes to live with Zoe who has three children, Yvonne (12), Veronica (10) and Scott (3). Zoe's rent on a three-bedroom council house is £45 a week. They do not receive HB. Even though it is Zoe who is legally liable for the rent, it is still an eligible cost.

Bob's exempt income is now:	£
Personal allowance	67.50
Housing costs	45.00
Total exempt income	**112.50**

Anita is now in paid employment. As long as she is not in receipt of working tax credit, her exempt income must be calculated. She lives with her two children, Carol (13) and David (8). Her mortgage is under £60,000 and the payments, including the capital repayments, are £70 a week.

		£
Personal allowances	Anita	67.50
	Carol	62.33
	David	62.33
Family premium		17.40
Mortgage payment (total)		70.00
Total exempt income		**279.56**

Anita marries Joe and together they buy a house, taking out a mortgage of £85,000. The interest payments are £495 a month and the endowment premium £108 a month – ie, £114.23 and £24.92 a week. However, as the CSA does not have information about how much of the premium is to cover the mortgage, the endowment premium is restricted to £23.55 (0.0277% x £85,000) (see p187).

		£
Personal allowances	Anita	67.50
	Carol	62.33
	David	62.33
Family premium		17.40
Mortgage payment	(£114.23 + £23.55)	137.78
Total exempt income		**347.34**

The excessive housing costs rule does not apply because there are children in the family, but Bob could consider seeking a departure (see p294) on the grounds that Joe can afford to contribute towards the mortgage.

4. Pre-April 1993 property settlements

In order for an allowance to be included in 'old rules' exempt income, the property or capital transfer must satisfy certain qualifying criteria (see below).[63] Departure can be sought where the allowance in exempt income does not properly reflect the effect of the settlement (see p295).

Unlike other elements of exempt income, this allowance applies to a parent with care only if she was the non-resident parent at the time the property was transferred.[64] If a parent with care transferred capital to the non-resident parent or the child(ren) and the non-resident parent also transferred capital, this 'compensating transfer' may be offset against that of the non-resident parent's 'qualifying transfer'.[65]

Qualifying transfer

A **'qualifying transfer'** is one which was made:[66]

- as part of a court order or written maintenance agreement made before 5 April 1993;
- when the non-resident parent and parent with care were living separately;
- between the non-resident parent and either the parent with care or a child for whom maintenance is being assessed;
- with the effect that the recipient was given the whole of the value of the transferred property (this condition can be met where the whole value of a part share in a property or asset is transferred);[67] *and*
- without its only purpose being to replace maintenance payments (either periodic or a lump sum) for the parent with care – ie, for herself as opposed to the child(ren) – and to compensate the parent with care for the loss of any right to apply for or receive such payments, or to compensate her for a reduction in such payments. 'Loss of any right' in this context should be taken to mean 'loss of any one right' rather than 'loss of all rights'.[68] This means that if a maintenance agreement for a low or nominal sum exists, it may still be the case that the only purpose of the transfer was to compensate the parent with care for this reduced maintenance, and therefore the transfer will not qualify.[69]

The types of evidence which might be considered when deciding whether a transfer should be excluded by the final condition listed above are likely to include a court order, written maintenance agreement, the transfer document, and/or confirmation from a building society, solicitor, accountant or property valuers. All evidence produced by either party should be considered, including any documents which might expressly state that the transfer was only to compensate the parent with care for the loss of some right to spousal maintenance. However, although decision makers may consider other evidence beyond the transfer agreement in order to determine the purpose of the transfer, the purpose must be 'clearly and explicitly' shown by the evidence and not inferred on the balance of probabilities.[70]

Certain transfers made under Scottish law can only be for the purpose of compensating the parent with care and, therefore, cannot be qualifying transfers,[71] but transfers made under a written maintenance agreement rather than a court order may still qualify.[72]

It is possible for the non-resident parent to transfer the whole of the asset to the parent with care, but for the lender to insist that the non-resident parent's name is retained on the mortgage – eg, if the amount of the mortgage is more than the parent with care can borrow. This does not negate the fact that the whole of the asset has been transferred to the parent with care. Even if the non-resident parent retains a partial beneficial interest in the property, it may still be considered a relevant transfer. If a charge is placed on the property to benefit the non-resident parent, this is deducted when calculating the allowance.

Property is defined as:[73]

- cash and savings in a bank, building society or equivalent account;
- a legal estate or an equitable interest in land (or in Scotland, an interest in land);
- an endowment or other insurance policy obtained in order to discharge the mortgage or charge on a property which was also being transferred;
- a business asset, whether in the form of money, land or otherwise, which, before it was transferred, was being used in the course of a business in which the non-resident parent was a sole trader, a partner or a participator in a 'close' company.[74]

It does not include other assets – eg, a car or contents of the home. The value of a trust or trust fund set up between the non-resident parent and parent with care, or the non-resident parent and the child, should be considered.

Providing evidence

Once a non-resident parent has notified the Child Support Agency (CSA) that he wants a property/capital settlement taken into account, he has to supply evidence within a reasonable time.[75] If the evidence is not produced within this time, the transfer is treated as having no value.[76]

The non-resident parent must send written evidence to the CSA of:[77]

- a court order or maintenance agreement which required the transfer of property (this evidence must be from the same time period as the court order or agreement);
- the fact of the transfer – eg, solicitors' or building society correspondence, or a copy of a Land Registry extract;

- the value of the property transferred at the date that the court order/written agreement was made (confirmed by a building society, insurance company or firm of property valuers); *and*
- the amount of any mortgage or charge outstanding at the date that the court order/written agreement was made (confirmed by a building society, bank, solicitor or accountant).

If the parent does not have this documentary evidence, it could be contained in solicitors' files, if still available. The most difficult information to obtain may be the historical value of the asset and a charge will usually be made for such a valuation.

When the non-resident parent applies for a property/capital settlement to be taken into account, the person with care is notified and asked for any relevant information.[78] Any allowance in exempt income is not calculated until 14 days after the person with care has been contacted.

Calculating the allowance

The qualifying value of a transfer of property, land or a business asset is calculated using the following formula:[79]

$$\text{qualifying value} = \frac{(VP - MCP)}{2} - (VAP - MCR) - (VCR)$$

Where:

- VP is the value of the property or business asset which is (wholly or in part) transferred.
- MCP is the amount of any mortgage or charge outstanding on the property immediately prior to the date of the agreement.
- VAP is the value of any interest in the property which continues to be beneficially owned by the non-resident parent – eg, if the non-resident parent transfers three-quarters of the interest in a house to the parent with care, VAP would be one-quarter of the total value.
- MCR is the amount of any mortgage or charge on the property for which the non-resident parent remains liable immediately following the transfer (this will be the same proportion of MCP as VAP is of VP).
- VCR is the value of any charge in favour of the non-resident parent on the property immediately following the transfer.

Any change in property, land or business prices since that time is irrelevant – the above figures are based on values at the agreement date. Land or property is valued on the basis that the parent with care and the child(ren) would vacate it on completion of a sale.[80] The total net value is used irrespective of whether or not the asset was previously in joint ownership.

The qualifying value in the case of a bank or building society account is half of the balance on the date of the order/agreement, and for an endowment policy, half of the surrender value at that date.[81]

If the evidence produced shows that the whole of the transfer was made in lieu of ongoing child maintenance, the qualifying value is twice that arrived at by the above formula (in the case of property, land or business assets)[82] or (in the case of money or endowment policies) the full value transferred.[83] If there has been more than one qualifying transfer, the qualifying values of the transfers are totalled.[84]

Transfers made by the parent with care to the non-resident parent or child(ren) which satisfy the qualifying criteria (see p192), except that they are made in the reverse direction, are called 'compensating transfers'.[85] In addition, there is provision for the whole amount of money raised by a parent with care (eg, by taking out a loan) after the date of the court order or written agreement in order that she or her child(ren) will be entitled to the whole of the property to be taken into account as a compensating transfer.[86] This applies if a non-resident parent transfers the matrimonial home to the parent with care on the condition that she buys out his interest in the property. Otherwise, compensating transfers are valued in the same way as qualifying transfers.[87]

The value of any compensating transfer is deducted from that of the qualifying transfer to give the relevant value.[88] The allowance included in the exempt income relates to this relevant value:[89]

Relevant value	*Weekly allowance*
Less than £5,000	Nil
£5,000 – £9,999	£20
£10,000 – £24,999	£40
£25,000 or more	£60

Remember that this is an allowance in the exempt income and, therefore, its inclusion does not mean that the resulting maintenance assessment will be reduced by a corresponding amount.

Example 10.3: pre-April 1993 property settlement allowance

Debbie and Steve divorced in 1991. The family home was transferred to Debbie. At the time of the court settlement, the property was worth £58,000 and the outstanding mortgage was £22,000. Almost all the contents of the house were left with Debbie, as was the car. Instead of Steve paying maintenance for Debbie, as part of the settlement, their joint savings account of £14,200 was transferred into Debbie's name. In addition, Steve gave each of the two children £3,000.

The house contents and the car do not come within the definition of property. The savings account is not a qualifying transfer as it was payment in lieu of maintenance for Debbie.

In this case, VP = £58,000 and MCP = £22,000 (see p194). VAP, MCR and VCR are nil. The qualifying value of the transfer of the house is therefore:

(£58,000 – £22,000) ÷ 2 = £18,000

The qualifying value of the cash to the children is the whole actual value – ie, 2 x £3,000 = £6,000

Total qualifying value = £24,000

There is no compensating value to offset.

As the relevant value is over £10,000 but less than £25,000, the allowance included in exempt income is £40.

If the savings transferred to Debbie were only £10,000 of the £14,200 and this was not for any specified purpose, this would have been another qualifying transfer valued at £5,000.

Total qualifying value = £29,000

Debbie has to pay Steve for the funds remaining in the joint account, so there is a compensating transfer with a value of £4,200 ÷ 2 = £2,100

Relevant value = £29,000 – £2,100 = £26,900

The allowance = £60

If Steve had transferred only three-quarters of the property to Debbie (retaining one-quarter interest himself), the qualifying value of the transfer of the home would be lower. VP = £58,000, MCP = £22,000, VAP = £14,500 (25% x VP) and MCR = £5,500 (25% x MCP). VCR is nil.

The qualifying value = (£58,000 – £22,000) ÷ 2 – (£14,500 – £5,500) = £18,000 – £9,000 = £9,000

In this case, if the house were the only asset transferred, the allowance included in exempt income would be £20.

5. Travel-to-work costs

An allowance towards travel costs can be included in 'old rules' exempt income for parents in employment who travel long distances.[90] It does not apply to self-employed parents.

As well as buying petrol or a ticket, travel-to-work costs include contributing to the costs of someone other than the employer who pays for transport, or paying someone else to provide the transport.[91] The allowance does not apply if an employer either provides transport (including a company car) for any part of the journey between home and the workplace, or pays for any part of the travel-to-work cost.[92] If an employer has made a loan to the parent, increases the amount of pay, or makes a payment which would be taken into account as part of net income (see p205), this is not classed as an employer paying for the transport.

Calculating the allowance

The parent must supply the required information.[93] The Child Support Agency (CSA) calculates or, where this is not possible, estimates:[94]

- the straight-line distance (ie, as the crow flies), rounded to the nearest kilometre, between the parent's home and workplace;
- the number of journeys made between home and the workplace over a period of whole weeks which it thinks is representative of the parent's normal pattern of work (disregarding any two journeys made between the home and workplace within a period of two hours); *and*
- the number of journeys multiplied by the distance and divided by the number of weeks in the period used.

No allowance is included if this figure comes to less than or equal to 240 kilometres. However, if it is over this, 6 pence is included for each kilometre over 240.[95]

If the allowance does not reflect the real travel costs, either party can apply for a departure direction (see p290 and p295).

Example 10.4: exempt income including travel costs

Steve has remarried and has a net income for child support purposes of £380 a week. He and his wife, Lisa, have a mortgage of just under £60,000 and make monthly interest and endowment premium payments totalling £416 a month. They have no children.

Steve commutes five days a week to London with a straight-line distance from home to work of 132.3km. 10 journeys x 132.3 km = 1,323 km a week.

Days of annual leave or sickness are ignored.

This is 1,083 kilometres more than 240 and thus the allowance is 1,083 x 6 pence = £64.98 a week.

Steve's exempt income:	£	
Personal allowance	67.50	
Mortgage in full*	96.00	
Property settlement allowance	40.00	(from the first part of *Example 10.3*)
Travel-to-work costs	64.98	
Total exempt income	**268.48**	

*Although the housing costs are over £80, they are not considered excessive as half of Steve's net income is £190 a week (see p190).

Parent who have more than one workplace

There are special rules to deal with parents who work at more than one workplace, whether for one employer or in more than one job.[96] If the pattern of work is irregular in a job, the CSA can select one of the workplaces or another location connected with the employment and assume that each day the parent travels to and from this deemed workplace.[97]

Otherwise, the CSA must calculate the straight-line distances between any of the workplaces between which the parent travels, as well as between the home and each of the workplaces.[98] The pattern of journeys is obtained over a representative period, as above. Each distance is multiplied by the number of times that journey is made over the period, and the total number of kilometres is divided by the number of weeks in the period.

6. Second families

The term 'second family' is used in this *Handbook* to describe the situation where a parent is living with a partner and children. The children may be her/his own and/or the partner's. The word 'second' is not precise, as the family could be a parent's third or fourth family, or indeed a first family – eg, where the qualifying children are children of a relationship formed after a marriage, and the parent continues to live with her/his spouse and children of the marriage.

Partners and children who are not the parent's children are not considered when including personal allowances and premiums at the exempt income stage. However, a child of the parent is included and that child may have another parent who is liable to maintain her/him. If the other parent is non-resident, the child is a qualifying child and there is the possibility of receiving child maintenance.

Alternatively, if the other parent is also living in the family, the 'old rules' exempt income calculation can be adjusted to recognise the other parent's liability to maintain the joint child. In other words, if a parent is living with her/his own child and the child's other parent, the partner may be able to help support the child. This will reduce the parent's responsibility for the joint child included in the exempt income calculation. If the partner has sufficient income, this will halve the amounts for the joint child in the exempt income calculation.

The partner can refuse to disclose her income, in which case it is assumed that she can afford to help support her child(ren) and the allowances are halved.

This assessment will need to be done not only where the non-resident parent has a second family, but also where a parent with care has had a child with a current partner. This is the only time in the formula that the income of the parent with care's partner is involved.

Can the partner afford to maintain a joint child?

Before including the full allowance and premiums for a joint child in the parent's exempt income, the net income of the partner must be assessed. The partner's net income is calculated in the same way as the parent's net income when working out her/his assessable income (see Chapter 11), with just one difference.[99] The income of any of the partner's own children is *not* included. This means that maintenance for any of her own qualifying children from their non-resident parent (ie, stepchildren in the second family) is ignored.

To assess whether a partner can help support a joint child(ren), compare the amount of her/his net income with the total of:[100]

- the income support (IS) personal allowance for a person aged 25 or over (£67.50); *plus*
- half the amount of the IS personal allowance for each child; *plus*
- if the child(ren) would qualify for the IS disabled child premium (see Appendix 2), half the amount of that premium for that child(ren); *plus*
- half the amount of the IS family premium, except where the family premium would be payable in respect of another child(ren) who is included in exempt income (£8.70); *plus*
- any contribution the partner is expected to make towards housing costs after a departure direction (see p294).

No personal allowances are included for any other children of the partner.

If the partner's net income is higher than the figure above, s/he can afford to contribute to their joint child's support. Therefore, the parent's exempt income will include only half the child's personal allowance, half of any disabled child premium, and (if there is no other child included in the exempt income) only half the family premium.[101]

Example 10.5: exempt income with a joint child

Bob and Zoe have a baby, Ricky. They are still living in the same house with a rent of £45 a week and Zoe's other three children (see *Example 10.2*).

Zoe stays at home full time. Her only income is child benefit and maintenance for Yvonne and Veronica, both of which are ignored. Therefore, Zoe cannot afford to contribute to Ricky's upkeep and Bob's exempt income will include the full allowances for Ricky.

Bob is not the father of Yvonne, Veronica and Scott, and therefore they are not included in the exempt income calculation.

Bob's exempt income:		£
Personal allowances	Bob	67.50
	Ricky	62.33
Family premium		17.40
Housing costs		45.00
Total exempt income		**192.23**

Zoe begins paid work and brings home £120 a week.

Her earnings are compared with:

Personal allowances	Zoe	67.50
	Ricky (half)	31.17
Family premium (half)		8.70
Total		**107.37**

Note: half the family premium is allowed in Zoe's means test as the family premium is only included in Bob's exempt income for Ricky. There is no other child included in exempt income.

Zoe's other three children are not taken into account.

No departure application has been made for Zoe's contribution towards housing costs.

As her earnings are higher than £107.37, Zoe is seen as being able to contribute to the maintenance of Ricky. Therefore, Bob's exempt income is adjusted.

Bob's exempt income:		£
Personal allowances	Bob	67.50
	Ricky (half)	31.17
Family premium (half)		8.70
Housing costs		45.00
Total exempt income		**152.37**

Family premium

If the only children who are included in the parent's exempt income are joint children with the current partner, whether or not the family premium is included in full or halved in the exempt income depends solely on the net income of the partner. When calculating whether the partner can afford to help support the children, half the family premium is included in the amount with which the partner's net income is compared, as in *Example 10.5*.

However, if there is another child in the family who is the parent's but not the partner's child, s/he will be included in the exempt income calculation of her/his parent. Therefore, the family premium is payable in full for this other child and the question of halving the family premium does not arise. The family premium is therefore excluded from the amount with which the partner's net income is compared when calculating whether she can support half the joint child.[102]

Example 10.6: exempt income with a joint child and a qualifying child

The situation is the same as in *Example 10.5,* except that Bob's daughter, Carol (15), has come to live with Bob and Zoe.

Zoe's earnings are now compared with:

		£
Personal allowances	Zoe	67.50
	Ricky (half)	31.17
Total exempt income		**98.67**

Half of the family premium is not included as Bob is entitled to the full family premium in his exempt income for Carol, and between the two partners there cannot be more than one family premium.

As her earnings are higher than £98.67, Zoe is seen as being able to contribute to half the maintenance of Ricky. Therefore, Bob's exempt income is adjusted.

Bob's exempt income:		£
Personal allowances	Bob	67.50
	Carol	62.33
	Ricky (half)	31.17

Family premium (in full)	17.40
Housing costs	45.00
Total exempt income	**223.40**

If Carol only comes to stay some of the time, her personal allowance may be included in Bob's exempt income, but at a reduced rate, depending on how often she stays with him (see Chapter 14).

For a detailed explanation of the family premium in exempt income where there is a joint child and a shared-care child, see p271.

Notes

1. **What is exempt income**
 1 Sch 1 para 5(4) CSA 1991; regs 10A and 10B CS(MASC) Regs
 2 Sch 1 para 5(4) CSA 1991; reg 10A CS(MASC) Regs

2. **How much is exempt income**
 3 Reg 10 CS(MASC) Regs
 4 Reg 9(5) CS(MASC) Regs
 5 Sch 1 para 5 CSA 1991; reg 9(1) CS(MASC) Regs
 6 Reg 10(b) CS(MASC) Regs

3. **Housing costs**
 7 Reg 14 and Sch 3 para 4(1)(b) and (c) CS(MASC) Regs
 8 Reg 40(7) CSDDCA Regs
 9 CCS/6741/1995; CCS/2852/1995
 10 Sch 3 para 4(2)(a) CS(MASC) Regs
 11 Reg 15(3) CS(MASC) Regs
 12 CSCS/8/1995; CCS/8189/1995
 13 CCS/13698/1996
 14 Reg 15(3) CS(MASC) Regs
 15 *JM v United Kingdom* (No.37060/06) ECtHR, 28 December 2010
 16 Sch 3 para 4(2)(b) CS(MASC) Regs
 17 Reg 15(4) CS(MASC) Regs
 18 CSCS/2/1994; CSCS/5/1995
 19 Sch 3 para 4(1)(a) CS(MASC) Regs
 20 Sch 3 paras 1, 2, 2A and 3 CS(MASC) Regs; CCS/12/1994 and CCS/2750/1995
 21 Reg 15(2) CS(MASC) Regs
 22 CSCS/3/1996
 23 CSCS/1/1994; R(CS) 3/96
 24 CCS/11252/1995
 25 CSCS/13/1995
 26 CCS/12897/1996
 27 Regs 9(1)(h) and 11(1)(i) CS(MASC) Regs
 28 CCS/11252/1995
 29 Reg 1(2) CS(MASC) Regs
 30 CSCS/8/1995; CCS/8189/1995
 31 CCS/19/1994
 32 CCS/4/1994; R(CS) 2/96
 33 CCS/4305/1995
 34 Regs 1(2), 9(1)(h) and 11(1)(i) CS(MASC) Regs
 35 Sch 3 para 5 CS(MASC) Regs
 36 Reg 15(2) CS(MASC) Regs
 37 Reg 15(2) CS(MASC) Regs
 38 Sch 3 para 3 CS(MASC) Regs
 39 Sch 3 para 3(4) CS(MASC) Regs; CCS/12598/1996
 40 Sch 3 para 3 CS(MASC) Regs
 41 CSCS/1/1994
 42 CCS/1321/1997
 43 R(CS)12/98; CCS/1418/2003; *SJ v CMEC* [2010] UKUT 355 (AAC)
 44 Sch 3 para 4 CS(MASC) Regs
 45 CCS/2750/1995
 46 Sch 3 para 3(5A) and (5B) CS(MASC) Regs
 47 Sch 3 para 3(5B) CS(MASC) Regs
 48 Sch 3 para 3(5) and (5A) CS(MASC) Regs

49 Sch 3 para 3(6) CS(MASC) Regs
50 CCS/9/1995
51 *NM v CMEC* [2010] UKUT 58 (AAC), reported as [2010] AACR 33
52 Sch 3 para 3(2A) CS(MASC) Regs
53 Sch 3 para 4A CS(MASC) Regs
54 Sch 3 para 6 CS(MASC) Regs
55 **IS** Sch 3 para 17(2) IS Regs
56 Sch 3 para 6(d) CS(MASC) Regs
57 Reg 16(1) CS(MASC) Regs
58 Reg 16(2)(d) CS(MASC) Regs
59 Reg 16(2) CS(MASC) Regs
60 Reg 18(2) CS(MASC) Regs
61 Reg 18(1) CS(MASC) Regs
62 CCS/6/1995

4. **Pre-April 1993 property settlements**
63 Reg 9(1)(bb) and Sch 3A CS(MASC) Regs
64 Reg 10(a) CS(MASC) Regs
65 Sch 3A paras 1, 8 and 9 CS(MASC) Regs
66 Sch 3A para 1(1) CS(MASC) Regs
67 Sch 3A para 1(1)(d) CS(MASC) Regs; CCS/14368/1997; CCS/97/1997
68 CCS/97/1997
69 Sch 3A para 1(1)(d) CS(MASC) Regs
70 CCS/97/1997
71 The Family Law (Scotland) Act 1985
72 CSCS/1/1998; CSCS/2/1998
73 Sch 3A para 1(1) and (2) CS(MASC) Regs
74 As defined by ss414 and 415 ICTA 1988
75 Sch 3A para 2(2) CS(MASC) Regs
76 Sch 3A para 2(2) CS(MASC) Regs
77 Sch 3A para 2(1) CS(MASC) Regs
78 Sch 3A para 3 CS(MASC) Regs
79 Sch 3A para 4(1) CS(MASC) Regs
80 Sch 3A para 4(2) CS(MASC) Regs
81 Sch 3A para 5 CS(MASC) Regs
82 Sch 3A para 6(a) CS(MASC) Regs
83 Sch 3A para 6(b) CS(MASC) Regs
84 Sch 3A para 7 CS(MASC) Regs
85 Sch 3A para 1 CS(MASC) Regs
86 Sch 3A para 8A CS(MASC) Regs
87 Sch 3A para 8 CS(MASC) Regs
88 Sch 3A para 9 CS(MASC) Regs
89 Sch 3A para 10 CS(MASC) Regs

5. **Travel-to-work costs**
90 Reg 9(1)(i) and Sch 3B CS(MASC) Regs
91 Sch 3B para 1 CS(MASC) Regs
92 Sch 3B paras 21-23 CS(MASC) Regs
93 Sch 3B para 2 CS(MASC) Regs
94 Sch 3B paras 3-6 CS(MASC) Regs
95 Sch 3B paras 7, 14 and 20 CS(MASC) Regs
96 Sch 3B paras 8-20 CS(MASC) Regs
97 Sch 3B paras 8(2) and 15(2) CS(MASC) Regs
98 Sch 3B paras 9-13 and 16-19 CS(MASC) Regs

6. **Second families**
99 Reg 9(2) CS(MASC) Regs
100 Reg 9(2)(c) CS(MASC) Regs
101 Reg 9(1)(f) and (g) CS(MASC) Regs
102 Reg 9(2)(c)(iv) CS(MASC) Regs

Chapter 11

Assessable income ('old rules')

This chapter covers:

1. What is assessable income

Assessable income is the parent's income that remains after basic living expenses (represented by exempt income – see Chapter 10) have been accounted for. A proportion of this remaining income is used to contribute towards child maintenance payments (see Chapter 12). In the case of the parent with care, this is a notional contribution which can have the effect of reducing the maintenance payable by the non-resident parent.

Assessable income is the parent's net income minus exempt income.[1]

This step of the formula is carried out in the same way for non-resident parents and parents with care[2] and, therefore, any reference to parent in this chapter applies to both. It does not apply to a person with care who is not the parent of the qualifying child.

It is useful to calculate the non-resident parent's assessable income first because if he has no assessable income there is no need to calculate that of the parent with care (see p222).

A parent who is in receipt of income support (IS), income-based jobseeker's allowance (JSA),income-related employment and support allowance (ESA) or pension credit (PC) is treated as having *no* assessable income.[3] If only the parent with care is on IS/income-based JSA/income-related ESA/PC, the assessable income step must be done for the non-resident parent alone. If the non-resident parent is on IS/income-based JSA/income-related ESA/PC, the formula calculation is not carried out at all and instead the non-resident parent may have a deduction from his benefit (see p397). If the benefit claim of one party is thought to be fraudulent, this can be challenged by the other party (see p344).

Parents with care who are on working tax credit (WTC) are treated as having no assessable income.[4] This, as for IS/income-based JSA/income-related ESA/PC, applies whether the benefit is being paid to the parent herself or to her partner. A non-resident parent on WTC is only treated as having no assessable income if he is also a parent with care and either there is a maintenance assessment in force for his qualifying child(ren) or an application for an assessment is being considered.[5] (But if a maintenance calculation is made as a parent with care, this will convert the non-resident parent's maintenance assessment to the 'new rules', under which WTC is included as income.)

2. What is net income

Net income under the 'old rules' is the total income of the parent taken into account when assessing how much child maintenance the parent can afford to pay.

Net income includes earnings, benefits and other income.[6] The types of income that come within each of these categories are defined in the Regulations.[7] Certain types of income are ignored, either in full or in part.[8] The rules about income are similar, but not identical, to those for income support (IS).

The net income of a parent's partner is calculated using these rules when assessing whether s/he can afford to contribute to the support of any joint child in the exempt income calculation (see p244).[9]

These rules for calculating net income are also used when working out the family's total income at the protected income stage of the formula (see Chapter 13). However, there are a few exceptions,[10] which are explained here and in Chapter 13.

If any income normally received at regular intervals is not received, it can be treated as though it has been received, as long it is due to be paid and there are reasonable grounds for believing that the payment will actually be made.[11]

Capital is not taken into account, although any income generated from the capital does count as income (see p217).

In certain cases, a parent can be treated as having income (or capital which is a source of income) which s/he does not possess if the Child Support Agency (CSA) believes the parent deprived her/himself of it with the intention of reducing her/his assessable income (see p220).

Verification of income is expected (see p69).

Whose income is included

A partner's income is *not* included in the net income when calculating assessable income. This is commonly misunderstood (see p250 for the way in which a partner's income may affect the assessment). If a source of income is held jointly and the proportions are not known or defined, the income available is divided equally between the people who are entitled to receive it.[12]

The income of the parent's own child living in the household can be treated as though it were the income of the parent (see p218).[13]

Relevant week

The concept of the 'relevant week'[14] is important in child support assessments, particularly when calculating income.

For the parent who is not the applicant, the relevant week is the seven days immediately before the date that the maintenance enquiry form (see p59) is sent to her/him. For the applicant, the relevant week is the seven days immediately before the maintenance application form (see p41) is submitted to the CSA. For the purpose of calculating earnings only, if the CSA has not been able to make an assessment (except perhaps an interim maintenance assessment – see p331), but is later supplied with the information required, the relevant week is the seven days immediately before the date on which the required information or evidence was received.[15]

If a decision is revised (or if it is superseded because of ignorance or a mistake about a material fact), the relevant week of the new decision is the same as that for the original decision. If a decision is superseded on other grounds, the relevant week is the seven days immediately prior to the application for a supersession (or the seven days prior to the date of notification if the CSA supersedes on its own initiative).[16] See Chapter 18 for more information on grounds for revision and supersession of decisions.

Earnings from employment

'Earnings' means 'any remuneration or profit derived from employment' and, as well as wages, includes:[17]

- payments for overtime;
- profit-related pay;
- any bonus or commission (including tips);
- holiday pay (except any payable more than four weeks after the job ends);
- payment in lieu of notice;
- statutory sick pay, statutory maternity pay, statutory adoption pay and statutory paternity pay;[18]
- payment for expenses not 'wholly, exclusively and necessarily incurred' in actually carrying out the job (these include payments made to cover travelling expenses from home to work and the care costs of any other member of the family);
- allowances paid to local councillors for local authority duties, as opposed to expenses 'wholly, exclusively and necessarily incurred';
- payment for duties as an auxiliary coastguard, part-time firefighter, or with the lifeboat services, territorial army or reserve forces relating to a period of less

than one year (such payments for a period of one year or more are disregarded);[19]
- awards of compensation for unfair dismissal;
- certain employment protection payments;
- any retaining fee;
- remuneration, but not share dividend or debenture interest (which is other income) paid to a director of a limited or unlimited registered and incorporated company (as opposed to a sole trader or partner who is self-employed – see p208).

If an employee is also a director of a company, money drawn from a director's current account or loan account could be either income or capital. If it is income, it may or may not be earnings, depending on whether it is 'derived from that employment'. A decision about this money needs to be fully explained following an investigation of the facts.[20]

The CSA should not simply adopt HM Revenue and Customs' (the Revenue's) estimate (eg, of expenses) and should carry out an independent examination of the facts, although CSA staff would have to consider carefully before taking a different position.[21] Non-taxable allowances are not automatically excluded as earnings for child support purposes.[22]

Earnings do *not* include:[23]
- occupational pension payments (these count as other income – see p214. For how payments made into a pension scheme are treated, see p208);
- payments for expenses 'wholly, exclusively and necessarily' incurred in carrying out the duties of the job;
- payments in kind;
- any advance of earnings or a loan made by an employer to an employee (such a payment is also disregarded as other income,[24] and any repayments made will be included as earnings, not deducted from them[25]);
- payments made after employment ends which relate to a specific period of time, provided that a period of equal length has elapsed since the payment was received;
- earnings from a previous job where they are paid in a week or a period that earnings from a second job are received;
- payments made by an employer when an employee is on strike;
- any tax-exempt allowance paid by an employer to an employee;
- a compensation payment negotiated and made on the termination of employment[26] (except any payment in lieu of notice – see p205);
- the value of free accommodation provided by an employer (although the CSA may consider the issue of notional earnings – see p220 – if the actual earnings are low in relation to the job performed).

Payments made by the parent for expenses can be deducted from her/his earnings if the employer did not reimburse them,[27] but only if the expenses were incurred 'in the performance of duties'. It is possible that part of a payment (eg, towards a telephone rental or travel costs) could be 'wholly, exclusively and necessarily' incurred.[28]

A local overseas allowance paid to members of the armed forces abroad is disregarded,[29] whereas a rent or mortgage allowance paid by an employer (eg, to a police officer,[30] an army major in the UK,[31] or a civil servant[32]) would normally be taken into account as earnings, except where the housing expenses are necessarily incurred in the performance of their duties.[33] For the same reason, meals allowances are treated as earnings.[34]

Calculating normal weekly earnings

Average earnings are used in the child support calculation.[35] When calculating or estimating average earnings for the relevant week (see p205), the CSA considers the evidence of the parent's earnings over any appropriate period, beginning no more than eight weeks before the relevant week and ending by the date of the assessment. It may also consider cumulative earnings to date in the tax year covering the relevant week.

If a parent has claimed or been paid working tax credit (WTC) or child tax credit (CTC) on any day during the eight weeks before the relevant week or up to the date the assessment is made, the CSA can use the amount of earnings taken into account in the WTC/CTC calculation even though those earnings may relate to a period outside that normally used for a child support assessment.

If the parent is a student (see p214), earnings are averaged over 52 weeks ending with the relevant week, or as many weeks as the parent has been a student if this is shorter.[36]

If the CSA believes that the amount of weekly earnings arrived at does not accurately represent the parent's normal earnings, any other period can be used, taking into account earnings received and those due to be received.[37] The CSA must first be satisfied that the calculation of earnings at the relevant week produces a figure which is not normal.[38] A future period can be used to ensure the usual pattern is reflected – eg, earnings from a job which has not yet begun. The CSA must also consider the expected duration and pattern of any employment. A parent may want to suggest an alternative period to the CSA, giving reasons, as the CSA cannot be expected to consider an alternative period without substantial grounds and a prompt by one of the parents.[39] The CSA must use one continuous period.[40]

If a bonus, commission or profit-related pay is paid separately from earnings or in relation to a longer period than other earnings during a year ending with the relevant week, those payments are totalled over the year and divided by 52 weeks.[41] Such a payment cannot be disregarded on the grounds that it distorts normal earnings.[42]

The CSA must take into account any change of circumstances it is aware of between the relevant week and the effective date (see p332).[43] However, it must first calculate earnings in the usual way for the relevant week in order to determine whether there has been a material change of circumstances.[44] For changes after this date, see p319.

The calculation of earnings is one of the areas where errors are frequently made and, therefore, should be checked carefully. A commissioner held that an appeal tribunal must enquire into whether the process used to determine income was correctly carried out and whether the period used for the averaging of earnings gave an accurate picture.[45]

Calculating net earnings

Net earnings from employment are counted as net income in full. Net earnings mean gross earnings *less*:[46]

- income tax;
- Class 1 national insurance (NI) contributions;
- half of any contributions made to an occupational pension scheme; *and*
- half of any contributions made towards a personal pension scheme (unless that scheme is intended partly to pay off a mortgage on the parent's home, in which case it is 37.5 per cent of such contributions). Certain retirement savings plans do not come within this provision,[47] but regular contributions under a retirement annuity contract may be deducted.[48]

The amount of tax and national insurance actually paid is usually deducted.[49] However, where earnings are being estimated, the amount to be deducted as income tax is calculated using the personal allowances and the tax rates applicable in the relevant week (see p205).[50] Similarly, the amount to be deducted as Class 1 NI contributions is calculated by using the appropriate percentage rate applicable in the relevant week.

Earnings from self-employment

From 1 August 2007, earnings from self-employment are based on taxable profits from self-employment, as defined for income tax.[51] (This means that capital allowances can be deducted from gross profits, and balancing charges applied to them.) A parent must, on demand, supply the CSA with a copy of the Revenue's tax calculation notice (and any revised notice). However, if there is evidence that the figures used in the tax calculation are not reliable, the CSA is not required to use the figures used by the Revenue.[52]

If the CSA is satisfied that it is not reasonably practicable for a parent to provide the tax calculation notice, earnings are calculated using the gross receipts of self-employment, with relevant deductions (see p209).[53]

The earnings taken into account are the taxable profit from self-employment less tax, NI and half of pension premiums (37.5 per cent of the premium where the scheme is intended to pay off a mortgage).[54] The tax, national insurance and pension premium deductions from self-employed earnings are calculated using the rates applicable at the effective date.

If self-employed earnings are assessed as above, those profits must relate to a period of not less than six months and not more than 15 months ending within two years of the relevant week.[55] If there is more than one such period, the figure used will be the taxable profits relating to the latest period.[56]

Before 1 August 2007, self-employed earnings were based on self-assessment forms or tax calculation notices, or where these were not available or not appropriate, via gross receipts. There were also other differences, including the fact that capital allowances were not deducted. For further information, see the 2007/08 edition of this *Handbook*.

If a parent's liability or maintenance received has changed to her/his disadvantage because of the way in which self-employed earnings are now assessed, s/he could raise the issue with her/his MP, or s/he may be able to complain to the CSA and ask for compensation.

Earnings from self-employment calculated from gross receipts

If the CSA is satisfied that it is not reasonably practicable for a parent to provide a tax calculation notice, earnings are calculated on the following basis.

In these cases, earnings mean the gross receipts of the business. They include any business start-up grant which is paid in respect of the same period for which earnings are determined.[57] Payments received for providing board and lodging accommodation are counted as other income (see p214) unless they provide the largest part of the parent's income, when they are treated as earnings from self-employment.[58] If a parent is a childminder, only one-third of her gross receipts count as earnings.[59]

Net earnings to be included as net income are the gross receipts of the business *less:*[60]

- income tax (calculated using the personal allowance and the tax rates applicable on the effective date – see p332);
- NI contributions (Class 2 and Class 4 contributions at the rates applicable on the effective date[61]);
- half of any premium on a personal pension scheme (unless that scheme is intended partly to pay off a mortgage on the parent's home, in which case 37.5 per cent of the contributions are deducted) or on a retirement annuity contract;
- any VAT paid in excess of VAT received in the same period as that over which the earnings are assessed;
- any expenses which are reasonably incurred for the purposes of the business. If the CSA is not satisfied that the full expense was appropriate or necessary to the business, it will allow that part considered reasonable. If an expense is part business and part private (eg, a car), the CSA has to decide on the breakdown between the two uses on the evidence available. If the CSA is not satisfied that

the full expense was appropriate or necessary to the business, it should be able to allow the part it does deem reasonable. It may apportion these in line with Revenue practice.

Business expenses include:[62]

- repayments of capital on loans used to replace or repair a business asset (but not for loans taken out for any other business purpose);
- any income used to repair a business asset;
- any payment of interest on loans taken out for business purposes (this does not include loans taken out to acquire a share of a business, nor to pay business tax liabilities).[63]

Business expenses do *not* include any capital expenditure nor any expenses incurred in providing business entertainment.[64]

A person may still be classed as a self-employed earner even if her/his profits are not taxable – eg, if s/he spends a significant amount of time gambling. In such a case, it may be difficult to calculate gross receipts and allowable deductions and, in practice, a person with care may have to consider applying for a departure direction on the grounds that a parent's lifestyle is inconsistent with her/his income (see Chapter 15).[65]

There are separate rules and guidance for share fishermen to reflect the different ways in which their expenses may be shared.[66]

If a profit and loss account is provided for a period of at least six months (but no longer than 15 months) which ended within the last two years, it can be used to calculate average weekly earnings.[67] The two years end on the date on which the assessment takes effect – ie, the effective date (see p332). The CSA may decide to wait if accounts will shortly be available and impose a Category C interim maintenance assessment in the meantime. However, it is important that accounts which include income received after the effective date are not used.[68]

The actual gross receipts relevant to the period covered by the profit and loss account are included, whether or not they were received during that period.[69]

If there is more than one profit and loss account covering different periods, the account covering the latest period will be used unless the CSA is satisfied that this latest account is not available for reasons beyond the parent's control.[70] Not being available includes where an accountant or another government department (eg, the Revenue) holds them without a date set for their return, the Official Receiver has the accounts, or they have been destroyed, lost or stolen.

The accounts do not need to be prepared by accountants, or even typed. However, if they do not contain the required information, the CSA may request other evidence of gross receipts.

If no appropriate profit and loss account is available, earnings for the self-employed are averaged over the previous 52 weeks or, if the person has been self-employed for less than a year, over the period during which s/he has been self-employed up to and including the relevant week (see p205).[71] The self-employed person may be asked to provide other evidence of business receipts and expenses, such as business books, receipts of bills sent and paid, bank statements, records of wages paid, Revenue forms and VAT bills.

If the CSA believes that either or both of the above calculations produce an amount which does not accurately represent the parent's true earnings, another period can be used.[72] This should not be used just because earnings fluctuate, receipts are irregular or come in a lump sum, trade is slow at times or work non-existent for a period, nor should a different period be used just because it is known that earnings will subsequently change.[73]

Self-employed parents on tax credits

If a self-employed parent has claimed or been paid WTC/CTC on any day during the eight weeks before the relevant week or up to the date the assessment is made, the CSA may use the amount of earnings taken into account in the WTC/CTC calculation even though those earnings may relate to a period different from those described on p210.[74]

Challenging self-employed earnings

There have often been delays in the self-employed parent producing all the information necessary to carry out the assessment. The CSA has discretion to impose a Category A or C interim maintenance assessment while waiting for the information (see p331). The person with care may want to request that this is done if there is a delay, and may want to consider complaining if the CSA refuses to do so (see Chapter 20). Interim maintenance assessments can be imposed even if the non-resident parent's failure to provide information is not his fault – eg, if he has not yet gone through the self-assessment process. In that case, a Category C interim maintenance assessment of up to £30 can be imposed.[75]

Many self-employed non-resident parents have, in the past, received low assessments, and some persons with care may allege that the self-employed non-resident parent, perhaps with the help of an accountant, has managed to disguise his true income. Once an assessment has been made, the person with care can seek a revision of the assessment (see p344) and ask the CSA to use an inspector (see p70) in order to obtain more detailed information. If the non-resident parent's accounts have been accepted by the Revenue, it is unlikely that the CSA would consider it worthwhile to undertake further investigations unless evidence can be provided that the figures are not reliable. The CSA may also refuse to revise the assessment if the person with care cannot substantiate her allegations. This refusal can be challenged if the belief that income is too low is reasonably held, as it is very difficult for one party to obtain definitive details of the other's income. The CSA is much better placed to do this.

If the person with care takes the case to the First-tier Tribunal, she will see details of the income in the appeal papers, and she may be able to argue that some of the expenses included are not reasonable or not wholly connected with the business (see p210). She should also consider the notional earnings rules (see p220) and, if relevant, suggest that the First-tier Tribunal make a finding on this. Alternatively, the First-tier Tribunal can estimate net earnings based on the available evidence, including oral evidence from the person with care.[76] It can also consider data about earnings in different sectors and in particular localities (eg, the *New Earnings Survey*) to estimate the likely self-employed earnings in particular jobs.[77]

The person with care can apply for departure from the assessment on the grounds that a person's lifestyle is inconsistent with his level of income or that assets which do not currently produce income are capable of doing so (see p293).

Benefits

Benefits paid by the Department for Work and Pensions count as income for the purposes of net income, although some of these are disregarded in full or in part.[78] Remember that if IS, income-based jobseeker's allowance (JSA), income-related employment and support allowance (ESA) or pension credit (PC) is received by the parent or her/his partner, the parent is treated as having no assessable income (see p204) and the formula is not used. See p213 for tax credits.

The amount of benefit to be taken into account is the weekly rate applying on the effective date (see p332).[79]

Whose benefit?

The income of a partner is not included when working out a parent's net income. Some non-means-tested benefits contain an extra amount for a partner, called an adult dependency increase. The amount paid in respect of that dependant is treated as the dependant's income, not the claimant's[80] – ie, if the parent is the claimant, s/he is treated as not receiving the adult dependency increase and, if the partner is the claimant, the parent is assumed to have income equal to the increase paid to the partner in respect of her/him. If a parent receives a non-means-tested benefit which includes an increase for a child, this is treated as the income of the child (see p218). These rules also apply to adult and child dependency increases paid with a war disablement, war widow's, war widower's or surviving civil partner's pension.[81]

Benefits ignored in full

The following benefits are ignored in full when working out net income:

- child benefit;[82]
- housing benefit;[83]
- council tax benefit;[84]
- disability living allowance (or a mobility supplement);[85]
- attendance allowance (or constant attendance allowance or exceptionally severe disablement allowance paid because of industrial injury or war injury);[86]

- social fund payments;[87]
- guardian's allowance;[88] *and*
- Christmas bonus.[89]

Payments made to compensate for the loss of benefits are also disregarded.[90] Special war widows' payments granted in 1990 are likewise disregarded in full.[91]

Benefits ignored in part

A total of £10 a week of a war disablement pension, war widow's or war widower's pension, or a payment made to a parent under the Armed Forces Compensation Scheme is disregarded.[92] However, only £20 a week in total can be disregarded from a combination of war pensions, student income (see p214) and regular charitable/voluntary payments (see p217).

Other income

Unless specified below, all other income is taken into account on a weekly basis by considering the 26-week period ending in the 'relevant week' (see p205).[93] If the income has been received during each week of the period, the total received over the 26 weeks is divided by 26. In other cases, the total received is divided by the number of complete weeks for which the payment was received. However, the CSA has the discretion to use a different period if the amount produced by the above calculation does not accurately reflect actual income. Furthermore, a change occurring between the relevant week and the effective date (see p332) must be taken into account by the CSA if it is aware of the change, in the same way as for earnings (see p208).

Other income includes any payments received on a periodic basis which are not earnings, benefits or a child's income, as well as the types of payments listed below. Periodical payments drawn down from capital are not income,[94] although interest is (see p217). However, if capital is being drawn down in this way, it may indicate that the parent should be treated as having notional income (see p220). Periodical payments do not include a non-resident parent's payments towards his share of a parent with care's housing costs.[95] Some payments are taken into account in full or in part, while others are ignored completely. Payments which are ignored as earnings cannot be taken into account as other income.

Working tax credit

WTC is usually treated as the income of the parent who qualifies for the payment through her/his normal engagement in remunerative work.[96] If a couple both meet the conditions for WTC, it is all treated as the income of the non-resident parent, provided his earnings are higher than his partner's during the period used to calculate earnings for the maintenance assessment. If the earnings are equal, half the amount of the WTC counts as the income of the non-resident parent. If the non-resident parent's earnings are less than the other person's, WTC is not counted as his income.

Child tax credit

All payments of CTC are ignored in full.[97]

Payments from occupational or personal pension schemes

These and any analogous payments are taken into account in full.[98]

Income from rent

Different provisions apply, depending on the type of income from the property.

- Payments made towards household expenses by a non-dependant (see p253) are completely ignored.[99]
- The first £20 a week of a payment from a boarder is disregarded, as is 50 per cent of any amount over £20 (as long as this is not the largest part of a parent's income, in which case it is treated as earnings from self-employment).[100] A boarder is someone who is liable to pay for board and lodging which includes at least one meal a day.
- Payments from a person who is liable to pay for accommodation in the parent's home (but who is not a lodger or a non-dependant) are treated as income. However, there is a disregard of £19.45 (or £4 if the payment is not inclusive of heating).[101]
- Payments for the use of a property which is not the parent's home are taken into account as other income, unless the parent is self-employed. In this case, the income is treated as part of the gross receipts of the business. If the parent is not self-employed, the amounts to cover income tax,[102] mortgage interest, interest on loans for repairs and improvements, council tax and water charges can be deducted from the amount received as rent.[103] It is not clear whether other expenses necessary to obtain the rental income (eg, servicing gas fires) may also be deducted.

Student income

A student is defined as someone following a full-time course of study at an educational establishment and, if under 19 years old, the course must be advanced education – ie, above A level or Scottish Higher.[104] This can include sandwich courses. There is no definition of full time and it does not relate to the number of hours the student actually attends. Once a course has begun, a person continues to be treated as a student until either the course ends or s/he leaves it.

Unless they have income in addition to an educational grant (including any contribution due) or student loan, students are treated as having no net income and are exempt from having to pay child maintenance.[105]

In other cases, income paid to a student as a grant, grant contribution, covenant income or student loan, is taken into account, except that which is:[106]

- intended to meet tuition fees or examination fees;
- intended to meet additional expenditure as a result of a disability;
- intended to meet expenditure connected with residential study away from the educational establishment;
- made on account of the student maintaining a home away from the educational establishment;
- intended to meet the cost of books and equipment, or, if not specified, £390 (amount for the 2009/10 academic year);
- intended to meet travel expenses.

The amount of a student's grant, covenant income and loan are apportioned equally between the weeks for which they are payable.[107] Five pounds a week can be deducted from covenant income and £10 a week from loan income, although not more than £10 a week can be deducted in total where both types of income are received.[108] Any amount disregarded under this provision counts towards the £20 disregard for war pensions (see p213) and charitable/voluntary payments (see p217).[109]

Financial assistance or awards from a local authority for courses of further education are disregarded.[110]

Schemes to help people back to work

Payments from an employer under the New Deal schemes are treated as earnings. This includes payments under the voluntary sector and environment task force options as well as the community task force (introduced in 26 April 2010). However, most New Deal participants will be in receipt of income-based JSA and are therefore not assessed under the formula. Payments received as part of a back-to-work scheme, such as the in-work credit, return-to-work credit and better-off-in-work credit are all disregarded as income.[111]

At the time of writing, it is not known whether there will be similar payments under the government's new Work Programme, due to begin in June 2011, and how they will be treated for child support purposes.

Training allowances

Training allowances are taken into account (but see below), except for the training premium, travelling expenses or any living away from home allowance.[112]

Work-based learning for young people

These training schemes for young people aged under 19 include apprenticeships, other work-based training and (in Scotland) Skillseekers training. Trainees who are not employees receive a training allowance or an education maintenance allowance, depending on where in the UK they are training. Young people on these schemes who have no income other than their training allowance or education maintenance allowance are taken to have no net income and are exempt from paying any child maintenance (see p169). Trainees who are employees have their earnings taken into account in the usual way (see p205).

Maintenance for a parent

This income is taken into account in full. There is a specific rule used to calculate the amount of maintenance to be taken into account. It is calculated by averaging the payments received in the 13 weeks preceding the assessment over the number of weeks for which a payment was due.[113] Caselaw has established that payments of maintenance to a parent with care by a non-resident parent cannot be counted as the parent with care's income.[114] However, the CSA may continue to treat such payments as income.

Child maintenance

Child maintenance from a non-resident parent for the qualifying child for whom the assessment is being carried out is ignored when calculating the income of the parent with care.[115]

Except at the protected income stage (see p251), the CSA treats maintenance paid to a parent for any other child as the child's income. This may still be included in net income, but there are separate rules covering when and how much of the child's income can be taken into account as the parent's income (see p218).

In the calculation of protected income, any maintenance being paid for other children under a court order is deducted from the liable person's income, as long as an application cannot be made to the CSA (see p35).[116] See p251 for further details.

Lump-sum maintenance

There is provision to disregard other maintenance payments in full, whether child support maintenance or other forms of maintenance, if they are not income.[117] However, as all payments received on a periodic basis are income, this disregard appears only to apply to irregular maintenance payments. It does not apply to maintenance payments made periodically.[118]

Payments made by a local authority towards a child's living costs

Payments made by a local authority, where it is looking after a child and has placed the child with a family, relative or other suitable person, including a foster parent, are ignored completely.[119] Payments made by local authorities to promote the welfare of children being looked after, or who were formerly in their care, are also ignored.[120]

Payments made as a contribution towards the maintenance of a child living with the family as a result of a residence order are ignored to the extent that they exceed the personal allowances and any disabled child premium included for the child in the exempt income calculation (see p182).[121]

Adoption allowances

A payment for an adopted child is disregarded:[122]

- to the extent that it exceeds the personal allowance and any disabled child premium for the child, if child maintenance is *not* being assessed for that particular child;
- only up to the amount of any income of the child which is included as income of the parent, if child maintenance is being assessed for that child.

Income from capital

A payment is capital and not income if it is not paid in respect of a particular period, it is paid without reference to any past payment, and it is not intended to form part of a series of payments. Such capital payments are not taken into account. However, the interest, dividend or any other income produced by capital is taken into account as income and is calculated by dividing the total received over 52 weeks by 52.[123] If this gives a figure which the CSA decides is not representative of the income produced, it can use another period. It is the actual income received that must be taken into account.

If capital is jointly held and the shares are unknown, any income from the capital is divided equally between the joint owners.[124] If capital is divided on divorce, dissolution of a civil partnership or separation and it is intended for the purchase of a new home or furnishings, income from that capital is ignored for one year.[125]

Prisoners' pay

Unless they have another source of income, prisoners receiving only prisoners' pay are assumed to have no net income and are exempt from paying child support.[126]

Regular charitable or voluntary payments

These are disregarded in full if they are intended and used for any items *other than* food, ordinary clothing, household fuel, housing costs or council tax.[127] There has to be a mutual understanding between the donor and the recipient about the purpose of the payment, but this does not need to be a formal agreement.[128] If the payment is for school fees, it is not counted as income at all even if part of the school fees relates to one of the specified items – eg, school meals.[129]

If the payment is for one of the above specified items, the first £20 will be disregarded, although no more than £20 in total can be disregarded from the total of a student's income (see p214), a war pension (see p213) and such voluntary payments.[130] See p251 for the position if the voluntary or charitable payment is made directly to a third party.

This provision does not apply to payments made by non-resident parents which are treated as maintenance (see p216).

Other disregarded income

The following are not taken into account as income:

- income tax payments;[131]
- payments in kind (except for self-employed earners);[132]
- payments made instead of Healthy Start vouchers;[133]
- all NHS health benefits, such as fares to hospital;[134]
- payments for prison visits;[135]
- payments made by a local authority to help a child take advantage of a course of study or educational facilities, including a scholarship, or an assisted place;[136]
- payments under a mortgage protection insurance policy to the extent that they exceed the interest, capital payments and any further mortgage protection premiums;[137]
- payments of expenses to unpaid voluntary workers (as long as the expenses cannot be treated as notional earnings);[138]
- payments made to assist a person with a disability to obtain or keep employment;[139]
- payments made to a person under the relevant community care provision to enable her/him to obtain community care services;[140]
- payments made by a local authority for welfare services or housing services;[141]
- payments made by a health authority, local authority or voluntary organisation for a person who is temporarily a member of the household in order to receive care;[142]
- compensation for personal injury and any payments made from a trust fund set up for that purpose;[143]
- payments from the Macfarlane Trust, Independent Living (1993) Fund or Independent Living (Extension) Fund;[144]
- payments from the Family Fund;[145]
- payments (other than those for lost earnings and benefits) made to jurors and witnesses for court attendance;[146]
- certain home income annuities purchased when aged 65 or over;[147]
- charges for converting payments in another currency than sterling;[148]
- amounts payable outside the UK where transfer to the UK is prohibited;[149] *and*
- payments to a person as a result of holding the Victoria or George Cross.[150]

Children's income

If the parent has a child of her/his own living with her/him for at least 104 nights a year, the income of that child may be included in the parent's net income.[151] This does not apply if the child is *not* a child of the parent whose income is being assessed. If a parent of the qualifying child has, for example, stepchildren or grandchildren living with her/him, the income of these children does not count when calculating net income at the assessable income stage, but it is taken into account at the protected income stage.

The child's income is taken to be her/his own parent's income when calculating both net income for assessable income purposes and total family income for protected income purposes. However, the child's income is *not* included when calculating the net income of her/his parent's partner in order to find out whether the partner can help support a joint child included in the exempt income (see p244).[152]

What counts as the child's income

Child maintenance already being received for a qualifying child who is the subject of the assessment being undertaken is ignored in full.[153] Child dependency increases in any benefit received by an adult are the income of the child, which is included in the parent's net income, if applicable.[154]

The following are *not* included when calculating the child's income and are, therefore, not part of a parent's net income:[155]

- a child's earnings;
- payments by a non-resident parent to the child for whom maintenance is being assessed;
- interest payable on arrears of child maintenance;
- payments from a discretionary fund which benefit the child, provided they do not cover food, ordinary clothing/footwear, household fuel or housing costs.

How much of the child's income counts as the parent's

The first £10 a week of any income of a child is ignored.[156] In addition, once the child's income is treated as that of her/his parent, the same disregards apply as for the parent's own income.[157]

How much of the child's net income is taken into account as her/his parent's income depends on whether the child is the subject of the maintenance assessment. If the child is *not* the subject of the maintenance assessment, her/his income up to the amount of the personal allowance (and any disabled child premium) included in the exempt income calculation in respect of that child is counted as the parent's income.[158] Income above that amount is disregarded.

If the child is the subject of the maintenance assessment, the child's income counts in full if s/he is the only child for whom an assessment is being made.[159] If there is more than one child, each child's income is counted up to the level of the child's proportion of the maximum child maintenance payment (see p235) – ie, a share of the maintenance requirement plus 1.5 times the basic rate of the family premium and the personal allowance.[160]

At the protected income stage of the formula, the rules on how much of the child's income is taken into account are different (see p251).

Notional income

Parents can be assumed to have income which they do not possess.[161] Such 'notional income' is treated in the same way as if it were actual income.[162] In practice, this provision is not used very often, and parents who are contesting the other party's income may want to remind the CSA that notional income should be considered.

Notional earnings

A person may have notional earnings if s/he has done some work without being paid or at an insufficient rate for the job for an employer who could afford to pay full wages. This cannot apply if the employer is a charity or voluntary organisation, or a member of the parent's family. The estimated foregone income is treated as earnings if the CSA decides that the principal purpose of the person doing the work without pay or for reduced pay was to reduce her/his assessable income. To estimate an appropriate level of foregone earnings the decision maker has to consider:

- the nature of the service from which the employer benefits;
- the comparable rate of pay;
- the means of the employer.

If the question of notional earnings is raised, the parent should let the CSA know her/his motives for doing the work. For example, notional earnings will be an issue if a parent is paid via a personal service company at less than the market rate.[163] In such a case, if the principal purpose was for business and tax reasons, notional income cannot be included.[164] If the CSA considers that a parent has notional earnings, it calculates the parent's net income as if her/his earnings included the notional amount.[165]

Deprivation of income or capital

If the CSA decides that a parent has intentionally deprived her/himself of income in order to reduce her/his assessable income, an amount equal to that income is included in her/his net income.[166]

This rule applies equally to capital which would have been a source of income – eg, if shares are given away or sold at less than their market value. Lump-sum voluntary contributions towards a retirement annuity contract may count as deprivation of capital.[167] The CSA estimates a notional income from the notional capital – eg, by using the rates of interest paid by high street banks and building societies. When the CSA has decided that a certain sum is notional capital, that capital is reduced after 52 weeks by an amount equal to the income which would have been generated from that capital over the year.

Deprivation refers both to income or capital that a person has disposed of or failed to obtain – eg, by failing to apply for a benefit. However, it does not apply to contribution-based JSA if IS is payable, nor to a payment from a discretionary trust or a trust set up with personal injury compensation.[168] If income would have been available to a parent on application, an estimated amount is included in her/his net income from the date on which it could be expected to have been paid.[169]

The CSA is most likely to identify a potential deprivation of income or capital if it finds that a source of income previously declared is no longer included. The first question to be considered is whether the parent has actually disposed of the income or capital, and the onus is on the parent to prove s/he no longer has the resource. Deprivation can apply to a parent who has transferred assets to a new partner or possibly to a self-employed parent who is paying her/his partner a reasonable salary but not drawing much her/himself, or who has entered a salary sacrifice arrangement in circumstances where the CSA considers that at least part of the intention was to reduce the amount of assessable income.[170]

Once it is shown s/he no longer possesses it, the intention behind the deprivation has to be examined, and on the balance of probabilities the CSA must decide whether the aim was to reduce assessable income for child support purposes.[171]

This rule is similar, but not identical, to that for means-tested benefits (see CPAG's *Welfare Benefits and Tax Credits Handbook*) and an adviser should, therefore, consider whether any social security commissioners' decisions could be cited as persuasive. It may be argued that the reduction of assessable income was not the only, or even principal, motive for the action. While the CSA may accept that there were also other motives for the parent's actions, it simply has to be able to show that it is satisfied that reduction of assessable income was at least one purpose of the parent's actions, even if there may also have been other motives. The test is whether the action was undertaken with the intention of reducing assessable income, even if this was not the dominant or primary purpose.[172] The onus of proof on this point remains with the CSA.[173]

If deprivation of capital is an issue, the CSA will consider whether the parent was aware that reducing capital would reduce the maintenance assessment.

This deprivation rule cannot be used against a parent who refuses an offer of employment,[174] but it might be applied to a non-resident parent who gave up his job.[175] It would have to be shown that by leaving the employment he had intentionally deprived himself of income, and that he did so with the intention of reducing his assessable income.

Deprivation is probably not applicable to a case where a parent has taken out a higher mortgage which reduces her/his assessable income.[176] A non-resident parent in this situation needs to consider the excessive housing costs rule (see p287). On the other hand, the use of capital as a deposit to buy a property could possibly be considered to be deprivation and motives would need to be examined.

If the CSA considers that a parent has deprived her/himself of income or capital, it will calculate the parent's net income as if it includes the gross amount. In the case of deprivation of income through a salary sacrifice arrangement, the income tax (but not the NI contributions) that would have been applicable to the earnings of which the parent has deprived her/himself can be deducted.[177]

Payments to third parties

If a payment is made on behalf of a parent or a child to a third party, it is only treated as the parent's income if it is a payment for food, ordinary clothing or footwear, household fuel, housing costs or council tax.[178] For example, if a grandparent paid the parent's fuel bill directly to the fuel company, this would be notional income, whereas paying the telephone bill would not. Some of this notional income can be disregarded as a voluntary payment if made regularly (see p217).

A payment made by a partner to meet her/his own liability (eg, for a mortgage to a building society) is not made on behalf of the parent or child.[179] The same applies to payments made by an ex-partner for his own liability towards the former joint home in which the parent with care remains, whereas payments made by him towards her part of the mortgage count as the parent with care's income (see also p216).[180]

3. Calculating assessable income

Assessable income is the parent's total net income less her/his exempt income. For details of exempt income, see Chapter 10.

If the parent's exempt income is higher than her/his net income, assessable income is taken to be nil.[181] If his assessable income is nil, the non-resident parent may still have to make the minimum payment of child maintenance. There is, however, no need to continue with the steps of the formula, as the maintenance due will either be the minimum payment of £6.80 or nil (see p168). If a non-resident parent's net income is itself less than £6.80, he is exempt from paying child maintenance.[182]

If the parent with care's assessable income is nil, the proposed maintenance step is carried out with just the non-resident parent's assessable income.

Example 11.1: assessable income of a non-resident parent

Bob is living in a bedsit on his own. His exempt income is £115.50 (see *Example 10.1*). His income is £154 a week in earnings after tax, national insurance (NI) and £12 weekly superannuation contribution. Only half his superannuation is taken into account when calculating Bob's net earnings for child support purposes, which are £154 + £6 = £160. Bob's net income is, therefore, his net earnings = £160.

	£
Net income	160.00
Less exempt income	115.50
Assessable income	**44.50**

Bob moves in with Zoe and her three children (see *Example 10.2*).

	£
Net income	160.00
Less exempt income	112.50
Assessable income	**47.50**

Bob is in receipt of long-term incapacity benefit (IB) of £108.05 and lives with his parents (see *Example 10.1*).

	£
Net income	108.05
Less exempt income	96.35
Assessable income	**11.70**

If Bob were receiving contributory employment and support allowance, including the work-related activity component, of £94.25 and disability living allowance (and was, therefore, still eligible for a disability premium in his exempt income), his assessable income would be nil. He would be exempt from the minimum payment (see p168) and would receive a nil assessment. No further calculation would be required.

Example 11.2 : assessable income of a parent with care

While Anita is on income support (IS) or working tax credit (WTC), she is automatically treated as having no assessable income.

Anita receives child benefit of £33.70 (this is ignored in net income). Bob has been paying £30.50 a week in maintenance for Carol (13) and David (8). This is not taken into account as income because it is maintenance for the qualifying children – ie, the children for whom the reassessment is being carried out.

Anita is now bringing home £280 a week (after tax, NI and a £15 superannuation contribution). She is entitled to child tax credit (CTC) (which is ignored as income) but not to any WTC. Only half of the superannuation payment can be taken into account (ie, £7.50) and, therefore, her net earnings for exempt income purposes are now £287.50 a week.

	£
Earnings	287.50
Total net income	287.50
Less exempt income (from *Example 10.2*)	279.56
Assessable income	**7.94**

Anita remarries. She brings home £195 a week after tax, NI and a £15 superannuation contribution. Her husband, Joe, earns £205 a week.

Net income is now £202.50. Joe's income is not taken into account.

	£
Net income	202.50

Less exempt income (from p191)	347.34
Assessable income	**Nil**

Example 11.3 : Bob and Zoe have a baby

Bob is now living with Zoe, their son Ricky and three stepchildren (13, 11 and 4). The exempt income is £192.23 (see *Example 10.5*). Bob is now working over 30 hours a week and has net earnings of £300 a week. Zoe is not in paid work. Any income that Zoe may have, including the maintenance of £20 a week for her daughters, is not taken into account. The couple receive £193 CTC a week, which is ignored.

	£
Earnings (Bob)	300.00
Total net income	300.00
Less exempt income	192.23
Bob's assessable income	**107.77**

Zoe begins paid work, bringing home £120 a week. The total net income remains at £300, as Zoe's earnings are not taken into account at this stage. However, her earnings have affected the exempt income (see *Example 10.5*), as she is now helping to support Ricky.

	£
Total net income	300.00
Less exempt income	152.37
Bob's assessable income	**147.63**

As the increase in their annual income is less than £10,000, it will not affect their final entitlement to CTC for the current tax year. In the next tax year, assuming no further changes in income, it will be taken into account and reduce their tax credits. In the meantime, if Zoe works 16 hours or more a week and they use eligible childcare, the tax credit calculation will be affected by the childcare element. This could mean that WTC becomes payable, which would be treated as Bob's income and would then affect assessable income, as well as affecting the calculation at the protected income stage.

Notes

1. **What is assessable income**
   1 Sch 1 para 5(1) and (2) CSA 1991
   2 Regs 8 and 10 CS(MASC) Regs
   3 Sch 1 para 5(4) CSA 1991; reg 10B CS(MASC) Regs
   4 Reg 10A CS(MASC) Regs
   5 Reg 10A(2) CS(MASC) Regs

2. **What is net income**

6 Reg 7(1) CS(MASC) Regs
7 Sch 1 CS(MASC) Regs
8 Sch 2 CS(MASC) Regs
9 Reg 9(2)(c) CS(MASC) Regs
10 Reg 11(2) CS(MASC) Regs
11 Reg 7(5) CS(MASC) Regs
12 Reg 7(4) CS(MASC) Regs
13 Sch 1 para 9(a) CSA 1991; reg 7(1)(d) CS(MASC) Regs
14 Reg 1(2) CS(MASC) Regs
15 Sch 1 para 2(3A) CS(MASC) Regs
16 Reg 1(2) CS(MASC) Regs
17 Sch 1 para 1(1) CS(MASC) Regs
18 Sch 1 para 1(1)(gg) CS(MASC) Regs
19 Sch 2 para 48B CS(MASC) Regs
20 CCS/2287/2006; CCS/3499/2004; CCS/3671/2002
21 CCS/2750/1995; CCS/318/1995
22 CCS/11364/1995; R(CS) 2/96; CCS/4/1994; CCS/10/1994; CCS/12598/1996; CCS/1321/1997; CCS/2320/1997; CCS/2561/1998; CCS/5352/1995
23 Sch 1 para 1(2) CS(MASC) Regs
24 Sch 2 para 6 CS(MASC) Regs
25 CCS/11252/1995; CCS/5352/1995
26 CCS/3182/1995
27 R(CS) 2/96 (CCS/4/1994)
28 CCS/12073/1996
29 CCS/318/1995
30 CCS/10/1994; CCS/12598/1996; CCS/1321/1997; CCS/2320/1997; CCS/2561/1998
31 CCS/5352/1995
32 CCS/11242/1995
33 CCS/12769/1996
34 CCS/6807/1995
35 Sch 1 para 2(1) CS(MASC) Regs
36 Sch 1 para 2(3) CS(MASC) Regs
37 Sch 1 para 2(4) CS(MASC) Regs
38 CCS/16/1994; CCS/11873/1996
39 CCS/511/1995
40 CCS/7312/1995; CCS/556/1995; CSCS/1/1996; CSCS/6/1996
41 Sch 1 para 2(2) CS(MASC) Regs
42 CCS/5079/1995
43 Reg 2(3) CS(MASC) Regs
44 CCS/2750/1995
45 CCS/556/1995
46 Sch 1 para 1(3) CS(MASC) Regs
47 CSCS/5/1994
48 R(CS) 3/00
49 Sch 1 para 1(3) CS(MASC) Regs
50 Reg 1(2A) CS(MASC) Regs
51 Sch 1 para 2A CS(MASC) Regs
52 *KB v CMEC* [2010] UKUT 434 (AAC)
53 Sch 1 para 2C CS(MASC) Regs
54 Sch 1 para 2A(2) CS(MASC) Regs
55 Sch 1 para 5A(1) CS(MASC) Regs
56 Sch 1 para 5A(2) CS(MASC) Regs
57 Sch 1 para 3 CS(MASC) Regs
58 Sch 1 para 3(2)(b) CS(MASC) Regs
59 Sch 1 para 4 CS(MASC) Regs
60 Sch 1 para 3(3) CS(MASC) Regs
61 Sch 1 para 3(6) CS(MASC) Regs
62 Sch 1 para 3(4)(a) CS(MASC) Regs
63 CCS/15949/1996
64 Sch 1 para 3(4)(b) CS(MASC) Regs
65 *HH v CMEC (CSM)* [2011] UKUT 60 (AAC)
66 Sch 1 para 3(7) CS(MASC) Regs
67 Sch 1 para 5(2) CS(MASC) Regs
68 CCS/1938/2006
69 Sch 1 para 5(2) CS(MASC) Regs
70 Sch 1 para 5(2A) CS(MASC) Regs
71 Sch 1 para 5(1) CS(MASC) Regs
72 Sch 1 para 5(3) CS(MASC) Regs
73 CCS/3182/1995; CCS/6145/1995
74 Sch 1 para 5(5) CS(MASC) Regs
75 Reg 8A(6) CS(MAP) Regs
76 CCS/7966/1995
77 CCS/13988/96; CCS/2901/02
78 Sch 1 para 6 CS(MASC) Regs; reg 10B CS(MASC) Regs
79 Sch 1 para 6(3) CS(MASC) Regs
80 Sch 1 para 7(1) CS(MASC) Regs
81 Sch 1 paras 9A and 22(1B) CS(MASC) Regs
82 Sch 2 para 16 CS(MASC) Regs
83 Sch 2 para 7 CS(MASC) Regs
84 Sch 2 para 7 CS(MASC) Regs
85 Sch 2 para 8 CS(MASC) Regs
86 Sch 2 para 9 CS(MASC) Regs
87 Sch 2 para 11 CS(MASC) Regs
88 Sch 2 para 48A CS(MASC) Regs
89 Sch 2 para 10 CS(MASC) Regs
90 Sch 2 paras 8 and 12-15 CS(MASC) Regs
91 Sch 2 para 40 CS(MASC) Regs
92 Sch 2 para 18 CS(MASC) Regs
93 Sch 1 para 16 CS(MASC) Regs
94 *Chandler v SSWP and Another* [2007] EWCA Civ 1211
95 Sch 1 para 15 CS(MASC) Regs
96 Sch 1 para 14B CS(MASC) Regs
97 Sch 2 para 48D CS(MASC) Regs
98 Sch 1 para 9 CS(MASC) Regs
99 Sch 2 para 35 CS(MASC) Regs
100 Sch 2 para 24 CS(MASC) Regs
101 Sch 2 para 22 CS(MASC) Regs
102 Sch 2 para 2 CS(MASC) Regs
103 Sch 2 para 23 CS(MASC) Regs
104 Reg 1(2) CS(MASC) Regs
105 Regs 7(3)(b) and 26(1)(b)(v) CS(MASC) Regs
106 Sch 1 paras 11 and 12 CS(MASC) Regs

107 Sch 1 para 16(3) CS(MASC) Regs
108 Sch 1 para 16(4) CS(MASC) Regs
109 Sch 2 para 20 CS(MASC) Regs
110 Sch 2 paras 36 and 36A CS(MASC) Regs
111 Sch 2 para 15a MASC Regs
112 Sch 2 para 21 CS(MASC) Regs
113 Sch 1 paras 14 and 16(2) CS(MASC) Regs
114 CCS/13698/1996; CCS/13923/1996
115 Sch 2 para 28 CS(MASC) Regs
116 Reg 11(2) CS(MASC) Regs
117 Schs 1 para 15 and 2 para 44 CS(MASC) Regs
118 CCS/4514/1995
119 Sch 2 para 29 CS(MASC) Regs. The payments are made under the CA 1989, the Social Work (Scotland) Act 1968 or the Boarding and Fostering Out of Children (Scotland) Regulations 1985.
120 Sch 2 para 31 CS(MASC) Regs. These payments are made under the CA 1989.
121 Sch 2 para 26 CS(MASC) Regs
122 Sch 2 para 25 CS(MASC) Regs
123 Sch 1 para 16(5) and (6) CS(MASC) Regs
124 Reg 7(4) CS(MASC) Regs
125 Sch 2 para 45 CS(MASC) Regs; CCS/4923/1995
126 Regs 7(3) and 26(1)(b) CS(MASC) Regs
127 Sch 2 para 19 CS(MASC) Regs
128 R(SB) 53/83; CCS/15/1994
129 Sch 1 para 31 CS(MASC) Regs
130 Sch 2 paras 19 and 20 CS(MASC) Regs
131 Sch 2 para 2 CS(MASC) Regs
132 Sch 2 para 46 CS(MASC) Regs
133 Sch 2 para 17 CS(MASC) Regs
134 Sch 2 para 33 CS(MASC) Regs
135 Sch 2 para 42 CS(MASC) Regs
136 Sch 2 para 36 CS(MASC) Regs
137 Sch 2 para 27 CS(MASC) Regs
138 Sch 2 para 48 CS(MASC) Regs
139 Sch 2 para 34 CS(MASC) Regs
140 Sch 2 para 48C CS(MASC) Regs
141 Sch 2 para 48D CS(MASC) Regs
142 Sch 2 para 30 CS(MASC) Regs. This refers to payments made under s93(1) and (2) Local Government Act 2000 or s91(1) Housing (Scotland) Act 2001.
143 Sch 2 para 5 CS(MASC) Regs
144 Sch 2 para 38 CS(MASC) Regs
145 Sch 2 para 47 CS(MASC) Regs
146 Sch 2 para 39 CS(MASC) Regs
147 Sch 2 para 37 CS(MASC) Regs
148 Sch 2 para 3 CS(MASC) Regs
149 Sch 2 para 4 CS(MASC) Regs
150 Sch 2 para 41 CS(MASC) Regs
151 Sch 1 Part IV CS(MASC) Regs
152 Reg 9(2)(c) CS(MASC) Regs
153 Sch 2 para 28 CS(MASC) Regs
154 Sch 1 paras 7 and 22 CS(MASC) Regs
155 Sch 1 para 23 CS(MASC) Regs
156 Sch 1 para 23 CS(MASC) Regs
157 Sch 1 para 24 CS(MASC) Regs
158 Sch 1 para 21 CS(MASC) Regs
159 Sch 1 para 19 CS(MASC) Regs
160 Sch 1 para 20 CS(MASC) Regs
161 Reg 7(1)(e) and Sch 1 Part V CS(MASC) Regs
162 Sch 1 para 32 CS(MASC) Regs
163 CCS/4912/1998
164 CCS/3675/2004
165 Sch 1 para 32 CS(MASC) Regs; *GR v CMEC* [2010] UKUT 436 (AAC)
166 Sch 1 para 27 CS(MASC) Regs
167 CCS/3542/1998
168 Sch 1 para 28 CS(MASC) Regs
169 Sch 1 para 29 CS(MASC) Regs
170 *GR v CMEC* [2010] UKUT 436 (AAC)
171 CCS/8172/1995
172 *AC v CMEC* [2009] UKUT 152 (AAC); *GR v CMEC* [2010] UKUT 436 (AAC)
173 R(SB) 38/85
174 CCS/7967/1995
175 CCS/4056/2004
176 CCS/6/1995
177 Sch 1 para 32 CS(MASC) Regs; *GR v CMEC* [2010] UKUT 436 (AAC)
178 Sch 1 para 31 CS(MASC) Regs
179 CCS/6/1995
180 CSCS/8/1995; CSCS/1/1996; CCS/8189/1995

3. **Calculating assessable income**
181 Sch 1 para 5(3) CSA 1991
182 Reg 26(1)(b)(v) CS(MASC) Regs

Chapter 12

Proposed maintenance ('old rules')

This chapter covers:

1. What is proposed maintenance

'Proposed maintenance' is not a term that is used in the legislation. It is used in this *Handbook* to describe the amount of child maintenance that, given the maintenance requirement and the assessable income of the parents, the non-resident parent could be expected to pay. There is no specific legal term for this amount; it is referred to in the legislation as 'the amount of the assessment'. However, the proposed maintenance step is not the end of the maintenance assessment. The protected income calculation still has to be done and this may reduce the amount of child maintenance payable. Therefore, a term is needed for this intermediate stage. The Child Support Agency uses the phrase 'the non-resident parent's notional assessment'.

Although the proposed maintenance figure may be reduced by the protected income calculation, it will never be increased. No non-resident parent ever pays more than the proposed maintenance figure.

There is misunderstanding about the way in which the income of a partner of the non-resident parent affects the maintenance assessment. At the protected income stage (see Chapter 13) the partner's income *is* taken into account in order to assess whether the family as a whole can afford the proposed maintenance.

However, the partner's income *cannot* increase the assessment above the proposed maintenance figure, which is arrived at using the non-resident parent's net income (see p204). The income of the partner is also used to decide whether she can help support their own children (see p198). If the partner objects to providing income details, the non-resident parent could consider the option of withholding the information and accepting a Category B interim maintenance assessment.

2. How much is proposed maintenance

Proposed maintenance is based on the assessable incomes of both parents. In some situations, a deduction rate of 50 per cent assessable income is used and, in others, a more complex calculation must be carried out. The 50 per cent calculation gives an amount of proposed maintenance which is smaller than the maintenance requirement figure (from Step 1). The additional element calculation applies where the parents have higher incomes and the maintenance requirement figure is met. The calculation for proposed maintenance becomes increasingly complex with more complex family situations.

To illustrate the principles of proposed maintenance, this chapter gives an overview of the calculation (see below). It then identifies the four situations, beginning with the most straightforward, in which the calculation of proposed maintenance varies:

- the 50 per cent calculation of proposed maintenance where the parent with care has no assessable income (see p229);
- the 50 per cent calculation of proposed maintenance where both parents have assessable income (see p230);
- the additional element calculation of proposed maintenance where the parent with care has no assessable income (see p232);
- the additional element calculation of proposed maintenance where both parents have assessable income (see p234).

These calculations are adapted if both parents are non-resident, or if there is more than one non-resident parent or more than one parent with care.

Overview of proposed maintenance

There are two alternative calculations.

– The 50 per cent calculation if the maintenance requirement is not met.

– The additional element calculation if the maintenance requirement is met.

To decide which to use, first do the 50 per cent calculation:[1]

– Add together both parents' assessable incomes (if the parent with care is on income support, income-based jobseeker's allowance, income-related employment and support allowance, pension credit or working tax credit, her assessable income is nil).

– Take 50 per cent of the joint assessable income.

– Compare the figure obtained with the maintenance requirement (from Step 1 in Chapter 9).

If 50 per cent of the joint assessable income is less than or equal to the maintenance requirement, the proposed maintenance is 50 per cent of the non-resident parent's assessable income.[2]

If 50 per cent of the joint assessable income is higher than the maintenance requirement, the additional element calculation must be done. This involves two components of proposed maintenance: a basic element and an additional element (see p232).[3] The end result is that the non-resident parent pays less than 50 per cent of his assessable income overall, but more than the maintenance requirement.

The general rule is that 50 per cent of the parents' assessable income goes towards child maintenance until the maintenance requirement is met.[4] Once the maintenance requirement is met, the non-resident parent continues to pay maintenance. However, only 15, 20 or 25 per cent of his remaining assessable income is paid as maintenance and only up to a maximum amount.[5]

Both parents are liable to maintain their child(ren) and, therefore, both their assessable incomes must be taken into account when calculating whether the maintenance requirement has been met. Although the assessable income of the parent with care may reduce the proposed maintenance, she will never end up paying child maintenance herself.

If the assessable income of the non-resident parent is nil, the proposed maintenance is nil and the minimum payment rules must be considered (see p168). The non-resident parent either pays £6.80 or is exempt. Similarly, if the proposed maintenance is less than £6.80, the non-resident parent pays the minimum payment of £6.80 unless he is exempt. In these cases, there is no need to calculate the protected income level as the proposed maintenance cannot be further reduced.

3. The 50 per cent calculation

Once assessable income has been calculated for both parents, the next step is to check whether the 50 per cent calculation is applicable.

The parent with care has no assessable income

In many cases the parent with care will have no assessable income – eg, because she is on income support (IS) or working tax credit (WTC). See Chapter 11.

50 per cent calculation if the parent with care has no assessable income

- Take 50 per cent of the non-resident parent's assessable income.
- Compare the figure obtained with the maintenance requirement (from Step 1 in Chapter 9).

If 50 per cent of the non-resident parent's assessable income is less than or equal to the maintenance requirement, the proposed maintenance is this figure – ie, the proposed maintenance figure is 50 per cent of his assessable income.[6]

If 50 per cent of the non-resident parent's assessable income is higher than the maintenance requirement, the additional element calculation is used to obtain proposed maintenance (see p232).

In these cases, the proposed maintenance calculation ends at this point, and the protected income calculation must now be done (see Chapter 13).

Example 12.1: 50 per cent calculation if the parent with care has no assessable income

Anita is on IS and therefore has no assessable income.

The maintenance requirement is £175.86 (see *Example 9.1*).

Bob is living on his own and has assessable income of £44.50 (see *Example 11.1*). As Anita has no assessable income, the first stage is to take 50 per cent of Bob's assessable income.

50 per cent of Bob's assessable income = 50% x £44.50 = £22.25

This is less than £175.86 (the maintenance requirement) and therefore £22.25 is the proposed maintenance for Carol and David.

Bob is living with Zoe and her three children. His assessable income is £47.50 (see *Example 11.1*).

50 per cent of Bob's assessable income = 50% x £47.50 = £23.75

This is less than £175.86 (the maintenance requirement) and therefore £23.75 is the proposed maintenance.

Note: the maintenance payable may be reduced by the protected income step.

The parent with care has assessable income

Even when the parent with care has assessable income, this income does not necessarily affect the proposed maintenance. If, together, the parents do not have enough joint assessable income for half of it to meet the maintenance requirement, the non-resident parent pays half of his own assessable income. This is exactly what he would have paid anyway had the parent with care had no assessable income.

50 per cent calculation if the parent with care has assessable income

– Add both parents' assessable incomes to give joint assessable income.

– Take 50 per cent of the joint assessable income.

– Compare the 50 per cent figure with the maintenance requirement (from Step 1 in Chapter 9).

If 50 per cent of the joint assessable income is less than or equal to the maintenance requirement, take 50 per cent of the non-resident parent's own assessable income to give proposed maintenance.

If 50 per cent of the joint assessable income is higher than the maintenance requirement, the additional element calculation must be done (see p233).

A parent with care's income does not reduce the maintenance she receives unless her notional contribution towards the maintenance requirement *plus* the non-resident parent's proposed maintenance is over the maintenance requirement. The level of the joint assessable income is the deciding factor. The higher the assessable income of a non-resident parent, the sooner the assessable income of the parent with care will reduce the maintenance payable (see p233).

Example 12.2: 50 per cent calculation if both parents have assessable income

Anita is now working full time and has assessable income of £7.94 (see *Example 11.2*).

Bob's assessable income = £44.50 (see *Example 11.1*)

Joint assessable income = £44.50 + £7.94 = £52.44

50 per cent of joint assessable income = 50% x £52.44 = £26.22

This is well below the maintenance requirement of £175.86 (see *Example 9.1*) and so Bob pays 50 per cent of his own assessable income (assuming the protected income calculation allows it).

Proposed maintenance = 50% x £44.50 = **£22.25** a week.

This is the same amount of proposed maintenance as when Anita had no assessable income (see *Example 12.1*). In this case, Anita takes home £280 a week. Although this is more than Bob, who takes home £154, her income still does not affect the level of proposed maintenance for David and Carol.

If Bob's earnings for child support were higher than £160, his assessable income would be more. For example, suppose his assessable income was £350.

Anita's assessable income = £7.94

Joint assessable income = £7.94 + £350 = £357.94

50 per cent of joint assessable income = 50% x £357.94 = **£178.97**

This is above the maintenance requirement of £175.86 and so the additional element calculation would have to be done to calculate the proposed maintenance (see *Example 12.4*). Anita's assessable income, although still £7.94, would now reduce the proposed maintenance. This is because Bob's assessable income is higher and together they meet the maintenance requirement.

4. The additional element calculation

An alternative calculation is used to obtain the proposed maintenance if half of the parents' joint assessable income is more than the maintenance requirement.

Proposed maintenance is composed of a basic element and an additional element. Likewise, the non-resident parent's total assessable income is composed of basic assessable income and additional assessable income.

The basic assessable income contributes towards the basic element at the rate of 50 per cent. The additional assessable income contributes towards the additional element at a lower rate, up to a maximum amount. The deduction rate is 15 per cent if there is one qualifying child, 20 per cent if there are two, and 25 per cent if there are three or more qualifying children in the assessment.[7]

The assessable incomes of both parents are taken into account in calculating the basic proposed maintenance. However, to illustrate the principle of what is a complex calculation, the situation where only the non-resident parent has assessable income is examined below.

The parent with care has no assessable income

If 50 per cent of the non-resident parent's assessable income is higher than the maintenance requirement, ignore the 50 per cent figure and continue as described below.

If the parent with care has no assessable income, the basic element equals the maintenance requirement.[8] As basic assessable income contributes towards the basic element at the rate of 50 per cent, the non-resident parent will (in order to meet the maintenance requirement) use up assessable income equal to twice the maintenance requirement. Additional assessable income which is not used up in meeting the maintenance requirement contributes towards the additional element at the rate of 15, 20 or 25 per cent.

The non-resident parent thus pays more than the maintenance requirement, but overall less than 50 per cent of his assessable income.

When proposed maintenance has been obtained using the additional element calculation, this figure must be compared with the maximum amount (see p235).

Additional element calculation if the parent with care has no assessable income

To calculate the proposed maintenance if only the non-resident parent has assessable income and the 50 per cent calculation has shown that it more than meets the maintenance requirement:

- Multiply the maintenance requirement (the basic element) by two to give the basic assessable income.
- Deduct the basic assessable income from the total assessable income to give the additional assessable income.
- Take:

  - 15 per cent if there is one qualifying child; *or*
  - 20 per cent if there are two qualifying children; *or*
  - 25 per cent if there are three or more qualifying children,

  of the additional assessable income to give the additional element.
- Add the basic element (the maintenance requirement) to the additional element to give the proposed maintenance.

Example 12.3: additional element calculation if the parent with care has no assessable income

Jeremy has just left his wife, Evie, who has no income of her own other than child benefit and child tax credit. They have four children, Francis (14), Georgina (12), Henry (8) and Isobel (4), who are all living with Evie.

The maintenance requirement is therefore:

Personal allowances		£
	Evie	67.50
	Francis	62.33
	Georgina	62.33
	Henry	62.33
	Isobel	62.33
Family premium		17.40
Sub-total		334.22
Less child benefit (see p174)		60.50
Maintenance requirement		**273.72**

Jeremy has an assessable income of £700 a week.

50% x £700 = £350

This is above the maintenance requirement of £273.72. Therefore, to calculate proposed maintenance, do the additional element calculation:

Basic element = £273.72 (the maintenance requirement)

Basic assessable income = 2 x £273.72 = £547.44

Additional assessable income = £700 – £547.44 = £152.56

Additional element = 25% x £152.56 = £38.14 (the 25 per cent deduction rate is applicable as there are four qualifying children)

Proposed maintenance = £273.72 + £38.14 = **£311.86**

Check whether this figure is above the maximum child maintenance payable (see *Example 12.5*).

The parent with care has assessable income

Both parents contribute towards the maintenance requirement if they can afford to do so, although in the case of a parent with care this is a notional transaction. If the parents together cannot meet the maintenance requirement, the income of the parent with care does not affect the maintenance assessment (see p230).

However, if 50 per cent of the parents' joint assessable income more than meets the maintenance requirement, the parent with care's assessable income reduces the non-resident parent's proposed maintenance. Each parent contributes towards the maintenance requirement in proportion to her/his assessable income. The parent with care's notional contribution towards the maintenance requirement reduces the amount of the non-resident parent's assessable income required to meet that maintenance requirement. Therefore, the non-resident parent begins paying at the lower deduction rate earlier than he otherwise would have done.

The additional element calculation is used to work out the proposed maintenance; the basic element does not now equal the full maintenance requirement, but only the proportion of the maintenance requirement that the non-resident parent has to contribute.[9] Once the basic element has been calculated, the rest of the calculation is the same as before.

The parent with care's assessable income can reduce the proposed maintenance below the maintenance requirement, but cannot reduce the non-resident parent's proposed maintenance to zero. The non-resident parent still pays at least some contribution towards the maintenance requirement and then a percentage of his additional assessable income.

Additional element calculation if parent with care has assessable income

To calculate proposed maintenance if the parents have joint assessable income, half of which more than meets the maintenance requirement:

- Add together both parents' assessable incomes to give their joint assessable income.
- Multiply the maintenance requirement by the non-resident parent's assessable income divided by the joint assessable income (ie, the non-resident parent's proportion of the joint assessable income) to give the basic element – ie, the non-resident parent's contribution to the maintenance requirement.
- Multiply the basic element by two to give the basic assessable income.
- Deduct the basic assessable income from the non-resident parent's total assessable income to give his additional assessable income.
- Take:
  - 15 per cent if there is one qualifying child; *or*
  - 20 per cent if there are two qualifying children; *or*
  - 25 per cent if there are three or more qualifying children,

  of the additional assessable income to give the additional element.
- Add the basic element to the additional element to give the proposed maintenance.

Example 12.4: additional element calculation if both parents have assessable incomes

Evie has now taken a paid job. Her exempt income is high as it includes allowances for the four children and a significant mortgage. Although she is earning £26,000 a year, her

assessable income is only £70 a week (she is not entitled to any working tax credit).
Jeremy's assessable income is still £700 a week.
The maintenance requirement is still £273.72 (see *Example 12.3*).
Joint assessable income = £70 + £700 = £770
50 per cent of the joint assessable income is £385, which more than meets the maintenance requirement. Therefore, the additional element calculation of proposed maintenance has to be done:
Basic element (the proportion of the maintenance requirement that Jeremy has to pay) = £273.72 x (£700/£770) = £248.84
Basic assessable income = £248.84 x 2 = £497.68
Additional assessable income = £700 – £497.68 = £202.32
Additional element = £202.32 x 25% = £50.58
Proposed maintenance = £248.84 + £50.58 = **£299.42**
Check whether this figure is above the maximum child maintenance payable (see *Example 12.5*).

5. Maximum child maintenance

There is an upper limit on the amount of child maintenance payable for a child under the child support formula.[10] No further child maintenance is deducted from assessable income once the maximum is being paid.

When the maximum is being paid, the parties could go to court to seek any further maintenance. The courts can consider further weekly child maintenance in the context of any other arrangements which have been made for the children (see p27).

Like proposed maintenance, maximum child maintenance is composed of a basic element and an additional element. The basic element is the same as the basic element of proposed maintenance, whereas the additional element relates to the number and age of the qualifying children.[11]

Again, like proposed maintenance, the calculation varies slightly if the parent with care has assessable income.

The parent with care has no assessable income

When the parent with care has no assessable income, the basic element of maximum child maintenance equals the maintenance requirement. The maximum amount of child maintenance equals the maintenance requirement plus the additional element.

The additional element equals 1.5 times the total of the income support (IS) personal allowance for each child and the amount of the IS family premium for each child.[12]

Example 12.5: maximum child maintenance if the person with care has no assessable income

Assuming Evie has no assessable income of her own, the maximum Jeremy would have to pay for the four children, Francis (14), Georgina (12), Henry (8) and Isobel (4), is as follows.

The maintenance requirement is £273.72 (see *Example 12.3*).

Additional element = 1.5 x [(4 x £62.33) + (4 x £17.40)]

= 1.5 x 318.92 = £478.38

	£
Basic element	273.72
Additional element	478.38
Maximum child maintenance	**752.10**

Therefore, the proposed maintenance of £311.86 (see *Example 12.3*) is less than the maximum.

In order to pay the maximum amount, Jeremy would have to have an assessable income of at least (£273.72 x 2) + (£478.38 x 4) = £2,460.96 a week.

The parent with care has assessable income

The non-resident parent is responsible only for paying the proportion of the maximum child maintenance which corresponds to his proportion of joint assessable income.

The basic element of the maximum child maintenance is the proportion of the maintenance requirement which the non-resident parent must contribute. It is calculated as for the additional element calculation for proposed maintenance – ie:

- *add* together both parents' assessable incomes to give their joint assessable income;
- *multiply* the maintenance requirement by the non-resident parent's assessable income divided by joint assessable income.

To calculate the additional element:

- multiply the total of the IS personal allowance for each child and the family premium for each child by 1.5; *then*
- multiply this figure by the non-resident parent's assessable income divided by the joint assessable income.

The maximum child maintenance equals the basic element plus the additional element.

Alternatively, there is a short cut for this calculation. Multiply the maximum amount (as calculated) where the parent has no assessable income by the non-resident parent's proportion of the joint assessable income.

Example 12.6: maximum child maintenance if the parent with care has assessable income

To check whether the proposed maintenance calculated in *Example 12.4* (£299.42) is above the maximum:

Evie's assessable income = £70

Jeremy's assessable income = £700

Joint assessable income = £770

The maintenance requirement is £273.72 (see *Example 12.3*).

Basic element = £273.72 x (£700/£770) = £248.84

Additional element =

1.5 [(4 x £62.33) + (4 x £17.40)] x (£700/£770) = £478.38 x (£700/£770) = £434.89

Maximum child maintenance = basic element plus the additional element =

£248.84 + £434.89 = **£683.73**

(Alternatively, multiply the maximum figure from *Example 12.5* by Jeremy's proportion of joint assessable income: £752.10 x (£700/£770) = £683.73)

Jeremy therefore pays proposed maintenance (*Example 12.4*) of £299.42.

Evie's income has reduced the assessment by just £12.44.

6. Both parents are non-resident

If the person with care is not a parent, this usually means that there are two non-resident parents. If an application is made for maintenance from both parents, an assessment is carried out for each non-resident parent. The same maintenance requirement is used in both assessments (see p177).

When calculating the proposed maintenance for each parent, the other non-resident parent's assessable income is used where the parent with care's income would normally be taken into account – ie, to give joint assessable income.[13] In other words, the parents will together contribute towards the maintenance requirement at the rate of 50 per cent of assessable income and, once the maintenance requirement is met, each will pay a lower percentage of their own additional assessable income.

Example 12.7: proposed maintenance if both parents are non-resident

Zoe is looking after her 17-year-old niece, Rebecca, whose parents have separated. Zoe's income is not taken into account as she is not Rebecca's mother.

The maintenance requirement is £47.83 (see *Example 9.4*).

50 per cent calculation

Assuming that the mother's assessable income is £14.50 and the father's is £23.90:

Joint assessable income = £38.40

50 per cent of joint assessable income = £19.20

This is less than the maintenance requirement.

Proposed maintenance from her mother = 50% x £14.50 = £7.25

Proposed maintenance from her father = 50% x £23.90 = £11.95

The additional element calculation

Assuming that the mother's assessable income is now £52 and the father's is £84:

Joint assessable income = £136

50 per cent of joint assessable income = £68

This is more than the maintenance requirement.

Therefore, the additional element calculation has to be done. The 15 per cent deduction rate is used as Rebecca is the only qualifying child in the assessment (see below).

Mother's proposed maintenance:

Basic element = £47.83 x (£52/£136) = £18.29

Basic assessable income = £18.29 x 2 = £36.58

Additional assessable income = £52 – £36.58 = £15.42

Additional element = £15.42 x 15% = £2.31

Proposed maintenance from mother = £18.29 + £2.31 = £20.60

Father's proposed maintenance:

Basic element = £47.83 x (£84/£136) = £29.54

Basic assessable income = £29.54 x 2 = £59.08

Additional assessable income = £84 – £59.08 = £24.92

Additional element = £24.92 x 15% = £3.74

Proposed maintenance from father = £29.54 + £3.74 = £33.28

Note: the basic proposed maintenance from both parents is the maintenance requirement – ie, £18.29 + £29.54 = £47.83

An application is made for maintenance from the mother only. The maintenance requirement is therefore halved to £23.92.

With assessable income of £14.50, the mother still cannot meet the maintenance requirement and, therefore, she pays 50% x £14.50 = £7.25. This is the same as in the 50 per cent calculation.

When the mother's assessable income increases to £52, the mother can now meet the maintenance requirement on her own (50% x £52 = £26). The basic element is the maintenance requirement of £23.92.

Basic assessable income = £23.92 x 2 = £47.84

Additional assessable income = £52 – £47.84 = £4.16

Additional element = £4.16 x 15% = £0.62

Proposed maintenance = £23.92 + £0.62 = £24.54

The total proposed maintenance for a child with two non-resident parents is the same as if there were one non-resident parent (with assessable income equal to the joint assessable income of the two non-resident parents) and a parent with care with no assessable income. However, with two non-resident parents, the total liability is split between the parents in proportion to their assessable incomes.

If an application is made for maintenance from both parents and the Child Support Agency (CSA) does not have the information about the other parent's income within the fortnight given to provide it (see p56), it is assumed that this second non-resident parent has no assessable income when calculating the first non-resident parent's proposed maintenance.[14] When this information is available, a fresh assessment will be carried out.[15]

The regulations do not distinguish between non-resident parents who live separately from one another and those who, although they are no longer living with their child, still live together as a couple. Therefore, in the case of a couple being assessed, two separate assessments would be carried out following the same basic rules up to this stage (ie, net income and exempt income would be calculated separately for each parent), even though between the two assessments the same housing costs would be included twice.

The person with care who is not a parent of the qualifying children may be looking after children who have different parents. For example, a grandmother may be looking after two grandchildren, one the child of her son and the other the child of her daughter. This involves two maintenance requirements. The proposed maintenance steps for the two children are completely separate and each can be carried out for both the non-resident parents of each child (see above). In theory, the grandmother could receive child maintenance from four non-resident parents.

7. **More than one person with care**

'More than one person with care' does not refer to the situation where a child is looked after for part of the time by one person and the rest of the time by another; this is called 'shared care' in this *Handbook* (see Chapter 14).

'More than one person with care' refers to the situation where different children of a non-resident parent are being looked after by different people. This includes where the non-resident parent has two or more families by different women with whom he does not live and also where the children of one family are split between two carers, perhaps with one child living with the mother and the other with grandparents. The non-resident parent is equally liable to maintain all the qualifying children and must pay child maintenance to each person with care who makes an application.[16]

The 'more than one person with care' situation involves applications for maintenance for *different* children from the *same* non-resident parent.

Sharing out the proposed maintenance

If the children of a non-resident parent are in the care of two or more people and a maintenance application has been made by more than one of those persons with care, the proposed maintenance has to be shared between the persons with care.[17] This is achieved by dividing the non-resident parent's assessable income between the maintenance assessments in the same proportions as their maintenance requirements.[18] If an allowance for a pre-April 1993 property settlement has been included in exempt income (see p192), an adjustment is made when apportioning the assessable income. The proposed maintenance step is then carried out separately for each application using the relevant portion of assessable income.

Only one protected income calculation (see Chapter 13) is carried out for the non-resident parent, using the total amount of proposed maintenance for all the assessments.[19] If the total maintenance worked out for all the persons with care is less than £6.80 (see p168), the minimum payment is divided between the persons with care in proportion to the maintenance requirements.[20]

Example 12.8: 50 per cent calculation if there is more than one person with care

Wayne is the father of Yvonne (12) and Veronica (10) who live with Zoe. Zoe has no assessable income. She has been receiving £20 a week child maintenance from Wayne. Zoe's maintenance requirement for Yvonne and Veronica is £133.41 (see *Example 9.3*).

Wayne and his girlfriend, Lauren, have a child together, Keith. Wayne is not living with Lauren, who is claiming income support (IS) as a single parent.

Lauren's maintenance requirement is:		£
Personal allowances	Lauren	67.50
	Keith	62.33
Family premium		17.40
Sub-total		147.23
Less child benefit		20.30
Total maintenance requirement		**126.93**

Joint maintenance requirement is £133.41 + £126.93 = £260.34

Wayne's total assessable income is assumed to be £40 a week.

For calculating Zoe's child maintenance, Wayne's assessable income =

£40 x £133.41/£260.34 = £20.50

For calculating Lauren's child maintenance, Wayne's assessable income =

£40 x £126.93/£260.34 = £19.50 (or £40 – £20.50 = £19.50)

Proposed maintenance = 50 per cent assessable income.

For Zoe: 50% x £20.50 = £10.25

For Lauren: 50% x £19.50 = £9.75

Subject to the protected income calculation, Wayne is paying £20 in total, but divided between the two parents with care.

When the Child Support Agency (CSA) makes a decision on Lauren's child maintenance, Zoe's child maintenance will be reduced from £20 to £10.25 a week.

By dividing the non-resident parent's assessable income in proportion to the different maintenance requirements, persons with care responsible for a larger number of children will usually receive a greater amount of child maintenance. However, in the above example, Zoe's maintenance requirement is smaller than would usually be expected for two children. She is receiving only half of certain allowances in the maintenance requirement, as her other child, Scott, has a different non-resident father (see p177).

The division in the proposed maintenance occurs only if both of the persons with care involved actually make an application for child maintenance from the same non-resident parent.[21]

Where one assessment is already in force when the second application involving the same non-resident parent is made (eg, when his second marriage breaks down) the first assessment is reduced from the date the assessment to the second person with care takes effect (see p323).[22]

Pre-April 1993 property settlements

Before dividing the non-resident parent's assessable income between the persons with care, any allowance for a pre-April 1993 property settlement (see p192) is added on to the assessable income.[23] Once this has been apportioned, the property settlement allowance (if any) relevant to that person with care is deducted from her portion of assessable income.

Example 12.9: more than one parent with care and a property settlement allowance

The situation is as in *Example 12.8* except that Wayne has an allowance of £20 included in his exempt income in recognition of the capital settlement he made to Zoe at the time of their divorce in 1992.

Assessable income to be apportioned = £40 + £20 = £60

For Lauren's child maintenance, Wayne's assessable income =

£60 x £126.93/£260.34 = £29.25

Proposed maintenance for Lauren = 50% x £29.25 = £14.63

For Zoe's child maintenance, Wayne's assessable income =

(£60 x £133.41/£260.34) – £20 = £10.75

Proposed maintenance for Zoe = 50% x £10.75 = £5.38

Wayne continues to pay £20 a week in total (£20.01, rounded up). Zoe sees her maintenance reduced from £20 to £5.38 when the CSA makes a decision on Lauren's child maintenance. Although this is less than the minimum of £6.80, it is not increased because the total amount payable by Wayne is more than £6.80.

The additional element calculation

The additional element calculation of proposed maintenance when there is more than one person with care is done in the same way as when there is only one person with care, except that a proportion of the non-resident parent's assessable income is substituted for his total assessable income.

Example 12.10: additional element calculation if there is more than one person with care

Jeremy has left his wife, Evie, who has no income of her own. Of their four children, Francis (14), Georgina (12), Henry (8) and Isobel (4), the three youngest are living with Evie, but Francis is living with Jeremy's brother and sister-in-law. Jeremy has an assessable income of £700 a week.

The income of Jeremy's brother is irrelevant as he is not Francis' parent. Francis now has two non-resident parents who are liable to maintain him. Evie is now a non-resident parent in respect of Francis, but as she is on IS, she has no assessable income. Because she has children living with her, she is exempt from the deductions from IS.

Jeremy must pay his brother child maintenance for Francis as well as paying Evie child maintenance for Georgina, Henry and Isobel. Both the brother and Evie have made applications for child maintenance.

Evie's maintenance requirement:		£
Personal allowances	Evie	67.50
	Georgina	62.33
	Henry	62.33
	Isobel	62.33
Family premium		17.40
Sub-total		271.89
Less child benefit		47.10
Total maintenance requirement		**224.79**

Francis' maintenance requirement:		
Personal allowances	Adult (half)	33.75
	Francis	62.33
Family premium		17.40
Sub-total		113.48
Less child benefit		20.30
Total maintenance requirement		**93.18**

(The adult personal allowance is halved since Francis, the only qualifying child in the assessment, is 14 years old – see p174.)

Joint maintenance requirement = £224.79 + £93.18 = £317.97

Jeremy's £700 assessable income has to be split between the two assessments in proportion to their maintenance requirements.

Evie's child maintenance:

Jeremy's assessable income = £224.79/£317.97 x £700 = £494.87

Proposed maintenance = 50% x £494.87 = £247.44

This is above the maintenance requirement of £224.79; therefore, the additional element calculation must be done (as on p232):

Basic assessable income = £224.79 x 2 = £449.58

Additional assessable income = £494.87 – £449.58 = £45.29

Additional element = £45.29 x 25% = £11.32

Proposed maintenance = £224.79 + £11.32 = £236.11

When Francis goes to live with his aunt and uncle, Evie's maintenance falls from £311.86 a week (see p232) to £236.11.

Note: if Evie had assessable income, then the additional element calculation would follow that on p236, using £494.87 as Jeremy's assessable income.

Child maintenance for Francis:

Jeremy's assessable income = £700 x £93.18/£317.97 = £205.13

Proposed maintenance = 50% x £205.13 = £102.57

This is above the maintenance requirement of £93.18; therefore:

Basic assessable income = £93.18 x 2 = £186.36

Additional assessable income = £205.13 – £186.36 = £18.77

Additional element = £18.77 x 15% = £2.82

Proposed maintenance = £93.18 + £2.82 = £96.00

Jeremy is paying £96.00 to his brother and £236.11 to Evie, a total of £332.11. This is £20.25 more than he paid to Evie when the four children were living together. The non-resident parent usually ends up paying more in total when there are two or more applications. This is because he is paying a larger amount of his assessable income at the 50 per cent rate, as he now has two or more maintenance requirements to meet.

8. **Divided families**

In this *Handbook*, the term 'divided family' is used to cover the situation where some children of a family are in the care of the mother and the others in the care of the father. The Child Support Agency may use the term 'split care'. This situation could involve two separate maintenance applications and assessments. If only one parent applies for maintenance, only that application is assessed. The calculations do not involve any variation from the basic formula.

This is not the same situation as where the care of the same child(ren) is shared between the parents ('shared care' – see Chapter 14).

Example 12.11: two proposed maintenance calculations for a divided family

Carol (now 15) does not like her stepfather, Joe, and decides that she wants to live with Bob and Zoe's family – Yvonne (14), Veronica (12), Scott (5) and Ricky (1). David (10) is still living with Anita and Joe.

Therefore, Anita is the non-resident parent for Carol, and Bob is the non-resident parent for David. Anita's net income is now £290.

Maintenance requirement for Carol (15) = £93.18

Maintenance requirement for David (10) = £126.93

Although Carol is older, her maintenance requirement is lower as the carer element is halved because she is over 14.

Anita's exempt income = £285.01

(Anita's exempt income is as in *Example 10.2*, but without the £62.33 for Carol.)

Anita's assessable income = £290 (net income) – £285.01 = £4.99

Bob's exempt income = £223.40 (see *Example 10.6*)

Bob's assessable income = £300 (net income) – £223.40 = £76.60

Joint assessable income = £4.99 + £76.90 = £81.89

50 per cent of joint assessable income = £81.59 x 50% = £40.80

The 50 per cent joint assessable income figure (£40.80) is lower than the maintenance requirement for David (£126.93) and that for Carol (£93.18).

Proposed maintenance from Bob = 50% x £76.60 = £38.30

Proposed maintenance from Anita = 50% x £4.99 = £2.50

The protected income calculation (see *Example 13.7*) shows that both Anita and Bob can afford these amounts. However, because Anita's proposed maintenance is less than the minimum amount, and she is not exempt from paying this, her maintenance will in fact be £6.80.

If either or both of the maintenance requirements had been lower than 50 per cent joint assessable income, the proposed maintenance would have been obtained using the additional element calculation (see p234).

9. More than one non-resident parent

A person with care may be looking after children of different non-resident parents. This section looks at the situation where the person with care is a parent of all the qualifying children. The situation where the person with care is not the parent of the qualifying child(ren) is dealt with on p237 – ie, both parents are non-resident.

If a parent with care is looking after children of different non-resident parents and applies for maintenance from more than one non-resident parent, more than one maintenance assessment has to be done. If the parent with care has no assessable income, the two (or more) assessments will not alter from the basic formula.

The parent with care has no assessable income

Example 12.12: proposed maintenance from more than one non-resident parent if the parent with care has no assessable income

Zoe has applied for maintenance from her ex-husband, Wayne, for Yvonne (14) and Veronica (12), and from Terence for Scott (5). She is living with Bob and has no income of her own other than child benefit and child tax credit. This means that her net income is nil and, therefore, her assessable income is nil.

Child maintenance from Wayne:

Step 1: Maintenance requirement = £133.41 (see *Example 9.3*)

Step 2: Exempt income

Wayne, Zoe's ex-husband, lives on his own in a rented flat. He earns £160 per week net and his rent is £65 a week.

	£
Personal allowance	67.50
Housing costs	65.00
Total exempt income	**132.50**

Step 3: Assessable income

Total net income	160.00	(net earnings)
Less exempt income	132.50	
Assessable income	**27.50**	

Step 4: Proposed maintenance = 50% x £27.50 = £13.75

This is below the maintenance requirement of £133.41.

Therefore, the proposed maintenance is **£13.75.**

(You may remember that Wayne had a son with Lauren. However, she has now married Sean and moved to the Republic of Ireland where the CSA has no jurisdiction.)

Child maintenance from Terence:

Step 1: Maintenance requirement = £91.38 (see *Example 9.3*)

Step 2: Exempt income

Terence is married to Dipa and, although they have three children, only Rana, 17 and still at school, counts as a dependant. Terence works 30 hours a week and earns £210 a week net. They have a mortgage of £34.18 a week. Dipa receives carer's allowance for looking after her mother, but this is not enough income to provide half of the support for Rana. They get working tax credit (WTC) of £19.33 and £59.62 child tax credit.

		£	
Personal allowances	Terence	67.50	
	Rana	62.33	
Family premium		17.40	
Housing costs		34.18	
Total exempt income		**181.41**	

	£	
Step 3: Assessable income	210.00	(net earnings)
	19.33	(WTC)
Total net income	239.33	
Less exempt income	181.41	
Assessable income	**57.92**	

Step 4: Proposed maintenance = 50% x £57.92 = £28.96

This is below the maintenance requirement of £91.38.

Therefore, the proposed maintenance for Scott is **£28.96**.

The protected income calculations now have to be done to see whether Wayne and Terence can afford these amounts (see *Example 13.5*).

The parent with care has assessable income

If the parent with care has assessable income and makes an application for child maintenance from more than one non-resident father, then a proportion of her assessable income is taken into account for each of the assessments. Her assessable income is divided between the maintenance assessments in proportion to the maintenance requirements.[24] This apportioning will only happen if an application is made for maintenance from more than one non-resident parent.

Example 12.13: more than one non-resident parent and the parent with care has assessable income

Jeremy left his wife, Evie, when he discovered that her youngest child, Isobel (4), was not his daughter.

Evie is also looking after their three children, Francis (14), Georgina (12) and Henry (8). Evie decided to apply for child maintenance from Isobel's father, Max, as well as from Jeremy.

Jeremy's assessable income is now £350. Max's assessable income is £42.50.

Maintenance requirement for Francis, Georgina and Henry:		£	
Personal allowances	Evie	33.75	(half of 67.50)
	Francis	62.33	
	Georgina	62.33	
	Henry	62.33	

Family premium		8.70	(half of 17.40)
Sub-total		229.44	
Less child benefit		47.10	
Total maintenance requirement		**182.34**	

Maintenance requirement for Isobel:

Personal allowances	Evie	33.75	(half of 67.50)
	Isobel	62.33	
Family premium		8.70	(half of 17.40)
Sub-total		104.78	
Less child benefit		13.40	
Total maintenance requirement		**91.38**	

Joint maintenance requirements = £182.34 + £91.38 = £273.72

Evie's total assessable income is £70. This has to be shared between the two assessments in proportion to the maintenance requirements.

Proposed maintenance from Max: 50 per cent calculation

Evie's assessable income used in this assessment = £70 x £91.38/£273.72 = £23.37

Max's assessable income is £42.50.

Max and Evie's joint assessable income = £23.37 + £42.50 = £65.87

50% x £65.87 = £32.94

This is less than the maintenance requirement of £91.38.

Therefore, proposed maintenance is 50 per cent of Max's own assessable income: 50% x £42.50 = **£21.25**

Proposed maintenance from Jeremy: additional element calculation

Evie's total assessable income is £70.

Her assessable income used in this assessment = £70 x £182.34/£273.72 = £46.63

Jeremy's assessable income is now £350.

Jeremy and Evie's joint assessable income = £46.63 + £350 = £396.63

50% x £396.63 = £198.32

This is more than the maintenance requirement of £182.34 and, therefore, an additional element calculation has to be done:

Basic element = £182.34/£396.63 x £350 = £160.90

Basic assessable income = £160.90 x 2 = £321.80

Additional assessable income = £350 – £321.80 = £28.20

Additional element = £28.20 x 25% = £7.05

Proposed maintenance = £160.90 + £7.05 = **£167.95**

Subject to the protected income stage, Evie will receive £21.25 from Max and £167.95 from Jeremy.

Notes

2. **How much is proposed maintenance**
   1 Sch 1 para 2(1) CSA 1991
   2 Sch 1 para 2(2) CSA 1991
   3 Sch 1 para 2(3) CSA 1991
   4 Sch 1 para 2 CSA 1991; reg 5 CS(MASC) Regs
   5 Sch 1 para 4 CSA 1991; reg 6 CS(MASC) Regs

3. **The 50 per cent calculation**
   6 Sch 1 para 2(2) CSA 1991

4. **The additional element calculation**
   7 Sch 1 para 4(1) CSA 1991; reg 6(1) CS(MASC) Regs
   8 Sch 1 para 3 CSA 1991
   9 Sch 1 para 3 CSA 1991

5. **Maximum child maintenance**
   10 Sch 1 para 4(2) CSA 1991
   11 Sch 1 para 4(3) CSA 1991
   12 Reg 6(2) CS(MASC) Regs

6. **Both parents are non-resident**
   13 Reg 19(2) CS(MASC) Regs
   14 Reg 19(3) CS(MASC) Regs
   15 Reg 19(4) CS(MASC) Regs

7. **More than one person with care**
   16 Reg 22(5) CS(MASC) Regs
   17 Reg 22(1) CS(MASC) Regs
   18 Reg 22(2) CS(MASC) Regs
   19 Reg 22(3) CS(MASC) Regs
   20 Reg 22(4) CS(MASC) Regs
   21 Reg 22(1)(a) CS(MASC) Regs
   22 Reg 22(1)(b) and (2A) CS(MASC) Regs
   23 Reg 22(2) CS(MASC) Regs

9. **More than one non-resident parent**
   24 Reg 23(4) CS(MASC) Regs

Chapter 13

Protected income ('old rules')

This chapter covers:

1. What is protected income

Protected income is income which cannot be used for paying child maintenance.[1] At the end of the protected income calculation, the amount of maintenance payable will be known. It will either be the proposed maintenance figure or a reduced amount. The non-resident parent never ends up paying more than the proposed maintenance. This step should be carried out for all non-resident parents. The only time it does not apply is when the proposed maintenance is £6.80 or less (see p168).

There are two forms of protection for a non-resident parent. One prevents him having to pay an excessive proportion of his own income as child maintenance, and the other considers the needs of his whole family.

The 30 per cent cap

A non-resident parent never has to pay more than 30 per cent of his net income (see p204).[2] His partner's income is ignored. If the proposed maintenance is greater than this, it will be reduced to 30 per cent of net income. In other words, 70 per cent net income is a protected level of income; all non-resident parents (except a few of those making the minimum payment) are left with at least 70 per cent of their own net income. This applies even where a non-resident parent is paying more than one Child Support Agency (CSA) assessment (see p258). Also, if a non-resident parent is paying maintenance for other children under a court order, whether inside or outside the UK, this can be deducted from net income at the protected income stage (see p251).[3]

Example 13.1

Bob is living with his parents, and is liable to pay maintenance for Carol and David. His net earnings are now £203 a week.

Step 1: Maintenance requirement = £175.86 (see *Example 9.1*)

Step 2: Exempt income (personal allowance) = £67.50

Step 3: Assessable income = £203 – £67.50 = £135.50

Step 4: Proposed maintenance = 50% x £135.50 = £67.75 (less than the maintenance requirement)

Step 5: Protected income = 30% x £203 = £60.90

The maintenance is therefore reduced to £60.90, before proceeding with the rest of the protected income step.

Bob is living with Zoe and her three children. His net income is now £160 (see *Example 11.1*), Bob's assessable income is now £47.50 and the proposed maintenance is £23.75 (£47.50 x 50%) (see *Example 12.1*).

30% x £160 = £48

The proposed maintenance is less than 30 per cent of net income and remains at £23.75.

Total protected income

This second part of the protected income calculation is intended to prevent the non-resident parent and his family being left below the income support (IS) level as a result of paying child maintenance.[4] The 'family' is the same as that used for means-tested benefits (see p25 for a definition).

Even if the proposed maintenance has been capped at 30 per cent of net income, this second protected income calculation is carried out, as the maintenance payable may be further reduced. When carrying out this second calculation, substitute the capped maintenance for proposed maintenance where the latter is more than 30 per cent of net income.

What is total family income

'Total family income' includes the incomes of all members of the non-resident parent's family (see p25).[5] The CSA calls total family income 'disposable income'. We do not use this term at this stage as disposable income is also used to specify the income remaining after proposed maintenance has been paid.

Income for total family income purposes is calculated in the same way as net income (see Chapter 11) except that:[6]

- child benefit is included in full as income;
- child tax credit (CTC) is included in full as income, whether it is payable to the non-resident parent or his partner;
- part of payments under a mortgage protection insurance policy which exceed the mortgage interest repayments are disregarded; *and*

- with the exception of child maintenance, which is counted in full as the parent's income, the income of any child is included as income up to the amount of the personal allowance for that child and any disabled child premium included in the protected income calculation. As at exempt income stage, children's earnings and the first £10 a week of other income are disregarded.

Child maintenance paid

If a non-resident parent or his partner is paying maintenance for a child under a court order where an application to the CSA cannot be made, the amount of that payment is deducted from total family income.[7] The effect is to protect the payments under the court order at the possible expense of the proposed maintenance resulting from the CSA application. This applies if the person with care receiving the maintenance under the court order is not the parent of the child or if she is not receiving one of the specified benefits (see p35). Arguably, it also applies if a parent with care on benefit has chosen not to make an application to the CSA (eg, to preserve the court order) and the non-resident parent is now being assessed for his liability to maintain other children. It also applies if the non-resident parent or his partner is paying any child maintenance due under a court order made outside Great Britain.[8] However, no account is taken of voluntary payments, whether made in this country or abroad. In the former situation, the non-resident parent should consider making an application to the CSA as he may be better off with two CSA assessments.

Example 13.2: total family income

The proposed maintenance from Bob to Anita for Carol and David is £53.89 (50% of his assessable income – see *Example 11.3*). Can he afford it?

Bob is living with Zoe and four children – Yvonne (14), Veronica (12), Scott (4) and Ricky (their baby). Bob has net earnings of £300. Zoe receives weekly maintenance of £20 for Yvonne and Veronica, CTC of £193 and child benefit of £60.50.

	£
Earnings (net)	300.00
Maintenance for Yvonne and Veronica	20.00
CTC	193.00
Child benefit	60.50
Total family income	**573.50**

What is total protected income

Total protected income is the level below which the non-resident parent's or second family's income must not fall. To make the calculation more manageable, here the total protected income level is split into basic protected income (see p252) and additional protected income (see p254).

The basic protected income is based on IS rates, and it includes personal allowances, premiums, an amount towards high travel-to-work costs, housing costs for all members of the non-resident parent's family, and £30 as a margin above IS. The family is allowed additional protected income of 15 per cent of any family income over and above the basic protected level.

Maintenance payable

The total protected income level is compared with the family's income remaining were the proposed maintenance, or capped maintenance if it is lower, to be paid. If the family's income would be brought below the total protected income level by paying the proposed maintenance, the maintenance due is reduced. The child maintenance is then payable at an amount which would leave the family with disposable income equal to the protected income level.[9] However, the maintenance due cannot be reduced to less than the minimum payment[10] unless the non-resident parent is exempt (see p169).

If the family would have income remaining over the protected income level after paying the proposed maintenance, the non-resident parent is due to pay the proposed maintenance, or the capped maintenance if that is lower. In other words, the non-resident parent pays the *lowest* of:

- 30 per cent of his net income; *or*
- the amount which would leave his family with disposable income equal to the total protected level; *or*
- the proposed maintenance from Step 4 (see *Example 3.1*).

2. **Basic protected income**

Basic protected income includes income support (IS) personal allowances and any relevant premiums for all the members of the family, whether the family receives IS or not (including if IS is received for adults but child tax credit is received for children). See Appendix 2 for the qualifying conditions and 2011/12 rates of the premiums.

Basic protected income is:[11]

- the amount of the IS personal allowance for someone aged 25 or over (£67.50) *or* if the non-resident parent has a partner, the IS personal allowance for a couple both aged 18 or over (£105.95); *plus*
- for each child in the family, the amount of the IS personal allowance for a child (£62.33);* *plus*
- the amount of any IS premiums for which the conditions are satisfied (note that, unlike at exempt income stage, pensioner premiums are included);* *plus*
- housing costs for the whole family (see p253); *plus*
- council tax liability less any council tax benefit (CTB – see p254); *plus*

- an allowance towards high travel-to-work costs of a non-resident parent (see p254); *plus*
- a standard margin of £30.

*A proportion of the full rate of the personal allowances and any premiums will be used if a child lives in the household for between two and six nights a week.[12]

Housing costs

The rules for assessing housing costs are the same as those used at the exempt income stage (see p185),[13] except that:

- if there is a mortgage, only interest payments are allowed;[14]
- if the non-resident parent is living as a non-dependant in someone else's house, an amount is included as housing costs (see below);[15]
- excessive housing costs are the higher of £80 or half the total family income.[16] Housing costs will be restricted to this figure unless the non-resident parent is exempt from that rule – eg, because the family includes a child (see p190).

The non-resident parent is a non-dependant

A non-resident parent may be a non-dependant if he lives in a household with people who are not 'family' (see p25). He is *not* a non-dependant if he, or a partner, is:[17]

- a co-owner or joint tenant of the home;
- employed by a charitable or voluntary body as a resident carer;
- liable to make a commercial payment in order to live in the home. It will not be considered a commercial arrangement if payments are made to a close relative in the household – ie, a a parent, son, daughter (including step-relatives and in-laws), brother and sister, and any of their partners.

The weekly amount to be included in protected income is given below.[18]

Working 16 or more hours a week and with a gross income of:	£
£387 or more	60.60
£310 to £386.99	55.20
£234 to £309.99	48.45
£180 to £233.99	29.60
£122 to £179.99	21.55
All others	9.40

Note: when calculating gross income, disability living allowance and attendance allowance are ignored.[19]

Council tax

If the non-resident parent is the only person, other than a partner, who is liable to pay council tax in respect of the home for which housing costs are included, the weekly council tax (less any CTB) is included in basic protected income. However, if there are other people resident in the home, the amount of council tax included is either:[20]

- the weekly liability divided by the number of liable people; *or*
- the weekly amount actually paid by the non-resident parent where he is required to pay more than his share because another liable person has defaulted.

If the non-resident parent lives in Northern Ireland, liability for rates replaces council tax. Likewise, if the person with care has applied to the Child Support Agency (Northern Ireland) but the non-resident parent lives in Great Britain, council tax is used.[21]

High travel-to-work costs

This allowance applies for non-resident parents who travel more than 240 kilometres a week to and from work.[22] The allowance is calculated in exactly the same way as at exempt income stage (see p196). It does not apply to partners.

3. Total protected income

In order to obtain total protected income, additional protected income has to be calculated. To do this, basic protected income must be compared with total family income.

If the total family income *exceeds* the basic protected income, an addition is made to the basic protected income.

Deduct the basic protected income from the total family income to give the excess family income. The additional protected income equals 15 per cent of this excess family income.[23] This figure is added to basic protected income to give total protected income.

If the total family income is *below* the basic protected income, there is no additional protected income. Any payment of child maintenance will bring the family's disposable income below the protected income level. Therefore, the non-resident parent will either pay the minimum amount (£6.80) or be exempt from paying child support (see p169).

Example 13.3: total protected income

The situation is the same as in *Example 13.1*, with Bob living with his parents and net earnings of £203 a week (£232 gross). He is contributing towards the household but is not a co-owner of the home, nor liable to pay council tax. He travels less than 240 kilometres a week to and from work.

	£
Basic protected income:	
Personal allowance	67.50
Housing costs (as a non-dependant)	29.60
Margin	30.00
Basic protected income	**127.10**
Additional protected income:	
Total family income	203.00
Less basic protected income	127.10
Excess family income	75.90
Additional protected income (15% x £75.90)	**11.39**
Total protected income:	
Basic protected income	127.10
Plus additional protected income	11.39
Total protected income	**138.49**

Two years later, Bob lives with Zoe and the situation is the same as in *Example 13.2*. Their rent is £45 a week and the council tax liability is £1,050.92 a year. Bob and Zoe are not entitled to housing benefit or council tax benefit.

		£
Basic protected income:		
Personal allowances	Couple	105.95
	Yvonne	62.33
	Veronica	62.33
	Scott	62.33
	Ricky	62.33
Family premium		17.40
Housing costs		45.00
Council tax liability		20.21
Margin		30.00
Basic protected income		**467.88**
Additional protected income:		
Total family income		573.50
Less basic protected income		467.88
Excess family income		105.62
Additional protected income (15% x £105.62)		**15.84**
Total protected income:		
Basic protected income		467.88
Plus additional protected income		15.84
Total protected income		**483.72**

4. The maintenance payable

There are two methods of calculating the maintenance payable. The full logic of the step is covered first, followed by a short cut.

The family's disposable income which would remain after paying child maintenance is obtained by subtracting the proposed maintenance (Step 4 – see *Example 3.1*) from the total family income. If the proposed maintenance has been capped at 30 per cent net income (see p249), this capped amount is used instead of the proposed maintenance.

If the disposable income is *higher* than the total protected income, the parent can afford to pay the full proposed/capped maintenance. Maintenance payable is the proposed/capped maintenance figure. If the proposed maintenance has been capped, it cannot be increased back to the originally proposed level.

If the disposable income is initially *below* the total protected income, the maintenance payable is reduced until the disposable income equals the total protected income.[24] Therefore, the maintenance payable is the total family income minus the total protected income.

The minimum payment rule still applies (see p168).[25]

The alternative way of arriving at the maintenance payable is to cut out the disposable income step and, in all cases, to deduct total protected income from total family income to give an alternative proposed maintenance. This is compared with proposed maintenance from Step 4 (see *Example 3.1*) and also 30 per cent of net income. The non-resident parent pays the lowest figure.

Example 13.4: maintenance payable

The proposed maintenance from Bob to Anita for Carol and David has been capped at £60.90 (see *Example 13.1*) and Bob's total protected income is £138.49 (see *Example 13.3*).

	£
Total family income	203.00
Less capped maintenance	60.90
Disposable income would be	**142.10**

As this is above the total protected income level, Bob can afford to pay the capped maintenance of £60.90.

Two years later, when Bob is living with Zoe, the proposed maintenance is £23.75 (see *Example 13.1*).

Total family income (from p251)	573.50
Less proposed maintenance	23.75
Disposable income would be	549.75

This is more than the total protected income of £483.72 (see *Example 13.3*) and therefore the proposed maintenance of £23.75 is paid.

Example 13.5: protected income from start to finish

A few months later, child maintenance from Zoe's ex-husband, Wayne, for Yvonne and Veronica, and from Terence for Scott is being assessed (see *Example 12.12*). The proposed maintenance from Wayne is £13.75 and from Terence £28.96. Can each of them afford it?

Wayne lives on his own in a rented flat. He earns on average £160 net a week and only travels a few kilometres to work. His rent is £65 a week and his council tax is £6 a week (see *Example 12.12*). He is not entitled to any council tax benefit or housing benefit. The 30 per cent cap does not reduce the proposed maintenance as: 30% x £160 = £48. Therefore, the proposed maintenance remains at £13.75.

Basic protected income:	£
Personal allowance	67.50
Housing costs	65.00
Council tax	6.00
Margin	30.00
Basic protected income	**168.50**
Total family income	160.00
Less basic protected income	168.50
Excess family income	0.00
Additional protected income (15% x £0)	**0.00**
Total protected income	**168.50**

Wayne's total family income is already slightly below his total protected income. Payment of the proposed maintenance of £13.75 would leave Wayne with a disposable income of £146.25, considerably below his total protected income. As Wayne's family income is below his total protected income, there is no disposable income from which to pay maintenance. However, Wayne is not exempt from the minimum maintenance payment and, therefore, he is liable to pay £6.80 a week.

Terence is married to Dipa and they have one dependent daughter, Rana (17), who lives with them. Their mortgage is £34.18 a week, half of which is capital repayments. Their council tax is £9.32 a week. Terence earns £210 net a week (see *Example 12.12*). Dipa receives carer's allowance of £55.55 and child benefit of £20.30 a week. They get £19.33 working tax credit (WTC) and child tax credit of £56.92 per week.

The 30 per cent cap does not reduce the proposed maintenance as: 30% x £229.33 (earnings plus WTC) = £68.80. Therefore, the proposed maintenance remains at £28.96 (see *Example 12.12*).

Basic protected income:		£
Personal allowances	Couple	105.95
	Rana	62.33
Family premium		17.40
Carer premium		31.00
Housing costs (mortgage interest)		17.09
Council tax		9.32

Margin	30.00
Basic protected income	**273.09**
Total family income:	
Net earnings	210.00
Carer's allowance	55.55
Child benefit	20.30
Working tax credit	19.33
Child tax credit	56.92
Total family income	**362.10**
Less basic protected income	273.09
Excess family income	89.01
Additional protected income (15% x £89.01)	**13.35**
Total protected income (£273.09 + £13.35)	**286.44**
Total family income	362.10
Less proposed maintenance	28.96
Disposable income	**333.14**

As disposable income is above the total protected income, the maintenance payable is the proposed maintenance of £28.96.

More than one person with care

If a non-resident parent is being assessed to pay child maintenance to two or more persons with care for different qualifying children, only one protected income step is carried out on the total proposed maintenance. Both the 30 per cent cap and the total protected income check are carried out for this total.[26] If the non-resident parent cannot afford the total proposed maintenance, the amount he can afford is divided between the persons with care in proportion to their proposed maintenance.

Example 13.6: protected income step for more than one person with care

Lauren has returned to the UK. She claims income support and applies for child maintenance for Wayne's son, Keith. Wayne is also the father of Zoe's daughters. His net wages are now £174, his rent is now £50.

Step 1: Maintenance requirement

	£	
Zoe	124.97	(see *Example 9.3*)
Lauren	126.93	(see *Example 12.8*)
Total	**251.90**	

Step 2: Wayne's exempt income = £117.50

Step 3: Wayne's assessable income = £56.50

(Neither parent with care has any assessable income.)

Step 4: Proposed maintenance

Zoe: (£56.50 x £124.97/£251.90) x 50% = £14.02

Lauren: (£56.50 x £126.93/£251.90) x 50% = £14.23

Total proposed maintenance = £14.02 + £14.23 = £28.25

Step 5: Protected income

Check whether the total proposed maintenance is more than 30 per cent net income: 30% x £174 = £52.20

The total proposed maintenance of £28.25 is less than this and, therefore, does not need to be capped. Now carry out the second protected income calculation.

	£
Personal allowance	67.50
Housing costs	50.00
Council tax	6.00
Margin	30.00
Basic protected income	**153.50**
Total family income	174.00
Less basic protected income	153.50
Excess family income	20.50
Additional protected income (15% x £20.50)	**3.08**
Total protected income (£153.50 + £3.08)	**156.58**
Total family income	174.00
Less total proposed maintenance	28.25
Disposable income	**145.75**

This is below the total protected income (£156.58), so Wayne cannot afford to pay the proposed maintenance.

Total family income	174.00
Less total protected income	156.58
Maintenance payable	**17.42**

The maintenance is split between Zoe and Lauren in proportion to their proposed maintenance:

Zoe: £17.42 x £14.02/28.25 = £8.65

Lauren: £17.42 x £14.23/£28.25 = £8.77

Note: Lauren ends up with a greater proportion of the maintenance, even though she has one young child and Zoe has two older children. In this case, as neither of them has assessable income, the difference is entirely due to the maintenance requirement rules.

5. Change of circumstances

An increase in the total family income of a second family on the protected income level can result in an increase in the maintenance payable to the first family. This arises because the total protected income level only increases by 15 per cent of any increase in family income. The net effect of a £1 a week increase in total family income is an 85 pence increase in the child maintenance payable to the first family. This begins as soon as the maintenance payable is £6.80 a week and only ceases once the maintenance due reaches the capped or proposed maintenance level.

This recycling effect is the same, irrespective of whether the income is the non-resident parent's or a partner's. There is no exception for income specifically meant for stepchildren in the second family – eg, child maintenance paid for them. The theory is that an increase in the income of the non-resident parent's partner means that she is better able to support herself and her own children. This in turn releases more of the non-resident parent's income away from supporting his partner and his stepchildren and into paying maintenance to his own children. However, this distinction may not be obvious to second families, who are likely to perceive it as unfair.

Once the proposed maintenance level is due, a £1 increase in the non-resident parent's income results in an increase of between 50 pence and 15 pence in the maintenance assessment. The partner's income then no longer increases the assessment at all (except to a limited extent in some instances where there is a joint child – see p198).

If the proposed maintenance has been capped, then increases in the partner's income do *not* increase the maintenance payable. While the maintenance remains capped, a £1 increase in the non-resident parent's own net income produces a 30 pence increase in the assessment.

Example 13.7: change in total family income

Zoe decides to take a job, earning £120 net a week. Bob is still taking home £300 a week. They are still entitled to £193 child tax credit (CTC) a week (Zoe's earnings will not affect their tax credits until the following tax year). Zoe now receives child maintenance as assessed in *Example 13.4*.

Step 1: Maintenance requirement = £175.86 (see *Example 9.1*)

Step 2: Bob's exempt income = £152.37

Step 3: Bob's assessable income = £147.63 (see *Example 11.3*)

Step 4: Proposed maintenance = 50% x £147.63 = £73.82

(Anita has no assessable income)

Step 5: Protected income.

To check whether the proposed maintenance is less than 30 per cent net income (see p222): 30% x £300 = £90

Therefore, the proposed maintenance remains at £73.82.

	£
Bob's earnings	300.00
Zoe's earnings	120.00
Maintenance from Wayne	6.80
Maintenance from Terence	28.96
Child benefit	60.50
CTC	193.00
Total family income	709.26
Less basic protected income (see p254)	467.88
Excess family income	241.38
Additional protected income (15% x £241.38)	**36.21**
Total protected income (£467.88 + £36.21)	**504.09**
If the proposed maintenance were paid, disposable income would be:	
Total family income	709.26
Less proposed maintenance	73.82
Disposable income	**635.44**

This is higher than the total protected income (£504.09) and, therefore, the proposed maintenance of £73.82 is the maintenance payable. Bob is now paying Anita £73.82 instead of £23.75 (see *Example 13.4*).

It would not be to Bob's advantage to ask for a supersession of the assessment on the grounds of a change of circumstances (see p350).

There are two reasons why not every change of circumstances will immediately affect the amount of child maintenance payable. First, the person concerned does not have to request a supersession if there is a change in her/his circumstances. It is optional. Second, if a supersession is requested and undertaken, the general rule is that the maintenance in payment will only be altered if the new assessment is at least £10 more or less than the assessment in force. However, a new assessment which is reduced by only £1 or more, or increased by £5 or more from the previous assessment, will always take effect if it leaves the non-resident parent's family on the protected income level.[27] Therefore, cases which involve a non-resident parent on the protected income level will be changing more frequently than cases where the full amount of the proposed maintenance is being paid.

Example 13.8: change in family composition

Bob's daughter Carol (now 15) moves, leaving Anita, to live with Bob and Zoe. Child benefit increases to £73.90. Child tax credit increases to £242.22. Otherwise, the situation is as in the previous example (*Example 13.7*).

David (10), Bob's son, still lives with Anita and her husband, Joe. Anita has net earnings of £290 and Joe has net earnings of £295. Anita's child tax credit entitlement is now £10.50.

Their mortgage interest payments are £114.23 a week, the endowment policy premium is £24.92 a week, and council tax £14.50 a week.

See *Example 12.11*:

Proposed maintenance from Anita for Carol = £2.50

Proposed maintenance from Bob for David = £38.30

Protected income calculation for Bob

The 30 per cent cap does not reduce the proposed maintenance as:

30% x £300 = £90

Basic protected income:		£
Personal allowances	Couple	105.95
	Carol	62.33
	Yvonne	62.33
	Veronica	62.33
	Scott	62.33
	Ricky	62.33
Family premium		17.40
Housing costs		45.00
Council tax liability		20.21
Margin		30.00
Basic protected income		**530.21**
Total family income:		
£516.26 (from *Example 13.7* without former CTC) + £242.22 (revised CTC) + £13.40 (extra child benefit)		**771.88**
Less basic protected income		530.21
Excess family income		241.67
Additional protected income (15% x £241.67)		**36.25**
Total protected income (£530.21 + £36.25)		**566.46**
Total family income		771.88
Less proposed maintenance		38.30
Disposable income		**733.58**

This is above the total protected income of £566.46 and, therefore, Bob can afford to pay the proposed maintenance of £38.30.

Protected income calculation for Anita

Basic protected income:		£
Personal allowances	Couple	105.95
	David	62.33
Family premium		17.40
Housing costs (mortgage interest only)		114.23
Council tax liability		14.50
Margin		30.00
Basic protected income		**344.41**

Total family income:	
Anita's earnings	290.00
Joe's earnings	295.00
Child tax credit	10.50
Child benefit	20.30
Total family income	**615.80**
Less basic protected income	344.41
Excess family income*	271.39

*At this point it is already clear that Anita will pay the proposed maintenance, but we continue with the calculation for completeness.

Additional protected income (15% x £271.39)	**40.71**
Total protected income (£344.41 + £40.71)	**385.12**
Total family income	615.80
Less proposed maintenance	2.50
Disposable income	**612.50**

This is well above the total protected income of £385.12 and, therefore, Anita can afford to pay the proposed maintenance. As the proposed maintenance is less than the minimum amount, it would usually be rounded up to £6.80. However, because Anita has a child living with her (David) for whom she gets child benefit, she is exempt from the minimum payment.

Note: the formula works in such a way as to leave Anita and Joe with disposable income of £612.50 when they have the care of one child, whereas Bob and Zoe are left with £733.58 when they are looking after five children.

Notes

1. **What is protected income**
   1 Sch 1 para 6 CSA 1991
   2 Regs 11(6)-(6A) and 12 CS(MASC) Regs
   3 Reg 12(1)(c) CS(MASC) Regs
   4 Reg 11(1)-(5) CS(MASC) Regs
   5 Regs 11(1)(l) and 12(1)(a) CS(MASC) Regs
   6 Reg 11(2) CS(MASC) Regs
   7 Reg 11(2)(a)(ii) CS(MASC) Regs
   8 Reg 11(2)(a)(v) CS(MASC) Regs
   9 Reg 12(2) CS(MASC) Regs
   10 Reg 12(3) CS(MASC) Regs

2. **Basic protected income**
   11 Reg 11(1)(a)-(kk) CS(MASC) Regs
   12 Reg 11(3) and (4) CS(MASC) Regs
   13 Reg 11(1)(b) CS(MASC) Regs
   14 Sch 3 para 3(1) CS(MASC) Regs
   15 Reg 11(1)(b) CS(MASC) Regs
   16 Reg 18(1)(b) CS(MASC) Regs
   17 Reg 1 CS(MASC) Regs; reg 3 HB Regs or reg 3 HB(SPC) Regs
   18 Reg 74(1) and (2) HB Regs or reg 55(1) and (2) HB(SPC) Regs
   19 Reg 63(9) HB Regs
   20 Reg 11(1)(j) CS(MASC) Regs

21 Sch 1 para 5(4) CS(NIRA) Regs
22 Reg 11(1)(kk) CS(MASC) Regs

3. **Total protected income**
23 Reg 11(1)(l) CS(MASC) Regs

4. **The maintenance payable**
24 Reg 12(2) CS(MASC) Regs
25 Reg 12(3) CS(MASC) Regs
26 Reg 22(3) CS(MASC) Regs

5. **Change of circumstances**
27 Reg 21(2) and (3) CS(MAP) Regs

Chapter 14

Shared care ('old rules')

This chapter covers:

1. What is shared care

The term 'shared care' is used in this *Handbook* to describe a situation where there is more than one person looking after a particular child and those people live in different households. If the people providing care live in the same household (see p21), this is not shared care.[1] The legislation only acknowledges shared care where more than one person has 'day-to-day care' of a child.

Day-to-day care

There is no definition of 'day-to-day care' in the Regulations for deciding whether someone is a person with care. Therefore, an everyday definition can be used (see p20). A person who is not a parent can apply to receive child maintenance only if s/he has day-to-day care of a child. Parents with care and non-resident parents can both apply for a maintenance assessment, although there are some exceptions (see p35) and rules governing which application takes precedence (see p44). There can be more than one person with care of a child.

The parent does not have to provide continuous care throughout a period of 24 hours, but must usually be providing care during the night.[2] If a non-resident parent looks after a child overnight at the home of the person with care, this can count as looking after the child for shared care purposes.[3]

For the purposes of shared care in the maintenance formula, a person is treated as having day-to-day care of a child only if s/he cares for the child for at least 104 nights in the 12-month period ending with the 'relevant week' (see p205 for a definition).[4] If 12 months have not passed since there was a shared care situation, or since the parents separated, this does not mean that there is no pattern (see below).[5]

Another period ending with the relevant week may be used if that would be more representative of the current arrangement.[6] The number of nights of care in that period must be in the same ratio as 104 nights is to 12 months – ie, 52 nights in six months, 26 nights in three months, 17 nights in two months, nine nights in a month. For example, a different period may be used if there is a recent relationship breakdown, a court ruling on residence or contact, or the person now providing day-to-day care has been abroad, in prison, in hospital, away from home or otherwise unable to provide care. If the arrangement has simply been re-negotiated between the two parents, written acceptance of this should be provided so that the Child Support Agency (CSA) knows this is now the current arrangement and not a temporary change. A future period cannot be used. The period should generally end with the relevant week, but does not have to.[7] If a change occurs after the relevant week, a supersession will usually have to be sought (see p350).

If a child is a boarder at boarding school or a hospital inpatient, whoever would otherwise have day-to-care is treated as providing care. The person who is treated as having day-to-day care for such periods need not be the person who pays the school fees.[8]

Parents should keep a note of the nights the child(ren) spends with them and, in case of dispute, be willing to supply further evidence – eg, a diary. The CSA and any subsequent First-tier Tribunal appeal must determine the amount of day-to-day care provided by each person on the basis of available evidence.[9]

Fewer than 104 nights in the year

If a non-resident parent is providing some care, but to a lesser extent than that described as day-to-day care, he is still liable to pay child maintenance and the level of care he provides is not acknowledged by the child support formula. Therefore, such a non-resident parent is expected to contribute the same amount of child maintenance as if he were not looking after the child at all. This means, for example, that fathers who have their children to stay every other weekend will pay the same level of maintenance as those who do not.

A father who looks after the child(ren) for all of the school holidays would not be accepted as a person with care if the time spent with the children was assessed over 12 months. However, the father could request a supersession during the summer holidays on the grounds that he is now a parent with care and a shorter period should then be used to calculate who has day-to-day care in order to reflect the current arrangement. It is unlikely that this would be grounds for a supersession if the six-week period had already been taken into account when averaging over the year for the current assessment. However, if the arrangement for the holiday had not been known at the time, this may be successful. If not, an appeal should be considered (see p360).

If day-to-day care were to be reassessed over this shorter period, the father would become the parent with care and the mother the non-resident parent. The father could then apply for maintenance from the mother. **Note:** the period used to assess day-to-day care ends with the relevant week which precedes the request for a supersession (see p350). Therefore, the request should not be made right at the beginning of the summer holiday.

If it is held that a supersession cannot take place, such a father technically remains the non-resident parent over the holiday when he has the child(ren) full time. He would be liable to continue paying the mother the full level of maintenance even for those weeks the children spend with him. Parents in such a situation could try to come to some voluntary arrangement whereby the mother pays back some or all of the maintenance, but this may not be financially possible.

More than one person with care

If there are two people in different households who both have day-to-day care of a qualifying child, either can make an application for child maintenance provided both or neither has parental responsibility (see p15) for the child.[10] If only one of them has parental responsibility, the person with that responsibility must be the applicant. This means that if the person with parental responsibility decides not to apply, the other person with care could lose out on child maintenance.

If both persons with care can, and do, make an application, only one will be accepted (see p44).[11] Which application is accepted is largely a technicality, as this does not change the status of the people involved nor the way in which the assessment is carried out. It does, however, affect who can cancel the assessment (see p327).

The basic formula is varied to take into account the fact that there is more than one person with care. The way in which the formula is adjusted depends on which people share the care.

2. Care shared between separated parents

If it is accepted that both parents have day-to-day care (ie, there is a shared care situation), one of the parents with care still has to be treated as a non-resident parent in order to make an assessment.[12] CPAG tried to challenge this rule in the past, but a child support commissioner decided that this is the correct interpretation of the law.[13]

If parents share care, only a parent who provides day-to-day care as defined above (ie, care of at least 104 nights out of 12 months or the equivalent – see p265) can be deemed non-resident (see p268). In almost all cases, the parents with care will both be providing care for at least 104 nights out of 12 months and, therefore, one has to be deemed non-resident. However, in some cases, although care is shared according to its everyday meaning, both parents are not providing day-to-day care according to the definition. For example, if the mother provides care during the day but the children sleep at their father's home, each cares for the children an equal number of hours a week, but because they are not providing day-to-day care, the shared care rules cannot be used to deem one of them non-resident. No maintenance assessment should be carried out. In a case like this, the Child Support Agency (CSA) may try to argue that the mother is the non-resident parent because she does not have day-to-day care. If this happens, she should appeal on the basis that the day-to-day care definition only legally has to be used in establishing whether there is shared care, not in deciding whether someone is a person with care, when a different definition can be used (see p265).

In cases where a parent with care is treated as non-resident, an assessment is carried out to find out how much child maintenance s/he has to pay to the other parent. As the remaining parent with care does not have to pay child maintenance, this can result in one parent paying child maintenance to another who has equal responsibility for the child.

Who is treated as the non-resident parent

The parent who provides day-to-day care to a 'lesser extent' is treated as the non-resident parent.[14] A '**lesser extent**' could be interpreted as meaning either for fewer *nights* per week on average or fewer *hours* per week on average. The number of nights will be considered first by the CSA, but it should be argued on the basis of hours if this would give a fairer result. Indeed, it could be said that nights involve less care than days. For example, if one parent had a school-age child from 4pm Friday to 8.30am Monday (three nights), this could be argued to be as much care as the other parent who is with the child from 4pm Monday to 8.30am Friday (four nights). It might be possible to argue that the degree of responsibility, as well as the amount of time, is relevant to determining the extent of the care – eg, who buys the child's clothes, who attends school functions or arranges visits to the dentist. These issues need not be raised if both parents agree that the number of nights of care fairly determines the question.

It is helpful if parents keep a record of the time the children spend in each household, especially if there are changes to the usual pattern of care. The extent of care is measured over the period explained on p265, usually the last year or since a change in the arrangements.

If the parents provide care for an equal amount of time, the parent who does *not* receive child benefit is treated as the non-resident parent.[15] As the right to receive child maintenance follows the receipt of child benefit, this may lead to competing claims for child benefit. If more than one person makes a claim for child benefit, an order of priority is used or, if this does not apply, HM Revenue and Customs makes a (non-appealable) decision.

For more information on the priority rules for child benefit, see CPAG's *Welfare Benefits and Tax Credits Handbook*.

If care is shared equally and neither parent receives child benefit, the CSA decides who is the principal carer.[16]

Example 14.1: shared care and a deemed non-resident parent

Marcia and Nathan are divorced. They have two children, Oscar (7) and Patrick (5). Every fortnight the children spend five nights with Nathan. The rest of the time they live with Marcia.

Marcia has the children nine out of every 14 nights = 234 nights a year.

Nathan has the children five out of every 14 nights = 130 nights a year.

Do both parents have day-to-day care? Yes.

But Nathan looks after the boys to a lesser extent. Therefore, Nathan is deemed a non-resident parent and an assessment is carried out to decide how much child maintenance he should pay to Marcia.

Marcia remains a parent with care and has no liability to pay child maintenance.

There may be cases where each child of a family spends a different amount of time with the two parents – ie, the mother may be deemed the non-resident parent for one child and the father for the other. If this is the case, the situation is similar to that of a divided family in which different children live full time with different parents (also known as 'split care' – see p243). Two completely separate assessments are carried out: if the mother cares for the daughter for the greater amount of time, the daughter's child maintenance will be assessed with the father as the deemed non-resident parent; child maintenance for the son, who spends more time with the father, will be assessed with the mother as the deemed non-resident parent.

Calculating child maintenance

When two parents share care, there is a remaining parent with care and a deemed non-resident parent (see p268). The five steps of the formula described in Chapters 9 to 13 are still applicable in calculating how much maintenance the deemed non-resident parent must pay. However, the standard formula is adjusted to take into account the time that the so-called non-resident parent looks after the child(ren).

Step 1: maintenance requirement

Only one maintenance requirement is calculated (see Chapter 9).

Example 14.2: maintenance requirement

The situation is as described in *Example 14.1*. Marcia has remarried and looks after Oscar (7) and Patrick (5) for nine nights every fortnight.

Maintenance requirement with Marcia as parent with care:

		£
Personal allowances	Marcia	67.50
	Oscar	62.33
	Patrick	62.33
Family premium		17.40
Sub-total		209.56
Less child benefit		33.70
Maintenance requirement		**175.86**

Step 2: exempt income

When calculating the exempt income of the parents, a proportion of the personal allowance for the child (plus any disabled child premium) is included to reflect the average number of nights a week the parent has care of the child.[17] Similarly, only a proportion of the family premium is allowed unless another of the parent's children lives in the household all week (see below for the situation where there is another child).[18] See *Example 14.10* if the care of more than one child is shared, but the children spend a different number of nights with the parent.

For full details of exempt income, see Chapter 10.

Example 14.3: exempt income for shared care when no child lives in the household for seven nights a week

Marcia looks after Oscar and Patrick for an average of 4.5 nights a week.

Nathan looks after Oscar and Patrick for an average of 2.5 nights a week.

Marcia married Gareth recently. Their mortgage payments are £120 a week.

Marcia's exempt income:		£	
Personal allowances	Marcia	67.50	
	Oscar	40.07	(for 4.5 days)
	Patrick	40.07	(for 4.5 days)
Family premium		11.19	(for 4.5 days)
Housing costs		120.00	
Total exempt income		**278.83**	

Nathan lives on his own when the children are not with him. His privately rented flat costs £60 a week. He lives within a few kilometres of his work.

Nathan's exempt income:		£	
Personal allowances	Nathan	67.50	
	Oscar	22.26	(for 2.5 days)
	Patrick	22.26	(for 2.5 days)

Family premium	6.21	(for 2.5 days)
Housing costs	60.00	
Total exempt income	**178.23**	

See *Example 14.10* for the apportionment of premiums where the children spend a different number of nights with each parent.

Premiums if there is a shared-care child and another child

This section only applies if there is a child who lives in the household all week, as well as child(ren) who are there part time. If the household includes only the children whose care is shared and stepchildren, the premiums are apportioned as above. Go to Step 3.

If another child of the parent lives in the household for seven nights a week, this child can be either another qualifying child or a joint child with a new partner. The family premium is either included in full or halved.[19] It will be included in full if:

- the parent qualifies for the family premium for the shared child(ren) – ie, receives child benefit for her/him, or if no one receives child benefit, has claimed child benefit or is the person with whom the child usually lives. This is referred to as shared-care children 'with child benefit'; *or*
- there is another qualifying child (of that parent) in the household; *or*
- a new partner cannot support the joint child (see p198).

The following outlines the various permutations.

- A lone parent with shared-care children (with or without child benefit) and another qualifying child: full family premium.
- A parent with shared-care children (with child benefit) and a joint child with a new partner: full family premium. Note that the personal allowance for the joint child is halved if the new partner can contribute to her/his support.
- A parent with shared-care children (no child benefit) and a joint child with a new partner: the family premium is halved if the new partner can contribute to the support of the joint child, but is included in full if the partner cannot (see p198). Note that the personal allowance for the joint child is also halved if the new partner can contribute to her/his support.

Example 14.4: exempt income if there is shared care and a joint child

Marcia still has the qualifying children, Oscar and Patrick, nine out of 14 nights (an average of 4.5 nights a week) and receives child benefit for them. Marcia and her husband, Gareth, now have a baby daughter, Megan. Gareth earns £450 a week. Their mortgage payments are £120 per week.

Marcia's exempt income:		£	
Personal allowances	Marcia	67.50	
	Oscar	40.07	(4.5 days)

	Patrick	40.07	(4.5 days)
	Megan (half*)	31.17	
Family premium (in full**)		17.40	
Housing costs		120.00	
Total exempt income		**316.21**	

* As Gareth earns £450 a week, he can afford to contribute to his daughter's maintenance and, therefore, only half of Megan's personal allowance is included (see p198 for details of the means test).

** Because Megan lives in the household all week, the family premium is not apportioned according to how many nights Oscar and Patrick stay. Instead, consideration has to be given to whether Marcia is entitled to the family premium as a result of looking after Oscar and Patrick. As she receives child benefit for them, she is entitled to the full rate of the premium. (If her ex-husband received the child benefit, Marcia would not be due the full family premium for them. Consideration would then be given to Megan and, since Gareth can afford to maintain half of Megan, the family premium would be halved.)

Step 3: assessable income

This step is exactly the same as for other situations (see Chapter 11).

Example 14.5: assessable income

Before the birth of her daughter, Marcia's income is net earnings of £145 a week. Her husband's earnings are not taken into account in the net income calculation and neither is any child benefit.

Marcia's assessable income:	£
Net income	145.00 (net earnings)
Less exempt income	278.83 (from *Example 14.3*)
Assessable income	**Nil**

Nathan takes home £220 a week, after £40 superannuation is deducted. Only half of the superannuation is taken into account (see p208).

Nathan's assessable income:	£
Net income	240.00 (net earnings)
Less exempt income	178.23 (from *Example 14.3*)
Assessable income	**61.77**

Step 4: proposed maintenance

The proposed maintenance step is carried out in full for each parent in order to obtain the proposed maintenance from the deemed non-resident parent and a notional proposed maintenance from the remaining parent with care.[20] When calculating the proposed maintenance from each parent, the assessable income of the other parent is taken into account in the same way as if both were non-resident parents (see *Example 12.7*).

The amount of the deemed non-resident parent's proposed maintenance and the notional amount of proposed maintenance from the remaining parent with care are then added together to give the joint proposed maintenance. The deemed non-resident parent is taken to have already contributed a proportion of the maintenance in kind. His assumed contribution is the proportion of the joint proposed maintenance that is equivalent to the proportion of time the children spend with him. The proportion of time the parent spends with his children is given in terms of the average number of nights per week divided by seven. The average number of nights per week does not have to be a round figure; it is calculated to two decimal figures – eg, if a deemed non-resident parent has the child one week in three, the average number of nights per week is 2.33. If there is more than one child, the total average number of nights per week is divided by the number of children – eg, if a father has one child two nights a week and another child four nights a week, the average number of nights per week is three.

This contribution in kind is then subtracted from the non-resident parent's proposed maintenance to give an adjusted proposed maintenance figure. If this produces a figure less than zero, no child maintenance is payable.[21] The non-resident parent has more than contributed his proportion of the total proposed maintenance in kind by providing a certain amount of care.

The minimum payment rule (see p168) applies to an adjusted proposed maintenance figure of between £0 and £6.80.[22] Therefore, all deemed non-resident parents calculated to pay child maintenance of up to £6.80 are exempt from the payment (as they have at least part of the family premium included in their protected income calculation).

Example 14.6: proposed maintenance

As Marcia has no assessable income, the proposed maintenance is 50 per cent of Nathan's assessable income (see *Example 14.5*):

50% x £61.77 = £30.89

This is less than the maintenance requirement of £175.86 (see *Example 14.2*), so £30.89 is the proposed maintenance.

As there is no proposed maintenance from Marcia, the joint proposed maintenance is also £30.89.

Nathan contributes a proportion of the care:

2.5 + 2.5/(7 x 2) nights in the average week = 35.71%

(2 represents the number of children for whom care is shared.)

As he contributes 35.71% of the care, he is taken as contributing 35.71% of the joint proposed maintenance in kind:

35.71% x £30.89 = £11.03

Nathan is deemed to have contributed £11.03 and is, therefore, due to pay the remainder of his proposed maintenance (if protected income allows).

Adjusted proposed maintenance = £30.89 – £11.03 = £19.86
(If the caring roles were reversed and Nathan had the children for 4.5 nights a week, the proposed maintenance from Marcia, as a deemed non-resident parent, to Nathan would be nil, as Marcia has no assessable income.)

The above example gives the most straightforward shared care situation where only the deemed non-resident parent has assessable income, but not enough to meet the maintenance requirement. See p281 for an example of the additional element calculation where both parents have assessable income.

However, any of the situations explained in Chapter 12 can apply to the assessments carried out for parents sharing care. In effect, two separate assessments are being carried out up to Step 4 to give a proposed maintenance from the deemed non-resident parent and a notional proposed maintenance from the parent with care. First, arrive at the proposed maintenance for each parent in the same way as for non-resident parents before adding together the two amounts of proposed maintenance to give the joint proposed maintenance. Only at this stage is the non-resident parent's proposed maintenance reduced in recognition of his payment in kind.

The shared care calculation is complicated, but there is a certain amount of logic to it. Both parents have a liability to maintain and, in theory, maintenance is due from each of them for the nights that the child spends with the other parent. For the child there is a notional amount of maintenance available per week. Imagine the joint proposed maintenance divided by seven to give a daily rate of maintenance. Each night of care provided is equivalent to having paid this amount of maintenance. A deemed non-resident parent has to make payments of child maintenance if the amount equivalent to the number of nights' care he contributes does not exceed his portion of the proposed maintenance.

However, the calculation can mean that the parent with a lower income who has the child for less time can end up paying maintenance to a parent with a higher income. Although this is equally true in standard cases, in cases of shared care the deemed non-resident parent may find that he does not have what he considers to be sufficient income left for those days when he is responsible for the child. In such a situation, the deemed non-resident parent on a low income will never receive any maintenance from a parent with care with a higher income. Parents may find this difficult to understand, and it may lead to competing claims for child benefit (see p268).

Step 5: protected income

Protected income is still the final stage of the calculation (see Chapter 13).[23] The deemed non-resident parent may not be able to afford the proposed adjusted maintenance. When assessing the basic protected income, the allowances for the child are adjusted as for exempt income (see p270) to represent the proportion of the average week that a child spends with the non-resident parent.[24] If there is more than one shared-care child and they spend different nights with the family, the family premium is usually included in proportion to the average number of nights per week that at least one qualifying child is in the household. However, if another child lives in the household on a full-time basis, the premium is included in full.

Example 14.7: shared care and protected income

Nathan lives on his own when his children are not with him. His rent is £60 a week and his council tax is £342 a year. He earns £240 net a week. He has Oscar and Patrick for five nights per fortnight. Can Nathan afford to pay the proposed maintenance of £19.86 (see *Example 14.6*)?

The 30% cap does not reduce the proposed maintenance as:

30% x £240 = £72

Therefore, the proposed maintenance remains at £19.86.

Basic protected income:		£	
Personal allowances	Nathan	67.50	
	Oscar	22.26	(for 2.5 days)
	Patrick	22.26	(for 2.5 days)
Family premium		6.21	(for 2.5 days)
Housing costs		60.00	
Council tax		6.58	
Margin		30.00	
Basic protected income		**214.81**	
Additional protected income:			
Total family income		240.00	(net earnings)
Less basic protected income		214.81	
Excess total family income		25.19	
(15% x £25.19)		3.78	
Total protected income		**218.59**	
(£214.81 + £3.78)			
Total family income		240.00	
Less proposed maintenance		19.86	
Disposable income		**220.14**	

This disposable income is above the total protected income level of £218.59. Nathan can pay the proposed maintenance of £19.86 a week.

3. Care shared between a parent and another person

Both the parent and the other person involved must provide day-to-day care (see p265) and live in different households. The way in which this situation is treated depends on which person with care provides day-to-day care to the lesser extent (see p268).

The parent provides care for less time

Where there are two persons with care but the one who is a parent of the child provides care for less time, for the purposes of the formula, the parent with care is deemed to be non-resident.[25] Therefore, there is no longer a parent with care, but a person with care and a deemed non-resident parent.

In most cases, the second parent will also be involved as a non-resident parent. For example, the grandmother has the child Monday night to Thursday night (the person with care), the mother has the child Friday to Sunday nights (the deemed non-resident parent) and the father has the child for only two weeks in the summer (the non-resident parent).

Both non-resident parents are liable to pay maintenance to the person with care. Therefore, two separate assessments are carried out, one for each of the liable parents, provided an effective application has been made in each case. The person with care who is actually going to receive the child maintenance cannot apply if she (eg, the grandmother) does not have parental responsibility while the deemed non-resident parent (eg, the mother) does have that responsibility (see p15).

How child maintenance is calculated

In the case of the non-resident parent who does not participate in the care of the child, the assessment is the same as it would be if there were no shared-care arrangement. The fact that the care of the child is shared between two people does not affect the amount that the non-resident parent can afford to pay. However, if an application is only made against the non-resident parent, and not the parent with care, the maintenance requirement is not halved as it would be when an application is made against one of two truly non-resident parents (see p176).[26]

At the proposed maintenance step of the calculation, the assessable income of the deemed non-resident parent is added to the actual non-resident parent's assessable income to give the parents' joint assessable income, in the same way as if both parents were truly non-resident (see p237).

The deemed non-resident parent's calculation follows that described above for a deemed non-resident parent sharing care with the other parent. The only difference is that instead of adding a notional proposed maintenance for the parent with care, the actual proposed maintenance of the non-resident parent is used to obtain joint proposed maintenance.[27] If there is no non-resident parent (eg, he has gone abroad or has died) or if the non-resident parent's assessable income is unknown (eg, he has not been traced), the deemed non-resident parent just pays child maintenance for those days for which she is not caring for the child(ren).[28]

Example 14.8: care shared between a parent to a lesser extent and another person to a greater extent

Gran, who is a widow, has Beverley (15) for four nights a week and her mother has her for the remaining three nights. As the mother looks after Beverley for less time than Gran, the mother is deemed to be non-resident. The mother has parental responsibility and receives child benefit. The mother earns £178.76 a week (net), has housing costs of £45 and travels less than 240 kilometres a week to and from work. The non-resident father earns £200 a week (net), has housing costs of £70 and also travels less than 240 kilometres a week to and from work.

The maintenance requirement is £93.18 (see *Example 9.2*).

The mother's assessable income is £32.09 a week. (When working out her exempt income, three-sevenths of the personal allowance for Beverley and three-sevenths of the family premium are included.)

The non-resident father's assessable income = £62.50

Parents' joint assessable income = £32.09 + £62.50 = £94.59

50% of joint assessable income = £47.30

This is below the maintenance requirement and, therefore, the 50 per cent calculation applies to each parent.

Father's proposed maintenance = 50% x £62.50 = £31.25

Mother's proposed maintenance = 50% x £32.09 = £16.05

Joint proposed maintenance = £31.25 + £16.05 = £47.30

The mother provides three out of seven nights' care = 42.86%

This is equivalent to paying 42.86% of £47.30 = £20.27 a week maintenance.

The mother's adjusted proposed maintenance = £16.05 – £20.27 = 0

As she is exempt from the minimum payment, she is not liable to pay any child maintenance as her contribution in kind outweighs the financial contribution.

Assuming the protected income calculation allows it, the father pays £31.25 week to the grandmother, but nothing to the mother.

See *Example 14.10* for an assessment where the parents have higher assessable incomes.

If the father emigrated or no application was made against him, the mother would pay four-sevenths of her proposed maintenance to the grandmother, assuming that the protected income calculation did not reduce this.

The mother's proposed maintenance would still be £16.05. She is still providing care three nights a week or 42.86% of the proposed maintenance in kind: 42.86% x £16.05 = £6.88

This leaves her with adjusted proposed maintenance of £16.05 – £6.88 = £9.17 a week to the grandmother. The protected income calculation has to be carried out and would include three-sevenths of Beverley's personal allowance and three-sevenths of the family premium.

Maintenance paid by a non-resident parent (who provides no care) cannot be split between two persons with care where one is a deemed non-resident parent. The entire amount of child maintenance from the non-resident parent is paid to the remaining person with care. In other words, a parent with care who shares care for the lesser amount of time can never receive child maintenance from a non-resident parent, no matter the size of the bill being paid.

This may seem illogical, particularly if the application has been made by the parent with care or if, although applications have been made by both persons with care, the application from the parent has been given priority (see p44). A parent with care who applies to the Child Support Agency (CSA) for maintenance from the non-resident parent, but ends up being deemed non-resident and paying maintenance, might therefore decide to have the assessment cancelled (see p327).

The parent provides care for more time

If a parent does a greater proportion of the caring than another person with care, she remains a parent with care for the purposes of the maintenance assessment.[29] This also applies if the parent provides care to the same extent as someone else, but the parent receives the child benefit. There is no deemed non-resident parent. Instead, there is usually a parent with care, another person with care and a non-resident parent. It can also cover the rare situation where a person cannot technically be a person with care even though s/he is providing care of at least two nights a week on average (see p19).

If only one of the persons with care has applied for a maintenance assessment, that person will receive all the child maintenance payable by the non-resident parent.[30] This also applies where both persons with care have made an application, but only one has been accepted. There is an order of priority on which applications will be accepted (see p45). It also covers cases where the second carer cannot make an application – eg, s/he does not have parental responsibility or s/he does not share a home with the child.

However, if a request is made to the CSA by *either* of the people looking after the child(ren), the child maintenance may be divided between the two of them in proportion to the day-to-day care provided.[31] The ratio of care provided does not have to be calculated on the basis of the number of nights a child spends with the carer. An alternative method could be argued for if this would give a fairer division of the maintenance (see p267).

There is no specific format needed for a request for maintenance to be divided. It is advisable to state in writing on the maintenance application form, or in a letter, that part of the maintenance should go to another person. There is no time limit for making the request.

The decision to share the child maintenance assessment between the persons with care is a discretionary decision made by the CSA. The CSA must consider the interests of the child, the current care arrangements and all representations received about the payment proposals.[32] The decision cannot be appealed.

The alternative is for the persons with care to come to a voluntary arrangement.

Example 14.9: care shared between a parent to a greater extent and another person to a lesser extent

If the caring responsibilities of the grandmother and mother in *Example 14.8* are swapped, so that the mother has Beverley for four nights a week, the calculation is as follows.

The mother now remains the parent with care and the grandmother is still a person with care. (This also applies where care is shared equally but the mother is in receipt of child benefit.)

The father's proposed maintenance remains £31.25 a week.

However, this time the mother will receive the full amount if she makes the application for maintenance and there is no request to split the payment. If there is such a request and it is granted, then the mother will receive four-sevenths (ie, £17.86) and the grandmother the remainder (ie, £13.39) a week.

4. Care shared between two people who are not parents

The situation may arise where two people living in different households each have day-to-day care (see p265) of a child of whom neither is the parent. The same rules apply as those where care is shared between a parent for the greater part of the time and another person for the rest of the time (see p278)[33] – ie, if a request is made by either person, the maintenance payable by each non-resident parent may be divided between the carers in proportion to the amount of care being provided. If no request is made, the full amount goes to the applicant.

In this situation, it is likely that there are two non-resident parents and, therefore, maintenance could be paid by both. If one of the persons with care chooses to apply for maintenance from only one of the non-resident parents, there is no reason why the second person with care cannot apply for child maintenance from the other non-resident parent.

5. Three persons with care

As a person with care has to look after the child for a minimum of two nights a week on average, there can be no more than three persons with care for any child.

However, there may be a combination of parents and others providing the care as follows (in each case, the first person provides the greatest amount of care and the third, the least).

- Parent, parent, other person – this situation is not covered specifically, although the intention must be to deem the second parent non-resident and for maintenance to be paid by him to the applicant.
- Parent, other person, parent – the second parent is deemed non-resident and maintenance is paid by him to the applicant.
- Other person, parent, parent – the first parent is deemed non-resident and maintenance is paid by him to the applicant, as well as by the second actual non-resident parent.
- Parent, other person, other person – the applicant receives maintenance from the non-resident parent or it may be apportioned on request.
- Other person, parent, other person – this is not explicitly covered, but we presume that the intention is that the parent would be deemed non-resident. There would, of course, be a second parent who is non-resident.
- Other person, other person, parent – the parent with care will be deemed non-resident and there would also be a second parent who is non-resident.
- Three other people – maintenance from both non-resident parents may be apportioned on request.

6. Care provided in part by the local authority

A local authority cannot be a person with care.[34] Therefore, if a child is in the care of the local authority for seven nights a week, no child maintenance is payable by the non-resident parents. There may be cases where a child is not being provided with care by the local authority all the time, but only for part of the time. If the care provided by the local authority amounts to less than day-to-day care (see p265), such a level of care can be ignored.

However, if the care provided by the local authority amounts to day-to-day care, child maintenance is not payable for any night when the child is in that local authority care.[35] Instead, the person with care who looks after the child for the remainder of the time receives reduced child maintenance from the non-resident parent. The maintenance payment is reduced to correspond to the number of nights per week that the child is in that person's care – eg, if the child is in local authority care for five nights a week, the person with care will receive two-sevenths of the amount of the maintenance assessment from the non-resident parent.

If there is more than one qualifying child and the local authority provides some day-to-day care for at least one of the children, again the maintenance payable is reduced.[36] For example, a person with care looks after two children: one spends the whole week with the person with care, the other child spends four nights in local authority care and three nights with the person with care. To work out the maintenance payable in these circumstances, calculate the total number of nights spent with the person with care per week, and divide this by seven times the number of qualifying children. In this case 10 (7+3) out of 14 (7x2) nights are spent with the parent with care. The maintenance payable is ten-fourteenths (or 71.43 per cent) of the maintenance assessed.

7. The maintenance requirement is met in full

The calculations described earlier in this chapter hold true when the maintenance requirement is met in full. If 50 per cent of the parents' joint assessable income is greater than the maintenance requirement, the additional element calculation has to be done. See Chapter 12.

Example 14.10: care shared by parents

This is the same family as in *Example 14.1*.

Oscar (now aged 9) now spends every other week with Nathan, while Patrick (6) still spends five days a fortnight with him. Marcia still receives child benefit for both boys and, therefore, Nathan is still deemed to be a non-resident parent of Oscar as well as Patrick. A calculation, therefore, has to be done to assess how much Nathan pays Marcia. However, in assessing Nathan's actual contribution, a notional contribution from Marcia has to be calculated.

Nathan's take-home earnings have risen to £500 a week and his superannuation contribution is now £50 a week.

Marcia has increased her hours and now earns £360 net a week. Her husband, Gareth, earns £450 net a week. Their mortgage payments are £120 a week. Their daughter Megan is two years old.

Step 1: the maintenance requirement = £175.86 (see *Example 14.2*)

Step 2: exempt income

Marcia's exempt income is as in *Example 14.4* except that Oscar's personal allowance is now included for 3.5 days (£31.17) instead of 4.5 days (£40.07), so now equals £307.31.

Nathan's exempt income:		£	
Personal allowances	Nathan	67.50	
	Oscar	31.17	(for 3.5 days)
	Patrick	22.26	(for 2.5 days)
Family premium*		8.70	(for 3.5 days)
Housing costs		60.00	
Total exempt income		**189.63**	

* The family premium is included in proportion to the average number of nights a week that care is provided for a child. In this case, Patrick stays with Nathan on nights that Oscar is there – ie, care is provided for at least one child for an average of 3.5 nights a week, and

for the other 3.5 nights Nathan is on his own. However, if the children stayed different nights, six-sevenths of the premiums would be included.[37]

Step 3: assessable income

Marcia's assessable income:		£
Net income	Earnings	360.00
Less exempt income		307.31
Assessable income		**52.69**

Nathan's assessable income:		
Net income	Earnings*	525.00
Less exempt income		189.63
Assessable income		**335.37**

* Only half of the superannuation is taken into account.

Step 4: proposed maintenance

Joint assessable income = £52.69 + £335.37 = £388.06

50% x £388.06 = £194.03.

This is above the maintenance requirement of £175.86 and, therefore, an additional element calculation must be done (see p233).

Marcia's notional proposed maintenance:

Basic element = £175.86 x £52.69/388.06 = £23.88

Basic assessable income = £23.88 x 2 = £47.76

Additional assessable income = £52.69 – £47.76 = £4.93

Additional element = 20% x £4.93 = £0.99

Notional proposed maintenance = £23.88 + £0.99 = £24.87

Nathan's proposed maintenance to Marcia:

Basic element = £175.86 x £335.37/£388.06 = £151.98

Basic assessable income = £151.98 x 2 = £303.96

Additional assessable income = £335.37 – £303.96 = £31.41

Additional element = 20% x £31.41= £6.28

Proposed maintenance = £151.98 + £6.28 = £158.26

Joint proposed maintenance = £24.87 + £158.26= £183.13

Nathan contributes in kind = $\frac{3.5 + 2.5}{7 \times 2}$ = 42.86% of the care.

This is equivalent to £78.49 (42.86% x £183.13).

Nathan's proposed maintenance after taking into account his portion of the care = £158.26 – £78.49 = **£79.77** a week.

This is below the maximum payment of £246.21.

The basic element of the maximum = £175.86 x 525/885 = £104.32

The additional element of the maximum = 1.5 [(2 x £62.33) + (2 x £17.40)] x 525/885 = £141.89 (see p235)

Step 5: protected income

This follows *Example 14.7*, except that now Nathan's income has risen, and half of Oscar's personal allowance and half the family premium are included (see p274).

There could be times when there is more than one child and because the care is shared in different ways for the different children, each parent would be the person with care for one child and the deemed non-resident parent for the other. In this case, two shared-care calculations would have to be carried out. This would happen in the situation described in the above example if Nathan were in receipt of the child benefit for Oscar.

Example 14.11: care shared between a parent and another person

Gran has Beverley (15) for four nights a week and her mother has her for the remaining three nights. The mother is, therefore, deemed to be a non-resident parent. When the mother's assessable income was £32.09 and the father's was £62.50, the mother's child maintenance liability was nil, while the father's proposed maintenance was £31.25 (see *Example 14.8*).

The mother's assessable income has increased to £140.

Joint assessable income = £140 + £62.50 = £202.50

50 per cent of joint assessable income = 50% x £202.50 = £101.25

This is above the maintenance requirement of £93.18 (see *Example 9.2*) and so an additional element calculation has to be done.

Father's proposed maintenance:

Basic element = £93.18 x £62.50/£202.50 = £28.76

Basic assessable income = £28.76 x 2 = £57.52

Additional assessable income = £62.50 – £57.52 = £4.98

Additional element = £4.98 x 15% = £0.75

Proposed maintenance = £28.76 + £0.75 = £29.51

Mother's proposed maintenance:

Basic element = £93.18 x £140/£202.50 = £64.42

Basic assessable income = £64.42 x 2 = £128.84

Additional assessable income = £140 – £128.84 = £11.16

Additional element = £11.16 x 15% = £1.67

Proposed maintenance = £64.42 + £1.67 = £66.09

Joint proposed maintenance = £29.51 + £66.09 = £95.60

The mother provides care three out of seven nights = 42.86% of the care. This is equivalent to paying 42.86% of £95.60 – ie, £40.97 a week maintenance. The mother's adjusted proposed maintenance = £66.09 – £40.97 = £25.12

Assuming the protected calculations allow these figures, Gran now receives £25.12 from the mother and £29.51 from the father, a total of £54.63 (instead of the £31.25 from the non-resident father).

If the non-resident father's assessable income had been £207 and the mother's £140 a week, again an additional element calculation would have been done.
Father's proposed maintenance would be £69.96.
Mother's proposed maintenance would be £47.31.
Joint proposed maintenance = £69.96 + £47.31 = £117.27
The mother provides care three out of seven nights = 42.86% of the care.
This is equivalent to paying 42.86% x £117.27 = £50.26 a week maintenance.
The mother, therefore, does not have to pay any maintenance as her contribution in kind (£50.26) outweighs her financial liability (£47.31). Despite the fact that her assessable income is the same, her liability has been reduced to nil as a result of the increased liability of the father.
The father still has to pay his proposed maintenance, assuming this does not bring his disposable income below the protected income level. The maintenance of £69.96 is paid to the grandmother.

Notes

1. **What is shared care**

1 Regs 20(1)(a) and 24(1)(a) CS(MASC) Regs
2 CCS/449/1995
3 R(CS) 7/08
4 Reg 1(2) CS(MASC) Regs
5 CCS/2885/2005
6 Reg 1(2) CS(MASC) Regs; CCS/6/1994
7 CCS/128/2001
8 CCS/12686/1996
9 CCS/11728/1996
10 s5(1) CSA 1991
11 s5(2) CSA 1991

2. **Care shared between separated parents**

12 Reg 20(2) and (3) CS(MASC) Regs
13 CCS/13455/1996
14 Reg 20(2)(a) CS(MASC) Regs
15 Reg 20(2)(b)(i) CS(MASC) Regs
16 Reg 20(2)(b)(ii) CS(MASC) Regs
17 Reg 9(4) CS(MASC) Regs
18 Reg 9(3) CS(MASC) Regs
19 Reg 9(1)(f) and (2)(c)(iv) CS(MASC) Regs
20 Reg 20(3) and (4) CS(MASC) Regs
21 Reg 20(5) CS(MASC) Regs
22 Reg 20(6) CS(MASC) Regs
23 Reg 20(6) CS(MASC) Regs
24 Reg 11(3) and (4) CS(MASC) Regs

3. **Care shared between a parent and another person**

25 Reg 20 CS(MASC) Regs
26 Reg 19(1) CS(MASC) Regs
27 Reg 20(4)(i) CS(MASC) Regs
28 Reg 20(4)(ii) CS(MASC) Regs
29 Reg 24(1) CS(MASC) Regs
30 Reg 24(2)(a) CS(MASC) Regs
31 Reg 24(2)(b) CS(MASC) Regs
32 Reg 24(2)(c) CS(MASC) Regs

4. **Care shared between two people who are not parents**
33 Reg 24 CS(MASC) Regs

6. **Care provided in part by the local authority**
34 Reg 51 CS(MAP) Regs
35 Reg 25 CS(MASC) Regs
36 Reg 25(3) CS(MASC) Regs

7. **The maintenance requirement is met in full**
37 Reg 9(3) and (4) CS(MASC) Regs

15

Chapter 15

Departures ('old rules')

This chapter covers:

The Child Support Agency can 'depart' from the standard formula (see Chapters 10–14) in special cases, but only once a maintenance assessment has been made (see Chapter 16).

A departure direction can only be made for one of the specified reasons (see p287), and only if it would be just and equitable to do so (see p300). Departure can mean changes to the amounts used in the standard formula to work out the assessment.

There can be no departure from a Category A or C interim maintenance assessment (IMA) (see p331).[1] A non-resident parent cannot request a departure from a Category D IMA.[2] Not all types of departure can be used with a Category D IMA where the person with care applies, or with a Category B IMA.[3]

There can be no departure if, on the date from which any departure direction would have effect (see p308):[4]

- the non-resident parent was being paid income support (IS), income-based jobseeker's allowance (JSA), income-related employment and support allowance (ESA) or pension credit (PC), or one of those benefits was being paid for him; *or*
- the person with care was being paid IS, income-based JSA, income-related ESA, PC or working tax credit, or one of those benefits was being paid for her. This only applies to a departure application by:
  - the person with care for special expenses (see p287); *or*
  - the non-resident parent on additional cases grounds (see p292).

1. Grounds for departure

Grounds for departure fall into three groups.

- **Special expenses** (see below) that the standard formula does not take into account – this is mostly used by non-resident parents.
- **Additional cases** (see p292) because of the underuse of available income/ assets or unreasonably high outgoings – this is mostly used by persons with care.
- **Property and capital transfers** made before April 1993 (see p295).

Special expenses

Departure is possible if the applicant has:[5]

- travel costs of contact with the child(ren) named in the assessment (see below);
- costs of supporting a stepchild and other children in the family (see p288);
- travel-to-work costs not taken into account in the assessment (see p290);
- costs of a long-term illness or disability (for himself or his dependant) (see p290);
- debts incurred before the couple separated (see p291); *or*
- pre-April 1993 financial commitments from which it would be impossible or unreasonable to withdraw (see p292).

The first £15 of the total of contact costs, travel-to-work cost, debts and pre-1993 financial commitments is disregarded.[6] Remember that there can be no departure for special expenses (or for any other reason) if the non-resident parent is on income support (IS), income-based jobseeker's allowance (JSA), income-related employment and support allowance (ESA) or pension credit (PC), or if the person with care is on IS or income-based JSA, income-related ESA, PC or working tax credit (WTC).

Contact costs

Only the non-resident parent's costs of contact with the child(ren) named in the assessment count.[7] The contact costs of a parent with shared care who is treated as a non-resident parent (see p268) are not treated as special expenses, and a departure would not be granted for such costs.[8]

Only travel costs count, not the cost of treats or overnight stays. Travel costs can be for the non-resident parent travelling to see the children, or the children travelling to see him. Costs incurred for the purpose of maintaining contact may include costs of some travel once the non-resident parent and child(ren) are together – eg, taking the child from the person with care's home to the non-resident parent's home. However, the cost of travel to, for example, the cinema from the person with care's home will not normally be considered.

Only the following count as travel costs:[9]

- the cost of a ticket by public transport – eg, train, coach, boat or plane;
- the cost of fuel by private vehicle – there is no allowance for repairs;
- the cost of taxi fares, but only for a non-resident parent whose disability or illness makes it impracticable for him to use another form of available transport.[10] Any financial assistance he receives towards contact costs is offset from the fare.[11]

Minor incidental costs also count. These may include bridge tolls, parking and ticket reservation fees.[12]

The costs are based on an established pattern of visits if one exists.[13] If there is no established pattern, the non-resident parent and person with care must have agreed a pattern of future contact. This will be used.[14]

The Child Support Agency (CSA) can decide that contact costs are unreasonably high or unreasonably incurred – eg, because the method of travel is too expensive, and may substitute lower amounts than those provided.

Where visits are frequent, the CSA may only allow travel costs of some of them. The CSA must allow enough costs for visits specified in a court order, as long as those visits are being made.[15] Non-resident parents who visit more often than the court order states may wish to change the order to reflect the true position.

Changes in contact may mean changes in any departure direction. If contact stops, even through no fault of the non-resident parent, the departure direction will be cancelled.[16]

The first £15 of these costs (or the total of these and other costs) is disregarded.

Costs of supporting a stepchild

If a non-resident parent or person with care supports a child who is part of her/his household (see p21), but of whom s/he is not the parent (see p15), an amount for those costs may be allowed.[17] This amount is set by a formula. This ground cannot be used by a departure applicant subject to a Category B interim maintenance assessment (IMA).[18]

A 'stepchild' is one who:[19]

- counts as a member of the applicant's family – ie:
  - a child of the applicant's current partner; *or*
  - a child of the applicant's former partner who lives in the applicant's household every night of the week;
- was part of the applicant's family and household before 5 April 1993; *and*
- remained part of that family and household from 5 April 1993 continuously to the effective date of the proposed departure direction (see p308).[20]

The effect of these conditions is that there will be very few children who can still be classed as 'stepchildren' for these purposes.

The expenses allowed depend on the support for the stepchild from her/his non-resident parent and, if the applicant's partner is the child's parent, from that partner. The **cost** of the stepchild is based on the amount excluded from exempt income and is the:[21]

- IS personal allowance for a child of that age; *plus*
- IS family premium if the family contains no children of whom the applicant is the parent. Where special expenses are sought for more than one stepchild, the family premium is divided equally between them;[22] *plus*
- IS disabled child premium if the stepchild would qualify.

If the care of the stepchild is shared between the applicant's current partner and the stepchild's other parent, the cost is reduced by the proportion of time the child spends away from the applicant's household.[23]

No expenses are allowed if maintenance payable to or for the stepchild by her/his non-resident parent is more than the cost of supporting the stepchild, whether the maintenance is a deduction from his benefits (see p170) *or* is under an order or written agreement for maintenance or a maintenance assessment.[24] The CSA can ignore maintenance payable (but not deductions due) if, for example, the stepchild's non-resident parent cannot be found.[25]

If maintenance is less than the cost, the **allowable amount** is the cost less any maintenance payable (unless ignored) or deductions.[26]

If the applicant's partner is *not* the stepchild's parent, the maximum special expenses allowed is the allowable amount.[27]

Where special expenses are sought for stepchildren of different parents, a separate allowable amount is worked out for each child (or group of children who have the same parents), and the allowable amount is the total of those amounts.[28]

If the applicant's partner is the stepchild's parent, her ability to support the child is taken into account in a similar way to the joint child calculation for exempt income (see p198). Her **net income** is worked out as if it were a non-resident parent's assessable income (see Chapter 11) plus child benefit for the stepchildren and any income the stepchildren have (except earnings) above £10.[29] Her **outgoings** are:[30]

- the IS personal allowance for a person aged 25 or over (regardless of the partner's actual age); *plus*
- the amount of any reduction in the applicant's exempt income because the partner can contribute to the costs of a joint child, as assumed under the standard formula (see p198); *plus*
- the allowable amount (see above); *plus*
- any partner's contribution to housing costs assumed under an existing departure direction (see p294).

If the partner's net income is more than her outgoings, no costs are allowed.[31] If it is less, maximum special expenses are the allowable amount.[32]

The definition of a 'stepchild' for these purposes means that there are likely to be very few cases where a new departure application on this ground could be made. For an example of how the costs of supporting a stepchild affect an assessment, see previous editions of this *Handbook*.

Travel-to-work costs

If the travel-to-work costs of a non-resident parent or person with care are not adequately covered by the broad-brush allowance in the formula (see p196), a departure can be made. As the formula allowance works on straight-line distances, those who travel around estuaries or mountains, or are in rural areas may benefit. Those whose reasonable public transport costs are more than 6 pence per straight-line kilometre may also benefit. Self-employed people can benefit for travel costs which are not tax-deductible.[33]

Travel costs allowable are the same as for contact costs (see p287), except that taxi fares are allowable regardless of disability, but only if the journey is unavoidably taken at a time when no other reasonable type of transport is available.[34] Minor incidental costs count. Costs can be reduced or refused where they are considered high or unreasonably incurred.[35]

The travel cost special expenses allowance replaces the formula allowance (see p196). There is a £15 disregard on the total of travel-to-work costs and certain other special expenses (see p287). Disabled people's parking costs should be claimed as costs of a long-term disability, rather than travel-to-work costs (see p287), in order to avoid the disregard.

Example 15.1

Steve (see *Example 10.4*) has an allowance of £64.98 included in his exempt income for travel to work. However, Steve's season ticket to London is £5,100 a year, or £98 a week. Even with the first £15 disregarded, this is greater than the allowance. The departure decision maker has decided that a direction is reasonable because Steve lives in Leicestershire in order to be near his two children and he has not been able to find an equivalent job nearer to home. The special expense of £83 replaces the broad-brush allowance of £64.98. See *Example 15.3* for the recalculated assessment.

Costs of a long-term illness or disability

Special expenses include costs of a long-term illness or disability of the non-resident parent or person with care and/or his/her dependant(s).[36] Long-term illness is one that is current at the date of the departure application and which is likely to last for a further 52 weeks or to be terminal.[37] 'Dependant' means:[38]

- the departure applicant's partner (see p25);
- a child (see p18) of the applicant or partner, living with the applicant, except a child named in the assessment to which the departure application applies (see also p30 for additional maintenance).

Costs allowable are the reasonable costs of:[39]

- personal care, attendance and communication needs;
- mobility;
- domestic help;
- medical aids which cannot be provided under the NHS;[40]
- heating, clothing and laundry;
- food essential for a diet recommended by a medical practitioner;
- adaptations to the applicant's home; *and*
- day care, respite care and rehabilitation.

Any financial help towards these costs from any source is deducted.[41] This includes disability living allowance (DLA) and attendance allowance (AA). If a DLA/AA claim has been made, the CSA will wait for that decision before deciding on departure.[42] If no claim has been made, but the CSA considers that the disabled person may be entitled, the CSA will notify the applicant, who has six weeks in which to claim. If no claim is made, the CSA deducts the highest rate of the appropriate component(s) of DLA (or AA if appropriate) from the costs.[43] The CSA has discretion to ignore DLA/AA awarded to a dependant of the applicant.[44] Applicants may want to ensure that this is considered.

Debts of the relationship

A non-resident parent or person with care may be repaying debts incurred *before* the non-resident parent became a non-resident parent (see p21) of the child named in the assessment (whether before or after April 1993). Repayments can count as special expenses, but only if the debt was incurred when the departure applicant and ex-partner were a couple (see p25) and was for the benefit of:[45]

- the departure applicant and an ex-partner, jointly;
- the ex-partner alone, if the applicant is liable for the repayments;
- a child (see p18) of the applicant and/or ex-partner, who lived with the applicant and ex-partner at the time the debt arose; *and/or*
- a child named in the assessment to which the departure application applies.

Ex-partner includes any ex-partner of the non-resident parent (not just the parent with care), but, if the person with care applies for departure, only the non-resident parent counts as an ex-partner.[46]

Loans only count if they are from a bank, building society or other registered lender, or from the departure applicant's current or former employer.[47] The following do *not* count as debts:

- debts incurred to buy something that the applicant kept after the relationship ended;[48]
- a debt for which the applicant took responsibility under a financial settlement with the ex-partner or a court order;[49]
- secured mortgage repayments; *and*

- endowment/insurance premiums,[50] except for mortgage/insurance incurred to buy or repair/improve (see p185)[51] the home of the parent with care and child named in the assessment.

The following also do *not* count as debts:[52]

- debts of a business or trade;
- gambling debts;
- legal costs of the separation, divorce or dissolution of a civil partnership;
- credit card repayments;
- overdrafts, unless taken out for a specified amount repayable over a specified period;
- fines imposed on the applicant;
- any debt incurred to pay off one of these (except for business/trade debts); *or*
- any other debt the CSA considers it reasonable to exclude.

Debts incurred to pay off a debt which would have counted also count.[53] However, any direction is based upon the repayment period and rate of the original debt.[54]

The first £15 of the total of allowable debts of the relationship and certain other special expenses is disregarded (see p287).

Any departure direction is for the debt repayment period.[55] If the applicant cannot meet the repayments, the direction can be extended, but only if the creditor agreed to extend time for repayment because of:[56]

- the applicant's unemployment or incapacity for work; *or*
- a substantial fall in the applicant's income.

Pre-April 1993 financial commitments

Special expenses can include other financial commitments of the non-resident parent – eg, hire purchase or school fees. Commitments like those on p291 do not count. The only commitments that count are those:[57]

- made before 5 April 1993;
- from which it would be impossible or unreasonable to withdraw; *and*
- where an order or written agreement for maintenance was made before 5 April 1993 for all the non-resident parent's children (see p18) (including at least one child named in the assessment) *and* that order/agreement was in force on both the date the commitment was made and on 5 April 1993.[58] There can be more than one order/agreement for different children.

The effect of these conditions is that there are likely to be relatively few cases where a new departure application on this ground could be made.

Additional cases

This can be used by a person with care who is not a parent. However, for convenience, we refer to 'parent'.

Grounds for departure are if:[59]

- a parent's lifestyle is inconsistent with the level of her/his income;
- a parent's assets could produce some or more income;
- a parent has diverted her/his income so it is not taken into account in the formula;
- the housing costs used in the formula are unreasonably high;
- it is reasonable for a parent's partner to contribute towards the couple's housing costs;
- travel-to-work costs used in the formula are unreasonably high; *or*
- travel-to-work costs should be disregarded completely.

There can be no departure on additional cases grounds if the non-resident parent is on IS or income-based JSA *or* if he is the departure applicant and the person with care is on IS, income-based JSA, income-related ESA, PC or WTC. However, it is possible that information about undeclared income will be passed to Jobcentre Plus (see p73) and/or the case referred to the CSA to consider whether there is notional income (see p220).

Example 15.2

A non-resident parent has a large well-furnished house in a stockbroker belt, with several cars in the drive and a lifestyle which suggests wealth. He is a director of his own company and pays a modest salary to himself and to his new partner. His declared income is only a few pounds above the mortgage so the assessment is nil. He is not subject to the excessive housing cost rule (see p190) nor to the minimum payment (see p168) as the couple have a child. The person with care could seek a departure on the grounds that:

– the non-resident parent's lifestyle is incompatible with his declared income;

– the non-resident parent's partner should contribute to housing costs; *and*

– the housing costs are unreasonably high.

If the new partner does not do much work for the business, the non-resident parent's income may have been unreasonably diverted to her.

Lifestyle inconsistent with income

Departure is possible where a parent's overall lifestyle requires substantially higher income than the amount of her/his income on which the maintenance assessment is based.[60] This cannot be done if the lifestyle is paid for:[61]

- from the parent's capital; *or*
- by her/his partner, unless the parent can influence the amount of the partner's income – eg, as employer. If s/he cannot, the CSA can consider whether the partner could contribute to housing costs (see p294).[62]

The CSA is unlikely to investigate a parent's lifestyle. If there appear to be grounds for investigation, it may refer the case to the First-tier Tribunal, which could direct the parties to provide evidence (see Chapter 18).

If departure is directed, notional extra income will be set (see p306).

Under-use of assets

A parent may be under-using her/his money or property. Departure can only happen if the total value of the assets found to be under-used (less any mortgage or charge) is £10,000 or more.[63] This can apply if s/he is the beneficiary of, or can control:[64]

- an asset which does not produce income but could do so;
- an investment producing less income than is reasonable;
- a claim to money (eg, a debt or legal action) which it is reasonable to enforce; *and/or*
- an asset which it would be reasonable to sell.

This also applies to any trust funds of which the parent is a beneficiary.[65]

The CSA can ignore assets which are to be used for a reasonable purpose.[66] The parent's home is not normally treated as an asset for the purpose of this ground, but any second or holiday home could be considered.

If an under-used asset exists, any departure direction will set the notional extra income which the asset could produce. The asset is assumed to produce income at the judgment rate: currently 8 per cent.[67] Any actual income from the asset is deducted from that notional income.

Diversion of income

Departure is possible where a parent can control her/his income *and* has unreasonably reduced her/his income (as worked out for the standard formula) by diverting it to other people or other purposes.[68] For example, a non-resident parent's company pays him no salary but pays his partner an inflated one.

Unreasonable housing costs

If a parent's housing costs are more than the amount normally allowed under the formula but s/he is exempt from that restriction (see p190), departure is possible if those costs are unreasonably high.[69] Departure only removes the exemption, so weekly housing costs still cannot be set at less than £80 or half the parent's net income, whichever is greater.[70]

Partner's contribution towards housing costs

Departure is possible if a parent has a partner who occupies the home and it is reasonable for that partner to contribute towards housing costs.[71] The CSA will decide what proportion the partner should pay, considering the parent's income and the partner's income.[72] This can be 100 per cent, especially if a Category B

IMA is in force and/or the parent is withholding information about her/his partner's income.[73]

Unreasonable travel-to-work costs/allowance

Departure is possible if travel costs allowed under the formula (see p196):

- are unreasonably high – eg, the parent shares a car;[74] *or*
- should not be allowed because the parent can pay maintenance assessed without an allowance for part or all of those costs.[75]

Property and capital transfers

The broad-brush formula allowance for pre-1993 property transfers (see p192) may not result in a proper reflection of the effect of that transfer in the amount of child support maintenance. Also, some parents cannot use that allowance – eg, because of lack of evidence. Departure allows for a more flexible approach. Property is not defined (as it is for the broad-brush allowance – see p192) so it includes things such as household items and shares. It is not a ground for departure, however, from a Category D IMA.[76]

Departure is possible if:[77]

- before 5 April 1993 a court order or written agreement was in force between the non-resident parent and the person with care and/or the child(ren) named in the assessment; *and*
- in connection with that order/agreement, property which the non-resident parent owned (or had the benefit of) was transferred to that person with care or that child, or to a trust for payment of the normal day-to-day living expenses of that child; *and either:*
  - that transfer reduced the non-resident parent's maintenance liability (not child support) *and* the effect of that transfer is not properly reflected in the current maintenance assessment; *or*
  - that transfer did *not* reduce the non-resident parent's maintenance liability (not child support) *but* the current maintenance assessment is reduced because of that transfer *and* that reduction is inappropriate because of the purpose of the transfer – eg, it was for spousal maintenance.

No departure can be made if:

- the change in maintenance would be less than £1;[78] *or*
- the transfer was temporary and ends before the effective date of the direction.[79]

To see if the broad-brush property allowance fairly reflects the child maintenance foregone, the CSA first works out the value of the transfer, ignoring any part which was not in lieu of child maintenance. Unless there is evidence to show otherwise, the CSA assumes that:[80]

- the property covered by the order/agreement was held in equal shares by the non-resident parent and person with care;

- if those parties had been married, half of the value of the transfer was for the person with care's benefit, and not for the child(ren);
- if those parties were *never* married, *none* of the value of the transfer was for the person with care's benefit.

The equivalent weekly value is then worked out. The number of years of liability is deemed to begin on the date of the order/agreement and to end on the date it sets for maintenance to end (for the youngest child if there is more than one), or, if no date is given, when the youngest child reaches 18.[81] Using that figure and the interest rate on judgment debts at the date of the order/agreement, a multiplier is given by a table.[82] That gives an equivalent weekly value which replaces the broad-brush allowance (see p192). If that would lead to a departed assessment of less than the child maintenance payable under the order/agreement, a lower weekly value can be set. The weekly value of a transfer of less than £5,000 is nil.[83]

The result is difficult to predict (see p305). The assessment may be increased or reduced, irrespective of who applied for departure.

2. Applying for departure

Once an assessment has been made, a person with care, non-resident parent or child applicant in Scotland may apply for a departure direction.[84] This applies to any assessment – whether made on initial application or after a revision or supersession – but not to all categories of interim maintenance assessment. Information about departure is provided with an assessment.

The Child Support Agency (CSA) can provide an application form on request, or a letter can be accepted if it has all the information required by the form.[85] The applicant should fill in the form as fully as possible. The date of the application is the date it is received by the CSA, unless there was unavoidable delay.[86] The date of the application affects the effective date of any direction (see p308).

If the application is not accepted because it is not properly made, the CSA can send it back (or send a form) to the applicant. If it is properly made within 14 days of the day the CSA sends it back, it counts as made when the defective application was made.[87]

An application cannot be made before the assessment is made.[88] Even if the reason for departure is in the maintenance application form or maintenance enquiry form, a separate application must still be made.

A departure applicant can be represented by any other person.[89]

A departure application can be withdrawn or amended by the applicant at any time before it is decided.[90] S/he may want to do this after seeing the other party's information. However, a person considering applying may want to try to work out what any departure would be *before* applying. This is because a departure may work against the applicant.

3. Procedure

Departure applications on several grounds or by both parties will be considered together to ensure that the outcome is just and equitable (see p300). Each party may have a departure direction granted (on multiple grounds) and applied to the assessment.

Preliminary consideration

The decision maker will carry out a preliminary consideration of each application before asking the other party for information.[91] If the application has no chance of success, it will be refused.[92]

The Child Support Agency (CSA) may ask the applicant for further information, which must be provided within one month (longer may be allowed if the CSA is satisfied that this is reasonable).[93] If it is not, and the decision maker is satisfied on the available evidence that a departure direction should not be given, the application may be refused without the other party being asked for information.[94]

Because the decision maker wants the assessment to be correct *before* departure is considered, s/he may pass the case to other CSA staff for revision or supersession before completing the preliminary consideration (see p309).

There is a right of appeal against refusal on preliminary consideration (see p311).

If the case passes the preliminary consideration, but the decision maker considers that a direction is unlikely to be given, s/he can decide the application without asking the other party for information.[95] However, if the decision maker then considers a direction should be made, s/he must ask for that information before making a decision (see below).[96]

Information

If the application passes the preliminary consideration, the CSA must (unless a direction is unlikely to be made) write to the other party (or parties if the maintenance application was by a Scottish child):[97]

- notifying her/him that the departure application has been made;
- sending details of the grounds for the application and any relevant information the applicant has given (but see below); *and*
- asking for representations about the application to be made within 14 days.[98]

If representations are sent, the CSA may send them to the applicant asking for comments.[99] However, this is only likely to happen if the evidence provided by another party contradicts that supplied by the applicant and the CSA cannot make a decision based on the evidence available. The contradictory evidence may then be copied to the other party for comments.[100] Any party can send further information to the CSA at any time. If a response cannot be made within 14 days, the information available should be sent with a request for more time to provide the rest. The CSA is unlikely to make its own enquiries, so each party must make their own case. (See Chapter 4 for further detail on the requirements and expectations for the CSA to investigate matters.) On appeal, the First-tier Tribunal can require information to be provided (see Chapter 18).

If one party does not know the whereabouts of another party or a child named in the maintenance assessment and that party has not agreed to disclosure, that address and any information which could reasonably be expected to lead to her/him being located will not be disclosed unless:[101]

- that address/information is necessary to decide the departure application; *and*
- there is no risk of harm or undue distress to that party/child if disclosure were made.

Undisclosed medical evidence will not be sent to a person if it would harm her/his health.[102]

Regular payments condition

If a non-resident parent applies for departure, the CSA can impose a regular payments condition (RPC).[103] This is intended to ensure that a non-resident parent does not use the fact that there is an outstanding departure application as a reason for not making regular payments of child support. An RPC will only normally be imposed if the non-resident parent has persistently failed to pay maintenance due, and only once the application has passed a preliminary consideration (see p297). A person with care who knows a departure application has been made can ask the CSA to make an RPC.

Consideration of an RPC may be initiated by the CSA debt management section, but the decision maker decides whether to impose it and the rate at which it should be paid. An RPC will usually be set at the rate of the current assessment.[104] The exception is where the departure application is for special expenses for travel costs, contact costs or illness/disability.[105] If this applies, the RPC will be set for a lower amount on the assumption that a departure direction has been made for those expenses, unless the non-resident parent has exaggerated or claimed unreasonable expenses.[106]

The CSA notifies the non-resident parent and person with care of any RPC and the effect of failing to comply.[107] If the non-resident parent fails to comply, he will usually be contacted and the RPC may be renegotiated.

If this does not work, the CSA can decide that the non-resident parent has failed to comply with the RPC. Written notice of this is sent to the non-resident parent and person with care. If the CSA decides that the non-resident parent has failed to comply with the RPC within 28 days of the notice, the departure application lapses.[108]

An RPC does not affect the amount of maintenance the non-resident parent is *liable* to pay. Even if he complies with the RPC, if this is less than the amount of the current assessment, there will be arrears if the departure application fails (see p402).

The RPC will end once the departure decision has been made or the application withdrawn.[109]

Revision or supersession of the assessment

A departure application can be made even if a revision or supersession of the existing assessment has been applied for.[110] An assessment can also be revised or superseded while a departure application is being considered. In a case where a fresh assessment is made on a revision or supersession, the decision maker may direct that the departure application lapse, unless the applicant asks for it to stand.[111] See Chapter 17 for revisions and supersessions.

If the application shows a ground for changing the assessment (eg, a mistake or a change of circumstances), the case will be considered for revision or supersession.

If an assessment is revised or superseded (see p309), the departure decision maker treats that fresh assessment as the current assessment when considering departure.

Decision on the application

If the decision maker decides the application (rather than referring it to the First-tier Tribunal), s/he must notify the parties of that decision and the reasons for it.[112] If the decision is to make a direction, the notification must state the way in which maintenance is to be worked out as a result. The CSA will then make a new assessment, taking into account the instructions in the departure direction (see p301). The decision on the departure direction and the maintenance assessment after the departure is taken into account can both be appealed. It is, therefore, important to be clear which decision is being appealed to the First-tier Tribunal. For more information on appeals, see Chapter 18.

Referral to the First-tier Tribunal

Once a departure application has passed the preliminary consideration and the parties' representations have been sought, a decision maker can refer it to the First-tier Tribunal instead of deciding it her/himself.[113] Although many departure cases are complex or difficult, they should normally be decided by a decision maker. A referral might be made if, for example:

- the case raises new points – ie, ones which have never arisen in a departure case before; *or*

- the case is very contentious – eg, both parties have solicitors and the evidence is completely contradictory; *or*
- only the First-tier Tribunal will be able to obtain the necessary evidence.

The First-tier Tribunal is subject to the rules which apply to a decision maker and will either give a direction or refuse to give one.[114] However, the procedure is similar to an appeal and the Tribunal's decision can be appealed on a point of law (see Chapter 18).

4. Considering departure

A departure direction can only be made if it would change the amount of the assessment by £1 or more.[115] The possible effect of 'old rules' phasing-in (see p322) is ignored.[116]

Discretion to make a direction

When considering whether and how to make a direction, the departure decision maker must:[117]

- treat parents as responsible for maintaining their children when they can afford to do so;
- treat parents as responsible for maintaining all their children equally;
- ignore the fact that all, or part, of the income of the person with care (or her partner) includes (or would, on departure, include) income support, income-based jobseeker's allowance, income-related employment and support allowance, pension credit, working tax credit, housing benefit or council tax benefit.

Just and equitable

Even though the grounds for departure are met and the assessment would change by £1 or more, a direction will only be made if it would be just and equitable to do so – ie, fair to all concerned.[118] The CSA must reach a positive conclusion on the evidence that it would be just and equitable to make the direction. It is not enough, in the absence of information on relevant matters, simply to conclude that there is no reason why it should not be just and equitable to make it.[119] The decision maker first works out what direction would be appropriate and how it would affect the assessment. When considering whether it would be fair to make that direction, the decision maker must consider:[120]

- the financial circumstances of the non-resident parent, including any liability to pay maintenance before the assessment's effective date;
- the financial circumstances of the person with care (but ignore her receipt of certain benefits);

- whether a direction would lead to the non-resident parent or person with care giving up employment;[121]
- if the application is for special expenses, whether the applicant could have made financial arrangements to cover those expenses, or could pay for them from money s/he is spending on non-essentials.

This may mean taking into account circumstances for which either party could have sought a direction, even if s/he did not. For example, since contact costs have an effect on the financial circumstances of the non-resident parent, it may be just and equitable to take these into account when deciding on departure, even if the departure application was about something else (and may have been made by the person with care).[122] However, if such circumstances are taken into account, it must be made clear to all parties on what basis the departure has been decided.

The decision maker must *not* take into account:

- the circumstances of the child's conception;
- the reasons for the breakdown of the relationship;
- the fact that either party is now involved in a new relationship;
- any contact arrangements;
- the failure of the non-resident parent to pay maintenance under the Child Support Agency (CSA) assessment or any previous arrangement; *nor*
- any representations made by a person other than the person with care, the non-resident parent or a Scottish child applicant.

Discretion should only rarely be used to refuse a departure direction outright. However, it may be used to reduce the amount of the direction. Both parties are seen as responsible for organising their lives so as to support their children. If parties have unreasonably taken on new responsibilities, failed to reduce outgoings (eg, reschedule debts) or failed to increase their income (eg, through work), the CSA may decide that it is not just and equitable for a departure direction to be made.

5. The departure direction

A direction is not a new assessment; it is a direction to reassess child maintenance on a different basis.[123] The Child Support Agency (CSA) must comply as soon as reasonably practicable.[124]

The direction cannot take maintenance above the formula maximum (see p235) or below the £6.80 weekly minimum (see p168).[125] A non-resident parent cannot fall below the protected income level (see Chapter 13), though the direction may change that level.[126]

Phased assessments

If the assessment is being phased in (see p322), special rules apply. If the effective date of the departure direction (see p308) is the *same* as that of the assessment, the direction is applied to the formula assessment.[127] The CSA then applies any phasing to that departed assessment.

If the effective date of the departure direction is *later* than that of the assessment, the direction is applied to the formula assessment. This proposed departed assessment is then compared with both the formula assessment and the phased assessment. If the proposed departed assessment is:[128]

- higher than the formula assessment, the difference between them is added to the phased assessment to give the actual departed assessment;
- less than the formula assessment but more than the phased assessment, departure has no effect and the phased assessment is used; *or*
- less than the phased assessment, the proposed departed assessment is used.

Special expenses directions

The direction states an amount for special expenses. The CSA includes this in the applicant's exempt income and any protected income.[129] Expenses for a stepchild do not change protected income because they are already included (see p258).[130] If the direction is for travel-to-work costs (see p290), any amount for those already included in exempt income or protected income is replaced by the amount stated in the direction.[131]

If the direction reduces the non-resident parent's assessable income, the departed assessment is *the lowest of*: [132]

- the assessment current on the direction's effective date (see p308);
- 50 per cent of his assessable income after departure (see Chapter 11); *or*
- the protected income level (see Chapter 13). This applies regardless of the maintenance requirement or the number of children.

If the direction would also change the figures to be used because of over-generous provision (see p292), the same calculation is done assuming those changes have taken effect.[133] For the rules if a direction for property/capital transfer is also made, see p305.

If a non-resident parent is liable to more than one person with care (see p239), his total liability is set by these rules.[134] The amount of each departed assessment will be the same proportion of total liability as it would be if liability were based on the maintenance requirements.[135]

Example 15.3: special expenses – debts and travel costs

Steve has been assessed to pay £59.26 a week to Debbie as maintenance for Paul (17), Grace (15) and Lewis (10). In July 2008, Steve applies for departure on the grounds of travel-to-work costs, debts of the relationship and pre-April 1993 commitments. He does not apply on the ground of the property settlement (see *Example 10.3*) as he wants first to ask his solicitor whether it would be to his advantage.

Steve is awarded special expenses of £83 travel-to-work costs (see *Example 15.1*). He divorced in 1991 and has already cleared some debts, but there remains one debt of the relationship and another commitment pre-dating the divorce. The total repayments amount to £34.60 a week: there is no £15 disregard as this has already been applied to the travel costs.

Debbie has net earnings of £300 and assessable income of £28.11. These were taken into account under the formula but, on departure, Steve simply pays 50 per cent of his own assessable income (as long as this is below the current assessment).

Steve's exempt income:		£
Personal allowance		67.50
Mortgage (in full – see *Example 10.4*)		96.00
Property settlement allowance		40.00
Travel-to-work costs		83.00
Debt repayments		34.60
Total		**321.10**
Steve's net income for child support purposes		380.00
Steve's assessable income		**58.90**
(£380 – £321.10)		
Proposed maintenance		**29.45**
(50% x £58.90)		
Protected income:		
Personal allowance	Couple	105.95
Mortgage (interest only)		78.46
Council tax		15.00
Travel-to-work costs		83.00
Debt repayments		34.60
Standard margin		30.00
Basic protected income		**347.01**

Total family income: Steve's new wife, Lisa, has net earnings of £280, so total family income = £380 + £280 = £660. This is far above protected income so Steve can afford the proposed maintenance of £29.45.

The departure direction has, therefore, reduced the assessment from £59.26 to £29.45. Because the 50 per cent taper applies right up the income range, there comes a point where a non-resident parent's income is too high to benefit from departure (see *Example 15.4*).

Example 15.4: special expenses and people with higher incomes

Jeremy has been assessed to pay £311.86 a week for his four children (see *Example 12.3*). He applies for departure for contact costs. The children stay with Jeremy every other weekend. He collects and returns them in his car. This is cheaper than four return train fares: the petrol used is £112 a weekend. As this is £56 a week, the £15 disregard leaves a special expense of £41.

Jeremy's exempt income is increased by £41.

His assessable income would be now £659 (instead of £700).

The proposed maintenance after the departure would be: 50% x £659 = £329.50. As this is higher than the current maintenance assessment of £311.86, no departure direction is given.

If, instead, Jeremy had net income of £1,050 a week and assessable income of £592.70 a week, the current assessment would be:

Basic element = maintenance requirement = £273.72 (see p233)

Basic assessable income = 2 x £273.72 = £547.44

Additional assessable income = £592.70 – £547.44 = £45.26

Additional element = £45.26 x 25% = £11.32

Proposed maintenance = £273.72 + £11.32 = £285.04

This is below the 30% protected income figure (£315), so the assessment is £285.04.

If Jeremy were awarded special expenses of £41, his assessable income would be £592.70 – £41 = £551.70.

Proposed maintenance = 50% x £551.70 = £275.85, which is less than the previous assessment of £285.04.

The protected income needs checking again as special expenses are now included:

	£
Personal allowance	67.50
Mortgage (interest only)	123.08
Council tax	21.00
Travel-to-contact costs	41.00
Standard margin	30.00
Basic protected income	**282.58**

His total family income = £1,050 net earnings

Excess income = £1,050 – £282.58 = £767.42

15% x £767.42= £115.11

Total protected income = £282.58 + £115.11 = £397.69

Jeremy can, therefore, afford to pay the £275.85 assessment without his disposable income falling below £397.69 a week.

Even if Evie applies for departure for excessive housing costs, none can be made because these are less than half Jeremy's net income.

Property/capital transfer directions

The direction states the weekly value of the transfer (see p295). Any property settlement allowance in exempt income (see p192) is removed, even if the weekly value is nil.[136] Proposed maintenance (see Chapter 12) is then reduced by the amount of any transfer value and the protected income level worked out again.[137] Maintenance payable cannot be below the £6.80 minimum (see p168).[138]

If a special expenses direction is also made, any property settlement allowance is removed from assessable income and the special expenses calculation is then carried out (see p302).[139] The result is then reduced by the transfer value (if any).[140]

If a non-resident parent is liable to more than one person with care (see p239), the transfer value is deducted from the assessment for the person with care or for the child for whom the transfer was made.[141]

The removal of the allowance from exempt income continues after the direction ends because it has compensated for the transfer.[142]

Where the transfer was to trustees and the weekly value is more than nil, any child maintenance from that trust is disregarded from the parent with care's assessable income.[143]

Example 15.5: property transfer direction

Hamish and Kirsty divorced in February 1993 when their only child, Angus, was two. At the time the departure is requested, Angus is over the age of 16. The house, then worth £31,000, was transferred to Kirsty with a mortgage of about £9,000. From April 1995, Kirsty's assessment was reduced when Hamish was given an allowance of £40 in his exempt income. Kirsty has remarried, has a baby and has no net income of her own. Hamish is single.

The current assessment is:

	£
Maintenance requirement	59.43
Hamish's exempt income:	
Personal allowance	67.50
Housing costs	45.00
Property settlement allowance	40.00
Total	**152.50**

Hamish's net income = £205 a week net earnings

Assessable income = £205 – £152.50 = £52.50

Proposed maintenance = £52.50 x 50% = £26.25 (less than the maintenance requirement)

Protected income shows that Hamish can afford this.

The purpose of the capital transfer was unspecified. Kirsty believes it was in lieu of spousal maintenance foregone and to provide a home for Angus. Hamish also had to pay £15 a week under a court order as maintenance for Angus. The departure decision maker decides that the property transfer in lieu of child maintenance was £6,000. Given that Angus was to be dependent for at least another 14 years from the date of the order, a transfer of

£6,000 does not amount to £20 a week child maintenance in advance as implied by the £40 allowance.

No date was set in the order for maintenance payment to end, so it is deemed to end when Angus turns 18. The number of years of liability is, therefore, 16. The interest rate for judgment debt was 14 per cent at the time of the order, so the table gives a multiplier of 0.00320: £6,000 x 0.00320 = £19.20. This is, therefore, the equivalent weekly value.

Hamish's exempt income = £67.50 + £45.00 = £112.50

Hamish's net income = £205 a week net earnings

Assessable income = £205 – £112.50 = £92.50

Proposed maintenance = (£92.50 x 50%) = £46.25 (less than the maintenance requirement of £59.43)

Therefore, proposed maintenance is £46.25.

Protected income shows that Hamish can afford this.

The amount under the departure direction is then deducted: £46.25 – £19.20 = £27.05

If Hamish's net income is £315, but exempt income the same (£152.50), the current assessment would be:

Assessable income = £315 – £152.50 = £162.50

£162.50 x 50% = £81.25 (more than maintenance requirement of £59.43)

Therefore, proposed maintenance =

£59.43 + 15% x (£162.50 – (£59.43 x 2)) = £59.43 + £6.55 = £65.98

Protected income shows that Hamish can afford this.

With a property transfer direction of £19.20 (where the £40 allowance in exempt income does not apply).

Assessable income = £315 – £112.50 = £202.50

Proposed maintenance = £59.43 + 15% x (£202.50 – (£59.43 x 2)) = £59.43 + £12.55 = £71.98

The amount under the departure direction is deducted:

£71.98 – £19.20 = £52.78

The departure has, in fact, ended up reducing the assessment by £13.20 (£65.98 – £52.78).

Additional cases directions

If departure is on the grounds of *lifestyle inconsistent with income*, *under-use of assets* or *diversion of income*, the direction states a figure of notional income to be added to net income (see p204) and so is also included in the income figures used in the protected income calculations (see p249).[144]

If *housing costs are unreasonably high*, the direction states the costs that are considered reasonable, and this replaces actual housing costs for exempt income (see p184) and protected income (see p253).[145] The limit of half income/£80 still applies.

If the *partner is to contribute to housing costs*, the direction states the proportion of costs by which housing costs are to be reduced (which may be 100 per cent).[146] Housing costs are reduced by that proportion for exempt income, but not for protected income (see p253). If the direction also states that housing costs are unreasonably high, housing costs used in exempt income are reasonable costs reduced by the stated proportion. The limit of half income/£80 still applies.

If *travel-to-work costs are unreasonably high or should be disregarded*, the direction states the amount of costs allowed (which may be nil). This replaces any travel costs included in exempt income or protected income.[147]

If a direction for special expenses has been given and one for over-generous provision is then sought (or *vice versa*), the case is reconsidered as if a single application were made on both grounds (see p292).[148]

Example 15.6: housing costs relating to the partner

A departure direction (see *Example 15.3*) reduced Steve's assessment from £59.26 to £29.45 a week. Debbie, his ex-wife, then applies for departure on the ground that Steve's second wife, Lisa, can contribute towards the couple's housing costs.

Lisa has net earnings of £280 compared with Steve's net earnings of £380. However, once Steve's travelling expenses of £83 a week are taken from his earnings, both partners have roughly the same amount to contribute towards the joint mortgage. Therefore, the departure decision maker decides Lisa can afford to contribute half the mortgage payments.

Therefore, Steve's exempt income is now:	£
Personal allowance	67.50
Mortgage (half of £96)	48.00
Property settlement allowance	40.00
Travel-to-work costs	83.00
Debt repayments	34.60
Total	**273.10**

Steve's assessable income =
£380 – £273.10 = £106.90

Proposed maintenance = 50% x £106.90 = £53.45

The protected income calculation remains as in *Example 15.3* and, therefore, Steve can afford £53.45 (which is still slightly below the original assessment).

Note: the 50 per cent calculation is used because of the special expenses departure; if only the housing costs departure had been made, proposed maintenance would have been calculated in the usual way (see Chapter 12).

Effective date of the direction

Normally, the effective date of a departure direction is:[149]

- the maintenance assessment's effective date, if the departure application is made within one month of the notification of the current assessment (see p321). If there was unavoidable delay, the CSA can treat the application as received in time;[150] *otherwise*
- the first day of the maintenance period in which the departure application was received.

However, if the reason for departure is a change of circumstances after the assessment's effective date, the effective date of the direction is:

- the first day of the maintenance period after the change of circumstances, if the departure application is made within one month of the notification of the assessment (see p321);[151] *otherwise*
- the first day of the maintenance period in which the departure application was received.[152]

If the direction is for contact costs and there was no established pattern of visits at the date of the application (see p296), the effective date is the first day of the first maintenance period after *either* the date the parents have agreed that pattern is to start *or*, if there is no agreed date, the date of the direction.[153]

Normally, a direction can only be made for the assessment that was current when the departure application was made. However, in some cases an application cannot be made while the assessment is current because notification was not sent until after the period covered by the assessment – eg, because it is made for a past period. The departure decision maker can still make a direction for that assessment, as if it were the current one, if:[154]

- a departure direction is given for the current maintenance assessment; *and*
- s/he considers that a direction would have been made for the assessment for the earlier period if an application had been made.

Duration of the direction

The direction may last for a specified period (eg, a 30-week repayment period) or until a specified event – eg, a child leaves school.[155] A direction may require the CSA to make a fresh assessment on a later change of circumstances and specify how that assessment is to be made.[156]

Changing the direction

The rules on changing a decision on departure are similar to those on changing a decision on the assessment itself (see Chapter 17). Any decision of the CSA (or one referred to the First-tier Tribunal) on departure can be revised[157] or superseded.[158] This would appear to include a decision that regular payments conditions have not been complied with. If it is considered that an application for departure is defective, there is no formal notified decision and this may only be challenged by judicial review. Refusal and rejection of applications may be revised. The 'test case' rules (see p385) also apply to revisions and supersessions of departure decisions.[159]

The rules on who can initiate a revision/supersession and on what grounds are summarised below.

Change of decision	*Grounds*	*Initiated by*	*Time limit*
Revision	Any	CSA/Any party*	1 month
Revision	Official error	CSA	No limit
Revision	Misrepresentation	CSA	No limit
Supersession	Change of circumstances	CSA/Any party*	No limit
Supersession	Erroneous in point of law	CSA/Any party*	No limit
Supersession	Ignorance/mistake as to fact	CSA/Any party*	No limit

*'Any party' includes any parent with care, non-resident parent or Scottish child applicant of the assessment to which the departure relates.

Disputing decisions

Any party to an assessment can apply to have a departure direction decision revised. This includes decisions made on referral to the First-tier Tribunal (see p299). The CSA can also act to revise a decision on any grounds within one month of notification of the original decision.[160] In addition, the CSA can also act to revise a decision at any time where that decision was made as a result of official error (see p347)[161] or where the original decision was wrong because a person misrepresented or failed to disclose a material fact (see p347) and the decision was, therefore, more advantageous to that person.[162] Revision cannot occur if a material change of circumstances has occurred (or is expected to occur) since the original decision.[163] In this case, supersession may be possible. Revision is not possiblle if the original decision is being appealed to the First-tier Tribunal and the revised decision (if made) would be less advantageous to the person making the appeal.[164]

An application for revision must normally be made within one month of notification of the decision.[165] If an application for revision is made and the CSA informs the applicant that the revision will not be made because there is insufficient evidence or information, the applicant has one month from the date of this notification to reapply with the required information.[166] The one-month time limit may be extended if the CSA accepts that it is reasonable to grant an extension. The application for the decision to be revised must have merit and there must have been special circumstances which meant that it was not practicable for the application to have been made within the one-month limit.[167]

The longer the extension requested, the more compelling the relevant special circumstances need to be.[168] An application for an extension must be made within 13 months of notification of the original decision.[169] When deciding whether to grant an extension, the CSA will take no account of an applicant's ignorance or misunderstanding of the law relating to her/his case, nor will account be taken of a commissioner's or court's new interpretation of the relevant law (see p346).[170] Applications for extension which are refused cannot be renewed.[171]

The revised decision normally takes effect on the same date as the original decision.[172] If the effective date from which the original decision takes effect is wrong, the revised decision takes effect from the correct date.[173] If, on revision of the decision, the CSA decides that a departure direction should not have been given, the direction will be cancelled.[174]

Supersession of a decision on departure

A decision relating to departure may be superseded if there has been a material change of circumstances since the original decision was made. Any party to the assessment can apply for a supersession on this ground or, if the CSA becomes aware of a relevant change of circumstances, it can act on its own initiative.[175] A party to the assessment can also apply for a supersession if s/he expects that a material change of circumstances is going to occur.[176] No supersession on a change of circumstances will be made if the amount of child maintenance payable would be changed by less than £1.[177] Decisions may also be superseded (either on application by a party or on the initiative of the CSA) if the original decision was made in ignorance of (or based on a mistake as to) a material fact[178] or (apart from decisions given on appeal) if the original decision was wrong in a point of law.[179] Decisions to refuse or reject an application for departure and decisions to cancel a departure direction cannot be superseded,[180] nor can any decision which can be revised (see p309).[181]

If, on supersession, the CSA decides that a departure direction should no longer have effect, the direction will be cancelled.[182]

A superseding decision normally takes effect on the first day of the maintenance period (see p327) in which the application for supersession is made.[183] This also applies if the CSA supersedes a decision on its own initiative on the basis of information or evidence contained in an unsuccessful application for a revision or supersession.[184] If an application is made because of an anticipated change of circumstances, the new decision takes effect from the first day of the maintenance period immediately after the maintenance period in which the change of circumstances is expected to occur.[185] If the CSA supersedes a decision on its own initiative because it becomes aware of a change of circumstances following a revision or supersession of a social security decision, the superseding decision takes effect from the first day of the maintenance period in which the social security decision maker became aware of the change of circumstances.[186]

Correction of accidental errors

A minor accidental error can be corrected by the departure decision maker at any time, without making a fresh direction. The parties must be notified and the normal time for appealing starts to run again (see Chapter 18).[187]

Change to the assessment

If the assessment is changed on revision or supersession, the direction normally applies to any fresh assessment. This may not mean there is a decision on departure that may be appealed at this stage. It has been recommended that the Secretary of State should always give a departure decision when making a new assessment to allow the party appeal rights.[188] If this does not occur and an appeal relates in part to the continuation of the departure direction, the First-tier Tribunal does not have jurisdiction to deal with the departure issue and should refer the case to the CSA as a request for supersession of the departure, which would lead to a decision that carried appeal rights.

In some cases, the CSA may replace the existing assessment with an interim maintenance assessment (IMA) (see p331). If the direction could not have been made for that IMA (see p286), the direction is suspended.[189] The suspension continues until the IMA is replaced by an assessment for which the direction could have been made.

If an assessment is cancelled or ceases to have effect (see p336), the direction normally ceases to have effect and does not apply to any later assessment.[190] However, if the cancellation is because of the CSA ceasing to have jurisdiction, and the CSA later gets jurisdiction again for the same parties and at least one of the same children, a property transfer direction has effect again from the effective date of any new assessment.[191] This only applies where a party moves away from the UK and then returns or where the parents reconcile but later split up.

Appealing the decision

Decisions on departure can be appealed to the First-tier Tribunal.[192] Any party to the assessment can appeal. The time limit and procedures for appealing are the same as for other appeals (see p363).[193] Any decision about a departure application can be appealed.[194] This includes a decision to refuse an application and one to make a direction. A decision that an application is defective can only be challenged via judicial review. If more than one departure direction is appealed and those departure directions relate to the same maintenance assessment, the First-tier Tribunal can consider both appeals at the same time.[195]

When making an appeal, it is important to distinguish whether the appeal is against the direction and/or any fresh maintenance assessment. See Chapter 18 for further details of appeals.

Notes

1 Reg 10(1)(a) CSDDCA Regs
2 Reg 10(1)(c) CSDDCA Regs
3 Reg 10(1)(b) and (c) CSDDCA Regs
4 Reg 9 CSDDCA Regs

1. **Grounds for departure**
5 Sch 4B para 2 CSA 1991
6 Reg 19 CSDDCA Regs
7 Reg 14(1) CSDDCA Regs
8 Reg 14(4) CSDDCA Regs
9 Reg 14(1) CSDDCA Regs
10 Reg 14(1)(c) and (6) CSDDCA Regs
11 Reg 14(5) CSDDCA Regs
12 Reg 14(1) CSDDCA Regs
13 Reg 14(1) CSDDCA Regs
14 Reg 14(7) CSDDCA Regs
15 Reg 14(3) CSDDCA Regs
16 Reg 32F(b) CSDDCA Regs
17 Reg 18 CSDDCA Regs
18 Reg 10(1)(b) CSDDCA Regs
19 Sch 4B para 2(6) CSA 1991; reg 18(8)(a) CSDDCA Regs
20 Reg 18(1) and (2)(a) CSDDCA Regs
21 Reg 18(4) CSDDCA Regs
22 Reg 18(4B) CSDDCA Regs
23 Reg 18(4A) CSDDCA Regs
24 Reg 18(2)(b) CSDDCA Regs
25 Reg 18(7) CSDDCA Regs
26 Reg 18(3) CSDDCA Regs
27 Reg 18(3) CSDDCA Regs
28 Reg 18(7A) CSDDCA Regs
29 Reg 18(5) CSDDCA Regs
30 Reg 18(6) CSDDCA Regs
31 Reg 18(2)(c) CSDDCA Regs
32 Reg 18(3) CSDDCA Regs
33 Reg 13(3) CSDDCA Regs
34 Reg 13(1) CSDDCA Regs
35 Reg 13(2) CSDDCA Regs
36 Reg 15(1) and (6)(a) and (b) CSDDCA Regs
37 Reg 15(6)(b) CSDDCA Regs
38 Reg 15(5) CSDDCA Regs
39 Reg 15(1) and (2) CSDDCA Regs
40 Reg 15(6)(c) CSDDCA Regs
41 Reg 15(3) CSDDCA Regs
42 Reg 15(4)(a) CSDDCA Regs
43 Regs 15(3)(b) and (4)(b) and 32(6) CSDDCA Regs
44 Reg 15(4A) CSDDCA Regs
45 Reg 16(1) CSDDCA Regs
46 Reg 16(5)(b) CSDDCA Regs
47 Reg 16(2)(k) and (5)(c) CSDDCA Regs; s376(4) ICTA 1988
48 Reg 16(2)(a) CSDDCA Regs
49 Reg 16(3) CSDDCA Regs
50 Reg 16(2)(h) and (i) CSDDCA Regs
51 Reg 16(5)(d) CSDDCA Regs
52 Reg 16(2)(a)-(g), (j) and (m) CSDDCA Regs
53 Reg 16(4) CSDDCA Regs
54 Reg 37(4) CSDDCA Regs
55 Regs 16(2)(l) and 37(3) CSDDCA Regs
56 Reg 37(3) CSDDCA Regs
57 Reg 17 CSDDCA Regs
58 Reg 17(1)(a) CSDDCA Regs
59 Sch 4B para 5 CSA 1991; regs 23-29 CSDDCA Regs
60 Reg 25 CSDDCA Regs
61 Reg 25(2) CSDDCA Regs
62 Reg 25(3) CSDDCA Regs
63 Reg 23(2)(a) CSDDCA Regs
64 Reg 23(1)(a) CSDDCA Regs
65 Reg 23(1)(b) and (c) CSDDCA Regs
66 Reg 23(2)(b) CSDDCA Regs
67 Reg 40(2) and (3) CSDDCA Regs
68 Reg 24 CSDDCA Regs
69 Reg 26 CSDDCA Regs
70 Reg 40(6) CSDDCA Regs
71 Reg 27 CSDDCA Regs
72 Reg 40(7) CSDDCA Regs
73 Reg 40(9) CSDDCA Regs
74 Reg 28 CSDDCA Regs
75 Reg 29 CSDDCA Regs
76 Reg 10(1)(c) CSDDCA Regs
77 Sch 4B paras 3(1) and 4(1) CSA 1991; regs 21(1) and (2) and 22(4) CSDDCA Regs
78 Reg 21(5)(a) CSDDCA Regs
79 Reg 21(5)(b) CSDDCA Regs
80 Reg 22(2) CSDDCA Regs
81 Sch para 1(3)(b) CSDDCA Regs
82 Reg 22(3) and Sch CSDDCA Regs
83 Sch para 3 CSDDCA Regs

2. **Applying for departure**
84 s28A(1) CSA 1991
85 s28A(2) and (3) CSA 1991; reg 4(1) CSDDCA Regs
86 Reg 2 CSDDCA Regs
87 Reg 4(4)-(8) CSDDCA Regs

88 s28A(1) CSA 1991
89 Reg 4(9) and (10) CSDDCA Regs
90 Reg 5 CSDDCA Regs

3. **Procedure**
91 s28B CSA 1991
92 s28B(2) CSA 1991; reg 7 CSDDCA Regs
93 Reg 6 CSDDCA Regs
94 Reg 8(4) CSDDCA Regs
95 Reg 8(1) CSDDCA Regs
96 Reg 8(4A) CSDDCA Regs
97 Reg 8(1) and (3) CSDDCA Regs
98 Reg 8(5) CSDDCA Regs
99 Reg 8(6) CSDDCA Regs
100 Reg 8(7) CSDDCA Regs
101 Reg 8(2)(b) CSDDCA Regs
102 Reg 8(2)(a) CSDDCA Regs
103 s28C(1) CSA 1991
104 s28C(2)(a) CSA 1991
105 Reg 45 CSDDCA Regs
106 Reg 45(1)-(3) CSDDCA Regs
107 s28C(3) CSA 1991
108 s28C(6)(b) CSA 1991; reg 45(4) CSDDCA Regs
109 s28C(4) CSA 1991
110 s28A(4) CSA 1991
111 s28B(6) CSA 1991
112 s28F(8) CSA 1991; reg 8(9)(a) and (10)(a) CSDDCA Regs
113 s28D(1)(b) CSA 1991
114 s28D(3) CSA 1991

4. **Considering departure**
115 s28F(4)-(5) CSA 1991; reg 7 CSDDCA Regs
116 Reg 44(4) CSDDCA Regs
117 s28E(2) and (4) CSA 1991; reg 12 CSDDCA Regs
118 s28F(1)(b) CSA 1991
119 R(CS) 3/01
120 s28F(2) and (3) CSA 1991; reg 30 CSDDCA Regs
121 Reg 1 CSDDCA Regs
122 CCS/1131/2005

5. **The departure direction**
123 s28F(6) CSA 1991
124 s28G(1) CSA 1991
125 Sch 1 paras 4(2) and (3) and 7 CSA 1991. A direction does not change the way these work.
126 Sch 4B para 6(6) CSA 1991
127 Reg 44(1) and (2) CSDDCA Regs
128 Reg 44(1) and (3) CSDDCA Regs
129 Reg 37(1) CSDDCA Regs
130 Reg 38(2) CSDDCA Regs
131 Regs 37(2) and 38(3) CSDDCA Regs
132 Reg 41(1)-(5) CSDDCA Regs
133 Reg 42A(1)-(6) CSDDCA Regs
134 Reg 43(1) CSDDCA Regs
135 Reg 43(2) CSDDCA Regs
136 Reg 39(1)(a) and (c) and (6) CSDDCA Regs
137 Reg 39(1)(b) CSDDCA Regs
138 Reg 39(2) CSDDCA Regs
139 Reg 42(1) and (2) CSDDCA Regs
140 Reg 42(3) CSDDCA Regs
141 Reg 43(3) CSDDCA Regs
142 Reg 39(5) CSDDCA Regs
143 Reg 39(3) CSDDCA Regs
144 Reg 40(2)-(5) CSDDCA Regs
145 Reg 40(6) CSDDCA Regs
146 Reg 40(7) CSDDCA Regs
147 Reg 40(10) CSDDCA Regs
148 Reg 42A(7) and (8) CSDDCA Regs
149 Reg 32(1)(a) and (2)(a) CSDDCA Regs. Different rules apply for assessments in force on 2 December 1996 if the application was made before 2 December 1997 – see the 1997/98 edition of this *Handbook*.
150 Reg 32(2)(b) CSDDCA Regs
151 Reg 32(1)(b) CSDDCA Regs
152 Reg 32(4) CSDDCA Regs
153 Reg 32(3A) CSDDCA Regs
154 Reg 46 CSDDCA Regs
155 s28G(2) CSA 1991
156 Sch 4A para 5 CSA 1991
157 Reg 32A CSDDCA Regs
158 Reg 32D CSDDCA Regs
159 s28ZA and Sch 4C para 1(a)(i) CSA 1991
160 Reg 32A(1)(f) CSDDCA Regs
161 Reg 32A(1)(c) CSDDCA Regs
162 Reg 32A(1)(d) CSDDCA Regs
163 Reg 32A(2)(a) CSDDCA Regs
164 Reg 32A(2)(b) CSDDCA Regs
165 Reg 32A(1)(a) CSDDCA Regs
166 Reg 32A(1)(b) CSDDCA Regs
167 Reg 32B(4) CSDDCA Regs
168 Reg 32B(5) CSDDCA Regs
169 Reg 32B(3)(a) CSDDCA Regs
170 Reg 32B(6) CSDDCA Regs
171 Reg 32B(7) CSDDCA Regs
172 s16(3) CSA 1991
173 Reg 32C CSDDCA Regs
174 Reg 32F(a) CSDDCA Regs
175 Reg 32D(2)(a) and (3)(a)(i) CSDDCA Regs
176 Reg 32D(3)(a)(ii) CSDDCA Regs
177 Reg 32D(6) CSDDCA Regs
178 Reg 32D(2)(b) and (4) CSDDCA Regs
179 Reg 32D(5) CSDDCA Regs
180 Reg 32D(10) CSDDCA Regs
181 Reg 32D(9) CSDDCA Regs
182 Reg 32F(b) CSDDCA Regs

183 s17(4) CSA 1991; reg 32E(2) CSDDCA Regs
184 Reg 32E(5) CSDDCA Regs
185 Reg 32E(4) CSDDCA Regs
186 Reg 32E(3) CSDDCA Regs
187 Reg 34A CSDDCA Regs. This does not say the error must be minor, but its terms suggest it does not cover major errors.
188 CCS/1641/2001
189 Reg 35(4) CSDDCA Regs
190 Reg 35(1) CSDDCA Regs
191 Reg 35(2) CSDDCA Regs
192 Sch 4C para 3(4) CSA 1991
193 Regs 31, 32 and 33 SS&CS(DA) Regs
194 Sch 4C para 3(1)(a) CSA 1991
195 Reg 45 SS&CS(DA) Regs

Part 5

Decisions, enforcement and challenges

Chapter 16

Maintenance decisions

This chapter covers:

This chapter does not contain information on the conversion of 'old rules' maintenance assessments to the new rules. For information on conversion decisions, see Chapter 7. For information on revision and supersession decisions, see Chapter 17.

If there are multiple applications under the 'old' and 'new' rules, the Child Support Agency decides which application to proceed with (see Chapter 3).

1. Making the initial maintenance decision

Once an effective maintenance application has been made and the Child Support Agency (CSA) has obtained, or tried to obtain, the necessary information, it can:[1]

- make a maintenance calculation;
- make a default maintenance decision (see p331); *or*
- refuse to make a maintenance calculation (p320).

Details of the case are entered onto the CSA computer and maintenance is calculated automatically.

Relationship with Child Support Agency Northern Ireland

For child support cases, there are two territories: Great Britain and Northern Ireland (see p7). If the person with care, non-resident parent and qualifying child do not all reside in the same territory, the application is dealt with by the CSA of the territory where the person with care lives.[2] If more than one application names the same non-resident parent, those applications are dealt with by the CSA of the territory where the person with care named in the first application received by the CSA lives.[3] If a case has been allocated to a CSA by these rules and the person with care applies again, naming a further non-resident parent, that application is dealt with by the CSA already dealing with the earlier case(s).[4]

These rules do not apply if an application is made by a child in Scotland (see p35). Instead, that application and any others naming the same non-resident parent are dealt with by the CSA for the territory where the person with care of the child applicant lives.[5]

Any calculation made under these rules must take into account the rules of the other territory.[6] Because the rules for the two territories are very similar, this should not make any difference.

Waiting for the calculation decision

If the person with care can provide contact details for the non-resident parent, the CSA aims to start gathering information from him within four weeks of the application. It aims to make an accurate decision within 12 weeks of an application, but some cases may take 26 weeks.[7] The CSA statistics show that almost 90 per cent of cases are cleared within 12 weeks.[8] If the CSA has to trace the non-resident parent, it is likely to take longer before it can make a decision.

Delays in dealing with applications

Even though it is intended that much of the contact with parents to collect and check information needed to make a maintenance calculation and collect payments is done by phone, there may still be a delay between the application and a decision.

Applicants are contacted at certain stages during the progress of the case – eg, to let them know about negotiations with the non-resident parent about collection or if they have made a complaint. The CSA has also said that it will do more to let its clients know about progress on a case, and it is reviewing and revising letters sent to clients so that they 'have a better understanding of what is happening with their case'.[9] However, a parent should continue to contact the CSA regularly for progress reports.

Delay after the non-resident parent is contacted about the application does not normally put off the starting date of any calculation (see p323), but the date of the decision on maintenance may be delayed. Liability under an order or agreement continues and these remain enforceable. Other non-resident parents should consider putting money aside or making voluntary payments (see p403). Parents who are already contributing voluntarily should check whether such payments might be used to offset initial arrears (see p399).

If the non-resident parent is not co-operating, the CSA should make a default maintenance decision (see p320) and may impose a criminal sanction. If the person with care is told by the CSA that the non-resident parent is causing the delay by failing to provide information and the CSA has not made a default maintenance decision, the person with care should write to the CSA requesting that one be made. If this does not happen, a complaint should be made (see p441).

Withdrawing the application

If an application is withdrawn or treated as withdrawn (see p43), the CSA cannot make a calculation. If a calculation *is* made after withdrawal, it can be challenged (see Chapter 18).

The application cannot be withdrawn after a decision has been made, but the applicant can ask the CSA to cease acting, in which case the calculation can be cancelled (see p327). In other cases, the decision may be revised or superseded (see Chapter 18).

Change of circumstances

Unlike under social security law, there is no general requirement to notify the CSA of changes. However, both the person with care and the non-resident parent are required to notify the CSA of some changes (see p71). Since October 2008, it is an offence for a non-resident parent not to notify the CSA of a change of address.[10] In addition, the non-resident parent must inform the CSA of changes when a deduction from earnings order is in force (see p417).

In practice, any party may want to tell the CSA of changes or new information about the case – eg, the parent with care may have discovered that the non-resident parent has a second job which she believes has not been disclosed to the CSA.

If the CSA is told about a change or given new information that relates to *before* the effective date (see p332), it has discretion on whether to take this information into account. This can be done in the initial calculation or by making two or more calculations for the different periods.[11]

If the date or period normally used is before the effective date (eg, for earnings) and the CSA knows about a relevant change which happened after that date or period but before the effective date, it must take that change into account.[12] If the change is after the normal 'relevant week' (see p205), the relevant week for each later calculation is the week before the date the CSA was notified of the relevant change.[13]

Any information about a change *after* the effective date but before the maintenance calculation can lead to a series of calculations in respect of different periods. The effective date of each such maintenance calculation will be the beginning of the maintenance period in which the change occurred or is expected to occur.[14]

Once a calculation is made, the person with care has a duty to notify the CSA of certain changes that happen after that (see p71). These may result in a revision or supersession, depending on when the change is notified and its significance (see Chapter 17).

Refusal to make a calculation

The CSA *must* refuse to make a calculation if:

- the application was made by a person who is *not* a non-resident parent, a person with care or, in Scotland, a qualifying child aged 12 or over (see p35);
- there is a pre-3 March 2003 court order (registered agreement in Scotland) or written agreement;
- there is a post-3 March 2003 court order (registered maintenance agreement in Scotland) that has been in force for less than one year;
- not all the parties are habitually resident in the UK (see p25);
- there is no non-resident parent, either because both parents live in the same household as the child (see p21) or because the CSA does not accept that the person named is a parent of the child (see p15); *or*
- there is no qualifying child (see p18).

The CSA can also delay making a calculation pending the outcome of a test case (see p385). Otherwise, the CSA must make a calculation.

If there is a change of circumstances so that one of these situations applies for a period beginning after the effective date (see p332), the CSA makes a calculation that ends on the date of the change.

If a child in respect of whom an application has been made dies before the calculation is made or notified to the parties, the CSA must treat the application as if it had not been made in respect of that child. If the only child or all qualifying children have died, the application will not go ahead.[15] The CSA cannot refuse to make a calculation just because it has insufficient information or because it may affect the welfare of a child.[16] The CSA may make a default maintenance decision (see below). If the CSA refuses to make a calculation, the applicant (and, if the applicant is a child in Scotland, any person with care or non-resident parent who had been notified of the application) must be notified in writing of the decision, the right of appeal (see Chapter 18) and how to seek a revision (see Chapter 17).[17]

A fresh application may be made after the refusal – eg, if there is a change of circumstances, such as the non-resident parent returning to live in the UK.

2. **Default maintenance decisions**

If the Child Support Agency (CSA) does not have enough information to make a maintenance calculation, or to revise or supersede a decision, it may make a default maintenance decision.[18] A default maintenance decision can also be made at conversion (see p143). (In 'old rules' cases prior to conversion, if there is not enough information to make a full assessment, an interim maintenance assessment may be made, see p331.)

The amount of the default maintenance decision is based on the number of qualifying children applied for:[19]

- £30 if there is one qualifying child;
- £40 if there are two qualifying children; *or*
- £50 if there are three or more qualifying children.

This amount may be apportioned if there is more than one person with care. Any relevant non-resident children are ignored.

Court order phasing may be applied to a default maintenance decision (see p322).

The effective date of a default maintenance decision is the same as it would have been for a maintenance calculation decision (see p332).

When a default maintenance decision ends

A default maintenance decision may be revised at any time – eg, when it is replaced by a maintenance calculation.[20] In practice, this only happens when the CSA has sufficient information to determine the case properly (ie, to make a maintenance calculation) from the effective date. If it does not have sufficient information to do this but has enough information from a later date, it can make a maintenance calculation that will take effect from the first day in the maintenance period in which the information is received.[21]

3. Notification of decisions

The Child Support Agency must notify the person with care, non-resident parent and Scottish child applicant once a maintenance calculation or interim maintenance decision has been made.[22] This also includes default maintenance decisions (but see p322). There are similar rules regarding notification of revision and supersession decisions (see Chapter 17).

The notification of the maintenance calculation or interim maintenance decision *must* include information on:[23]

- the effective date (see p332);
- where relevant, the net weekly income of the non-resident parent;
- the number of qualifying children;
- the number of relevant other children;
- the weekly rate;
- any variations;

- any adjustments for apportionment, shared care by the non-resident parent or part-time local authority care, or maintenance to another relevant non-resident child; *and*
- revision, supersession and appeal.[24]

Notification of a default maintenance decision must state the effective date, the default date, the number of qualifying children, details of any apportionment and the information needed to make a maintenance calculation.[25] It should also include details of rights to request a revision, supersession or an appeal.[26]

Unless there is written permission, a notification should not contain:[27]

- the address of anyone else other than the recipient or information that could lead to her/him being located; *or*
- information on anyone other than persons with care, non-resident parents or qualifying children.

If there are errors or someone disagrees with the decision, s/he may seek a revision (see p344) or appeal (see Chapter 18).

If there is a court order for maintenance, the court is notified of the calculation (see p30). In addition, where court order phasing applies, the amount due may be replaced by a transitional amount (see p323).

4. Court order phasing of calculations

If weekly liability under the calculation is higher than under an existing court order or agreement, the calculation can be introduced in up to three stages.

A calculation may *only* be phased in if:[28]

- a court order or maintenance agreement (see below) in relation to one or more qualifying children was in force on 4 April 1993 and remained in force until the date the calculation was made;
- the calculation exceeds that due under the old order/agreement; *and*
- either the non-resident parent is a member of a family (see p25) or there is a reduction for shared care to the basic or reduced rate.

Any payments in kind or to third parties are ignored when determining the old amount.[29] Arrears are also ignored – it is the weekly amount that should have been paid that counts.[30]

Maintenance agreements which count for phasing must have been:[31]

- made in writing (see p36); *or*
- evidenced in writing.

Court orders which count for phasing must have been made under:[32]

- one of the provisions listed in Appendix 3 for court maintenance orders;
- section 151 of the Army Act 1955;

- section 151A of the Air Force Act 1955; or
- Articles 1(b) or 3 of the Naval and Marine Pay and Pensions (Deductions for Maintenance) Order 1959.

The Child Support Agency is likely to seek verification of the order or written maintenance agreement.

If court order phasing applies, instead of the calculation amount, a transitional amount is paid.[33]The transitional amount is:[34]

- for the first 26 weeks, the old amount *plus* the greater of £20 or one-quarter of the difference between the calculation and the old amount;
- for the next 26 weeks, the old amount *plus* the greater of £40 or one-half of the difference between the calculation and the old amount; *and*
- for the last 26 weeks of the phasing-in period, the old amount *plus* the greater of £60 or three-quarters of the difference between the calculation and the old amount.

The maintenance payable becomes the calculation amount if the transitional amount would be larger than that.[35] Therefore, it is only where the difference between the old amount and the calculation amount is more than £60 a week that the phasing-in period lasts the full 18 months.

Revision and supersession where there is phasing

Where phasing applies and there is a subsequent decision, the following amount is payable:[36]

- if the amount of the subsequent decision is less than the calculation amount and less than or equal to the transitional amount, the subsequent decision amount;
- if the amount of the subsequent decision is less than the previous calculation but more than the transitional amount, the transitional amount;
- if the amount of the subsequent decision is higher than the previous calculation, the transitional amount is increased by the same amount as the increase between the calculation and the subsequent decision amount.

5. When the first maintenance calculation begins

The date a maintenance calculation takes effect is called the **'effective date'** (see p324).[37] There are different rules for effective dates after a supersession (see Chapter 17), for calculations replacing default maintenance decisions (see p320) and if there is conversion of an 'old rules' case (see p326). For effective dates in 'old rules' cases prior to conversion, see p332.

The effective date

Unless there is a maintenance order in force in relation to all the qualifying children (see below), the effective date of the calculation depends on who made the application. If there is, or has been, a maintenance calculation (or 'old rules' maintenance assessment) in force, special rules may apply (see p325).

If the application is made before 3 March 2003 but the effective date under the 'old rules' is after 3 March 2003, the case is dealt with as a 'new rules' case (unless the linking rules apply). However, the effective date remains that worked out under the 'old rules'.[38]

If the application was made by the person with care or a Scottish child applicant, the effective date is:[39]

- the date the non-resident parent is notified of the application; *or*
- if the non-resident parent has intentionally avoided notification, the date on which notification would have been given but for the avoidance.

The non-resident parent is normally notified of the application by phone. In some cases, a maintenance enquiry form may be issued (see p51). In this case, notification is treated as given or sent on the day it is given or posted.[40] Notification is treated as occurring if the maintenance enquiry form is sent to the non-resident parent at his last known or last notified address. A commissioner's decision has stated that it is for the Child Support Agency (CSA) to decide whether an address is sufficiently reliable to send a maintenance enquiry form; it does not have to be beyond reasonable doubt that it is the non-resident parent's current address.[41]

The non-resident parent cannot delay the effective date of a calculation by disputing paternity. The CSA does not make a calculation until the issue of paternity is resolved (see p17) but, if it later decides that the alleged non-resident parent is the father, the calculation is backdated to the effective date.

If the non-resident parent made the application, the effective date of the first calculation is the date of the effective application (see p332).[42]

If there are multiple applications for child maintenance and these are treated as a single application (see p44), the effective date is set by the earlier or earliest application.[43]

Court orders

The effective date is two months and two days after the date on which the application is made if:[44]

- there is no maintenance calculation in force for either the parent with care or the non-resident parent;
- there is a maintenance order in force for all of the qualifying children named in the calculation (this means that if the court order covers some, but not all, of the qualifying children, this rule will not apply);
- the maintenance order was made on or after 3 March 2003; *and*
- the maintenance order has been in force for at least one year.

If the maintenance order ceases to be in force after the application but before the effective date worked out under the above rule, the effective date is the day after the maintenance order ceased to be in force.[45]

Liability for maintenance continues until the order stops being in force, so the non-resident parent should continue making payments while waiting for the calculation. If a calculation is made following a voluntary application, an order made on or after 3 March 2003 has been in force for at least a year, and the non-resident parent makes payments due under the order but after the effective date of the maintenance calculation (and so will have been making them retrospectively after the order ceased to have effect), these will be treated as payments of child support maintenance (see also p403).[46] For collection and enforcement of arrears, see Chapter 19.

Effective dates in special cases

The effective date may be set earlier or later than under the normal rules in certain circumstances where there is, or has been, a maintenance calculation in force.

Condition	*Effective date*
A maintenance calculation is in force, the non-resident parent in the new application is the non-resident parent in the current calculation and the application is in respect of a different person with care and qualifying child.	The beginning of the maintenance period in the existing case in which the non-resident parent is notified of the new calculation.[47]
A maintenance calculation is in force and the non-resident parent in that calculation is the person with care in the new application .	The beginning of the maintenance period in the existing case which is not more than seven days after the non-resident parent in the new application is notified of that application.[48]
A maintenance calculation was in force within eight weeks of the application in relation to the same non-resident parent and qualifying child(ren) but a different person with care.	The date on which the previous maintenance calculation ceased to have effect.[49]
A maintenance calculation is in force, a new application is made in respect of the same non-resident parent but a different parent with care and the previous maintenance calculation ceases to have effect before a decision is made on the new application.	If the non-resident parent has been notified before the previous calculation ceases to have effect, the day after it ceases to have effect. If the non-resident parent is not notified until after the previous calculation ceases to have effect, the date of notification.[50]

A maintenance calculation was in force within the eight weeks preceding the application and the parent with care and non-resident parent have swapped roles in relation to all the qualifying child(ren) concerned – ie, the person with care in the old calculation is the non-resident parent in the new application and *vice versa*.	The date on which the previous maintenance calculation ceased to have effect.[51]

If there is, or has been, an 'old rules' maintenance assessment in force

If an 'old rules' maintenance assessment is, or has been, in force, the case may be dealt with under the 'old rules' or 'new rules' depending on who is involved and when the application is made.

Applications for a maintenance calculation after 3 March 2003 but within 13 weeks of an assessment being in force involving the same person with care, non-resident parent and qualifying child(ren) may be treated as an application for a maintenance assessment.[52] In these circumstances, the effective date is set under the 'old rules'.

Otherwise, the effective date of the new maintenance calculation is dealt with under the:

- normal effective date rules; *or*
- special cases rules explained above, as if references to the calculation which is, or was, in force were to the assessment.[53]

However, if there is a maintenance assessment in force that converts to the 'new rules' early (eg, because of an application from another person with care), there are special rules for working out the effective date of the conversion decision for that existing assessment (see Chapter 7).

Effective dates if there was a previous calculation in force

The effective date rules described above are modified if there was previously a maintenance calculation in force for the same non-resident parent (regardless of whether it was in respect of the same qualifying children) and which is no longer in force at the date the decision on the new maintenance calculation is made. In this situation, the effective date will be up to six days later, so that the first day of each maintenance period falls on the same day of the week as the first day of each maintenance period in the previous calculation.[54]

Example

Steve pays maintenance for his two children who live with his first wife. Each new maintenance period begins on a Tuesday. This maintenance calculation then ceases but, following an application from his second partner who is the parent with care of his baby son, a new maintenance calculation is made. The effective date for this new application would normally be Friday 2 July 2010. However, it is moved to the following Tuesday 6 July 2010, so that Steve's liability for maintenance continues to begin on a Tuesday.

Maintenance periods

Child maintenance is calculated on a weekly basis, although it is not always paid weekly (see p395). It is payable in respect of successive seven-day periods, with the first period beginning on the effective date.[55]

After a supersession, any fresh calculation comes into effect on the first day of the maintenance period (see p354).

6. When a maintenance calculation ends

A maintenance calculation continues until the Child Support Agency (CSA):

- cancels it following a request. In effect, this is a supersession decision due to a change of circumstances – ie, there has been a change in what the applicant wishes the CSA to do (see below);
- supersedes it because it has ceased to have effect (see p328);
- revises it (see p344); *or*
- supersedes it for another reason (see p350).

In some circumstances, this will mean that the calculation is replaced by another; in others, no further calculation will be made. When the cancellation takes effect will depend on the grounds on which the supersession or revision was made, or the nature of the request (see p329). Any arrears remaining after a calculation ends may still be collected (see Chapter 19). If an application is made for a child(ren) of the non-resident parent who is not named in the existing calculation, the new calculation replaces the old one.

Request to cancel a calculation

A maintenance calculation must be cancelled when the applicant requests that the CSA ceases acting.[56]

The request may be made verbally or in writing. If the request is made, the CSA must stop all action, including collection and enforcement of arrears, though the person may, if s/he wishes, specifically ask for action for arrears to continue.

Living together

When the request is made, reasons need not be given. However, if the reason is because the parent with care and non-resident parent are living together, the CSA should be told. This is because, once all the parties share a household, the non-resident parent is no longer non-resident (see p21), so the child is no longer a qualifying child and the calculation ceases to have effect (see below).

The calculation ceases to have effect

Some changes of circumstances lead to a termination of the maintenance calculation, whether or not a request is made. The CSA may be aware of a change from, for example, a request or a notification by the parent with care under her duty to do so (see p71) or from the Department for Work and Pensions. The CSA *must* supersede the decision and cancel a calculation (including a default decision) if the calculation ceases to have effect. The calculation will cease to have effect if:[57]

- the non-resident parent or person with care dies;
- the only, or all, qualifying child(ren) is (are) no longer a qualifying child(ren); *or*
- the non-resident parent ceases to be a parent of the only, or all, qualifying child(ren).

This means cancellation occurs, for example, when:

- a child aged 16 or over leaves school or becomes too old to count as a child;
- the qualifying child, non-resident parent and parent with care start living together;
- the qualifying child goes to live with someone else and as a result the person with care no longer counts as a person with care;
- the qualifying child is adopted, in which case the non-resident parent is no longer a parent; *or*
- the non-resident parent is no longer considered a parent because of the results of a DNA test or a declaration of parentage.

In 'new rules' cases, a calculation may cease to have effect because of a reconciliation during which the parent with care and non-resident parent are living together, since this will mean that the non-resident parent is no longer a non-resident parent and the child is no longer a qualifying child. How soon this happens will depend on the circumstances – eg, the nature of the reconciliation and the intentions of the parties. It may mean that the calculation ceases to have effect immediately.

In 'old rules' cases, an assessment ceases to have effect if the parent with care and non-resident parent have been living together for a continuous period of six months. There is conflicting caselaw on whether the assessment should be cancelled if there is a shorter period of cohabitation.[58]

Other cancellations

The CSA must cancel the calculation if the person with care, non-resident parent or qualifying child is no longer habitually resident in the UK (see p25).[59]

A non-resident parent who has successfully contested paternity will have any maintenance calculation cancelled and, if he has paid maintenance, may obtain a refund.

If an applicant fails to provide the CSA with enough information to make a revision or supersession decision, the CSA *may* cancel the calculation.

Date cancellation has effect

Cancellation of a calculation requires a decision by the CSA, either at its own initiative or following a request or application (see p327).[60] If the calculation is cancelled because it ceases to have effect or because of another relevant change, the cancellation takes effect from the first day in the maintenance period in which the change occurred. This includes where:

- the person with care is no longer the person with care for the child(ren) named in the calculation;[61] *or*
- a party is no longer habitually resident in the UK;[62] *or*
- the qualifying child dies or ceases to be a qualifying child;[63] *or*
- the non-resident parent ceases to be a parent.[64]

If the cancellation is because the non-resident parent is not considered to be the parent because of a DNA test or declarator of parentage, the effective date is the date of the original maintenance calculation.[65]

Cancellation following a request

A calculation is cancelled with effect from the first day of the maintenance period in which the request was received *or* a different date depending on the reason for the cancellation.[66] A later date may be appropriate if an applicant has asked that the calculation ends on a later date.

Notification of the cancellation decision

When the CSA cancels a calculation or refuses to cancel one, it must notify the non-resident parent, person with care and child applicant in Scotland of that decision, and must also provide information on the right of appeal and on revisions and supersessions.[67]

If the maintenance calculation has been made following an application from a child in Scotland and that child is no longer a qualifying child, the CSA must notify the person with care, non-resident parent and other children over 12 who are potential child applicants that the calculation has been cancelled.[68]

7. How child maintenance affects means-tested benefits

From 12 April 2010, child maintenance is fully disregarded as income when calculating all means-tested benefits. For the effect of child maintenance on benefits before 12 April 2010, see earlier editions of this *Handbook* and CPAG's *Welfare Benefits and Tax Credits Handbook*.[69]

8. Taxation of child maintenance

Person with care

Child support maintenance is not taxable income.

Non-resident parent

From 6 April 2000, maintenance (including child support maintenance) no longer qualifies for tax relief.

9. Existing 'old rules' cases

Existing cases continue to be dealt with under the legislation prior to reform, except for some provisions for parents with care on benefit – eg, they can ask the Child Support Agency (CSA) to cease acting in both 'new' or 'old' cases. For full details of the 'old rules', see Chapter 14 in the 2002/03 edition of this *Handbook*.

This section outlines the areas where there are differences between the 'new rules' and 'old rules' on maintenance decisions and provides an overview of the relevant provisions.

The following are minor differences between the 'old' and 'new' rules.

- Notifications under the 'old rules' are treated as given or sent by the CSA on the second day after the day of posting (unless this day is a Sunday or bank holiday),[70] apart from the issue of a maintenance enquiry form, which is treated as given or sent on the day that it is posted.
- Cancellations are now possible by 'old rules' parents with care on income support (IS)/income-based jobseeker's allowance (JSA)/income-related employment and support allowance (ESA) – ie, they can opt out. There are several other differences for parents with care on benefit).

Some provisions are completely different.

- Interim maintenance assessments (IMAs – see p331) are made under the 'old rules' where there is insufficient information to make an assessment. Default maintenance decisions apply to 'new rules' cases only. At conversion, an IMA may convert to a maintenance calculation or default maintenance decision (see p320).

- The effective dates of a maintenance assessment or IMA have different rules (see p332).

Interim maintenance assessments

If the CSA does not have sufficient information to make a full assessment using the formula, or to decide whether to revise or supersede a decision, it may make an IMA rather than a full assessment.[71] The decision to make an IMA is discretionary, so the CSA must take into account the welfare of any child(ren) affected by the decision (see p23).

For IMA commencement, see p334, for cancellations, see p336, and for revisions and supersessions, see Chapter 17.

There are four types of IMA.[72]

Interim maintenance assessments

Category	*When it is applied*	*How it is worked out*
A	A non-resident parent has failed to provide information about his own circumstances (not any new partner).	One-and-a-half times the maintenance requirement.
B	Either the person with care or non-resident parent has failed to provide information about the income of her/his new partner, or about other members of their family.	Calculated as a full assessment except that in exempt income it is assumed a new partner can help maintain a joint child and there is no protected income calculation, although the 30 per cent cap may apply.
C	The non-resident parent is self-employed and is unable to provide information about earnings.	Normally £30, but may be less.
D	A Category A IMA is in force but, on the information available, it appears that a full assessment would be higher.	Calculated as a full assessment, except: – there is no protected income, nor a 30 per cent cap;

- no housing costs are allowed;
- exempt income is the adult personal allowance only; *and*
- when working out income, there is no disregard of payments to personal or occupational pension schemes or to pension schemes intended to provide capital sums to discharge a mortgage.

For full information, see the 2002/03 edition of this *Handbook*.

The effective date of an assessment

Under the 'old rules' there are different rules on setting the effective date of assessments, IMAs and maintenance assessments replacing IMAs. In some cases the CSA may set an interim effective date.

Effective date of assessments

Circumstances	*Effective date*
Application by person with care or qualifying child in Scotland.[73]	Eight weeks from the date on which the maintenance enquiry form (MEF) is given or sent to a non-resident parent, as long as, within four weeks of being sent the MEF, he returns it with his name, address and written confirmation that he is the parent of the child(ren) named in the maintenance application form (MAF). *Otherwise,* the date the non-resident parent was actually given or sent the MEF.
Application by non-resident parent.[74]	Eight weeks from the date on which the application was received by the CSA, as long as the non-resident parent provides his name, address and written confirmation that he is the parent of the child(ren) named in the MAF as part of the MAF or provides these details within four weeks of the date of the application. *Otherwise,* the date an effective MAF (see p42) is received.

In either case where there is a court order in force for at least one of the qualifying children on the date the assessment is made.[75]	Two days after the date the assessment is made. The order for maintenance ceases to have effect from the effective date (see p29).[76]
The court order ceases (not because of an IMA) before the assessment is made and after the MEF/MAF is received, depending on the applicant.[77]	The day after the order ceased to be in force.
Another assessment is already in force and an application by a different person with care is then made.[78]	The CSA may treat the new application as received up to eight weeks earlier than the date it was actually received, but no earlier than the date on which the previous assessment ended.[79]
An assessment made following an application from a qualifying child in Scotland has been cancelled at the child's request or because s/he is no longer a child and an application for children who were qualifying children under the previous assessment has been made.[80]	The CSA may treat the new application as received up to eight weeks earlier than the date it was actually received, but no earlier than the date on which the previous assessment ended.[81]
An assessment is in force for a non-resident parent and a different person with care then applies for child maintenance.	The first day of the first maintenance period (see p327) not more than seven days after the parties are notified of the second assessment.[82] If this would make the effective date fall within the eight-week period and the non-resident parent meets the rules for that period (see p332), the effective date is the first day of the first maintenance period after the eight-week period.[83]

There is a previous maintenance calculation in relation to the same non-resident parent, which is no longer in force.	The effective date of a maintenance calculation can be aligned with the first day of the maintenance period of a maintenance calculation or assessment that has previously been, but has ceased to be, in force in relation to the non-resident parent. The previous maintenance assessment does not have to be in relation to the same person with care. In this situation, the effective date will be within six days of the new assessment and on the same day of the week on which the previous maintenance assessment began.[84]

If there are multiple applications for child maintenance and these are treated as a single application, the effective date is set by the earlier or earliest application.[85]

Effective date of interim maintenance assessments

Circumstances	*Effective date*
Category A or C unless there is a court order in force.	The first day after it is made which falls on the same day of the week as the day the MEF was actually given or sent to the non-resident parent or, where the non-resident parent is the applicant, the day the MAF was received by the CSA (but see the exception below).[86]
Category B unless there is a court order in force.	The date the MEF was actually given or sent to the non-resident parent or, where the non-resident parent is the applicant, the day the MAF was received by the CSA (but see the exception below).[87]
There is a court order in force.	See normal effective date rules.
Superseding IMA with another Category A, C or D IMA.	The first day of the maintenance period in which the CSA decides to make the new IMA.[88]

Superseding IMA is a Category B IMA.	Where the cancelled IMA (or the first cancelled IMA, if there is more than one) had caused a court order to cease to have effect, the effective date of that (or that first) IMA.[89] *Otherwise,* the day the MEF was actually given or sent to the non-resident parent or, where the non-resident parent is the applicant, the day the MAF was received by the CSA.[90]

The exception to these rules is that, if the effective date set by them would fall within the eight-week period and the non-resident parent meets the rules for that period for a full assessment (see p323), the effective date is set by those rules.[91]

Effective date of a maintenance assessment replacing an interim maintenance assessment

If the CSA:

- has sufficient information to make a full assessment for the *whole of the period* beginning with the usual effective date (see p332), the IMA ceases to have effect on the first day of the maintenance period (see p327) in which the CSA received the information.[92] The CSA revises (see p344) the IMA decision.[93] The amount payable under the IMA becomes that of the full assessment;[94] *or*
- has sufficient information to make a full assessment for *only part of that period,* the IMA ceases to have effect on the first day of the maintenance period in which the CSA received the information.[95] The CSA supersedes the IMA decision.[96] The effective date of the full assessment is also that date.[97] The amount payable under the IMA remains that of the IMA.[98]

If the information which enables the CSA to make a full assessment is that IS/income-based JSA/income-related ESA/pension credit has been awarded, the CSA is treated as receiving that information on the day benefit became payable.[99]

Interim effective date

If the CSA does not have sufficient information to make a full assessment from the usual effective date (see p332), but has enough to make one running from a later date, it can make a full assessment from that later date.[100] The interim effective date is the first day of the maintenance period (see p334) in which the CSA received the information.[101]

If the CSA later receives sufficient information to make a full assessment from the usual effective date, the assessment already made for the later period then has effect from the usual effective date instead.[102]

Cancelling assessments

The information on ending assessments is the same as that under the 'new rules' except for the following.

- From 3 March 2003, any applicant (including a parent with care on benefits) under the 'old rules' may ask the CSA to stop acting. The calculation will be cancelled, although until 14 July 2008 a parent with care on IS or income-based JSA may have had a reduced benefit decision made and imposed.
- Under the 'old rules', if a Scottish child applicant is no longer habitually resident in Scotland, the assessment is cancelled.[103] This takes effect from the first day in the maintenance period in which the change occurred.
- Under the 'old rules', the CSA had discretion, in some cases, on when to set the effective date of the cancellation – eg, if the person with care and non-resident parent are living together.[104] However, we understand that this discretion is now exercised to set the effective dates of cancellations to the same date that would apply if it were a new rules case.
- Before cancelling an assessment, the CSA must, if possible, give written notice to the person with care, non-resident parent and any Scottish child applicant of its intention to cancel the assessment, and allow 14 days from the date the notice is sent before cancelling.[105]
- The full amount of the assessment is due for the maintenance period in which the cancellation date falls,[106] except if a Category A or D IMA is cancelled, when it is only due to the cancellation date.[107]
- An IMA must be cancelled when the CSA has enough information to make a full assessment. Otherwise the only provision for cancellation is when the CSA accepts that the non-resident parent was unavoidably delayed in providing the information. The effective date of the maintenance assessment is as under the normal rules. However, where the new decision is another category of IMA, the date is:[108]
  - for a Category A or D IMA, the first day of the maintenance period in which the CSA decides to make the new IMA; *or*
  - for a Category B IMA, the day the MEF was given or sent to the non-resident parent, or if the non-resident parent is the applicant, the day the MAF was received by the CSA.

Court order phasing of assessments

The definition of maintenance agreement and court order are the same as in court order phasing for 'new rules' cases, but the legislative references are slightly different.[109] Evidence of the order must be provided.

In the Regulations there are two similar types of phasing, which we call 'original phasing' and '1994 phasing' in this *Handbook*. As phasing can last for a maximum of 18 months, it should only apply to 'old rules' cases which have had considerable delays in assessment, or for which there is still an IMA.

For full information on court order phasing and supersession of decisions where court order phasing applies, see the 2002/03 edition of this *Handbook*.

Original phasing

This has existed since April 1993 and the reduced amount payable is known as the **'modified amount'**.[110] It does not apply to a Category A IMA.[111] It applies where:[112]

- the old maintenance order/agreement covered all the children named in the assessment; *and*
- the non-resident parent is responsible for maintaining a child (see p18) living with him who is not named in the assessment; *and*
- the assessment is £60 or less.

The weekly modified amount is the weekly amount due under the old order/agreement *plus* £20.[113] This continues for a year, but ends before that if one of the above conditions is no longer met.

1994 phasing

This was introduced on 7 February 1994 and the reduced amount payable is known as the **'transitional amount'**.[114] It does not apply to a Category A or D IMA.[115] It applies if:[116]

- the old maintenance order/agreement covered at least one child named in the assessment; *and*
- the non-resident parent was a member of a family (see p25) which included at least one child on the effective date (see p332) and is still a member of a family with a child; *and*
- original phasing does not apply;[117] *and*
- the assessment does not replace a Category A or D IMA made after 22 January 1996.[118]

If the assessment is £60 or less, the transitional amount is the amount under the old order/agreement *plus* £20.[119] This lasts for 52 weeks.

If the assessment is more than £60 a week, the transitional amount is:[120]

- for the first 26 weeks, the old amount *plus* the greater of £20 or a quarter of the difference between the assessment and the old amount;
- for the next 26 weeks, the old amount *plus* the greater of £40 or half of the difference between the assessment and the old amount; *and*
- for the last 26 weeks of the phasing-in period, the old amount *plus* the greater of £60 or three-quarters of the difference between the assessment and the old amount.

The maintenance payable becomes the assessment amount if the transitional amount would be larger than that. Therefore, it is only where the difference between the old amount and the assessment amount is more than £60 a week that the phasing-in period lasts the full 18 months.

Which type of phasing applies

CSA guidance covers only 1994 phasing, implying that original phasing cannot be applied. However, the provisions remain in force.[121] This is only likely to matter if a Category D IMA is made or replaced, because only original and not 1994 phasing can apply to a Category D IMA. If the wrong (or no) phasing is applied, an appeal can be made (see Chapter 18).

Revisions and supersessions

If original phasing applies and the assessment decision is revised (see p344) or superseded (see p350) and the conditions for phasing are still met, phasing continues until the 52-week period ends.[122]

If 1994 phasing applies (or if original phasing applies and there is a change of circumstances), the following amount is payable:[123]

- if the fresh assessment is less than the modified/transitional amount, the fresh assessment;
- if the fresh assessment is less than the previous assessment but more than the modified/transitional amount, the modified/transitional amount;
- if the fresh assessment is higher than the previous assessment, the modified/transitional amount is increased by the same amount as the increase between the two formula assessments.

Notes

1. **Making the initial maintenance decision**
   1 s11 CSA 1991
   2 Sch 1 Art 5(5) CS(NIRA) Regs
   3 Sch 1 Art 5(1) CS(NIRA) Regs
   4 Sch 1 Art 5(3) CS(NIRA) Regs
   5 Sch 1 Art 5(2) and (6) CS(NIRA) Regs
   6 Sch 1 Art 5(4) and (7) CS(NIRA) Regs
   7 www.csa.gov.uk/en/setup/applying.asp
   8 CMEC/National Statistics, *CSA Quarterly Summary Statistics*, March 2011
   9 CSA Operational Improvement Plan 2006-2009
   10 s14A(3A) CSA 1991
   11 Sch 1 para 15 CSA 1991
   12 Reg 2(4) CS(MCSC) Regs; CCS/2750/1995
   13 Reg 1(2) CS(MCSC) Regs (see the exception to definition (c) of 'relevant week')
   14 Reg 25(5) CS(MCP) Regs
   15 Reg 6 CS(MCP) Regs
   16 R(CS) 2/98
   17 Reg 10(1) and (4) CS(MAP) Regs

2. **Default maintenance decisions**
   18 s12(1) CSA 1991
   19 Reg 7 CS(MCP) Regs
   20 s16(1B) CSA 1991; reg 3A(5) SS&CS(DA) Regs
   21 Reg 29A CS(MCP) Regs

3. **Notification of decisions**
22 Reg 23 CS(MCP) Regs
23 Reg 23(1) CS(MCP) Regs
24 Reg 23(4) CS(MCP) Regs
25 Reg 23(2) CS(MCP) Regs
26 Reg 23(4) CS(MCP) Regs
27 Reg 23(3) CS(MCP) Regs

4. **Court order phasing of calculations**
28 Reg 30 CS(TP) Regs
29 Reg 29(2) CS(TP) Regs
30 Reg 29(1) CS(TP) Regs
31 Reg 30(a)(iii) CS(TP) Regs
32 Reg 30(a)(i) and (ii) CS(TP) Regs
33 Reg 31 CS(TP) Regs
34 Reg 31(2) CS(TP) Regs
35 Reg 31(3) CS(TP) Regs
36 Reg 32 CS(TP) Regs

5. **When the first maintenance calculation begins**
37 Reg 1(2) CS(MCP) Regs
38 Reg 31(2) CS(MCP) Regs
39 Regs 1(2) and 25(3) and (4) CS(MCP) Regs
40 Reg 2 CS(MCP) Regs
41 CCS/2288/2005
42 Reg 25(2) CS(MCP) Regs
43 Reg 4(3) CS(MCP) Regs
44 Reg 26 CS(MCP) Regs
45 Reg 28 CS(MCP) Regs
46 Reg 8A CS(MAJ) Regs
47 Reg 7B and Sch 3B para 7 SS&CS(DA) Regs
48 Reg 29(1)(b) CS(MCP) Regs
49 Reg 29(1)(a) CS(MCP) Regs
50 Reg 29(1)(d) CS(MCP) Regs
51 Reg 29(1)(c) CS(MCP) Regs
52 Reg 28(1) CS(TP) Regs
53 Reg 31(1) CS(MCP) Regs
54 Reg 29B CS(MCP) Regs
55 s4A CSA 1991

6. **When a maintenance calculation ends**
56 ss4(5) and 7(6) and Sch 1 para 16(2) CSA 1991
57 Sch 1 para 16 CSA 1991
58 *SM v CMEC* [2010] UKUT 435 (AAC) followed *SL v CMEC* [2009] UKUT 270 (AAC) in holding that cancellation should occur after six months of cohabitation; R(CS) 8/99, followed by CCS/1740/2005, held that even a short period of cohabitation would mean that the relevant child ceased to be a qualifying child, leading to the assessment ceasing to have effect.
59 s44(1) CSA 1991
60 *SM v CMEC* [2010] UKUT 435 (AAC); *GR v CMEC* [2011] UKUT 101 (AAC)
61 Sch 3D para 3(b) SS&CS(DA) Regs
62 Sch 3D para 3(c) SS&CS(DA) Regs
63 Sch 3D, para 3(a) SS&CS(DA) Regs
64 Sch 1 para 16(1)(c) CSA 1991
65 s16(3) CSA 1991
66 s17(4) CSA 1991
67 Reg 15C(5) and (9) SS&CS(DA) Regs
68 Reg 15C(5)(b) SS&CS(DA) Regs; reg 24 CS(MCP) Regs

7. **How child maintenance affects means-tested benefits**
69 **IS** Sch 9 para 73 IS Regs
JSA Sch 7 para 70 JSA Regs
ESA Sch 8 para 60 ESA Regs
PC Reg 5 SPC Regs
HB Sch 5 para 47A HB Regs; reg 29 HB(SPC) Regs
CTB Sch 4 para 48A CTB Regs; reg 19 CTB(SPC) Regs
CTC/WTC Reg 19 Table 6 para 10 TC(DCI) Regs

9. **Existing 'old rules' cases**
70 Reg 1(6) CS(MAP) Regs
71 s12(1) CSA 1991
72 Reg 8 CS(MAP) Regs
73 Reg 30(2)(a) CS(MAP) Regs
74 Reg 30(2)(b) CS(MAP) Regs
75 Reg 3(5) CS(MAJ) Regs
76 Reg 3(6) CS(MAJ) Regs
77 Reg 3(8) CS(MAJ) Regs
78 Reg 3(1) CS(MAP) Regs
79 Reg 3(3) CS(MAP) Regs
80 Reg 3(2) CS(MAP) Regs
81 Reg 3(3) CS(MAP) Regs
82 Reg 33(6) and (7) CS(MAP) Regs
83 Reg 33(9) CS(MAP) Regs
84 Reg 30A(8) and (9) CS(MAP) Regs
85 Reg 4(3) CS(MAP) Regs
86 Reg 8C(1)(a) CS(MAP) Regs
87 Reg 8C(1)(b) CS(MAP) Regs
88 Regs 9(4) and 23(13) CS(MAP) Regs
89 Reg 9(5) and (6) CS(MAP) Regs
90 Reg 9(3) CS(MAP) Regs
91 Reg 8C(1)(d) CS(MAP) Regs
92 Reg 8D(5) CS(MAP) Regs
93 Reg 17(3)(a) CS(MAP) Regs
94 Reg 30A(2) CS(MAP) Regs
95 Reg 8D(6) CS(MAP) Regs
96 Reg 20(6) CS(MAP) Regs
97 Reg 30A(1) CS(MAP) Regs
98 Reg 8D(2) CS(MAP) Regs
99 Reg 8D(8) CS(MAP) Regs
100 Reg 30A(4) CS(MAP) Regs
101 Reg 30A(3) CS(MAP) Regs

102 Reg 30A(6) CS(MAP) Regs
103 Sch 1 para 16(5) CSA 1991; reg 7(1) CS(MAJ) Regs; reg 32A(1) CS(MAP) Regs
104 Sch 1 para 16(7) CSA 1991
105 Reg 32B CS(MAP) Regs
106 Reg 33(5) CS(MAP) Regs
107 Reg 8D(4) CS(MAP) Regs
108 Reg 9(1) CS(MAP) Regs
109 Sch para 7(1)(a)(iii) CSA(Comm3)O; reg 7(1)(a) CS(MATP) Regs
110 Sch para 6 CSA(Comm3)O
111 Sch para 7(2) CSA(Comm3)O
112 Sch para 7(1) CSA(Comm3)O
113 Sch paras 6 and 8 CSA(Comm3)O
114 Reg 6(1) CS(MATP) Regs
115 Reg 7(2)(a) CS(MATP) Regs
116 Reg 7(1) CS(MATP) Regs
117 Reg 7(2)(b) CS(MATP) Regs
118 Reg 7(2)(c) CS(MATP) Regs
119 Reg 8(2)(a) CS(MATP) Regs
120 Reg 8(2) CS(MATP) Regs
121 Reg 7(2)(b) CS(MATP) Regs
122 Sch para 8 CSA(Comm3)O
123 Sch para 12 CSA(Comm3)O; reg 11 CS(MATP) Regs

Chapter 17

Revisions and supersessions

This chapter covers:

This chapter does not include information on revisions and supersessions outstanding at conversion. These are covered in Chapter 7. Conversion decisions themselves may be revised or superseded as described in this chapter.[1] However, the amount of any maintenance to be paid (eg, any transitional amount) will be worked out using the rules described in Chapter 7.

Note: the detailed rules described in this chapter on when a decision can be revised or superseded and the date from when a supersession takes effect apply to 'new rules' cases. While revisions and supersessions of 'old rules' cases are broadly similar, there are some small differences.[2]

1. Changing decisions

Most decisions can be changed or challenged by revision or supersession. However, there are some decisions that cannot (see p343).

A supersession or revision is a decision which changes an earlier decision. As with all decisions, they are made by decision makers who work for the Child Support Agency (CSA) and who make decisions in the name of the Child Maintenance and Enforcement Commission (CMEC). A revision or supersession normally happens because the decision maker is told that something is wrong or has changed since the initial decision was made. A decision maker may also initiate a revision or supersession her/himself.

The table on p342 is a quick guide to when decisions are revised and superseded. The main difference between a revision and supersession is that:

- a revision means the decision which is wrong or has been challenged is itself changed, and the revised decision normally takes effect from the date the original decision had effect;

- a supersession means that a new decision is made that takes effect from a later date.

If a decision is challenged within one month, it may be revised. Outside this time period, a decision can only be revised if a late application for revision is accepted (see p346) or in special circumstances – eg, if there has been official error (see p347). If these special circumstances are not met, the decision may be superseded instead.

If the original decision is not incorrect, but the CSA has not dealt with the case properly in some way, a complaint can be made at any time (see Chapter 20). In addition, in some cases where the original decision is wrong (eg, where maladministration has led to an official error), it may be appropriate to make a complaint as well as applying for the decision to be revised.

Quick guide to revisions and supersessions

Why is the decision being challenged?	*When?*	*What can be done?*
The decision is wrong for any reason.	Within a month of being told the decision.	The decision can be revised.
The CSA made a mistake ('official error'), was misled, did not know about something that would have affected the decision or someone was not a parent of a child to whom a calculation relates.	At any time.	The decision can be revised. If the CSA did not know something or was misled, the decision can only be revised in certain circumstances (see p345). If these do not apply, the decision can be superseded.
The decision is wrong for any reason (other than one of the reasons in the above row).	Later than one month after being told the decision.	The decision may be superseded, but the person can make a late application for a revision to be considered (see p346).
Something that affects the decision has changed.	At any time.	The decision can be superseded.

Variations are an element of the calculation. This means that any change relating to a variation can lead to a revision or supersession of the maintenance calculation. See Chapter 6.

For changing decisions on deductions of maintenance from benefits, see CPAG's *Welfare Benefits and Tax Credits Handbook*.

Decisions of the First-tier Tribunal and the Upper Tribunal (see Chapter 18) can also be superseded or revised, but only in certain circumstances (see pp345 and 350).

If a non-resident parent thinks the revision/supersession may reduce the amount of his calculation, he may try to negotiate lower payments pending the decision, although this is usually difficult (see p406).

Challenging decisions that cannot be revised or superseded

Decisions that cannot be revised or superseded are mainly in the areas of information gathering, collection and enforcement, and others such as refusals to make an interim or default maintenance decision.

Further information can be given to the CSA and the decision maker can be asked to reconsider. If the decision maker refuses to change the decision, a complaint can be made. There may be other occasions that do not involve a decision, but where the behaviour of CSA staff or others acting for CMEC is unsatisfactory – eg, if there is intimidating or unnecessarily intrusive questioning, or unwarranted demands for evidence and documentation. In these cases, a complaint can be made.

Complaints should initially be made through the CSA's own complaints system before being taken further if necessary – eg, to the Independent Case Examiner (see Chapter 20).

Deduction from earnings orders can be appealed to a court (see p415). Judicial review may also be possible (see below).

Judicial review

Judicial review is the legal procedure that allows a court to examine the way in which a public body has exercised its discretionary decision-making power to ensure that it has done so for the lawful purpose of the power.[3] A person affected by a decision or action of a public body or one of its officers can ask the High Court (or Court of Session in Scotland) to carry out a judicial review of the decision or action.

Judicial review is about the validity of the process by which a decision was made rather than the actual result of the decision.

The court can 'set aside' the decision and also order the decision maker to consider it again in a lawful way. Judicial review cannot usually be brought if there is a right to raise the issue in an appeal to the First-tier Tribunal, Upper Tribunal or court. Otherwise, judicial review of a decision of the CSA may be sought – eg, on enforcement. Legal advice *must* be taken as soon as possible after the decision is made. Legal aid may be available.

Judicial review can succeed if:[4]

- the decision maker makes an error in law ('illegality') – eg, does something s/he has no power to do; *or*

- a decision maker fails to have regard to a relevant matter or has regard to an irrelevant matter, or where a decision is 'so outrageous in its defiance of logic or of accepted moral standards that no sensible person who had applied his mind to the question could have arrived at it' (irrationality); *or*
- there has been procedural unfairness.

Challenging decisions about benefit entitlement

Some CSA decisions depend on a decision of Jobcentre Plus or the Pension Service. For example, a non-resident parent in receipt of income support, income-based jobseeker's allowance, income-related employment and support allowance, or the guarantee credit of pension credit will pay the minimum rate (see p168) or the flat rate (see p81) of child support. As long as Jobcentre Plus or the Pension Service pay one of these benefits, even if the non-resident parent has other income, there can be no application for a variation on additional income grounds (see p119). A parent who believes that the other parent should not be allowed to claim a benefit (eg, because s/he is working full time) cannot directly challenge a Jobcentre Plus/Pension Service decision to award it. However, s/he can raise the issue with the CSA, which will contact Jobcentre Plus or the Pension Service, which then investigates. Jobcentre Plus/the Pension Service reports the result to the CSA, but not to the person who made the allegation. That person cannot appeal to the First-tier Tribunal against the Jobcentre Plus/Pension Service decision,[5] although judicial review could be sought.

2. **Revisions**

The decision maker can revise a decision if a person applies within one month or applies for a variation within one month (provided the grounds for variation existed from the date of the decision under revision), or if the decision maker her/himself initiates the revision within one month of the original decision. The decision maker can also revise a decision if a person applies for, and is granted, an extension of time (see p346).

In addition, there are certain situations where the original decision was wrong in such a way that it can be revised at any time (see p346). A revised decision normally takes effect from the date the original decision had effect.

If a person thinks that a decision is wrong, s/he does not have to seek a revision and can appeal directly to the First-tier Tribunal instead if it is a decision against which there is a right of appeal (see Chapter 18). There are advantages and disadvantages to both approaches.

Decisions that can be revised

Most child maintenance decisions can be revised, including:[6]

- a decision made by the Child Support Agency (CSA) that makes a maintenance calculation (including a variation on a calculation), an interim decision or a default maintenance decision (see p331);
- a decision made by the CSA not to make a maintenance calculation, unless the decision maker has instead made an interim or default maintenance decision (in which case, it is that decision which can be revised). A refusal to make an interim or default maintenance decision cannot be revised;[7]
- a decision of the First-tier Tribunal to make, or refuse to agree, a variation to a maintenance calculation following a referral by the CSA.[8] However, a decision to make, or to refuse to make, a variation made by an appeal tribunal before 3 November 2008 (when appeal tribunals were replaced by the First-tier Tribunal) cannot be revised;
- any supersession decision made by the CSA (see p350);[9]
- a decision which has previously been revised if any of the above circumstances apply to the revised decision.[10]

When a decision can be revised

The decision maker can revise a decision if, within a month of notification of the decision:[11]

- s/he starts action leading to a revision;
- a person (person with care, non-resident parent or child applicant in Scotland) applies for a revision; *or*
- a person applies for a variation.

'Month' means a complete calendar month from the date of notification.[12]

If this one-month time limit is missed, a person can seek to make a late application (see below).[13]

Outside this one-month time period, the decision maker can revise a decision if:

- an appeal is made in time (or within the time allowed for late appeals if the application meets those conditions and the appeal has not yet been determined.[14] If an appeal is lodged, the decision maker checks to see whether the decision should be revised (see above);
- there has been 'official error' (see p347);[15]
- the decision is wrong because of a misrepresentation or failure to disclose a material fact (see p347) and, because of this, the decision is more advantageous to the person who misrepresented or failed to disclose than it would otherwise have been;[16]
- it was made pending a test-case decision, which has now been given (see p385);[17]

- the person applied for a revision within a month of the decision but it was refused because there was insufficient information or evidence to carry out a revision and the person has provided the further information within a month (or such longer period as is reasonable in the circumstances) of being notified of the refusal;[18] *or*
- the decision is wrong because a person with respect to whom the maintenance calculation has been made was not, at the time the calculation was made, a parent of a child to whom the calculation relates.[19]

A decision *cannot* be revised because of a change in circumstances after the date the decision was made, or because of an expected change.[20] Instead, the decision may be superseded (see p350) or a new application should be made.

For revisions of default maintenance decisions, see p321.

Under the test case rules (see p385), the decision maker may refuse to follow the law as decided by the Upper Tribunal or the courts, or even suspend a decision on revision while an appeal is being brought in another case.

Late applications

Because a supersession (see p350) cannot usually lead to a decision being backdated to the original effective date, a late application for a revision may need to be made. However, in case it should not be accepted, an application for a supersession can be made at the same time, if appropriate. For example, a decision may be based on the wrong mortgage payment details. If the person concerned missed the deadline for applying for a revision, s/he can make a late application (giving special reasons – see below) and also apply for a supersession on the grounds that there has been a mistake of fact (see p350). S/he should also file a late notice of appeal if still within the maximum time limit for doing so (see p363). This is because the circumstances in which a late appeal can be accepted by the First-tier Tribunal are wider than those in which a late applicatiions for a revision can be accepted.

The decision maker can extend the one-month period for applying for a revision if s/he considers that:[21]

- it was not practicable to apply within one month because of 'special circumstances' (see below);
- the application for revision has merit; *and*
- it is reasonable to grant the application.

'Special circumstances' are not defined, but they are not the same as the special circumstances needed for the decision maker to admit a late appeal (see p363). However, ignorance of, or a mistake about, the law, including time limits, or a new interpretation of the law by the Upper Tribunal or court are *not* special circumstances and must be ignored when considering the application.[22] The person applying for a revision must apply for an extension within 13 months of the notification.[23] However, if s/he has asked for written reasons for the decision s/he is seeking to revise, the 13 months can be extended. If the statement of reasons is provided within one month of notification of the decision, the 13-month period is extended by 14 days. If the statement of reasons is provided after one month, the 13 months plus 14 days runs from the date it is provided.[24] The longer the delay in applying for a revision, the more compelling the special circumstances must be.[25]

An application for an extension must identify the decision that it seeks to revise and explain why an extension should be granted.[26] An application that is refused may not be renewed,[27] although the decision maker may have power to reconsider a refusal to extend.[28] There is no right of appeal against a refusal to allow a late application for revision. Instead, a person can try to make a late appeal against the original decision (see Chapter 18). Judicial review of a refusal to extend the time limit for making a revision may also be possible (see p343).

Official error

'Official error' is a mistake made by an officer of the CSA, Child Maintenance Enforcement Commission (CMEC), Department for Work and Pensions, HM Revenue and Customs, or a designated authority, which was not caused or contributed to by anyone outside one of these bodies.[29] This includes mistakes of law (see p352), except those only shown to be an error by a decision of the Upper Tribunal or court, as well as mistakes of fact, such as:

- a mistake of arithmetic;
- a wrong assumption about a person's circumstances where there was no evidence for it;
- a mistake made because CSA or CMEC staff did not pass information or evidence to the officer who made the decision, when they should have done.

Misrepresentation and failure to disclose

A **'misrepresentation'** is a written or spoken statement of fact which is untrue.[30] This applies to an untrue statement, even if the person making it believes it to be true ('innocent misrepresentation').[31]

There is only a **'failure to disclose'** a fact if there is a legal duty to report that fact to the CSA or CMEC.[32] Therefore, a person who is asked to give information, but does not, has failed to disclose that information. However, if a person is not asked for the information, there can be no failure to disclose unless it is one of the facts that a parent with care or non-resident parent must always report. There is no general duty to report all changes of circumstances to the CSA, but there are some changes which must be reported (see p71).

The decision that the decision maker wishes to revise must have been wrong because of a fact that was misrepresented or not disclosed and the decision was more advantageous to the person who misrepresented or failed to disclose.[33] Therefore, if a decision maker ignored that fact or if that fact made no difference, the decision maker cannot base a revision on misrepresentation or failure to disclose.

Example 17.1

When Amy applied for maintenance, she also applied for a variation on the grounds that Shaun had assets over £65,000. However, the variation was not agreed and her maintenance calculation was made without this element, based on the information Shaun provided. A few months later Amy discovers that Shaun had inherited a property from his aunt a few weeks before her application for maintenance. She informs the CSA, it investigates and confirms that he failed to disclose this when he was asked to provide information for the variation element. Because he failed to disclose the inheritance, his maintenance calculation is less than it would have been with the variation element. Since there was failure to disclose that resulted in a decision that was more advantageous to him, the decision maker revises the original maintenance calculation.

However, had Shaun only inherited the property some time after he was asked for information in relation to the variation application, the decision maker could not decide that he had failed to disclose information. In this case, the maintenance calculation could not be revised, but it may be superseded if Amy asked for a variation to be considered.

Procedure for revising

A notification of a decision sets out how to ask the decision maker to revise that decision.[34] The revision request may be made by telephone. However, unless the issue is straightforward, it is best to follow up any telephone call with a letter to the CSA confirming the reason for the request.

There is no general requirement for the decision maker to notify the parties that s/he is considering a revision or to inform one party that the other has applied for a revision. However, if an application for variation has passed preliminary consideration[35] or there is a request for a revision of a calculation with a previously agreed variation,[36] the other parties will be contacted and asked for their representations.

The rules about disclosure apply to the information given in any notification (see p72).

If a revision has been requested, the burden of proof is on the applicant.[37] In cases where a revision is sought within one month or a late application is accepted, a person does not have to show any specific grounds for the revision. It is enough that s/he simply thinks that the decision is wrong, although a full explanation of reasons for seeking the revision, and any supporting information or evidence, should always be provided.

In cases where the applicant fails to provide sufficient information to make a decision, the decision maker notifies her/him that there is insufficient information or evidence to make a decision. The applicant may be invited to reapply, usually within one month of this notification, providing sufficient information or evidence. The time limit may be extended if the decision maker considers this is reasonable.[38]

The decision maker may decide to:

- revise the decision; *or*
- make a default maintenance decision; *or*
- refuse to revise the decision.

If a default decision would be less than the current maintenance calculation, the decision maker may refuse to revise rather than make a default maintenance decision. For further information on default maintenance decisions, see p320.

If a revision is considered because an appeal has been lodged, unless the revised decision would be worse for the person appealing (the appellant), the revision is carried out and the appeal lapses.[39] The appellant can then decide to appeal against the revised decision, within the usual time limits. The CSA should try to inform all the relevant persons that the appeal has lapsed.[40] If the revised decision does not benefit the appellant, it is still carried out and the appeal does not lapse but continues against the decision as revised.[41]

The revised decision

The revised decision normally has the same effective date as the decision it replaces.[42] However, if the effective date of that decision was wrong, the revised decision has the effective date that the replaced decision should have had.[43]

Notification

If the decision is revised, whether or not this results in a fresh or new maintenance calculation (including a default maintenance decision), the parties must be notified of the decision and given the usual details (see p321).[44] If there is more than one person with care in relation to a non-resident parent, this means all must be notified. The normal rules on information disclosure apply (see p72).[45]

If the request for revision is refused, only the applicant will be informed, unless the other parties have been contacted – eg, where there has been a request for a variation. Notification of the decision must include reasons for refusal and details of appeal rights.[46]

The time limit for appealing against a decision that has been revised runs from the date of the notice of the revised decision. If the request for a revision is refused, the time limit for appealing runs from the date on which this refusal is notified only if the request was made within a month of the original decision being notified or a late application for revision was accepted.[47]

3. Supersessions

The decision maker can supersede a decision at any time if certain rules are met, with or without an application. Usually a decision is superseded because of a change in circumstances. The main difference between a revision and a supersession is that, as a general rule, a superseded decision takes effect from the date on which it is made (whereas a revision generally takes effect from the effective date of the decision being revised). However, there are numerous exceptions to this general rule. Unlike social security cases, there is no duty to tell the Child Support Agency (CSA) of all changes of circumstances (see p71 for changes that must be notified).

Future changes

When the new system of calculating child maintenance starts in 2012 (see Chapter 1), the amount will usually be fixed for a year. There are likely to be Regulations to restrict the situations in which a supersession can be made – eg, whether a particular change in circumstances can result in a supersession during the year.[48]

Decisions that can be superseded

Most child support decisions (whether made by the CSA, the First-tier Tribunal or the Upper Tribunal) can be superseded. However, a decision made before 3 November 2008 (when the new tribunal system was introduced) by an appeal tribunal or the child support commissioners cannot now be superseded. Decisions that can be superseded include:[49]

- a decision to make a maintenance calculation (including a variation on a calculation), an interim decision or a default maintenance decision (see p321);
- a decision of a First-tier Tribunal on a CSA referral of a variation application (see p299);
- a decision to make, or refuse to make, a departure direction;[50]
- any decisions made on revision (see p345).

It may also be possible to supersede other CSA decisions, depending on how the CSA (and the First-tier Tribunal and Upper Tribunal) interprets the rules. For decisions which may be possible to revise, see p345.

When a decision can be superseded

The decision maker can *normally* supersede a decision if:[51]

- it is a decision of the CSA, the First-tier Tribunal or the Upper Tribunal and there has been a relevant change of circumstances since the decision had effect or it is expected that there will be such a change and there would be a significant change in the amount of the calculation;

- it is a decision of the CSA, the First-tier Tribunal or the Upper Tribunal and the decision was made in ignorance of, or was based on a mistake about, a material fact;
- it is a decision of the CSA, the First-tier Tribunal or the Upper Tribunal and there is an application for a variation to the calculation; *or*
- the decision was made by the CSA and it is wrong in law (see p352). If a person thinks that a decision of the First-tier Tribunal or Upper Tribunal is wrong in law, s/he needs to appeal against it.[52]

Any information or evidence on which a superseding decision is to be based must be known to the CSA and not be based on supposition.[53] If a change of circumstances has taken place or is expected, this must be based on fact and not on probability.

When the CSA is notified of a change of circumstances, it does not have to consider anything not raised by the application (or if the CSA is acting on its own initiative, anything which did not cause it to act).[54] This means that the CSA does not have to investigate whether all the other circumstances are still correct. However, the CSA might decide to incorporate the supersession action into a case check, which could result in other changes or errors being identified, and subsequent revisions or supersessions being carried out.

Under the test case rules, the decision maker may refuse to follow the law as decided by the Upper Tribunal or courts, or even suspend a decision on supersession, while an appeal is being brought in another case. See p385 for details.

When a decision cannot be superseded

A decision maker cannot supersede a decision:

- which can be revised instead (see p344);[55]
- refusing to make or cancelling a maintenance calculation.[56] A further application for a maintenance calculation should be made instead.

A decision cannot be superseded on the basis that there has been, or it is anticipated that there will be, a change of circumstances relating to the net income of the non-resident parent unless there is a change of 5 per cent or more in the net income used in the calculation.[57] The CSA refers to this as the 'tolerance level'. However, this does not apply if the superseding decision:[58]

- is on the outcome of a variation application;
- affects a variation ground in a maintenance calculation, or a revised/superseded decision on this;
- is made on an interim maintenance decision, or on the revised/superseded decision;
- is made by the decision maker acting on her/his own initiative on the basis of information or evidence which was also the basis of a decision of the

Department for Work and Pensions on a claim for benefit or a revision or supersession of a decision on a claim or an award of benefit;[59]
- is made following an application on more than one ground, and the grounds which do not relate to the net income of the non-resident parent lead to a superseding decision. The change in income can also be taken into account.[60]

There is a different 'tolerance level' that applies to supersessions in 'old rules' cases. See p260, and for further information, see the 2002/03 edition of this *Handbook*.

The tolerance rule is not applied to other changes of circumstances – eg:
- relevant children joining or leaving the household;
- applications for other qualifying children;
- changes in shared care arrangements;
- changes notified by a third party – eg, Jobcentre Plus;
- the person with care, non-resident parent or qualifying child are no longer habitually resident in the UK; *or*
- the person with care and non-resident parent start living together.

If an application for a supersession is made to which the tolerance rule would apply and a further application is then made on a ground(s) that does not relate to the net income of the non-resident parent, a superseding decision can be made as if the two applications had been made at the same time – ie, so that the change in income can be taken into account.[61]

If, when making a supersession in circumstances where the tolerance rule is satisfied (ie, net income changes by 5 per cent or more), the CSA will make decisions on additional outstanding changes of circumstances of which it is aware without applying the tolerance rule to each of the additional changes. The government has announced its intention to amend the Regulations to make this clear.[62]

Wrong in law

As well as providing grounds for a supersession, a decision being wrong in law can constitute an official error and be grounds for a revision (see p347).

A decision of the CSA is wrong in law if:[63]
- when making the decision, the CSA misinterpreted or overlooked part or all of an Act of Parliament, a regulation or relevant caselaw;
- there is no evidence to support the decision;
- the facts are such that no reasonable person applying the law could have come to such a conclusion;
- there is a breach of natural justice – ie, the procedure used led to unfairness, or the officer who took the decision appeared to be biased;[64]
- the CSA has not given sufficient reasons for the decision;

- when exercising its discretion, the CSA took into account something irrelevant or ignored something relevant – eg, the welfare of the child (see p23).[65]

A decision is wrong in law if the Regulation under which it is made was not made lawfully. Such a Regulation is said to be *ultra vires* (outside the powers). The courts and tribunals can decide that a Regulation is *ultra vires*,[66] and the First-tier and Upper Tribunals have done so in benefit cases.

A decision is also wrong in law if it is contrary to European law – ie, European Union (EU) law and the European Convention on Human Rights (ECHR). EU law will rarely be relevant to child support issues. Commissioners have decided that European law on the equal treatment of men and women in social security matters does not apply to child support.[67]

ECHR law is more likely to be relevant. The CSA, courts and the First-tier and Upper Tribunals are required to interpret Acts of Parliament consistently with the ECHR as far as it is possible to do so.[68] They cannot use the ECHR to overrule an Act of Parliament, but the courts can issue a 'declaration of incompatability'.[69] However, courts and the Tribunals can use the ECHR to override Regulations which are incompatible with the provisions of the ECHR. It is unlawful for the CSA, courts or the Tribunals to act in a way which is incompatible with an ECHR right.[70] In practice, however, few challenges using these principles have succeeded.

Otherwise, the CSA, Jobcentre Plus, First-tier and Upper Tribunals cannot override or ignore the Acts or Regulations.

Procedure for superseding

A party to the calculation can apply for a supersession at any time. There are no time limits, but any superseding decision will run from the beginning of the maintenance period in which the application is made , unless one of the special situations described on p354 applies. If an application is made, the decision maker must consider it and supersede if the conditions set out above are met.

The decision maker can initiate a supersession her/himself. S/he must take into account the welfare of the child (see p23) when considering whether or not to do so. The decision maker learns of some changes automatically from the Jobcentre Plus or may do so from a third party.

If the decision maker is considering a supersession on her/his own initiative in a 'new rules' case, s/he must notify the relevant parties – ie, the person with care, non-resident parent and/or child applicant in Scotland.[71] The supersession cannot take effect until 28 days after this notice has been given, unless it is a decision based on information which was also used to make a benefit decision.[72]

If the supersession is in relation to an application for a variation that has passed preliminary consideration (see p125),[73] or a supersession of a previously agreed variation,[74] the other relevant parties will be contacted and notified of the grounds of the application and any relevant information or evidence the applicant has given. They will not be notified about the details of any long-term illness or disability of a relevant other child (if the application for variation was made on that basis), or about harmful medical evidence or about the address of a relevant person or qualifying child if that would cause a risk of harm or undue distress.[75]

Otherwise, the other party may not be notified of the application for a supersession. The normal rules about disclosure apply to the information given in any notification (see p72).[76]

The decision maker does not have to check all the facts again so can (and usually will) limit her/his consideration to the issues raised in the application.[77] An application for a supersession should, therefore, include all available information and evidence that supports the case for the decision to be changed. Information provided may need to be verified in the normal way (see Chapter 4). Remember that some changes will not lead to a supersession because of the 'tolerance rule' (see p351).

The superseding decision

The decision maker may decide that:

- there are no grounds for supersession and so refuse to supersede;
- there are grounds for supersession but the maintenance calculation remains unchanged;
- there are grounds for supersession and the maintenance calculation is changed; *or*
- the maintenance calculation should be cancelled.

Effective date of the superseding decision

The general rule is that a supersession takes effect from the first day in the maintenance period in which the decision is made or the application for the supersession/variation was made.[78] However, the effective date may be different in certain circumstances, as shown in the table below. This does not cover all circumstances in which a calculation is cancelled (see p327). The rules about the effective date for supersessions in 'old rules' cases are a little different and are not covered in this table.

Circumstances	*Effective date*
An application for an anticipated change in circumstances.	The first day in the maintenance period in which the change is expected to occur.[79]
The relevant circumstance is that a variation ground is expected to occur.	The first day in the maintenance period in which the ground is expected to occur.[80]
A qualifiying child dies or ceases to be a qualifying child.	The first day in the maintenance period in which the change occurred.[81]

The person with care ceases to be a person with care in relation to a qualifying child.	The first day in the maintenance period in which the change occurred.[82]
The person with care, non-resident parent or a qualifying child ceases to be habitually resident in the UK.	The first day in the maintenance period in which the change occurred.[83]
The non-resident parent begins to be liable or stops being liable to pay for half of the flat rate – ie, the following set of circumstances start to apply or stop applying to the non-resident parent: – his partner is also a non-resident parent; – there is a maintenance application in force in respect of the partner; *and* – either he or his partner receive income support, income-based jobseeker's allowance, income-related employment and support allowance or pension credit.	The first day in the maintenance period in which the change occurred.[84]
The decision maker has acted on her/his own initiative.	If the decision maker acts on information or evidence which also led the Jobcentre/ Pension Service to make a decision on a claim for or an award of benefit, the effective date is the first day in the maintenance period in which the CSA became aware of the information or evidence.[85] In all other cases, the decision takes effect from the first day of the maintenance period which includes the date 28 days after the date on which notice that s/he is proposing to supersede is given to the relevant persons.[86]
There is a further qualifying child in relation to the same non-resident parent and person with care.	If this is brought to the attention of the CSA by the non-resident parent, the first day of the maintenance period in which the CSA are told about the child.[87] If this is brought to the attention of the CSA by the person with care, the first day of the maintenance period in which the non-resident parent is given notification of the application for that child.[88]

A non-resident parent has another qualifying child with a different parent with care and an application for maintenance is made by either the non-resident parent or the new parent with care.	The beginning of the maintenance period in which notification of the calculation is given to the non-resident parent.[89]
A non-resident parent or person with care applies for a supersession and the decision maker decides when superseding that different amounts of child maintenance need to be calculated in respect of different specified periods.	The beginning of the maintenance period in which the change of circumstances to which the calculation relates occurred or is expected to occur, unless that change occurred before the date of the application for supersession and was notified after that date. In which case, the effective date is the date of application for supersession.[90]
The decision maker is superseding a decision of the First-tier Tribunal or the Upper Tribunal given following the decision maker having served notice that a test case which could have affected that decision was pending before the Upper Tribunal or a court.	The beginning of the maintenance period following the date on which the decision of the First-tier Tribunal or Upper Tribunal would have taken effect had it been decided in accordance with the decision in the test case.[91]
The decision maker is superseding a decision of the First-tier Tribunal or the Upper Tribunal on the ground that it is wrong because of a misrepresentation about or a failure to disclose a material fact and the decision is more advantageous to the person who misrepresented or failed to disclose than it would otherwise have been but for that error.	The date on which the First-tier Tribunal or Upper Tribunal decision took or was to take effect.[92]
A decision of a decision maker is superseded because it is shown to have been wrong as a result of an Upper Tribunal or court decision in which the CSA lost.	The date of the relevant Upper Tribunal or court decision.[93]

There is currently no provision to backdate the effect of a supersession on the grounds that a relevant other child has ceased to be a child for child maintenance purposes (eg, s/he has reached age 19 or otherwise left the household). The government has announced its intention to amend Regulations to enable supersession in such cases to take effect from the first day in the assessment period in which the change occurred.[94]

Notification

If the decision results in a supersession, whether or not a new maintenance calculation is made (including an interim maintenance decision or default maintenance decision), the parties must be notified of the decision and given the usual details (see p321).[95] The notice must also state how to seek a revision, supersession and appeal.[96]

If the decision is to refuse to supersede, notification will be given including the reasons for refusal and appeal rights.[97]

A party can ask for a supersession decision to be revised or, if the decision is one against which there is a right of appeal, can appeal to the First-tier Tribunal (see Chapter 18).

If the CSA intends to cancel the case it must notify each party and, where the reason for cancellation is a child applicant in Scotland ceasing to be a qualifying child, inform other potential child applicants.[98]

Whether to request supersession

Before requesting a supersession because of a change of circumstances, a parent should try to work out whether a fresh calculation would be higher or lower. S/he need only tell the CSA about the changes in her/his favour. If the change only relates to one party, the CSA may not tell the other person, but if it does, that party might tell the CSA about other changes. These may cancel out the effect of the changes which led the other to ask for a supersession.

If a person believes that another person's circumstances have changed (eg, a non-resident parent no longer has children living with him), s/he can ask for a supersession and for the CSA to investigate (see Chapter 4). The CSA does not have to, but any changes it is aware of must be taken into account when it decides whether or not to supersede.

Notes

1 Reg 4(1)(a) CS(TP) Regs
2 Reg 17-24 CS(MAP) Regs contain the detailed rules on supersessions and revisions for 'old rules' cases.

1. **Changing decisions**
3 *West v Secretary of State for Scotland*, 1992 SC 385, 1992 SLT 636 (reported as *West v Scottish Prison Service*, 1992 SCLR 504)
4 *Council of Civil Service Unions v Minister for the Civil Service* [1984] 1 WLR 1174, [1984] 3 All ER 935
5 s12(2) SSA 1998 and reg 25 SS&CS(DA) Regs

2. **Revisions**
6 s16 CSA 1991
7 Reg 3A(8) and (9) SS&CS(DA) Regs
8 Reg 3A(3) SS&CS(DA) Regs
9 s16(1A)(a) and reg 3A(3) SS&CS(DA) Regs
10 Reg 3A(3) SS&CS(DA) Regs
11 Reg 3A(1)(a) and (d) SS&CS(DA) Regs
12 R(IB) 4/02
13 Regs 3A(1)(a) and 4 SS&CS(DA) Regs
14 Reg 3A(1)(cc) SS&CS(DA) Regs
15 Reg 3A(1)(e) SS&CS(DA) Regs
16 Reg 3A(1)(c) SS&CS(DA) Regs
17 Reg 3A(5A) SS&CS(DA) Regs
18 Reg 3A(1)(b) SS&CS(DA) Regs
19 Reg 3A(1)(f) SS&CS(DA) Regs
20 Reg 3A(2) SS&CS(DA) Regs
21 Reg 4(4) SS&CS(DA) Regs
22 Reg 4(6) SS&CS(DA) Regs
23 Reg 4(3)(b) SS&CS(DA) Regs
24 Reg 4(3)(b) SS&CS(DA) Regs
25 Reg 4(5) SS&CS(DA) Regs
26 Reg 4(3)(a) SS&CS(DA) Regs
27 Reg 4(7) SS&CS(DA) Regs
28 See CIS/93/1992
29 Reg 1(3) SS&CS(DA) Regs
30 R(SB) 9/85
31 R(SB) 2/92 (*Page and Davis v CAO*)
32 CCS/15846/1996
33 Reg 3A(c) SS&CS(DA) Regs
34 Reg 23(4) CS(MCP) Regs
35 Reg 9 CS(V) Regs
36 Reg 15B SS&CS(DA) Regs
37 R(I)1/71
38 Reg 3A(1)(b) SS&CS(DA) Regs
39 s16(6) CSA 1991; reg 30(1) and (2)(f) SS&CS(DA) Regs
40 Reg 15C(12) SS&CS(DA) Regs
41 Reg 30(3) SS&CS(DA) Regs
42 s16(3) CSA 1991
43 Reg 5A SS&CS(DA) Regs
44 Reg 15C SS&CS(DA) Regs
45 Reg 15C(3) SS&CS(DA) Regs
46 Reg 15C(9) and (10) SS&CS(DA) Regs
47 r23(1) and Sch 1 TP(FT) Rules

3. **Supersessions**
48 s17 CMOPA 2008
49 s17(1) CSA 1991
50 s28H and Sch 4C para 1(a) CSA 1991
51 Reg 6A(2)-(6) SS&CS(DA) Regs
52 Reg 6A(2)(c) SS&CS(DA) Regs
53 CCS/162/2006
54 s17(2) CSA 1991
55 Reg 6A(5) SS&CS(DA) Regs
56 Reg 6A(6) SS&CS(DA) Regs
57 Reg 6B(1) SS&CS(DA) Regs
58 Reg 6B(4) SS&CS(DA) Regs
59 Regs 6B(4)(e) and Sch 3D para 4 SS&CS(DA) Regs
60 Reg 6B(3) SS&CS(DA) Regs
61 Reg 6B(5) SS&CS(DA) Regs
62 CMEC consultation on draft Child Support (Miscellaneous Amendment) Regulations 2010, March 2010
63 R(A) 1/72; R(SB) 11/83
64 *R v Gough* [1993] AC 646, [1993] 2 WLR 883, [1993] 2 All ER 724
65 *Wednesbury Corporation v Ministry of Housing and Local Government (No.2)* [1965] 3 WLR 956, [1965] 3 All ER 571
66 *CAO v Foster* [1993] AC 754, [1993] 2 WLR 292, [1993] 1 All ER 705
67 R(CS) 3/96; R(CS) 2/95; CCS/17/1994. These concerned the application of Art 141 of the EC Treaty (formerly Art 119), and Council Directives 75/117 and 79/7. The Sex Discrimination Act 1975 also has no effect. CCS/6/1995
68 s3 HRA 1998
69 s4 HRA 1998
70 s6 HRA 1998
71 Reg 7C SS&CS(DA) Regs
72 Sch 3D para 9 SS&CS(DA) Regs

73 Reg 9 CS(V) Regs
74 Reg 15B SS&CS(DA) Regs
75 Reg 15B(2) SS&CS(DA) Regs
76 Reg 15B SS&CS(DA) Regs
77 s17(2) CSA 1991
78 s17(4) CSA 1991
79 Sch 3D para 2 SS&CS(DA) Regs
80 Sch 3D para 2 SS&CS(DA) Regs
81 Sch 3D para 3(a) SS&CS(DA) Regs
82 Sch 3D para 3(b) SS&CS(DA) Regs
83 Sch 3D para 3(c) SS&CS(DA) Regs
84 Sch 3D para 3(d) SS&CS(DA) Regs
85 Sch 3D para 4 SS&CS(DA) Regs
86 Sch 3D para 9 SS&CS(DA) Regs
87 Sch 3D para 6(a) SS&CS(DA) Regs
88 Sch 3D para 6(b) SS&CS(DA) Regs
89 Sch 3D para 7 SS&CS(DA) Regs
90 Sch 3D para 8 SS&CS(DA) Regs
91 Sch 3D para 10 SS&CS(DA) Regs
92 Sch 3D para 11 SS&CS(DA) Regs
93 Sch 3D para 12 SS&CS(DA) Regs
94 CMEC consultation on draft Child Support (Miscellaneous Amendments) Regulations 2010, March 2010
95 Reg 15C SS&CS(DA) Regs
96 Reg 15C(4) SS&CS(DA) Regs
97 Reg 15C(9)-(11) SS&CS(DA) Regs
98 Reg 15C(5) SS&CS(DA) Regs

Chapter 18

Appeals

This chapter covers:

This chapter does not include information on appeals outstanding at conversion (see Chapter 7). However, conversion decisions themselves can be appealed as described in this chapter.[1]

Most child maintenance decisions made by a decision maker in the Child Support Agency (CSA) or Child Maintenance Enforcement Commission (CMEC) can be appealed to an independent appeal tribunal: the First-tier Tribunal (Social Entitlement Chamber). An application for a variation can also be referred to the First-tier Tribunal by the decision maker.[2] The First-tier Tribunal looks at all the evidence in the case and gives a new decision. This decision replaces the decision of the decision maker. A First-tier Tribunal decision can be appealed on a question of law to the Upper Tribunal (Administrative Appeals Chamber).

On 1 April 2011, the Tribunal Service, which administers both the First-tier Tribunal and the Upper Tribunal, became part of a new body known as HM Courts and Tribunals Service, an agency of the Ministry of Justice.

The rules described in this chapter relate to the tribunal system introduced from 3 November 2008. For details about the rules that applied before this date, see previous editions of this *Handbook*. If an appeal was made before 3 November 2008 and is still ongoing, the First-tier Tribunal or Upper Tribunal can apply the old procedural rules if this would be fair.[3]

Many aspects of appealing and appeal procedure are explained in more detail in CPAG's *Welfare Benefits and Tax Credits Handbook*.

1. Decisions that can be appealed and who can appeal

Usually, any relevant person (ie, person with care, non-resident parent or a child applicant in Scotland) has the right to appeal.[4] However, there are some exceptions to this. The rules are covered in this table.

Decisions that can be appealed	*Who can appeal*
A decision (as originally made or as revised), including default and interim maintenance decisions, about whether maintenance is payable and, if so, how much or, in 'new rules' cases, a decision to supersede a calculation.	Any relevant person.[5]
A refusal to make a maintenance calculation (including default and interim maintenance decisions) or, in 'new rules' cases, a refusal to supersede.	Any relevant person.[6]
In 'old rules' cases, a decision to cancel or to refuse to cancel a maintenance assessment or interim maintenance assessment, and a decision to make, or refuse to make, a maintenance assessment or departure direction.	Only the person who made the application can appeal against a decision to refuse to make a maintenance assessment.[7] In all other situations, any relevant person.
A decision to impose penalty payments or payment of fees.	In these cases, only the parent required to pay the penalty or person required to pay the fees can appeal.[8]
An adjustment, or cancellation of an adjustment, of the amount paid because of an overpayment of maintenance or voluntary payments.	Any relevant person.[9]
A supersession decision, whether as originally made or as revised. Conversion decisions can therefore be appealed, since these are supersession decisions.	Any relevant person.[10]

The Child Support Agency (CSA) may also refer a variation application to the First-tier Tribunal in certain cases. The First-tier Tribunal can also consider departures in 'old rules' cases.

Person with right of appeal dies

If a relevant person with a right of appeal dies, the executor or administrator of her/his estate can exercise the right of appeal that s/he had and can continue with any appeals that are already underway.[11] If a non-resident parent dies and an appeal is ongoing at that time, the CSA must appoint the administrator or executor as the person to proceed with the appeal unless there is no such person, in which case the CSA can appoint someone it thinks fit to proceed in the place of the deceased.[12]

Decisions that cannot be appealed

Only decisions and, in some cases, refusals to make decisions, can be appealed. It is not possible to appeal if no decision has been made – eg, because of a delay. Instead, a complaint (see Chapter 20) or application for judicial review could be considered. Similarly, decisions about the method of collection or the enforcement of payment cannot be appealed. If you are uncertain whether you can appeal against a decision, you should seek advice straight away.

Parentage disputes

If the appellant denies s/he is the parent of a child named in the maintenance application, the appeal is not dealt with by the First-tier Tribunal, but by a court.[13] If there are other grounds for appeal apart from the dispute about parentage, the First-tier Tribunal will deal with those issues and the parentage issue will be dealt with at court. An appeal involving a dispute about parentage is made in exactly the same way as any other appeal.[14] If the appeal is sent by the CSA to the First-tier Tribunal and it involves a denial of parentage, the First-tier Tribunal should transfer that issue to the court.[15] For parentage disputes that arise before the appeal stage is reached see p18 and p61.

2. Appealing to the First-tier Tribunal

When the decision maker makes a decision, each relevant person must be sent a notice of that decision and information on the right of appeal.[16]

An appeal is started by a person with a right of appeal sending a 'notice of appeal' to the Child Support Agency (CSA) office that issued the decision.

Regardless of who makes an appeal, all parties have the same rights, except that only the person making the appeal (the appellant) can ask to withdraw the appeal. Because an appeal can be withdrawn without the consent of any other party (see p373), it is best for each party who wishes to challenge the decision to bring her/his own appeal. The appeals can be heard together.

There is a CSA form that can be used to make an appeal (CSL307). The notice of appeal must include:[17]

- the name and address of the person making the appeal;
- the name and address of that person's representative (if s/he has one);
- an address to which documents about the appeal may be sent or delivered to the person making the appeal;
- details of the decision being appealed;
- the grounds of the appeal.

There are strict time limits for making an appeal (see below), which can only be extended in certain circumstances (see below). If the notice of appeal does not include sufficient information or is not made on the approved form, see p364.

Time limits

An appeal must be received at the relevant CSA office within one month of the notice of the decision being sent to the appellant.[18]

If a written statement of reasons for a decision was requested within one month of that decision, the time limit for appeal is 14 days after the later of:

- the end of that month; *or*
- the date on which the written statement of reasons was provided.[19]

If the appellant is appealing against a refusal to revise a decision following a late application for a revision (see p346) where time was not extended, this one-month time limit runs from the date of the original decision being notified, not the date on which the CSA notified her/him of its refusal to revise. However, if the CSA refused to revise a decision following an application for a revision that was made within the time limit (see p345) or the extended time limit, the one-month time limit runs from the date on which the notice of refusal to revise was issued. Similarly, if a decision is revised, the time for appealing runs from the date on which the revised decision is sent to the appellant.[20]

A notice of a decision counts as having been sent to the person on the day it is issued by the CSA.[21]

'Month' means a complete calendar month from the day of notification.[22]

When calculating time, if something has to be done by a certain day, it must be done by 5pm that day. If a time limit ends on a day other than a working day, it must be done by the next working day to meet the time limit.[23]

Late appeals

In certain situations, the above time limits can be extended. However, the period in which an appeal must be made can never be extended by more than 12 months from the time limit that applied.[24]

If a notice of appeal is submitted outside the time limit, in addition to the information listed above, it must also include the reasons why it is late.[25]

A decision maker can extend the time limit for appealing, but only if s/he is satisfied that it is in the interests of justice.[26] It will be in the interests of justice to extend the time for appealing if it was not practicable to make the application in time because of special circumstances – ie:[27]

- the applicant, her/his partner or dependant has died or has a serious illness;
- the applicant is not resident in the UK;
- normal postal services were disrupted; *or*
- other wholly exceptional special circumstances.

The later the appeal, the more compelling the special circumstances must be.[28] When considering whether there are special circumstances, the decision maker must not take into account any mistake made by the applicant (or her/his representative) about the law (including about a time limit), or an interpretation of the law by the Upper Tribunal, a commissioner or a court, which is different from the way the CSA had understood and applied the law.[29]

If the decision maker does not think it is in the interests of justice for the appeal to be admitted, s/he should still send the appeal to the First-tier Tribunal. If the decision maker objects to the First-tier Tribunal admitting the appeal or believes the appeal is outside the maximum extension of 12 months, s/he should refer the case immediately to the First-tier Tribunal, indicating that s/he objects to its admission.[30] If the decision maker does not object, the First-tier Tribunal *must* admit the appeal unless it is made outside the maximum 12-month extension period.[31] If the decision maker objects to the appeal being admitted, the First-tier Tribunal *may* (provided the appeal is not outside the maximum 12-month extension) still admit the appeal if it believes that it is fair and just to do so – ie, it does not have to be satisfied that there are special reasons.[32]

If the First-tier Tribunal decides that an appeal cannot be admitted because it was made outside the absolute time limit for appealing, an appeal can be made to the Upper Tribunal (see p381) against this decision.[33]

The appeal form or letter has insufficient information

The CSA can forward to the First-tier Tribunal a written appeal which is not on the appeal form (or which is, but is not fully completed) if it contains sufficient information for the appeal to proceed.[34] However, if the form is not properly completed, or the letter contains insufficient information, the CSA may return it to the appellant for completion or ask for further information.[35] If the appellant returns the completed form/information within 14 days of the CSA request (or a longer period if the CSA accepts), the appeal is treated as having been made on time.[36] If the appellant does not do this, the CSA refers the appeal form/letter (with any relevant documents or evidence) to the First-tier Tribunal for it to decide if it meets the rules.[37] Any information received by the CSA after the referral is made but before the First-tier Tribunal's decision must be referred to the First-tier Tribunal, which must take it into account.[38]

After an appeal is made

After an appeal is made, a decision maker looks at the decision again and may revise it. See p348 for further information about what may happen if the decision is revised.

The decision maker should prepare a 'response' to the appeal. This should be sent to the First-tier Tribunal and to the parties to the appeal as soon as reasonably practical after receiving the notice of appeal.[39] The response should state:[40]

- the name and address of the decision maker;
- the name and address of the decision maker's representative (if any). These are known as 'presenting officers';
- an address where documents for the decision maker can be sent or delivered;
- the name and addresses of any other respondents and their representatives (if any).

The response should explain (or have attached documents which explain) what parts of the grounds put forward for the appeal the decision maker disagrees with, and why.[41]

The response may also indicate whether the decision maker thinks the case requires a hearing or could be decided by just considering the papers.[42]

The response should have attached to it:[43]

- a copy of any written record of the decision being appealed;
- copies of all documents relevant to the case that the CSA has;
- a copy of the notice of appeal, together with any documents submitted by the appellant.

If a person with care or non-resident parent has told the CSA that s/he would like her/his address, or the address of the child, to be kept confidential, the decision maker should take steps to ensure that this is not revealed to the other party(ies).[44]

3. The appeal procedure

Once an appeal has been made, the First-tier Tribunal deals with the case. The First-tier Tribunal will not be aware of the case until it receives the response from the decision maker (or a referral of a late appeal if that is sent before the response). If there is a delay in the decision maker sending the response to the First-tier Tribunal which is causing hardship, the appellant could apply to the First-tier Tribunal for a direction telling the Child Support Agency (CSA) to provide the papers.

When the regional office of HM Courts and Tribunals Service receives the appeal papers, it sends the appellant a questionnaire (called an enquiry form) asking whether s/he wants an oral hearing. For further information about oral and paper hearings, see p375.

Both the First-tier and Upper Tribunal have procedural rules, setting out their powers and how they should deal with cases. There are also Practice Directions and Practice Statements, which set out how they should conduct themselves in various situations. The rules are similar for both the First-tier and Upper Tribunal and so this section applies to both (and explains where there are differences). The rules about hearings and decisions are also part of the procedural rules, but are dealt with on p375 and p377. See p380 for challenging and p381 for appealing against a First-tier Tribunal decision.

The overriding objective: fair and just

The overriding objective of the rules is to enable the Tribunal to deal with cases 'fairly and justly'.[45] Whenever the Tribunal exercises a power under the rules (eg, to admit or not admit a late appeal, or to strike out an appeal), it must have regard to whether it would be fair and just. Similarly, when the Tribunal interprets what the rules mean or what the Practice Directions say, it must try to come to the interpretation which meets the overriding objective – ie, to enable a case to be dealt with in a way which is fair and just.[46]

It is therefore important to bear in mind the overriding objective in any dealings with the Tribunal about the conduct of the proceedings – eg, directions that should be given, witnesses to be summoned, a child giving evidence, asking for an adjournment, asking for more time to give submissions or get evidence, and objecting to the decision maker being given more time to get evidence. It may be worthwhile explaining to the Tribunal why doing what you want would be fair and just.

The rules set out some of the things that must be taken into account when deciding whether a particular interpretation of the rules is fair and just or in deciding whether it would be fair and just to exercise a power conferred by the rules in a particular way.[47] The Tribunal should:

- deal with the case in a way which is proportionate to its importance, the complexity of the issues, the anticipated costs and the resources of the parties;
- avoid unnecessary formality and be flexible in the proceedings;
- ensure, so far as practicable, that the parties are able to participate fully in the proceedings;
- use any special expertise of the Tribunal effectively; *and*
- avoid delay, so far as it is compatible with the proper consideration of the issues.

Note: the list on p366 is not exhaustive. Matters that are not listed can still be taken into account when considering what is fair and just in a particular case.[48]

The parties to an appeal have a duty to assist the Tribunal in dealing with cases fairly and justly.[49]

Applying for directions

Tribunals can give a wide range of directions in order to manage cases. When doing so, the Tribunal must ensure that its action is consistent with the overriding objective (see p366).

A direction can be given at any time, either on the initiative of the Tribunal or following an application by a party to the proceedings.[50]

An application for a direction can be made either orally at a hearing or by writing to the Tribunal. The application must include the reason for seeking the direction.

The Tribunal must, unless it considers there is a good reason not to do so, send a written notice of the direction to every party and to anyone else affected by it.

If a party is unhappy with a particular direction, s/he can use this same procedure to apply for another direction which amends, suspends or sets aside the earlier direction.

If a party fails to comply with a direction, the case could be struck out (see p370) or the party barred from any hearing (see p371).

It may sometimes be possible to appeal to the Upper Tribunal about the content of a particular direction – eg, to exclude harmful evidence or to include certain evidence.[51]

General case management powers

In particular, the Tribunal can give directions to:

- extend or shorten the time for complying with any rule, Practice Direction or direction. This is the only rule there is on extending time. It is relevant to any late application – eg, to appeal, for a statement of reasons or to set aside. Importantly, it does not contain any upper limit (although there is an upper limit of a 12-month extension for late appeals);
- consolidate or hear together two or more sets of proceedings (or parts of proceedings) raising common issues, or treat a case as a lead case;
- permit or require a party to amend a document;
- permit or require a party or another person to provide documents, information, evidence or submissions to the Tribunal or a party. There are more specific powers to obtain evidence (see p368);
- deal with an issue in the proceedings as a preliminary issue – eg, to decide precisely what decision is under appeal or whether the Tribunal has jurisdiction;

- hold a hearing to consider any matter, including a case management issue. This could include, for example, a preliminary hearing to decide what further evidence is needed and who should provide it, how much time the final hearing needs or whether the appeal should be struck out because of a failure to comply with a direction;
- decide the form of any hearing – eg, the order in which parties speak or give evidence and who questions the appellant. If the Tribunal consists of more than one member, this is decided by the presiding member (see p375);[52]
- adjourn or postpone a hearing;
- require a party to produce a 'bundle' (an indexed set of documents and legal authorities relating to the case) for a hearing. Because the Tribunal must take into account the resources of the parties when issuing a direction and the fact that there is a disparity of resources between a typical parent with care/non-resident parent and the CSA, it will be rare for anyone but the CSA to be required to produce a bundle;
- 'stay' (or, in Scotland, 'sist') proceedings. This allows the Tribunal to put the case on hold pending the outcome of another case in which it is expected legal issues will be decided which are relevant to the outcome to be given in the stayed case;
- transfer proceedings to another court or tribunal if that has jurisdiction in relation to the proceedings. This can happen where there has been a change of circumstances since the proceedings were started and the Tribunal no longer has jurisdiction, or if the Tribunal considers the other court or tribunal to be more appropriate to determine the case. For example, if a non-resident parent denies parentage for the first time in the proceedings, the Tribunal would no longer have jurisdiction. Similarly, if a denial of parentage had not been noted by the CSA and the Tribunal becomes aware of it, the Tribunal would have to transfer the case;
- suspend the effect of its own decision pending the determination of an application for permission to appeal against (and any appeal or review of) that decision.

Evidence

The Tribunal can give directions about:[53]

- issues on which it requires evidence or submissions;
- the nature of the evidence or submissions it requires;
- whether the parties are permitted or required to provide expert evidence;
- any limit on the number of witnesses whose evidence a party may put forward, whether in relation to a particular issue or generally;
- the manner in which any evidence or submissions are to be provided;
- the time at which any evidence or submissions are to be provided.[54]

The Tribunal can exclude evidence if:

- it was not provided within a time limit in a direction or Practice Direction;
- it does not comply with a direction or a Practice Direction in some other way;
- it would be unfair to admit the evidence.

Harmful evidence

If a person with care or non-resident parent has told the CSA that s/he would like her/his address, or the address of a child, to be kept confidential, the decision maker should take steps to ensure that the address is not revealed to the other party(ies).[55] In addition, the Tribunal can order that documents or information relating to the proceedings are not to be disclosed or that any matter which could allow members of the public to identify the people involved should not be disclosed.[56]

The Tribunal can also direct that a particular person does not get a document or information if:[57]

- disclosure would be likely to cause her/him or some other person serious harm; *and*
- weighing up that potential harm against the interests of justice, it is proportionate not to disclose the information.

If a party thinks the Tribunal should direct that a particular document or piece of information should be withheld from another party, s/he must not give the document or information to that party. Instead, s/he must write to the Tribunal with a copy of the document or information and explain why it should not be disclosed.[58]

The Tribunal can, however, disclose the document or information to the party's representative if it is satisfied that s/he will not disclose the document to another person without the consent of the Tribunal and that such disclosure is in the interests of justice.[59]

Witnesses

The Tribunal has a power to summons (in Scotland, cite) witnesses and to order other documents to be produced.[60] The Tribunal may require any person (this extends to all people and not just to one of the parties to the appeal, including companies) to:

- attend as a witness at a hearing at the time and place specified in the summons (citation in Scotland);
- to answer any questions which relate to the proceedings;
- to provide any documents in her/his possession or control which relate to the proceedings.

The Tribunal must give the person summoned at least 14 days' notice of the hearing (or a shorter period if the Tribunal directs this). If the person summoned is not a party to the proceedings, her/his expenses will be paid.

If the person has not already had an opportunity to object to being summonsed or ordered, the summons/order should state that s/he can apply to the Tribunal to vary or set aside the summons/order. The summons must state the consequences of failing to comply. The First-tier Tribunal can refer the person to the Upper Tribunal if s/he fails to comply (see p381).[61]

Note: the Tribunal cannot summons a child if this would be detrimental to her/his welfare.

Costs

Neither the First-tier Tribunal nor the Upper Tribunal when hearing an appeal (other than in a judicial review) can award costs.[62]

Failure to comply with rules

If there has been a failure to comply with the rules, a Practice Direction or a direction, the Tribunal may take any action which it considers just, including:[63]

- waiving the requirement;
- requiring the failure to be remedied;
- striking out the appeal;
- the First-tier Tribunal referring the matter to the Upper Tribunal;
- restricting a party's participation in the proceedings;
- fining or committing someone to prison (Upper Tribunal only).

The Upper Tribunal has the same powers as the High Court (the Court of Session in Scotland) concerning the attendance and examination of witnesses and the production and inspection of documents.[64] It can therefore commit (imprison) a person who does not comply with its rules (eg, if s/he does not obey a summons) or impose a fine.

The First-tier Tribunal does not have this power, but can refer a person to the Upper Tribunal in order for the Upper Tribunal to deal with her/him under its own powers as if s/he had failed to comply with one of its own rules or directions.[65] The First-tier Tribunal can only refer someone if s/he has failed to:

- attend at any place to give evidence;
- otherwise make her/himself available to give evidence;
- swear an oath in connection with giving evidence;
- produce a document;
- facilitate the inspection of a document or any other thing (including premises).

Striking out an appeal and barring

In certain circumstances, the Tribunal can 'strike out' (ie, dismiss without considering the decision under appeal) an appeal, or part of an appeal.

The Tribunal *must* strike out an appeal, or part of an appeal, if:

- the appellant has failed to comply with a direction which stated that the appeal, or that part of the appeal, *would* be struck out for failure to comply;[66] *or*
- it does not have jurisdiction to decide the appeal (or that part of it) and it has not transferred the appeal (or part of the appeal) to another tribunal or court.[67]

The Tribunal *may* strike out an appeal, or part of an appeal, if:

- the appellant has failed to comply with a direction which stated that the appeal, or that part of the appeal, *could* be struck out for failure to comply; *or*
- the appellant has failed to co-operate with the Tribunal to such an extent that the Tribunal cannot deal with the proceedings fairly and justly;[68] *or*
- it considers that the appeal has no reasonable prospects of success.[69]

The Tribunal must give a written notice of its decision to strike out an appeal, or part of it. A party to the appeal can ask for a written statement of reasons for the decision and can seek permission to appeal against the striking-out decision to the Upper Tribunal.[70]

If an appeal, or part of an appeal, is struck out because the appellant has failed to comply with a direction, s/he may apply in writing for the appeal, or that part of it, to be reinstated.[71] This should be received by the Tribunal within one month of the Tribunal sending the appellant notice of the striking out.[72] This one-month time limit can be extended if the Tribunal considers it is fair and just to do so.[73]

It is not possible for an appeal, or part of it, to be reinstated if it is struck out for a reason other than a failure to comply with a direction. However, the Tribunal cannot strike out an appeal for one of these reasons unless it has first invited the appellant to make representations about whether or not it should do so.[74]

The rules for striking out an appeal apply to the CSA in exactly the same way that they apply to the appellant, except that references to 'striking out' are to 'barring'. When the Tribunal 'bars' the respondent, it need not consider any response or other submission made by that respondent, and can determine any or all issues against that respondent.

Sending and receiving documents

If there is a time limit for a party to provide a document, this starts to run from when the Tribunal sends the request. The time limit is met when the Tribunal receives the response.

Anything that has to be done by a particular day must be done by 5pm on that day.[75]

If the final day of any time limit for doing something is not a working day (ie, Saturday, Sunday, Christmas Day, Good Friday or a Bank Holiday), the act will be treated as being in time if it is done on the next working day.[76]

Documents can be sent to the Tribunal by pre-paid post (or fax) to the address (or number) specified for the proceedings. The Tribunal may give directions permitting documents to be sent by other methods.[77]

If a party provides a fax, email address or other method for receiving documents electronically, s/he must accept delivery of documents by that method unless s/he has explicitly stated that this is not acceptable.[78]

If a document is sent electronically, the recipient can request a hard copy and the sender must supply it (this also applies to appellants and their representatives). The request for a hard copy should be made as soon as reasonably practicable after receiving the document electronically.[79]

Each party should assume that the address provided by another party remains valid unless s/he has received written notice to the contrary.[80]

Representatives

A party has a right to appoint a representative (whether legally qualified or not) to represent her/him in the proceedings. Once appointed, a representative can do anything permitted or required to be done by the party (except sign a witness statement).[81]

The Tribunal should notify all other parties when a representative has been appointed. When a person (including the Tribunal itself) receives the notice of the appointment of a representative, s/he must provide her/him with any documents required to be issued to the represented party and need not send the documents to that party.[82] The enquiry form (see p365), however, is not a document that has to be issued to all parties and is generally sent by HM Courts and Tribunals Service only to the appellant.[83]

It should be assumed that the representative continues to act unless notice to the contrary from either the representative or the represented party is received.

Even if a party has not appointed a representative, s/he can still be accompanied at the hearing. Her/his companion may, with the permission of the Tribunal, act as a representative or otherwise assist in presenting the case at the hearing.[84]

Withdrawing an appeal

A party can withdraw all or part of her/his case.[85]

In the First-tier Tribunal, a case may be withdrawn either by writing to the Tribunal before the hearing, or orally at a hearing. If a party waits until a hearing to withdraw, s/he can only do so with the Tribunal's consent.[86] In the Upper Tribunal, consent is always needed to withdraw an appeal (even if the request is made in writing), unless the case is still at the stage of awaiting permission to appeal.[87]

Once a case has been withdrawn, it can be reinstated if the party writes to the Tribunal requesting this within one month of the notice of withdrawal being received by the Tribunal, or within a month of the date of the hearing at which the case was withdrawn.

When a case is withdrawn, the Tribunal must notify each party.

If an appellant or her/his representative wishes to stop an appeal proceeding before it has been referred to the First-tier Tribunal, s/he can simply write to the CSA, which discontinues the action.[88]

4. **Preparing a case**

The First-tier Tribunal may be the first chance for an independent evaluation of the decision under appeal. It may also be the last chance because there can only be an appeal to the Upper Tribunal on a point of law. Therefore, each party should make sure that the First-tier Tribunal knows the facts and arguments about the case.

Considering the facts and law

Each party should:

- read the response from the Child Support Agency (CSA) and any other documents to see whether the decision maker now accepts some of the arguments previously rejected or ignored. However, just because the decision maker accepts part of a person's case does not mean that the Tribunal will, especially if the other party disputes it;
- check the law using this *Handbook* and other sources (see Appendix 5). If the CSA quotes a decision of the commissioners or the Upper Tribunal, consider getting a copy. HM Courts and Tribunals Service does not have copies of unreported decisions. If an unreported decision is to be relied on by the decision maker, a copy should be supplied to the parties and to the First-tier Tribunal. If a party wishes to quote an unreported decision, s/he should supply copies to everyone, preferably by sending a copy to the Tribunal clerk in advance of the hearing. A party (including the decision maker) can quote the CSA's internal procedural guidance, but it is important to remember that this guidance is not legally binding;
- check the documents attached to the response. If anything relevant is missing, write to the First-tier Tribunal asking it to direct the decision maker to provide it.

If the CSA delays producing its response to an appeal, the appellant can write directly to the First-tier Tribunal and ask for a direction that the appeal be heard. This may mean that the First-tier Tribunal will not have all the evidence the decision maker has. However, a party can ask the First-tier Tribunal to direct the CSA (see p367) to provide copies of all the papers, explaining why those papers are needed.

Further evidence

Each party should consider:

- whether s/he has (or can get) any further relevant written evidence. This can be sent to the First-tier Tribunal at any stage, but it is best to do this soon after the response is sent out so papers can be copied to the other parties. If evidence or unreported commissioners'/Upper Tribunal decisions are produced at the hearing or sent in shortly before, this may cause a postponement or an adjournment;
- how to tell the First-tier Tribunal about the facts and law at the hearing. A party can 'give evidence' – ie, say what s/he has seen and heard. For example: 'I look after the child from Friday night to Monday night' may be the best evidence of those facts;
- whether to call any witnesses at the hearing (see p369).

Information relating to court proceedings concerning children heard in private or ancillary relief proceedings (ie, dealing with money and property) can be disclosed to the First-tier Tribunal by any party to the proceedings without permission being sought, as long as the court does not direct otherwise.[89] This means that one parent can supply information about the finances of the other parent, to which s/he admitted in the course of divorce proceedings.

Obtaining information and evidence

A party may want another person to provide further information or documents. The party can write to the First-tier Tribunal requesting that the other person be directed to provide these. It is best for the party to send a prepared list to HM Courts and Tribunals Service which is as precise as possible and explains why the documents are needed. For example, the parent with care may believe the non-resident parent has received a pay increase; she decides to ask for 'pay slips from February to May 2009 (inclusive)'. A person who is not a party (eg, an employer) cannot be directed to provide evidence, but can be ordered to attend as a witness and produce documents (see p369). This should be done before the full hearing so the parties can consider that evidence.

If a person fails to comply without a good explanation, the First-tier Tribunal may decide that s/he has something to hide and so may not believe that person's evidence. If the person is the appellant, the appeal can be struck out (see p371).

5. Hearings

This section applies to both the First-tier and Upper Tribunal.

'Hearing' means an oral hearing (including one conducted by video link, telephone or other instant two-way electronic communication).[90]

When must a hearing be held

The rules about when a hearing must be held are different for the First-tier and Upper Tribunal.

The **First-tier Tribunal** must hold a hearing before making a final decision in a case unless:[91]

- it is exercising its powers to strike out the proceedings;
- each party has consented to, or has not objected to, the matter being decided without a hearing and it considers it is able to decide the matter without a hearing;
- it is deciding whether to admit an application for permission to appeal, set aside a decision or correct a decision;
- it is disposing of the proceedings through a consent order.

The **Upper Tribunal** may decide any case without a hearing, but must consider any views expressed by a party when making a decision on whether or not to hold a hearing.[92]

If there is not a hearing, the Tribunal makes its decision by considering what has been said on the appeal form, any other evidence provided by the appellant and any other party, and the decision maker's response. This is known as a paper hearing.

Notice

The Tribunal must give reasonable notice of the time and place of the hearing and of any changes to the arrangements.[93] This period of notice must be at least 14 days, although shorter notice can be given with the parties' consent or in urgent or exceptional circumstances (if shorter notice is given, it must still be reasonable).[94]

Attending a hearing

Generally, all hearings must be held in public and a party has a right to attend. There are limited exceptions to these general principles: the Tribunal may direct that a hearing, or part of it, is to be held in private and may determine who is allowed to attend.

Even in a public hearing, the Tribunal may exclude from all or part of it:[95]

- anyone whose conduct is disrupting, or is likely to disrupt, the hearing;

- anyone whose presence is likely to prevent another person from giving evidence or making submissions freely;
- anyone who should be excluded in order to prevent her/him hearing information that is likely to cause harm;
- anyone whose attendance would defeat the purpose of the hearing;
- a witness in the proceedings.

If a party fails to attend a hearing and the Tribunal is satisfied that s/he has been notified or that reasonable steps to notify her/him have been taken, it may proceed with the hearing if it is in the interests of justice.[96]

Composition of the Tribunal

When the First-tier Tribunal deals with a case involving a child support decision, it will usually consist of a single member called a 'tribunal judge'.[97] The judge is a person qualified as a lawyer.[98] If the appeal raises difficult issues about financial accounts, the First-tier Tribunal can include a financially qualified member (a 'tribunal member') – ie, a chartered or certified accountant.[99] The President of the Social Entitlement Chamber of the First-tier Tribunal formally decides who is on the panel and who hears each appeal but, in practice, this is delegated to a senior tribunal judge.[100] If a First-tier Tribunal is composed of other members in addition to the tribunal judge, the judge is the 'presiding member', can regulate the proceedings and has the casting vote if there are an even number of members.[101]

The Upper Tribunal almost always consists of a single judge, who is legally qualified. If the case is of particular difficulty or there is conflicting caselaw, there may be a three-judge panel.

The venue

There should normally be separate waiting rooms available at the hearing venue for the non-resident parent, parent with care and presenting officer. A party who is worried about this should check with HM Courts and Tribunals Service whether there are separate waiting areas available before the hearing and, if not, explain any problems this may cause. If another party or witness could become violent, the Tribunal clerk should be told as soon as possible and asked what steps will be taken.

The hearing is usually held in the appellant's area. Expenses, including travel expenses, subsistence and some compensation for loss of earnings, are paid to those who attend as a party, witness or unpaid representative. The clerk pays travel and subsistence on the day, unless these are high. Travel expenses can be paid in advance.

A party for whom it is difficult to attend the hearing (eg, because of disability) should inform the clerk. An alternative venue may be possible, but convenience to the other parties to the appeal will also have to be considered.

Conduct of the hearing

The First-tier Tribunal attempts to be informal. Its member(s) usually sit on one side of a table. The clerk to the Tribunal (who does not take any part in making the decision) shows the parties into the room and they usually sit on the other side of the table, with the presenting officer between them. The judge introduces everyone and explains the Tribunal's role. If anyone's role is unclear, the judge should be asked for clarification.

Every party has the right to address the Tribunal, give evidence, call witnesses and put questions to any other party, the presenting officer or witnesses. The order in which the parties present their cases is up to the judge. The Child Support Agency (CSA) is there to explain the decision, not to argue for the CSA. The presenting officer has a role, for example, to inform the Tribunal about CSA procedures. It is rare for the presenting officer to call any witnesses. The Tribunal may require any witness, including a party, to take an oath or affirmation.

It is HM Courts and Tribunals Service policy to arrange an interpreter, if requested in good time. This should be requested on the pre-hearing enquiry form. The Tribunal should not place itself in the position of being seen to assist one of the parties make her/his case.[102]

The First-tier Tribunal can adjourn a hearing at any point – eg, if more documents are needed. If evidence has been taken, a new panel hearing the case must be made up of either exactly the same, or entirely different, members. Hearings can take one hour or longer.

6. Decisions

After the hearing, the First-tier Tribunal considers the case and makes its decision. If the appeal is allowed, the decision of the First-tier Tribunal replaces that of the Child Support Agency (CSA). If the appeal is dismissed, the decision of the CSA remains in force. Similarly, the Upper Tribunal may replace the decision of the First-tier Tribunal (or can direct that the case be reconsidered by a new First-tier Tribunal).

Decisions of the First-tier Tribunal

In making its decision, the First-tier Tribunal looks afresh at the situation up to the date of the CSA decision under appeal.[103]

When deciding the appeal, the First-tier Tribunal cannot take into account any change of circumstances that occurred after the date of the decision under appeal.[104] If it decides to allow the appeal because the decision was wrong on the facts at the time it was made, it cannot go on to direct how the decision maker should deal with a later change of circumstances. Supersession could be sought instead.

The First-tier Tribunal can consider any evidence and arguments, including those rejected or overlooked by the decision maker and those which have not been used before.[105] The First-tier Tribunal has no duty to consider any issue not raised in the appeal.[106] However, it is 'inquisitorial', which means it can consider legal arguments and factual questions on its own initiative, if appropriate.[107] The First-tier Tribunal must decide what it believes are the relevant facts by evaluating all the relevant available evidence. The Tribunal is not bound to find the same facts as found on the same issue in a different case (eg, a finding about the income of a non-resident parent in ancillary relief proceedings in the county court), but may take them into account as evidence.[108]

If the First-tier Tribunal reaches a different conclusion from that of the decision maker, it allows the appeal. **Note:** it may make a decision that is less advantageous to the appellant than the decision which has been appealed.[109]

If the appeal is against a refusal to revise/supersede, the First-tier Tribunal must decide whether a revision/supersession can be carried out. When considering this, it looks at the facts as they were when the decision maker refused to supersede, or at the date of the original decision in the case of a refusal to revise, even if the decision maker did not know those facts.[110] Unless there was a basis for a revision/supersession at that time, a later change of circumstances is irrelevant.[111] A request for a supersession on the basis of the later change should be made instead.

It is possible for the First-tier Tribunal to make a provisional decision, which will become final in specified circumstances. A provisional decision may be given, for example, as a case management technique in circumstances where the First-tier Tribunal wishes to give one last chance to a non-compliant party to provide certain information within a specified time. The time limit for any further appeal runs from the date of the final decision.[112]

Decision notices

Usually, at the First-tier Tribunal, the parties are invited to wait outside the hearing room and then asked to come back in to get the result. A First-tier Tribunal is also obliged to give a decision notice to the parties (unless it decides to withhold harmful information) as soon as reasonably practicable, stating:[113]

- its decision;
- any right to apply for reasons for the decision;
- any right of appeal against the decision, together with information about the time and manner in which such an appeal must be made.

The First-tier Tribunal can decide to issue a full statement of the reasons for its decision, either orally at the hearing or in writing to each party.[114] If it does not do this, a party can apply for a written statement of reasons , provided this is received by the Tribunal within a month of the party being given or sent the decision notice.[115]

If a party has applied for a written statement of reasons (subject to the rules about withholding harmful information), the Tribunal must, unless the decision was a consent order (see below), send them within one month of receiving the application, or as soon as reasonably practicable after that.[116] The one-month limit, although not absolute, provides a useful guideline on how long to expect to wait for a statement of reasons.

Decisions of the Upper Tribunal

The Upper Tribunal may announce its final decision orally at a hearing (although this is far less common than in the First-tier Tribunal) and must then (subject to the harmful information rule) provide the parties with a notice stating its decision and details of any onward rights of review and appeal. The Upper Tribunal must always give reasons for its decision unless the decision was made with the consent of the parties or the parties have consented to a decision being given without reasons.[117]

Record of proceedings

The presiding member of the First-tier Tribunal must keep a record of proceedings. This should include any evidence taken, submissions made and any procedural issues – eg, if a party asked for an adjournment.[118]

The record can be in any form determined by the presiding member and must be kept by HM Courts and Tribunals Service for at least six months from either the date of the decision, the date the reasons for the decision were given, the date the decision was corrected, the date a refusal to set aside was made or the date of the determination of an application for permission to appeal (unless the documents are sent to the Upper Tribunal before the six months expire), whichever is the later. A party can apply to the First-tier Tribunal for a copy of the record of proceedings within this six-month period and it must be sent to her/him.

In the Upper Tribunal, if the proceedings are recorded, this should be kept for six months. A party can apply for a transcript, but will have to pay for it unless s/he intends to or has challenged the decision of the Upper Tribunal, the transcript is necessary in order to bring that challenge, and the Upper Tribunal is satisfied that s/he cannot afford to pay.

Consent orders

If all the parties agree, they can request that the Tribunal makes an order disposing of the proceedings by their consent. It is not bound to do so and will only make a consent order if it considers it is appropriate.[119] It may simply make a decision on the appeal in the usual way.

If a consent order is made, there does not have to be a hearing and no reasons for the order need to be given. Independent advice should be sought *before* agreeing to request a consent order.

7. Changing a First-tier Tribunal decision

A First-tier Tribunal decision can be changed by:[120]

- correcting an accidental error (see below);
- setting aside the decision (see below);
- reviewing the decision (see p381);
- allowing an appeal to the Upper Tribunal (see p381).

Note: an application for any of the first three options can be treated by the First-tier Tribunal as an application for either of the other two options.

Correcting an error

The First-tier Tribunal can, at any time, correct a clerical mistake or accidental slip or omission in a decision, direction or any document it produces by sending notice of the amended decision or direction to all parties.[121]

Setting aside the decision

A decision, or part of a final decision, can be set aside by the First-tier Tribunal if it considers it is in the interests of justice to do so and:[122]

- a document relating to the proceedings was not sent to or received by the First-tier Tribunal, a party or representative at an appropriate time; *or*
- a party or representative was not present at the hearing; *or*
- there has been some other procedural irregularity.

An application for a set-aside must be received within one month of being sent the decision by the First-tier Tribunal. However, it appears that the Tribunal may exercise this power without receiving an application – ie, of its own volition.

The rules state that the First-tier Tribunal, on setting aside a decision, can then 'remake' the decision – ie, give a new final decision. Presumably, if the ground for a set-aside was that a party was not present, this would require the First-tier Tribunal to hold a hearing to avoid perpetuating the problem. Furthermore, presumably it would not be right to remake a decision if new documentary evidence or submissions were to be put before the First-tier Tribunal, unless the parties had been given an opportunity to comment on the significance of the new documents.

In addition, if following an application for permission to appeal, all parties argue the decision is in error of law, it will be set aside and referred to a differently constituted First-tier Tribunal to determine.[123]

Reviewing a decision

The power of the First-tier Tribunal to 'review' a decision was not something that could be done by an appeal tribunal under the rules that applied before November 2008.[124] Broadly speaking, it combines the previous power to set aside a decision on the grounds that there had been an error of law,[125] with a new power to then remake the decision. The First-tier Tribunal is required to consider whether to review its own decision before considering whether to grant permission to appeal and so, in practice, every application for permission to appeal is *de facto* an application for a review.

The First-tier Tribunal may only review a decision if an application for permission to appeal has been made and it considers that there is an error of law in the decision. However, given that an application for a correction of an accidental error or set-aside can be treated as an application for permission to appeal, there is some scope for the power to be exercised in a slightly wider way.

The First-tier Tribunal is required to notify the parties of the outcome of any review and of any right of appeal against it.

Note: a decision which has been reviewed can still be appealed to the Upper Tribunal.

8. Appealing to the Upper Tribunal

Any party (including the decision maker) can appeal to the Upper Tribunal against a final decision of the First-tier Tribunal. An appeal will only succeed if there is an error of law in the First-tier Tribunal's decision. See p352 and CPAG's *Welfare Benefits and Tax Credits Handbook* for information about when a decision contains an error of law. It is not an error of law for the First-tier Tribunal simply not to have believed what one of the parties said, provided that decision is one which a reasonable tribunal could have arrived at, is properly explained and is based on all the evidence.

The Upper Tribunal can give the decision it thinks the First-tier Tribunal should have given. Alternatively (particularly if it thinks the First-tier Tribunal did not find all the relevant facts or consider the evidence properly), it may refer the case back to the First-tier Tribunal for a new decision to be made. Making findings of fact is reserved to the First-tier Tribunal. If a case is referred back, the new First-tier Tribunal must find the necessary facts itself and apply the interpretation of the law as explained to it by the Upper Tribunal.

Before the appeal can be dealt with by the Upper Tribunal, permission to make the appeal needs to be obtained. This permission must first be sought from the First-tier Tribunal. If permission is refused, an application for permission can be made directly to the Upper Tribunal. Permission should only be granted if it is arguable that there is an error of law in the First-tier Tribunal decision.

The procedural rules set out above also apply in the Upper Tribunal (except where stated).

Applying for permission to appeal from the First-tier Tribunal

An application for permission to appeal against a final decision of the First-tier Tribunal must be in writing and be received by the Tribunal within one month of being sent the following, whichever is the latest:[126]

- a written statement of reasons for the decision;
- notification of the amended reasons for, or correction of, the decision following a review;
- notification that an in-time (either within the month or such longer period as was allowed) application for a set-aside was refused.

The application must state:[127]

- the decision of the First-tier Tribunal to which it relates;
- the alleged errors of law in the decision;
- the result sought by the party making the application.

If the application is made late, it must also include a request for an extension of time and explain why it was not made in time.[128] The First-tier Tribunal cannot consider a late application unless it has extended the time for applying.

Usually, it is necessary to have obtained the full statement of reasons for a decision before seeking permission to appeal. If no request for a statement of reasons has been made, the First-tier Tribunal must treat the application as an application for a statement of reasons rather than as an application for permission to appeal.[129] If reasons are issued, the party will then need to make a new application for permission to appeal. If a request for a statement of reasons has been refused because it was made late, the First-tier Tribunal can only grant permission to appeal if it is in the interests of justice to do so.[130]

When considering an application, the First-tier Tribunal must consider whether to review its decision (see p381).[131] If it has not changed the decision (or part of it) on review, it must consider whether to grant permission to appeal in respect of its decision, or the unchanged part of it.

The First-tier Tribunal must send a record of its decision on the application for permission to appeal to the parties.[132] If permission is refused in full or in part, the notice must include the reasons for this. It must also include notice of the right to apply directly to the Upper Tribunal for permission to appeal, the time within which this must be done and the method for making such an application.[133]

It is possible for the First-tier Tribunal to grant permission to appeal in respect of part of a decision. A party may then wish to file that appeal with the Upper Tribunal and also to seek permission to appeal directly from the Upper Tribunal in respect of the parts of the decision for which permission has not been granted by the First-tier Tribunal.

Applying directly to the Upper Tribunal for permission to appeal

If permission to appeal has been refused (in whole or in part) by the First-tier Tribunal, an application can be made to the Upper Tribunal. An application can only be made to the Upper Tribunal if the First-tier Tribunal has refused permission to appeal or has refused to admit an application.[134]

The application to the Upper Tribunal must be made in writing and within one month of being sent the refusal of permission. If made late, the application must include an explanation for why it is late, and it will not be considered unless the time limit is extended by the Upper Tribunal. If the earlier application for a written statement of reasons to the First-tier Tribunal or the application for permission to appeal to the First-tier Tribunal was made late, an explanation must also be given and can only be considered if the Upper Tribunal considers it in the interests of justice to do so.

The application must include details of:[135]

- the name and address of the appellant;
- the name and address of the representative (if any);
- an address for sending/delivery of documents;
- details (including a full reference) of the decision challenged;
- the grounds on which the appellant is relying;
- whether the appellant wants a hearing of the application.

The application must include copies of:[136]

- the written record of the decision challenged;
- the written statement of reasons for the decision (where it exists);
- the First-tier Tribunal's notice of refusal of permission to appeal or refusal to admit the application.

Using Form UT1, *Application for Permission to Appeal and Notice of Appeal from First-tier Tribunal (Social Entitlement Chamber)*, available online, should ensure that applications are correctly made.[137]

The Upper Tribunal must send the appellant (but not the respondent) reasons for refusing an application.[138] There is no right of appeal against a decision of the Upper Tribunal to refuse permission to appeal.[139]

The Upper Tribunal must send notice of permission to appeal to all the parties.[140] If this happens, generally the application for permission will be treated as the notice of appeal. The Upper Tribunal will send a copy of this application to all the parties and explain that it is treating the application for permission as the actual appeal.[141] If the parties agree, the Upper Tribunal can determine the appeal without a need for any further response from them.[142]

Notice of appeal

If the First-tier Tribunal grants permission to appeal, the appellant should send a notice of appeal to the Upper Tribunal. If the appellant has received permission to appeal directly from the Upper Tribunal, this will be treated as the notice of appeal.[143]

If needed, the notice of appeal must be received by the Upper Tribunal within one month of the party being sent the notice of permission to appeal by the First-tier Tribunal.[144]

The same information and documents must be included with the notice of appeal as for an application for permission to appeal (except that the appellant will be sending the notice of grant and not refusal of permission).[145]

Late notices of appeal must include a request for an extension of time and the reasons why the notice was not provided in time, and cannot be admitted unless time is extended.[146]

The Upper Tribunal must send a copy of the notice of appeal and accompanying documents to each respondent.[147]

Responses and replies

A response to the appeal can be provided by the other party, but does not have to be unless the Upper Tribunal so directs.[148]

A response must be in writing and received by the Upper Tribunal within one month of being sent the notice of appeal (or the notice of a grant of permission to appeal where that is treated as the notice of appeal). Late responses must include an application for an extension of this time limit and an explanation for why they are late.[149]

The response must state:[150]

- the name and address of the respondent;
- the name and address of her/his representative (if any);
- an address for sending/delivery of documents;
- whether the respondent opposes the appeal;
- the grounds on which the respondent intends to rely in the appeal;
- whether the respondent wants a hearing.

The Upper Tribunal must provide a copy of the response to the appellant and the other parties.[151]

The appellant may then reply to the response, but does not have to unless the Upper Tribunal so directs. The reply must be received within one month of being sent the response and is then copied to each of the other parties by the Upper Tribunal.[152]

Challenging decisions of the Upper Tribunal

Note: legal advice should always be sought when considering whether to challenge an Upper Tribunal decision.

Upper Tribunal decisions can be changed by:

- correcting an accidental error (see p380);[153]
- setting aside the decision (see p380);[154]
- appealing to the Court of Appeal (in Scotland, the Court of Session), for which permission is needed.[155] This is similar to the procedure for applying for permission from the First-tier Tribunal, except the time limit is three months, not one month. The Upper Tribunal must also consider a review (see below) before deciding whether to grant permission. Permission can only be granted if the Upper Tribunal considers the appeal would raise an important point of principle or practice, or there is some other compelling reason to grant it.[156] If the Upper Tribunal refuses permission, the request can be put before the Court of Appeal/Court of Session;
- reviewing the decision (see p381). The procedure is as for the First-tier Tribunal except that the Upper Tribunal can only exercise this power if, when making its decision, it overlooked a legislative decision or binding authority which could have affected the decision or, since giving its decision, a court has made a decision which could have affected its decision.[157]

The Upper Tribunal may treat an application for a decision to be corrected, set aside or reviewed, or an application for permission to appeal against a decision, as an application for any one of these things.[158]

9. Test case rules

Special rules apply if a court or Upper Tribunal decision on a 'test case' is pending or an Upper Tribunal or court decision on a test case has been made. A 'test case' is one in which a person is challenging the Child Support Agency's (CSA's) interpretation of the law, even if it is the CSA's own appeal and even if the person does not consider the case to be a test case.

These rules apply to maintenance calculation decisions, revision and supersession decisions and appeals in relation to a different matter by the Upper Tribunal or courts.

Test case pending

If a test case is decided against the CSA, normally the CSA has to follow the law as decided in that case in all other cases. However, if an appeal is pending before the Upper Tribunal or a court, in any case which might be affected by the decision to be given in that appeal, the CSA can:[159]

- suspend a decision on the application, revision or supersession until the test case appeal has been decided; *or*

- make a decision on the assumption that the test case appeal has already been decided and has been decided against the person who applied for the decision (ie, the calculation, revision or supersession), but only if:[160]
  - prior to 12 April 2010, the CSA would otherwise have had to have made a calculation (including one on revision or supersession) leading to the parent with care becoming entitled to income support (IS) or a higher rate of IS; *or*
  - the non-resident parent is employed or self-employed.[161]

An appeal is 'pending' before a court if:[162]

- an appeal (including a judicial review) about child support has been made to the High Court, Court of Appeal, Court of Session or Supreme Court but has not been determined;
- an application for permission to make such an appeal (or judicial review) has been made, but has not been determined;
- the CSA has certified in writing that it is considering making such an appeal or application and the time for appealing/applying has not expired, and the CSA considers that the appeal might result in the non-resident parent having no, or less, liability for child maintenance.[163]

An appeal also counts as pending if a court (but not the Upper Tribunal) has referred a question to the European Court of Justice (ECJ) for a preliminary ruling.

If the CSA does not make an application/appeal in time, it can no longer suspend making a decision. The time limits for making applications/appeals are as follows:

- applying to the Upper Tribunal for permission to appeal to the Court of Appeal/Court of Session: three months from the date the Upper Tribunal decision is issued;[164]
- applying to the Court of Appeal/Court of Session for permission to appeal from the Upper Tribunal to it (or appealing to one of those courts with permission of the Upper Tribunal): six weeks from the date the Upper Tribunal decision is issued;
- applying to the Court of Appeal/Court of Session for permission to appeal to the Supreme Court: this is usually done at the end of the hearing in which the court gives its judgment;
- applying to the Supreme Court for permission to appeal to it: 28 days from the date of the order of the court below;[165]
- appealing to the Supreme Court with permission of the Court of Appeal/Court of Session: 42 days from the date on which permission is given;[166]
- applying to the High Court/Court of Session for permission to apply for judicial review: three months from the date of the decision for High Court challenges. There is no time limit to apply to the Court of Session, but an application should be made as soon as possible.

A decision to suspend or make a decision on the assumption that the CSA will win the test case is a discretionary one. The CSA must, therefore, have regard to the welfare of the child when making it.

Test case decisions

If a decision of the Upper Tribunal or court interprets child support law, the CSA normally has to apply that interpretation of the law in the period before that decision was given. This usually requires the CSA to supersede all decisions which are affected.

However, if the Upper Tribunal/court rejected the CSA's interpretation of the law, that test case decision only has effect from the date it is given by the Upper Tribunal/court.[167] For the period before that date, the CSA (and either Tribunal) assumes that it was right in its interpretation of the law when making the original decision which led to the appeal.[168] This includes cases where the test case appeal began with a First-tier Tribunal decision on a referral of an application for a variation to the maintenance calculation. This rule applies:

- to maintenance calculations and reduced benefit decisions;[169]
- even if the application for a revision or supersession was made before the test case decision was given and regardless of whether the person applying raised that issue of law;[170]
- even if the Upper Tribunal/court decides that a regulation is *ultra vires*.[171] If this decision is made because the regulation is inconsistent with the European Convention on Human Rights, this rule may also breach that Convention;[172]
- even to decisions of the ECJ.[173] This rule is unlawful under European Union law, except in a case where the ECJ has itself decided that its decision only has effect from the date it is given.[174]

This rule does not apply to:

- an application for maintenance made before 1 June 1999 or a reduced benefit decision;[175]
- a revision of any decision made before 1 June 1999;[176]
- a supersession of any decision made before 1 June 1999;[177]
- a decision in a case where the CSA had suspended a decision under the test case pending rules (see p385);[178]
- a revision or supersession decision in a case where the CSA had required the First-tier or Upper Tribunal to refer the case to the CSA, or deal with it on the assumption that the test case had already been decided against the appellant.[179]

Test case rules affecting appeals

If a test case pending before a court may affect a similar case awaiting a decision from the First-tier Tribunal or Upper Tribunal, or there is a possibility that the CSA may appeal, the CSA may:[180]

- direct the Tribunal to refer the similar case to the CSA. The CSA makes no decision until the test case is decided. It then revises the CSA decision under appeal or supersedes the Tribunal decision under appeal; *or*
- direct the Tribunal to deal with the case itself. The Tribunal must then either:
  - 'stay' the appeal (ie, postpone its decision) until the test case is decided; *or*
  - decide the appeal on the assumption that the test case appeal has already been decided and has been decided against the person who appealed in the similar case. If the test case is later decided in that person's favour, the CSA supersedes the Tribunal decision in the similar case.

Notes

1 Reg 4(1)(b) CS(TP) Regs
2 s28D(1)(b) CSA 1991
3 Sch 3 para 4 TTFO

1. **Decisions that can be appealed and who can appeal**

4 Reg 1(3) SS&CS(DA) Regs
5 s20(1)(a) and (2)(a) CSA 1991
6 s20(1)(b) and (2)(b) CSA 1991
7 s20(1) CSA 1991, as it has effect without the substitution made by s10 CSPSSA 2000
8 s20(1)(d) and (2)(c) CSA 1991
9 Reg 30A SS&CS(DA) Regs
10 s20(1)(a) and (2)(a) CSA 1991
11 Reg 12(1) CS(MPA) Regs
12 Reg 34(1) SS&CS(DA) Regs
13 **EW** Arts 3 and 4 CSA(JC)O 2002
S Arts 2, 3 and 4 CSA(JC)(S)O 2003
14 **EW** Art 5 CSA(JC)O 2002
S Art 5 CSA(JC)(S)O 2003
15 r5(3)(k) TP(FT) Rules

2. **Appealing to the First-tier Tribunal**

16 s20(3) CSA 1991; reg 23 CS(MCP) Regs; reg 15C SS&CS(DA) Regs
17 r23(6) TP(FT) Rules
18 r23(2) and Sch 1 TP(FT) Rules
19 Sch 1 TP(FT) Rules
20 s16(5) CSA 1991
21 Reg 2(b) SS&CS(DA) Regs
22 R(IB) 4/02
23 r12 TP(FT) Rules
24 r23(5) and (8) TP(FT) Rules
25 r23(3) TP(FT) Rules
26 Reg 32(2) and (4) SS&CS(DA) Regs
27 Reg 32(5) and (6) SS&CS(DA) Regs
28 Reg 32(7) SS&CS(DA) Regs
29 Reg 32(8) SS&CS(DA) Regs
30 r23(7) TP(FT) Rules
31 r23(4) and (5) TP(FT) Rules
32 rs2(1), (2) and (3)(a) and 5(3)(a) TP(FT) Rules
33 *LS v London Borough of Lambeth (HB)* [2010] UKUT 461 (AAC)
34 Reg 33(4) and (5) SS&CS(DA) Regs
35 Reg 33(3) SS&CS(DA) Regs
36 Reg 33(7) SS&CS(DA) Regs
37 Reg 33(8) SS&CS(DA) Regs
38 Reg 33(9) SS&CS(DA) Regs
39 r24(1)(b) TP(FT) Rules
40 r24(2)(a)-(d) TP(FT) Rules
41 r24(2)(e) TP(FT) Rules
42 r24(3) TP(FT) Rules
43 r24(4) TP(FT) Rules
44 r19(3) TP(FT) Rules

3. **The appeal procedure**

45 r2 TP(FT) Rules; r2 TP(UT) Rules
46 r2(3) TP(FT) Rules; r2(3) TP(UT) Rules
47 r2(2) TP(FT) Rules; r2(2) TP(UT) Rules
48 *MS v SSWP* [2009] UKUT 211 (AAC)
49 r2(4) TP(FT) Rules; r2(4) TP(UT) Rules
50 r6(1) TP(FT) Rules; r6(1) TP(UT) Rules
51 *LM v London Borough of Lewisham* [2009] UKUT 204 (AAC)

52 Practice Statement, *Composition of Tribunals in Social Security and Child Support Cases in the Social Entitlement Chamber on or after 3 November 2008*, para 12. Practice Statement, *Composition of Tribunals in Relation to Matters that Fall to be Decided by the Administrative Appeals Chamber of the Upper Tribunal on or after 3 November 2008*, para 8
53 r15 TP(FT) Rules; r15 TP(UT) Rules
54 *LM v London Borough of Lewisham* [2009] UKUT 204 (AAC)
55 r19(3) TP(FT) Rules
56 r14(1) TP(FT) Rules; r14(1) TP(UT) Rules
57 r14(2) TP(FT) Rules; r14(2) TP(UT) Rules
58 r14(3) TP(FT) Rules; r14(3) TP(UT) Rules
59 r14(5) and (6) TP(FT) Rules; r14(5) and (6) TP(UT) Rules
60 r17 TP(FT) Rules; r17 TP(UT) Rules
61 r7(3) TP(FT) Rules
62 r10 TP(FT) Rules; r10 TP(UT) Rules
63 r7 TP(FT) Rules, r7 TP(UT) Rules
64 s25 TCEA 2007
65 r7(3) and (4) TP(UT) Rules
66 r8(1) TP(FT) Rules
67 r8(2) TP(FT) Rules
68 r8(3)(b) TP(FT) Rules
69 r8(3)(c) TP(FT) Rules
70 *Synergy Child Services Ltd v Ofsted* [2009] UKUT 125 (AAC)
71 r8(5) TP(FT) Rules
72 r8(6) TP(FT) Rules
73 rs2(1) and (3)(a) and 5(3)(a) TP(FT) Rules
74 r8(4) TP(FT) Rules
75 r12(1) TP(FT) Rules; r12(1) TP(UT) Rules
76 r12(2) and (3) TP(FT) Rules; r12(2) and (3) TP(UT) Rules
77 r13(1) TP(FT) Rules; r13(1) TP(UT) Rules
78 r13(2) and (3) TP(FT) Rules; r13(2) and (3) TP(UT) Rules
79 r13(4) TP(FT) Rules; r13(4) TP(UT) Rules
80 r13(5) TP(FT) Rules; r13(5) TP(UT) Rules
81 r11(5) TP(FT) Rules; r11(3) TP(UT) Rules
82 r11(6) TP(FT) Rules; r11(4) TP(UT) Rules
83 *MP v SSWP (DLA)* [2010] UKUT 103 (AAC)
84 r11(7) and (8) TP(FT) Rules; r11(5) and (6) TP(UT) Rules
85 r17 TP(FT) Rules; r17 TP(UT) Rules
86 r17(1)(b), (2) and (3)(b) TP(FT) Rules
87 r17(1) and (2) TP(UT) Rules
88 Reg 33(10) SS&CS(DA) Regs

4. **Preparing a case**
89 r5 Family Proceedings Courts (CSA 1991) Rules; r10.21A Family Proceedings Rules

5. **Hearings**
90 r1(3) TP(FT) Rules; r1(3) TP(UT) Rules
91 r27 TP(FT) Rules
92 r34 TP(UT) Rules
93 r29(1) TP(FT) Rules; r36(1) TP(UT) Rules
94 r29(2) TP(FT) Rules; r36(2)(b) TP(UT) Rules. The only other exception to this is when the Upper Tribunal is conducting a hearing of an application for permission to bring judicial review, in which at least two working days' notice must be given. Such proceedings are outside the scope of this *Handbook*.
95 r30 TP(FT) Rules; r37 TP(UT) Rules
96 r31 TP(FT) Rules; r38 TP(UT) Rules
97 Art 2 FT&UT(CT)O and Practice Statement, *Composition of Tribunals in Social Security and Child Support Cases in the Social Entitlement Chamber on or after 3 November 2008*, para 6
98 Sch 2 para 1(2) TCEA 2007
99 Practice Statement, *Composition of Tribunals in Social Security and Child Support Cases in the Social Entitlement Chamber on or after 3 November 2008*, para 7
100 Practice Statement, *Composition of Tribunals in Social Security and Child Support Cases in the Social Entitlement Chamber on or after 3 November 2008*, para 9
101 Practice Statement, *Composition of Tribunals in Social Security and Child Support Cases in the Social Entitlement Chamber on or after 3 November 2008*, para 12; Art 8 FT&UT(CT) Order
102 CSCS/16/07

6. **Decisions**
103 s20(7) CSA 1991
104 s20(7)(b) CSA 1991
105 CCS/16351/1996; *MB v CMEC* [2009] UKUT 29 (AAC), para 16
106 s20(7)(a) CSA 1991
107 R(IB)2/04; *A P-H v SSWP (DLA)* [2010] UKUT 183 (AAC)
108 *RC v SSWP* [2009] UKUT 62 (AAC), para 57
109 R(IB)2/04
110 CSCS/2/1994; CSCS/3/1994
111 CCS/511/1995
112 *AB v CMEC (CSM)* [2010] UKUT 385 (AAC)

113 r33 TP(FT) Rules
114 r34(2)(b) TP(FT) Rules
115 r34(3) and (4) TP(FT) Rules
116 r34(5) TP(FT) Rules
117 r40 TP(UT) Rules
118 Practice Statement, *Record of Proceedings in Social Security and Child Support Cases in the Social Entitlement Chamber on or after 3 November 2008*
119 r32 TP(FT) Rules; r39 TP(UT) Rules

7. **Changing a First-tier Tribunal decision**
120 Not including judicial review of non-appealable decisions.
121 r42 TP(FT) Rules
122 r43 TP(FT) Rules
123 s23A CSA 1991
124 Introduced by s9 TCEA 2007; see also r40 TP(FT) Rules
125 Under s13 SSA 1998

8. **Appealing to the Upper Tribunal**
126 r44 TP(UT) Rules
127 r38(6) TP(FT) Rules
128 r38(5) TP(FT) Rules
129 r38(7) TP(FT) Rules
130 r38(7)(c) TP(FT) Rules
131 r39(1) TP(FT) Rules
132 r39(3) TP(FT) Rules
133 r39(4) TP(FT) Rules
134 r21(2) TP(UT) Rules
135 r21(4) TP(UT) Rules
136 r21(5) TP(UT) Rules
137 Form UT1 is available from www.justice.gov.uk
138 r22(1) TP(UT) Rules
139 *Cart and Ors, R (on the application of) v The Upper Tribunal and Others* [2009] EWHC 3052 (Admin), 1 December 2009
140 r22(2)(a) TP(UT) Rules
141 r22(2)(b) TP(UT) Rules
142 r22(2)(c) TP(UT) Rules
143 r23(1) TP(UT) Rules
144 r23(2) TP(UT) Rules
145 r23(3) and (4) TP(UT) Rules
146 r23(5) TP(UT) Rules
147 r23(6) TP(UT) Rules
148 r24(1) TP(UT) Rules
149 r24(2) and (4) TP(UT) Rules
150 r24(3) TP(UT) Rules
151 r24(5) TP(UT) Rules
152 r25 TP(UT) Rules
153 r42 TP(UT) Rules
154 r43 TP(UT) Rules
155 rs44 and 45 TP(UT) Rules
156 **EW** Art 2 AUTCAO
S para 41.59 Rules of the Court of Session 1994
157 r46 TP(UT) Rules
158 r48 TP(UT) Rules

9. **Test case rules**
159 s28ZA(1) and (2) CSA 1991
160 Reg 23(3) and (5) SS&CS(DA) Regs
161 As defined in s2(1) SSCBA 1992
162 s28ZA(4) and (5) CSA 1991
163 s28ZA(4)(c) CSA 1991; reg 23(4) SS&CS(DA) Regs
164 r44(3) TP(UT) Rules
165 r11(1) SCR
166 r19(2) SCR
167 s28ZC(1) and (3) CSA 1991; reg 7B(10) SS&CS(DA) Regs
168 s28ZC(1) and (6) CSA 1991
169 s28ZC(3) CSA 1991
170 s28ZC(5) CSA 1991
171 s28ZC(4) CSA 1991
172 Art 13 ECHR requires an effective remedy for violations
173 s28ZC(6) CSA 1991
174 *Commission v France,* C-35/97 [1998] ECR I-5325
175 s28ZC(1)(b)(i) CSA 1991
176 s28ZC(1)(b)(ii) CSA 1991
177 s28ZC(1)(b)(iii) CSA 1991
178 s28ZC(2)(a) CSA 1991
179 s28ZC(2)(b) CSA 1991
180 s28ZB CSA 1991

Chapter 19

Collection and enforcement

This chapter covers:

The legal power to collect and enforce the payment of child support now rests with the Child Maintenance and Enforcement Commission (CMEC). In particular, new enforcement powers (such as lump-sum and regular deduction orders) were granted directly to CMEC. However, at the time of writing, CMEC's powers are operated via the Child Support Agency (CSA) and it is the CSA with which most parents will have contact. The CSA, rather than CMEC, is therefore referred to in this chapter.

The CSA can arrange the collection and enforcement of child support maintenance[1] and certain other maintenance payments (see p401).[2] This service has been free to all CSA clients since April 1995.[3] However, fees are expected to be introduced by CMEC some time in the future (see Chapter 1).

Once the decision on liability and calculation has been made, a collection schedule is set up. If the payment schedule breaks down and arrears accrue, debt management procedures may be put in place, or the CSA may decide to take enforcement action.

Within the limits of the Regulations, decisions about how payment is enforced are discretionary, and so should be made taking account of all the circumstances of the individual case. This should allow scope for negotiation between the CSA and the individuals involved. The CSA does not publish the guidance used by its decision makers. It is, however, possible to make a Freedom of Information request to the CSA to see its guidance on the use of its collection and enforcement powers (see Chapter 1). It may be useful to point out phrases from the guidance to remind the CSA of helpful principles. If the guidance is not helpful, the CSA can be reminded that it is not binding. There is some evidence of cases where the CSA has not fully investigated the circumstances to allow it to exercise its discretion appropriately.[4]

As the decisions are discretionary, the welfare of any child likely to be affected must be taken into account by the CSA (see p23).

The amount of maintenance calculated cannot be altered except by revision, supersession, appeal or variation (departure under the 'old rules'). The CSA does not suspend current collection just because the non-resident parent states that he cannot afford to pay. However, the CSA may agree to lower payments if a decision on a revision, supersession, appeal or variation/departure is pending (see p406).

There is no right of appeal to the First-tier Tribunal about a decision concerning collection and enforcement (see p361 for which CSA decisions can be appealed).[5] A deduction from earnings order (see p415) can, in limited circumstances, be appealed to a magistrates' court (see p415) and orders to deduct amounts from current or savings accounts (see p425) can be appealed in the county court (England and Wales) or the sheriff court (Scotland). Judicial review may be possible for other decisions (see p343). Once the CSA's internal complaints procedure has been followed (see Chapter 20), complaints about the CSA's exercise of discretion can be made to the Independent Case Examiner (see p446). For regular payment conditions imposed because a departure application has been made, see p298.

1. Payment of child maintenance

If a maintenance calculation has been made and the Child Support Agency (CSA) is collecting and enforcing the maintenance, it has discretion to decide:
- the method by which the non-resident parent pays;[6]
- the person to whom it is paid;[7]
- if payments are made through the CSA or someone else, the method by which payment is made to the person with care;[8]
- the timing of payments;[9] *and*
- the amount of payments towards arrears.[10]

Before making these decisions, the CSA must, as far as is possible, give the non-resident parent and the person with care an opportunity to make representations and must take these into account.[11] In every case, the CSA must notify the non-resident parent in writing of the amounts and timing of payments due, to whom he must make payment, how he must pay and details of any amount that is overdue and remains outstanding.[12] This notice is sent as soon as possible after the calculation is made and again after any change in the details in the notice.[13] A copy is sent to the person with care. If the payments are to be made directly between the two parties, the CSA takes no further action regarding collection unless the person with care notifies the CSA that the non-resident parent has failed to comply as directed. Therefore, the parties can agree between them to use another method or frequency of payment.

If there are arrears and the CSA has imposed a penalty payment, see p411.

Who is paid

The CSA can require the non-resident parent to pay child maintenance:[14]

- directly to the person with care;
- directly to a Scottish child applicant;
- to, or via, the CSA (the CSA can only provide the collection service at the request of one of the parties to the calculation[15]); *or*
- to, or via, another person.

The person with care can agree to have maintenance paid directly to her. In this situation, once the CSA has calculated the amount of maintenance owed, the parties make their own arrangement about how payments will be made. This is known as 'maintenance direct'. Letters are sent by the CSA telling each parent about the amount of arrears and the date regular payments should start. These direct payments are not monitored by the CSA. If the payment arrangement breaks down, the person with care can ask to use the collection service (see below).

The CSA can treat certain payments made to a third party (eg, a mortgage lender) as payments of child support. This can include voluntary payments made between the effective date and the date of the calculation (used to offset any initial arrears – see p403) and, from 25 January 2010, payments made after the effective date (see p400).[16]

The collection service

When child support payments are to be made to or via the CSA, this is referred to as the collection service. Any party to a case can request that payment be via the CSA.[17]The CSA normally provides the collection service if a party requests it, even if the other party does not.

If the non-resident parent is on benefit, the person with care may use the collection service to secure direct deductions from his benefit. This is particularly useful if a voluntary arrangement cannot be reached.

The collection service can be requested at a later date – eg, if payments become irregular. The request can be made verbally or in writing.

If payments are made to the CSA, only those actually received by the CSA can be passed on. The CSA aims to make the first payment to the person with care within six weeks of making initial payment arrangements with the non-resident parent. The CSA also aims to transfer child support payments to the person with care within one week of receiving them from the non-resident parent.[18]

Using the collection service can have a number of advantages.

- It removes the need for direct contact between the non-resident parent and person with care.
- It is supposed to ensure regular payments by starting enforcement action (see p414) as soon as payments are missed, although this does not always happen.

Using the collection service can also have a number of disadvantages.

- A payment statement is only issued periodically or on request (see p398) and these are often considered to be inaccurate. The parties should, therefore, always keep their own records and evidence of payments. The majority of accounts are in arrears and many persons with care and some non-resident parents are unhappy with the level of service from the CSA.
- The CSA negotiates collection and arrears schedules with the parents and may agree to an arrears arrangement, not withstanding any objections from the person with care.

If someone is both a person with care and a non-resident parent

In some child support maintenance calculations, a person might be both a person with care and a non-resident parent at the same time. This may arise where the qualifying children from a relationship live with different parents after the relationship has ended. In this situation, both parents may be liable to pay child support to each other. From 25 January 2010, if the collection service is being used, the CSA can offset their liabilities.[19]

Example 19.1

Ali and Nazia were married. They have two children, Mohammed and Faisal. When they separate, Mohammed lives with Ali and Faisal lives with Nazia. Both parents apply to the CSA to use the collection service. Ali works full time and is liable to pay child support of £60 a week. Nazia works part time and is liable to pay child support of £20 a week.

Instead of the CSA collecting and distributing two sets of payments, it deducts Nazia's liability from Ali's, so that Ali pays less child support and Nazia does not pay any.

£60 – £20 = £40

Ali pays Nazia £40 per week. Nazia does not pay anything.

Payments can only be offset if the collection service is being used.[20] However, it is understood that, although the CSA has the ability to offset payments, the current computer system is unable to process the arrangement. If parties to a calculation insist on offsetting payments, it is likely to mean that their case will have to be dealt with manually ('clerical cases'). This can cause considerable delay for both parties to the calculation at all stages of its implementation, including the use of enforcement measures if these are required in the future. Parents whose cases are already treated as clerical should be able to request that offsetting is applied.

Before 25 January 2010, if both parties to a child support calculation were non-resident parents and persons with care and both fell into arrears, the CSA had to pursue each party separately. From this date, any arrears can also be offset so that the CSA only has to pursue the party with the largest debt.[21]

Person with care on benefits

Arrears of child support may be retained by the CSA if they are in respect of a period during which the person with care (or her/his partner) was in receipt of income support (IS), income-based jobseeker's allowance (JSA), income-related employment and support allowance (ESA) or pension credit (PC) and child maintenance was not fully disregarded for these benefits.[22]

Note: from 12 April 2010, all child maintenance is fully disregarded when working out these benefits and so the CSA should not retain any child support in respect of periods on or after this date.

The amount retained is equal to the difference between the amount of benefit paid to the person with care and the amount that would have been paid if the non-resident parent had kept to the maintenance arrangement during the relevant period.

Before 27 October 2008, if payments were made via the CSA, the person with care received one credit transfer from Jobcentre Plus that included both IS/income-based JSA/PC and child support. If the non-resident parent did not make a payment to the CSA, the person with care's benefit was still paid, but there was no child support element. From this date, the CSA has paid all child support collected directly to the person with care. This is paid into the same account as the one into which benefits are paid, unless the CSA is notified otherwise.

It is the responsibility of the person with care to notify Jobcentre Plus of any child support received. Although child support is now fully disregarded for IS/income-based JSA/income-related ESA/PC, Jobcentre Plus still requests that claimants inform it if they receive child support. This is to allow Jobcentre Plus to disregard child support income where appropriate and to check whether any of it would fall under the capital rules. It is possible for child support payments to build up and exceed the capital rules for IS/income-based JSA/income-related ESA/PC, although this is unlikely to be the case for most claimants. If Jobcentre Plus is not notified promptly, the person with care could be accused of causing an overpayment by failing to disclose a material fact, particularly if s/he is found to have unexplained income in a bank account. The reason why child support has to be declared in this way is not always fully explained to claimants.

Method of payment

The non-resident parent can make payments by standing order, direct debit, automated credit transfer, credit card, debit card, cheque, postal order, bankers draft, voluntary deductions from earnings arrangements or cash.[23] A debit card means one that can be used as a substitute for a cheque – ie, where the non-resident parent's bank account is debited instantly, such as with a Switch card.[24] If the collection service is being used, the CSA prefers payment by direct debit.[25] The CSA can direct a non-resident parent to take all reasonable steps to open a bank or building society account.[26] However, there is no penalty if he fails to open an account and the CSA can discuss alternative payment arrangements.[27] Non-resident parents who wish to pay by a method other than direct debit may have to insist on doing so. So long as payments are made when due, a deduction from earnings order should not be made.

When deciding the method of payment, the CSA must take into account any representations from all the parties.

If the non-resident parent is receiving certain benefits, the CSA will normally deduct the amount for child support directly from the benefit before he receives it (see below).[28]

If payment is made via the CSA, the person with care is paid by automated credit transfer wherever possible, and if not, by cheque.[29] The person with care is asked to provide details of a bank, building society or Post Office account. If she does not have an account, or experiences difficulty opening one, she should contact the CSA national helpline on 0845 713 3133.

Deductions from benefit: new rules

If a non-resident parent on benefit is required to pay child support at the flat rate (see Chapter 5), the CSA may request Jobcentre Plus to make a deduction for maintenance.[30] Deductions can be made from:[31]

- IS;
- income-based JSA;
- contribution-based JSA;
- maternity allowance;
- bereavement benefits;
- widows' benefits;
- retirement pension;
- incapacity benefit (IB);
- contributory ESA;
- income-related ESA;
- carer's allowance;
- severe disablement allowance (SDA);
- industrial injuries schemes benefits;
- war disablement pension;
- PC.

If someone should pay at the flat rate but a variation has been made which results in the reduced or basic rate being payable, deductions can be made towards the new amount of child support calculated.

If a non-resident parent and his partner are:[32]

- on IS, income-related ESA, income-based JSA or PC; *and*
- each is a non-resident parent,

the £5 flat-rate deduction will be split between them so that each contributes £2.50 to their respective persons with care.[33] (In polygamous relationships where there is more than one new partner who is also a non-resident parent, the £5 is apportioned between all the non-resident parents.[34])

The CSA requests the deduction and Jobcentre Plus must make it in full wherever possible. The parent must be left with at least 10 pence a week.[35] Partial deductions will not be made. In addition, priority debt rules do not apply to deductions for child support maintenance under the 'new rules'. This means the deduction for child support is always made, whatever other deductions are due.

Both the person with care and non-resident parent are notified that deductions are to be made.

If there are arrears of child support, a £1 deduction towards arrears may be made from the benefits listed on p396, except IS, income-based JSA, income-related ESA or PC (see p407).

Deductions from benefit: old rules

When an application is received by the CSA and it is found that the non-resident parent is on IS/income-based JSA/income-related ESA/PC, both parties will be notified about whether or not deductions from benefit are possible. If the non-resident parent is not exempt from deductions, the Department for Work and Pensions (DWP) will be sent notification requesting that a deduction is made. This is binding on the DWP, unless there are other deductions being made from the benefit which take precedence.[36]

Direct deductions for contributions of child support cannot be made from any benefit other than IS/income-based JSA/income-related ESA/PC, unless contribution-based JSA, IB, SDA or retirement pension are paid together with IS/income-based JSA/income-related ESA/PC.[37] After the deductions are made, the claimant must be left with at least 10 pence a week.[38]

There is a maximum amount which can be deducted from IS/income-based JSA/income-related ESA/PC for various payments.[39] The contribution for child support has a lower priority than any of the other possible deductions.[40] Therefore, in some cases where non-resident parents have other deductions, it will not be possible to deduct the full £6.80 for the contribution to child maintenance. The DWP can deduct half of the £6.80 contribution.[41] For more information about deductions from benefits, see CPAG's *Welfare Benefits and Tax Credits Handbook*.

If full deductions from IS/income-based JSA/income-related ESA/PC are not possible, arrears of child maintenance contributions do *not* accrue.

The DWP will tell the CSA whether deductions are possible. The CSA, in turn, notifies the non-resident parent and the person with care if deductions are going to begin. The £6.80 is paid to the person with care via the CSA.[42] The CSA notifies her of the way in which the payments will be made.

If there are arrears of maintenance, these can be deducted from contribution-based JSA or contributory ESA only (see p407).

Timing of payments

The CSA decides the day and frequency of payments,[43] but asks for the non-resident parent's preference. When deciding the day and the interval for payment by the non-resident parent, the CSA must also take into account:[44]

- the day on which, and the interval at which, the non-resident parent receives his income;
- any other relevant circumstances of the non-resident parent;
- time for cheques to clear, if applicable, and for payments to be transferred to the person with care; *and*
- any representations by the parties.

Unless undue hardship would be caused to the non-resident parent or the person with care, the frequency of payments to the person with care will be the same as the frequency set for the non-resident parent's payments (but see p416 for deduction from earnings orders).[45]

Unless payments are to be by direct debit or standing order, the non-resident parent is advised to make each payment three to four days before the due date in order to ensure that payments are received on time and to avoid arrears. Clearance times are allowed for each method of payment, but the CSA aims to make payments to the person with care within a week of receiving them from the non-resident parent.[46] If a delay in payments is caused by maladministration on the part of the CSA, the person with care may be entitled to compensation. She will need to make a complaint first.[47] See Chapter 20 for more information.

Records and evidence of payments

It is important for both the non-resident parent and the person with care to keep records of the payments made and received, particularly given the high level of errors on CSA accounts. Records can be in the form of bank statements, or receipts if payments are made in cash. If a person with care, non-resident parent or child in Scotland disputes the amount that the CSA says is owed, s/he could ask the CSA to provide a statement of transactions and a breakdown of its calculations.

Overpayments

An overpayment can arise either because the amount of the maintenance due for a past period has been reduced, there has been a CSA error or the non-resident parent has paid more than the regular payment due. The CSA has a discretion about allocating the overpayment,[48] including setting it against any arrears of child maintenance resulting from a previous calculation.[49]

If there is a surplus remaining after current child support, arrears and other liabilities have been met, the non-resident parent may have the amount he pays adjusted or a refund made. An adjustment is the preferred option.

If the CSA receives an unexpected payment from the non-resident parent, it should check to determine the reason for this – eg, it could be for an overdue collection to offset arrears or an amount towards a future collection. Following this investigation, the amount may be allocated to reduce arrears arising under a previous calculation or, if there are no arrears, it can be used to reduce the amount payable under the current calculation. If the current calculation is to be reduced, the CSA should consider the amount by which it is appropriate for it to be reduced given the circumstances of both the parent with care and the non-resident parent (see below).[50] The decision to reduce a calculation may also be influenced by the amount of the overpayment and the period over which it would be reasonable to adjust the amount payable in order to rectify it.[51]

Refunds are only usually made if there are no overdue collections or arrears on the case.

The CSA should refund overpayments made because of CSA error – eg, if a person was told to pay more than the calculation required. In such cases, the non-resident parent may also wish to complain and seek compensation (see Chapter 20).

Adjustments

If an overpayment remains after offsetting it against regular child support, arrears and other liability, the CSA can reduce the amount payable to compensate the non-resident parent for the overpayment.[52] Adjustments may also be made where there are overpayments of voluntary payments in the initial payment period.[53] When making this discretionary decision, the CSA must consider, in particular:

- the circumstances of the non-resident parent and person with care;
- the welfare of any children (see p23);
- the amount of the overpayment in relation to the amount of the current calculation; *and*
- the period over which it would be reasonable to recoup it.

An adjustment of the amount payable in relation to the current child support calculation may reduce the amount to nil.[54] This means that the parent with care would not receive any more child support until the overpayment had been recovered.

Recovery of overpayments from the person with care

If the CSA reimburses an overpayment to a non-resident parent, it can recover from the person with care any maintenance overpaid to her.[55] This includes overpaid voluntary payments that the CSA has refunded to the non-resident parent.[56] The CSA cannot enforce the recovery of overpayments because of its own administrative error, but the person with care will be asked if she is prepared to repay them.

Recovery of overpayments is a discretionary decision, so the welfare of any children likely to be affected by reimbursement must be taken into account (see p23).

The overpayment is usually collected from any current child support payments.[57]

Payments made to a third party

If the person with care agrees to receive payments from the non-resident parent outside of the usual child support collection service, these may be offset against the amount of child support owed by the non-resident parent. For example, this situation may occur if a non-resident parent agrees to pay an urgent utility bill on behalf of the person with care.[58] The amount paid towards the utility bill can be offset against any arrears owed by the non-resident parent, or from his ongoing liability if there are no arrears.

For the offsetting rule to apply, the payment must have been agreed by the person with care and must be for one of the following in relation to the home in which the qualifying child lives:[59]

- a mortgage or loan either to purchase the property or to pay for essential repairs to it;
- rent on the property;
- mains-supplied gas, water or electricity charges;
- council tax payable by the person with care;
- essential repairs to the heating system; *or*
- essential repairs to 'maintain the fabric' of the home.

Offsetting can only be used if child support maintenance is collected by the CSA's collection service on behalf of the person with care. This means that the non-resident parent must be paying money to the CSA, rather than directly to the person with care. Those with a direct maintenance arrangement can reach their own offsetting agreement, but the CSA will not monitor it.[60]

If the CSA intends to reduce ongoing payments of maintenance to the person with care, it should take into account the circumstances of all the people involved in the calculation and the period over which it would be reasonable to adjust the payments.[61] An adjustment of the current maintenance calculation may reduce the amount payable to nil.[62]

The decision to apply offsetting is discretionary. The regulations make no provision to appeal against the decision to offset any payments, which are said to have been made in lieu of child maintenance. Problems may therefore occur if the person with care denies that she agreed to payments being made to third parties. CMEC's intention is to keep decisions out of the appeals system that are not concerned with the actual maintenance calculation or the underlying liability to pay child maintenance.[63] However, a party could complain about how the CSA has exercised its discretion.

The above provisions apply to both 'old rules' and 'new rules' cases. In addition, for 'old rules' cases, the CSA has a non-statutory discretion to accept certain payments made by the non-resident parent as voluntary payments to be set against the amount assessed as child support. These payments do not have to fall into the types of payments listed above. In exercising its discretion on whether payments may be offset, the CSA must give weight to the view of the person with care but must take into account all the circumstances of the individual case.[64]

2. Collection of other payments

The Child Support Agency (CSA) can collect and enforce other forms of maintenance if child support maintenance is being collected.[65]

The power to collect other maintenance is discretionary. However, the CSA may agree to requests to collect other types of maintenance for parents with care. The CSA can only collect other maintenance that falls due after the CSA gives the non-resident parent written notice that the other maintenance will be collected.[66]

The following payments under a court order (see p30) can be collected by the CSA:[67]

- additional child maintenance in excess of the CSA maximum;
- maintenance for a child's education or training;
- maintenance paid to meet the expenses of a child with a disability;
- maintenance paid for a stepchild – ie, a child living with the person with care who used to live with the non-resident parent and was accepted by him as a member of his family;
- spousal or civil partner maintenance for a person with care of a child for whom child support maintenance is being collected.

The methods used by the CSA for collecting and enforcing other types of maintenance are the same as for child support maintenance.[68] If a non-resident parent is paying more than one type of maintenance and pays less than the total amount required, he should stipulate how the amounts are to be allocated. The CSA will allocate as requested, except that where arrears of child support maintenance are specified, current child support maintenance will be paid before arrears. If the non-resident parent does not stipulate, the CSA will make the payment of child support a priority.[69]

Collection of court costs and penalty payments

Fees have not been charged for CSA services since April 1995. From 5 August 2008, the requirement to pay any outstanding fees from years before 1995 has also been removed.[70]

If the CSA applies to the court for a decision on whether a person is a parent and the court decides that he is, the court can order him to pay the CSA's costs in bringing the case, including the cost of any DNA tests which have been carried out (see p65). Also, a non-resident parent may have agreed to pay DNA test fees to the CSA without a court order (see p65).

The CSA may also have imposed a penalty payment on the non-resident parent for failure to pay.

The CSA will negotiate with the liable person about payment of these other liabilities. It will initially request the full amount due, but payments by instalment may be agreed.

Payment of fees and costs can only be enforced through court action. The rules for enforcement of maintenance (see p414) do not apply. The relevant court is the county court in England and Wales or the sheriff court in Scotland. If the case is contested, a hearing is arranged in the court with jurisdiction for the area in which the parent lives. A money judgment can be enforced by the usual debt enforcement procedures.

3. Arrears

The Child Support Agency (CSA) acts on arrears only if child maintenance is arranged through it.[71] If the collection service is being used, the CSA can take action immediately when payments are missed. If the parties made an application to the CSA but agreed that the non-resident parent would pay maintenance directly to the person with care (maintenance direct), the person with care will need to notify the CSA that payments have stopped.[72] The CSA will otherwise not be aware that maintenance direct payments have stopped and so cannot take action to pursue arrears. The CSA cannot take action on non-payment of maintenance in a private agreement. If a private agreement breaks down, the person with care can apply to the CSA for child support instead. The CSA can pursue all arrears from the date the child support maintenance calculation is requested.[73]

Initial arrears

As the first calculation is usually made after its effective date, there are usually always initial arrears. If a court order made on, or after, 3 March 2003 has been in force for more than a year and there is an application to the CSA, the effective date is two months and two days from the date of the application. If the non-resident parent has continued to make payments due under the order beyond the effective date, these payments will be treated as payments of child support.[74] This helps to avoid additional liability for child support if, for whatever reason, it takes the CSA longer than two months and two days to make the child support maintenance calculation, so that when it is made, its effective date (and, therefore, the date the court order ceases to have effect) is in the past. If the payments made under the court order are at a higher rate than those due under the calculation, this will be treated as an overpayment of child support and the calculation can be adjusted accordingly.

The CSA will draw up a collection schedule, which shows payments for the following 12 months, including initial arrears.[75] The non-resident parent can request and negotiate changes to the schedule. Written confirmation of the collection schedule is issued once the non-resident parent has agreed to it.[76]

The written notification states:[77]

- the amount due and to whom it is to be paid;
- how it is to be paid – ie, method, day and interval between payments;
- any amounts that are overdue and outstanding.

The CSA may request payment of the initial arrears as a lump sum. If a non-resident parent cannot pay this all at once, he may negotiate an agreement to pay in instalments or a collection schedule to cover both the initial payment and ongoing liability (see p405).

A parent who fails to make payment of the outstanding arrears within seven days of written notification of the amount due may face financial penalties and further enforcement action.

A parent who thinks the calculation is wrong may be able to seek a revision or make an appeal. If he objects to the way the CSA is dealing with collections, he may make a complaint (see Chapter 20).

Voluntary payments made in the initial period

Voluntary payments made by the non-resident parent through the CSA (or, if the CSA agrees, direct to the person with care or a third party) after the effective date, but before the calculation is made and notified, may be offset against arrears of child maintenance.[78] The CSA may seek the views of the parties when considering whether a payment is to be classed as a voluntary payment.[79] As this is a discretionary decision, the CSA must consider the welfare of any child likely to be affected.

Only the following types of payment can be offset:[80]

- in lieu of child support maintenance;
- in respect of a mortgage or loan on the child's home, or for repairs or improvements to the property;
- rent on the child's home;
- mains gas, water or electricity at the child's home;
- council tax payable at the child's home;
- repairs to the heating system at the child's home; *or*
- repairs to the child's home.

Payments can be made by cash, standing order, cheque, postal order, debit card or other method/arrangement from an account of the non-resident parent or on his behalf – eg, credit card.[81]

If the payments are made to the CSA, they will be passed on to the person with care. Once the calculation has been made, the voluntary payments will be offset against the initial arrears.

If the payments are made directly to the person with care or a third party, the CSA will check with the person with care whether payments have been made.[82] This is normally done by phone. If the person with care confirms the payments were made, this is usually accepted without any further need for proof. If there is a dispute about whether a payment has been made, the CSA will ask the non-resident parent to provide proof. Payment can be verified by bank statements, duplicates of cashed cheques, receipts, paid bills/invoices, or a written or oral statement from the person with care.[83] It is in the interests of both parties to ensure payments are recorded, and the CSA should explain to the non-resident parent the importance of keeping a record and provide a form on which to do so.

If either party disagrees with a decision about offsetting, a complaint can be made (see Chapter 20).

If offsetting means that there is an overpayment, the calculation may be adjusted to compensate the non-resident parent or a refund may be made (see p399).

If payments are made by the non-resident parent outside the usual collection service after the calculation is made (eg, if a non-resident parent pays an urgent bill on behalf of the parent with care), see p400.

Arrears notice

If the non-resident parent has missed one or more child support payments, the CSA must send him an arrears notice itemising the amounts owed. The notice also explains the rules about arrears and requests payment of the outstanding amount.[84] The CSA then contacts the non-resident parent to discuss the issue.

The non-resident parent should check that the amount owed is correct and tell the CSA of any mistakes. There have been high levels of mistakes on accounts in the past. Therefore, if there is a concern that the balance is incorrect, the non-resident parent should ask for a payment statement (see p398) and compare this with his own record. While doing this, it is important that he keeps the CSA informed so that a penalty payment or a deduction from earnings order is not imposed in the meantime.

The non-resident parent can contact the CSA to negotiate payment by instalments (see p405). Once an arrears notice has been served, another does not have to be sent if arrears remain uncleared, unless the non-resident parent has paid all arranged payments for a 12-week period.[85]

Negotiating an arrears agreement

An arrears notice will be sent to the non-resident parent, requesting payment of all outstanding arrears. The non-resident parent should get in touch with the CSA to negotiate an agreement to deal with the arrears.

Negotiations with the CSA may begin on notification of the collection schedule or at a later date if the non-resident parent has difficulty making ongoing payments. However, the CSA does not normally agree to defer payment of current liability, though it may do so if a revision, supersession or appeal is pending.

Limitations on the level of payments or how quickly the arrears must be cleared are not specified in child support law. Although CSA staff always begin by requesting full payment of the outstanding arrears, an arrears agreement may be reached to pay the amount in instalments.

In making this discretionary decision, the CSA must take into account the welfare of any child likely to be affected by the decision and should consider the:

- needs of the non-resident parent or any new family;
- representations of the non-resident parent about hardship; *or*
- needs of the person with care and the qualifying child.

If a non-resident parent has other priorities (eg, fuel) or other large debts, he should seek independent money advice. Preparing a financial statement and sending it to the CSA may assist in reaching an agreement. However, existing arrangements with other creditors may have to be renegotiated to take into account the CSA calculation. It is important to keep the CSA informed so that it does not assume that the non-resident parent is refusing to come to an agreement.

The CSA can use other methods of recovery, such as a deduction from earnings order (see p415). Therefore, CSA staff are unlikely to agree to a non-resident parent making low payments over a very long period. It is in his interests to come to an agreement if he wishes to avoid further payment penalties and enforcement action. If he has children living with him, their welfare must be taken into account.

It is understood that the CSA aims to collect arrears within two years,[86] at a rate of up to 40 per cent of a non-resident parent's income.[87] CSA staff can use their discretion and take into account the non-resident parent's particular circumstances, where appropriate to do so.[88]

A plan to pay arrears by instalments that lasts more than two years may be accepted, but the CSA is likely to obtain a liability order if there will be more than £1,000 outstanding at the end of two years. A liability order gives the CSA discretion to use other methods to enforce payment, should the plan not be completed. The CSA may also consider other methods of recovery which do not require a liability order.

Repayments spread over several years may help non-resident parents who are in financial hardship, but this means that the person with care will receive payments very late and may want to make representations to the CSA. No interest will be paid to the person with care in respect of arrears, even though the arrears may have accrued because of CSA delay or error, and/or the non-compliance of the non-resident parent. If arrears have accrued because of CSA delay or error, the person with care (or a child applicant in Scotland) may, however, wish to consider making a complaint and requesting compensation (see Chapter 20).

The person with care and qualifying children are not consulted about the level at which arrears are collected, but will be informed when the decision has been made. This practice may be contrary to the European Convention on Human Rights' protection of private property,[89] but there has been no reported caselaw on this point (see also p413 on the fact that a person with care cannot directly enforce the payment of child support).

Revision, supersession or appeal pending

The CSA can suspend collection of arrears if a decision on a revision, supersession, variation or appeal is pending. If the calculation is likely to be reduced, the CSA may agree to suspend collection of some of the ongoing payments. However, this does not happen often; the CSA prefers to speed up its consideration of the case.

A non-resident parent who requests a revision, supersession or appeal and is having problems paying current child support or any arrears should make representations to the CSA for lower regular payments.

Payment of arrears

Arrears do not have to be paid by the same method as ongoing child support payments. For example, arrears could be collected via the CSA, while ongoing payments are made directly to the person with care. However, in practice the CSA prefers to use the same method of payment for both.

Arrears of child support may be retained by the CSA if they are in respect of a period prior to 12 April 2010 during which the person with care (or her partner) was in receipt of income support (IS), income-based jobseeker's allowance (JSA), income-related employment and support allowance (ESA) or pension credit (PC).

From this date, all child maintenance is fully disregarded when working out the amount of benefit.

The CSA can keep any arrears payments that would not have been passed to the person with care had the child support maintenance been paid when due.[90] That is, the CSA can retain an amount equal to the difference between the amount of IS/income-based JSA/income-related ESA/PC that was paid to the person with care and the amount that would have been paid had the non-resident parent not been in arrears.[91] Payments of arrears are allocated between the CSA and person with care in the same way as overpayments (see p399).

Collection of arrears from a non-resident parent on benefit

In 'new rules' cases, if the non-resident parent is in receipt of one of the following contribution-based benefits, a deduction of £1 may be made towards arrears. This is in addition to a deduction for flat-rate child support. These deductions are separate to other deductions made from benefit and are not affected by priority rules on which deductions should be made first. The £1 deduction can be made from the following benefits, except where IS, income-based JSA, income-related ESA or PC are also being paid to the non-resident parent or his partner:[92]

- contribution-based JSA;
- maternity allowance;
- bereavement allowance;
- widowed parent's allowance;
- war widow's pension;
- widow's pension;
- widowed mother's allowance;
- reduced earnings allowance;
- industrial death benefit and retirement allowance;
- retirement pension;
- incapacity benefit;
- contributory ESA;
- carer's allowance;
- severe disablement allowance;
- industrial injuries benefits;
- war disablement pension.

This means that arrears action in 'new rules' cases will be suspended against non-resident parents on IS/income-based JSA/income-related ESA/PC. If a person with care believes that the arrears action should be pursued in some other way, she should contact the CSA and explain her reasons. If the CSA is unwilling to take action, a complaint may be made (see Chapter 20).

In 'old rules' cases, a deduction for arrears can only be made from contribution-based JSA/contributory ESA, at a maximum of one-third of the age-related amount payable – eg, £22.50 a week for a non-resident parent aged 25 or over in

2011/12.[93] In 'old rules' cases, the priority rules on deductions from benefit apply and, therefore, the deduction may not be made if certain other deductions take priority – eg, for arrears of council tax. For more information on the priority rules on deductions from benefit, see CPAG's *Welfare Benefits and Tax Credits Handbook*.

Offsetting arrears

'Offsetting' is a way of balancing payments or arrears that are owed by persons with care and non-resident parents to each other, so that the CSA only has to pursue arrears from one party. Similarly, the amount of child support a non-resident parent is required to pay can be reduced to take account of arrears owed to him by the other party for a period when he was a person with care.

Offsetting therefore reduces any arrears of child support due under any current or previous maintenance calculation made in respect of the same relevant persons – ie, a person with care, non-resident parent and child applicant in Scotland.[94]

Arrears may be offset if:

- a non-resident parent becomes a parent with care (see below); *or*
- arrears are owed by both parties to a calculation (see p409).

A non-resident parent becomes a parent with care

From 25 January 2010, when a qualifying child for whom child support is payable moves households, so that the non-resident parent becomes the parent with care and *vice versa*, the CSA has the power to offset the new non-resident parent's liability to pay child maintenance against arrears of maintenance owed to her/him by the other parent.[95] The amount payable in relation to the current maintenance calculation by the new non-resident parent can be reduced to nil.[96]

Before 25 January 2010, a new non-resident parent may have found that s/he had to pay child maintenance to someone who still owed them arrears. From this date, the amount of maintenance that the new non-resident parent has to pay is reduced as a way of recovering the arrears owed to her/him.

Example 19.2

Stephen and Zoe divorced five years ago. They have one child, Luke, who has lived with Zoe since the divorce. Zoe applied to the CSA and used the collection service. However, Stephen has not paid her regular maintenance for the past few years. Luke decides that he wants to live with Stephen, who becomes the parent with care. Zoe is now the non-resident parent. If Stephen applies to the CSA for child support, the amount of maintenance that Zoe has to pay to Stephen each week can be reduced as a way of recovering the arrears still owed to her.

Arrears are owed by both parties to a calculation

From 25 January 2010, offsetting can also be used if the parties to a calculation owe each other arrears.[97]

Example 19.3

Luke has now lived with his father, Stephen, for two years. Zoe makes regular maintenance payments for the first year, but when Stephen moves in to live with his new partner, she starts to miss payments. Luke then decides to return to live with Zoe, who becomes the parent with care again. At this time, Zoe owes Stephen £1,000 in arrears. However, there are still £500 arrears that are yet to be recovered from when Stephen was the non-resident parent and did not make regular payments to Zoe. Rather than pursue both sets of arrears, the CSA deducts Stephen's arrears from Zoe's.

Zoe has to pay Stephen £500 in arrears. Only Zoe is pursued for arrears. Stephen's liability for child maintenance under the current calculation could be reduced to recover these.

Offsetting of arrears may also apply if the qualifying children from a relationship live with different parents. In this situation, both are parents with care and non-resident parents in relation to different children.

If both are liable to pay child maintenance, but one falls into arrears, the ongoing payments of the other parent can be reduced.[98]

Example 19.4

Tariq and Ann are separated. They have two children, Dina and Noreen. Dina lives with Tariq and Noreen lives with Ann. Both Tariq and Ann are liable to pay child maintenance to each other and use the CSA's collection service. Tariq fails to make regular payments of child maintenance to Ann. As a result, the amount of maintenance Ann has to pay each week is reduced to take account of the arrears owed to her by Tariq.

If Ann and Tariq fail to make regular maintenance payments to each other and Ann owes Tariq £300 in arrears and Tariq owes Ann £1,000, instead of the CSA pursuing both Ann and Tariq for arrears, the amount owed by Ann is deducted from what she is owed by Tariq.

When offsetting can be applied

Offsetting can only be applied when the collection service is being used. Those with a maintenance direct arrangement can reach their own offsetting agreements, but the CSA will not monitor them.[99]

Offsetting is a discretionary power. The decision to offset does not require the agreement of either parent,[100] but the CSA should take into account her/his wishes.[101] The CSA should notify all relevant parties to the calculation when it is considering offsetting and ask for their views. Parties have 14 days in which to respond. The CSA should also have regard to the welfare of any child likely to be affected by the decision.[102]

If there are no arrears of child support due, or an amount remains to be offset after any arrears have been taken into account, the CSA can reduce the amount payable under the current maintenance calculation. When reducing ongoing payments of child support to the person with care, the CSA should take into account the circumstances of the people involved in the calculation and the period over which it would be reasonable to adjust maintenance payments. Payments can be reduced to nil.[103]

If the current child support calculation is reduced, either the person with care or the non-resident parent can contact the CSA at any time to ask that it be reviewed. The CSA should then discuss with both parties alternative ways of collecting any outstanding arrears.[104]

Arrears may be retained by the CSA if they are in respect of a period prior to 12 April 2010 during which the person with care (or her partner) was in receipt of IS, income-based JSA, income-related ESA or PC. From that date, all child maintenance is fully disregarded when working out the amount of benefit.[105]

Starting recovery action

The CSA may begin to consider recovery action when:

- a payment from the non-resident parent to the CSA is not received; *or*
- the person with care notifies the CSA that a payment due has not been received.

The CSA contacts the non-resident parent to investigate the situation. Contact is normally initially by telephone and followed up in writing if no response is received. The non-resident parent may request an appointment at a local office if he wishes to discuss payment face to face with CSA staff.

If the non-resident parent intends to pay the amount, the CSA may:

- accept a delayed payment, setting a time limit by when payment must be received; *or*
- reschedule the amount to include it within the arrears.

If the non-resident parent indicates that a change of circumstances is causing difficulty in making the payments, the CSA may collect information to check whether or not there should be a supersession.

If the non-resident parent refuses to pay, the CSA will inform him of its powers to collect and enforce maintenance. The CSA may discuss imposing a penalty payment (see p411) to encourage him to pay the child support due. A non-resident parent can also be fined up to £1,000 for failing to provide required information or providing false information.[106]

To avoid other methods of recovery, the non-resident parent should come to an agreement (see p405) as soon as possible and comply with it. The CSA has discretion on the agreements reached with non-resident parents about debt recovery. However, if a non-resident parent fails to come to a voluntary arrangement or breaks it, the CSA may enforce a deduction from earnings order (DEO) at up to 40 per cent of net income and/or take further enforcement action.

At the time of writing, it is understood that the CSA aims to take prompt action on new debts, allowing 12 weeks from the date of a missed payment in which to reach an agreement with the non-resident parent or to obtain payment via non-legal means – eg, a DEO. If an arrangement has not been reached at the end of 12 weeks, legal enforcement should begin. This policy does not apply to exisiting debts where more than 12 weeks has passed since the first missed payment. This 12-week strategy is a policy decision and is not set in the legislation.

When the non-resident parent defaults

If the non-resident parent fails to keep to an arrears agreement:

- a penalty payment may be imposed; *and*
- a DEO (see p415) or other method of enforcement may be considered (see p414).

In all cases, a non-resident parent who wants to co-operate should try to renegotiate an agreement in good time before a change in his circumstances – eg, redundancy. If the non-resident parent has paid regularly and the change would produce a reduction in the amount due, the CSA may accept a lower amount. The non-resident parent could also try to negotiate a suspension in payments if his personal circumstances make it difficult or insensitive to enforce recovery – eg, if he is unemployed, sick or in prison.

Penalty payments

In 'new rules' cases, the power exists to impose a penalty payment on a non-resident parent who is in arrears with his child support payments.[107] In practice, this power does not appear to be used at present. All references to late payment penalties have been removed from CSA leaflets and letters to its clients.[108]

Delays in collection and enforcement

Despite CSA steps to avoid debts building up, many cases may accumulate arrears. The current intention is for the CSA to take action more quickly in response to a non-resident parent's failure to pay and impose financial penalties to encourage payment or establish arrears agreements. The Operational Improvement Plan that ran from 2006 to 2009 stated that the CSA would take 'quicker and firmer action' if non-resident parents default. This included increasing the use of DEOs and the number of non-resident parents brought to court, which has had some success in increased collection rates.[109] There is evidence in recent years that the CSA is taking enforcement action earlier, and pursuing a more vigorous approach to enforcement.[110] However, performance continues to be hindered by the increasing number of cases which have to be processed outside the main computer system.[111] The additional administration required in these cases can lead to increased delays in both collection and enforcement. It is likely that the problem will not be fully solved until the new scheme for child maintenance is introduced.[112]

A person with care who is concerned about the speed of pursuit and who wants quicker action should contact the CSA. A person with care may want to explain the effects of the lack of arrears action on the welfare of the child(ren). In particular, a person with care may want to request that a DEO be issued and, if there is undue delay, make a complaint (see Chapter 20). If a DEO or another form of enforcement is refused, the person with care should be given the reasons for this.

Note, however, that enforcing the obligation to pay child support maintenance is at the discretion of the Secretary of State and not at the discretion of the person who requested its enforcement.[113] This means that the person with care cannot decide which method of enforcement is used. If a person with care believes that there has been undue delay by the CSA, or that it has not used its discretion reasonably or rationally, she can make a complaint (see Chapter 20). It is possible that judicial review (see p343) could also be considered. Parents with care should seek specialist advice before considering an application for judicial review.

If there are arrears of over £100 that have built up because of CSA maladministration, the person with care may be eligible for an advance payment (see below). This may be in addition to any payment of compensation (see p436).

Advance payments

An advance payment of child support is not compensation. The payment is to ensure the person with care is not worse off as a result of maladministration by the CSA. Essentially, it is advance payment of arrears that the CSA is collecting from the non-resident parent. The decision on whether or not to make an advance payment is discretionary and there are no guidelines laid down in legislation. In fact, the CSA can choose to withdraw the scheme at any time.[114]

For an advance payment to be considered, there must be clear evidence of maladministration by the CSA. Maladministration may include:[115]

- rudeness;
- delay;
- refusal to answer reasonable questions;
- knowingly giving advice which is misleading or inadequate;
- incompetence;
- bias because of, for example, gender or ethnicity; *or*
- disregard of guidance that should be followed.

A request for advance payments could also be considered even if the CSA is not able to recover the arrears from the non-resident parent. This could apply if arrears of child support have become unenforceable – eg, because enforcement action was not taken within the time limits, or the non-resident parent has subsequently moved abroad and thus outside the CSA's jurisdiction. If the arrears could have been collected had the CSA taken timely action, a request for advance payments can be made. Although the power is discretionary, the Independent Case Examiner has recommended payment in such cases.[116]

The CSA may consider an advance payment on its own initiative or at the request of the person with care. If an advance payment is to be made, the amount is the arrears of child support that would have been due but for the maladministration. Allowances are made for normal processing time, so only that time over and above this is considered.

If a decision is made not to make a payment, there is no right of appeal. The person with care may provide further information to support her case, complain (see Chapter 20), contact her MP or possibly seek judicial review (see p343). If a complaint is made, the CSA may still refuse to make an advance payment. However, both the Independent Case Examiner and the Ombudsman have the power to recommend advance payments, so it may be worthwhile moving to the next stage of the complaints procedure if the person with care has reasonable grounds.

Where maladministration has occurred, there is also provision for the CSA to pay compensation or a consolatory 'special payment' as recognition of the effects of error (see p443).

Enforcement by the person with care

Although there is no provision in child support legislation for the parent with care to bring her own court action against the non-resident parent for the child support maintenance due, it may be possible to raise an action to recover the amount owed to her. In practice, however, such action may be difficult. The European Court of Human Rights has confirmed that a lack of direct access to the courts by a person with care to enforce child support payments from a non-resident parent does not breach the right to a fair hearing under the European Convention of Human Rights.[117]

If the person with care has lost out because of CSA delay or maladministration, it may be possible to sue the CSA for negligence. Anyone considering doing either of the above should seek legal advice. Using the complaints procedure is more likely to be an effective means of obtaining redress within a reasonable timescale (see Chapter 20).

Interest

From 5 August 2008, interest is no longer added to child maintenance arrears and any outstanding liability for interest has been removed.[118]

4. Enforcement

Future changes

Further enforcement powers, in addition to the current powers of the Child Support Agency (CSA), have been provided by legislation but have not yet been brought into force. These provisions include powers for the CSA to:

- obtain an administrative liability order to take control of goods without having to apply to a court;
- apply to a court for an order disqualifying a parent from holding or obtaining travel authorisation;
- apply to a court for a curfew order; *and*
- disqualify a non-resident parent from holding a driving licence or passport without having to apply to a court.[119]

The government previously announced that, during 2010/11 it intended to introduce the ability to apply for curfew orders and to disqualify non-resident parents from holding a driving licence or passport without having to apply to a court.[120] At the time of writing, however, these powers have not yet been brought into force and it is expected that they will form part of a package of reforms to be introduced from 2012 (see Chapter 1).

A case should usually be considered for enforcement action as soon as it is clear that the non-resident parent has failed to keep to the agreed payment arrangements and has not responded to warnings. Court action may also be taken for criminal offences relating to the supply of information (see Chapter 4).[121]

When making any discretionary decision about enforcement, the CSA must consider the welfare of any children likely to be affected (see p23).

In many cases, in order to pursue enforcement, the CSA must first obtain a **liability order** from the county court/sheriff court (see p422). However, for an increasing number of enforcement options, the CSA does not need a liability order and no court action is required.

A liability order is not required for:

- a deduction from earnings order (DEO). This is usually appropriate when the non-resident parent is employed (see p415);
- deductions to be made from bank/building society accounts. This is likely to be used if the non-resident parent is not an employee (see p425);
- collecting arrears from a deceased person's estate (see p429).

However, the CSA must first obtain a liability order if it wants to:

- use bailiffs (see p424);
- disqualify the non-resident parent from driving (see p432);
- imprison the non-resident parent (see p432).

Deduction from earnings orders

The CSA may make a DEO. This is an order to the non-resident parent's employer to make deductions from his earnings and pay them to the CSA.[122] The CSA does not need to go to court to make a DEO. A DEO is the principal enforcement tool for non-resident parents who are employed and cannot provide a good reason for the arrears, or who have failed to agree a method of payment with the CSA.[123]

A non-resident parent can choose a voluntary DEO, even if he is not in arrears (see p395).

Persons with care have complained in the past that the CSA is slow to make DEOs. However, as part of the Operational Improvement Plan 2006–2009, the CSA planned to increase the use and effectiveness of DEOs, using this method earlier and more frequently, for either non-resident parents who default or those who 'indicate that they are unlikely to pay'.[124] Around 65,000 DEOs were issued in 2009/10, a slight decrease on each of the previous two years, but achieving a higher percentage compliance than previously.[125]

A DEO may not be made if there is good reason not to use that method of payment.[126] For what is considered 'good reason', see p421.

The best way for a non-resident parent to avoid a DEO is to negotiate an arrears agreement (see p405) and keep to it wherever possible. However, making ongoing payments in full may be enough to prevent a DEO being made. Any objection to a DEO by a non-resident parent is likely to be outweighed if it is unlikely that regular payments would be made using a different method.

The decision to make a DEO is discretionary and the welfare of any children must be considered (see p23).[127] If warned of a DEO, the non-resident parent should tell the CSA, preferably in writing, how any child(ren) would be affected. If a DEO is made, the non-resident parent can appeal to the magistrates' court in England and Wales, or sheriff court in Scotland (see p421).

A DEO can be made while the non-resident parent is waiting for a decision on a revision, supersession or appeal. The CSA should consider the grounds of the revision, supersession or appeal before making a DEO. A non-resident parent can also make representations about the amount and method of payments (see p395 and p402). The CSA may accept lower payments, but may still impose a DEO.

A DEO cannot be made if the employer is based outside the UK and has no place of business in the UK, but a DEO can be made in Great Britain against an employer in Northern Ireland and *vice versa*.[128]

A DEO cannot be made if the non-resident parent is in the armed forces. Instead, the CSA can request the armed forces to make deductions for child maintenance under armed forces law, known as a deduction from earnings request (DER), which sets limits on the amounts which can be deducted.[129]

If the full amount requested by the CSA cannot be deducted from earnings, the CSA uses other methods to collect and enforce the remainder.

If a deduction from earnings order is made

A DEO is an instruction to the employer of a non-resident parent to make deductions from his earnings.[130] A copy of the DEO must be served on the employer and the non-resident parent.[131] The employer has to comply with the DEO within seven days of receiving it.[132] An employer can be fined up to £1,000 if it provides false or misleading information, or deliberately withholds information from the CSA.[133]

The DEO must state:[134]

- the name and address of the non-resident parent;
- the name of the employer;
- the non-resident parent's place of work, the nature of his work, his employee number and national insurance (NI) number (if known by the CSA);
- the normal deduction rate(s) (see p435) and the date on which each takes effect;
- the protected earnings proportion;
- the address to which the deductions are to be sent.

The CSA national helpline (see Appendix 1) provides further information for employers. The CSA leaflets *What is My Role in Helping My Employees Pay Child Maintenance?* (CSL313) ('new rules') and *Advice for Employers* (CSA2002) ('old rules') also provide guidance to employers on deductions. If an employer is implementing a DEO incorrectly and the non-resident parent is disputing this, the non-resident parent should ask the CSA to intervene.

Date of payment

The employer must pay the CSA monthly by the 19th of the month following the month in which the deduction is made.[135] This means that there is always a delay before the person with care receives the first payment from the CSA. Because the employer makes monthly payments, the person with care receives monthly payments, even if the non-resident parent is having weekly deductions made. These monthly payments may not always be for the same amount (see p419 and p436).

The payment by the employer may be made by credit transfer, cheque or any other method to which the CSA agrees.[136] The DEO reference number must be given so that the CSA can identify the person with care.

It is an offence punishable by a fine of up to £500 for an employer to fail to take all reasonable steps to pay the CSA on time.[137]

Providing information

Information sent to the CSA is treated as having been given or sent on the day that it is received.[138]

Any notice that is sent from the CSA will be treated as though it was given or sent on the day that it was posted.[139]

Failure to take all reasonable steps to comply with any of the following requirements to provide information to the CSA is an offence punishable by a fine of up to £500.[140]

The non-resident parent

The non-resident parent must provide the name and address of his employer, the amount of earnings and anticipated earnings, place of work and the nature of work within seven days of being asked to do so in writing by the CSA.[141] Once a DEO is in force, a non-resident parent must inform the CSA within seven days of leaving employment or becoming employed or re-employed.[142]

The employer

An employer must inform the CSA in writing within 10 days of being served with a DEO if s/he does not, in fact, employ the non-resident parent.[143] If a non-resident parent who is subject to a DEO leaves his job, the employer must notify the CSA within 10 days of his leaving.[144] If an employer finds out that a DEO is in force against an employee (eg, on becoming his employer), s/he must notify the CSA within seven days of becoming aware of this information.[145]

The employer must inform the non-resident parent in writing of the amount of each deduction no later than the date of the deduction or, if not practicable, by the following payday.[146] Although child support law imposes no penalty on an employer who fails to do this, employment protection law requires the employer to give the non-resident parent a written statement of deductions on or before the payday.[147] If the deduction will always be the same amount, this can be done by a standing statement given at least annually.[148] If the employer does not give notice of the deduction, the non-resident parent may complain to an employment tribunal, which can order the employer to pay the non-resident parent a fine up to the total amount of the unnotified deductions, even if paid to the CSA.[149] This fine would not affect deductions already paid to the CSA.

For other duties about providing information, see p53.

Earnings

Earnings include wages, salary, fees, bonus, commission, overtime pay, occupational pension or statutory sick pay, any other payment made under an employment contract and a regular payment made in compensation for loss of wages.[150] Earnings do not include a payment by a foreign government or the government of Northern Ireland,[151] or a payment to a special member of a British reserved armed force.[152] Net earnings means, in this context, the amount remaining after tax, NI and contributions towards a pension scheme have been deducted.[153]

How much is deducted

The DEO states a **normal deduction rate** and a **protected earnings proportion**.[154] These rates should usually correspond to the pay periods of the non-resident parent – ie, at a weekly rate if paid weekly, and a monthly rate if paid monthly.[155] More than one normal deduction rate can be set, each applying to a different period.[156]

Normal deduction rate

The normal deduction rate is the amount that will be deducted each payday provided net earnings are not brought below the protected earnings proportion. The normal deduction rate can include not only the current child support liability but also an amount for any arrears, penalty payments and fees due. There are no special rules on how quickly the CSA should seek to clear the liability, although often the maximum deduction rate of 40 per cent is applied (see p405). Non-resident parents may wish to discuss with the CSA how it has chosen to apply its discretion.

Protected earnings proportion

The protected earnings proportion is the level below which earnings must not be reduced by the deductions. The protected earnings proportion is 60 per cent of net earnings.[157]

Administering a deduction from earnings order

The employer can deduct a charge for administrative costs each time a deduction is made under the DEO.[158] This means that employees paid weekly can be charged more for administrative costs. The additional amount must not exceed £1 per deduction and can be made even if this would bring earnings below the protected earnings proportion.

Each payday the employer should make a deduction from net earnings at the normal deduction rate plus any administration charge, unless deducting the normal deduction rate would reduce net earnings below the protected earnings proportion. If this would be the case, the amount of the deduction is the excess of net earnings over the protected earnings proportion. In addition, an administration charge may be deducted.[159]

If the employer fails to make a deduction, or the deduction is less than the normal deduction rate, arrears build up and are deducted at the next payday in addition to the normal deduction, applying the same rules for protected earnings.[160]

If, on a payday, the non-resident parent is paid for a period longer than that for which the normal deduction rate is set, the deduction is increased in proportion to the length of the pay period.[161]

Such fluctuations in deductions may mean that the person with care receives irregular payments.

Example 19.5

The non-resident parent is due to pay child maintenance of £48 a week and his net earnings are £240 a week. When a DEO is considered, there are arrears of £432 and penalty payments of £26.40. The DEO shows a normal deduction rate of £60 (maintenance due plus 5 per cent net income) and a protected earnings proportion of £144. His employer can deduct £1 administrative costs for weeks in which a deduction is made.

Payday	*Net pay*	*Child support due*	*Deduction*	*Pay*	*DEO unpaid*
	£	£	£	£	£
5/7	240	60	61	179	
12/7	250	60	61	189	
19/7	160	60	17	143	44
26/7	160	104	17	143	88
2/8	240	148	97	143	52
9/8	250	112	107	143	6
16/8	250	66	67	183	
23/8	240	60	61	179	
30/8	120	60	Nil	120	60
6/9	240	120	97	143	24
13/9	240	84	85	155	
20/9	250	60	61	189	
27/9	240	60	61	179	

In the week 19/7 the full deduction cannot be made, as this would take income below the protected earnings proportion. A deduction is made of £16 plus a £1 administration fee. The amount of the DEO outstanding is added to the next amount due on 26/7. As earnings are again low, the full deduction cannot be taken and is carried forward.

In the week 30/8, earnings are too low for a deduction to be made and, therefore, there is no deduction and no administrative charge.

Payment to the person with care

The employer has to pass the month's payments to the CSA by the 19th of the following month.[162] When these have reached the CSA's account, they should be passed on to the person with care within approximately 10 days. If the person with care was on income support, income-based jobseeker's allowance, income-related employment and support allowance or pension credit in the period to which the arrears relate, some of the payments may be retained in lieu of benefit paid.[163] This only applies to arrears of child support payments which were due to be made before 12 April 2010. The person with care should receive the full amount of any arrears which relate to the period after 12 April 2010, when child maintenance became fully disregarded for all means-tested benefits.

Example 19.6

Following on from the previous example where there are arrears of £432, the parent with care would receive the following payments.

Month	*Payment to CSA by the 19th of the month*	*Current liability paid (£48 a week due)*	*Arrears paid (assigned to oldest debt)*
	£	*£*	*£*
July		Nil	Nil
August	156	156	Nil
September	328	192	136
October	300	192	108

By the time the parent gets her first payment from the DEO in August, she is owed £624 (£432 + £192 (July)), but because of the fluctuating earnings of the non-resident parent, she will receive less than the maintenance due. It is only in September that she begins to obtain arrears of maintenance, even though the DEO was put into place in July.

Priority of orders

A DEO takes priority over an attachment of earnings order for a judgment or administration debt (non-priority debts), and any arrestment of earnings under Scottish law.[164] In England and Wales, when a DEO is served on an employee who is already subject to an attachment of earnings order for a priority debt (eg, council tax or fine), the earliest order has priority.[165]

Any deductions under a lower priority order are taken from the net earnings left after deductions under the first order have been made.[166]

Reviews, cancellations and lapsed orders

The CSA must **review** a DEO if there is a change in the amount of the calculation or if any arrears, penalty payments (interest in some cases – see p413) and fees included have been paid off.[167] This does not apply if a normal deduction rate that takes into account the change has already been specified (see p435). A DEO can be changed on this review.[168] The employer must comply with the change within seven days of a copy of the new DEO being served on her/him.[169] The usual penalties for failure to comply apply.

The CSA can **cancel** the DEO if:[170]

- no further payments are due under it;
- the DEO is ineffective or there appears to be a more effective way of collecting the payments;
- the DEO is defective (see p421) or does not comply with some other procedural provision in the legislation;
- the CSA did not have, or has ceased to have, jurisdiction to make a DEO; *or*
- a DEO being used to enforce a default maintenance decision or interim maintenance decision is no longer appropriate given the compliance or attempted compliance of the non-resident parent.

The CSA must send written notice of cancellation to the non-resident parent and employer.[171]

A DEO **lapses** when a non-resident parent leaves the employment.[172] The CSA can revive it if he finds a new job with the same or a different employer.[173] If it is revived, copies of the notice must be served on the non-resident parent and new employer.[174] Any shortfall under the DEO prior to the revival cannot be carried over to the revived DEO.[175]

Appeals

A non-resident parent can appeal against a DEO to the magistrates' court in England and Wales or sheriff court in Scotland.[176] The appeal must be made within 28 days of the DEO being made (56 days if the non-resident parent is not resident in the UK).[177] An appeal can only be made on the grounds that the order is defective (see below), or that the payments made to the non-resident parent are not earnings (see p417),[178] or that there is 'good reason' not to use a DEO.[179]

When determining whether there is good reason not to use a DEO, the CSA must consider whether making the order is likely to result in the disclosure of the parentage of a child and the likely impact of that disclosure on the non-resident parent's employment or on any relationship between the non-resident parent and a third party.[180] The impact of a third party becoming aware of the non-resident parent's DEO will not be considered as a good reason in any circumstances other than in connection with the disclosure of the parentage of a child.[181]

A good reason for not imposing a DEO may also exist if a family member of the non-resident parent or parent with care is employed by the same employer as the non-resident parent and that family member's employment is such that s/he is likely to acquire knowledge of the DEO. If the consequence of this is that the non-resident parent's employment status or family relationships may be adversely affected, there should be good reason not to impose a DEO.[182]

The fact that a non-resident parent may prefer a different method of payment or would prefer for his employer not to be informed about his child support liability are not considered good reasons to refrain from using a DEO.[183]

If the CSA has not properly exercised its discretion in making a DEO, judicial review can be sought (see p343) and/or a complaint made first to the CSA and then, if not resolved, to the Independent Case Examiner (see Chapter 20).

A DEO is **defective** if it is impracticable for the employer to comply with it because it does not include the correct information required.[184] Many DEOs have included incorrect information (such as errors in names, addresses and dates), but an appeal will not succeed on this basis if the employer can still comply with the DEO. Although some early appeals were upheld because the DEO was unsigned, there is no requirement in the Regulations for a signature.

In Scotland, the form of the application for an appeal is laid out in the sheriff court child support rules.[185] In England and Wales, a complaint is made against the Secretary of State for Work and Pensions (who acts through the CSA). As there is no specific form given, we suggest that the Scottish wording is followed as an example, but including, 'This complaint is made under section 32(5) of the Child

Support Act 1991 and regulation 22 of the Child Support (Collection and Enforcement) Regulations 1992.'

Once the complaint or application is made, the court notifies the CSA. The CSA checks the DEO and contacts the employer to check the earnings. If the DEO is based on the wrong amounts, the CSA varies and reissues it. If the case does get as far as a court hearing, the magistrates/sheriff may quash the DEO or specify which payments, if any, constitute earnings.[186] The court cannot question the maintenance calculation itself.[187]

Even if the court quashes the DEO, it cannot order the CSA to repay deductions to the non-resident parent.[188] For this reason, if deductions are being made from payments that are not earnings, or on the basis of an incorrect normal deduction rate or protected earnings proportion, it may be better to challenge the DEO by judicial review.

Either party can be represented by a lawyer. The CSA can (and does) instead appoint its own staff to conduct DEO appeals and appear at related hearings before magistrates in England and Wales or a sheriff in Scotland.[189] The non-resident parent can also be represented by a lay person, if the sheriff accepts s/he is suitable. An authorised lay representative does not have the full rights of a legal representative, but may be entitled to expenses.

Obtaining a liability order

If a DEO is inappropriate (eg, because the non-resident parent is not employed) or one has been made but proved ineffective, the CSA may apply to the magistrates' court in England and Wales, or sheriff court in Scotland, for a liability order.[190] (Alternatively, the CSA may seek a deduction order to take money directly from a non-resident parent's current or savings bank account. This does not require a liability order or any other court order (see p425). A deduction order may be sought if a non-resident parent is self-employed and a DEO is not possible.)

A liability order provides the CSA with legal recognition of the debt, and allows the CSA to take further enforcement measures.

If the court decides that the payments are due but have not been made, it must make the order.[191] The court cannot question the maintenance calculation itself.[192] When making a liability order, the court is, however, entitled to take into account payments made by the non-resident person by a method other than that specified by the CSA for the payment of the child support liability.[193]

An order (including one made in Northern Ireland) can be enforced anywhere in the UK.[194]

Either party can be represented by a lawyer. The CSA can (and does) instead appoint its own staff to apply for liability orders and appear at related hearings before magistrates in England and Wales or a sheriff in Scotland.[195] The non-resident parent can also be represented by a lay person, if the sheriff accepts s/he is suitable. An authorised lay representative does not have the full rights of a legal representative, but may be entitled to expenses.

If the court makes the order, it can (and usually will) order the non-resident parent to pay the CSA's legal expenses.

Time limits for obtaining and using a liability order

Since 12 July 2006, there has been no time limit for applying for a liability order. Debts that were older than six years on 12 July 2006 (ie, that became due on or before 12 July 2000) cannot be enforced and will be recovered by other methods, such as a DEO.[196] The six years do not begin to run until the non-resident parent is notified of the assessment or calculation. Although an assessment can be backdated, liability does not exist until the assessment is made.[197]

The CSA does not need to act on a liability order immediately after it is granted. If a liability order is made in time, there may be a long delay before the CSA takes any further action. For actions that directly aim to recover money (eg, levying distress), there is a time limit of six years from the date of the liability order in which to act.[198]

For actions that do not themselves recover money, such as imprisonment or disqualification from driving, the six-year time limit does not apply and the CSA may be able to take action after this date.[199]

England and Wales

The CSA must give the non-resident parent seven days' notice of its intention to seek a liability order (28 days if the non-resident parent is not resident in the UK).[200] The notice must state the amount of child support outstanding, including any penalty payments.

The non-resident parent will be sent a summons giving 14 days' notice of the hearing. The magistrates decide whether or not to issue the liability order, but cannot consider whether the non-resident parent is liable or the assessment/calculation has been properly made.[201] If an appeal against the CSA on those issues is pending, however, the magistrates' court might decide to adjourn.

The magistrates may decide not to issue an order if the non-resident parent appears to be co-operating. However, the CSA may still ask for the order to be granted on the understanding that it will not be enforced if the non-resident parent continues to co-operate. If the non-resident parent does not attend the court, the CSA may still obtain the order unless the application has not been properly made. It is relatively unusual for a non-resident parent to attend a liability order hearing. If the non-resident parent does attend, the court may adjourn and arrange another hearing to ensure that there is sufficient time for the non-resident parent to speak.

The form of the court order in England and Wales is set out in the Regulations. The order must specify the outstanding amounts of child support maintenance, penalty payments, fees (interest in some cases – see p413) and other forms of maintenance.[202]

Scotland

A CSA litigation officer can sign the liability order application instead of a solicitor.[203] Court officials serve notice of the application on the non-resident parent.[204] The non-resident parent has 21 days to object to the liability order being made. This should be done in writing by returning the notice stating the grounds of the objection and enclosing evidence. If objections are received, a hearing is held. Even if the non-resident parent does not attend, the sheriff must still consider his objections.[205] As in England and Wales, the sheriff court cannot consider whether the non-resident parent is liable, nor whether liablity has been correctly calculated. An extract of the liability order may be issued 14 days after the order is actually made. All the forms used in this procedure are included in the sheriff court child support rules.[206]

Enforcing a liability order

In **England and Wales**, the CSA can decide to levy distress (see below) or take action in the county court (see p425). The Operational Improvement Plan stated that the CSA will use the full range of sanctions available, including driving licence removal, imprisonment or seizure of assets, where appropriate.[207]

In **Scotland**, a liability order can be enforced by 'diligence'.[208] The form of the demand for payment sent by the sheriff court is given in that court's child support rules.[209] It states the sum owed, including court charges, and specifies that further action will be taken if payment is not made within 14 days (28 days if the non-resident parent is outside the UK). Otherwise, there are no procedures specific to child maintenance. The procedures are the same as for any other debt enforced in Scotland following the granting of a liability order.

The liability order may be enforced by inhibition of sale of property and arrestment of bank accounts.[210]

Distress

If a liability order has been made, the amount specified on the order can be enforced in England and Wales by distress – ie, the seizure and sale of goods.[211] The bailiff levying distress must either carry written authority to hand to the non-resident parent, or leave at the address where distress is to be levied a copy of the relevant Regulations and a memorandum setting out the amount to be levied.[212] If payment is made in full, the levy of the goods or the subsequent sale will not take place.[213]

Certain items cannot be seized. These are:[214]

- tools, books, vehicles and other items necessary for work; *and*

- clothing, bedding, furniture, household equipment and provisions necessary to meet the basic domestic needs of the non-resident parent and any member of his family who lives with him; *and*
- any money, promissory notes, bond or other securities for money belonging to the non-resident parent.

Charges can be made at each of the stages involved in distress proceedings.[215]

Any person can appeal to the magistrates' court by making a complaint to the court.[216] If the court is satisfied that the levy was irregular, it may order the goods to be returned if they have been seized, and order compensation in respect of any goods sold.

County court action

Once a liability order has been made, the CSA can arrange for the county court to record the order as if it were a judgment debt.[217] This record is publicly available and damages the non-resident parent's credit rating. The CSA can also use the county court to recover any amount that remains unpaid.[218]

A **charging order** allows a debt to be registered against certain assets, such as land, stocks, shares and any interest the non-resident parent may have in a trust. If a charge is registered and the assets are sold, the debt due under the liability order can be recovered from the proceeds of the sale. In some cases it may not be possible to register a charge, in which case a caution against dealings may be obtained to prevent the property from being sold without the CSA's knowledge. Once a charge or caution has been registered, the CSA can consider applying to the court for an order of sale.

A **third-party debt order** can be obtained by the CSA if it is aware that the non-resident parent has a bank account or is owed money by a third party. The order freezes funds in the account and requires that person to release funds to the CSA up to the amount of the liability order.

Deductions from bank accounts

Since 3 August 2009, the CSA has had the power to make deductions from current or savings accounts without the consent of the non-resident parent.[219] This includes accounts with banks, building societies and credit unions. To exercise this power, the CSA does not need to apply to court or obtain a liability order. The deductions can be either regular or made as a lump-sum payment.[220] Technically, as soon as a non-resident parent is in arrears, a deduction order becomes possible as a method of enforcement.

In a review of the first year of operation of this power, the Child Maintenance and Enforcement Commission (CMEC) has said that it 'has pursued an extremely careful approach to implementation to ensure that deduction orders are used correctly and proportionately'. It intends to make procedural improvements that will ensure that the use of orders is considered as standard for all appropriate cases where there are arrears.[221]

If a non-resident parent has failed to pay child support, the CSA can make an order requiring a bank or building society with which the non-resident parent has an account to make deductions from that account and pay the CSA. The CSA has discretion to choose the most suitable account from which to make deductions. Generally, regular deduction orders will be directed at current accounts and lump-sum deduction orders at savings accounts. CMEC has said that, following careful implementation of the powers, it may now consider the use of deduction orders on more complex accounts, such as notice accounts or stocks and shares accounts.[222]

A lump-sum or regular deduction order cannot be made in respect of an account which is used wholly or partly for business purposes. This does not apply if a regular deduction order is made in respect of an account that relates to a non-resident parent who is a sole trader.[223] The powers to make deduction orders in respect of joint accounts have not yet been brought into effect by Regulations.[224]

In the first year of operation, 3,430 cases were considered for deduction order action, with 500 deduction orders made. The average value of funds received from successful orders was £2,200, with significantly more funds being gathered by lump-sum deduction orders than by regular deduction orders.[225]

The bank or building society is able to take an amount from the non-resident parent's account to cover the administrative costs of setting up and paying a deduction order. The maximum amounts that can be charged are:[226]

- £10, in the case of each deduction made under a regular deduction order;
- £55, in the case of each deduction made under a lump-sum deduction order.

Regular deduction orders

A regular deduction order can be used to collect both arrears and ongoing child support payments that will become due under the calculation that is in place.[227]

When a regular deduction order is made, a copy is served on both the deposit taker and the non-resident parent. The order must specify the amount of the regular deduction and the dates on which regular deductions are due to be made.[228]

If there is a current child support maintenance calculation, or arrears are being collected for a maintenance arrangement which is no longer in force, the maximum that can be deducted is 40 per cent of the non-resident parent's net weekly income. If a default maintenance decision has been made, the maximum that can be deducted is £80 a week.[229]

Before a regular deduction can be made from a joint account, each of the account holders should be given an opportunity to make representations on the making of the order and the amounts to be deducted.[230] **Note:** the powers to make deductions from a joint account have not yet been brought into effect (see above).

A deduction cannot be made if the amount of credit in the relevant account is below a certain level on the date a deduction is due to be made. The minimum amounts are:

- £40, if deductions are made monthly;
- £10, if deductions are made weekly;
- if deductions are made for any other period, £10 for each whole week in that period plus £1 for each additional day in that period.

In addition to these amounts, there must be sufficient funds in the account to pay the administrative costs charged.[231]

If the non-resident parent's account is subject to other deduction orders, such as third-party debt orders and garnishee orders, these will generally be paid first before a regular deduction order is dealt with. The exception to this is where a third-party debt order or garnishee order is served on the deposit taker after the regular deduction order but on or before the date a payment is due to be made under the deduction order. In this case, the deduction order will be paid first on that occasion, unless the deposit taker has already taken steps to process the other orders. For future payments, it is assumed that the third-party debt order or garnishee order will take priority.[232]

It is an offence for a person not to comply with the requirements of a regular deduction order and failure to do so can lead to a fine of up to £500. However, there is a defence if the person can show that all reasonable steps were taken to comply with the order or regulation.[233]

Reviews and variations of regular deduction orders

A non-resident parent or a bank or building society can apply to the CSA for a review of a regular deduction order if:[234]

- the non-resident parent or deposit taker can satisfy the CSA that the non-resident parent does not have a beneficial interest in some or all of the amount of money in the account that is subject to the order; *or*
- there has been a change in the amount of the maintenance calculation in question; *or*
- any amounts payable under the order have been paid; *or*
- there has been a change in the non-resident parent's net weekly income; *or*
- because of an official error, an incorrect amount has been specified in the order.

A regular deduction order can be varied to change the amount that is deducted if:[235]

- the CSA accepts that the non-resident parent has made a payment of child support and no alternative method of payment of child support maintenance is in place; *or*

- there has been a successful appeal against a child support maintenance calculation; *or*
- the order has been changed following a successful review.

Lump-sum deduction orders

If it is established that the non-resident parent owes arrears of child support, the CSA will consider whether a lump-sum deduction order is the most appropriate method of recovering them.

Once the CSA has decided to make a lump-sum deduction order, it serves an interim order on a 'deposit taker' (the non-resident parent's bank or building society, or other third party). The interim order acts as an instruction to secure funds up to the amount of the order in a specified account until further notice. The bank or building society is expected to prevent the funds from being moved or reduced below the amount that is ordered or, if funds are already below this amount, not to allow them to decrease further.

Once funds have been secured, a copy of the order is served on the non-resident parent. Both the deposit taker and the non-resident parent have 14 days from the date the order was served in which to make representations to the CSA. The order is treated as having been served on the non-resident parent at the end of the day on which the copy is posted to his last known address.[236]

When issuing the order and instructing the deposit taker to secure funds, the CSA should have regard to:[237]

- any hardship that may be caused to the non-resident parent's partner or a relevant child;
- any written, contractual obligations regarding the money that were made prior to the lump-sum deduction order being made;
- any other circumstances that the CSA considers appropriate in the particular case.

The CSA should also ensure that the amount deducted from a joint account does not exceed an amount that is fair, given all the circumstances, especially the amounts contributed to the account by each of the account holders.[238] **Note**: the powers to make deductions from a joint account have not yet been brought into effect (see p425).

In addition to this 14-day period, a non-resident parent or deposit taker can ask the CSA to use its discretion to vary the order in certain circumstances. These include if:[239]

- the CSA accepts the non-resident parent's agreement to make a payment;
- there has been a revision or supersession of, or a successful appeal against, the maintenance calculation that is the subject of the order;
- there has been an appeal to the county court (or sheriff in Scotland) against the making of an order, or against a refusal by the CSA to consent to funds being moved or reduced;

- the CSA agrees that hardship may be caused to the non-resident parent's partner or a relevant child;
- the non-resident parent is under a written contractual obligation, made before the lump-sum deduction order was made.

Priority of payments

In **England and Wales**, if there is a final lump-sum deduction order and other interim third-party debt orders or garnishee orders *nisi*, a deposit taker must comply with them in the order in which they were served on the deposit taker. If an interim lump-sum deduction order is served after an interim third-party debt order or garnishee order *nisi*, the final versions of these other orders will take priority.[240]

In **Scotland**, a deposit taker must give priority to the lump-sum deduction order and any other orders, according to the order in which they were served on the deposit taker.[241]

Minimum amounts

A deduction should not be made if the amount of credit in the relevant bank account is below a minimum level. The current minimum level is £55 plus the amount of administrative costs charged by the bank or building society. The administrative costs must not be more than £55 for a lump-sum deduction order.

Appeals

A non-resident parent has the right to appeal against a lump-sum deduction order or a regular deduction order and related decisions made by the CSA. The appeal is made to the county court in England and Wales or the sheriff court in Scotland.

The non-resident parent can appeal against:

- the making of a regular deduction order;
- any decision by the CSA in relation to a request to review a regular deduction order;
- a refusal to consent to the waiving of the requirement to freeze or protect funds which are the subject of an interim lump-sum deduction order;
- the making of a final lump-sum deduction order.[242]

There is a time limit of 21 days from the date the final lump-sum deduction order is received in which to appeal against it being made. The non-resident parent is considered to have received the final lump-sum deduction order two days after it was posted. If, after 21 days has expired, no appeals have been made, the CSA will instruct the deposit taker to pay the funds to the CSA.

Recovery of arrears from an estate

From 25 January 2010, the CSA has had powers to request the payment of arrears from a deceased person's estate. This is a discretionary power. The person must have died on or after 25 January 2010. Any arrears for which the deceased was liable immediately before his death become a debt payable to the CSA from his estate.[243] The CSA can contact the administrator or executor of the deceased's estate to request payment.

The administrator or executor has the same rights of appeal, following the same procedures and time limits, as the deceased person had prior to his death. The CSA must appoint the administrator or executor to proceed with any appeal or, if there is no such person, the CSA can appoint someone it thinks fit.[244]

The CSA must disclose relevant information to enable the administrator or executor of the deceased's estate to make a decision about whether to pay or appeal the arrears. The CSA has discretion to decide if the information requested is essential and, therefore, whether it should be disclosed.[245] Any application for information should be in writing and give reasons. The address of any person involved in the case should not be disclosed by the CSA, unless the person concerned has given written consent. The CSA should also prevent the disclosure of any information that could lead to the person with care, or any other relevant person, being located.[246]

It is intended that child support arrears will be treated in the same way as other debts – eg, unpaid utility or council tax bills. It does not appear that they will take priority over other payments.

Concerns have been raised about possible inaccuracies in calculating the correct amount of child support that may be owed by a deceased non-resident parent. Before making a claim on an estate, the CSA should thoroughly check the amount of outstanding debt, including completing any outstanding reassessments relating to periods before his death.[247] Administrators of the estate should check that the CSA has carried out this process and that the amount of debt to be recovered is accurate.

When arrears should not be recovered

The CSA should not pursue arrears from a deceased person's estate without seeking the consent of the person with care. If the person with care does not wish to pursue the arrears, the CSA should not take any further action.[248] The CSA also has a duty to take into account the welfare of any child likely to be affected by its decision.[249] This includes children of the deceased person who may not have been the subject of the maintenance calculation, or other dependent children who would otherwise benefit from his estate. When the CSA registers its claim against the estate, it may not be aware of other children or the potential implications for them. If the CSA later becomes aware of any potentially adverse impact on other children, it should reconsider whether to pursue the arrears.[250]

If the arrears recovered from an estate would be retained by the CSA in lieu of any benefit paid, they should not be pursued if to do so would have a detrimental effect on a person with care or a qualifying child. This only applies to arrears relating to a period before 12 April 2010, when child maintenance became fully disregarded for all means-tested benefits. The CSA should contact the person with care to establish what impact the recovery would have before approaching the administrators of the estate.[251]

Using the power

CMEC has expressed an intention to avoid legal action where possible when using this power and not to delay or obstruct the administration of an estate.[252] In the first 11 months of 2010/11, this recovery action was pursued in 840 cases.[253]

It is understood that the CSA will be notified electronically when other government departments are informed of the death of a non-resident parent. However, the person with care may also wish to inform the CSA of the death of a non-resident person who owes arrears of child support.

Orders preventing the disposal of assets

From 6 April 2010, the CSA has had powers to take action to prevent a non-resident parent disposing of his assets, from which the CSA could recover the arrears.[254] The CSA may apply to the High Court (England and Wales) or the Court of Session or sheriff court (Scotland) if a non-resident parent has:

- arrears of child support; *and*
- has disposed of, or is about to dispose of, assets with the intention of avoiding paying child support.

These powers apply only to disposals made on or after 6 April 2010.

Disposing of assets includes any conveyance, assurance, or gift of property of any description. It does not include assets transferred under a will or codicil.[255]

If the asset has already been disposed of, the Court can make an order to 'set the transaction aside' or, in Scotland, to 'reduce the disposition' – ie, to reverse the disposal.[256]

If the non-resident parent is about to dispose of an asset, the Court can make a restraining order (England and Wales) or an interdicting order (Scotland) to prevent this.[257]

The Court can review any disposal of assets by the non-resident parent, except if the asset was given as part of a contract with an innocent party who acted in good faith.[258] For example, if the non-resident parent disposes of a sum of money to purchase goods from an individual, who had no knowledge of his intention to avoid paying child support, the transaction cannot be reversed. An asset transferred to another as part of a marriage agreement can, however, be reviewed by the Court.[259]

If the Court is satisfied that the CSA would be able to take action to recover arrears from the asset in question, the burden of proof is on the non-resident parent to show that he did not dispose of, or was not about to dispose of, the asset with the intention of avoiding paying maintenance.[260] If an order is made in

Scotland, the non-resident parent can apply to the Court to have it reviewed, varied or recalled at any time.[261]

Disqualification from driving or imprisonment

The CSA may take action to disqualify the non-resident parent from driving or to imprison him (but not both) if all other methods of recovery have failed.[262]

Before taking action, every attempt must be made to contact the non-resident parent. If no phone contact has been successful during the enforcement action, a face-to-face visit may be appropriate. These powers are only used as a last resort.[263] Suspended prison sentences and suspended disqualifications from driving are significantly more common than actual commitals and disqualifications.[264]

As with the exercise of all discretionary powers, when deciding whether to take this action, the CSA should consider the welfare of any children likely to be affected.

Action for committal or disqualification from driving

In England and Wales, if distress and/or county court proceedings have been tried or, in Scotland, diligence via arrestments or inhibitions on sale, but an amount is still due under the liability order, the CSA can apply to the magistrates' court or sheriff court to issue either a warrant committing the non-resident parent to prison or an order disqualifying him from driving.[265]

The hearing must take place in the presence of the non-resident parent.[266] The court can summon him to appear in court and produce his driving licence.[267] If he does not appear, the court may issue a warrant (citation in Scotland) for his arrest.[268] The CSA can make representations to the court on whether to issue a warrant or order disqualification.[269] The non-resident parent may reply to these.

The court must enquire into the non-resident parent's means, whether he needs a driving licence to make a living and whether there has been 'wilful refusal or culpable neglect' on his part.[270] Only if there has been, can the court commit the non-resident parent to prison or disqualify him from driving;[271] the decision whether to do so is at the discretion of the court. A non-resident parent should seek advice in preparing a statement of his income and outgoings.[272] A written statement from an employer will be accepted as proof of earnings.[273] The CSA can appoint its own staff to apply for committal and appear at related hearings before magistrates in England and Wales or a sheriff in Scotland.[274]

Imprisonment

If the court decides that there has been wilful refusal or culpable neglect and committal is appropriate, a warrant for imprisonment will be issued.[275] A warrant for imprisonment cannot be issued against a non-resident parent who is under 18.[276]

Instead of immediate committal, the court usually fixes a term of imprisonment and postpones it on conditions, usually of regular payments.[277] A warrant of commitment is issued stating the total amount outstanding, including child support, penalty payments, fees (interest in some cases – see p413), court costs and any other charges.[278] If the amount is paid in full, the non-resident parent will not be imprisoned.

The maximum period of imprisonment is six weeks.[279] If, after the warrant has been issued, part-payment is made, the period of imprisonment is reduced by the same proportion as that by which the debt has been reduced.[280]

If the non-resident parent is imprisoned, he can secure his immediate release by arranging for the liability order debt to be paid in full. If part of the liability order debt is paid, the prison sentence can be reduced.[281] Advisers should check whether the payment needs to be made to the prison or to the CSA.

The court cannot write off the arrears, so if full payment is not made, arrears will still exist following the period of imprisonment. If a warrant is not issued or the court does not fix a term of imprisonment, the CSA can renew the application at a later date on the grounds that the non-resident parent's circumstances have changed.

The ability to apply to court for a warrant for imprisonment is not a one-off power. If the non-resident parent builds up a new debt, for example by not keeping up with current child support payments, the CSA can go back to court to request a warrant in respect of each new debt.[282]

Disqualification from driving

If the court decides that there has been wilful refusal or culpable neglect and disqualification from driving is appropriate, an order will be issued.[283] The order may be issued but its implementation suspended on conditions – eg, regular payments. The order will state the amount outstanding, including child support, interest, court costs and any other charges.[284] If the amount is paid in full, the order is revoked.

The maximum period of disqualification is two years.[285] If, after the order has been issued, part-payment is made, the period of disqualification may be reduced.[286] If the amount is paid in full, the order must be revoked. If at the end of the period of disqualification the arrears have not been paid in full, the CSA may apply again for imprisonment or disqualification.[287]

Note: legislation provides powers for the CSA to disqualify a non-resident parent from driving without the need for a liability order or having to apply to court. These powers have not yet been brought into force but it is expected that they will form part of a package of reforms to be introduced from 2012 (see Chapter 1).

Bankruptcy

The CSA does not pursue bankruptcy (sequestration in Scotland), but a non-resident parent may have child support maintenance arrears when he is made bankrupt. The CSA is not a creditor that is capable of being bound by an individual voluntary arrangement (ie, in England and Wales, a binding compromise agreement with creditors to avoid the consequences of bankruptcy) made by a non-resident parent who has failed to pay child support maintenance. The clear purpose of the legislation is to exclude liability to pay child support maintenance from the consequences of bankruptcy. Any liability for arrears of child support cannot, therefore, be reduced by means of an individual voluntary arrangement.[288] The Welfare Reform Bill introduced in February 2011 includes a clause which seeks to make this position clear.

The CSA is unable to take enforcement action while a non-resident parent is being made bankrupt. Therefore, if the CSA is notified of bankruptcy, any ongoing enforcement action must cease until the bankruptcy order has been made.

In either case, the CSA may decide not to enforce the order because it may not be practical – eg, a charging order/inhibition of sale may not be effective, as any property may already have been sold to pay off creditors. The CSA may secure a liability order to remind the non-resident parent that he cannot avoid his maintenance responsibility.

As part of bankruptcy proceedings, the non-resident parent can inform the court of his maintenance liabilities. If this is done, the administrator of the bankruptcy should take child support liability into account when deciding how much money the non-resident parent needs to meet basic living expenses. This decision is made before any available funds are distributed among creditors.

Bankruptcy/sequestration may not prevent the CSA considering further enforcement measures, such as committal to prison or disqualification from driving. For example, further action may be pursued if the non-resident parent has a steady income. In these circumstances, the non-resident parent will need to show that he cannot afford to meet his child support liability. This may be more difficult if the administrator of the bankruptcy has already made provision for his current maintenance payments when deciding how much money the non-resident parent needs to meet his basic living expenses.

5. Existing 'old rules' and conversion cases

Existing 'old rules' maintenance assessments are collected and enforced in much the same way as 'new rules' maintenance calculations – involving negotiations, deduction from earnings orders, liability orders and action for committal or disqualification from driving. Some differences are indicated in the rest of this chapter – eg, how deductions from benefit can be made. However, there are some other important differences, which are outlined here.

The legislation applied to existing 'old rules' is that prior to its reform by the Child Support, Pensions and Social Security Act 2000 and associated Regulations. On conversion, the case comes under the reformed legislation.

Penalty payments do not apply to 'old rules' cases. Once the case converts, the 'new rules' penalty payments may be applied. This means that penalty payments can only be made in respect of missed or late payments after the date of conversion (see p411).

Voluntary payments are governed by the same statute as 'new rules' cases.[289]

Deduction from earnings orders (DEOs) are calculated and applied in a slightly different way. At conversion, any old arrears uncollected under the previous order may be included in a new one issued under the 'new rules'.

Certain non-resident parents with a maintenance assessment used to be able to make a deferred debt agreement under the **temporary compensation scheme**. This agreement can continue in force after conversion. If it was discharged, the person with care may have been eligible for a **deferred debt compensation payment** (see p436).

Deduction from earnings orders

Deductions made are based on the **normal deduction rate** and the **protected earnings rate.**

Normal deduction rate

The normal deduction rate is the amount that will be deducted each payday as long as net earnings are not brought below the protected earnings rate. The normal deduction rate can include current maintenance liability and amounts for arrears and interest due. No arrears or interest can be included if they would have brought the non-resident parent's disposable income, on the date the current assessment was made, below the protected income level (not the protected earnings rate) *minus* the minimum payment (see p168).[290] This does not apply if the current assessment is an interim maintenance assessment (IMA – see p331). See Chapter 13 for protected income level and disposable income.

Protected earnings rate

The protected earnings rate is the level below which earnings must not be reduced by the deductions. Unless a Category A or D IMA is in force, it is set at the exempt income level (see Chapter 10).[291] If a Category A or D IMA is in force, the protected earnings rate is either:[292]

- if the CSA knows something of the non-resident parent's circumstances:
  - the income support (IS) single or couple personal allowance;
  - the IS personal allowance for any children under 16 living with him;
  - any relevant IS premiums (see Appendix 2); *plus*

  - £30; *or*
- otherwise, the IS adult personal allowance plus £30.

If there is no assessment in force, the protected earnings rate is the exempt income level for the last assessment. If the non-resident parent satisfies the CSA that his circumstances have since changed, the protected earnings rate is the exempt income level he would have if his assessment were superseded.[293] If the last assessment was a Category A or C IMA, the protected earnings rate is still worked out as for IMAs.

If the non-resident parent has more than one employer and a deduction order is made in respect of more than one of them, the protected earnings rate for each order is divided proportionally between the non-resident parent's earnings with each employer.[294]

Administering a deduction from earnings order

The rules are almost identical to those described in this chapter – ie, each payday the employer:

- should make a deduction from net earnings at the normal deduction rate. If this reduces earnings below the protected earnings rate, the deduction is adjusted and the unpaid amount is carried forward to the next payday;[295]
- may deduct up to £1 as an administrative charge. This can be made even if this would bring earnings below the protected earnings rate.[296]

However, in addition to these rules, if on any payday net earnings are below the protected earnings rate, no deduction or charge can be made. When this occurs, the difference between net earnings and protected earnings is carried over and treated as additional protected earnings on the next payday.[297] For an illustration of how this operates in practice, see *Example 18.1* in the 2001/02 edition of this *Handbook*.

If two or more DEOs have been issued, the employer should deal with the earliest first.[298]

Temporary compensation payment scheme (deferred debt)

From 31 January 2001, a temporary compensation payment scheme was introduced to allow the CSA to reduce the arrears liability of a non-resident parent in certain circumstances.[299] The CSA referred to these arrears as a deferred debt. The scheme only applied to parents with assessments made before certain dates (the latest being 1 April 2005) and who had at least six months' arrears, at least half of which were caused because of unreasonable delay by the CSA.

If a non-resident parent entered and kept to an agreement to pay regular maintenance and repay the arrears, the CSA could reduce the amount of arrears to be repaid.[300] Agreements could only be made before 1 April 2005 and all had to expire before 1 April 2006.[301] Although technically the deferred debt was not written off, it was not enforced by the CSA if the non-resident parent kept to the agreement for the full period. The CSA could make a compensatory payment to the person with care in respect of part or all of the arrears that were not collected.

For more information about this scheme, see the 2006/07 edition of this *Handbook*.

Notes

1 s29(1) CSA 1991
2 s30(1) CSA 1991
3 Reg 3(3A) CSF Regs as revoked by reg 4 CS(CEMA) Regs
4 *Independent Case Examiner's Annual Report 2009/10*
5 *KA v CMEC* [2009] UKUT 99 (AAC)

1. **Payment of child maintenance**
6 Reg 3 CS(C&E) Regs
7 Reg 2 CS(C&E) Regs
8 Reg 5 CS(C&E) Regs
9 Reg 4 CS(C&E) Regs
10 Reg 4 CS(MPA) Regs
11 Reg 6 CS(C&E) Regs
12 Reg 7(1) CS(C&E) Regs
13 Reg 7(2) CS(C&E) Regs
14 s29 CSA 1991; reg 2 CS(C&E) Regs
15 s29(1)(b) CSA 1991
16 Regs 6 and 7 CS(MPA) Regs
17 *What is Child Maintenance and How Does it Affect Me?* CSL301, April 2010
18 CSA Business Plan 2008/09 and *What is Child Maintenance and How Does it Affect Me?* CLS301, April 2010
19 Reg 5 CS(MPA) Regs
20 s41C(3) CSA 1991
21 Reg 7 CS(MPA) Regs
22 Reg 8 CS(AIAMA) Regs
23 Reg 3(1) CS(C&E) Regs
24 Reg 3(1A) CS(C&E) Regs
25 *What is Child Maintenance and How Does it Affect Me?* CLS301, April 2010
26 Reg 3(2) CS(C&E) Regs
27 *How Do I Pay Child Maintenance?* CSL305, April 2010
28 *How Do I Pay Child Maintenance?* CSL305, April 2010
29 Reg 5(1) CS(C&E) Regs
30 s43 CSA 1991
31 s43 CSA 1991; Sch 9B SS(C&P) Regs
32 Sch 4 para 4(2) CSA 1991; reg 4(2) CS(MCSC) Regs
33 Reg 4(3)(a) CS(MCSC) Regs
34 Reg 4(3)(b) CS(MCSC) Regs
35 Reg 35(l) SS(C&P) Regs; Sch 9B SS(C&P) Regs
36 Sch 9 para 7A(1) SS(C&P) Regs
37 Sch 9 paras 1 and 2(1)(f) SS(C&P) Regs
38 Sch 9 para 2(2) SS(C&P) Regs
39 Sch 9 para 8 SS(C&P) Regs
40 Sch 9 para 9 SS(C&P) Regs
41 Sch 9 para 7A(4) SS(C&P) Regs
42 Sch 5 para 9 CS(MASC) Regs
43 Reg 4(1) CS(C&E) Regs
44 Regs 4(2) and 6 CS(C&E) Regs
45 Reg 5(3) CS(C&E) Regs
46 CSA Business Plan 2008/09 and *How Will I Receive Child Maintenance?* CSL314, April 2010
47 *How Do I Complain About the Service I Get from the Child Support Agency?* CSL308, April 2010
48 Reg 8 CS(MPA) Regs
49 Reg 8 CS(MPA) Regs
50 Reg 8 CS(MPA) Regs
51 Reg 8(2)(b) CS(MPA) Regs
52 Reg 8 CS(MPA) Regs
53 Reg 9 CS (MPA) Regs
54 Reg 9(3) CS(MPA) Regs
55 s41B CSA 1991
56 s41B(7) CSA 1991
57 s41B(6) CSA 1991; regs 8 and 9 CS(MPA) Regs
58 Reg 6 (1) CS(MPA) Regs
59 Reg 6(3)(a)-(f) CS(MPA) Regs
60 s41C(3) CSA 1991
61 Reg 7(2) CS(MPA) Regs
62 Reg 7(3) CS(MPA) Regs

63 CS(MPA) Regs, Explanatory Memorandum, para 7.11
64 *Green v SSWP* [2010] EWHC 1278, 16 July 2010

2. **Collection of other payments**
65 s30 CSA 1991; CS(CEOFM) Regs
66 Reg 5 CS(CEOFM) Regs
67 Reg 2 CS(CEOFM) Regs
68 Regs 3 and 4 CS(CEOFM) Regs
69 s30(3) CSA 1991
70 s43 CMOPA 2008

3. **Arrears**
71 *What Action Can the CSA Take if Parents Don't Pay?* CSL306, April 2010
72 www.csa.gov.uk/en/case/payment-problems.asp
73 *What Action Can the CSA Take if Parents Don't Pay?* CSL306, April 2010
74 Reg 8A CS(MAJ) Regs 1992
75 *How Do I Pay Child Maintenance?* CSL305, April 2010
76 *How Do I Pay Child Maintenance?* CSL305, April 2010
77 Reg 7 CS(C&E) Regs
78 s28J CSA 1991
79 Reg 2(2) CS(VP) Regs
80 Reg 3(b) CS(VP) Regs
81 Reg 3(a) CS(VP) Regs
82 Regs 2(2) and 4(b) CS(VP) Regs
83 Reg 4(a) CS(VP) Regs
84 Reg 3(3) CS(MPA) Regs
85 Reg 3(4) CS(MPA) Regs
86 CMEC Corporate Plan 2009/10 and *Independent Case Examiner's Annual Report 2008/09*
87 *Independent Case Examiner's Annual Report 2008/09*
88 *Independent Case Examiner's Annual Report 2008/09*
89 First protocol, Art 1 ECHR
90 s41(2) and (2A) CSA 1991; reg 8 CS(AIAMA) Regs
91 Reg 8 CS(AIAMA) Regs
92 s43 CSA 1991; Sch 9B SS(C&P) Regs
93 Sch 9 para 7B SS(C&P) Regs
94 Reg 7(1) CS(MPA) Regs
95 Reg 5 CS(MPA) Regs
96 Reg 7(3)(2) CS(MPA) Regs
97 Reg 5(2) CS(MPA) Regs
98 Reg 5(2) CS(MPA) Regs
99 *Child Maintenance and Other Payments Act Summary of Responses to the Consultation on Draft Regulations*, CMEC, November 2009, para 3
100 *Child Maintenance and Other Payments Act Summary of Responses to the Consultation on Draft Regulations*, CMEC, November 2009, para 3
101 *Child Maintenance and Other Payments Act Summary of Responses to the Consultation on Draft Regulations*, CMEC, November 2009, para 3.4
102 *Child Maintenance and Other Payments Act Summary of Responses to the Consultation on Draft Regulations*, CMEC, November 2009, para 3.4
103 Reg 7(3) CS(MPA) Regs
104 *Child Maintenance and Other Payments Act Summary of Responses to the Consultation on Draft Regulations*, CMEC, November 2009, para 3.5
105 s41(2) CSA 1991
106 s14(A) CSA 1991 and *What Action Can the CSA Take if Parents Don't Pay?* CSL306, April 2010
107 s41A CSA 1991
108 *Independent Case Examiner's Annual Report 2006/07*
109 CSA Operational Improvement Plan 2006-2009
110 *Independent Case Examiner's Annual Report 2009/10*
111 CMEC Business Plan 2010/11 and *Independent Case Examiner's Annual Report 2009/10*
112 CMEC Business Plan 2010/11
113 *Kehoe v UK* [2009] 48 EHRR, [2008] 2 FLR 1014
114 CSA Annual Report and Accounts 2006/07
115 *How Do I Complain About the Service I Get From the Child Support Agency?* CSL 308, April 2010
116 *Independent Case Examiner's Annual Report 2008/09*
117 *Kehoe v UK* [2009] 48 EHRR, [2008] 2 FLR 1014
118 s43 CMOPA 2008

4. **Enforcement**
119 s51 Welfare Reform Act 2009
120 CMEC Business Plan 2010/11, March 2010
121 *What Action Can the CSA Take if Parents Don't Pay?* CSL306, April 2010; s14A CSA 1991
122 s31 CSA 1991
123 *What Action Can the CSA Take if Parents Don't Pay?* CSL 306, April 2010
124 CSA Operational Improvement Plan 2006-2009

125 CMEC/National Statistics, *CSA Quarterly Summary Statistics*, March 2011
126 Reg 29(4)(a) CSA 1991
127 *R v Secretary of State for Social Security ex parte Biggin* [1995] 2 FCR 595, [1995] 1 FLR 851
128 Sch 1 para 10 CS(NIRA) Regs
129 CSA(CA)O; Army Act 1955; Air Force Act 1955; Naval Forces Act 1947; Merchant Shipping Act 1970
130 s31(5) CSA 1991
131 s31(6) CSA 1991
132 s31(7) CSA 1991
133 *What is My Role in Helping My Employees Pay Child Maintenance* CSL313, April 2010
134 Reg 9 CS(C&E) Regs
135 Reg 14(1) CS(C&E) Regs; see also *What is My Role in Helping My Employees Pay Child Maintenance*, CSL313, April 2010
136 Reg 14(2) CS(C&E) Regs
137 s32(8) and (11) CSA 1991; reg 25(aa) CS(C&E) Regs
138 Reg 1(3)(a) CS(C&E) Regs
139 Reg 1(3)(b) CS(C&E) Regs
140 s32(8) and (11) CSA 1991; reg 25(ab) and (b) CS(C&E) Regs
141 Reg 3 CS(MA) Regs 2008
142 Reg 15(2) CS(C&E) Regs
143 Reg 16(1) CS(C&E) Regs
144 Reg 16(2) CS(C&E) Regs
145 Reg 16(3) CS(C&E) Regs
146 Reg 13 CS(C&E) Regs
147 s8(2)(b) ERA 1996
148 s9 ERA 1996
149 s12(3)-(5) ERA 1996
150 Reg 8(3) and (4) CS(C&E) Regs
151 Reg 8(4)(a) CS(C&E) Regs
152 Reg 8(4)(b) CS(C&E) Regs
153 Reg 8(5) CS(C&E) Regs
154 Reg 9 CS(C&E) Regs
155 Regs 10(1) and 11(1) CS(C&E) Regs
156 Reg 9(d) CS(C&E) Regs
157 Reg 11(2) CS(C&E) Regs
158 Reg 12(6) CS(C&E) Regs
159 Reg 12(20) CS(C&E) Regs
160 Reg 12(4) CS(C&E) Regs
161 Reg 12(3A) CS(C&E) Regs
162 *How Do I Pay Child Maintenance?* CSL305, April 2010 and *What is My Role in Helping My Employees Pay Child Maintenance?* CSL313, April 2010
163 Reg 8 CS(AIAMA) Regs
164 Reg 24(2)(a) CS(C&E) Regs
165 Reg 24(2)(b) CS(C&E) Regs
166 Reg 24(2)(a) and (3) CS(C&E) Regs
167 Reg 17 CS(C&E) Regs
168 Reg 18 CS(C&E) Regs
169 Reg 19 CS(C&E) Regs
170 Reg 20(1) CS(C&E) Regs
171 Reg 20(2) CS(C&E) Regs
172 Reg 21(1) CS(C&E) Regs
173 Reg 21(4) CS(C&E) Regs
174 Reg 21(5) CS(C&E) Regs
175 Reg 21(6) CS(C&E) Regs
176 Reg 22(1) CS(C&E) Regs
177 Reg 22(2) CS(C&E) Regs
178 Reg 22(3) CS(C&E) Regs
179 Reg 22(3A) CS(C&E) Regs
180 Reg 3(4) CS(C&E) Regs
181 Reg 3(6)(c) CS(C&E) Regs
182 Reg 3(5) CS(C&E) Regs
183 Reg 3(6) CS(C&E) Regs
184 Reg 8(1) CS(C&E) Regs
185 r5 and Form 6 AS(CSR)
186 Reg 22(4) CS(C&E) Regs
187 s32(6) CSA 1991
188 *Secretary of State for Social Security v Shotton* [1996] 2 FLR 241
189 ss48 and 49 CSA 1991; r6 AS(CSR)
190 s33 CSA 1991
191 s33(3) CSA 1991
192 s33(4) CSA 1991
193 *Bird v SSWP* [2008] EWHC 3159 (Admin), 19 December 2008
194 Reg 29 CS(C&E) Regs; r3 AS(CSR)
195 ss48 and 49 CSA 1991; r6 AS(CSR)
196 Reg 28(2) and (2A) CS(C&E) Regs
197 *R Sutherland (on the application of) v SSWP* [2004] EWHC 800 (Admin), 25 March 2004
198 s9 Limitation Act 1980
199 *CMEC v Mitchell* [2010] EWCA Civ 333
200 Reg 27 CS(C&E) Regs
201 *Farley v CSA and another* [2006] UKHL 31, 28 June 2006
202 Reg 29(1) and Sch 1 CS(C&E) Regs
203 *Secretary of State for Social Security v Love* [1996] SLT 78
204 r2 AS(CSR)
205 *Secretary of State for Social Security v Nicol* [1996] SLT 34
206 Forms 1-4 AS(CSR)
207 CSA Operational Improvement Plan 2006-2009
208 ss38(1)(a) and 58(9) CSA 1991
209 r4 and Form 5 AS(CSR)
210 s38(1)(b) CSA 1991
211 s35 CSA 1991
212 Reg 30(2) CS(C&E) Regs
213 Reg 30(4) and (5) CS(C&E) Regs
214 s35(3) and (4) CSA 1991
215 Reg 32 and Sch 2 CS(C&E) Regs
216 Reg 31 CS(C&E) Regs
217 s33(5) CSA 1991
218 s36 CSA 1991

219 ss32A and 32F CSA 1991
220 Reg 25A CS(C&E) Regs
221 CMEC Research Report No.2, *Deduction Order Review*, March 2011, pp2 and 4
222 CMEC Research Report No.2, *Deduction Order Review*, March 2011, p16
223 Reg 25X CS(C&E) Regs
224 CMEC Research Report No.2, *Deduction Order Review*, March 2011, p15
225 CMEC Research Report No.2, *Deduction Order Review*, March 2011, p5
226 Reg 25Z CS(C&E) Regs
227 s32A CSA 1991
228 Reg 25B(1) CS(C&E) Regs
229 Reg 25C CS(C&E) Regs
230 s32B CSA 1991
231 Reg 25D CS(C&E) Regs
232 Reg 25H CS(C&E) Regs
233 s32D CSA 1991
234 Reg 25G CS(C&E) Regs
235 Reg 25I CS(C&E) Regs
236 Reg 25A(3)(b) CS(C&E) Regs
237 Reg 25N(1) CS(C&E) Regs
238 s32F(3)(b) and (4) CSA 1991
239 Regs 25R and 25N CS(C&E) Regs
240 Reg 25P(1) and (2) CS(C&E) Regs
241 Reg 25P(6) CS(C&E) Regs
242 Reg 25AB CS(C&E) Regs
243 Reg 11 CS(MPA) Regs
244 Reg 12 CS(MPA) Regs
245 Reg 13 CS(MPA) Regs
246 Reg 13(3) CS(MPA) Regs
247 *CMOP 2008: Summary of Responses to the Consulation on the Draft Regulations*, CMEC, November 2009, para 4.11
248 *CMOP 2008: Summary of Responses to the Consulation on the Draft Regulations*, CMEC, November 2009, para 4.6
249 *CMOP 2008: Summary of Responses to the Consulation on the Draft Regulations*, CMEC, November 2009, para 4.8
250 *CMOP 2008: Summary of Responses to the Consulation on the Draft Regulations*, CMEC, November 2009, para 4.8
251 *CMOP 2008: Summary of Responses to the Consulation on the Draft Regulations*, CMEC, November 2009, para 4.7
252 *CMOP 2008: Summary of Responses to the Consulation on the Draft Regulations*, CMEC, November 2009, para 4.9
253 CMEC/National Statistics, *CSA Quarterly Summary Statistics*, March 2011
254 s32L CSA 1991
255 s32L(8) CSA 1991
256 s32L(2) CSA 1991
257 s32L(1) CSA 1991
258 s32L(5) CSA 1991
259 s32L(5) CSA 1991
260 s32L (7) CSA 1991
261 s32L(11)(b) CSA 1991
262 s39A CSA 1991
263 *What Action Can the CSA Take if Parents Don't Pay?* CSL306, April 2010
264 CMEC/National Statistics, *CSA Quarterly Summary Statistics*, March 2011
265 ss39A(2) and 40(1)-(11) CSA 1991
266 s39A(3) CSA 1991
267 Reg 35(1) CS(C&E) Regs
268 s40(11) CSA 1991
269 s39A(4) CSA 1991
270 s39A(3) CSA 1991
271 s40A(1) CSA 1991
272 ss40(5) and 40A(3) CSA 1991
273 ss40(11) and 40A(8) CSA 1991; reg 35(2) CS(C&E) Regs
274 ss48 and 49 CSA 1991
275 ss40 and 40B CSA 1991
276 ss40(5) and 40A(3) CSA 1991
277 ss40(3) and 40B(1) CSA 1991
278 Sch 3 CS(C&E) Regs
279 ss40(7) and 40A(5) CSA 1991
280 Reg 34(5) and (6) CS(C&E) Regs
281 *What Action Can the CSA Take if Parents Don't Pay?* CSL306, April 2010
282 *What Action Can the CSA Take if Parents Don't Pay?* CSL306, April 2010
283 s40B CSA 1991
284 Reg 35(4)-(5) and Sch 4 CS(C&E) Regs
285 s40B(1) CSA 1991
286 s40B(5) CSA 1991
287 s40B(7) CSA 1991
288 *CMEC v Beesley* [2010] EWCA Civ 1344, 24 November 2010

5. Existing 'old rules' and conversion cases

289 Reg 2(2) CS (MPA) Regs
290 Reg 10 CS(C&E) Regs
291 Reg 11(2) CS(C&E) Regs
292 Reg 11(3) CS(C&E) Regs
293 Reg 11(4) CS(C&E) Regs
294 Reg 11(6) CS(C&E) Regs
295 Reg 12(4) CS(C&E) Regs
296 Reg 12(2) CS(C&E) Regs
297 Reg 12(5) CS(C&E) Regs
298 Reg 24(1) CS(C&E) Regs
299 Reg 2(2) CSPSSA(Comm 13)O
300 s27(3) CSPSSA 2000
301 s27(5) CSPSSA 2000

Chapter 20

Complaints

This chapter covers:

There are many reasons why people using the Child Support Agency (CSA) may wish to complain. Complaints are appropriate in situations where there has been rudeness, discrimination, poor administration (eg, lost papers) and delays. They may also be appropriate in situations where the CSA has a discretion about how to act – eg, where enforcement action is not taken.

A complaint is a separate process to an appeal or revision and does not necessarily lead to a decision being changed. However, it may be appropriate if the decision is one with no right of appeal. In some of these cases, judicial review may also be possible (instead of, or as well as, making a complaint). Legal advice should be sought if a judicial review is being considered (see also p343). In some cases, an appeal may be appropriate as well as a complaint – eg, if a parent thinks a maintenance calculation has been wrongly calculated and appeals against the decision but also wishes to complain about the delay in making the calculation.

It is important to be clear which organisation has caused the problem. In most cases, this will be the CSA. However, problems concerning the deduction of payments from benefits may be caused by Jobcentre Plus. Complaints about any Jobcentre Plus function should be directed to Jobcentre Plus. If a parent (or qualifying child in Scotland) has appealed, and there are delays or poor administration on the part of HM Courts and Tribunals Service, the complaint should be directed to HM Courts and Tribunals Service. For information about making complaints to HM Courts and Tribunals Service, see CPAG's *Welfare Benefits and Tax Credits Handbook*.

1. Complaining to the Child Support Agency

Most complaints involving child support are made to the Child Support Agency (CSA). Complaints are likely to be about either:

- standards of service, including delays, staff communications, poor administration and lost papers;
- how discretionary decisions are made – eg, failure to follow guidance, following it too strictly or failing to take all the relevant circumstances into account. It may be appropriate to seek advice on whether judicial review is also possible.

A parent (or qualifying child in Scotland) should begin her/his complaint by contacting the person who has been dealing with her/his case, or her/his manager. This information should be on letters sent by the CSA. The complaint can be made either by telephone, in writing, or by using the online complaint form on the CSA website. Records of all communications should be kept in case it is necessary to take the complaint further.

If the CSA officer or her/his manager cannot resolve the complaint, the parent can take things further by contacting the complaints resolution team at the office handling the case. Contact details of CSA regional offices are in Appendix 1, or on the CSA website. Contact details should also be given on any letters sent.

If a parent is not satisfied with the outcome of the complaints resolution team or if there has been an unreasonable delay, s/he can ask for a review. The complaints review team can check whether the complaint was dealt with properly and if anything else can be done. Contact details for the complaints review team should be given on the letter received from the complaints resolution team.

More information about the complaints procedure is given in the leaflet *How Do I Complain About the Service I Get From the Child Support Agency?* produced by the CSA (leaflet CSL308).[1]

If, after going through this procedure, a complainant is not satisfied that the complaint has been resolved, s/he can contact the Independent Case Examiner (see p446). A complainant can only do this if:

- s/he has been through all of the stages in the CSA's internal complaints procedure; *and*
- s/he has received a final reply from the CSA; *and*
- no more than six months have passed since s/he received that final reply.

The final stage of the complaints procedure is the Parliamentary and Health Service Ombudsman (see p447).

Standards of service

When complaining to the CSA, it may be useful to quote its standards of service. These may also be useful when considering whether, or at what point, to make a complaint. A summary of standards of service used to be in the CSA's Client Charter, which was last updated in 2007.[2] However, since the establishment of the Child Maintenance and Enforcement Commission (CMEC), this has not been replaced and is no longer in use. It is understood that there are no immediate plans to update the Charter.

Some of the service standards can be found in the CSA's Business Plan 2008/09. The CSA did not publish a Business Plan for 2010/11 and service standards were not included in CMEC's Business Plan for 2010/11. Limited information can be found on the CMEC website.[3] A complainant can refer to both the website and the service targets in the CSA's 2008/09 Business Plan on the assumption that targets will not have been lowered. These include the following service standards. This is not an exhaustive list.

- The CSA aims to start gathering information from the non-resident parent within four weeks of a maintenance application, if it has contact details.
- The CSA aims to make an accurate decision on an application within 12 weeks (but in some cases a decision may take up to 26 weeks).
- If the collection service is being used, the CSA aims to make payments to the person with care within a week of receiving the money from the non-resident parent.
- The CSA aims to take action to use a deduction from earnings order, where appropriate, within four months of when a non-resident was first informed of his liability.
- The CSA aims to answer telephone calls within one minute.
- The CSA aims to respond to letters, and either resolve complaints or agree on the next course of action, within three weeks of receiving them.

Compensation

If a parent (or qualifying child in Scotland) has lost out because of CSA error, delay or standard of service, it may be appropriate to request compensation or a consolatory payment (see p444) when making a complaint. *Ex gratia* payments can be made if someone has experienced an actual financial loss, significant delay or has been caused severe distress or inconvenience.

The *Special Payments Guide* is the CSA's own guidance on whether financial compensation should be paid to complainants and, if so, how much is appropriate. It is available on the CSA website or on request from the CSA.[4]

A complainant has no legal right to these payments, but it can sometimes be useful to make it clear that financial compensation would help to resolve the complaint. A Court of Appeal judgment concluded that no duty of care can be imposed on the CSA in order to recover damages in negligence and that the complaints system (together with the ability to seek judicial review if the CSA acts, or does not act, unreasonably) offers sufficient redress.[5]

Compensation payments may be appropriate if there has been:

- significant delay in issuing forms, making calculations or reviewing liability. It is useful to refer to the service standards when assessing how severe the delay has been;
- delays or errors in enforcement;
- delays in passing maintenance to the person with care;
- wrong identification of non-resident parents;
- financial loss because of CSA error – eg, in bank, postal or telephone charges;
- other examples of gross inconvenience, embarrassment, breach of confidentiality or severe distress.

If a complainant is not offered compensation and believes that it should have been offered, or s/he is not offered as much as s/he thinks is appropriate, s/he can consider taking the complaint further – ie, to the Independent Case Examiner or the Ombudsman.

Consolatory payments

Consolatory payments are smaller payments that can be made if actions by the CSA have caused serious inconvenience because the same mistakes were made more than once, or they caused severe embarrassment or humiliation.

Evidence of the complainant's (or a family member's) health being affected as a result may also be considered if it can be shown to be a direct result of errors made by the CSA.[6]

Consolatory payments are made in recognition of the effect of an error on the complainant's life and, therefore, it is possible to claim them even if there is no financial loss.

The CSA recognises that many of its users will experience inconvenience and frustration, and this alone is not enough to secure a consolatory payment. The CSA's actions must have caused serious inconvenience because the same mistakes were made more than once, or have caused severe embarrassment or humiliation.[7]

The CSA will make separate decisions on whether to award compensation or a consolatory payment, based on the facts of each case. In some cases, it may pay both.[8] The *Special Payments Guide* covers both compensation and consolatory payments.

2. Complaining to the Child Maintenance Options service

The complaints process for the Child Maintenance Options service is similar to that for the Child Support Agency (see p442). A complaint should be started by talking to the person dealing with the enquiry, or to her/his manager. If the matter cannot be resolved in this way, a complaint should be made to the complaints resolution team. A complaint can be made over the phone, in writing or by email via the website www.cmoptions.org. If a complaint is made by email or letter, Child Maintenance Options will write to the complainant to let her/him know it has been received.[9]

If a complainant is not satisfied after following this procedure, s/he can ask for a review. The complaints review team should look at the complaint again to see if there is more that can be done. The review team aims to resolve complaints within 15 days.[10]

Further details of the complaints process can be found in the publication *How Can I Complain About the Child Maintenance Options Service?*, which is available from the above website or by telephoning 0800 988 0988 (in Northern Ireland, 0800 028 7439).

If a complainant has gone through every stage of the Child Maintenance Options complaints procedure and is still not satisfied, s/he can complain to the Independent Case Examiner (see p446), or, via her/his MP, to the Parliamentary and Health Service Ombudsman.

3. Complaining to Jobcentre Plus

It is important to remember that some decisions about benefits carry the right of appeal and an individual can request a revision or appeal against them. It may be necessary to do this as well as, or instead of, complaining.

As part of the Department for Work and Pensions (DWP), Jobcentre Plus has a similar complaints procedure to the Child Support Agency (CSA). Non-resident parents may want to complain about the way in which their maintenance payments have (or have not) been deducted from their benefit. However, a non-resident parent receiving benefits who disagrees with the rate of maintenance he should be paying (and therefore with the deduction being made from his benefit) should appeal to the CSA about the maintenance decision, not to Jobcentre Plus. A complaint to Jobcentre Plus can be made if it is about the administration of the deductions.

Note: the CSA may not automatically know if a non-resident parent or a parent with care is in receipt of benefits. Caselaw has established that, although the Secretary of State for Work and Pensions is ultimately responsible for administering both Jobcentre Plus and the CSA, knowledge gained by her/him in one role should not be attributed to her/his other area of responsibility.[11]

The Jobcentre Plus complaints procedure is described in the leaflet *Our Service Standards*.[12] Complainants may also wish to refer to the DWP customer charter.[13] A complainant should begin by speaking to the person s/he has been dealing with, or her/his manager. If this does not resolve matters, the district manager or delivery manager for the office concerned should be contacted. The third stage of the process, if the complaint is still not resolved, is to write to the Chief Executive of Jobcentre Plus. The Chief Executive should ensure that the complaint is fully considered by an appropriate senior officer.

Like the CSA, Jobcentre Plus can make compensatory payments if these are seen as appropriate. More information about compensation payments is provided in CPAG's *Welfare Benefits and Tax Credits Handbook*.

If a complainant has gone through every stage of the Jobcentre Plus complaints procedure and is still not satisfied, s/he can complain to the Independent Case Examiner (see below), or, via her/his MP, to the Parliamentary and Health Service Ombudsman.

4. Complaining to the Independent Case Examiner

The Independent Case Examiner's (ICE) office is a body set up to help resolve the situation where people believe that certain government agencies have not dealt with them fairly or resolved complaints to their satisfaction. ICE is an independent referee, completely separate from the Child Support Agency (CSA), the Child Maintenance Options service or any other government department. ICE was set up to deal with complaints about the CSA but, since April 2007, it has also dealt with complaints about several other government agencies and businesses, including Jobcentre Plus and the Northern Ireland Social Security Agency.

A complainant can only go to ICE after using the CSA's (or other agency's) complaints procedure in full. A final response from the agency is normally a reply from the Chief Executive or on her/his behalf – eg, from a senior manager. The complaint to ICE should be made within six months of the CSA's final response. ICE cannot look at complaints made after this date.

ICE cannot consider a complaint which is being investigated, or which has been investigated, by the Parliamentary and Health Service Ombudsman (see p447). A complainant may have the choice of complaining directly to the Ombudsman via an MP, but the Ombudsman's office will usually encourage people to use ICE first.

Complaints can be made in writing or by telephone on 0845 606 0777. A complaint form can be found on the ICE website. It can be printed, or completed online. Hard copies of the complaint form can be obtained from the helpline number above. The complainant should include all relevant facts, including the CSA office s/he is complaining about, details of the complaint and the CSA's response. ICE can give complainants further advice on making their complaint, or appoint a representative to act on their behalf, if required.

ICE will investigate and decide whether or not it can accept the complaint. If it can, the first attempt will be to settle the complaint by suggesting ways in which the CSA (or other agency) and the complainant can come to an agreement. Over 60 per cent of cases are resolved this way. If this fails, ICE prepares a formal report setting out how the complaint arose and how it believes it should be settled. In 2009/10, ICE upheld almost 70 per cent of the complaints on which it reached findings and conclusions.[14] If it makes a recommendation of action to the agency, this is almost always followed. ICE aims to clear 55 per cent of cases within six months and 90 per cent within 12 months (although it falls significantly short of these, particularly on the six-month target).[15] Other details of its standards of service are available in the leaflet *Our Standards of Service* or at www.ind-case-exam.org.uk.

5. **Using an MP**

It may be appropriate for a complainant to consult her/his MP at any stage of the complaints process. An MP may be able to provide advocacy or other support to get the matter resolved more quickly. However, consulting an MP is particularly important if the complainant has been through the complaints process of the Child Support Agency (or Child Maintenance Options or Jobcentre Plus) without a satisfactory resolution, and even more so if s/he has used the Independent Case Examiner but still wants to take matters further.

An MP may be able to advise on whether taking the complaint further is worthwhile. It may be that the complainant is unhappy about an aspect of child support law, in which case a complaint is not appropriate. Whether the issue concerns law or procedure, an MP may be willing to take matters further to try and get legislation changed or practice improved. The MP may also (or in addition) refer the complaint to the Parliamentary and Health Service Ombudsman (see below).

Anyone can find out who her/his MP is by using a constituency locator on the internet, by ringing the House of Commons Information Office on 020 7219 4272 or emailing it at HCinfo@parliament.uk. Most MPs have surgeries held locally where they meet constituents. Alternatively, the complaint can be passed to the MP in writing. Contact details, including email addresses, for MPs are available on the Parliament website.[16]

6. **Complaining to the Ombudsman**

The Parliamentary and Health Service Ombudsman investigates complaints about a range of government departments and other public bodies.

The complainant should first give the organisation a full chance to respond to the complaint and put things right. For complaints about the Child Support Agency, Child Maintenance Options and Jobcentre Plus, a complainant has the option of first using the Independent Case Examiner (ICE) – see p446. A complainant does not need a referral from her/his MP to use ICE. The Ombudsman's office will encourage people to use ICE first.

The first stage of using the Ombudsman is for the complainant to send the complaint to the relevant MP, who will decide whether or not to pass it on to the Ombudsman. Normally, the Ombudsman will not investigate if the complaint is passed to an MP more than 12 months after the complainant became aware that s/he had a good reason to complain – ie, that there was a need to take the complaint further.

If the complaint is investigated, the MP will be sent a full report. The Ombudsman may recommend an apology and possibly compensation. Ombudsman reports can also lead to changed practices and procedures in the agencies under investigation.

More information about the Ombudsman is available at www.ombudsman.org.uk, or from the helpline on 0345 015 4033.

Notes

1. Complaining to the Child Support Agency

1 Available from www.csa.gov.uk/en/PDF/leaflets/new/CSL308.pdf
2 CSA Client Charter 2007
3 www.childmaintenance.org/en/about/standards.html
4 www.csa.gov.uk/en/case/special-payments.asp
5 *Rowley and Others v SSWP* [2007] EWCA Civ 598, 19 June 2007
6 *How Do I Complain About the Service I Get From the Chlld Support Agency?* CSL308, April 2010
7 *How Do I Complain About the Service I Get From the Chlld Support Agency?* CSL308, April 2010
8 *How Do I Complain About the Service I Get From the Chlld Support Agency?* CSL308, April 2010

2. Complaining to the Child Maintenance Options service

9 *How Can I Complain About the Child Maintenance Options Service?* October 2008
10 *How Can I Complain About the Child Maintenance Options Service?* October 2008

3. Complaining to Jobcentre Plus

11 *R(Rew) v SSWP* [2008] EWHC 2120 (Admin), 13 June 2008
12 Available from www.dwp.gov.uk/docs/dwp1018.pdf
13 Available from www.dwp.gov.uk/about-dwp/customer-delivery

4. **Complaining to the Independent Case Examiner**

14 *Independent Case Examiner's Annual Report 2009/10*

15 Independent Case Examiner, *Our Standards of Service 2010/11*; *Independent Case Examiner's Annual Report 2009/10*

5. **Using an MP**

16 www.parliament.uk/mps-lords-and-offices/mps

Appendices

Appendix 1

Useful addresses

Department for Work and Pensions

www.dwp.gov.uk

Child Maintenance and Enforcement Commission

The Commissioner and Chief Executive
Noel Shanahan
PO Box 239
Leeds LS11 1EB
www.childmaintenance.org

Child Maintenance Options

Tel: 0800 988 0988
(England, Wales and Scotland)
www.cmoptions.org
Tel: 0800 028 7439 (Northern Ireland)
www.nidirect.gov.uk/choices

Child Support Agency

PO Box 55
Brierly Hill
Dudley
West Midlands DY5 1YL
Tel: 0845 713 313
Textphone: 0845 713 8924
www.csa.gov.uk

Child Support Agency regional offices

(including for first-stage complaints) Further contact details are available at: www.csa.gov.uk/en/contact/index.asp

Hastings

Child Support Agency
PO Box 258
St Leonards on Sea TN38 1GP

Offices covered:
Acton, Brixton, Lewisham, Tunbridge Wells, London Highgate, Croydon, Bloomsbury, Bromley, Ilford, Canterbury, Colchester, Basildon, Wandsworth, Woolwich

Plymouth

Child Support Agency
PO Box 43
Plymouth PL95 8DL

Offices covered:
Bristol, Crownhill (Plymouth), Exeter, Gloucester, Guildford, Hounslow, Isle of Wight, Poole, Portsmouth, Southampton, Swindon, Taunton, Truro, Weymouth, Worthing

Dudley

Child Support Agency
PO Box 36
Birmingham B99 1DW

Offices covered:
Birmingham, Chester, Hanley, Lichfield, Stockport, Banbury, Milton Keynes, Shrewsbury, Telford

Birkenhead

Child Support Agency
PO Box 31
Chester CH70 8DN

Offices covered:
North West: Barrow-in-Furness, Blackpool North, Bury, Carlisle, Huyton (Liverpool), Kendal, Lancaster, Penrith, Salford, Skelmersdale, St Helens, Wirral, Workington
Wales: Aberystwyth, Anglesey, Caernarfon, Cardiff, Haverfordwest, Holyhead, Newport, Pontypridd, Rhyl, Swansea, Wrexham

Belfast (GB)

Child Support Agency
PO Box 30
Newtonabbey BT58 1AF

Offices covered:
Ipswich, Cambridge, Peterborough, Great Yarmouth, Kings Lynn, Norwich, St Albans, Northampton, Leicester, Nottingham, Lincoln, Sutton-in-Ashfield, Doncaster, Huddersfield, Bradford, Hull, Scarborough, Pontefract, Grimsby

Falkirk

Child Support Agency
PO Box 20
Edinburgh EH91 5BD

Offices covered:
Aberdeen, Campbeltown, Darlington, Dundee, Edinburgh, Falkirk, Galashiels, Inverness, Irvine, Leeds, Middlesborough, Mosspark, Newcastle upon Tyne, Northshields, Oban, Sunderland, Wick

Northern Ireland

Child Maintenance and Enforcement Division
Great Northern Tower
17 Great Victoria Street
Belfast BT2 7AD

Local rate telephone lines

National enquiry line (for general enquires)	0845 713 3133
Welsh language enquiry line	0845 713 8091
Hastings:	
'old rules'	0845 713 4000
'new rules'	0845 609 0052
Plymouth:	
'old rules'	0845 713 7000
'new rules'	0845 609 0072
Dudley:	
'old rules'	0845 713 1000
'new rules'	0845 609 0062
Birkenhead:	
'old rules'	0845 713 8000
'new rules'	0845 609 0082
Belfast (GB):	
'old rules'	0845 713 2000
'new rules'	0845 609 0092

Falkirk CSAC:	
'old rules'	0845 713 6000
'new rules'	0845 609 0042
Belfast	
Northern Ireland CMED:	
'old rules'	0845 713 9896
'new rules	0845 608 0022

HM Courts and Tribunals Service

The President of the Social
Entitlement Chamber
Fox Court
14 Grays Inn Road
London WC1X 8HN
Tel: 0203 206 0619

The President (Northern Ireland)
Cleaver House
3 Donegall Square North
Belfast BT1 5GA
Tel: 028 9051 8518

The offices detailed below are the regional offices for social security and child support appeals. To find your nearest tribunal venue see www.tribunals.gov.uk/qasvenuefinder.aspx

Leeds

York House
York Place
Leeds LS1 2ED
Tel: 0113 389 6000
Textphone: 0113 389 6070
sscsa-leeds@tribunals.gsi.gov.uk

Liverpool

36 Dale Street
Liverpool L2 5UZ
Tel: 0151 243 1400
Textphone: 0151 243 1450
sscsa-liverpool@tribunals.gsi.gov.uk

Newcastle

Manorview House
Kings Manor
Newcastle upon Tyne NE1 6PA
Tel: 0191 201 2300
Textphone: 0191 201 2350
sscsa-newcastle@tribunals.gsi.gov.uk

Sutton

Copthall House
9 The Pavement
Grove Road
Sutton
Surrey SM1 1DA
Tel: 020 8652 2300
Textphone: 020 8652 2366
sscsa-sutton@tribunals.gsi.gov.uk

Birmingham

Administrative Support Centre
PO Box 14620
Birmingham B16 6FR
Tel: 0845 408 3500
Textphone: 0121 634 7218
ascbirmingham@tribunals.epgsi.gov.uk

Cardiff

Eastgate House
Newport Road
Cardiff CF24 0YP
Tel: 0300 123 1142
Textphone: 0300 123 1264
sscsa-cardiff@tribunals.gsi.gov.uk

Glasgow

Wellington House
134–136 Wellington Street
Glasgow G2 2XL
Tel: 0141 354 8400
Textphone: 0141 354 8413
sscsa-glasgow@tribunals.gsi.gov.uk

Offices of Adminstrative Appeals Chamber of the Upper Tribunal

www.justice.gov.uk/about/hmcts/tribunals.htm

England

5th Floor
Chichester Rents
81 Chancery Lane
London WC2A 1DD
Tel: 020 7911 7085
TypeTalk: 18001 020 7029 9850
www.justice.gov.uk/guidance/courts-and-tribunals
adminappeals@tribunals.gsi.gov.uk

Wales

Civil Justice Centre
2 Park Street
Cardiff CF10 1ET
Tel: 029 2066 2257

Scotland

George House
126 George Street
Edinburgh EH2 4HH
Tel: 0131 271 4310
www.justice.gov.uk/guidance/courts-and-tribunals
ossc@ossc-scotland.org.uk

Northern Ireland

3rd Floor
Bedford House
16–22 Bedford Street
Belfast BT2 7FD
Tel: 028 9072 8731
www.courtsni.gov.uk/en-GB/services/tribunals

Independent Case Examiner

PO Box 155
Chester CH99 9SA
Tel: 0845 606 0777
Textphone: 0151 801 8888
www.ind-case-exam.org.uk
ice@dwp.gsi.gov.uk

The Parliamentary and Health Service Ombudsman

Millbank Tower
Millbank
London SW1P 4QP
Tel: 0345 015 4033
www.ombudsman.org.uk
phso.enquiries@ombudsman.org.uk

Appendix 2

Income support premiums

Premiums are added to income support (IS) personal allowances to help with extra expenses becuase of age, children and disability. The premiums are used in the child support formula irrespective of whether the parent is in receipt of IS, although not all apply at each stage. **Note:** although some of the rules below no longer apply to all IS claimants, they are still relevant for working out 'old rules' assessments.

Family premium	£17.40
Disabled child premium	£53.62
Carer premium (per carer)	£31.00
Disability premium	
Single	£28.85
Couple*	£41.10
Severe disability premium	
One qualifies	£55.30
Two qualify*	£110.60
Enhanced disability premium	
Single	£14.05
Couple*	£20.25
Child	£21.63
Pensioner premium	
Single*	£69.85
Couple*	£103.75

*These amounts are only ever used at the protected income stage.

Family premium

A person is entitled to family premium if her/his family includes a child, even if s/he is not the child's parent. It does not matter how much capital a child has. For child support purposes, a child is taken to be a member of the household if the adult has 'day-to-day care' of that child. If a child does not live in the household full time, a proportion of the family premium can be included in exempt income and protected income (see Chapter 14). Only one family premium is payable regardless of the number of children a person has.

If a child who is in the care of or being looked after by a local authority, or who is in custody, comes home for part of a week, a proportion of the premium is payable, according to the number of days the child is at home.

Disabled child premium

A person is entitled to a disabled child premium for each child who gets disability living allowance (DLA) or who is blind. A child is treated as blind if s/he is registered as blind and for the first 28 weeks after s/he has been taken off the register on regaining her/his sight. For how to qualify for DLA, see CPAG's *Welfare Benefits and Tax Credits Handbook*.

If DLA has stopped because the child is in hospital, this premium continues as long as the child continues to be treated as a member of your family. See CPAG's *Welfare Benefits and Tax Credits Handbook* for more details. If the child does not live in the household full time, a proportion of the premium is included in exempt income and in protected income (see Chapter 14).

If a child has over £3,000 capital, there is no entitlement to this premium.

Carer premium

A person qualifies for this if s/he or her/his partner is getting carer's allowance (CA), or would get it but for the overlapping benefit rules – ie, because s/he is receiving another earnings replacement benefit paid at a higher rate. For example, a woman getting CA who is awarded retirement pension at a higher rate than CA continues to qualify for the premium as long as the person being cared for continues to get the higher or middle rate care component of DLA or either rate of attendance allowance (AA).

A double premium is awarded if both the person concerned and her/his partner satisfy the conditions for it.

See CPAG's *Welfare Benefits and Tax Credits Handbook* for more details on the premium and conditions of entitlement for CA.

Disability premium

A person can get a disability premium if s/he is under the qualifying age for pension credit and:

- s/he (or her/his partner) is getting a qualifying benefit. These are DLA (or an equivalent benefit paid to meet attendance needs because of an injury at work or a war injury), disability or severe disability element of working tax credit, war pensioner's mobility supplement, incapacity benefit (IB) paid at the long-term rate or when terminally ill, or severe disablement allowance (SDA). A person or her/his partner must be getting the benefit for her/himself, not on behalf of someone else – eg, as a parent or an appointee. In some situations, entitlement to the premium continues after the person stops receiving the qualifying benefit – see CPAG's *Welfare Benefits and Tax Credits Handbook*;

- s/he (or her/his partner) is registered as blind with a local authority (England and Wales) or regional or islands council (Scotland); if sight is regained, s/he will still qualify for 28 weeks after s/he is taken off the register;
- s/he (or her/his partner) has an NHS invalid trike or private car allowance because of disability;
- s/he is 'incapable of work' (or exempt from the 'all-work test') and either entitled to statutory sick pay or has been incapable for at least:
  - 196 days if certified as 'terminally ill' – ie, it can reasonably be expected that s/he will die within six months due to a progressive disease;
  - 364 days in all other cases, provided s/he has claimed IB (it is not necessary to send in medical certificates).

  Breaks in incapacity/entitlement of up to 56 days (104 weeks if a 'welfare to work beneficiary') are included in these periods. For more on incapacity for work, see CPAG's *Welfare Benefits and Tax Credits Handbook*.

Entitlement to the disabilty premium stops when someone has been in hospital for more than 52 weeks.

At the protected income stage of the child support calculation, couples get the disability premium at the couple rate, provided either of them qualifies under one of the first three of the above rules. They only get the premium under the last condition if the person who qualifies is the parent being assessed for child maintenance.

Severe disability premium

A person can get this premium if:

- s/he is receiving AA (or the equivalent war pension or industrial injury benefit), or the higher or middle rate care component of DLA (or extra-statutory payments to compensate for not receiving any of these). If s/he is part of a couple, they must both be getting one of these benefits or the partner who does not get AA/DLA must be registered or treated as blind; *and*
- no non-dependant aged 18 or over is living with her/him (see below); *and*
- no one is getting CA for looking after her/him.

A couple who are both severely disabled only get the single rate if someone is getting CA in respect of one of them or one of them qualifies only because s/he is registered or treated as blind.

Non-dependants aged 18 or over

The following people living with a person do not count:

- a partner (but s/he must be getting AA/DLA or be blind);
- anyone aged under 18;
- anyone staying in a person's home who normally lives elsewhere;

- a person (who may be her/his partner) employed by a charitable or voluntary body as a resident carer for a person or her/his partner if s/he pays for that service (even if the charge is only nominal);
- a person receiving AA or the higher or middle rate care component of DLA;
- a person who is registered blind or treated as blind;
- a person, or her/his partner, who jointly occupies her/his home and is either a co-owner with the person or her/his partner, or jointly liable with her/him to make payments to a landlord in respect of occupying it;
- a person, or any member of her/his household, who is liable to pay on a commercial basis for occupying the dwelling (eg, tenant or licensee), unless s/he is a close relative;
- a person, or any member of her/his household, to whom a person or her/his partner is liable to make such payments on a commercial basis, unless s/he is a close relative.

If someone (other than those listed above) comes to live with a person in order to look after her/him or her/his partner, her/his severe disability premium will only remain in payment for the first 12 weeks.

For more detail of these rules, see CPAG's *Welfare Benefits and Tax Credits Handbook*.

Enhanced disability premium

The enhanced disability premium applies if the person or a member of her/his family receives the highest rate of the DLA care component and is aged under 60.

The following people cannot qualify:

- children or young people with more than £3,000 in capital;
- a claimant who has been a hospital inpatient for more than 52 weeks; *or*
- a claimant whose partner has been a hospital inpatient for more than 52 weeks.

Pensioner premium

There are three pensioner premiums, all paid at the same rate:

- pensioner premium if a person or her/his partner is aged 60–74 inclusive;
- pensioner premium (also known as an enhanced pensioner premium) if a person or her/his partner is 75–79 inclusive;
- higher pensioner premium if a person or her/his partner is aged over 80 or satifies other conditions detailed below.

Each of these can be paid at a couple rate if one partner fulfils the age condition. If a person or her/his partner is sick or disabled, check to see if the higher pensioner premium described on p461 applies.

Higher pensioner premium

A person can get this if:

- s/he or her/his partner is 80 or over; *or*
- s/he was getting a disability premium as part of her/his IS at some time during the eight weeks (104 weeks for 'welfare to work beneficiaries') before s/he was 60 and has continued to get IS since the age of 60 (breaks of up to eight (or 104) weeks are ignored). Couples can qualify under this rule regardless of which partner meets the condition; *or*
- s/he or her/his partner is aged 60–79 *and* either of them receives a qualifying benefit (as for the disability premium but including AA), is registered blind, or has an NHS trike or private car allowance. If a person stops getting IB or SDA to change to retirement pension, the higher pensioner premium still applies if there is a continuous entitlement (apart from breaks of eight weeks (104 weeks for 'welfare to work beneficiaries') or less) to IS.

Entitlement to the higher pension premium stops if someone has been a hospital inpatient for more than 52 weeks.

For more details on the premium and who is a 'welfare to work beneficiary', see CPAG's *Welfare Benefits and Tax Credits Handbook*.

Appendix 3

Statutes

A man is assumed to be the father of a child for child support purposes if he is found to be the father by a court in England or Wales in proceedings under the following.

s42 National Assistance Act 1948
Affiliation Proceedings Act 1957
s6 Family Law Reform Act 1969
Guardianship of Minors Act 1971
Children Act 1975
Child Care Act 1980
Children Act 1989
s26 Social Security Act 1986
s4 Family Law Reform Act 1987
s105 Social Security Administration Act 1992

A maintenance order only prevents a s4 or s7 application to the Child Support Agency if it was made in proceedings under the following. In addition, a variation for property/capital transfers can only be made if the transfer was made under the following.

Conjugal Rights (Scotland) Amendment Act 1861
Court of Session Act 1868
Sheriff Courts (Scotland) Act 1907
Guardianship of Infants Act 1925
Illegitimate Children (Scotland) Act 1930
Children and Young Persons (Scotland) Act 1932
Children and Young Persons (Scotland) Act 1937
Custody of Children (Scotland) Act 1939
National Assistance Act 1948
Affiliation Orders Act 1952
Affiliation Proceedings Act 1957
Guardianship of Minors Act 1971
Part II Matrimonial Causes Act 1973

Guardianship Act 1973
Children Act 1975
Supplementary Benefits Act 1976
Domestic Proceedings and Magistrates' Courts Act 1978
Part III Matrimonial and Family Proceedings Act 1984
Family Law (Scotland) Act 1985
Schedule 1 Children Act 1989
Social Security Act 1986
Social Security Administration Act 1992
Schedule 5, 6 or 7 Civil Partnership Act 2004

The court order usually states the legal provisions under which it was made.

Appendix 4

Information and advice

It is often difficult for unsupported individuals to get a positive response from the Child Support Agency. You may be more successful if you have taken advice about your rights or have an adviser assisting you. The following agencies may be able to help.

- Citizens Advice Bureaux (CAB) and other local advice centres provide information and may be able to represent you. You can find your nearest CAB from www.citizensadvice.org.uk.
- Law centres can help with advice and representation, but may not cover child support problems and may limit their help to people who live and work in certain areas. You can check whether you are near a law centre from www.lawcentres.org.uk
- Solicitors can give free legal advice to people on low incomes under the 'legal help' scheme (advice and assistance scheme in Scotland). This does not cover the cost of representation at an appeal hearing, but can cover the cost of preparing written submissions and obtaining evidence such as medical reports. However, solicitors do not always have a good working knowledge of the child support rules and you may need to shop around until you find one who does.
- http://legaladviserfinder.justice.gov.uk (0845 345 4345) can be used to find high quality legal advisers in England and Wales, including advice agencies and solicitors.
- Local authority welfare rights workers provide an advice and representation service for benefit claimants in many areas.
- Lone-parent organisations may offer help and advice about child support, or it may help to talk to other parents about their experiences. For details of your local group and for helpline advice contact: Single Parent Action Network (0117 951 4231; www.spanuk.org.uk); Gingerbread (single parent helpline 0808 802 0925; www.gingerbread.org.uk); One Parent Families Scotland (helpline 0808 801 0323; www.opfs.org.uk).
- There are some groups supporting parents who may be able to provide advice. These include the National Association for Child Support Action, PO Box 4454, Dudley, West Midlands DY1 9AN. For general enquiry support you can write or email enquiries@nacsa.co.uk. A telephone advice line is available to subscribers.
- Many trade unions provide advice to members on child support.

- Local organisations for particular groups may offer help – eg, unemployed centres, claimants' unions, centres for people with disabilities.

Representation at the First-tier Trbunal

Some parents may find it difficult to obtain representation at appeal hearings. Although many parents, especially with the help of Chapter 18, will be perfectly able to present their own cases, it can be invaluable to obtain objective independent advice which draws on the legislation. An advice centre which has a copy of the legislation (see Appendix 5) and experience of representing at tribunals in other sorts of cases (eg, social security) may be able to provide a representative for a child support appeal.

Child Poverty Action Group

Unfortunately, CPAG is unable to deal with enquiries, either from advisers or members of the public, on child support issues.

Appendix 5

Useful publications

Stationery Office books are available from Stationery Office bookshops or can be ordered from The Stationery Office, Post Cash Department, PO Box 29, Norwich NR3 1GN (tel: 0870 600 5522; fax: 0870 600 5533; email: customer.services@tso.co.uk; web: www.tso.co.uk). Many publications listed are available from CPAG. See below for order details, or order from www.cpag.org.uk/publications/.

1. Caselaw and legislation

Social Security Case Law – Digest of Commissioners' Decisions
D Neligan (Stationery Office, looseleaf in two volumes).

CPAG's Welfare Benefits and Tax Credits Law Online
(CPAG) Includes all social security and tax credits legislation, updated and consolidated throughout the year; over 3,500 decisions of the commissioners and Upper Tribunal, with summaries and commentary from CPAG's *Welfare Rights Bulletin* where available; over 300 court cases; the *Welfare Benefits and Tax Credits Handbook* updated throughout the year with links to the relevant legislation, Upper Tribunal decisions and caselaw. £53 + VAT per concurrent user (bulk discounts available). More information at http://onlineservices.cpag.org.uk.

CPAG's Child Support Law Online
(CPAG) Includes all child support legislation, updated and consolidated throughout the year, with expert commentary from *Child Support: the legislation* (Jacobs); the *Child Support Handbook* updated once a year in line with the print edition, with links to the relevant legislation, Upper Tribunal decisions and caselaw. £65 + VAT per concurrent user (bulk discounts available). More information at http://onlineservices.cpag.org.uk.

CPAG's Housing Benefit and Council Tax Benefit Law Online
(CPAG) Includes complete housing benefit and council tax benefit legislation, updated and consolidated throughout the year; commentary from *CPAG's Housing Benefit and Council Tax Benefit Legislation* (Findlay), updated twice a year in line with the print edition, with links to Upper Tribunal decisions, court cases and other relevant material. £110 + VAT per

user (bulk discounts available). More information at http://onlineservices.cpag.org.uk.

The Law Relating to Social Security
(Stationery Office, looseleaf, 12 volumes) All the legislation but without any comment. Known as the 'Blue Book'. Also available at www.dwp.gov.uk/advisers.

The Law Relating to Child Support
Consolidated legislation without any commentary. Shows the law as it applies both before and after the 'new rules' changes come into force for a particular case. Also known as the 'Orange Volumes'. Available at www.dwp.gov.uk/advisers.

Social Security Legislation, Volume I: Non-Means-Tested Benefits
D Bonner, I Hooker and R White (Sweet & Maxwell) Legislation with commentary. 2011/12 edition (October 2011): £95 for the main volume.

Social Security Legislation, Volume II: Income Support, Jobseeker's Allowance and the Social Fund
P Wood, R Poynter, N Wikeley and D Bonner (Sweet & Maxwell) Legislation with commentary. 2011/12 edition (October 2011): £95 for the main volume.

Social Security Legislation, Volume III: Administration, Adjudication and the European Dimension
M Rowland and R White (Sweet & Maxwell) Legislation with commentary. 2011/12 edition (October 2011): £95 for the main volume.

Social Security Legislation, Volume IV: Tax Credits, Child Trust Funds and HMRC-administered Social Security Benefits
N Wikeley and D Williams (Sweet & Maxwell) Legislation with commentary. 2011/12 edition (October 2011): £95 for the main volume.

Social Security Legislation – updating supplement to Volumes I, II, III & IV
(Sweet & Maxwell) The spring 2012 update to the 2011/12 main volumes: £58.

CPAG's Housing Benefit and Council Tax Benefit Legislation
L Findlay, R Poynter, S Wright, C George, M Williams (CPAG) Legislation with detailed commentary. 2011/12 (24th) edition (December 2011): £100 including updating Supplement. Also available as part of *CPAG's Housing Benefit and Council Tax Law Online*.

Child Support: the legislation
E Jacobs (CPAG) 10th edition main volume (summer 2011): £87.

2. Periodicals
Welfare Rights Bulletin
(CPAG, bimonthly). Covers developments in social security law, including decisions of the courts and the Upper Tribunal, and updates CPAG's *Welfare Benefits and Tax Credits Handbook*. The annual subscription is £33 but it is sent automatically to certain categories of CPAG member (contact CPAG or see www.cpag.org.uk/membership for details).

Articles on social security can also be found in *Legal Action* (Legal Action Group, monthly magazine), *The Adviser* (Citizens Advice, bi-monthly magazine) and the *Journal of Social Security Law* (Sweet & Maxwell, quarterly).

3. Child Support Agency publications
A full list of CSA leaflets is available on the CSA website. Leaflets and most other CSA publications can be obtained from the national enquiry line: 08457 133 133. Many leaflets and other publications are also available at www.csa.gov.uk. The following is only a selection of the publications available. Some of the leaflets listed have 'old rules' equivalents with different titles and numbers.

Child Maintenance and Enforcement Commission Business Plan 2010/11

How Can I Appeal Against a Child Maintenance Decision? (CSL307)

How Do I Complain About the Service I Get From the Child Support Agency? (CSL308)

What Action Can the CSA Take if Parents Don't Pay? (CSL306)

What Happens if Someone Denies They Are the Parent of a Child? (CSL304)

What is My Role in Helping My Employees Pay Child Maintenance? (CSL313)

4. Other publications: child support
This section lists other publications on child support, including some relevant leaflets, but only includes the most recent research, reports and commentary. For earlier research and reports on child support, please see previous editions of this *Handbook*.

Independent Case Examiner's Office: Our Service

Our Standards 2010/11: Independent Case Examiner (ICE)
(both available from www.ind-case-exam.org.uk)

Independent Case Examiner For The Child Support Agency Annual Report 2009/10 (available from www.ind-case-exam.org.uk)

House of Commons Select Committee for Work and Pensions, Third report of 2009/10, *Child Support Reform*, February 2010 (available from www.parliament.uk)

N Wikeley, *Child Support Law and Policy*, Hart Publishing, 2006

5. Other publications: general

Welfare Benefits and Tax Credits Handbook
£39/£9 for claimants (2011/12, April 2011). Also available as part of *CPAG's Welfare Benefits and Tax Credits Law Online.*

Personal Finance Handbook
£16.50 (3rd edition, November 2009)

Paying for Care Handbook
£19.50 (6th edition, March 2009)

Student Support and Benefits Handbook: England, Wales and Northern Ireland
£13.50 (9th edition, autumn 2011)

Benefits for Students in Scotland Handbook
£13.50 (9th edition, autumn 2011)
Available free online at www.scottishhandbooks.cpag.org.uk, funded by the Scottish Government.

Council Tax Handbook
£17 (9th edition, summer 2011)

Debt Advice Handbook
£22 (9th edition, September 2010)

Fuel Rights Handbook
£19 (15th edition, February 2011)

Benefits for Migrants Handbook
£23 (5th edition, January 2011)

Children's Handbook Scotland: a benefits guide for children living away from their parents
£13 (4th edition, autumn 2011)

Disabled Children: a legal handbook
£40 (1st edition, October 2010)
Published by Legal Action Group.

Tribunal Practice and Procedure
£50 (2nd edition, summer 2011)
Published by Legal Action Group.

Children in Need: local authority support for children and families
£45 (1st edition, April 2011)
Published by Legal Action Group.

Guide to Housing Benefit and Council Tax Benefit 2011/12
£27 (summer 2011) Published by Shelter/CIH.

Disability Rights Handbook
£28.50 (May 2011) Published by Disability Alliance.

For CPAG publications and most of those in Sections 1 and 5 contact:
CPAG, 94 White Lion Street, London N1 9PF, tel: 020 7837 7979, fax: 020 7837 6414. Online shop at www.onlineservices.cpag.org.uk/shop. Postage and packing: free for orders up to £10 in value; for order value £10.01–£100 add a flat rate charge of £3.99; for order value £100.01–£400 add £5.99; for order value £400+ add £9.99.

Appendix 6

Abbreviations used in the notes

AAC	Administrative Appeals Chamber	FCR	Family Court Reports
AC	Appeal Cases	FLR	Family Law Reports
All ER	All England Reports	HC	High Court
App	Appendix	HL	House of Lords
Art(s)	Article(s)	para(s)	Paragraph(s)
CA	Court of Appeal	QB	Queen's Bench Reports
CCR	County Court Rules	r(s)	Rule(s)
Ch	Chapter	Reg(s)	Regulation(s)
col	Column	s(s)	Section(s)
DC	Divisional Court	SCLR	Scottish Civil Law Reports
ECJ	European Court of Justice	Sch(s)	Schedule(s)
ECR	European Court Reports	SLT	Scots Law Times
EHRR	European Human Rights Reports	UKUT	United Kingdom Upper Tribunal
FamD	Family Division	Vol	Volume
		WLR	Weekly Law Reports

Acts of Parliament

Unless information in this *Handbook* specifically relates to 'old rules' cases, legislative references are for 'new rules' cases only. Provisions for 'old rules' cases are as the law stood before the Child Support, Pensions and Social Security Act 2000 came into force. Full legislative referencing for 'old rules' cases can be found in the 2001/02 and 2002/03 editions of this *Handbook*.

A&CA 2002	Adoption and Children Act 2002
A&C(S)A 2007	Adoption and Children (Scotland) Act 2007
CA 1989	Children Act 1989
CMOPA 2008	Child Maintenance and Other Payments Act 2008
CPA 2004	Civil Partnership Act 2004
CSA 1991	Child Support Act 1991
C(S)A 1995	Children (Scotland) Act 1995

CSPSSA 2000	Child Support, Pensions and Social Security Act 2000
DPMCA 1978	Domestic Proceedings and Magistrates Courts Act 1978
ERA 1996	Employment Rights Act 1996
FL(S)A 1958	Family Law (Scotland) Act 1958
FLRA 1969	Family Law Reform Act 1969
HF&EA 1990	Human Fertilisation and Embryology Act 1990
HF&EA 2008	Human Fertilisation and Embryology Act 2008
HRA 1998	Human Rights Act 1998
ICTA 1988	Income and Corporation Taxes Act 1988
LR(PC)(S)A 1986	Law Reform (Parent and Child) (Scotland) Act 1986
MCA 1973	Matrimonial Causes Act 1973
MO(RE)A 1992	Maintenance Orders (Reciprocal Enforcement) Act 1992
SSA 1998	Social Security Act 1998
SSAA 1992	Social Security Administration Act 1992
SSCBA 1992	Social Security Contributions and Benefits Act 1992
TCA 2002	Tax Credits Act 2002
TCEA 2007	Tribunals, Courts and Enforcement Act 2007

Regulations and other statutory instruments

Unless information specifically relates to 'old rules' cases, legislative references in this *Handbook* are correct for 'new rules' cases only. Most 'new rules' statutory instruments have 'old rules' equivalents. For example, the CS(MAP) Regs are the 'old rules' equivalent of the CS(MCP) Regs. Full legislative referencing for 'old rules' cases can be found in the 2001/02 and 2002/03 editions of this *Handbook*.If you are unsure of the correct 'old rules' legislative reference, seek advice.

AS(CSA)(AOCSCR)	The Act of Sederunt (Child Support Act 1991) (Amendment of Ordinary Cause and Summary Cause Rules) 1993 No.919
AS(CSR)	The Act of Sederunt (Child Support Rules) 1993 No.920
AUTCAO	The Appeals from the Upper Tribunal to the Court of Appeal Order 2008 No.2834
C(AP)O	The Children (Allocation of Proceedings) Order 1991 No.1677
CB&SS(FAR) Regs	The Child Benefit and Social Security (Fixing and Adjustment of Rates) Regulations 1976 No.1267
CP(PSS&CS)(CP)O	The Civil Partnership (Pensions, Social Security and Child Support) (Consequential, etc. Provisions) Order 2005 No.2877
CPA 2004(RACP)O	The Civil Partnership Act 2004 (Relationships Arising Through Civil Partnership) Order 2005 No.3137

CS(AIAMA) Regs	The Child Support (Arrears, Interest and Adjustment of Maintenance Assessments) Regulations 1992 No.1816
CS(APD)	The Child Support (Applications: Prescribed Dates) Regulations 2003 No.194
CS(C&E) Regs	The Child Support (Collection and Enforcement) Regulations 1992 No.1989
CS(C&E)(DO)(A) Regs	The Child Support Collection and Enforcement (Deduction Orders) Amendment Regulations 2009 No.1815
CS(CEMA) Regs	The Child Support (Collection and Enforcement and Miscellaneous Amendments) Regulations 2000 No.2001/162
CS(CEOFM) Regs	The Child Support (Collection and Enforcement of Other Forms of Maintenance) Regulations 1992 No.2643
CS(D&A)(A) Regs	The Child Support (Decisions and Appeals) (Amendment) Regulations 2000 No.3185
CS(IED) Regs	The Child Support (Information, Evidence and Disclosure) Regulations 1992 No.1812
CS(IEDMAJ)(A) Regs	The Child Support (Information, Evidence and Disclosure and Maintenance Arrangements and Jurisdiction) (Amendment) Regulations 2000 No.2001/161
CS(MA) Regs	The Child Support (Miscellaneous Amendments) Regulations 2008 No. 536
CS(MA) Regs 2009	The Child Support (Miscellaneous Amendments) Regulations 2009 No.8947
CS(MA)(No.2) Regs	The Child Support (Miscellaneous Amendments) (No.2) Regulations 2008 No.1042
CS(MA)(No.2) 2009	The Child Support (Miscellaneous Amendments) (No.2) Regulations 2009 No.2909
CS(MAJ) Regs	The Child Support (Maintenance Arrangements and Jurisdiction) Regulations 1992 No.2645
CS(MAP) Regs	The Child Support (Maintenance Assessment Procedure) Regulations 1992 No.1813
CS(MASC) Regs	The Child Support (Maintenance Assessments and Special Cases) Regulations 1992 No.1815
CS(MATP) Regs	The Child Support (Miscellaneous Amendments and Transitional Provisions) Regulations 1994 No.227

CS(MCA) Regs	The Child Support (Miscellaneous and Consequential Amendments) Regulations 2009 No.736
CS(MCP) Regs	The Child Support (Maintenance Calculation Procedure) Regulations 2000 No.2001/157
CS(MCSC) Regs	The Child Support (Maintenance Calculation and Special Cases) Regulations 2000 No.2001/155
CS(MPA) Regs	The Child Support (Management of Payments and Arrears) Regulations 2009 No.3151
CS(NIRA) Regs	The Child Support (Northern Ireland Reciprocal Arrangements) Regulations 1993 No.584
CS(TCPS)(MA) Regs	The Child Support (Temporary Compensation Payment Scheme) (Modification and Amendment) Regulations 2002 No.1854
CS(TP) Regs	The Child Support (Transitional Provisions) Regulations 2000 No.3186
CS(V) Regs	The Child Support (Variations) Regulations 2000 No.2001/156
CS(V)(MSP) Regs	The Child Support (Variations)(Modification of Statutory Provisions) Regulations 2000 No.3173
CS(VP) Regs	The Child Support (Voluntary Payments) Regulations 2000 No.3177
CSA(CA)O	The Child Support Act 1991 (Consequential Amendments) Order 1993 No.785
CSA(JC)O	The Child Support Appeals (Jurisdiction of Courts) Order 1993 No.961
CSA(JC)O 2002	The Child Support Appeals (Jurisdiction of Courts) Order 2002 No.1915
CSA(JC)(S)O	The Child Support Appeals (Jurisdiction of Courts)(Scotland) Order 2003 No.96
CSC(P) Regs	The Child Support Commissioners (Procedure) Regulations 1999 No.1305
CSDDCA Regs	The Child Support Departure Directions and Consequential Amendments Regulations 1996 No.2907
CSF Regs	The Child Support Fees Regulations 1992 No.3094
CSI Regs	The Child Support Information Regulations 2008 No.2551
CSMA Regs	The Child Support Miscellaneous Amendments Regulations 2007 No.1979

CSPSSA(Comm3)O	The Child Support, Pensions and Social Security Act 2000 (Commencement No.3) Order 2000 No.2994
CSPSSA(Comm12)O	The Child Support, Pensions and Social Security Act 2003 (Commencement No.12) Order 2003 No.192
CSPSSA(Comm13)O	The Child Support, Pensions and Social Security Act 2000 (Commencement No.13) Order 2003 No.346
CTB Regs	The Council Tax Benefit (General) Regulations 2006 No.215
CTB(SPC) Regs	The Council Tax Benefit (Persons who have Attained the Qualifying Age for State Pension Credit) Regulations 2006 No.216
FT&UT(CT)O	The First-tier Tribunal and Upper Tribunal (Composition of Tribunal) Order 2008 No.2835
HB Regs	The Housing Benefit (General) Regulations 2006 No.213
HB(SPC) Regs	The Housing Benefit (Persons who have Attained the Qualifying Age for State Pension Credit) Regulations 2006 No.214
HB&CTB(D&A) Regs	The Housing Benefit and Council Tax Benefit (Decisions and Appeals) Regulations 2001 No.1002
IS Regs	The Income Support (General) Regulations 1987 No.1967
JSA Regs	The Jobseeker's Allowance Regulations 1996 No.207
SCR	The Supreme Court Rules 2009 No.3
SS(C&P) Regs	The Social Security (Claims and Payments) Regulations 1987 No.1968
SS(CMB) Regs	The Social Security (Child Maintenance Bonus) Regulations 1996 No.3195
SS(CMP)A Regs	The Social Security (Child Maintenance Premium) Amendment Regulations 2004 No.98
SS(CMPMA) Regs	The Social Security (Child Maintenance Premium and Miscellaneous Amendments) Regulations 2000 No.3176
SS(PAOR) Regs	The Social Security (Payments on Account, Overpayments and Recovery) Regulations 1988 No.664
SS&CS(DA) Regs	The Social Security and Child Support (Decisions and Appeals) Regulations 1999 No.991

TP(FT) Rules	The Tribunal Procedure (First-tier Tribunal)(Social Entitlement Chamber) Rules 2008 No.2685
TP(UT) Rules	The Tribunal Procedure (Upper Tribunal) Rules 2008 No.2698
TTF Order	The Transfer of Tribunal Functions Order 2008 No. 2833

Index

How to use this Index

Entries against the bold headings direct you to the general information on the subject, or where the subject is covered most fully. Sub-entries are listed alphabetically and direct you to specific aspects of the subject.

CSA	Child Support Agency
ESA	employment and support allowance
IS	income support
JSA	jobseeker's allowance
PC	pension credit
WTC	working tax credit

Child Support Law Online

This online service is a one-stop resource for anyone working with the child support scheme. Contents include:

- the full text of the ***Child Support Handbook***, updated annually in line with the print version, with links from the text to child support legislation, regulations etc.
- all child support legislation, together with expert commentary, updated throughout the year
- commissioners' and Upper Tribunal decisions, reported and unreported, with CPAG commentary where available
- relevant court cases, taken from CPAG's ***Welfare Rights Bulletin***

Annual subscription £65 + VAT per user (discounts available for bulk subscriptions of 10+ users)

For more information about this and other online services from CPAG, visit the website **http://onlineservices.cpag.org.uk**

Published by Child Poverty Action Group, 94 White Lion St, London N1 9PF
Tel: 020 7837 7979
Email: bookorders@cpag.org.uk
Website: www.cpag.org.uk/publications

Training at CPAG

CPAG courses provide comprehensive rights training for advisers and detailed coverage of up-to-the minute legislative changes. Our tutors are expert in their areas of work and draw on the extensive training experience of CPAG's own welfare rights specialists. Courses include:

- Child support: liability and enforcement
- An introduction to welfare rights
- Dealing with debt
- Moving into work
- Welfare reform.

For full course information and online booking please see our website (details below). Our courses can also be tailored to meet the needs of specific groups, including those not normally concerned with welfare rights. To assess your training needs, we are happy to discuss your requirements for 'in-house' training to meet the internal needs of your organisation.

CPAG's London-based courses are Law Society and Bar Council accredited and carry continuing education points. They are also approved by The Institute of Legal Executives and the UK College of Family Mediators. Courses in Scotland have Law Society Scotland accreditation.

Contacts for further information:

London Judy Allen, Training Co-ordinator,
tel: 020 7812 5228 email: jallen@cpag.org.uk
website: www.cpag.org.uk/training

Scotland Pauline Chalmers, Training Administrator
Tel: 0141 552 3420 email: pchalmers@cpagscotland.org.uk
website: www.cpag.org.uk/scotland/training

CPAG Handbooks order form

Use this form to get more copies of this or other CPAG handbooks – or visit our online shop at www.onlineservices.cpag.org.uk/shop

	Title	Price £	Total £
	Welfare Benefits and Tax Credits Handbook 2011/12	39.00	
	Council tax Handbook 9th edition (due autumn 2011)	17.00	
	Child Support Handbook 2011/12)	27.00	
	Student Support & Benefits Handbook: England, Wales and N. Ireland 2011/12 (due autumn 2011)	13.50	
	Benefits for Students in Scotland Handbook 2011/12 (due autumn 2011)	13.50	
	Children's Handbook Scotland 4th ed. (due autumn '11)	13.00	
	Fuel Rights Handbook 15th edition (February 2011)	19.00	
	Benefits for Migrants Handbook 5th ed. (January 2011)	23.00	
	Debt Advice Handbook 9th edition (September 2010)	22.00	
	Personal Finance Handbook 3rd ed. (November 09)	16.50	
	Paying for Care Handbook 6th edition (March 2009)	19.50	
		Subtotal £	
	Add P&P: order value £10.01—£100, add £3.00; £100.01—£400, add £5.99; order value £400+, add £9.99	**P&P £**	
	Optional donation towards CPAG's work against child poverty	**£**	
		Grand total £	

I enclose a cheque/PO for £__________ payable to Child Poverty Action Group

Title ______ First name ________________ Second name ________________

Organisation ____________________________ Dept ________________

Address ____

____ Postcode ____________

Email ____

Return form with payment to:

Child Poverty Action Group, 94 White Lion St, London N1 9PF

Tel: 020 7837 7979 Email: bookorders@cpag.org.uk

Debt Advice Handbook

9th edition

The **Debt Advice Handbook** contains all the essential information needed by advisers dealing with debt problems, and explains the key stages and issues in money advice in England and Wales.

It has guidance on interviewing clients; dealing with emergencies; establishing liability for debts; income maximisation; prioritising debts; preparing financial statements and negotiating with creditors. There are sections covering business and student debts, and court action by creditors to recover debts and repossess property/goods. Further sections deal with enforcement in magistrates' courts, bailiffs, and insolvency.

As well as outlining the debt advice process, the book helps advisers choose the most effective strategies and deal with unacceptable debt collection practices.

Every edition is revised and updated to cover recent changes to legislation, caselaw, court procedures and practice. The book is fully indexed and cross-referenced to other relevant publications and articles as well as to caselaw, legislation and the rules of court.

> *This book continues to provide welcome support for advisers and consumers. CPAG are to be congratulated on meeting this need.*
> **Institute of Money Advisers**

> *Quite simply, if you give debt advice, you must have this book.*
> **The Adviser (Citizens Advice)**

Price £22.00 September 2010 ISBN: 978-1-906076-46-7

Published by Child Poverty Action Group, 94 White Lion St, London N1 9PF
Tel: 020 7837 7979
Email: bookorders@cpag.org.uk
Website: www.cpag.org.uk/publications
Online shop: www.onlineservices.cpag.org.uk/shop

Child Support: the legislation

10th edition

This volume contains all the primary and secondary legislation relating to child maintenance, together with the rules for both Tribunals.

The author gives authoritative analysis of decisions made by the courts, the Child Support Commissioners and Upper Tribunal, to show how the law governing child support has been interpreted and applied.

This book will enable tribunal judges and members, parents and their representatives to deal with cases under all versions of the child support legislation.

Author Edward Jacobs is a Judge of the Upper Tribunal. He is a barrister and was formerly a full-time chairman of child support appeal tribunals and a Child Support Commissioner

Price £87.00 Summer 2011 ISBN: 978-1-906076-56-6

Published by Child Poverty Action Group, 94 White Lion St, London N1 9PF
Tel: 020 7837 7979
Email: bookorders@cpag.org.uk
Website: www.cpag.org.uk/publications